THE KINDNESS
OF STRANGERS

The KINDNESS of STRANGERS

❖ ❖ ❖

THE ABANDONMENT OF CHILDREN
IN WESTERN EUROPE
FROM LATE ANTIQUITY
TO THE RENAISSANCE

JOHN BOSWELL

VINTAGE BOOKS

A DIVISION OF RANDOM HOUSE, INC.

NEW YORK

First Vintage Books Edition, February 1990

Copyright © 1988 by John Boswell

All rights reserved under International and Pan-American Copyright Conventions. Published in the United States by Vintage Books, a division of Random House, Inc., New York, and simultaneously in Canada by Random House of Canada Limited, Toronto. Originally published, in hardcover, by Pantheon Books, a division of Random House, Inc., New York, in 1988.

Library of Congress Cataloging-in-Publication Data
Boswell, John.
The kindness of strangers : the abandonment of children in Western Europe from late antiquity to the Renaissance / John Boswell. — 1st Vintage Books ed.
p.   cm.
"Originally published in hardcover by Pantheon Books . . . in 1988" —T.p. verso.
Includes bibliographical references.
ISBN 0-679-72499-0
1. Abandoned children—Europe—History.   2. Child welfare —Europe—History.   3. Europe—Social conditions—To 1492.
I. Title.
[HV887.E8B67   1990]
362.7'3'094—dc20   89-40117
                                                                       CIP

Manufactured in the United States of America
10 9 8 7 6 5 4 3 2 1

This book is dedicated
to all loving families,
adoptive and natal,
especially to my own mother and father,
sister and brothers,
and to Elsie, Gram, Sally, Rob,
Jamie John, and Jennifer,
who adopted me
though I was not abandoned

We enjoin thee . . . that thou carry
This female bastard hence, and that thou bear it
To some remote and desert place, quite out
Of our dominions; and that there thou leave it,
Without more mercy, to its own protection
And favour of the climate. As by strange fortune
It came to us, I do in justice charge thee,
On thy soul's peril, and thy body's torture,
That thou commend it strangely to some place,
Where chance may nurse or end it. Take it up.

Shakespeare, *The Winter's Tale*, 2.3.172–81

❖   ❖   ❖

Contents

❖   ❖   ❖

LIST OF ILLUSTRATIONS

❖   ❖   ❖

ABBREVIATIONS

*(Full references for works cited in footnotes by author and
title only, without publication data, can be found in
Frequently Cited Works.)*

AASS   *Acta sanctorum,* ed. J. Bollandus. Paris, 1863–1948.
ADH   *Annales de démographie historique.*
AHR   *American Historical Review.*
Annales   *Annales: Économies-Sociétés-Civilisations.*
ANRW   *Aufstieg und Niedergang der römischen Welt. Geschichte
            und Kultur Roms im Spiegel der neueren Forschung,* ed.
            Hildegard Temporini. Berlin, 1972–.
ASOB   *Acta sanctorum ordinis sancti Benedicti,* ed. J. Mabillon.
            Mâcon, 1935–.
CCCM   *Corpus Christianorum continuatio mediaevalis.*
CCSL   *Corpus Christianorum series latina.*
CIC   *Corpus iuris canonici,* ed. Emil Friedberg. Leipzig,
            1879.*
CIL   *Corpus inscriptionum latinarum,* Berlin, 1888.
CSEL   *Corpus scriptorum ecclesiasticorum latinorum.*
Dig.   Digest of Justinian: in *Corpus iuris civilis* (*see* JC).

*I cite from both the *Decretum* and from canon law in the most obvious way—
i.e., division numbers in order from largest to smallest, as one would identify
sections from any other large, subdivided work. This makes it possible for non-
specialists to check references and should pose no barrier to experts, who can readily convert to old-style (e.g., my citation "*Decretum* 2.22.5.14" = Decretum, Part
2, Cause 22, question 5, canon 14 = old style c14.C22.q5). I also supply column
numbers from Friedberg.

L'Enfant 1	*L'Enfant*. 1. *Antiquité—Afrique—Asie,* in *Recueils de la Société Jean Bodin,* 35. Brussels, 1975.
L'Enfant 2	*L'Enfant*. 2. *Europe médiévale et moderne,* in *Recueils de la Société Jean Bodin,* 36. Brussels, 1976.
IF	*Íslenzk Fornrít.* Rejkyavik, 1933–.
ILCV	E. Diehl, *Inscriptiones latinae christianae veteres.* Zurich, 1925–1961.
JB	*Jerusalem Bible.*
JC	Code of Justinian: in *Corpus iuris civilis,* ed. T. Mommsen, P. Krueger. Berlin, 1866, and many subsequent editions.
JFH	*Journal of Family History.*
LAMPC	J. C. Russell, *Late Ancient and Medieval Population Control.* Philadelphia, 1985.
LCL	*Loeb Classical Library.*
LMIR	*Late Medieval Icelandic Romances,* ed. Agnete Loth. Editiones Arnamagnaeanae, Series B, vols. 20–24. Copenhagen, 1962–1965.
LSJ	Henry Liddell, Robert Scott, and Henry Jones, *A Greek-English Lexicon.* Oxford, 1968.
LV	*Leges Visigothorum,* ed. K. Zeumer. Hannover, 1902 (in MGH LL, q.v.).
LXX	Septuagint.
MGH	*Monumenta Germaniae historica.* Hannover, 1826–.
	AA *Auctores antiquissimi.*
	Const. *Constitutiones et acta publica imperatorum et regum.*
	Epp. *Epistolae.*
	LL *Leges.*
	PLAC *Poetae latini aevi carolini.*
	SS *Scriptores.*
	SSRRGG *Scriptores rerum germanicarum in usum scholarum.*
	SSRRLL *Scriptores rerum langobardarum.*
	SSRRMM *Scriptores rerum merovingicarum.*
MHSSC	*Monumenta Hispaniae sacra,* serie canónica, ed. Gonzalo Martínez Díez, Felix Rodríguez. Madrid, 1966–.
NGL	*Norges gåmle Love indtil 1387,* ed. R. Keyser and P. A. Munch. Christiania, 1846–1895, 5 vols.
OLD	*Oxford Latin Dictionary,* ed. P. G. W. Glare. Oxford, 1982.

OP   *Oxyrhynchus Papyri*, ed. B. P. Grenfell and A. S. Hunt. London, 1898–.

PG   *Patrologia, Series graeca*, ed. J. P. Migne.

PL   *Patrologia, Series latina*, ed. J. P. Migne.

RE   A. Pauly, G. Wissowa, and W. Kroll, *Real-Encyclopädie der klassischen Altertumswissenschaft*, 1893–.

Recueil   *Recueil des documents concernant le Poitou contenus dans les registres de la Chancellerie de France*, ed. Paul Guérin, in *Archives historiques du Poitou* (Société des Archives historiques du Poitou).

SSRRII *Rerum italicarum scriptores*, ed. Ludovico Muratori. Milan, 1723–1751.

TAPA   *Transactions of the American Philological Association*.

TC   Theodosian Code: *Theodosiani libri xvi cum constitutionibus Sirmondianis*, ed. T. Mommsen. Berlin, 1905.

VSH   *Vitae sanctorum Hiberniae*, ed. Charles Plummer. Oxford, 1910.

PREFACE

AND

ACKNOWLEDGMENTS

THE TITLE of this book was inspired by the happy resolution of a problem of translation. A number of the Latin legal, ecclesiastical, and literary texts discussed below use the expression *aliena misericordia* to describe the motivation of the persons who rescued abandoned children. For a long time I had trouble rendering this phrase into idiomatic English. At first glance it seems to mean "strange kindness," or "foreign mercy," but this seemed to me an odd and inelegant way to describe such generosity. Because the phrase occurs often, and in important contexts, I worried long over finding an effective translation, and when it finally occurred to me that it is the Latin equivalent of "the kindness of strangers," I decided to use this evocative phrase in the title. As will be seen, the "kindness of strangers" who found and reared the children is as prominent a theme in this study as the sadder issue of the abandonment itself.

Because the subject of this study may be of interest to persons of widely differing backgrounds and points of view, I have made an effort to provide basic information about some aspects of the topic which experts may find unnecessary. The Introduction, for example, is largely addressed to those who have not had occasion to ponder the relationship between "literary" and "historical" sources, and who might wonder about some of the issues raised in the main body of the book. Historians may wish to skip this discussion and begin on page 22 with "Words and Numbers," which deals with more technical historiographical problems.

The notes are largely written for readers who wish to consult the sources or enter the somewhat involved scholarly debates that rage about many issues and details. Readers who skip them risk missing only ancillary data and qualifications of specific points: the central argument and the broad outlines of my story stand without them.

This book was begun many years ago, and it is no longer possible to recall all those who have generously provided assistance. First and foremost, I owe an incalculable debt to Ralph Hexter of the Yale Classics Department, who substantially improved the whole text with critical comments and suggestions. Giles Constable of the Institute for Advanced Study at Princeton, Elizabeth Archibald of King's College, Cambridge, Ruth Mazo Karras of the History Department at the University of Pennsylvania, Robert and Robin Stacey of the History Department of the University of Washington, and James Schultz of the University of Illinois (Chicago), all very kindly offered me the benefit of their expert advice on portions of the manuscript. I acknowledge my gratitude as well to Suzanne Roberts, Lucy Freeman Sandler, George Greenia, Elizabeth Meyer, Diana Moses, Barbara Bachman, Edward Segal, and Leo Hickey.

I thank the staff of the Bibliothèque Nationale (Paris), the British Library (London), the Bodleian Library at Oxford, and the Biblioteca Apostolica Vaticana for their help with the project over the past six years.

I hope that any others who have helped me and whom I have forgotten to thank by name will forgive the oversight and accept my gratitude anonymously: it is no less heartfelt for its absent-mindedness.

New Haven, Connecticut
February, 1988

THE KINDNESS
OF STRANGERS

INTRODUCTION

My third child was thus deposited in a foundling home just like the first two, and I did the same with the two following: I had five in all. This arrangement seemed to me so good, so sensible, so appropriate, that if I did not boast of it publicly it was solely out of regard for their mother. . . . In a word, I made no secret of my action . . . because in fact I saw no wrong in it. All things considered, I chose what was best for my children, or what I thought was best. . . .

Jean-Jacques Rousseau, *Confessions*[1]

A PUZZLE

THIS BOOK began as the investigation of a mystery, and in writing it I have tried to preserve some aspects of the mystery, both because I have not, in the end, entirely solved it, and because the context in which I originally gathered the material seems the most authentic framework for presenting it to others.

While collecting information about early Christian sexual mores for a previous study,[2] I came across the argument by several prominent theologians of the early church that men should not visit brothels or have recourse to prostitutes because in doing so they might unwittingly commit incest with a child they had abandoned. "How many fathers," asked Clement of Alexandria, "forgetting the children they abandoned, unknowingly have sexual relations with a son who is a prostitute or a daughter become a harlot?"[3] "Those who use the services [of prostitutes]," Justin Martyr warned, "may well commit incest with a child, a relative, or a sibling."[4]

---

1. *Confessions,* 8, ed. Jacques Voisine (Paris, 1964), p. 424. Rousseau did subsequently regret his actions: see below, note 42.
2. Boswell, *Christianity,* pp. 143–44.
3. *Paedagogus* 3.3 (PG 5.585); discussed more fully in chapters 2 and 3.
4. 1 *Apology* 27 (PG 6.369–72); further discussion in chapters 2 and 3.

4 · *The Kindness of Strangers*

At first I was stunned by how peculiar and oblique an argument this was against prostitution; but in the end I found even more surprising the implication that the writers' contemporaries abandoned children so commonly that a given father was likely to encounter his own child in a brothel.[5] Was this possible? Although the "exposure" of children was a part of the standard litany of Roman depravities, I had understood that they were left to die on hillsides. I never imagined that it was a widespread or common practice, and certainly had not thought that Christians abandoned babies. Indeed, I had been led to believe that Christians rescued such children. Was the warning predicated on a remote possibility worth mentioning simply because it would be so dreadful if it did happen? It would hardly work as an admonition, it would seem, if listeners did not believe it possible: if Christian fathers did not abandon their children, they would hardly be dissuaded from visiting brothels by the threat of incest.

If children were abandoned in infancy by many couples—pagan or Christian—how would we know? Would they leave any sort of mark in the historical record? Would it be possible to obtain information which not only individuals but society as a whole might wish to hide? Criminals have an interest in disguising their activities, but society usually has a counter-interest in exposing them, and the historian can often obtain information about them by consulting legal records. But what of something everyone wanted to hide? Obviously the writers warning fathers against frequenting brothels expected that the children had been abandoned surreptitiously, and that neither parent nor child would recognize the other. This made sense to me: the point of abandoning a child, it would seem, would be to negate parental obligations, and in most societies such ties are regarded as largely irrevocable. The only way to achieve such a break would be to avoid any public awareness of the relationship and, hence, of the abandonment. How then might one find out about it?

Conjugal relations, reproduction, and the interior life of the family are, in fact, among the most reclusive and private aspects of human existence, jealously guarded from public view in most cultures, and less likely than almost any other interpersonal activity to

---

5. Although in fact Minucius Felix and Tertullian specifically contrast Christian morality, which is not likely to result in the problem of incest, with that of pagans, which is.

leave written records. Even the birth of children, obviously a communal event to some degree, was shrouded in secrecy in certain premodern cultures. Custom, personal sentiment, and folk tradition have doubtless been controlling influences on perception and practice in all these areas throughout Western history, and all three are unusually resistant to modern investigative techniques. It is relatively easy to discover what civil or ecclesiastical laws stipulate about conjugal relations, but it would be fatuous to assume that these necessarily determined or reflected popular behavior.

Historians have long been accustomed to playing the paleontologist—collecting, cleaning, analyzing, and arranging for display the bones of the species they study, in this case those aspects of human society which happen to leave hard remains in the sediments of time: birth certificates, death notices, tax lists, laws, records of public events. But the great bulk of any organic entity is too soft to survive as fossil: the flesh that provided size and shape, the skin and hair that determined appearance, the viscera that governed metabolism and growth, the brain that directed movement and invested life with meaning—all these are leached from the sediments. In the case of the human family, what is missing is the "flesh and blood" in its most literal sense: children. The fossil remains of ancient and medieval populations are almost entirely of adults; children left impressions too fragile to survive, or no imprints at all.

Even in the relatively rare instances of fully preserved specimens (e.g., a census) the sample can at most capture as static entities organisms that changed and grew throughout their existence: learning in detail how families appeared to a census taker in 1400 may reveal much less than knowing, even roughly, the changes they had undergone the year before or were to experience in the following twelve months. If many couples were recorded as having three children at the moment of the count, the historian might conclude that this was a common pattern, but would be misled about parent-child relations and reproductivity if three was the ideal number of children in the eyes of contemporaries and many parents took measures to achieve it: those who had six, for example, might abandon two or three who would then be reared by couples with fewer children or none. Simply counting the "bones" of such a society might produce a rough indication of how many living beings it comprised, but it would hardly illuminate even the most basic outlines of the lives of its individual members.

There are, however, not even enough bones to count. From all of Europe during the whole of the Middle Ages, at most a half dozen reliable bits of demographic data survive,[6] and they are so widely scattered in time and place that it is nearly impossible to know whether they are typical or peculiar, indicative of continuity or change, meticulously reliable or grossly misleading. So much of the skeleton is missing that it is difficult to place individual pieces, or even to be confident that they belong to the specimen.

Here the historian has one advantage over the paleontologist, and his task might be better compared to that of a detective, because he can often supplement material evidence with the testimony of witnesses. Unfortunately in the case of children, even narrative and personal documents from late antiquity and the Middle Ages are strikingly reticent: "Of all social groups which formed the societies of the past, children, seldom seen and rarely heard in the documents, remain for historians the most elusive, the most obscure."[7]

The testimony of humans, moreover, poses special problems: unlike fossil remains, eyewitnesses may deliberately or inadvertently change facts in the process of reporting them. There is, for example, one fairly copious source of information on abandonment in ancient and medieval Europe, but there is reason to suspect its veracity. Abandoned children are everywhere in imaginative literature, from Moses to Tom Jones. One might infer from this that abandonment was a familiar social reality, and is therefore reflected in creative writing; but it is also possible that authors introduced as a convenient plot device something that fascinated precisely because of its improbability.

Dozens of movies and novels I have seen or read, from Saturday westerns to *Lawrence of Arabia* to *Blazing Saddles,* use quicksand as a plot device: to get rid of good characters with pathos, bad ones with justice, or simply to provide an episode of exciting action. Quicksand is, in fact, such a familiar part of fictional landscapes that I know a good deal about it: for example, that struggling only makes it worse, and that the best way to rescue someone caught in quicksand is to have him lie flat and extend a board to him.

6. The problem of medieval demography is addressed in more detail below.
7. Herlihy, "Medieval Children," p. 109. Laslett, *The World We Have Lost:* "These crowds and crowds of little children are strangely absent from the written record. . . . There is something mysterious about the silence of all these multitudes of babes in arms, toddlers and adolescents, in the statements men made at the time about their own experience" (p. 104).

I do not, however, know whether any real person has ever actually died in quicksand, or even needed to be rescued from it. I have never met a person with a friend, relative, or casual acquaintance who has been incommoded in any way by quicksand, despite its pivotal role in the lives of many citizens of fiction. I suspect that it is its imaginative force and dramatic convenience that cause it to appear so frequently in stories, and that these have no relation to its role in actual lives.[8]

Since abandonment offers irresistible opportunities for hilarious misprisions of identity, titillating near-misses of incest, and joyful turns of plot when slave girls turn out to be nubile aristocrats or long-lost children, it may well be a "quicksand problem." The occurrence of life crises related to quicksand in many genres of modern fiction should not be construed as a useful datum by future historians attempting to assess the difficulties of life in the nineteenth and twentieth centuries; and the frequency of abandonment in ancient and medieval literature, one might suspect, should not be taken seriously by historians trying to understand the family in earlier societies.

But then there is the case of adultery: it, too, provides the substance of imaginative writing of every sort, and it, too, is such a convenient plot device (offering excuses for jealousies, murders, touchingly false suspicions, new groupings of major characters, etc.) that one imagines it might have been invented for fiction whether it occurred in real life or not. And, indeed, most adults probably imagine that adultery is more common in fiction than in real life.

The case is nearly the reverse. Most fictional occurrences of adultery are limited to key characters in the story; the rest of the population is presumed—by implicit contrast if not explicit description—to be faithfully married. Moreover, the moral, emotional, legal, and social crises provoked by adultery in nineteenth- and twentieth-century fiction would certainly suggest that it was an event of major traumatic and stressful consequences which most married persons avoided. In real life, however, adultery is not limited to leading characters and can hardly be considered uncommon, whatever its emotional or social consequences. (Even in

8. This is not to say that quicksand does not exist, or is never a problem for humans: simply that its role in fiction is not a realistic reflection of its importance.

the 1940s, long before the current sexual revolution, about half of all married men in the United States had intercourse with women other than their wives.)[9]

Mysteries related to adultery may be particularly apt parallels to those surrounding the abandonment of children, because the participants in extramarital affairs generally have an interest in seeing that no record of them survives. Indeed, the greatest difference between fictional and real adultery is probably the fact that in fiction *someone always knows:* it advances the plot when a spouse discovers it, and this provokes conjugal realignments, struggles, or at least revelations of feeling and character. Even if the spouse is unaware, the whole concept of adultery in the realms ruled by authors is subtly skewed by the fact that so many people—at the very least, the writer and all his readers—know all about it.

In nonfictional lives, unless the published data are entirely incorrect, the majority of instances of adultery are not silently observed by large audiences, and do not lead to crimes of passion, major social crises, or even divorce. Most instances apparently pass unnoticed,[10] and in any given community a very large amount of extramarital sexuality takes place without giving rise to colorful developments or transformations of character, much less to any record the historian could discover.

The same may be true of abandonment: a major difference between fictional accounts of abandonment and its reality in premodern societies is that in fiction *someone always knows* about the abandonment, and this knowledge almost always has a major impact on the lives of those involved. This fictional representation of both adultery and abandonment probably betrays a genuine anxiety on the part of society about the propriety, morality, or consequences of both acts, and is itself an important datum. Involvement in adulterous relationships causes people stress as a result of guilt or

9. See Kinsey, *Sexual Behavior in the Human Male*, pp. 583–94, esp. p. 585: ". . . it is probably safe to suggest that about half of all the married males have intercourse with women other than their wives, at some time while they are married." For more recent data, see Blumstein and Schwartz, *American Couples*, pp. 267–306, esp. p. 274, where it is suggested that 68 percent of husbands and 57 percent of wives have had sexual relations outside the marriage. Adultery as a theme of eighteenth- and nineteenth-century novels has been the subject of two recent studies: Judith Armstrong, *The Novel of Adultery* (London, 1976), and Tony Tanner, *Adultery in the Novel: Contract and Transgression* (Baltimore, 1979).

10. See discussion of this in Blumstein and Schwartz, esp. pp. 268–71.

fear about what might happen *if people knew.* The investigator should be aware that such results usually do not attend instances of adultery, but must also recognize in fictional accounts the traces of the potent fear that they might, and be prepared to assess what this reveals about attitudes and feelings.

Abandonment would hardly have worked as a social mechanism if the parents believed that their actions were invariably observed or that some turn of fate would inevitably disclose the child's relationship to them. But the fear—or hope—that this was the case may be one of the forces behind its regular occurrence in literary treatments of the subject. Literature in this case provides essential information almost in spite of itself—like a witness whose nervousness is more revealing than his testimony—and is a kind of evidence which would rarely if ever occur in purely historical sources.

A subtler analogue occurs in treatments of murder and abortion in twentieth-century fiction. Both are the objects of real and urgent moral, emotional, and legal concerns among American citizens. Yet murder is depicted vastly more often than abortion: it is the single most common plot device in whole genres of imaginative literature—novels, movies, and television. Abortion occurs much less often as a plot device even in novels, and almost never in movies or on television. Is this because murder is a familiar part of most Americans' lives and abortion is not? Or because Americans are more likely to be affected by a murder than by an abortion? Or because murder is less horrible and disapproved than abortion?

On the contrary: there are enormously more abortions in the United States than murders,[11] and vastly more members of the reading public are affected by abortion than by homicide (unless, of course, one categorizes abortions as "murders," but it is still not the act on which the bulk of mystery or action plots turn). Moreover, although substantial elements of the population are categorically opposed to it, many Americans do not regard abortion as immoral. Precisely because murder, although a real social problem, is horrible enough and sufficiently removed from everyday life to provide the excitement of the extreme and perverse, it makes a useful sub-

---

11. In the United States in 1978, according to government figures, there were 1.4 million *legal* abortions—a figure doubtless much lower than the number of abortions of all kinds—as compared to 19,600 murders for the same year, including "nonnegligent homicides" (U.S. Dept. of Commerce, Bureau of the Census, *Statistical Abstract of the United States: 1980: National Data Book and Guide to Sources* [Washington, 1980], pp. 69 and 182).

ject for fiction, whereas abortion raises problems which are too familiar, too troubling, too ambivalent, and not sufficiently exotic to afford the same satisfaction in reading.[12]

It would be convenient if there were a way for the historian—or the detective—to articulate in advance a foolproof methodology for distinguishing false from reliable testimony, but human consciousness and behavior vary so extremely from individual to individual that no system could predict either the intentions and actions of all those leaving clues or the responses and understanding of all those assessing them. Sound history, like good detective work, must in the end take account of all kinds of evidence and rely on the skill of the investigator and the perspicacity of the reader (or jury) to separate the spurious from the real clues.

"Facts" often prove as difficult to interpret as fictional clues. Many of the more lurid aspects of abandonment are today reported as "facts," particularly in organs of print that specialize in the sensational. One reads of mothers who unknowingly marry sons they had abandoned, or brothers sisters.[13] If true, these stories disclose little about modern family life: the abandonment of children, though known in the West, is by no means a major social problem.[14] Since

12. In addition, the fact that abortion is so controversial makes it a risky subject for a medium designed to appeal to a general audience. Partisans of any point of view are likely to take exception to—possibly even action against—a work that depicts abortion from a perspective they oppose, and it is safer for writers to avoid such topics in a culture in which commercial success affects artistic considerations. In assessing such analogies the modern reader needs to bear in mind that neither the history nor the literature of the past was composed for a general audience. The number of the literate was much smaller before the twentieth century, the cost of books vastly greater before the invention of printing, and most ancient and medieval writers had in mind a more specific and limited audience than their modern counterpart would. During some of the periods addressed by this investigation, furthermore, public dissent from orthodox views on matters of Christian morality rendered one liable to criminal sanctions, even capital punishment, and this also skews the possible uses and interpretation of both literary and historical writing.

13. E.g., a Portuguese woman unwittingly married her own son forty-five years after she abandoned him: "Mom Weds Her Own Son," *New York Sun,* February 11, 1986, p. 29. A few weeks' perusal of several tabloids will unfailingly turn up a case or two of this sort. Oral accounts of such phenomena are also common, and perhaps more reliable: a woman who overheard me describing this study to a fellow passenger on a flight to Paris told me that the pastor of her church, in applying for a passport, discovered he had been abandoned and adopted. He managed to locate his six natal siblings, and two of them were members of his own congregation.

14. It probably is a major social problem in other areas of the world, but rarely attracts attention. Vast numbers of apparently abandoned children roam the urban streets of many South American nations, and even in the Soviet Union there is a

these are "false clues" to the frequency and importance of abandonment today, the researcher might be tempted to discount similar tales from premodern societies, even when recorded as "facts."[15] But this would be a mistake. Most modern reports are actually good evidence of what they purport to show: remarkable individual incidents, possibly factual, but certainly unlikely. Not only do the accounts themselves make no suggestion that they are reporting instances of widespread practice; they are predicated on and derive their interest from the singularity of the event. Most ancient references to abandonment, by contrast, give equally clear indication that they concern a common and familiar problem.

---

surprisingly high rate of abandonment (see, e.g., Sophie Quinn-Judge, "The Soviet Union's Unwanted Children," *Christian Science Monitor,* Aug. 14, 1987, pp. 25–26).

15. At least three quite different types of "facts" can often be recognized: "historical," which the writer believed actually happened and related as information (e.g., the sack of Rome by the Vandals); "likely," which he used to impart an aura of reality or verisimilitude in a story, either real or fictional (e.g., the hero puts on his armor before battle); and "wondrous," which is designed to seem marvelous to the audience (e.g., the Virgin Birth: Christian authors and audiences took it as "factual" in premodern Europe, but not at all "likely"—it was precisely its unlikelihood that made it important). Such distinctions are ancient. For example, the pseudo-Ciceronian *Rhetorica ad Herennium* distinguishes comparably among *fabula, historia,* and *argumentum* (ed. Harry Caplan [Cambridge, Mass., 1958] [LCL] 1.8.13, pp. 22–25). The corresponding Greek triad, frequently met, is ἱστορία, πλάσμα, and μῦθος (see, e.g., Sextus Empiricus, *Adv. mathematicos* 1.263, and LSJ s.v. πλάσμα).

It would be naïve to think that ancient and medieval historians recorded "historical" truths, while imaginative writers addressed the "wondrous," or that those attempting to commemorate "historical" events are inherently less likely to stretch the truth than those who compose tales for polemical (e.g., religious) purposes or entertainment. In fact, it is a question of degree only. A historical investigation itself prejudices its findings: no action of the mind is neutral or fails to affect its own representation. All historical writing is fictive in what it chooses to record and explain, just as all fictional writing is historical to the extent that it records and explains human thoughts and feelings. Much history is an effort to make the wondrous seem historical, and nearly all historical writing prior to the twentieth century focuses to a considerable extent on the remarkable rather than the ordinary, for a variety of reasons. The "wondrous," moreover, is not necessarily nonfactual—wondrous events do occur—and is a useful vehicle for conveying accurate information about human culture (at the very least, by implicit contrast with the normal). It is, nonetheless, the "likely" which is of most use to historians, both because of its comparative preponderance as background and because it is, of the three, the least subject to conscious manipulation and distortion. In both historical and fictive writing the involuntary expectations of the audience control it to a large degree: elements that stray too far from these will not function as "likely."

Child abuse is probably both a closer and better parallel. Until the last two decades it was infrequently spoken or written about in the modern West except when some sensational incident brought it briefly to the attention of the public. One might, indeed, conclude on the basis of the proportion of silence to discussion about it that it was a "quicksand problem" or at least a rare event, notable precisely for its singularity. Even now, information about child abuse is erratic and anecdotal, but it strongly suggests that the problem occurs on a wide scale in a large number of homes, and affects a substantial portion of the population.[16] Looking only at the frequency and intuitive likelihood of the data rather than at their content, one might well infer that laws about and mentions of child abuse occur because the theoretical possibility or very rare instance is so horrible that it must be severely provided for, not because it is actually a broad social problem. But it actually is a common social problem, as careful reading of the sources plainly demonstrates.

The "intuitive likelihood" of a phenomenon is itself largely an artifact of historical circumstance. To ancient readers whose knowledge and experience did not extend beyond the temperate regions of the Mediterranean, Procopius's precise description of the seasonal extremes of darkness and light in Scandinavia must have seemed improbable, especially since Procopius himself could offer no convincing explanation for it.[17] Widespread abandonment of children by their parents may seem equally unlikely to residents of modern industrial nations, accustomed to economies of surplus, reasonably effective and widely available contraception, and a general acceptance of prenatal family planning or abortion, all of which tend to focus social concern on the responsible rearing of a relatively small number of children.[18] Especially when the tragedy of missing or

16. For a recent study of just one aspect of this problem, see Judith Herman and Lisa Hirschman, *Father-Daughter Incest* (Cambridge, Mass., 1981). An interesting case of the obverse—something believed to be more common than it actually is—is assessed in Peter Schneider, "Lost Innocents: The Myth of Missing Children," trans. Joel Agee, *Harper's Magazine* (Feb. 1987), pp. 47–53.

17. *History of the Wars,* ed. and trans. H. B. Dewing (London, 1968) [LCL] 6.15, p. 416.

18. On the general issue of human reproductivity and population, see A. Coale, "The History of Human Population"; Nathan Keyfitz, "The Population of China"; or Mary Douglas, "Population Control in Primitive Groups," *British Journal of Sociology* 17 (1966) 263–73. Cf. Jack Goody, *Production and Reproduction: A Comparative Study of the Domestic Domain.* For a broad survey of historical change, one might consult D. V. Glass, *Population in History,* or Peter Marcy, "Factors Affecting the Fecundity and Fertility of Historical Populations: A Review," *Journal*

stolen children is poignantly depicted on milk cartons and bus plac-
ards, it may be difficult to imagine circumstances under which parents would voluntarily dispose of children.

In the more precarious ecologies and fragile social structures of
premodern Europe, a couple without such resources or expectations, whose marriage might produce eight to fifteen children in ten
to twenty years, had to face harsher realities.[19] If as many as a third

---

of Family History (hereafter JFH) 6, 3 (1981) 309–26; for overviews of premodern
Europe, see J. C. Russell, *Late Ancient and Medieval Population Control;* Herlihy,
Medieval Households; Flandrin, *Families in Former Times;* Laslett and Wall, *Household
and Family in Past Time;* or Richard Wall, ed., *Family Forms in Historic Europe* (Cambridge, Mass., 1983). Most of these are surveys of demographic data; for studies
attempting to interpret systems and structures of family organization and reproductive strategy see, e.g., Gary Becker, *A Treatise on the Family;* Jack Goody,
The Development of the Family and Marriage in Europe; Alexander Murray, *Germanic
Kinship Structure: Studies in Law and Society in Antiquity and the Early Middle Ages;*
and Herlihy, "The Making of the Medieval Family." More specialized studies can
be traced through these works, and by consulting the journals *Annales de démographie historique* (esp. 1981, "Démographie historique et condition féminine"; and
1983, "Mères et nourrisons"), and *Population Studies: A Journal of Demography,*
which are entirely devoted to such research.

19. Russell (LAMPC, p. xiii) assumes for ancient and medieval Europe an
average of 4.2 children per married woman, but no generalizations are possible
about length of marriage or gross reproductive rate per mother that would be applicable beyond specific time and place. Flandrin (*Families,* p. 53) rejected the
"child per year" assumption of some demographers, but Garden suggests that urban women in Lyons in the seventeenth and eighteenth centuries did bear a child a
year (Garden, *Lyons et les Lyonnais au XVIIIe siècle,* pp. 95–107), although even in
the neighboring countryside there were longer intervals between birth, occasioned
in part by the practice of the urban mothers of sending their children to rural wet-
nurses, who then did not conceive as quickly. Flandrin (*Families,* pp. 53 and 217)
posited death through childbirth (for about 10 percent of mothers), premature sterility, and late marriage as reasons to assume a relatively short period of fertility
among married women during this period, and believed that six to eight was the
normal number of children per married woman, a figure supported by D. Sabean
("Famille et tenure paysanne: aux origines de la guerre des paysans en Allemagne
[1525]," AESC 27 [1972] 903–22), who found that on the eve of the Peasants' War
the average peasant wife after sixteen years of marriage had produced eight children, of whom five survived to age fifteen. Volker Hunecke ("Les enfants trouvés,"
pp. 21–23), however, cites many instances of more than a dozen children per
mother only a little farther south in Europe. David Nicholas (*The Domestic Life of a
Medieval City,* p. 151) observes that "the individual conjugal family was a fleeting
phenomenon, for few married couples survived as a unit until their children were
adults." On marriage, see also J. Hajnal, "European Marriage Patterns in Perspective," in *Population in History: Essays in Historical Demography,* ed. D. V. Glass and
D. Eversley (London, 1965), pp. 101–43.

of the infants died,[20] the parents would still be left with more mouths than most people could feed in subsistence economies.[21] Indeed, if the demographer's estimate of 2.2 children per couple[22] is in fact the level of reproduction needed to maintain a stable preindustrial population, six or more children in many households would severely strain whole societies as well as families. Abandonment would provide an obvious solution to these problems and to others as well—for example, the need to adjust the sex ratio of offspring to meet difficulties of inheritance or the marriage market.[23] By contrast, some percentage of married couples—between 10 and 25 percent[24]—in the same society would lack any children due to infertility or high infant mortality, or would desire a child of a specific gender. They would be likely to rear abandoned children, and awareness of such prospective adopters could influence decisions by fertile couples with more offspring than they could support.

In fact, it is not necessary to imagine such scenarios or to draw on the trust of Procopius's audience to argue for the *possibility* of massive abandonment, since it can be empirically demonstrated in

20. Infant mortality rates are particularly dependent on temporal and geographic variables: see pp. 47–48, below. Family size is impossible to express even for a given time and place without careful attention to subgroups within the population, and enormous variations can take place within a few miles or years: Laslett (*Household and Family*) shows an average of 4.73 persons per household in early modern England, but this comprises a range from 7.22 per household in some areas to 3.63 in others, and is therefore almost meaningless in terms of understanding the dynamics of individual family life. Herlihy's figures for Florence vary by nearly a hundred percent within a little over a century (3.8 per household in 1427, 5.66 in 1552).

21. Or too many heirs for any but the very rich in societies with partible inheritance (division among heirs): on the role of inheritance in abandonment, see pp. 318–21. Even parents who could afford many children might find it onerous to forego conjugal relations, as most Western societies expected, again and again during a nursing period of two or three years after each child.

22. See sources cited in note 18.

23. The biological male-to-female ratio of births is 1.05 (Coale, "History," p. 43), but many factors, both biological and social, can alter this, from the timing of intercourse (see, e.g., Susan Harlap, "Gender of Infants Conceived on Different Days of the Menstrual Cycle," *New England Journal of Medicine* 300 [1979] 1445–48, or Marcia Guttentag and Paul Secord, *Too Many Women? The Sex Ratio Question* [Beverly Hills, 1983]) to medical conditions such as *Trichomonas vaginalis* or *bacteroides* (see *Science News* 128, 10 [September 7, 1985], p. 153). Although it is probably fair (if depressing) to say that most premodern European societies have valued male heirs over females, individual couples often desire female children for personal reasons.

24. See, e.g., Goody, *Production*, p. 134.

some periods. The absence of precise demographic data for ancient and medieval Europe makes it impossible to argue that any other age constitutes a particularly apt point of comparison, but it seems reasonable to consider as a point of reference the first century with extensive records, since it was also the last before advances in industrial and agricultural technology could support a much larger population—and before techniques of contraception rendered abandonment less necessary than it had been. Some of the figures available for this period (the eighteenth century) are so startling that they themselves might have inspired my investigation into earlier epochs had I encountered them before the moral mystery which ultimately led me to them.[25]

In Toulouse in the eighteenth century the rate of *known* abandonment as a percentage of the number of *recorded* births varied from a mean of 10 percent for the first half of the century to a mean of 17 percent in the second half, with the final decades consistently above 20 and sometimes passing 25 percent for the whole population of the city. That is, in the late eighteenth century in Toulouse, one child in every four was *known* to have been abandoned.[26] In poor quarters the rate reached 39.9 percent; even in rich parishes the rate was generally around 15 percent.[27] In Lyons between 1750 and 1789 the number of children abandoned was approximately one-third the number of births.[28] During the same period in Paris children *known* to have been abandoned account for between 20 and 30 percent of the registered births.[29] In every city in France in the eigh-

25. For contemporary comparison with another culture the interested reader might consult Angela Kiche Leung, "L'Accueil des enfants abandonnés dans la Chine du Bas-Yangzi aux XVIIe et XVIIIe siècles," *Études chinoises* 4.1 (1985) 15–54.

26. I.e., if the abandoned children were counted at birth or baptism; Wolff (see following note) is not clear about this. If they were not counted, about one in five was abandoned.

27. Wolff, Labrousse, et al., *Histoire de Toulouse,* pp. 338–40.

28. Garden, *Lyons,* p. 85 (Table 2: Births/Baptisms 1750–1785) and p. 86 (Table 3: Children given to hospices, 1750–1789). I have subtracted estimated totals for the years 1786–1789 from the figures in table 3 in making the calculations.

29. This is a very conservative reckoning, based on the cautious analysis of Jean Meyer, "Illegitimates and Foundlings in Pre-Industrial France," pp. 252–53. Giovanni Da Molin ("Les enfants abandonnés dans les villes italiennes aux XVIIIe et XIXe siècles," p. 106) places the number at 40 percent, following the detailed study of Claude Delasselle ("Les enfants abandonnés à Paris au XVIIIe siècle"). P. Guillaume and J.-P. Poussou, *Démographie historique* (Paris, 1970), p. 173, also favor 40 percent.

teenth century where it is known, the rate of abandonment was 10 percent or better.[30] In Florence it ranged from a low of 14 percent of all baptized babies at the opening of the eighteenth century to a high of 43 percent early in the nineteenth. In Milan the opening of the eighteenth century witnessed a rate of 16 percent; by its closing it was 25.[31]

Comparable figures are not available for other nations, although fragmentary evidence suggests very similar urban abandonment rates ranging from 15 to 30 percent of registered births.[32] (The contrast with the twentieth century may be clearer if one considers that fewer than fifty thousand children—1.5 percent of the recorded births—become available for adoption in the United States each year, even though more than two million couples are seeking to adopt.) France and Italy were comparatively prosperous countries:

30. This is evident, e.g., in Meyer's essay (see preceding note), although it requires careful reading to elicit the figures. Meyer fails to distinguish bastards (who were not necessarily abandoned) from abandoned children in some contexts, and in others distinguishes foundlings from either legitimate or illegitimate children left in hospices, giving a misleading impression of the number of children—legitimate and illegitimate—"abandoned" in this sense. The rate of "abandonment" as defined in the present study, regardless of legitimacy, was, according to Meyer, 10 percent even in St. Malo, which had exceptionally low rates of illegitimacy and abandonment. For more recent work, see, e.g., Jean-Pierre Bardet, "Enfants abandonnés et enfants assistés à Rouen dans la seconde moitié du XVIIIe siècle," *Sur la population française au XVIIIe et au XIXe siècles: Homages à Marcel Reinhard* (Paris, 1973) 19–47; P.-F. Aleil, "Enfants illégitimes et enfants abandonnés à Clermont dans la seconde moitié du XVIIIe siècle," *Cahiers d'histoire* 21 (1976) 307–33; Sonoko Fujita, "L'Abandon d'enfants légitimes à Rennes à la fin du XVIIIe siècle," ADH (1983) 151–62; Carlo Corsini, "L'Enfant trouvé: Note de démographie differentielle," ADH (1983) 95–102.

31. Da Molin, "Enfants," pp. 105–6. For more detail, see Da Molin, *L'Infanzia abbandonata in Italia nell'età moderna: Aspetti demografici di un problema sociale* (Bari, 1981), and Carlo Corsini, "Materiali per lo studio della famiglia in Toscana nei secoli XVII–XIX: gli Esposti," *Quaderni storici* 11, 33 (1976) 998–1052.

32. María Carbajo Isla, "Primeros resultados cuantitativos de un estudio sobre la población de Madrid (1742–1836)," *Moneda y Crédito* 107 (1968), pp. 79–80, finds that admissions to Madrid's Inclusa foundling hospital ranged from a low of 14.1 percent of recorded baptisms in the city in 1765 to 26.2 percent during the period 1801–1807. Cf., e.g., Hunecke; León Carlos Alvarez Santaló, *Marginación social y mentalidad en Andalucía occidental: Expósitos en Sevilla (1613–1910)* (Seville, 1980); Joan Sherwood, "El niño expósito: cifras de mortalidad de una inclusa del siglo XVIII," *Anales del Instituto de Estudios madrileños* 18 (1981) 299–312; Tomás Eiras Roel, "La Casa de expósitos del Real Hospital de Santiago en el siglo XVIII," *Boletín de la Universidad Compostelana* 75–76 (1967–68) 295–355; Ruth McClure, *Coram's Children: The London Foundling Hospital in the Eighteenth Century.*

there is no reason to suspect that their populations were particularly unable to support their offspring.[33]

Moreover, I have emphasized the words "known" and "recorded" because all of these numbers were obtained by comparing records of children admitted to foundling hospitals with official registers of births or baptisms. It is virtually certain that the numbers do not represent all the children abandoned. There is every reason to suspect that, owing to the very nature of child abandonment, secrecy would in many cases disguise it and distort the numbers downward.[34] (This may be partly offset, however, by the fact that birth and baptismal records were probably also underrepresentative, and for similar reasons: parents would not report the child's birth or have him baptized, either out of shame or fear of interference if they subsequently abandoned him, or simply because in most of Europe it was customary to pay a priest to baptize.)[35] Some

33. But d'Angeville, using the records of foundling hospitals, estimated the national rate at 3.5 percent of all births: Adolphe d'Angeville, *Essai sur la statistique de population française, considerée sous quelques-uns de ses rapports physiques et moraux.*

34. Motives and causes for abandonment in early modern Europe varied according to time and place, and the evidence is unreliable, since information about the parents is available only for a very small percentage of abandoned children. Various attempts have been made to correlate aspects of the food supply—such as urban grain prices—with rates of abandonment (e.g., Alvarez Santaló, as above, note 32, although he also adduces plague [p. 51] and other factors; compare the argument of Delasselle, note 29, above). D'Angeville (p. 32) felt that legitimate children comprised a very substantial proportion of the exposed, whereas Meyer (p. 253) estimated that in Paris in the nineteenth century, 83 percent of foundlings were bastards; in other cities he thought the figure closer to 60 percent. Wolff et al. reject the possibility that most of the abandoned in Toulouse were illegitimate, and regard the legitimate poor as a more likely source for most (pp. 338–40), and Hunecke also thinks that most children abandoned in the nineteenth century were legitimate offspring of impoverished parents (e.g., pp. 9–10). Hunecke's opinion is particularly persuasive because his documents allow verification in many cases of the identity of the parents, and show that many married couples in Milan abandoned not only one but several children (p. 21), sometimes reclaiming a few. In one of his cases a man abandoned six of the seven children he had with his first wife and all five of the children he and his second wife produced, although she subsequently tried to reclaim some; another man abandoned eleven of his twelve legitimate children (born in thirteen years of marriage!): pp. 21–23. Legitimacy was probably of less concern among the very poor, whose liaisons were often irregular to begin with, and they may have constituted the largest group of abandoning parents. During periods of great social stress—widespread famine, plague—illegitimacy would presumably be a minor factor occasioning abandonment.

35. Failure to baptize abandoned children was a substantial moral problem in the High Middle Ages: see chapters 9 and 11, below.

percentage of children would have been abandoned without being
sent to a foundling hospital, and would therefore not appear in such
statistics.[36]

Even if these figures represent a high point for early modern Europe,[37] they are nonetheless significant, both as indication of what a

36. The sources themselves provide abundant evidence that they are not precise. Meyer (p. 255) acknowledges that before the decree of 1779 (which prohibited transportation of foundlings) perhaps one quarter of the children abandoned in Rennes failed to appear in the town's statistics, although he then neglects to take this into account in any of his numerical projections. See Hunecke (p. 21) on the inability of police and hospital officials to know how many children parents had abandoned, even though elsewhere Hunecke takes hospital records as precise and complete. Garden (p. 85, n. 4) acknowledges that the apparently detailed birth records of Lyons can be quite misleading. Of the children admitted to the Hôtel-Dieu there the baptismal status of two-thirds was unknown (p. 85): hence they might well not have been registered anywhere if they had not entered the hospital. Santaló found that only 30 percent of the children admitted to the Casa Cuna of Seville in the eighteenth century had documents: the rest would have left no trace at all if not received at the home. An eighteenth-century delegate in Fougères told an *intendant* that there were only thirty to thirty-five foundlings a year in the town, but that "three times more go to Paris" (Meyer, p. 255). "Going to Paris" did not necessarily mean being processed through any official channel and clearly distorted the town's own statistics severely. Meyer, p. 261: "The enquiry [of 1779] also revealed the commerce in abandoned children in the north of the country. . . . These children came mostly to Paris where they were sometimes resold or redirected to the country. . . ." This was true also in Italy: see Da Molin, "Enfants," p. 107.

37. There is no doubt that the rate of *recorded* abandonment increased in France and Italy throughout the eighteenth century (see, e.g., Meyer and Da Molin; also, *inter alia,* Jean-Claude Peyronnet, "Les enfants abandonnés et leurs nourrices à Limoges au XVIIIe siècle," and Jean-Claude Perrot, *Génèse d'une ville moderne: Caen au XVIIIe siècle* [Paris, 1975] 2.846–53). But there is considerable doubt about whether an increase in the official rate corresponds to a quantitative change or simply to an improvement in regulation and recording. Even if the rates for the period 1750–1850 were much higher than those for the previous hundred years, it would not be clear that this represented an "increase" over a "normally" lower rate, since prior to the seventeenth century there is enormously less quantifiable data, and after it, changing conditions render comparison meaningless. (Indeed, it may be unrealistic to evaluate any rates apart from particular historical conditions.) Contemporary social reformers found the rates unacceptably high, as might be expected, but apart from discussion of the statistics themselves there is little indication of a general perception that abandonment was more common than it had been previously: for example, lurid accounts in newspapers focused on the rate of mortality in hospices for abandoned children rather than on the rates of abandonment. In debates over foundling hospitals, which were perceived to be part of the problem, it was frequently argued that to remove the hospices would result in massive infanticide or anonymous abandonment—i.e., both sides assumed that the rate itself would remain more or less constant. By contrast, most of the ferment in Spain

reasonably prosperous society might experience or tolerate in the absence of effective means of contraception, and as counterpoise to the incredulity the subject provokes when viewed from the peculiar vantage of the twentieth century. This incredulousness is especially pronounced, and misdirected, in relation to early modern art and literature.[38] Modern audiences enjoy as an imaginative contrivance the scene in *Le Nozze di Figaro* (act 3) in which Figaro suddenly discovers that Marcellina and Bartolo are his long-lost mother and father. The moment is ironic, but the power of its cynical humor derives from a bleak *reality* of the society for and about which it was composed, not from its improbability: Mozart's opera and the Beaumarchais play on which it was based[39] were written during the

---

during the same period focused on efforts to utilize the human resources the foundling homes represented: see, e.g., Tomás de Montalvo, *Práctica y política de expósitos* (Granada, 1701) and Pedro Joaquín de Murcia, *Discurso político sobre la importancia y necesidad de los hospicios, casas de expósitos y hospitales que tienen todos los Estados y particularmente España* (Madrid, 1798).

38. If the eighteenth century experienced a steady increase in abandonment, as some have argued (see preceding note), was this the result of greater fecundity, a decrease in ability or willingness of parents to rear their children, social catastrophe, or some interaction of all three? In Lyons the fecundity rate fell from 4.32 children per household in 1700 to 4.02 during mid-century, to 3.42 during the decade 1776–86 (Garden, p. 83); such a drop could, in fact, be largely explained by the abandonment of children at a rate of 20 to 30 percent. (On fertility rates generally during this period, see, in addition to the works cited in note 18, above, Marcel Lachiver, "Fécondité légitime et contraception dans la région parisienne," in *Hommage à Marcel Reinhard* [cited in note 30, above] 383–401; Edward Shorter, "Female Emancipation, Birth Control, and Fertility in European History," AHR [June 1973] 605–40; E. A. Wrigley and R. S. Schofield, "English Population History from Family Reconstitution: Summary Results, 1600–1799," *Population Studies* 37 [1983] 157–84, an update and summary of their *The Population History of England* [London, 1981]. The older article by Wrigley, "Family Limitation in Pre-Industrial England," *Economic History Review* 1 [1966] 82–109, is also still useful.) Social and economic conditions alone might have induced more parents to abandon children in 1780 than in 1680, or the expansion of public facilities for abandoned children might have inspired more abandonment, as contemporary appeals to terminate state support of foundling homes suggest (e.g., d'Angeville, pp. 31–37, an impassioned plea to close French foundling hospitals). But it is also likely that improved public assistance simply made the matter more open and recognizable, and that the basic problem had long existed and was previously handled without public awareness or intervention. (And it is not an either/or proposition: rates of abandonment may have varied as well as techniques of recording, and both may have been affected by the presence or absence of foundling homes.)

39. *Le Mariage de Figaro,* act 3, scene 16.

second half of the eighteenth century, when one of every three or four children was abandoned in many French, Italian, and Spanish cities.[40] Figaro naïvely believes that he was stolen by bandits from noble parents, but contemporary audiences, knowing the realities of abandonment, doubtless saw a grim humor in his delusion: his mother and father were unmarried, and he had been conveniently outfitted with symbols of his status and an identifying mark noted before the "theft."[41] Nor is it an unlikely detail that a child would be abandoned by prosperous persons as opposed to the desperate poor: Jean-Jacques Rousseau abandoned all five of his children to foundling homes, not even bothering to keep a record of their birth dates.[42]

40. In the countryside the rate was lower, although precise data are wanting and the known interaction between country and city greatly complicates efforts to make distinctions: poor girls came to the city to have illegitimate children, or shipped newborns to city hospitals, but both parents and officials also shipped children out of major cities to nurse, sometimes abandoning them in the process. "Of the 13,000 to 14,000 foundlings registered each year in Lyons, over 6,000 came not from the Département du Rhône in which the city lies but from the Département de l'Ain" (Meyer, p. 253); Hunecke considers that thirty to forty percent of the children abandoned in Paris were actually from the provinces (p. 4). Such complications make it very difficult to assess the apparent difference between rural and urban rates of abandonment, as well as comparatively low national figures such as the 3.5 percent given by d'Angeville for France as a whole. On the sending of children out to nurse, see Meyer, pp. 260–62, and Trexler, treated below.

41. For the leaving of tokens with children even at foundling hospitals, see below, p. 418.

42. See note 1, above, where Rousseau boasted of this. He subsequently regretted it, however: later in the *Confessions* (Book 12, p. 702) he admitted that this action weighed so heavily on him that in *Émile* (Book 1) he made what amounted to a public confession, and he admonished his readers that "He who cannot fulfill the duties of a father has no right to become one. No poverty, no career, no human consideration can dispense him from caring for his children and bringing them up himself." The reference to career was especially pointed, since his profession as a poorly paid but important writer was one of his justifications for abandoning his children. Admirers have tried to argue that (1) the children were not actually his, (2) he did not abandon as many as five, or (3) he did not abandon any at all—the story was a "parable." No modern scholars take this last defense seriously, and the first is completely unprovable: Rousseau himself clearly did not doubt that they were all his, so it would make no moral difference in any case. Arguments about the second arise from the fact that his friends were uncertain about how many children he had, and Rousseau himself only mentioned four specific birthdates. But in a letter of June 12, 1761 (*Correspondence générale,* ed. Théophile Dufour [Paris, 1924] 6.146–49) he admitted that he had kept no record of their birthdates, so it is hardly surprising that his friends should have been somewhat ill-informed. In this

Child abandonment looms large in early modern culture, from comic recognition in Mozart to the poignant setting for the Dublin Foundling Hospital version of Handel's *Messiah,* from Spanish picaresque novels to Fielding's *Tom Jones.* It is a curious turn of history that the difficulties of conjugal life and childrearing have been so profoundly eased during the twentieth century that the dark backdrop they provided for audiences of previous ages has come to seem comic fancy to viewers in more fortunate circumstances.

Like a beleaguered detective—or a fortunate one, depending on one's point of view—I thus discovered that I had not one but many mysteries to contend with. Abandonment on a wide scale was clearly a possibility, judging from the evidence of the eighteenth century; but this hardly demonstrated that it was in fact common among ancient and medieval Europeans, whose world was so profoundly different from that of their early modern descendants. Would the evidence, when gathered, collated, and carefully analyzed, indicate that it was a familiar reality for them, accidentally or deliberately omitted from historical records, or would it show that it was a "quicksand problem" employed mainly for artistic purposes? If they did abandon their children, what became of them? How did neighbors, civil and religious institutions, and the parents and children themselves feel about it? Beneath these were even larger areas of uncertainty: Were the shape and structure of the family significantly different in premodern Europe? Was it possible to obtain records of something inherently clandestine? What was (and is) the relationship between the kinds of evidence that do survive—that is, to what extent can historians rely on literary records?

Some of these are classic components of detective stories: a single mystery which develops into several related ones, shadowy characters who turn out to be other than they seem, a struggle to uncover evidence deliberately obscured by those with something to hide, and the problem of distinguishing false clues from real ones. In fictional mysteries all of the important details are eventually dis-

letter he asks his friend Mme. de Luxembourg to try to locate the eldest child, a girl whose birthdate he can recall only within a couple of years, but whose swaddling clothes he had marked before giving her up, retaining a copy of the mark. Finding her was, of course, impossible, since the foundling hospitals of Paris accepted in excess of four thousand children a year.

closed; the climax reveals everything necessary to convince the authorities—and, more importantly, the reader—that the guilty party and his motive and method have been correctly identified. In real life this is often not the case: actual judicial truth is rarely unmistakable and satisfying. Most judges and juries must content themselves with probabilities and "reasonable doubt." Historians have, to some extent, a choice in the matter: they can arrange their material so that the questions they posed are all answered, the necessary facts all presented, and all doubt apparently resolved; or they can simply write down the results of their investigation, propose their interpretation of the facts, and leave the reader to judge the merits and demerits of the case.

I do not pretend that the following pages provide satisfying answers to all the questions I set out to investigate. Uncertainties remain; new facts will come to light; different judges will interpret my findings in different ways. Fortunately for the historian, the court to which his evidence is submitted has no fixed term; interesting cases can be argued before it indefinitely. The jury can remain out for as long as it takes to gather the requisite data and come to a sound decision. Nor is there a prohibition of double jeopardy: the historian can watch with delight or consternation as the case is tried and retried by others, who may prove his hunches right or wrong, untangle knots he could not, set aside his evidence as inadmissible, or call surprise witnesses to the stand. If the original motivation was simply a desire to get to the bottom of a mystery, future revelations will bring satisfaction and delight.

WORDS AND NUMBERS

In reporting his findings a good investigator must separate what is material to the case from what is not: too many extraneous or unimportant details becloud rather than clarify a sound case. Almost no ancient or medieval source is genuinely irrelevant to a subject as extensive in time and space as the family in ancient and medieval Europe, and studies of demography and the family now appear at a pace so rapid that several journals are devoted exclusively to them.[43] Of this vast literature, both ancient and modern, I

43. E.g., *The History of Childhood Quarterly, The Journal of Family History,* and *Annales de Démographie Historique,* in all of which articles of relevance to this study will likely have appeared between the time it goes to press and its actual publication.

have reported only a sampling. Many potentially apposite sources have had to be given short shrift, some ignored.[44] Were it even possible to locate and present every strand of relevant evidence, the effect on the reader would be stupefaction rather than illumination.

I have tried, however, to provide depth as well as breadth, and this has occasioned some difficult choices. I have addressed the Jewish tradition, for example, during the first centuries of the Christian era, when Jewish influence on Christianity was still pronounced and when Jewish writing, often reflecting general conditions in Mediterranean cities, constitutes a valuable part of the social record. To pursue Jewish legal and theological literature through the many changes and singular vicissitudes experienced by the Jewish communities of the Middle Ages would greatly enlarge, complicate, and alter this study; only a few points of comparison with the Jews of later periods are therefore offered. Similarly, Norse-Icelandic legal and literary traditions are adduced as a focal point for investigating abandonment in medieval Scandinavia: Swedish, Danish, and Finnish materials might also have been relevant, but to sustain a detailed analysis of their differences and similarities would have completely shifted the focus of the work as a whole. Abandonment was so widespread in premodern Europe, and the subject has attracted so little previous attention, that a single survey cannot do justice to its fullness and variety.

It has been my aim to present my sampling of the evidence in a brief, manageable, and clear form. To offset the inevitably distorting effect of the selection process, I have also tried to record findings and investigative techniques as distinct from conclusions, so that the reader can formulate a different interpretation of the case without having to repeat my labor. For example, I do not discern a valuable division between "fictional" and "historical" sources, as noted in the preceding discussion, but recognizing that some other scholars do rely on such distinctions, I have attempted to separate materials drawn from traditional historical sources (e.g., law codes, narrative accounts, epigraphy) from analysis of abandonment in imaginative literature. For two periods (imperial Rome and the

---

44. Moreover, this book could have been made much larger without increasing its value proportionally. A survey of the use of the theme of the abandoned child in spiritual writings of the Middle Ages, for example, would yield many instances but few insights. Similarly, although a much more detailed description of the later medieval foundling homes—their officials, their operations, their funding, their residents—would have been appropriate, it would simply have repeated material already available in several modern monographs.

High Middle Ages) the literary material is so abundant that this could be done in chapters focusing individually on "history" and "literature," though the separation cannot be neat. For other periods the fictional sources are less plentiful, and have been adduced within each chapter as complements to other information. The point of this strategy is not to make a statement about the relative reliability or accuracy of the two types of sources, but simply to facilitate viewing the subject from two somewhat distinct perspectives, each inspiring its own particular modes of analysis.

All translations in text and notes, unless otherwise identified, are my own, and I have reproduced the original language in all cases where the translation was significantly ambiguous or difficult. Because language itself determines understanding to an almost irresistible degree, I have devoted considerable attention to etymological and philological questions, attempting to expose conceptual frameworks hidden behind or complicating the function of language—my own as well as that of others.

For example, "abandonment," as used here, refers to the voluntary relinquishing of control over children by their natal parents or guardians, whether by leaving them somewhere, selling them, or legally consigning authority to some other person or institution.[45] This is a modern concept, both more and less precise than the rubrics employed in ancient and medieval documents, which usually referred to specific modes of abandonment rather than the general phenomenon. The closest equivalent to "abandonment" in Greek is ἔκθεσις; in Latin, *expositio*.[46] These terms are commonly

45. The last is the most difficult category of discrimination, and the one used least frequently hereafter. Indenturing could be regarded as consigning authority to another person, as could marrying a young daughter to another family in a distant location. I have not treated these or similar phenomena as "abandonment," although I have tried to adduce them as close parallels when they help to clarify the context of other parental actions. For an example of the consigning of authority that does seem like abandonment, see the discussion on "fostering" among Visigoths, in chapter 4, below.

46. Other Greek terms include synonyms such as ἀποτίθημι, "put out"; more intense or specific words, such as ἐκβάλλω, "throw out"; expressions for specific modes of abandonment, such as ἐγχυτρίζω, "to expose in earthenware vessels"; or designations of a general kind, like χαμεύρετος, "lying on the ground" (used to translate *expositus* in Justinian's Novel 153). For a detailed discussion of Attic usage, somewhat earlier than the materials treated below, see Mark Golden, "Demography and the Exposure of Girls at Athens," pp. 330–31. Latin also employs terms for "toss out," like *projicere* (Seneca the Elder, *Controversiae* 10.4.16, where it is contrasted with *exponere* although in reference to abandonment), *abicere* (e.g.,

translated as "exposure," but this conveys a sense of risk or harm—"exposure" to danger, dying of "exposure"[47]—which is absent from the ancient terms. Whether "exposed" children actually died as a consequence of *expositio* is one of the historical mysteries addressed below; linguistically, the Latin and Greek words were not associated with injury or risk. Both meant simply "putting out" or "offering"; "exposition" (e.g., as a display, or as the elaboration of an argument) is closer to their connotations than "exposure" in the sense of "suffering" (which was *patientia* in Latin; πάθος in Greek). English "exposure" has a related meaning only in regard to publicity: "exposure" of the facts, or "exposure" for a celebrity. "Exposing" a child was simply placing him outside the home, usually in a public place, where he would be noticed.[48] Other ancient and medieval languages exhibit comparable expressions for anonymous abandonment of this sort, usually words for "putting outside" or "taking out."[49] I have rendered these words either literally or as "exposing," which should be understood as a particular form of the broader phenomenon "abandonment."[50]

Modern languages also exhibit nuances and conceptual variations which both reflect and determine attitudes and expectations

---

Suetonius, *Claudius* 27); much earlier one finds a bland "put out," or "hand over": *prodere* (Terence, *Hecyra* 672).

47. The two concepts often occur together, utterly conflated: when Barbara Hanawalt (*The Ties That Bound*), in her treatment of infanticide and abandonment, writes that "none of the seventy-eight babies were described as dying from drowning or exposure" (p. 102), it is impossible to know precisely what she means.

48. Note the contrast in Seneca (above, note 46) between "exposing" in this sense and "tossing out" in a sense closer to the modern misprision: "quos parentes sui proiciunt magis quam exponunt." Although in some of the Romance languages the connotations of "exposed" in relation to children have become focused on the act of abandonment rather than the possibility of recovery, in others the original connection is still apparent. The Catalan *Pal·las Diccionari català il·lustrat* (Barcelona, 1962) defines *expòsit* as "a newborn left in a public place so that someone will rescue him" (p. 280).

49. E.g., in Old Norse the normal expression is *barna útburðr,* "carrying out a child."

50. Herlihy (*Medieval Households*) writes of "exposing or abandoning unwanted babies" without explaining the difference. Jean Meyer ("Illegitimates and Foundlings in Pre-Industrial France," in *Bastardy and Its Comparative History,* pp. 249–63) uses "abandoned" to describe children left anonymously, as opposed to legitimate children deposited by parents in foundling homes or illegitimate children left by the mother.

about abandonment. English and French conventionally designate abandoned children in terms of their recovery—"foundling," *enfant trouvé* ("found child")[51]—while Italian and Spanish focus on the abandonment—*gettatello* ("tossed out"),[52] *expósito* ("exposed"). In ordinary speech the distinctions may not be crucial; it is clear enough what is at issue. But they can be important to careful analysis: the difference between the number of children "exposed" and the number "found" might be quite significant.[53] I have tried to convey as precise a sense of the original as possible in such cases through accurate translation, explanation of context, and, where necessary, accompanying notes.

"Child" is itself not an uncomplicated term. Among ancient and modern writers, conceptions of "childhood" have varied widely, posing considerable lexical problems for investigators. Even the bases of distinction change: sometimes the root concept arises from chronological boundaries (to age twenty-one, to age seven, etc.), sometimes from associated aspects such as innocence, dependency, mental incapacity, or youthful appearance. Should "the abandonment of children" be understood to apply to those whom ancient and medieval writers regarded as "children" or to those we would so designate? Sending a nine-year-old daughter to be married in a distant place or apprenticing an eight-year-old son to a knight in another county might constitute abandonment in the eyes of a modern parent, while to the medieval father or mother it could have

51. In Middle High German the nouns *fundeling* or *funtkind* for abandoned children also emphasize this outcome, and medieval Hebrew designates such children in terms of their being "gathered": אסופי; Arabic has both *laqīt*, "found," and the Qur'anic "children of the way." Sometimes medieval French used *enfant geté*, but this was uncommon.

52. There is also an Italian term *trovatello*, but it is both less common and less ancient than *gettatello* or *esposito*, the classic nouns for abandoned children. Da Ponte's *trovato* translates Beaumarchais's *trouvé*.

53. Technically, an orphan could be an *enfant trouvé*, so that figures for *enfants trouvés* might be misleading for a study of abandonment. In fact, the term is rarely used of orphans unless they were abandoned by those who were supposed to care for them. Early modern French sources (and historical writings based on them) sometimes distinguish between *enfants trouvés* and *enfants illégitimes*, although logically the former category would seem to include the latter if such children were abandoned and found. Bernard-Benoît Remacle (*Des Hospices d'enfans* [sic] *trouvés en Europe, et principalement en France*) employs *enfant trouvé* for children whose parents are not known, and *enfant abandonné* for those whose parents are known but not locatable (cf. Meyer, as above, note 50).

been a normal, responsible parental gesture—"childhood" being over at this point in the eyes of contemporaries.[54]

Two sets of problems overlap: the semantic variability of terms for children and childhood, and historical changes in social structures and expectations regarding both. Each deserves a separate study, although they cannot be treated adequately in isolation. They are often inseparable. Terms for "child," "boy," and "girl," for example, are regularly employed to mean "slave" or "servant" in Greek, Latin, Arabic, Syriac, and many medieval languages.[55] This is both a philological subtlety and a social one. In modern Western democracies everyone of sound mind achieves independent adult status on attaining a prescribed age: the primary distinction in social and political capacity is between children and adults, and everyone normally occupies each position in succession. But during most of Western history only a minority of grown-ups ever achieved such independence: the rest of the population remained throughout their lives in a juridical status more comparable to "childhood," in the sense that they remained under someone else's control—a father, a lord, a master, a husband, etc. It is tempting to infer from this linguistic connection that literal children frequently occupied posi-

54. Many societies establish chronological limits for parental authority, but few seem to imagine that the parent-child relationship actually terminates: "Is there an age at which one ceases to be a son?" (Seneca the Elder, *Controversiae* 3.3).

55. Syriac, for example, has two plurals for the adjective "young": one (*telāye*) refers to boys or children and the other (*telayā*) to slaves or servants. Pollux's second-century (A.D.) *Onomasticon* of fourth-century (B.C.) Athenian usage notes that "slaves are called children [παῖδες] among the Athenians even if they are older" (ed. E. Beche [Leipzig, 1900], 3.78, p. 179): on this see Mark Golden, "*Pais*, 'Child,' and 'Slave,'" *L'Antiquité classique* 54 (1985) 91–104. Latin employs overlapping concepts related to status and age of unusual, almost impenetrable, richness and complexity. *Pueri* designates children (either free or servile) and slaves; *liberi,* children (usually free) and the free. (There is no single widely accepted explanation of the latter relationship.) *Filii* could be either free or slave. *Familia* refers to all those members of a household dependent on its head, including *liberi* who will ultimately be *sui juris.* Nonetheless, *famuli* would normally apply only to those who could not be free themselves. For a sampling of literary overlap of these concepts in classical Greek, see LSJ, s.v. παῖς; for classical Latin, OLD, s.v. *puer.* This usage was conveyed to the Middle Ages through the Christian scriptures as well as Roman legal and literary muniments: in Matthew 14.1, for example, the Vulgate uses *puer* (Greek παῖς) for a slave, although where Galatians 4.22 uses παιδίσκη for "maidservant" Jerome used *ancilla,* and he resolved the ambiguity of Matthew 9.15 (υἱοὶ τοῦ νυμφῶνος) in favor of the less likely interpretation *filii* (cf. KJV and JB interpretations as servants of some sort).

tions of servitude, but the verbal correlation is more likely related to the fact that the social roles themselves (slave, serf, servant, etc.) were those of "children" in terms of power and juridical standing, whether the person discharging them was young or old. Words for "children" designate servile adults well into the High Middle Ages, and it is often impossible to be sure, without adequate context, whether the appellation is based on age or status, or both.[56] ("Boy" is still used in English in the United States to disparage an adult male, particularly as a racial slur. In premodern Europe it was not precisely an insult, but it was a negative and disempowering observation.)

Connotations even further removed from biological relation also tangle the strands of meaning. In most Western cultures objects of sexual or romantic desire are addressed or referred to in language associated with youth, childhood, or even infancy ("baby," "cutie pie," "sweetie," etc.).[57] Terms for "boy" and "girl" are standard designations of the beloved in ancient romantic literature as well, even when they are not chronologically appropriate,[58] and this

---

56. Sometimes *pueri* are clearly slaves, as one can often deduce in Gregory of Tours (see the *Index verborum* in the MHG edition s.v. *puer, puella*) or in Boniface of Mercia (MHG, Epp., 3.1 [Berlin, 1892], no. 99, p. 387); but there can also be exquisite ambiguity. Cf. Caesar of Heisterbach, *Dialogus miraculorum* 12.42: "servi vero sive pueri . . ." Very occasionally contemporaries recognized the need to resolve such ambiguity, e.g., Eusebius, *De martyribus Palaestinae* 9.2 (PG 20.1491): ὑπομαζίοις παισί—apparently as distinct from παισί as slaves (though related even here to the οἰκέταις). Even in legal documents, where one might anticipate precision, such terms are often loose or misleading: a French royal remission of 1476 mentions "jeunes enfans, nouvellement mariez," who are called "povres jeunes hommes" in the same sentence (Archives nationales, Register JJ 204, 170, folio 106, published in *Recueil des Documents concernant le Poitou contenus dans les Registres de la Chancellerie de France*, in *Archives Historiques du Poitou*, vol. 41, p. 139).

57. Doubtless in large measure because (1) love is envisioned as a preoccupation principally of young, unmarried members of society; (2) the young are thought to possess in greater degree the physical attributes that inspire love: Agathon in Plato's *Symposium* argues this explicitly as the reason that Love is himself a young god; (3) the kind of intense tenderness associated with erotic love is also inspired by babies.

58. Παῖς, "child," or παιδικά, "childlike, relating to children," are the normal designations for the male object of male sexual desire in Greek, which many historians have interpreted to mean that homosexual relations normally involved an adult "lover" and a younger "beloved." These terms are clearly conventional, however, and, at least by late antiquity, often apply to adults (e.g., Dio Cassius, *Roman History* 59.11.1; Plutarch, *Dialogue on Love* 9, 11, etc.; Pseudo-Lucian 36), so this is a questionable inference, even when buttressed by pictorial representations of male couples, which normally depict one partner as a youth. In modern homo-

usage persists in the Western tradition throughout the period of this analysis,[59] rendering many words for "youth" or "child" less clear than they might at first appear. And in a number of specific social and religious contexts other nonliteral uses of age-related words are important enough to skew interpretation of the category "child" in the original language.[60]

Close lexical analysis of age-related terms is necessary but not sufficient.[61] Words which occur in some writings as specific to a par-

---

erotic art there is also a tendency to portray couples as differentiated according to some easily recognizable polarity, either of age or appearance—experienced with innocent, or dark-haired with blond are especially common—and while such conventions bear some relation to popular fantasies and preferences, they are more directly related to artistic and dramatic schemes, and should certainly not be taken as an indication that such pairings are standard among gay males in the twentieth century. No modern scholars, in any event, would take παῖς in these contexts literally as "child": at the very youngest it refers to adolescents. Those who still doubt might wish to consider whether future historians should take expressions like "my old man" or "hot mama" to indicate widespread intergenerational incest among the American population of the twentieth century.

59. In the twelfth century, Marbod, the bishop of Rennes, uses *puer* of himself apparently as the paired obverse of *amans* in a love poem (PL 171.1717; translated in Boswell, *Christianity*, p. 370; for context, see ibid., pp. 247–49). Aelred of Rievaulx refers to the monk he loves as *puer,* although they are both adults of roughly the same age (*Speculum caritatis,* ed. A. Hoste and H. Talbot [Turnhout, 1971], 1.34.102; for commentary on this relationship, see Boswell, *Christianity,* pp. 221–23). Aelred subsequently says of Simon that he was father, brother, son and friend (104). Of course, age may be disregarded in the opposite direction as well, and in medieval vernacular literature (e.g., Provençal lyric, or Middle High German poetry) even very young lovers are conventionally designated as "lady" or "lord."

60. The layers of complexity in Latin become ponderous. All humans were designated in the Latin Bible as the *pueri* of God (e.g., Isaiah 8:18, Wisdom 12:7, Hebrews 2:13), meaning both "children" and "slaves," drawing deliberately on the conflations underlying the word. Lay brothers living in monasteries were especially apt to be referred to as *pueri,* even if they were adults: see discussion in Ursmer Berlière, "Les Écoles claustrales au Moyen Age," p. 552. And since monasteries might also have slaves, called *pueri,* and children as oblates, also called *pueri,* it can be ferociously difficult to be sure who is meant by *pueri.* Context is often not sufficient to decipher the meaning of the word: see, e.g., the thoroughly ambiguous reference to *puer* in MGH, Epp., 3.1, 5.2.2, p. 204.

61. For studies of medieval terminology, see, *inter alia,* Adolf Hofmeister, "Puer, Iuvenes, Senes: Zum Verständnis der mittelalterlichen Alterbezeichnungen," *Papsttum und Kaisertum, Paul Kehr zum 65 Geburtstag dargebracht,* ed. Albert Brackman (Munich, 1926), pp. 287–316; Joseph de Ghellink, "Iuventus, gravitas, senectus," *Studia mediaevalia in honorem admodum reverendi patris Raymundi*

ticular stage of life will appear in others in much more general or even opposed senses,[62] or a writer may employ them interchangeably.[63] Scholarly discussions of chronological classification are not necessarily tied to social attitudes. Isidore of Seville articulated a categorization that was followed, with variations, by much of the learned literature of the Middle Ages. According to him, up to 6 years constituted infancy; 7 to 13, childhood; 14 to 27, adolescence; 28 to 48, youth; 49 to 76, maturity (*senectus*); and 77 to death, old age. But as an encyclopedist his aim was to have a place for everything and everything in a place.[64] Civil and religious laws

---

Josephi Martin (Bruges, 1948) 39–59; Pierre Riché, "L'Enfant dans le Haut Moyen Age"; Pierre-André Sigal, "Le vocabulaire de l'enfance et de l'adolescence dans les recueils de miracles latins des XIe et XIIe siècles"; Micheline de Combarieu, "Enfance et demesure dans l'épopée médiévale française," *L'Enfant au Moyen Age* (Paris, 1980), pp. 407–17. It would be only a slight oversimplification to say that these studies as a whole report no consistent system of terminology at any period in the Middle Ages. Richard Lyman, "Barbarism and Religion: Late Roman and Early Medieval Childhood" (p. 77), sums up: "the term 'child' seems to refer to anyone, depending on context and literary convention, from infancy to old age." Cf. Mary McLaughlin, "Survivors and Surrogates: Children and Parents from the Ninth to the Thirteenth Centuries," p. 144, nn. 31 and 32. Approaches to concepts of childhood through literary depictions have not been much more successful, with the notable exception of Alexandre-Bidon and Closson, cited below.

62. Plautus uses *adulescens,* usually "adolescent," of an adult slave (*Menaechmi* 1024), and calls a traveling merchant *adulescentulus* (*Cistellaria* 158). Terence characterizes the adult hero of *Heautontimoroumenos* as *adulescens;* Parthenius describes a male old enough to be having sexual relations with women as παῖς (ed. Stephen Gaselee [Cambridge, Mass., 1916] 17; also cf. 32); a *iuvenis* in Apuleius's *Metamorphoses* (10.23–24) is married; Dionysius of Halicarnassus (16.4) uses μειράκιον, "adolescent," of a soldier; Alcuin addresses a drunkard as *puer* (MGH *Poetae* 1.270)—could he actually be a "boy"?

63. Parthenius characterizes a school-aged boy as both παῖς and μειράκιον (ed. Gaselee 7.1–2); Heliodorus uses παῖς, νεανίας, and ἐφηβεύων interchangeably of Cnemon, the hero of his *Aethiopica;* Lucian has characters in his *Lucius* address the hero as τέκνος, νέος, νεανίσκος, μειράκιον, etc. Longus calls Daphnis παῖς, νεανίσκος, and μειράκιον (*Daphnis and Chloe*); Paul the Deacon of Merida uses both *puer* and *adolescens* of the same person at the same time (*De Vita et miraculis patrum Emeritensium,* ed. Henrique Florez, in *España Sagrada* 13 [Madrid, 1782], chap. 5, pp. 348–49; cf. p. 336, where *puer, puerulus,* and *ephoebus* appear to mean the same thing).

64. *Origines* 11.2 (ed. W. M. Lindsay [Oxford, 1911]); cf. Gregory the Great, *Moralia* 11.46, where the same system is outlined, presumably following the received wisdom among Latin lexicographers (e.g., comments in the Digest quoted below). Augustine considered "youth" to last until thirty, after which old age began (*City of God* 22.15). For later discussions, see, e.g., Philippe de Novarre, *Les*

evince a more complex and variegated picture. Among Romans, "minority" extended from puberty, which occurred by statute at fourteen, to age twenty-five. During this period freeborn "minors" had legal capacity to act on their own, although even as adults Romans were not freed from paternal authority.[65] Anglo-Saxon law considered males to be adults at ten, at least in terms of responsibility for their actions;[66] the sixth-century Salic law made this distinction at twelve.[67] Contemporary ecclesiastical laws from the same parts of Europe, however, drew the line between child and adult somewhere between fifteen and twenty, and referred to ten-year-olds as "young children."[68] In Byzantium, although children did not officially become adults until age twenty-five, ecclesiastical law adopted a wide variety of ages as points of reference for moral responsibility, and boys were allowed to marry at fifteen, girls at thirteen.[69] In the long debate in Western Europe over the practice of parents' donating their children to monasteries, one of the few points on which all sides agreed was that by the age of twelve, fe-

---

quatre ages de l'homme, ed. Marcel de Fréville (Paris, 1889) (*Société des anciens textes français* 27) 5.188–92 (pp. 102–65). Michel Salvat ("L'Accouchement dans la littérature scientifique médiévale," in *L'Enfant au Moyen Age,* p. 104) discusses a similar system by Bartholomew the Englishman (early thirteenth century). David Herlihy, "The Generation in Medieval History," *Viator* 5 (1974) 347–64, treats Dante's views and those of other high and later medieval writers. See also discussion in Sigal, "Vocabulaire," p. 144; Riché, "L'Enfant," p. 95 (with further bibliography); and Elizabeth Sears, *The Ages of Man: Medieval Interpretations of the Life Cycle.*

65. On "minority" see, e.g., Dig. 4.4, 26.7.8. For the power of the *paterfamilias,* see discussions in chapters 1 and 2, below.

66. E.g., Laws of Eadric 6, and Laws of Ine 7.2, both in *Laws of the Earliest English Kings.* But by the tenth century, the Laws of Aethelstan draw the line at age twelve, at least in regard to theft: II Aethelstan 1 (ibid., pp. 126–27).

67. *Pactus legis Salicae,* ed. Karl A. Eckhardt (Hannover, 1962) MGH LL 1.41, sec. 24.7.

68. E.g., the Penitential of Cummean (ca. 650) 10.3 (ed. Ludwig Bieler, *The Irish Penitentials* [Dublin, 1963]); cf. Excarpsus Cummeani 2.14 (H. J. Schmitz, *Die Bussbücher und die Bussdisciplin der Kirche* 1.611–45). For "young child" (*puer parvus*), see Penitential of Cummean 10.9. The seventh-century Penitential of Theodore grants boys of fifteen and girls of sixteen or seventeen the power to make decisions (e.g., about entering religious life) without the consent of their parents (2.12.36–37), in John McNeill and Helena Gamer, *Medieval Handbooks of Penance,* p. 211.

69. See H. Antoniadis-Bibicou, "Quelques notes sur l'enfant de la Moyenne Epoque Byzantine," esp. pp. 77–78, and Evelyne Patlagean, "L'Enfant et son avenir dans la famille byzantine," esp. p. 88.

males should be considered responsible for their own decisions, and males by fourteen.[70]

Canon lawyers of the High Middle Ages were divided on the issue of precisely when persons became morally responsible: some favored seven, the age at which children were thought to be able to distinguish right from wrong ("capable of a lie" was the classic formulation) and could consent to marriage; others argued that genuine culpability only accompanied puberty, believed to occur at twelve for females and fourteen for males.[71] Gregory IX, while agreeing that sexual maturity accompanied adolescence and began at about this age, denied that this was the sole locus of moral responsibility or that children differed from adults in regard to "innocence":

> Some are unwilling to attribute sin to children younger than fourteen, when puberty begins. We could accept this if there were no sins other than those associated with the genitals. Who will have the audacity to claim that theft, lies, and deceit are not sins? Childhood is full of these, even if it seems that children should not be punished as older persons.[72]

Males were considered capable of discharging most obligations in twelfth-century England at fifteen.[73] A male "of sixteen winters"

---

70. Arguments to this effect are briefly summarized in Livario Oliger, "De pueris oblatis in ordine minorum," p. 415. For more detailed discussion, see chapters 5 and 8, below.

71. So, e.g., the *Liber Poenitentialis* of Robert of Flamborough, one of the first moral manuals of the thirteenth century to incorporate Gratian's *Decretum*: "The age of discretion—the capacity to lie—is said to occur at age seven; according to others at age fourteen . . ." (2.3.52, p. 86). The text of the *Decretum* cited in support of the first view (2.22.5.14; Friedberg 1.886–87) does not, in fact, mention an age, but seven is given as the earliest age of consent to marriage at 2.30.2 (Friedberg 1.1099–1100).

72. Gregory IX, *Decretalium* 5.23.1 (Friedberg 2.824). For further discussion of canonistic views (and the conclusion that they are not precise), see René Metz, "L'Enfant dans le droit canonique médiéval: Orientations de recherche," in *L'Enfant* 2.9–96, esp. pp. 17–23.

73. E.g., Glanvil and Bracton set this as majority for sokeman; twenty-one remains the majority for military tenants: Glanvil, in *De Legibus Anglie* 7.9; S. E. Thorne, *Bracton on the Laws and Customs of England* 2.250–51. Cf. *Fleta* 1.9. The classic article on "youth" and knighthood is Georges Duby, "The 'Youth' in Twelfth-Century Aristocratic Society." More recently, Stephen Wailes ("The Romance of Kudrun," p. 359) reports on the basis of literary evidence that boys be-

could establish his own household in Iceland by the High Middle Ages; a female had to be twenty.[74] Frederick II's *Constitutions of Melfi* for Sicily set maturity at eighteen—where most modern states would place it[75]—but in the neighboring state of Valencia, twenty was the age of majority.[76] By the later Middle Ages many civil codes differentiated adulthood variously according to context: taxation, criminal responsibility, inheritance, etc. In Castile, for example, seven was the minimum age for betrothal; ten and a half for discerning right from wrong (except in sexual matters); twelve the earliest a girl, and fourteen a boy, could marry; seventeen the age at which one could practice law; and twenty the minimum age to be a judge.[77]

Few of these regulations are derived from Roman law or traditional sources; most appear to reflect functional local ideas of maturation. Law is, nonetheless, by nature formulaic and may not reflect social experience accurately. Literary evidence suggests that Roman males, for example, often experienced puberty later than the age set by their statutes,[78] whereas females were frequently regarded as

---

come knights at about eighteen or twenty, whereas women of the same class begin their adventures (usually erotic) at puberty or even younger. But this may depend on location or literary conventions. In *Jómsvíkinga saga* the Vikings are generally eighteen or twenty, but Vagn leaves home at twelve to join them (chap. 22), and contemporary sagas like *Hrólfs saga Kraka* also show young men leaving home at twelve to seek their fortune as adults, whereas in the later and more chivalric sagas, eight seems to mark the transition to adulthood (see cases cited in Jürg Glauser, *Isländische Märchensagas,* p. 239)—possibly because twelve has come to seem normal and fiction demands the extraordinary.

74. *Laws of Early Iceland: Grágás* 1, p. 126. But to count as an adult laborer a male only had to be twelve: see ibid., sec. 89, p. 150.

75. Title 42 (ed. Jean Huillard-Bréholles, *Historia diplomatica Friderici II* [Paris, 1852–61]; trans. James Powell, *The Liber Augustalis or Constitutions of Melfi* [Syracuse, 1971]).

76. See, e.g., *Furs de València* 2.13.1 (p. 215): "Menor sia dit tro a xx ans, e aquella cosa metexa sia entesa e dita de tot menor, haje muller o no muller." Liability for crime, however, began at seven, the age of discretion according to the law (2.13.6, p. 217). Unmarried sons appear to be minors regardless of age (3.22.4, p. 272), although it seems doubtful whether this really affected their social position. Orphans could manage their own affairs at twelve on much of the Iberian peninsula, regardless of majority statutes for others: see, e.g., *Fuero de Béjar,* pp. 267 and 269.

77. *Las Siete Partidas* 1.16.3, 4.1.6; 3.4.5, 7.2, 16.9; 7.1.9.

78. Chaerea in Terence's *The Eunuch* is able to pass for a eunuch because he has no beard and is apparently prepubescent, although he is sixteen (line 693); Daphnis in Longus's *Daphnis and Chloe* is not bearded at seventeen; in Apuleius's *Metamor-*

suitable objects of erotic desire, and therefore capable of discharging a major "adult" role of their gender, long before menarche.[79] The age of puberty varies not only with individuals but apparently over time in whole populations according to nutrition and other

---

phoses a young man just getting his beard has been the captain of a great band of thieves for some time and has "wasted" Macedonia (7.5). On the other hand, the arrival of the beard may not be a reliable guide; beardlessness is erotically desirable in some cultures, and may be projected onto romantic characters in fiction without conscious implication of age or maturity: a male old enough to be committing adultery with a married woman has no beard and is characterized as a *puer* by Apuleius (*Metamorphoses* 9.16 and 9.22); and Psyche characterizes her husband as a *iuvenis* without a beard (ibid., 5.8 and 5.13, where his cheeks are just like hers). Burchardus de Bellevaux, in *Apologia de barbis* (ed. E. P. Goldschmidt [Cambridge, 1935], p. 32, or, more recently in *Apologiae duae,* ed. R. B. C. Huygens [Turnhout, 1985] [CCCM, 62]) opines in the twelfth century that beards begin to grow in adolescence and that it is characteristic of "youths" ("juvenes") to have beards, but aesthetic attitudes probably affect public perceptions as much as the age of puberty. In high medieval martial epics like the *Song of Roland* or the *Poem of the Cid* a showy beard is a heroic attribute, but in romantic literature beardlessness is often preferred even in warriors: Gahmuret, King Clamide, and Parzival himself are all admired by ladies and praised by the author as beardless in Wolfram von Eschenbach's *Parzival.* The problem is further compounded by the ambiguity of the concept "beardless" in Latin and other medieval languages, as in English: it could apply either to inability to grow a beard or to having shaved, although *imberbis* more commonly implies the former. On the general issue of beards and their significance, see Giles Constable, "Beards in History," pp. 47–150, in *Apologiae duae,* as cited above.

79. Men are sexually attracted to Charicleia in Heliodorus's *Aethiopica,* for example, when she is only seven years old. P. A. Brunt (*Italian Manpower, 225 B.C.–A.D. 14,* pp. 137–38) finds that upper-class Roman girls during the period of his study marry between twelve and fourteen (poor girls much later—perhaps at twenty), even though there are other indications that women were not considered fully grown at this age. (Alimentary foundations for children, for example, supported girls to thirteen or fourteen and boys to eighteen: ibid., p. 137.) By contrast, late teens seem to be the earliest age thought suitable for the marriage of males in the ancient world: see Brunt's discussion for Rome, ibid., and the more general treatment in Sarah Pomeroy, *Goddesses, Whores, Wives, and Slaves: Women in Classical Antiquity.* Aristotle recommended that Greek males marry at thirty-seven and females at eighteen (*Politics* 7.14.6, 1335a), but Mark Golden found that upper-class Athenian men married at around thirty, women between fourteen and eighteen ("Demography and the Exposure of Girls at Athens," pp. 322–23). On early Christian ages of first marriage, see Cyrille Vogel, "L'Age des époux chrétiens au moment de contracter mariage d'après les inscriptions paléo-chrétiennes," *Revue de droit canonique* 16 (1966) 355–66. For other ancient commentary, see, e.g., Ninus, Fragment AII, ed. Stephen Gaselee (in Longus, *Daphnis and Chloe*; and Parthenius [Cambridge, Mass., 1916]).

factors,[80] and psychological maturity responds to an array of variables of almost impenetrable complexity. "Maturity" and "adulthood" are highly subjective concepts, and may be applied to different persons differently by the same speaker. The Greek word ἡλικία, for example, usually refers to "maturity" of strength and judgment in males, but only to the ability to bear children in females.[81] These boundaries are not consistent with each other or with the category "adult" from a modern perspective: a female could become pregnant while still a child from a twentieth-century perspective, and a male might have ceased being a child for quite a time before achieving "maturity."

The concept of "child," in short, is perplexing and analytically inadequate, and in assessing the abandonment of children older than infants, close attention must be paid to historical context to determine whether parents are forfeiting responsibility for a "child" or simply forwarding a young person to the ordinary next stage of life according to contemporary expectations.[82] By and large I have considered as abandoned children persons who were so designated in the sources, whose age at the time of the abandonment corresponded to prevailing notions of childhood, or who appear to have been ten years old or less. But no analytical apparatus can clear away entirely the layers of conceptual and historical debris cover-

80. "Full puberty" (τελεία ἐφηβότης) is thought by Byzantine writers of the High Middle Ages not to occur until eighteen, although their forebears in antiquity had set it at fourteen: see Antoniadis-Bibicou, p. 78. Little work has been done on this problem for the Middle Ages. See the article by Vern Bullough and C. Campbell, "Female Longevity and Diet in the Middle Ages," *Speculum* 55 (1980) 317–25, or, more recently, Bullough, "Age at Menarche: A Misunderstanding," *Science* 213 (July 17, 1981) 365–66, with further bibliography, arguing that menarche (the onset of menstruation, and therefore fertility) during the Middle Ages generally took place between twelve and fourteen. Most of the argument relies on prescriptive regulations, which were probably based on observation in some societies, but are not necessarily applicable to others.

81. So used of Sarah, for example, in Hebrews 11:11; for its more common application to males, ubiquitous in Hellenic literature, see LSJ s.v. ἡλικία.

82. Even more troubling for the historian is the fact that some "children" may not "exist" at all because of their gender: Herodotus describes someone as dying "childless, leaving an only daughter named Gorgo" (5.48: ἀπέθανε ἄπαις, θυγατέρα μόνην λιπών, τῇ ὄνομα ἦν Γοργώ). While it is conceivable that she was adopted, and he meant "no natural children," it is more likely that the force of ἄπαις is "without a son." Abel Hugo reported that in the Limousin in the nineteenth century, mothers without sons would say they had no "children" even if they had several daughters (*La France pittoresque* [Paris, 1835] 1.266).

ing and complicating the recovery of "childhood" as an idea or a phenomenon.

Indeed, it has been argued in the past few decades that there was no concept of "childhood" in premodern Europe, and that parent-child relations in previous ages were for this and other reasons (such as the high infant mortality rate) inherently and categorically different from those in the modern West.[83] This proposal would seem to fit in well with the subject under investigation: if parents did abandon children on a large scale in ancient and medieval Europe, a fundamental difference in affective bonds within the family or in the conceptualization of childhood might provide a valuable explana-

83. The classic statement of this is Philippe Ariès, *L'Enfant et la vie familiale sous l'ancien régime.* Of many assessments by medievalists, one might recommend those of Shulamith Shahar (*The Fourth Estate: A History of Women in the Middle Ages,* esp. p. 236), who contrasts Ariès's theory with a variant by E. LeRoy Ladurie, and that of David Herlihy ("Medieval Children," pp. 110–11), who sagely discounts the views of Ariès. For other replies, see, e.g., Jacques Le Goff, "Petits enfants dans la littérature des XIIe–XIIIe siècles," ADH (1973) 129–32; Paul Spagnoli, "Philippe Ariès, Historian of the Family," JFH 6, 4 (1981) 434–41; and Caroline Bynum, reviewing Donald Weinstein and Rudolph Bell, *Saints and Society: The Two Worlds of Western Christendom, 1000–1700* (Chicago, 1982) in *Speculum* 59 (1984), p. 459. Jean-Claude Schmitt (*The Holy Greyhound: Guinefort, Healer of Children Since the Thirteenth Century,* p. 84), finds Ariès's theory "fundamentally correct," in that although relatives felt affection for children they did not evince a notion of "childhood." For support of the artistic base of Ariès's theory, derived largely from the "absence" of ideas of "childhood" in medieval art and literature, see, e.g., Béatrix Vadin, "L'absence de représentation de l'enfant et / ou du sentiment de l'enfance dans la littérature médiévale," and F. Garnier, "L'Iconographie de l'enfant au Moyen Age," ADH (1973) 135–36; but for a much more sensible approach, including scores of medieval illustrations of children *qua* children, see Danièle Alexandre-Bidon and Monique Closson, *L'Enfant à l'ombre des cathédrales,* who express cautious disagreement with Ariès. Jean-Louis Flandrin ("L'Attitude à l'égard du petit enfant et les conduites sexuelles dans la civilisation occidentale") questions the assumption that the Middle Ages were heedless of children, but argues that their well-being was a low priority before the twelfth century; in *Families in Former Times,* pp. 130 and 138, he places the "rise" of concern with children even later, in the sixteenth century. For other "discoveries" of childhood or some aspect of it, see, e.g., Pierre Riché, "Découverte de l'enfant," in *De l'éducation antique à l'éducation chevaleresque: Questions d'histoire* (Paris, 1968), or Elisabeth Badinter, *L'amour en plus: Histoire de l'amour maternel (XVIIe–XXe siècles)* (Paris, 1980), English trans. Roger DeGaris, *Mother Love: Myth and Reality: Motherhood in Modern History* (New York, 1981). On the issue of maternal affection in general, see the many articles in ADH (1983): "Mères et nourrissons." Note that in the 1920s, German scholars argued that the Hellenistic age "invented" the child: S. Herter, "Das Kind im Zeitalter des Hellenismus," *Bonner Jahrbücher* 132 (1927) 250–59.

tory principle as either the cause or the consequence of such a practice.

But such theories do not account well for the available evidence. In regard to abandonment, Hunecke wryly notes that the greatest known increase in the exposing of children occurred "at the point when, as Philippe Ariès has shown, Europe began to discover childhood."[84] Obviously the degree of parental attachment to children will vary in a given population; neglectful or callous parents doubtless occur in all societies.[85] Whether or not the particular parents who abandoned children felt a notable lack of affection for them is assessed in subsequent chapters according to specific time and place. It is clear, however, that there was no *general* absence of tender feeling for children as special beings among any premodern European peoples.[86] Everywhere in Western culture, from religious literature

84. "Les enfants trouvés," p. 3: "A l'époque où la vieille Europe commençait à découvrir l'enfance, comme Philippe Ariès l'a montré, un nombre croissant de nouveau-nés, nombre jamais atteint jusque-là, furent exposés et abandonnés dans l'Occident chrétien."

85. B. Vadin (p. 368) cites Philippe de Novarre's urging parents to love their children as comprising a demonstration of lack of "natural" parental feeling, but moralists of the twentieth century are equally likely to upbraid parents for their coldness or inattention. She also adduces the reply of a noble who, when threatened with the death of his son, a hostage, says that he can easily produce a better one (p. 369). This, too, is misleading, since it was probably a bluff intended precisely to obviate the killing of his son, and would be, in any event, a somewhat unusual circumstance from which to draw conclusions about fatherly devotion. Hostages have not been treated in this study as a form of abandonment, although they provide interesting parallels and revealing clues to attitudes toward children (see, e.g., examples in Sidney Painter, *William Marshall: Knight-Errant, Baron, and Regent of England* [Baltimore, 1933], p. 16). A treatment of this theme is much needed.

86. Documenting parental affection is somewhat like documenting the existence of parents—i.e., impossible precisely because nearly all documents are apposite. On affection for children among the Jews, see (in addition to the Hebrew scriptures, *passim*), René Voeltzel, "L'Enfant chez les Hebreux," in *L'Enfant* 1.131–83. Little Astyanax in Hector's arms was (and is) a justly celebrated moment in the *Iliad*. Euripides, who knew how to pull out all the emotional stops, has Hercules exit with the lines, "The best of mortals, and those who are not, love children; they may differ in means, the haves and have-nots, but all love children" (*Hercules Furens* 634–36). That in his ensuing madness he then kills his own children is the height of pathos. For Romans and early Christians, see discussion in chapters 1–3, below, or Jerome's letters 107 and 128, which are filled with maudlin sentiment about young children. For the early Middle Ages, *inter alia*, Walafrid to Liutger in "Ad Liutgerum clericum," MGH PLAC, ed. Ernst Dümmler (Berlin, 1881–84) 2.385, no. 31. The twelfth-century bishop Etienne de Fougères com-

to secular poetry, parental love is invoked as the ultimate standard
of selfless and untiring devotion, central metaphors of theology and
ethics presuppose this love as a universal point of reference, and language must devise special terms to characterize persons wanting in
this "natural" affection.[87] Many different notions of childhood op-
erated in the Western tradition throughout antiquity and the Middle
Ages, as has been shown, but no Western societies evince a complete
lack of interest in the question of childhood and its boundaries.

The comparative absence of artistic depictions of young children
has been exaggerated by Ariès and his followers as demonstration
of their thesis,[88] but even if they assessed it accurately they would be
missing a fundamental point. Art, like other forms of human communication, directs its attention to matters of interest to someone—
to the artist, to the public, to the patron. Many of the most basic
components of daily life, precisely because they are so familiar and
mundane, are of little interest to most people and often absent from
the pictorial or literary record. People eat infrequently in medieval
fiction[89] and almost never eliminate bodily waste, but an inference
from this that medieval Europeans were unaware of such things or

---

plained that parents were rendered "insane" by infants in their arms and were
driven by their immoderate tenderness to rob and steal for their children (discussed
in J. Batany, "Regards sur l'enfance dans la littérature moralisante," ADH [1973]
123–29, p. 124); cf. Gauthier de Coincy, *Les miracles de Nostre Dame* 1.131: "vit
bien et solt / ques'ame estoit en grant peril / por l'amor qu'avoit a son fil." Wolfram
von Eschenbach's *Parzival* depicts such excess of maternal affection in narrative
(e.g., verses 3248–3281; pp. 65–67 in the translation by A. T. Hatto [London,
1980]), as do numerous other high medieval romances (e.g., *Guillaume d'Angleterre,* verses 450–490; cf. Jacques de Caluwe, "L'Enfant dans *Daurel et Beton,*" in
L'Enfant au Moyen Age, 317–34, pp. 322–23). In Scandinavian literature, even parents who expose their children are often said to love them very much (e.g., *ynni
mikit* of Thorgerd's feeling for the newborn she must expose in *Finnboga saga hins
Ramma* (chap. 2, p. 4; cf. chap. 6, p. 12); for other examples of great parental tenderness, see *Hrólfs saga Kraka,* pp. 1 and 73; or *Flateyjarbok: En Samling af Norske
Konge-Sagaer* 1.419; or, in LMIR 2 (1963), "Sigurðar saga þogla," chap. 2, p. 98, or
vol. 4 (1964), "Vilmundar saga Viðutan," chap. 1, p. 142.
   87. See below, p. 92.
   88. For example, of 166 illustrations in the Utrecht Psalter, an illuminated
manuscript of the ninth century, 46—more than a quarter—depict children. See
discussion in Patricia Quinn, "Benedictine Oblation: A Study of the Rearing of
Boys in Monasteries in the Early Middle Ages," chap. 4. Scores of medieval illustrations of children *qua* children appear in Danièle Alexandre-Bidon and Monique
Closson, *L'Enfant à l'ombre des cathédrales.*
   89. Except at formal banquets or in religious ceremonies.

that they were less important then than they are now would be un-warranted and probably erroneous. Abandonment by free parents is very common in classical literature, exposing by slave parents al-most unheard of: this is certainly not because slaves did not abandon children, but because writers were not interested in the abandoned children of slaves. Parental affection in and of itself, while amply attested in premodern writings, was not often of particular interest to artists. One might, in fact, wonder whether it was not more taken for granted during those periods than later, when it became a subject of greater note, although the increase in pictorial and liter-ary art of every sort in early modern Europe is probably sufficient explanation for this.

HISTORIOGRAPHY

Previous historical writing on abandonment in late antiquity and the Middle Ages has been meager.[90] Several articles on found-lings at the close of the Middle Ages have recently appeared,[91] but there is virtually nothing modern on abandonment as a historical phenomenon between imperial Rome and the Renaissance.[92] A few nineteenth-century monographs surveyed the history of the prac-tice, usually as introduction to commentary on contemporary social problems.[93] Some indication of the scant attention they paid to the

90. Compare this paucity with the considerable bibliography on the subject for ancient Greece (note 96, below) and early modern Europe (notes 25–33, above). Even very detailed studies of closely related issues often ignore abandonment. Keith Hopkins ("Contraception in the Roman Empire," pp. 125–28) finds that Romans had less than three children per family, which he regards as subnormal fertility. To explain this he considers abortion, infanticide, and effective contracep-tion, although proof for the last is wholly wanting; he does not even mention aban-donment, for which Roman evidence is abundant.

91. See chapter 11, below.

92. There are some literary studies of the theme in the Middle Ages, notably Charles Dunn's treatment of the foundling motif in *The Foundling and the Werewolf. A Literary-Historical Study of Guillaume de Palerne.* See also the preliminary com-parison of exposing and oblation in my earlier "*Expositio* and *Oblatio:* The Aban-donment of Children and the Ancient and Medieval Family."

93. Remacle, *Des Hospices;* Jean Terme and J.-B. Monfalcon, *Histoire des en-fants trouvés;* S. Hügel, *Die Findelhäuser und das Findelwesen Europa's, ihre Geschichte, Gesetzgebung, Verwaltung, Statistik und Reform;* M. Martin-Doisy, "Enfants trouvés, abandonnés et orphelins pauvres"; Ernest Semichon, *Histoire des enfants abandonnés depuis l'antiquité jusqu'à nos jours;* L. Lallemand, *Histoire des enfants abandonnés et de-laissés;* Antoine Duguer, *Essai sur l'histoire des enfants trouvés.* A number of more

Middle Ages is conveyed by the fact that one devotes less than two pages to the twelfth century and another offers four paragraphs on the thirteenth.[94] Much attention has been focused on early modern abandonment in recent years, but none of its students have attempted to trace its antecedents into the Middle Ages, and some have evinced remarkable naïveté about its premodern history.[95]

Even for comparatively well studied periods such as Greece[96]

---

general works on children, infanticide, or hospitals and charity touch on the subject. For the first, see, e.g., Klaus Arnold, *Kind und Gesellschaft in Mittelalter und Renaissance,* or older studies such as George Payne, *The Child in Human Progress;* for the second, see note 98, below; for the third, see chapter 12, below. Unfortunately, Alexandre-Bidon and Closson in their otherwise excellent *L'Enfant à l'ombre des cathédrales* scarcely mention abandonment except to claim that parents did not abandon newborn infants during the Middle Ages (p. 73).

94. Hügel on the twelfth (pp. 46–47); Semichon on the thirteenth (pp. 78–79). Moreover, the citations in most of these works are of little use, as they had to rely on unreliable editions (often now unavailable), and some simply catalogue "references" without analyzing them or even indicating their precise relevance to the topic (e.g., Hügel, especially on Christian writings, pp. 30–32).

95. Meyer, for example, opines, "This practice, so prevalent in seventeenth- and eighteenth-century France, would appear to go back to the middle ages [*sic*] and to have arisen from the habit of putting children out to nurse" ("Illegitimates and Foundlings in Pre-Industrial France," in Laslett, ed., *Bastardy and Its Comparative History,* p. 249).

96. The subject was established by G. Glotz, "L'Exposition des Enfants," who believed that abandonment was widespread among the Greeks, but this view was opposed by La Rue van Hook, "The Exposure of Infants at Athens." He was followed by H. Bolkestein, "The Exposure of Children at Athens and the ἐγχυτρίστριαι," and, more fully, by A. Cameron, "The Exposure of Children and Greek Ethics," whose tone exemplifies the contentious aspect of this literature: "The parents who are willing to leave their child to perish by cold or hunger or by the attack of wild beasts are . . . untroubled, clearly, by any moral or theological scruples" (p. 107). A. W. Gomme, *The Population of Athens in the Fifth and Fourth Centuries B.C.* (Oxford, 1933), Note C (appendix), concluded that there is no reason to suppose "that infanticide by exposure [N.B.] was at all common, was in any sense a regular practice"; but R. Tolles, "Untersuchung zur Kindesaussetzung bei den Griechen" (Ph.D. diss., Breslau, 1940), made a sound case that abandonment was common among Athenians. G. van N. Viljoen, "Plato and Aristotle on the Exposure of Infants at Athens," came to the conclusion that "after the fourth century B.C. [N.B.] the exposure of infants became increasingly frequent throughout the Greek world, and that in the course of time it was freely and arbitrarily practised by parents to get rid of unwanted children after birth, even and especially from purely economic motives and in particular with regard to baby daughters" (p. 58). W. K. Lacey, *The Family in Classical Greece,* argued against frequent abandonment, using such questionable specifics as, e.g., the fact that Aeschines mentioned that some Athenians had eye trouble—hence, according to Lacey, "con-

and early modern France, the subject has been hampered both by moral prejudice and failure to make or maintain crucial distinctions. Bennet opined of abandonment at Rome that it was "another vice which the Romans first learned from the Greeks"—as if the upright and dull-witted Italians would have had no thought but to rear all their children if they had not learned this naughty stratagem from the ingenious Greeks.[97] Much previous writing has conflated exposing with infanticide, hindering accurate assessment of either.[98] Ob-

---

genitally defective" children were not abandoned (p. 164). Of course, visual difficulties usually manifest themselves after infancy, even when they are congenital. Louis Germain also denied that abandonment was widespread among the Greeks in "L'Exposition des enfants nouveau-nés dans la Grèce ancienne: Aspects sociologiques" (*L'Enfant* 1.211–46). He was particularly critical of Glotz for using "literary sources," among which he apparently included epigraphy (e.g., p. 215), and introduced (pp. 229–30) the troublesome issue of affection, first raised by Ariès. Mark Golden replied to Donald Engels' article ("The Problem of Female Infanticide in the Greco-Roman World") on Greece in "Demography and the Exposure of Girls at Athens," arguing that Engels assumed what he set out to prove: the low rate of increase in the population of the ancient world. The low rate was itself, according to Golden, the result of efforts at population control (p. 320). He added that Athenians must have exposed 10 percent of females, or there would have been a severe surfeit of females at certain age levels. By "expose," he appears to mean "kill," which greatly clouds his argument: the abandoning of girls might remove them from certain marriage pools or population groups but not others, and a much subtler analysis of "exposing" is required. Sarah Pomeroy, "Infanticide in Hellenistic Greece," and "Copronyms and the Exposure of Infants in Egypt," employed more reliable data and subtler analysis than these, but did not resolve the larger issues. Cynthia Patterson, "'Not Worth the Rearing': The Causes of Infant Exposure in Ancient Greece," surveys previous literature but adds little new.

97. H. Bennet, "The Exposure of Infants in Ancient Rome," p. 351. It seems unlikely, on the basis of historical evidence, that humans need to be taught any but the most arcane vices; it is, nonetheless, a recurrent theme of historiography that ancient peoples "learned" unseemly behavior from others. See, e.g., discussion of this motif in relation to homosexuality in Boswell, *Christianity*, p. 52. (It is unclear to me whether "learning" a vice from someone else makes its practice more or less reprehensible, and if so, why.)

98. On infanticide itself, a related but distinct topic, see the overview by W. Langer, "Infanticide: A Historical Survey," with bibliography, or more specialized studies by epoch, such as Pomeroy, "Infanticide"; R. Étienne, "La Conscience médicale antique et la vie des enfants"; Lyman, "Barbarism and Religion"; Emily Coleman, "Infanticide in the Early Middle Ages" and "L'Infanticide dans le haut moyen âge"; McLaughlin, "Survivors and Surrogates"; Barbara Kellum, "Infanticide in England in the Later Middle Ages"; Richard Helmholz, "Infanticide in the Province of Canterbury during the Fifteenth Century"; Richard Trexler, "Infanticide in Florence: New Sources and First Results"; and Yves Brissaud, "L'Infanticide à la fin du moyen âge, ses motivations psychologiques et sa répression."

viously the two may be related, either theoretically or empirically
(this relationship is considered at length in subsequent chapters),[99]
but to treat one as *a priori* a subset of the other is both a conceptual
and a historical error. Even the most ardent ancient opponents of
abandonment usually argued that it might become infanticide if the
child died, presupposing that at the outset the two were distinct.[100]
Modern historians have not been so careful.[101] Some have inferred
that the death of the child was anticipated or even desired by the
exposing parent.[102] Others have argued, despite an utter lack of
proof, that abandonment necessarily or usually resulted in death,
whether the parents intended it or not.[103] In his otherwise lucid survey of family limitation at Rome, Eyben asserts it as "a fact" about
exposed children "that many—perhaps the majority—did not survive. They succumbed to hunger or cold or both, or were devoured
by dogs or birds of prey."[104] Where this "fact" is recorded is not

99. Especially chapters 2, 3, and 11.

100. See below, pp. 131–32, 157–60.

101. But Yvonne Knibiehler and Catherine Fouquet, *L'Histoire des mères du
moyen-âge à nos jours* (Paris, 1980), p. 133, do recognize the difference in the seventeenth century: ". . . l'acte d'abandon doit être compris comme une chance de sur-
vie offerte à l'enfant." The irony, as they recognize, is that by this time most
abandoned children did die: see chapter 11, below.

102. "La mort, voilà donc le destin assez probable de tout enfant abandonné.
C'est celui que prévoient les parents" (Glotz, "L'Exposition des enfants," p. 212).
Note that on pp. 199–200 Glotz cites instances of children being exposed with the
clear intention on the part of their parents that they be saved, and on pp. 202–3 he
concedes that Greek literature implies that nearly all abandoned children would be
rescued. Cf. the remarks of the usually perspicacious J.-L. Flandrin, "L'Attitude à
l'égard du petit enfant" (p. 168): "Chez les Grecs et les Romains l'exposition des
nouveau-nés était généralement une manière hypocrite de faire mourir un enfant
indésirable . . ." This is not to say that the exposing parents never aimed at the
death of the child: occasionally they did. Astyages of Media clearly wished to have
Cyrus killed (see sources in note 79 of chapter 1, below); and in the thirteenth-
century poem *Wolfdietrich* A (ed. Hermann Schneider) a pagan king of Greece actually orders his child killed. But such instances are rare, even in literature, which
often depicts extremes, and certainly do not justify the inference that exposing parents invariably intended the death of the child.

103. E.g., Terme and Monfalcon: "L'infanticide et l'exposition de part dif-
féraient assez peu chez les anciens, ils avaient ordinairement le même but: donner la
mort au nouveau-né" (*Histoire des enfants trouvés,* p. 21). Payne observes (p. 199)
that "the Greeks who exposed their children hoped, as a rule, they might possibly
be saved by others, and precautions were frequently taken to this end," but then
adds (p. 217) that "nearly always the exposed child died"—without documenting
either statement.

104. Emil Eyben, "Family Planning in Graeco-Roman Antiquity," p. 19.

disclosed, but it follows closely a reference (his note 54) to a statement by Justin Martyr, a contemporary observer, that "nearly all such children, boys as well as girls, will be used as prostitutes"—leaving one to wonder whether Eyben has chosen to disbelieve this testimony or assumes an unusual incidence of necrophilia among the Roman population.

Others simply conflate infanticide and abandonment as if they were evidently interchangeable. Brunt notes that "those who lacked the means to procure abortion . . . could still resort to infanticide by exposing the newborn child; it might then be picked up and reared by the chance finder, either as his child or, more probably, as his slave."[105] One wonders what meaning Brunt assigns to "infanticide" if a child who was its victim could be picked up and reared, whatever his subsequent social standing. Golden agrees that exposing was not the same as infanticide, and that the conflation should be avoided, but then assumes throughout his arguments that exposed children necessarily died and that abandonment therefore had exactly the same demographic consequences as infanticide, even though many of his references explicitly acknowledge that exposed children were rescued and survived to adulthood.[106]

Part of the difficulty is lexical—conflation of terms for abandonment and infanticide occurs in many contexts, ancient and modern, for a variety of reasons (some addressed above).[107] On another level,

---

105. P. A. Brunt, *Italian Manpower*, p. 148. Similar conflation occurs in Bennett, "Exposure," p. 341 and *passim;* and Cameron, "Exposure of Children and Greek Ethics," p. 112 and *passim*.

106. E.g., Golden, "Demography," n. 34. Golden even equates exposing with abortion: e.g., pp. 330–31. Patterson distinguishes carefully and correctly between infanticide and "exposure" (pp. 104–7) but explicitly views and treats them as a single subject (p. 103, n. 1).

107. For conflation of the concepts in treatment of a later period, see Juha Pentikäinen, *The Nordic Dead Child Tradition,* pp. 74–75. In my *"Expositio"* (p. 13, n. 3), I noted that Pentikäinen incorrectly translates Old Norse "um utslato barns" as "concerning the abandonment of a child" (p. 82) instead of "concerning the killing of a child." I failed, however, to point out that Richard Cleasby and Gudbrand Vigfusson (*An Icelandic-English Dictionary,* 2nd ed. [Oxford, 1975], p. 670) indicate that *út-slátta* is synonymous with *útburðr* ("abandonment"), citing a passage from Norwegian law as substantiation. The ambiguity of this law is discussed below, and I remain unconvinced, in spite of the arguments adduced by Carol Clover in her article on female infanticide and frontier migration in *Scandinavian Studies,* forthcoming as of this writing. Although she claims it is a "mystery" how I could have arrived at my conclusion that abandonment and infanticide can be distinguished, she herself concedes that "every description [of abandonment] we have

the misprision often involves confusing the "wondrous" and the "likely."[108] If cases of abandoned children who died are mentioned in literary or historical sources in terms and contexts resembling those for infanticide, a historian might infer that (1) exposed children generally died, and (2) infanticide and abandonment were more or less equivalent, both conceptually and in terms of their actual consequences. But these would be mistaken conclusions if it was in fact the unanticipated and *unusual* death of such a child which brought it to light and induced the writer to compare it to infanticide: abandonment itself, normally not fatal, could be an ordinary and accepted part of life in the same society.[109]

Conflation of abandonment and infanticide not only obscures the history of the former, which was the *alternative* to infanticide in much of Europe, but also seriously blunts the possibility of accurate demographic assessment of the impact of either one.[110] The few

---

ends with the infant's being found and saved. . . ." Her major arguments are that persons exposing children sometimes appear to intend their deaths (citing two sagas in which they do not in fact die) and that analysis of sex ratios, especially from cemetery remains, suggests female infanticide. The latter is a particularly treacherous methodology, for reasons detailed elsewhere in this study. Abandonment also skews sex ratios in most societies, even where most of the children survive, because *expositi* may be much less likely to be recorded or buried in family plots.

108. See note 15, above.

109. For example, the remission granted by the French crown to two men who had exposed a baby which then died (discussed in chapter 11, below) might inspire the inference that infants often died as a result of such abandonment, but in fact the evidence *in toto* indicates precisely the opposite. Other documentation from the period indicates widespread and regular abandonment without any legal actions against the abandoning relative in any of the published remissions. It was obviously the *unusual* death of the infant that brought this case to light.

110. Or moral analysis: Eyben consistently collapses ethical distinctions about forms of family limitation—e.g., arguing that "orthodox Christianity sharply opposed exposure, abortion, and contraception" (p. 62), while providing evidence only for the latter two (n. 188), as if they necessarily included the first; cf. a similar statement on pp. 72–73 that "all forms of family planning" were regarded as murder, with references to contraception and abortion as substantiation. The claim that in all early councils "abortion and infanticide or exposure are usually mentioned together and incur the same punishment" (p. 73) is simply untrue: see discussion, below, chapter 3. Possibly Eyben's own views affect this analysis: note the peculiarly moralizing tone of remarks about Ovid (p. 52), or the effusive praise of the ascetic attitudes of Musonius Rufus (p. 40: "from this humane philosopher come the most beautiful words on matrimony antiquity has bequeathed us").

credible statistics on the relative frequency of infanticide and abandonment in societies where both were common indicate that abandonments outnumbered infanticides by factors ranging from several hundred to nearly a thousand.[111] Killing children is, moreover, not only morally different from leaving them in a place where they might be picked up and reared; it also entails dramatically different demographic consequences. If even a small percentage of abandoned children were rescued, abandonment would have a less drastic effect on the next generation than an equal rate of infanticide. If a majority were saved and survived to adulthood, the impact on the population would be entirely different: the reduction in the size of the exposed children's natal families would be the same, but there would be little or no reduction in the age cohort as a whole. There would, in fact, be *more* families with children if infertile couples adopted them, and the subsequent reproductive effects would be nothing like those of comparable rates of infanticide.

I assume throughout the following chapters that death might or might not result from abandonment, that this cannot be predicted or assessed independently of particular local and temporal circumstance, and that careful analysis of the actual likelihood of death for abandoned children is essential to understanding the phenomenon.

DEMOGRAPHY

The absence of detailed demographic analysis in a work of this nature may surprise, even disappoint some readers, and will probably annoy demographers. The omission is deliberate, the consequence of three factors in particular: (1) With few exceptions, the meager statistical data from ancient and medieval Europe are so uncertain and controverted that detailed analysis of them reduces their value from great uncertainty to certain absurdity. Often it is not precision but gross relation to reality that is in question, and even the most sophisticated numerical uses of such materials can be seriously misleading. Experts in demography realize full well that the "facts" on which they rely for statistical analysis are inevitably ar-

---

111. E.g., Remacle, *Des Hospices,* finds that in the nineteenth century, French departments that have at most one recorded infanticide per year (p. 215) have annual rates of recorded abandonment ranging from 391 (Loiret) to 724 (Bouches-du-Rhône) to 928 (Gironde) (p. 189).

rived at by the same personal judgments about the nature and value of the sources that underlie traditional historical interpretation, but for the reader who has not seen the sources the alembic of purely mathematical procedures seems, deceptively, to remove the element of human intuition. No matter how cautiously the historian presents them, statistical conclusions often appear not only more reliable, but more "scientific" and "objective" than traditional inferences in which the element of personal exegesis and guesswork is not obscured by arithmetical overlay. "About a third of the cases" sounds much less precise than 32.8 percent, although the latter may be based on exactly the same reading of ambiguous data as the first.[112] The difficulty of identifying the dividing line between the reporting of facts and the making of judgments is thereby greatly exacerbated, because—for the reader, at least—the line is hidden behind calculations he often does not fully understand, or is placed out of critical reach by appeal to "statistical significance."

(2) Given the nature of the historical record, moreover, the most that statistics could provide would be, to adopt again the language of the paleontologist, a detailed description of skeletal remains, which alone leave data hard enough to be analyzed in this way. But it is precisely because the skeleton cannot remain forever the locus of inquiry that I have pursued my investigation into the more mysterious—but potentially revealing—organic parts missing from the fossil record of the ancient and medieval family. Until the relative proportion of these to the extant skeleton is established, statistical quantification of the latter is of limited value and has been employed in what follows in very limited ways. References to other works which make greater use of such methods are provided in the notes.[113]

(3) One would, of course, like to know how many parents abandoned children, how many children they abandoned, how many of these found homes, how many died, etc. But since we do not know, and probably will never know, how many parents there were or

112. The figures from the 1427 *catasto* of Florence, for example, because of their quantity and detail, are often contrasted as comparatively "hard" evidence with ostensibly "softer" deductions about areas and times for which there is much less data, but their foremost analyst, David Herlihy, allows that the census might be off by as much as 20 percent (e.g., in *Tuscans and their Families: A Study of the Florentine Catasto of 1427,* with Christiane Klapisch-Zuber [New Haven, 1985], p. 25). This reduces the apparent precision of much of his (excellent) statistical analysis to sophisticated guesswork.

113. See, e.g., the works cited in note 18, above.

how many children were born in ancient and medieval Europe, it would be futile to hope for numbers or mathematical ratios for abandoned children. Propositions of likelihood, based chiefly on nonnumerical evidence (e.g., historical or literary indications that families of a given area, time, and social class usually had a certain number of children and abandoned a certain percentage of them) are possible, but will not inspire wide agreement.

There is, indeed, remarkably little certainty about the most basic biological aspects of human population and its reproduction, and lively disagreement about the significance of what little is known. It is not possible to say what are "natural" fertility rates for couples,[114] what is "normal" growth for a given population and what rate of reproductivity is necessary to maintain it,[115] what are average rates of infant mortality: all of these are dependent on particulars of climate, nutrition, social structures, and economic realities as much as they are on any biological attributes of the species.[116] Even aspects of reproductivity one might guess are constant and predictable at the population level—the effect of nursing on fertility, the age of menarche, the average incidence of sterility[117]—turn out to be vari-

114. For a good introduction to these problems and some of the current literature, see Coale and Keyfitz, as cited in note 18, above.

115. Noble families have been thoroughly studied for many periods, and their rate of growth is often known in detail: e.g., Michel Parisse (*Noblesse et chevalierie en Lorraine médiévale: Les familles nobles du XIe au XIIIe siècle,* p. 296) finds that during each century of the High Middle Ages Lorraine lost about one-third of its old noble families and gained about half again as many new ones, resulting in a growth rate of some 20 percent per century. But this discloses virtually nothing about the population as a whole, and is not very useful for this study even in regard to the nobility, because by the High Middle Ages the wealthy probably abandoned few children, for reasons discussed below. For other studies of noble families and their reproductivity, see chapters 6 and 9, below.

116. Some researchers give the impression, nonetheless, that a great deal is known with certainty. Becker (*A Treatise on the Family*) states matter-of-factly that "prior to the nineteenth century, even in advanced countries, no more than about half of all live births survived to age ten. Therefore modest changes in age at marriage, frequency of coition, and breast feeding—combined with coitus interruptus—would have reduced the average number of surviving children to only three or less" (pp. 100–101). He offers no support for these statements, and many of the specific facts he adduces on p. 101 contradict them. Even for intensively studied and highly specific cultures like Periclean Athens this level of assurance is unattainable: see note 96, above.

117. Of the many studies on these subjects, see, e.g., J.-P. Habicht et al., "The Contraceptive Role of Breastfeeding"; Ulla-Britt Lithell, "Breast-Feeding Habits and Their Relations to Infant Mortality and Marital Fertility"; and J. N. Hobcraft,

able, not only from person to person but over time and according to place. This is not surprising: biological factors will obviously be affected by temporary conditions such as famine and plague, and social and cultural pressures such as preference for offspring of one gender or another. Limitations on inheritance, for example, may influence parents to take measures to alter or override "natural" patterns of reproductivity.[118] It is as likely that historians will assist demographers in understanding human reproductivity by providing a view of specific earlier patterns and parameters as it is that demographers will offer historians reliable models on which to base generalized conclusions.

Comparisons to the industrial democracies of the nineteenth and twentieth centuries, for which much more detailed demographic evidence is available, would be misleading. The same factors that have led to accurate population statistics have so profoundly altered patterns of reproduction and family life that it would be injudicious to extrapolate from them to preindustrial societies in Europe. Even nonindustrial societies of the twentieth century receive external aid and forms of medical assistance from developed nations which render them unsuitable as points of comparison with ancient or medieval Europe. In the ancient world even the most prosperous societies subsisted in precarious balance with natural disaster and uncertain food supplies, and no generally effective means of contraception (except abstinence) was known to any social class.

Moreover, the possibility of abandonment introduces a loop into the demographic problem, rendering inference about family size in the past exquisitely difficult. If there was widespread abandonment, a record of the number of children in the families of a given ancient or medieval population will not yield an accurate view of the number or distribution of offspring, since abandoned children will be counted in the "wrong" family, or not at all.

Records of the eighteenth century, as noted previously, suggest that from ten to forty percent of urban children were abandoned,

---

J. W. McDonald, and S. O. Rutstein, "Demographic Determinants of Infant and Early Child Mortality: A Comparative Analysis," *Population Studies* 39, 2 (July 1985) 213–32.

118. The connection between family limitation and inheritance is discussed in detail in subsequent chapters, and has attracted substantial attention from previous writers: see, e.g., Flandrin, *Families,* chap. 2; Goody, *The Development of the Family and Marriage in Europe;* and Gary Becker, *A Treatise on the Family.*

and, flawed as such indications are, they may be worth considering as a point of reference in the absence of any comparable data from earlier periods. But the enormous impact of local and temporal factors on all aspects of family life and reproduction should make one cautious about extrapolating from these, especially since in ancient and medieval societies abandonment took forms fundamentally different from those of early modern Europe. Foundling homes, for example, for which the great majority of exposed children were destined in the eighteenth century, were not known in the ancient world or through most of the Middle Ages. They first became widespread in the fourteenth century, and their appearance introduced a curious and unexpected twist to the story of abandonment and its mysteries, a turn addressed in the final chapter of this study. Prior to this, the history of abandonment was more complex and variegated, and to survive, a child would have to be rescued by the kindness of strangers.

PART I

◆ ANCIENT PATTERNS

1

❖   ❖   ❖

ROME: THE
HISTORICAL
SKELETON

Aside from the fact that they prostitute their daughters, the
Lydians live pretty much as the Greeks . . .
Herodotus 1.94

OF THE MANY muniments of imperial Roman civi-
lization[1] that make reference, often in passing, to the abandonment
of children, few have been carefully examined by previous writers
and many have not even been noticed.[2] This is partly because the

1. The discussion that follows deals primarily with the Roman world of the
central Mediterranean (including the Roman provinces of North Africa) during the
first three centuries of the present era. This frame of reference does not justify an
inference of uniformity, but it does avoid straddling some prominent discon-
tinuities of Roman history (such as the transition from republic to empire). It has,
nonetheless, seemed sensible to bring to bear material from adjacent periods and
places—earlier law and drama, for example, or Germanic customs—when we have
evidence that Romans knew about them. Republican literature and Greek philosophy made up part of the cultural and political world of imperial citizens.

2. The secondary literature on abandonment in the ancient world is larger than
that dealing with any other historical period except the eighteenth century, but
even so, it amounts to a sampling of journal articles mostly replying to each other
on particular aspects of the problem, and few deal specifically with Rome. Most,
like E. Weiss, "Kinderaussetzung," RE 11.1 (1921) 463–72, concentrate on Greek
evidence. Pierre Chuvin's somewhat sensationalized "Antiquité: Le scandale des
enfants abandonnés," L'Histoire 72 (November 1984) 30–38, though insightful,
addresses all of "antiquity"—Greek, Roman, Egyptian, and even Jewish—in eight
pages, and extrapolates generously from a very small sampling of evidence. Of the
general works on abandonment cited in the introduction, none has been taken seriously by classicists. Bennett, "The Exposure of Infants in Ancient Rome," was
querulously criticized by Max Radin, "The Exposure of Infants in Roman Law and
Practice," on almost every single point. Jérôme Carcopino, "Le droit romain d'ex-

subject itself has been neglected, and partly because comments on the issue tend to be brief and scattered and to occur in contexts that make them difficult to gather and assess. Accounts of abandonment in narrative history are rare; casual allusions in legal, epigraphical,

---

position des enfants et le Gnomon de l'Idiologue," addressed the particular questions raised by the discovery early in this century of a set of second-century Egyptian laws. More sophisticated approaches to family limitation were applied by John Noonan, *Contraception: A History of Its Treatment by the Catholic Theologians and Canonists,* and Keith Hopkins, "Contraception in the Roman Empire." Hopkins concluded that no contraceptive technique, including *coitus interruptus,* played a large role in Roman family limitation, but paid no attention to the possibility of abandonment. Brunt, in *Italian Manpower,* the standard work on Roman demography through Augustus, summarized Hopkins on contraception, but did briefly consider abandonment (pp. 148–54, *passim*). Unfortunately, he conflated infanticide and abandonment so assiduously that it is difficult to trust his observations, since the two would have different demographic results. Donald Engels disagreed with Brunt's conclusion that female infanticide was common. A "high rate of female infanticide in antiquity was demographically impossible," Engels argued, because of the (very low) rate of increase in the population: even killing 20 percent of newborn girls would reduce the whole population by half in 57.75 years ("The Problem of Female Infanticide," pp. 118–19), and he concluded that "the rate almost certainly never exceeded more than a few percent of female births in any era" (p. 120). (His argument assumes that female infanticide would have been more common than male, which must therefore have been even less significant.) Of course, a much higher percentage of girls could be *abandoned* without reducing the population so drastically, but Engels does not consider this. Many ancient references to abandonment are ably surveyed by Eyben, "Family Planning in Graeco-Roman Antiquity" (see esp. pp. 22–23), although with curious errors of interpretation, especially in regard to Egyptian and early Christian legal materials; these are noted *in situ,* below. William Harris replied to Engels on Greece and Rome in "The Theoretical Possibility of Extensive Infanticide in the Graeco-Roman World," arguing that infanticide was common, and responding both to his statistical analysis and to his use of previous historiography (which was quite limited). Engels somewhat indirectly rebutted the statistical points in "The Use of Historical Demography in Ancient History," *Classical Quarterly* (1984) 386–93. Roman legal enactments are treated in considerable detail by Maria Bianchi Fossati Vanzetti, "Vendita ed esposizione degli infanti da Costantino a Giustiniano," although with odd omissions and misprisions (e.g., her claim that the *patria potestas* did not include the right to sell children). The most recent contribution (as of this writing) is Beryl Rawson, "Children in the Roman *Familia,*" which makes excellent use of epigraphical materials, particularly as regards *alumni,* but tends to conflate imperial legislation as if half a millennium had not elapsed between Augustus and Justinian. More specialized studies (e.g., dealing with *alumni* or slavery) are cited below. See also Edyth Binkowski and Beryl Rawson, "Sources for the Study of the Roman Family" (in Rawson, ed., *The Family in Ancient Rome,* pp. 243–57).

philosophical, and literary works are common. Epigraphical data often lack context and lend themselves to widely differing interpretations; philosophical texts may reflect ideals or minority views rather than social reality. The general difficulty of relating "literature" to "history" has been sketched above, and the specific value of Roman literature on the subject of abandonment is examined at some length in the following chapter. "Historical" reports are also often unreliable, partly because imperial historians had relatively few sources to draw on for much earlier periods, and because, like modern writers, they sometimes subordinated factual accuracy to other agendas.[3]

Laws, too, can be misleading. The fact that statutes are enacted or decrees issued does not mean that they are enforced, or even taken seriously,[4] but the corpus of imperial Roman law was large, complex, and varied, and can often be employed as a check on contemporary historical and literary accounts. Roman juridical sources contain not only edicts and rulings which may or may not have been enforced or realistic, but also summaries of actual cases, legal opinions citing custom and practice, complaints about the failure of previous enactments, and many remarks and observations about legal and social structures introduced as incidental factual premises rather than arguments—and they are revealing for precisely this reason.

Legal materials have therefore been privileged in the treatment of abandonment at Rome both thematically and structurally. The first point addressed is the legality of various forms of abandonment, both because it is fundamental to discussion and because it affords a temporal and thematic overview of the subject. Moral and ethical writings are considered next. Whether they influenced practice or not, they frequently reflect (sometimes by opposing) the attitudes of the populace. Narrative and epigraphical sources, the former few in number and the latter poor in context, are used as supplements to these when appropriate. Literary materials are gen-

---

3. Some ancient historians, moreover, followed conventions of "accuracy" which may confuse or mislead modern audiences, such as the tendency to "report" speeches which the writer did not hear but simply composed around the themes he believed to have been covered.

4. Laws often reflect degree of disapproval more than frequency of occurrence: a single case of marriage contracted unwittingly between brother and sister might inspire horrified legislators to draft a law to deal with such a circumstance. This may be the explanation for some laws dealing with cases of accidental incest, as in *Mosaicarum et Romanarum legum collatio,* ed. M. Hymanson (London, 1913), p. 90.

ally considered separately. This should not be taken to indicate a low estimation of their reliability: on the contrary, the arrangement is, in part, designed to show, by introducing less controversial genres first, that the literary materials confirm and corroborate them, and vice versa. Because the social realities of the Roman world were not static and the development of laws and attitudes is as important as their final form, within each subdivision the materials are introduced in chronological order (as far as this is known).

Such a schematization cannot be neat and has therefore not been given priority over common sense or organizational clarity. The corpus of Latin writings, for example, comprises genres which are neither clearly historical nor clearly literary, and which might sensibly be considered both. To this group belong the "declamations" and "controversies";[5] they are cited where thematically apposite,

---

5. Although they contain valuable information about many social issues, few scholars have made use of them, partly because they have been rarely translated or commented on, and partly because there is no consensus about their relationship to social or legal reality. Models of rhetorical debate about legal points, they present the best arguments that could be made on one or both sides of a given case. Whether all or any of the cases were actual incidents is unclear; even some legal principles cited may be fictive. Some fictional elements, however, do not demonstrate that these collections are generically untrustworthy in relation to law, any more than errors in Plutarch mean he cannot be trusted as a historian. Most of their content is informed by a knowledge of Roman judicial procedure and statute, a point one of their authors, Quintilian, addresses specifically, and in regard to children: "For the scholastic themes concerned with the disowning of children are on exactly the same footing as the cases of sons disinherited by their parents, which are tried in the public courts, or of those claims for the recovery of property, which are tried in the centumviral court . . ." (*Institutio* 7.4.11, cited in E. Patrick Parks, "The Roman Rhetorical Schools as Preparation for the Courts under the Early Empire," *The Johns Hopkins University Studies in Historical and Political Science* 63, 2 [1945], p. 91). Moreover, in relation to issues of parental control and abandonment, they are very reliable, even if previous authors have misunderstood their import. D. L. Clark (*Rhetoric in Greco-Roman Education* [New York, 1957], p. 231) opines of one of Seneca's cases, for example, that its legal basis was "fictional": "only under school law could a parent disown a child for disobedience." But this is wrong: while there may not have been a specific statute authorizing parents to disown children, the *patria potestas* included this power within the father's *vitae necisque potestas* over his children. (This is one of the principles Quintilian cites specifically, above, as corresponding to legal practice; cf. S. F. Bonner, *Roman Declamation in the Later Republic and Early Empire* [Berkeley, 1949], pp. 312–14.) Clark also brands as fiction (p. 233) the legal principle in Quintilian that to recover an abandoned child a parent had to repay the cost of his rearing, which, whether statutory or not, was unquestionably a genuine legal requirement, as discussed below.

generally after legal texts but before other genres.[6] The evidence of imaginative writing is adduced where it clarifies aspects of legal or moral materials. In general, however, the aim has been to present abandonment first as it appears in "historical" (including ethical) materials, and then to compare this with the "literary" picture. This approach is helpful methodologically (it facilitates comparison of types of sources not ample enough to be thus juxtaposed in treatments of later periods) but has the disadvantage of presenting initially a rather skeletal overview of the subject: the "flesh and blood" are much clearer in literary records. Those who prefer to understand the more visceral aspects first—who was abandoned, and how, and why—may wish to begin by reading chapter 2 and return to the judicial overview subsequently.

Modern states have legislated about abandonment chiefly out of concern for the child, or in acknowledgment of parental responsibility. Roman government, by contrast, had little interest in regulating

6. Scholarly opinion about the accuracy of the content of these works has undergone enormous change over time. H. Bornecque (*Les Déclamations et les déclamateurs d'après Sénèque le père* [Lille, 1902], p. 73) maintained that only twenty of the elder Seneca's seventy-four *controversiae* turned on actual Roman law, but the more comprehensive subsequent work of Bonner (*Roman Declamation*) showed that most of the *controversiae* were derived from real juridical principles, even if they were not always entirely up-to-date about niceties of practice. A further shift toward regarding them as useful sources is evident between two works of D. L. Clark: in 1922 in *Rhetoric and Poetry in the Renaissance: A Study of Rhetorical Terms in English Renaissance Literary Criticism* (New York), p. 39, he dismissed the "utter unreality and hollowness of such rhetoric"; whereas he took them quite seriously in *Rhetoric in Greco-Roman Education* (esp. pp. 213–66, in the course of which he discussed several of the specific *controversiae* treated below). Parks ("The Roman Rhetorical Schools," as above, esp. pp. 88–101) also concludes that they were largely reliable. For more recent commentary, consult the cautious introduction to the *Declamationes* of Quintilian by their most recent editor, Michael Winterbottom (Berlin, 1984), or the more general approach of S. F. Bonner, *Education in Ancient Rome* (Berkeley, 1977), chapter 21 ("Declamation as a preparation for the lawcourts"); also, ANRW II.31.1 and 4, and D. A. Russell, *Greek Declamation* (Cambridge, 1983), chap. 2. Even if they were not entirely accurate about juridical niceties, they would still offer valuable insights into contemporary moral values and social practice: in the preface to his *Controversiae* Seneca mentions that they include in addition to legal and moral matters general statements on "fortune, cruelty, the times, wealth"—i.e., everyday life. And regardless of theory, they may well reflect the *de facto* operations of the Roman legal system, which was not bound by judicial precedent in the same way its modern descendants are (on this see Bruce Frier, *The Rise of the Roman Jurists: Studies in Cicero's "Pro Caecina"* [Princeton, 1985]).

personal moral behavior, and formulated laws primarily to enforce public obligations to the state, or to facilitate civil litigation regarding status, property, or damages.[7] Romans were not legally required to keep any of the children born to them. One of the duties citizens had to the state, at least from the time of Augustus, was to produce heirs, but the point of this obligation was to increase the numbers of the privileged classes, not to encourage a love of children.[8] Social critics of the time, in fact, complained that laws to this effect had a detrimental effect on the quality of family life, since people married and begot children simply to acquire legal advantages, not out of respect for parenthood.[9]

It is difficult to imagine how Roman law could have penalized abandonment, or even infanticide, since within the *familia* (which included slaves as well as wife and lineal descendants) the authority of the Roman father (*paterfamilias*) was absolute.[10] It extended to life

7. Arguable exceptions to this are Augustus's moral legislation, which was considered novel by contemporaries, and Dig. 25.3.4, on parental responsibility for children (which is addressed below).

8. There was a fine for celibacy (remaining unmarried) in Cicero's day: see, e.g., Cicero, *De legibus* 3.3. Brunt (*Italian Manpower*) catalogues the disappearance of many Roman noble lines (p. 142, n. 1), and suggests that this was due chiefly to family limitation and normal mortality. Livy speaks of governmental efforts to encourage Romans to have children (5.30.8; cf. 27.9.11). Three were considered the necessary contribution to the state, and for this, special privileges were granted: the *ius trium liberorum* (right of three children—for freedmen, four were required). Its benefits were sometimes granted by emperors as a favor to those with fewer than three children (e.g., Augustus's wife Livia, mother of two; she was also accorded the title *univira*, though Augustus was her second husband) or even to the unmarried. Both the *Lex julia de maritandis ordinibus* (18 B.C.) and the *Lex Papia Poppaea* (A.D. 9) were directed against the childless and celibate, and both were confirmed or expanded in subsequent legislation. For an overview of such issues under the early empire, see L. Raditsa, "Augustus's Legislation Concerning Marriage, Procreation, Love Affairs, and Adultery," ANRW 2.13 (1980) 278–339. For Roman commentary see Aulus Gellius, 1.6; Propertius 2.7; Pliny, *Natural History* 14.5; Suetonius, *Augustus* 34, 89; for legal references, Dig. 35.1.64.1, 50.5.2; JC 5.66.1; cf. TC 8.16, 9.42.9, 8.17.1–3. Paulus discusses having children as a requirement of an heir, and includes childlessness with being unmarried and committing murder(!) in a list of conditions "against the law, against imperial decrees, or against good manners" (*Sententiae* 3.4b.2).

9. E.g., Plutarch, *De amore prolis* 493E.

10. The *familia* is legally defined in Dig. 50.16.195.1–4; for useful modern discussion, see Richard Saller, "*Familia, domus,* and the Roman Conception of the Family," *Phoenix* 38 (1984) 336–53. Saller draws more careful distinctions than Herlihy (*Medieval Households,* chap. 1).

and death, and Roman society through the time of Vergil appears to have accepted without question the right of a father to execute even a grown son.[11] The only ancient evidence suggesting legal barriers to abandonment[12] is the testimony of the historian Dionysius of Halicarnassus, who twice refers to a law of Romulus requiring Romans to rear all their male children. But his account is self-contradictory,[13] based on no known source, written seven centuries after the alleged event, and supported by no other documentation, legal, historical, or literary. He may have derived the idea from confusion with laws attributed (perhaps also falsely)[14] to Sparta or

11. Lucius Junius Brutus, for example, was considered a great patriot in Vergil's day for having killed his own sons in the cause of Roman freedom (*Aeneid* 6.823), but was called "unnatural" by Servius in the late fourth century (*Servianorum in Vergilii carmina commentariorum,* ed. E. K. Rand et al. [Lancaster, Pa., 1946–65] ad loc. cit.), in part due to great reductions in the power of the *paterfamilias.* The effectively absolute power of the *paterfamilias* in republican times renders curious the provision of the Twelve Tables that apparently "allows" the killing of deformed children; Cicero, *De legibus* 3.8. Dionysius of Halicarnassus, a less reliable authority, attributes this to Romulus. Greeks were shocked by the extent of the *patria potestas:* see, e.g., the remarks by Dionysius, cited below, p. 119. Due to his conflation of abandonment and infanticide, it is impossible to know exactly what Brunt (p. 148) means when he observes, apparently of the latter, that "Its legality is beyond doubt: it was perhaps practiced in shame and secrecy." On the *patria potestas* in general, see W. K. Lacey, "*Patria potestas,*" in Beryl Rawson, ed., *The Family in Ancient Rome: New Perspectives* (Ithaca, 1986), pp. 121–44; see also older bibliography cited there.

12. With the possible exception of Dig. 25.3.4.

13. At 9.22 he says they must rear *all* children born to them, at 2.15 only the males and the firstborn female. He says that a deformed child could be exposed if five neighbors examined it and agreed to its abandonment. Ulpian makes no reference to such a practice when he renders the opinion that parents of monstrous or deformed children should "benefit" from them—i.e., enjoy the *ius liberorum:* Dig. 50.16.135.

14. Plutarch, *Lycurgus* 16.1–2. For discussion, see P. Roussel, "L'exposition des enfants à Sparte," *Revue des études anciennes* 45 (1943) 5–17. It might also be a conflation with the measures of Phillip, discussed in note 39, below. Aelian says that exposing was prohibited at Thebes in the third century (see chapter 3), although the parents could sell a baby of either gender; this may have been the case earlier as well, but Greek practice was not sufficiently uniform to justify extrapolation to Rome: an inscription from Delphi allows manumitted women to strangle or rear newborn infants, but not to sell them—presumably because this would return the family to servile status (*Bulletin de Corréspondance Hellénique* [1893], p. 383, n. 80, discussed in Glotz, pp. 216–17, G. van N. Viljoen, p. 62, and Eyben, p. 22, n. 65).

Thebes, but it could also be a fantasy about a simpler time when people behaved more responsibly.[15]

Even in Dionysius's account[16] it would be legal for parents to abandon girls beyond the first daughter, and early imperial writings assume both that it was legal for parents to abandon children and that many did so, although some of the texts are of arguable authority and easily misread.[17] A *controversia* of the elder Seneca concerns a man who collects exposed children and cripples them so that they will be more effective at begging.[18] Most of those involved in the debate are understandably horrified by the cruelty of the man's actions, and several speakers suggest that it would have been better for the children to die; but neither horror nor blame is focused on

15. Attributions to archetypal lawgivers of wished-for measures about family life are common in ancient literature. Both Sextus Empiricus (*Outlines of Pyrrhonism* 3.24) and Hermogenes Rhetor (Περὶ εὑρέσεως 1.67 and 2.7) attribute to Solon, eight centuries before they wrote, laws permitting infanticide (for discussion, see van N. Viljoen, "Plato and Aristotle"), while Plutarch, a little before, related that Solon had prohibited selling children (see preceding note). Whatever the legality of infanticide or the selling of children in Greek states, the Code of Gortyn (ed. R. F. Willetts, *The Law Code of Gortyn* [Berlin, 1967]), the fullest surviving pre-Hellenistic Greek code, specifically allows divorced women to abandon children their husbands will not accept (3.44–4.23).

16. In one of them, anyway. Bennett ("The Exposure of Infants"), although he agrees that this cannot be taken as historical, concludes that it reflects the absence of infanticide among the ancient Romans (pp. 343–44). He does not explain why he is inclined to credit the tenor of the account while rejecting its authority. The editors of *Ancient Roman Statutes* (Allan Johnson, Paul Coleman-Norton, and Frank Bourne [Austin, 1961]) consider this and other "laws of Romulus" to be indicative of ancient custom (p. 3). Tertullian (late second century A.D.) says that no laws are violated with greater security or impunity than those against infanticide (*Ad nationes* 1.15, in CSEL 20.85 or CCSL 1.33), but it is far from clear what this should be taken to mean. The text is uncertain (cf. CSEL "sub omnium conscientia unius aetatis tabellis" and CCSL "sub omnium conscientia unius aeditui tabellis"), and it is entirely possible that he meant "law" in some overarching sense (as the "laws of nature," or "laws of mankind"). Even Dionysius's statements do not indicate a blanket prohibition of infanticide, since at the least the deformed could be killed. Tertullian thinks abandonment is morally equivalent to infanticide (ibid.), but it is less clear whether he understands it to be subject to any penalty.

17. Especially true of the *Controversiae* and *Declamationes:* see comments above, notes 5 and 6.

18. Note that crippling is elsewhere associated with abandoned children as an identifying sign—e.g., in the case of Oedipus—and it seems quite possible that children with some deformity were particularly likely to be abandoned in the first place. None of the speakers in the debate alludes to either of these facts.

the action of the abandoning parents. One side even argues that the state is harmed through the man's behavior because of the injury *to* the parents, who cannot take action themselves.[19] This is the more striking because the *Controversiae* are as concerned with moral as with legal values, and often exaggerate to the extent of condemning behavior which was commonly tolerated and even expected.[20] It was, moreover, not long after this that the emperor Claudius declared that slaves who were abandoned because of *old* age or infirmity were automatically free,[21] while children of any class could apparently be abandoned to a life of cruelty and suffering.

In another *controversia* a father who had abandoned twin sons locates them and offers to repay the foster father the cost of their upbringing if he will return them. The discussants assume throughout that this is the sole requirement for the natal father to reassert his authority over the children. The foster father wanted to keep one of the boys, however, and constrained the father to agree to this as the price of the other, the legality of which constituted the subject of the case. One speaker—specifically characterized as "harsh"—does suggest that the father was cruel to abandon the twins, but even he does not imply that it violated the law: the only issue is whether the bargain the father made to accept one child legally obstructs his subsequent desire to have both.[22]

A set of declamations attributed to Quintilian includes six cases about exposed children, in all of which an abandoning parent appears: it is never hinted that he or she is in any way liable or wrong for having exposed a child.[23] On the contrary, in one of the cases the father claims paternal right to a reward the son had earned while under the care of a foster parent. The presumption in all the cases is that a natal parent may reclaim an exposed child with impunity, so long as he repays the cost of the child's upkeep, and this is specifically stated as a point of law in Quintilian's most famous work:

19. Seneca, *Controversiae* 10.4.

20. One of the speakers, for example, complains that his interlocutors pity the crippled children for not having limbs while they do not pity men forced into gladiatorial service for having them; he is praised for inveighing against the "vices of the age"—but no one declaims against the practice of abandonment.

21. Suetonius, *Claudius* 25. Their masters were liable to prosecution for murder if they tried to kill them.

22. Seneca, *Controversiae* 9.3.

23. Summarized below, in note 120 of chapter 2.

"Anyone who can identify an abandoned child may reclaim him if he repays the cost of his rearing."[24] It is hardly credible that under such circumstances abandonment itself could be illegal, or even generally regarded as reprehensible.

There was, however, an aspect of abandonment that was troublesome to Romans and eventually required the intervention of the state (although without restricting the right of parents to abandon). Rome was a slave society, in which the distinction of status between the slave and free populations was fundamental to both the social and economic order. In the cases adduced by Seneca and Quintilian[25] all of the children (except possibly the crippled *expositi*) seem to have remained in free status, but it was possible that an abandoned child would be reared and used as a slave.[26] Allowing exposed children of the free classes to pass casually into slavery was conceptually dangerous and personally horrifying to most Romans, although it clearly happened with considerable frequency. At the opening of the second century, Pliny the Younger wrote to the emperor Trajan from the province of Bithynia in Asia Minor to ask him what was to be done about freeborn Roman citizens abandoned as children who were brought up as servants or slaves by those who found them. This was, he noted, a "great problem affecting the whole province."[27] It was not a new issue: he had seen a number of

24. "Expositum qui agnoverit, solutis alimentis recipiat" (*Institutio* 7.2.14). A similar statement in *Declamationes minores* 278 ("Recipere illum nisi solutis alimentis non potuisti. Lex tibi dicit: 'alienus est, et tibi ut pater esse incipias emendus'" [Winterbottom, p. 87]) has a slightly different emphasis, suggesting that the adopting parent has a prior right *until* such payment is made. This position was eventually sustained by Constantine: see below. Glotz had argued (pp. 208–9) that foster parents had no legal rights over children unless natal parents specifically disinherited them, but did not adduce legal evidence for this. Repaying the cost of upbringing is pictured much earlier, in Terence (*Heautontimoroumenos*, lines 835–36: "minas quidem iam decem habet a me filia, / quas pro alimentis esse nunc duco datas"), but this may reflect a Greek custom in his model (note *minas*).

25. For convenience I use "Quintilian" to refer to the *Institutio*, which is unquestionably authentic, and "Quintilian(?)" for the *Declamationes minores*, which may be Quintilian's.

26. Probable in the view of Brunt: "except in the realm of romance . . . most foundlings must have remained slaves, unless or until they were manumitted" (p. 148). See Iza Bieżuńska-Małowist, "Die Expositio von Kindern als Quelle der Sklavenbeschaffung im griechisch-römischen Ägypten," and discussion below.

27. "Magna, domine, et ad totam provinciam pertinens quaestio est de condicione et alimentis eorum, quos vocant θρεπτούς," Pliny, *Letters* 10.65. (On θρεπτός, see below.) Glotz (p. 211) cited this exchange as proof that natal parents could re-

rulings from former emperors on the subject, but these applied to other provinces and he was not certain his copies were accurate. Trajan replied to him that

> the problem of persons born free and abandoned, then picked up by someone and brought up in slavery has often been discussed, but nothing can be found in the rescripts of the rulers before me which applies to all provinces. . . . I should think therefore that a declaration of free status should not be withheld from those who might be liberated in this way, nor should their freedom have to be purchased by repaying their upkeep.[28]

Trajan's reply makes clear that this was and had been a problem in many provinces other than Bithynia.[29] The principle he articulates did not, obviously, abridge the right of parents to abandon free children: it simply denied the finder the right to retain them as slaves if their free status could be proven, whether or not they or their parents were in a position to repay their upkeep.[30] Since children were in a fairly real sense the property of the *paterfamilias,* it made sense, in a way, that abandoned children, as "unclaimed objects" (*res vacantes*), should become the property of whoever found them, but, at least from Trajan's time, the law limited this by insisting that freeborn natal status was irrevocable.[31]

Relationship to natal parents, like free status, survived abandonment under Roman law. The second-century jurist Scaevola re-

---

claim children and that foster parents had no legal rights over them, but in fact it only indicates that the children themselves could regain free status if they had been born free. This was a right even of those who had sold themselves into slavery (so long as they had not profited thereby): Dig. 40.12.7 (Ulpian). Nani's discussion of the exchange ("ΘΡΕΠΤΟΙ," pp. 67 ff.) is more sensible, although she also appears to have missed the latter point.

28. Nani, p. 66.

29. "There are letters of Domitian to Avidius Nigrinus and Armenius Brocchus which should perhaps be observed, but Bithynia is not among the provinces to which he directed them." Ibid.

30. Eyben (p. 30, n. 90) appears to misread this, perhaps influenced by Radice's translation, which he quotes. The Latin is (probably deliberately) phrased so that it is unclear *who* sues for the child's liberty or might have to reimburse the *nutritor;* Eyben thinks it must be the father.

31. A speaker in Seneca's *Controversiae* (10.4.13) had argued that all exposed children were servile ("Licuit, inquit; expositi in nullo numero sunt, servi sunt"), but this cannot outweigh the other evidence.

ferred to a case in which a boy was abandoned by his mother when her husband divorced her.[32] He was called by his father's name, although neither father nor mother knew that he was alive. After the father's death his mother and paternal grandmother identified him and he succeeded as heir. Abandonment was not at issue in the legal proceedings, which dealt with the question of authority over the father's slaves during the period before the boy was recognized: the problem was not whether the parents had the right to abandon, but whether once they had done so the child was still legally the heir, even during the time he was not under their roof. (The law concluded that he was.)

The jurist Ulpian articulated in the third century the principle that parents must support their children and vice versa,[33] but the question was not whether action could be taken against parents who did not rear all the children born to them. It was, rather, how to assess responsibility and claims for support in relation to estates, income, and inheritance. The existence of a body of precise rules about fathers acknowledging legitimate children meant that an abandoned child, if he could later prove his relationship, would have strong grounds to sue for maintenance or his share of an estate. But no laws prescribed or even suggested action against the parents for abandoning the child in the first place.[34] "Between fathers and sons," went a maxim, "the courts recognize reasonableness as the only law."[35]

32. Dig. 40.4.29.

33. Dig. 25.3.5.

34. At least from the early third century (Dig. 25.3). The point at which a child *became* officially his father's is arguable. Many authors (e.g., Herlihy, "Medieval Children," p. 113) assume as a juridical process the "taking up" and placing on his knee of a newborn infant by the father—hence *ingenuus* and "genuine." But this practice belongs more to the realm of custom than law. The verb *tollere*, for example, is often thought to constitute the technical term for recognition in this way, along with the noun *susceptio*, but *tollere* and *suscipere* were regularly used for "picking up" children in many other ways: e.g., theft (Dig. 47.2.68; JC 1.4.24; Plautus, *Menaechmi* 25), or collecting *expositi* (Plautus, *Cistellaria* 186, where it is a slave who does so, so it could hardly have juridical significance; cf. Seneca, *Controversiae* 6.3, and Terence, *Andria* 401–464, where illegitimate children are at issue). Even within the family, *tollere* does not necessarily relate to the *patria potestas*, as many references make clear: e.g., Terence, *The Mother-in-Law* (*Hecyra*) 571, where the mother-in-law is to do it, or *Heautontimoroumenos* 627–28, where it is the wife (although this may be a metaphorical play on the normal prerogatives of the father).

35. "Inter patres et filios id solum iudex putat licere quod oportet"—attributed to Pollio in Seneca, *Controversiae* 4.5.

A rescript of Diocletian indicates that a father could enforce paternal authority (*patria potestas*) even over a child he had abandoned: a man who reared an abandoned girl wished to marry her to his own son, but the natal father was known,[36] and so far was he from having lost any rights (much less incurred any penalty) that he could legally prevent the marriage if he wished—but he must then repay the foster father for having reared his daughter.

In the eyes of Roman law, in fact, all natal status survived abandonment: children born as slaves also remained slaves, even if their parents abandoned them and someone else reared them as free. The *paterfamilias* owned them and could reclaim them, according to a ruling of Alexander Severus in 224, so long as he repaid expenses incurred by the person who had picked them up.[37]

Roman parents might also sell their children, a common form of abandonment with its own legal intricacies.[38] According to the Laws of the Twelve Tables (redacted apparently in the mid-fifth century B.C. and regarded as the foundation of Roman jurisprudence) a father could sell a son up to three times, after which he lost paternal authority over him.[39] Although such sales were sometimes em-

36. JC 5.4.16.
37. JC 8.51(52).1.
38. Such sales were sometimes simple—i.e., the child became the property of the buyer (though prohibited in later law: see below, n. 43)—but sometimes involved *nexum,* debt servitude. Officially enslavement for private debts was terminated by the *Lex Poetelia Papiria* in the early fourth century B.C., but such measures are difficult to enforce; cf. note 41, below.
39. 4.2, cited by Ulpian (*Liber singularis regularum*) 10.1: "sed filius ter mancipatus, ter manumissus sui iuris fit; id enim lex duodecim tabularum iubet his verbis: SI PATER FILIUM TER VENUNDUIT, FILIUS A PATRE LIBER ESTO"; cited also by Gaius (*Institutes* 1.132, 4.79) and by Dionysius of Halicarnassus (2.27). Dionysius appears to find it shocking that Roman parents could sell children, but Greeks are known to have sold theirs, at least before Solon, who, according to Plutarch, prohibited the sale of daughters unless they were no longer virgins (Plutarch, *Solon* 13, 23). Livy, usually more reliable than either of these, notes that Phillip of Macedon, to restore the war-reduced population of his kingdom, ordered the people (ca. 185 B.C.) to have and rear children ("cogendis omnibus procreare atque educare liberos," 39.24), implying that there had been no previous requirement to this effect, although this remark was probably not intended as a juridical statement, and there is no reason to doubt Plutarch. Indeed, the right of fathers to sell children appears to have been widespread in the ancient world: the Code of Hammurabi (117) recognized it, as did the unusually restrictive family legislation of the Jews. For modern commentary on this law, which has been interpreted in widely varying ways, see, e.g., the recent discussion by Alan Watson, *Rome of the XII Tables: Persons and Property* (Princeton, 1975), pp. 118–19, or R. Yaron, "Si pater filium ter venum duit," *Tijdschrift voor Rechtsgeschiedenis* 36 (1968) 57–72.

ployed simply to emancipate sons from the *patria potestas*,[40] there is
no evidence that this was the original intent of the law or common
practice in the early empire, and much indication of real sale of
children.[41]

Despite its traditional legality, the emperor Antoninus (137–
161) opined that the sale by a Roman father of his freeborn children

40. Imperial legislation does not appear to have taken note of pseudo-sales
used to emancipate before Diocletian (JC 8.48[49].1), and even this reference is
ambiguous. Augustus may have used this method to adopt two of his grandsons—
"adoptavit domi per assem et libram emptos a patre Agrippa" (Suetonius, *Augustus*
64)—but the legal complexities of Roman "adoption" are immense, to some degree unclear, and far too detailed to be considered here. Two basic forms were
known: *adrogatio,* the voluntary submission of an independent (*sui iuris*) person to
the *patria potestas* of another; and *adoptio,* the taking up of a *filius familias* by a new
family. Like most writers of English, I use "adoption" for both, although I have
provided the original language in cases where it is relevant. Because of the variations of these forms over time and by locality, and because of the complexity of
their relations with other customs (such as testamentary adoption), it would require a separate study to treat adoption properly, even in relation to such specific
questions as the extent to which it could affect the *ius trium liberorum.* For a theoretical approach to the question, see the writings of Jack Goody, especially "Adoption in Cross-Cultural Perspective," and E. N. Goody, "Forms of Pro-Parenthood:
The Sharing and Substitution of Parental Roles," in *Kinship,* ed. Jack Goody (London, 1971), pp. 331–45. For more technical materials on Rome, see John Crook,
"*Patria potestas,*" *Classical Quarterly* NS 17 (1967) 113–22; Marek Kuryłowicz,
"*Adoptio Plena* und *Minus Plena,*" *Labeo* 25 (1979) 163–82; Carlos Rosenfeld, "La
adopción en el derecho romano," *Revista del Notariado* 766 (1979) 1349–55; or general texts on Roman law, especially Alan Watson, *The Law of Succession in the Later
Roman Republic* (Oxford, 1971) and *The Law of Persons in the Later Roman Republic*
(Oxford, 1967). A large-scale study of adoption is needed. Often it was purely political (e.g., the use of adoption in order to stand for plebeian office by Clodius
Pulcher), for which, see Marcel-Henri Prévost, *Les Adoptions politiques à Rome sous
la République et le Principat* (Publications de l'Institut de Droit Romain de l'Univer-
sité de Paris) 5 (1949).

41. A famous case of a son's being enslaved for his parents' debts gave rise to
legislation to protect minors, although the details of both the original incident and
the law which resulted are unclear and much disputed: the sources are Valerius
Maximus 6.1.9, Livy 8.28 (note that Livy says "se dedisset"—he gave himself up),
and Dionysius of Halicarnassus 16.9. For discussion, see Boswell, *Christianity,*
pp. 65–68. For many other indications of the sale of children, see following discussion, and Ludwig Mitteis, *Reichsrecht und Volksrecht in den östlichen Provinzen des
römischen Kaiserreichs* (Leipzig, 1891), pp. 358–64. Brunt tersely observes that "the
sale of a free child, invalid in law, might be effective in practice" (p. 131, n. 4),
offering no specific evidence for his opinion, which appears to be wrong. By the
time of the *Institutes* of Justinian (A.D. 533) Roman law itself viewed the triple sale
as simply a ruse (see 1.12.6), but this is not necessarily a historically accurate view.

was an "illicit and shameful thing," which could not be binding on the children,[42] and a century later (in 294) Diocletian rendered the opinion that it was "an evident principle of law" that parents could not sell, pawn, or give away their own offspring,[43] nor could children be forced into servitude to pay their parents' debts.[44] These were not efforts to forbid abandonment. To a modern reader, "selling a child" suggests a questionable financial arrangement between natal parents and someone wishing to obtain a son or daughter, a transfer of authority rendered slightly distasteful by the intrusion of commerce. In the ancient world, selling a person meant making him or her a slave, the property of another person—irrevocably. It was not simply a change of guardianship but of personhood, and much Roman legislation, as noted, was designed to prevent the wrongful enslavement of free citizens and their offspring. Antoninus and Diocletian were, in fact, making clear what had *not* been clearly defined before:[45] that free children could not be enslaved by their parents deliberately any more than they could be by chance; even the *patria potestas* did not enable fathers to make slaves of freeborn offspring.[46]

The practice had been widespread not only in Rome but throughout the Hellenistic Mediterranean. Indeed, earlier in the century, Aelian had praised as "exceptionally just and humane" a Theban law that prohibited exposing children or abandoning them to death in deserted places but allowed genuinely poor parents to sell babies of either gender under official supervision to the *lowest bidder* (presumably to prevent profiteering). The child then became, through

---

42. "Rem quidem illicitam et inhonestam admisisse confiteris, quia proponis filios ingenuos a te venumdatos. Sed quia factum tuum filiis obesse non debet . . ." JC 7.16.1.

43. JC 4.43.1. Cf. 2.4.26, where he says that it is "well known" that mothers cannot make their children slaves.

44. JC 4.10.12. It is not clear whether this is a new law or the recognition of an older one. Diocletian also ruled that children could not legally be given in pledge for goods, although the wording of the rescript makes it plain that people do so: JC 8.17.6.

45. The wording of the passage in the Twelve Tables (see note 39, above) leaves ambiguous exactly what status the sold child acquires after the sale or emancipation. The clarification by Dionysius of Halicarnassus (cited ibid.) should be viewed with caution.

46. Mothers probably never had the right to enslave their children: see note 43, above.

legal covenant, the slave of the purchaser, who was entitled to its labor in return for supporting it.[47]

Imperial proscription of such arrangements constituted a rare intrusion into Roman family life and evinces the extent of the horror free Romans felt about servitude: slavery was not simply a fate "worse than death"—it *was* death in the eyes of the law, since slaves were legally not persons. It may seem odd that the state would intervene against selling children into slavery, "legal death," while permitting a father to execute a child. It is essential to notice that the rulings did not *prohibit* or penalize such sales, but simply declared them *invalid*: if the child (or a relative) wished subsequently to reclaim his freedom, he could do so, and the fact of the sale could not be invoked by the buyer to retain him. This is made clear by the wording of the laws,[48] as well as by contemporary legal materials. Diocletian wrote that if a man sold his free son to his son-in-law neither could accuse the other of a crime, since the son-in-law could not possibly be ignorant of the son's status.[49] The issue was not whether parents were meeting obligations of childrearing, but whether sales that entailed the enslavement of free Romans—even by those with the power of life and death over them—should be honored when challenged.

The underlying reality—that parents could and did sell their children, but that the state was unwilling to allow free Romans to be reduced to slavery—is neatly expressed in the *Sentences* of the jurist Paulus: "Anyone who, faced with extreme necessity or to ob-

---

47. *Varia historia* 2.7. "There is an exceptionally just and humane Theban law that no Theban man can expose a child or leave it to die in a desert place. But if the father is desperately poor, he should bring the baby, whether boy or girl, with its swaddling clothes to the officials as soon as it is born. They will then give it to the person offering the lowest price, and make a covenant and agreement with him that in return for supporting and rearing the child he is to have him or her as a slave. . . ." Aelian is by no means an unimpeachable source, but this description seems consistent with other data about the sale of children by free parents, discussed below.

48. "Nor under the pretense of ignorance on the part of the buyer" (JC 4.43.1) could only refer to the matter of free status, since the purchaser could hardly claim to have been ignorant that it was a *child* he was buying if the difficulty lay in the age of the party.

49. JC 7.16.37. This whole instance seems extremely odd. It could perhaps be related to the feigned sale of children as a means of emancipating them (see "Cum inspeximus . . ." JC 8.48[49].6), but it is difficult to imagine why any charges might then be considered.

tain food, sells his own children, does not prejudice their status as freeborn; for no price can be put on a free person."[50] The very wording suggests, if anything, sympathy for the parents.[51]

Through the third century the law intervened in cases of abandonment only to preserve natal status or to uphold the permanence of paternal authority. At the opening of the fourth century, however, the irrevocability of natal status was abruptly abrogated, more or less permanently, by Constantine, the first Christian emperor. He had been uncertain at first how to deal with the increasingly common and troublesome problems of status occasioned by abandonment: in 313 he recognized the legitimacy of a sale of a child by his parents and demanded that in order to reclaim him as their own they repay the woman who had bought him, or replace him with

50. *Sentences* 5.1.1. Fossati Vanzetti ("Vendita ed esposizione," pp. 206–7) argues that this must be a later interpolation to Paulus's text, since the principle on which it rests was not established until the fourth century, but as has been shown above, it is perfectly consonant with the tenor of other third-century pronouncements, most of which Fossati Vanzetti does not consider.

51. This is one of many reasons to doubt the attribution to Paulus of the opinion (cited in the sixth-century *Digest* of Justinian) that "a person is considered to have killed a child not only when he smothers it, but also if he casts it away or denies it food or leaves it in a public place, expecting [sc., from others] a compassion he himself lacked" (Dig. 25.3.4). If this judgment was in fact Paulus's, it is curious that he should have entertained such dramatically different views of the morality of the two most common forms of abandonment (sale and exposure); and its juridical significance must be viewed in context: there was no law against parents killing their children until 318 (JC 9.17), and even the latter was not intended to discourage infanticide, but to limit the *patria potestas*. It is directed against "parricide" and specifies children killing parents as well as parents killing children; in the latter case it does not employ the words used for "infant" in Roman law, but the general terms for children of any age (*filii* and *liberos*). Killing of parents by children, however, had probably always been prosecutable (see Seneca, *Controversiae* 5.4). The texts of Paulus are uncertain and controverted; the most reliable portions of the *Sententiae* are contained in the *Lex romana Visigothorum,* in which this opinion does not occur. Moreover, it is clear that no subsequent Roman ruler or legislator considered that abandonment incurred any penalty, at least until 374— more than two hundred years after Paulus. Modern scholarship tends to regard this statement as a Christian interpolation—see B. Biondi, *Il diritto romano cristiano* (Milan, 1954) 3.25–26, and Eyben, p. 31—relevant as an indication of later attitudes but not those of Paulus or his contemporaries. Even later Christian law, however, did not adopt positions this clear-cut. Fossati Vanzetti even doubts the attribution to Paulus of the denial of a parent's ability to sell children (above), arguing that the legal principle on which it rests was not established until the fourth century (pp. 206–7), but I disagree.

another.[52] But when it subsequently came to his attention that parents in the provinces were selling and pawning their newborn children in great numbers, he responded by directing that state funds be made available for the needs of such families,[53] and in the following year he reverted to the principle that the sale of freeborn children was not valid.[54] (As with previous legislation, however, the regulation was not intended to hinder such sales: it simply resolved particular legal issues arising when "a freeborn person is sold while a minor.")[55]

But in 329 he began to dismantle, irrevocably, the protections his predecessors had set up for freeborn children. First he decreed that although those who sell children can alienate only their service, not their freedom, the buyer nonetheless has a clear right to this service and the parents or masters must reimburse him for it if they wish to reclaim the child. This applied both to sale and to exposing. In one version the decision emphasizes poverty as a motivation of parents:

> If overcome by dire poverty or need anyone should sell an infant son or daughter for nourishment, the buyer in this case acquires a legitimate right only to [the child's] labor. The person who sold or gave the child away—or anyone else, for that matter—may, however, undertake to regain the child's freedom if he either repays what he is worth or provides a substitute.[56]

52. *Iuris anteiustiniani fragmenta quae dicuntur Vaticana,* ed. Theodor Mommsen (Berlin, 1861) Fragment 34, pp. 8–9. The child was a citizen, but from 212 all inhabitants of the empire were citizens, and this does not necessarily imply freeborn status. On the other hand, it is difficult to imagine the emperor intervening if the parents did not enjoy at least a modest social position.

53. TC 11.27.1 (A.D. 315 or 322) and JC 11.27.2 (A.D. 322). These are probably the same rescript, although it is not certain.

54. "Freedom was of such import to our ancestors, that it was not permitted to fathers to deprive their children of it, although fathers had once enjoyed the power of life and death over them" (JC 8.46.10); the same statement is repeated in TC 4.8.6, which, however, deals with a separate issue (as discussed below). The principle is also adduced in Vatican Fragment 33 (also A.D. 315): "Ingenuos progenitos servitutis adfligi dispendiis minime oportere etiam nostri temporis tranquillitate sancitur, nec sub obtentu initae venditionis inlicite decet ingenuitatem infringi" (Mommsen, as above, p. 8). Fossati Vanzetti does not notice this.

55. Although kidnapping was a problem, the statute does not seem to have had this in mind.

56. JC 4.43.2.

But another version does not mention poverty:

> According to the laws of earlier emperors, if anyone legiti-
> mately purchases or undertakes to rear a newborn infant, he ob-
> tains thereby the right to his labor, so that if after the passage of
> years someone should seek to recover his freedom or reclaim
> him as his servant, he must offer either a substitute or the
> amount he is worth.[57]

What earlier edicts Constantine had before him is unclear. In 331,
not claiming any precedent, he permanently altered Roman juridical principles regarding the abandonment of children by declaring:

> Anyone who picks up and nourishes at his own expense a little
> boy or girl cast out of the home of its father or lord with the
> latter's knowledge and consent may retain the child in the posi-
> tion for which he intended it when he took it in—that is, as
> child or slave, as he prefers. Nor may those who willingly and
> knowingly cast out of their home newborn slaves or children
> bring any action to recover them.[58]

This edict changed the legal position of abandoned children not
only among Romans but throughout the realms in which Roman
law would be known for the next millennium.[59] It does not recognize the *patria potestas,* or rights of natal parents, which had previously been paramount in discussions of abandonment or sale of
children; it upholds as inviolable the claim of those who took in the
children, even if it is their intention to employ them as slaves; and in
so doing, it suggests that abandoned children retain neither natal
status nor any legal relation to their biological parents once they
have been abandoned. The children of the upper classes could now
become slaves through abandonment, and vice versa.

It did not, obviously, limit the right of parents to abandon, and
it probably simply brought the law into more realistic correspon-

57. TC 5.10.1. Fossati Vanzetti argues (pp. 196–99) that this ruling deals not
with abandoned children in general, but only with the sale of slave children. It is
unlikely, she contends, that Constantine would have reversed himself only two
years later (see below) if he had intended this to apply to all children.

58. TC 5.9.1.

59. Justinian effectively abolished it within Byzantine territory, as noted below, but it is difficult to know how effective his legislation was; see chapter 4.

dence with actual circumstance, reflected perhaps in the Theban statute cited by Aelian. But Constantine further undermined the legal safeguards for children and most likely occasioned an increase in abandonment by decreeing in 336 that no one could inherit from an unmarried mother, overturning the previous recognition in Roman law of a mother's duty to illegitimate offspring.[60] This may have been offset to some extent by his prescribing capital punishment for the making of eunuchs, doubtless a major outlet for abandoned boys.[61] Zosimus (considerably after the fact) specifically accused Constantine of inducing the sale of many children through his onerous tax on commerce—suggesting that the selling of children would be an obvious recourse for parents burdened by increases in taxation.[62]

Why would the first emperor to favor Christianity issue an edict consigning abandoned children to perpetual slavery, after centuries of judicial pronouncements insisting that children could not be reduced to servile status simply because their parents could not afford to maintain them? The most likely explanation is the almost obsessive interest in stability and permanence characteristic of fourth-century legislation in general. By the opening of the century, political, social, and economic insecurity were so great throughout the empire that Constantine had to employ desperate measures to stabilize and maintain what appeared to him to be the status quo. Diocletian had already taken steps to ensure that most occupations and social positions became hereditary under pain of law, and every child had to follow the profession and status of his father. Constantine continued this: under his reign, for example, farmers were tied to the land on which they were born.[63] Although it seems ironic to deny the importance of natal heritage in a century so preoccupied with heredity, it is consistent with a pointedly conservative policy of freezing imperial social and economic structures; abandoned children, like the rest of society, were to remain where they were. Allowing them to be reclaimed or to regain freedom

---

60. TC 5.27.1. For a summary of obligations under earlier imperial rulings, see Dig. 25.3.5. The position of illegitimates grew steadily worse under Christian influence: see JC 5.27.2, TC 4.6.6, Novels 18.5 and 89.12.4–6.

61. CJ 4.42.1.

62. *History* 2.38.3.

63. For such provisions see, e.g., TC 7.22.1 (A.D. 313 or 319), 13.4.1 (A.D. 314), and 5.17.1 (A.D. 332).

might further weaken the delicate balance of social classes: it would reduce the shrinking work force and discourage masters or even foster parents from rescuing children in the first place, and thus put a greater burden on the fisc or the towns or the natal parents, all struggling to survive already. (A subsequent emperor, though attempting to undo Constantine's legislation about status, went to great lengths not to discourage buyers of children; see below, p. 117).

Constantine was the last ruler of an empire that was sufficiently stable and organized to support an elaborate bureaucracy, and his imperial acts are the latest that may be considered reflective of widespread conditions in antiquity (as opposed to opinion confined to imperial legislative circles; for later Roman law, see chapter 3, below). Their stipulations regarding abandonment and servitude survived in many abridgments of Roman law despite their official amendment or abrogation by subsequent rulers.[64]

During the first three centuries of the present era the major concerns of Roman civil and imperial jurisprudence in relation to abandonment were to safeguard the status of the freeborn by defining as invalid sales of free children by parents, to clarify issues of inheritance involving the abandoned, and to uphold the property rights of masters whose slaves abandoned their own children.[65] Only in the first half of the fourth century did this change, when Constantine denied the previously supreme right of parents and owners to re-

64. See chapter 4, below.

65. There were doubtless variations according to locality in the general picture presented here. A second-century law in Roman Egypt confiscated to the government one-quarter of the estate of anyone who made a foundling his heir (*Fontes Iuris Romani Anteiustiniani* 1 [Florence, 1940] 99.41). This has given rise to many odd speculations. Eyben, for example, claims (p. 200, n. 51) that "In Roman Egypt the adoption of male foundlings was forbidden," which is certainly untrue. The point of the law appears to have been simply confiscatory: much of the collection in which it occurs consists of inheritance penalties which will produce revenue for the state. But the right of Egyptian women to abandon had been specifically guaranteed by law in 10 B.C. (*Berliner griechische Urkunden: Ägyptische Urkunden aus den Königlichen Museen zu Berlin* [Berlin, 1912], 4:1104; discussed in R. Taubenschlag, *The Law of Greco-Roman Egypt in the Light of the Papyri, 332 B.C.–640 A.D.* [Warsaw, 1955], p. 151). This may indicate that Egypt had a particular tradition about abandonment, since such a right was generally assumed elsewhere in the ancient world. Foundlings also could not be priests (see below). On abandonment in Egypt, see Bieżuńska-Małowist, "Expositio."

claim, and granted to foster parents or new owners absolute rights over children they picked up. But at no point was the right of parents to abandon their children abridged or denied, and the great wealth of legislation covering many different aspects of the practice makes clear that it was quite common.

If the law seems heartless, it must be viewed against the backdrop of the age. Many provisions make pointed references to the desperate circumstances of the parents who sold or abandoned their children. The same rulings speak of the "miserable deprivation" inflicted on parents by kidnappers, and punish the offense with extreme penalties, all capital.[66] (And children were often stolen: they were valuable.)[67] People who had abandoned children frequently tried and managed to reclaim them.[68] And those who picked them up often reared them with great care and affection as foster children (*alumni*).[69] It was considered appropriate—though more for women than for men—to manumit *alumni* who were not free.[70] Both legal and literary texts suggest that a common reason for picking up abandoned infants was to pass them off as biological heirs; although this was fraudulent, it presumably resulted in a decent life for the child.[71]

66. Commitment to the mines, being thrown to beasts, or execution by sword: JC 9.20.16.

67. JC 47.2.68(67).2; Dig. 40.12.12.

68. The reclaiming of abandoned or sold children is discussed, assumed, or implied in JC 4.43.2, 5.4.16, 8.51(52).1; Paulus, *Sententiae* 5.1.1; Vatican Fragment 34; TC 3.3.1, 4.8.6, 5.9.2 and 12, and 5.10.1; Sirmondian Constitutions, 5; and Valentinian's Novel 33, all of which are discussed in the text above or below; and in *Declamationes* of Quintilian and *Controversiae* of Seneca, also discussed below.

69. On *alumnus* as "foster child," see below. Many cases of inheritances left to foster children occur in the codes; often they disclose that the testator had natal children of his own: Dig. 34.1.15 records a second-century legacy for the care of an infant *alumnus* until he was twenty, to be supervised by the testator's son and wife; similar and very generous bequests are mentioned in Dig. 34.1.14.1 and 36.3.26.

70. Dig. 40.2.14; *Institutes* 1.6.5.

71. Substitution (*suppositio*) was banned or regulated by numerous laws (e.g., Dig. 3.2.15, 48.10.19.1; JC 9.22.1); it must have been a considerable problem. Ulpian noted in the second century that "It is in the public interest that children not be substituted, to preserve the dignity of orders and families" (Dig. 25.4.1.13). Nonetheless, it was not a crime against the state; only the affected family members could prosecute: Dig. 48.10.30.1. For literary treatments, see below. Such children used to be called "supposititious," but as this word is difficult for the English eye, ear, and tongue, I have preferred the more accessible and equally clear "substituted."

It was, nonetheless, a slave society, in which the major source of energy was human labor; the slave population was immense and controlled by strict laws and structures designed to maintain its status, and owners of slaves enjoyed usufruct from infancy.[72] Children who were in the possession or control of persons other than their parents could be prostituted (Roman law allowed for concubines of twelve years or older, though slaves of any age could presumably be employed sexually) or put to labor at any age. Laws mention children placed in charge of taverns.[73]

THE MORALITY OF ABANDONMENT

What the law allowed could be a far cry from what a society accepted or approved—especially in a state like the Roman one, which generally acknowledged the chief function of legal structures to be safeguarding the common weal rather than upholding a specific moral code. Many of the principles and cases cited here imply general equanimity (on the part of lawmakers, at least) about abandonment, and a widespread assumption that parents gave up children for understandable reasons. But these do not necessarily demonstrate that the practice was regarded as morally indifferent or acceptable. Three sources of moral and ethical viewpoints can be used in analyzing Roman attitudes toward abandonment: religious, philosophical, and literary.

In some societies religious laws or prohibitions reflect or determine common practice, or at least instill a clear sense of the norms that are being violated when people perform acts disparaged by them. Few Roman religions, however, were understood as ethical systems until relatively late in Roman history. And Greco-Roman mythology,[74] the "revelation" of ancient paganism, was a repository of so many competing value systems, and derived from such varied

72. On usufruct, see Dig. 7.1.55.
73. Dig. 14.3.8. "Child," however, must be understood cautiously: see Introduction.
74. I have attempted in the following discussion to limit analysis of Greek materials to those which would actually have been familiar to Romans, although it is not always possible to distinguish, at this remove, the aspects of cult or mythology that were international from those that were local.

and disparate periods and places, that it does not necessarily represent Roman ethical values. It is, nonetheless, worth considering as an influence on Roman moral views, since it provided ideas, archetypes, and, above all, a common discourse about behavior, both human and divine.

The founding of the Roman state was, according to one of the most widely dispersed of Roman myths, the happy result of the abandonment of children. In Livy's account, a vestal virgin who had been raped bore twin sons, and the harsh monarch Amulius ordered them abandoned on the Tiber. Left in a basket which floated ashore, they were found by a wolf and suckled by her until a shepherd took them home to his wife and the couple brought them up as their own.[75] This tale has many of the most common elements of the abandonment motif in classical myth and literature: the children are of lofty though complicated ancestry;[76] a male figure orders the abandonment, to the regret of the mother; they are actually taken away and left by servants; they are found by shepherds and reared by foster parents; they subsequently rise to greatness.

These same or similar elements were familiar to Romans in a variety of venerable sources; some were originally Greek, but by the time of the empire had become a part of Roman culture. Oedipus was abandoned at the order of his father (because of a prophecy), was found by a shepherd and reared by a childless king, and rose to greatness, though he came to a tragic end.[77] The eponymous founder of the Ionians, Ion, was abandoned by his mother (because he was illegitimate) with a token for later recognition, brought up in the temple of Apollo, and was miraculously reunited with his mother when she and her (new) husband came to the temple to pray

---

75. Livy 1.4. Cf. Plutarch, *Romulus* 3–5, and shorter accounts: Livy 1.6.3; Cicero, *De Republica* 2.2; Servius 1.274; Strabo, *Geography* 5.3.2 (where he says that such exposure was τι πάτριον, an "ancestral custom"); and Dionysius of Halicarnassus 2.56. Both Livy and Plutarch report speculation that the myth arose because "she-wolf" was an expression for a woman of loose character, a designation appropriate for the twins' foster mother.

76. Their mother said that Mars was the father; Plutarch (4) says that Amulius himself had ravished her.

77. Oedipus is alluded to or mentioned at length in such an array of European literature, from Homer to Freud, that it would be pointless to offer bibliographical guidance. For an overview with speculations on the origins of the myth, see M. Delcourt, *Oedipe ou la légende du conquérant* (Paris, 1944), or, more recently, V. Propp, *Edipo alla luce del Folklore* (Torino, 1975). See index, s.v. *Oedipus*.

for a son.[78] Cyrus, the founder of the Persian empire, had been abandoned and brought up by a herdsman and his wife, according to Herodotus;[79] as had Paris, who began the Trojan War, which ultimately led to the founding of the dynasty overthrown by Romulus and Remus.[80] Telephus, a king of Mysia in Greece, and Habis, a ruler of the Cunetes in Spain, had both been exposed as children, according to tradition.[81] Jupiter himself had been abandoned as a child, and his twin sons, Zethus and Amphion, were exposed, as were Poseidon, Aesculapius, Hephaistos, Attis, and the goddess Cybele.[82]

In some of these tales the abandonment is a central issue; in most it is not. Euripides recounts the exposing of Ion five times in the play bearing his name—which was read and studied by educated Romans of the early empire—and devotes considerable attention to its emotional aspects. A servant can hardly believe that Creusa would abandon her child, even though he is illegitimate, and Ion himself considers it "frightful" ($\delta\varepsilon\hat{\iota}\nu\alpha$, 1497) that his mother would

78. This story in its Attic form is told in Euripides' play, *Ion*.

79. In response to a dream warning that he would rule all of Asia, the grandfather had ordered the child murdered; the steward entrusted with the task could not bear to do it, and gave the baby to a herdsman to expose in the forest. The herdsman was also too tenderhearted to do this, and took the infant home to his wife, substituting for it their own stillborn son: Herodotus 1.108–30. On this theme, see G. Binder, *Die Aussetzung des Königskindes: Kyros und Romulus*. It is less likely that Romans knew the Babylonian hero Sargon (exposed in a basket like Moses: see "The Legend of Sargon," trans. E. A. Speiser, *Ancient Near Eastern Texts Relating to the Old Testament*, ed. J. B. Pritchard [Princeton, 1950], p. 119), or the legend that Zoroaster had been exposed (not even evident in Persian literature until the twelfth century).

80. Paris was also exposed to obviate infanticide after a dream: Hyginus 91; cf. Apollodorus 3.148 ff.

81. The childhood of Telephus is related in Diodorus Siculus 4.33; that of Habis in Justinus's epitome of the work of Trogus (*Epitoma historiarum Philippicarum Pompei Trogi,* ed. Otto Seel [Leipzig, 1935] 44.4, pp. 229–301).

82. Most of these incidents are recounted in a number of mythological sources: for Jupiter, see Apollodorus, *On the Gods* 1.1.5–7; Hesiod, *Theogony* 453–67; Hyginus, *Poeticon astronomicon* 2.13 and *Fabula* 118; for Zeus's twins, Hyginus 7 and Dio Chrysostom, *Discourse* 15; for Hephaistos, Apollodorus, *Bibliotheca* 1.3.5; for Poseidon and Aesculapius, Pausanius 8.8 and 8.28, respectively; Attis's history is told in Pausanius 7.16; and Cybele's infancy is discussed in Pausanius 7.17. Other mythical exposings are catalogued in Donald Redford, "The Literary Motif of the Exposed Child," and L. Gernet, "Fosterage et légende," in *Mélanges Gustave Glotz*, 1 (Paris, 1932) 385–95.

have left him in a cave. He is terrified that the mother will turn out to be a slave if he finds her, which would be worse than not having a mother at all (1382–83); but he also complains that his life has no value unless he can locate his mother (670). When he does find her their reunion is quite emotional (1433ff.). By contrast, the abandonment in extant versions of the Oedipus legend is important chiefly because it leads to his famous incestuous marriage, and has relatively little specific emotional import.[83]

In most mythical cases abandonment turns out happily; in some, the ultimate end is disaster, although even in the latter (e.g., Oedipus) the abandonment is usually a means of avoiding outright infanticide. And even at its most heartless, abandonment is clearly a benign reaction to troublesome children when compared to other responses of Greco-Roman divinities: Kronos devoured his own children; Pelops was cooked and served to the gods as a meal by his father; the children of Thyestes were served to him by his brother. It is with bitter sarcasm that Tertullian writes of Saturn's devouring his children, "better he than wolves, if he had exposed them":[84] none of the childhood possibilities for mythic heroes was very pleasant. Abandonment usually turned out to be, in both the literal and figurative sense, providential.

Some of these stories may have grown out of real circumstances and reflect actual practices or psychological aspects of abandonment: sacrificing children to gods, for example, is attributed retrospectively by Roman, Jewish, and Christian writers to a number of Mediterranean peoples.[85] But the development and sources of mythology are far too uncertain to justify extrapolation from its particulars. What can be deduced with reasonable assurance is that Roman religious and political mythology presented abandonment

83. Cicero mentions him in the context of matrimonial incest (*De finibus* 5.3), Suetonius as a figure of blindness (*Nero* 21), Plautus as the interpreter of the riddle of the Sphinx (*Poenulus* 443).

84. *Ad nationes* 2.12.

85. Both Plutarch (*Superstition* 171, *Sayings of Kings* 175) and Diodorus Siculus (20.14) describe in detail the Punic custom of sacrificing children to Kronos, and Diodorus says specifically that the myth of Kronos eating his children arose from the cultic practice, rather than vice versa. Diodorus may have been hostile to Carthage, but there is no reason to doubt Plutarch's corroboration, and the first settlers of Carthage had reportedly come from the area of the Middle East where sacrifice of children to Moloch was common. For Moloch, see below, chapter 3. Sacrifice of children was also known in the Mediterranean in political contexts, as in the famous tale of the Minotaur (Plutarch, *Theseus* 15).

as a *common* and *ordinary* reaction of both human and divine parents
to unwanted children. In Seneca's *controversia* about the man who
cripples abandoned children the speakers are poignantly aware of
the myth of Rome's origin and the ironies it holds for the situation.
One remarks that it is fortunate for Rome that such a man did not
find its founders.[86] In *Daphnis and Chloe* two abandoned children,
reared by shepherds, fall in love and are eventually reunited with
their natal parents. When one character makes fun of Daphnis for
having been exposed and nursed by a goat, he proudly replies that
this is something he shares with Jupiter.[87] Arguing against the importance of noble descent, a speaker in Dio Chrysostom's discourse
on slavery chides another that he would have taken Zeus's abandoned twins for slaves and contemned them before their identity
became known.[88]

Mythology enshrined cruelty and wantonness as well as kindness and heroism, and the frequency with which it included abandonment may attest only to the latter's familiarity and associations.
But the idea that the founders of most of the great dynasties known
to Romans—and even Zeus and his children—had been abandoned
and reared (usually quite humbly) by other people could not but
affect Roman views of the practice.

Cultic and superstitious aspects of Roman religion may also have
contributed to acceptance of abandonment, or even have prompted
it. Evil omens are known to have occasioned instructions to expose
infants among the Greeks,[89] and probably did so among Romans as
well. Citizens of the empire abandoned children as a symbolic ritual
of grief when Caligula died.[90] An inscription of the second century
A.D. from Smyrna prescribes a purification period of forty days before someone who has exposed a child can enter the temple;[91] but
purification was also required after birth or miscarriage in this as in

86. Seneca, *Controversiae* 10.4.9.

87. 1.16: ἐμὲ αἲξ ἀνέθρεψεν ὥσπερ τὸν Δία.

88. Discourse 15.

89. In the fifth century B.C., Herodotus recorded the counsel given to Hippo-
crates, ruler of Athens, by Chilon the Lacedaemonian in response to an omen (vessels containing meat and water boiled without fire): that he not take home a
childbearing wife or if he chanced to have one to divorce her, and if there was a son
to disown him (Herodotus 1.59).

90. Suetonius, *Caligula* 5.

91. In J. Keil, ed., "Inschriften aus Smyrna," *Anzeiger der österreichischen Akademie Wien,* 90 (Vienna, 1953) 1; discussed in Martin Nilsson, *The Dionysiac Mysteries of the Hellenistic and Roman Age* (Lund, 1957), pp. 133–35.

many other Mediterranean cultures, so it is unlikely that the rule indicates moral disapproval as opposed to ritual "impurity." A child abandoned on a dung heap could not be a priest in Egypt, but this was certainly a rule of purity rather than an ethical objection to abandonment, since it was the child who incurred the disadvantage.[92] Zosimus describes a Sabine father who believed the gods were angry with his children and who offered himself and his wife as sacrifices in their stead: the story evinces both the threat to children sometimes posed by religion and the fact that parental sentiment might nonetheless triumph over it.[93]

Astrological beliefs about human destiny constituted a considerable portion of the religion of antiquity; these must have contributed to a certain amount of resignation about abandonment, if they did not provide direct inspiration for it. Julius Firmicus Maternus describes several dozen heavenly constellations which will result in the exposing of newborn infants;[94] they will determine as well whether the child will die shortly afterward (often with the mother), be recovered by strangers and reared as their own child[95] or as a slave,[96] not be given food (7.2.21,22), be torn to pieces by dogs (7.2.9,11,12, etc.), or perish on water (7.2.10,11, etc.).[97] It is difficult to assess the "likelihood" of these scenarios: although astrology was intended to elucidate and anticipate the quotidian lives of its devotees, some of the events discussed in ancient lore of this sort seem likely to have been singular and rare occurrences, so it would be rash to infer from such provisions that these were all familiar aspects of abandonment.

Educated Romans would also have had acquaintance with a considerable body of ethical literature, both Greek and Roman, in which abandonment occurred as a moral issue, although never very

92. *Fontes Iuris Romani Anteiustiniani* (see note 65, above) 99.92.

93. *History* 2.1.2.

94. *Iulii Firmici Materni Matheseos Libri VIII,* ed. K. Ziegler (Stuttgart, 1968) 7.2 ("De expositis et non nutritis").

95. "Si vero his sic constitutis benivola stella coniunctionem Lunae venientis exceperit, expositi ab aliis colligentur, et libertati redditi in filiorum loco nutrientur" (ibid., 7.2.7). Cf. 7.2.14: "expositus ab alio collectus nutrietur," and 7.2.16 and 18.

96. "Expositis et nutriti laqueis servilibus inplicantur" (ibid., 7.2.18).

97. All of the children were apparently to be exposed immediately after birth, although 7.2.10 mentions children "nursed a few days and then cast out" ("paucis diebus nutriti proicientur").

prominently. The extent to which such writings provided models of behavior is difficult to determine, and they are notably ambivalent about abandonment. Several issues, easily conflated because of their superficial similarity to each other, must be carefully distinguished to understand the basis of antique moral opinion on the subject. For modern sensibilities the two paramount ethical considerations would be (1) the welfare of the child, and (2) parental responsibility. These are related but separable: one might believe, for example, that all parents have an obligation to support and rear the children they engender, while recognizing that in some cases it would be better for the child to be placed in another home.

Few of the various ethical objections to abandonment in ancient Europe, however, acknowledged either of these as significant principles. Most focused their attention on two other questions which are much less prominent in modern societies: (3) procreative purpose, and (4) civic duty to have (or not have) children. The former is straightforward: some antique philosophies (e.g., strains of neo-Platonism, of Stoicism, and of Christianity) held that procreation was the sole legitimate function of sexuality. A moral parent could therefore not have accidental or unwanted children: the only reason to indulge in sexual intercourse, even within marriage, was to produce a child. Such a philosophy might be expected to have made distinctions about what parents did with a child they had produced "wrongly," but few did. The actual fate of the child was much less important in assessing blame than the inferred self-indulgence of the couple, who must have had conjugal relations for pleasure alone.

Civic duty was somewhat more complex, comprising presumed obligations either to a family unit (immediate or extended) or to the state. In the first case, the duty was generally to preserve or enhance the genealogical grouping through the production of heirs. Duties to the state, by contrast, might be either to contribute to its population (e.g., the *ius trium liberorum*) or to refrain from doing so—or, as a combination of the two, to produce precisely so many children and no more. An obligation of either sort to produce heirs could result in condemnations of abandonment which seem like generic disapproval, but which are in fact rooted in principles quite different from modern concerns, and often, for example, had little or no relation to notions of parental responsibility or the welfare of the child.

Writings of both Plato and Aristotle known to Romans express concerns about procreative purpose and civic duty. In the *Republic*

Plato urged that parents not have more children than they could
support,[98] that the poor not rear any children at all,[99] and that the
state "hide away in a secret and unknown place" defective children
or those of "inferior" parents.[100] Some commentators have taken the
second and third to be euphemisms for infanticide, but probably incorrectly.[101] What Plato meant, as is clear both from the wording
and from a cross-reference in the *Timaeus* (19A),[102] is that such children should be brought up outside of both their natal homes and
public view. All of the children in the *Republic* are, in fact, to be
"abandoned" in the sense under discussion here, since their parents
are to give them up as infants to the control of others and to have no
personal contact with or responsibility for them. It is an organized
transference in the case of most children—anonymous exposing is
recommended only for cases of incest[103]—but it suggests, nonetheless, a low estimation of the desirability of or need for direct parental involvement in childrearing.[104]

The *Laws*—on this as on most matters—appears to be more realistic. It suggests as a means of maintaining a stable population that
parents rear a single son as heir; other sons should be given to childless couples, "ideally for free"—presumably as opposed to a sale.[105]
(Compare the Theban law regarding the lowest bidder.) The ideal
number of children is two[106]—one boy and one girl, although more
girls may be allowed.[107] (This prescription matches closely the de-

98. *Republic* 2.12 (372B).

99. *Republic* 5.8 (459E): τῶν μὲν τὰ ἔκγονα τρέφειν, τῶν δὲ μή.

100. *Republic* 5.9 (460C): ἐν ἀπορρήτῳ τε καὶ ἀδήλῳ κατακρύψουσιν. The translation of this passage in the LC edition (trans. Paul Shorey [Cambridge, Mass.,
1953] 1.463) as "they will properly dispose of in secret" is entirely misleading.
Κατακρύπτω means simply "to hide," not "to dispose of."

101. This is well discussed in G. van N. Viljoen, "Plato and Aristotle on the
Exposure of Infants at Athens."

102. See more detailed discussion in van N. Viljoen, pp. 64–65.

103. *Republic* 5.9 (461C): οὕτω τιθέναι, ὡς οὐκ οὔσης τροφῆς τῷ τοιούτῳ.

104. Athenaeus claimed that the Etruscans actually did rear their children in
common in this way (*Deipnosophistae* 12.518), but this is doubtful.

105. Κατὰ χάριν μὲν μάλιστα. R. G. Bury's translation renders this as "by a
friendly arrangement if possible" in the LC edition (*Laws* [Cambridge, Mass.,
1952] 1.365), but this seems to me unlikely. The sale of children was as common in
the Greek world as it was in the Roman: see Plutarch, *Solon* 13.5, 33.2; Xenophon,
Agesilaos 1.21.

106. *Laws* 11.930D.

107. *Laws* 5.470B, 11.923C.

scription Polybius gave of the many wealthy Greeks who would not bring up more than one or two "out of a larger number" born to them.)[108] The *Laws* further suggests that sexuality be directed exclusively toward procreation (825E–842C). The combination of these two requirements—exclusively procreative sexuality and a maximum family size of two children—would require either extraordinary popular restraint or abandonment on a large scale. Plato clearly prefers the former, but would tolerate the latter.

In the *Theaetetus* (160E–161A) Socrates compares the process of assessing the value of a new idea to deciding whether to keep or abandon a newborn infant.

> Shall we say that this [new idea] of yours is a kind of newborn infant, and I the midwife? . . . And after the birth . . . we must not fail to ascertain whether what has been born is worth bringing up, and not idle or false.[109] Or do you imagine that any child of yours should necessarily be reared and not abandoned? And will you be able to stand overseeing the decision, and not take it ill if it is disposed of, even though it is your firstborn?

The implicit question here is not whether it is morally acceptable to abandon children (or ideas)—this is presumed—but how one should make a determination in a particular case. Some students of the text have been shocked by its casual acceptance of exposing—to the point of arguing that the metaphor is not to be taken seriously—but it accords well with Plato's other comments on the subject.[110]

Aristotle objected strongly to the family communism Plato had

108. Polybius 36.17.7.

109. The idea, of course, at the most obvious level, but probably also a paronomastic reference to substituted children.

110. See, e.g., against taking it seriously, pp. 225–28 in Louis Germain, "L'Exposition des enfants nouveau-nés dans la Grèce ancienne: Aspects sociologiques," in *L'Enfant* 1. 211–46, and Engels, "The Problem of Female Infanticide." In addition to the fact that Plato has elsewhere recommended a policy of family limitation, one might note that (1) the analogy would hardly work if Plato's contemporaries would *not* have considered abandoning a newborn; (2) all of the other analogies in the *Theaetetus* are quite realistic and familiar (wax tablets, birds in aviary, etc.); (3) earlier in the text (151A–D) in another metaphor about a midwife and birth Plato specifies exactly where the metaphor becomes unrealistic, as if its accuracy were an important part of his argument. Note, too, that this passage makes reference to the child's being "taken away" from the mother, which could be a reference to a father's decision to abandon.

recommended in the *Republic,* particularly the common rearing of children, and devoted a section of his *Politics* (2.1) to showing why it could not work. Among his arguments were the likelihood that people in charge of them would abuse children they did not know to be their own, and that no one would know whether his child had been "saved" (σωθῆναι) or not: he assumed, that is, that the system would not obviate abandonment (or killing?) of children. The *Politics* also includes a brief comment about population control whose textual uncertainty has given rise to much disagreement about whether Aristotle believed that local custom either did or might prohibit the exposing of children.[111] Almost any reading indicates that Aristotle himself would approve of abandonment as a means of population control.[112]

Aristotle also repeated two curious zoological data about abandonment which had considerable impact on those traditions inclined to look to animal models of sexuality as "natural."[113] He adduced as true the widely disseminated belief that eagles laid three eggs, hatched two, and reared only one of these, ejecting the other one from the nest; the abandoned eaglet was then taken in and brought up by another species of bird.[114] And he reported, accurately, that the cuckoo "substituted" her young in the nest of other birds, an image of sufficient impact on the popular imagination to

111. In the *Nicomachean Ethics* (7.5) Aristotle condemned, not surprisingly, the murder or eating of children, customs practiced, according to him, by barbarians.

112. *Politics* 7.14.10 (1335B). The difference hinges on the readings of fourteenth- and fifteenth-century manuscripts, and we can have no firm idea what text was available to Romans. The controversy is discussed at length in nearly all treatments of Greek abandonment: e.g., Eyben, pp. 37–38; van N. Viljoen, pp. 66–69.

113. On animals and the "natural," see Boswell, *Christianity,* esp. pp. 137–43, 152–56, 313–15, 319–21.

114. *Historia Animalium* 6.6 and 9.34,44. The species of bird that rescues the exposed eaglet is called a φήνη, which cannot be identified with certainty. Pliny says it is another species of eagle (*Natural History* 10.4). This is not exactly the "brood parasitism" actually common among cuckoos (see following note), where birds lay their eggs in the nest of another species, and modern naturalists have not described this behavior among eagles. But Aristotle was normally circumspect in treating popular zoological legends (especially those used as moral examples: see Boswell, *Christianity,* pp. 138–40), and this account may be related to the variation of "brood parasitism" recently discovered to take place among swallows, who transfer six percent or more of eggs already laid to the nests of other swallows: see R. Monastersky, "Swallows Keep Eggs in Several Baskets," *Science News* 133, 2 (Jan. 9, 1988), p. 22.

have given rise to the English "cuckold."[115] Pliny perpetuated the story about the eagle among Roman readers,[116] and although neither he nor Aristotle drew moral conclusions about human abandonment from it, Christian writers who knew it were quite troubled by its moral implications, and it may have subtly affected the attitudes of other ancient writers as well.[117]

By contrast, the roughly contemporary Athenian orator Isocrates, also familiar to educated Romans, railed against the "outrageously perverse and horrid crimes" perpetrated by Greeks of other (N.B.) times and places depicted on the stage every year. He included the "abandonment of the newborn" along with murder, incest, drownings, and blindings—a context of severe disapproval—but he offered no insight into the exact nature of his objections to the practice.[118]

Of philosophers actually writing at Rome, only two objected to abandonment. Both were Stoics. Epictetus, writing (in Greek) during the first century of the Christian era, criticized the earlier Greek philosophical schools for their attitudes toward childrearing. He complained that Epicurus had objected to the rearing of one's own children because they were often an occasion of sorrow.[119]

> "Let us not rear our children," [Epicurus] says. A sheep will not abandon its young, nor a wolf—but a human should abandon his? Would you have us be as simple as sheep? But they do not

115. *Historia animalium* 11.29 (618A). "Brood parasitism" occurs in about one-third of the 150 species of cuckoos. Joel Welty, *The Life of Birds* (New York, 1979), p. 323: "This characteristic, a nasty and subversive one by human standards, but perfectly natural and biologically 'moral' by avian standards, is practiced by representatives of five families. . . . Birds of various genera among these families lay their eggs in nests of other species and abandon them to the care of their foster parents."

116. Adding details, such as the species of rescuer (as above), and the fact that the eagle persecutes the abandoned offspring even when they grow up. Pliny also gives the number of exposed as two or even three.

117. For comparable legends among Jews about ravens and jackals abandoning their young, see L. Ginzberg, *The Legends of the Jews,* 1.30, 5.56 and 142 (n. 31).

118. *Panathenaicus* 122.

119. Herodotus claimed that Persian fathers did not see their sons before the age of five, to avoid unhappiness if they died (1.136; note that in the same place he makes reference to substituted children, and although he does not make the connection, it would seem that this system would make such substitutions particularly easy).

abandon their offspring. As wild as wolves? But they do not abandon, either.[120] Come—who will listen to you when he sees his child fallen down and crying? Even if your mother and father had been able to guess that you would say such things, I do not believe they would have abandoned you![121]

He also berated the Cynics for their support of detachment from the duties of life, using parental responsibility to children as an example of an unavoidable obligation.

Doesn't one have to provide cloaks for his children? Doesn't he have to send them to school with tablets, writing tools, notebooks? Doesn't he have to turn down their beds? They can't be Cynics as they come from the womb. If he does not do these things, it would be better to throw them out [ῥῖψαι] than to kill them [i.e., thus by neglect].[122]

This appeal to the welfare of the child is almost unique in antique ethical writing, but even Epictetus does not insist that parents are obliged to rear all children born to them, only that a minimum level of concern is necessary to discharge responsibility for those kept. Without this, the children might as well be abandoned. Whether abandonment would be justified if parents are unable to provide this sort of care remains unclear.

Musonius Rufus, a contemporary of Epictetus (who attended his lectures in Rome), left behind a work whose title poses precisely that question: "Should every child that is born be reared?"[123] This was not, however, the real subject of the essay; at no point does Musonius even articulate, much less insist upon, a principle that parents are responsible for every child born to them. His concern is largely civic: Romans should strive to have large families. Appealing to laws designed to increase population and to the admiration

120. The story of Romulus and Remus, whose statue stood over the forum, provides an ironic backdrop for this sarcasm.

121. *Discourses* 1.23.

122. *Discourses* 3.22.74.

123. Εἰ πάντα τὰ γινόμενα τέκνα θρεπτέον. Such titles were often added to ancient writings by later copyists, but Stobaeus quotes the work specifically by this title (*Florilegium,* ed. C. Wachsmuth and O. Hense [Berlin, 1884–1923] 4.24.15, p. 605), so it is at least ancient, if not original, and interesting either way. It is translated as section 16 in Cora Lutz, *Musonius Rufus, "The Roman Socrates."*

one feels on seeing parents with many children—both implying that such families were rare—he adduces two reasons that parents actually limit the size of their families: poverty or wealth. To the former he holds up the example of birds:

> "I am poor and lack means; if I have many children how will I support them all?"
>
> "How do little birds, much poorer than you—swallows and nightingales and larks and blackbirds—support their young? Are they of greater understanding than humans? . . . Of greater strength and power?"

(Note that he does not mention eagles or cuckoos.) To the latter— the rich who refuse to bring up the children born later to them, so that the first few will inherit more[124]—he makes the argument that siblings are more valuable than wealth:[125] "I consider it right for us to try to bequeath to our children siblings rather than wealth, as an inheritance providing greater means of good." This may be predicated on concern for the welfare of the child, although other interpretations are possible.

That these were minority opinions is stated explicitly by Hierocles, a second-century Stoic, who opined that

> the rearing of all or at least most children born to one is in accord with nature and proper respect for marriage. But the majority of people appear to ignore this advice for a reason which is not particularly laudable: out of love of wealth and the conviction that poverty is the greatest evil. . . .[126]

Hierocles subjoins to this argument, based on procreative purpose, the issue of civic duty: he maintains that one has an obligation to

124. All legitimate children had equal share in an intestate parent's estate; Brunt believed that most Romans died without a will (p. 141).

125. Although Musonius considers this "frightful" or "shocking" (δεινότατον, the word most commonly used by Greek critics of abandonment: cf. Euripides' *Ion,* above), Lutz's translation of κακῶς εἰδότες as "such a deed of wickedness" (p. 101) overstates the opinion: "badly devising" would be closer to the sense, since κακῶς connotes inferiority as much as (if not more than) "wickedness," a concept somewhat corrupted by anachronistic modern associations of absolute right and wrong.

126. Stobaeus, 4.24.14 (Wachsmuth, 4.603).

ancestors, friends, and the state to engender posterity. But he includes also a consideration not part of any traditional ethical speculation on the matter (and arguably not an "ethical" point): anyone
who fails to rear children deprives himself of support in old age.

Even Hierocles' ideal parent might only bring up "most" of his
children, and hence would abandon some. Most ancient moral writings evince indifference toward or acceptance of abandonment.
Gellius, who excoriates abortion as an act "worthy of public contempt and general hatred,"[127] and even rails against the evils of
mothers' not nursing their own children, mentions abandonment as
a common and normal occurrence without any suggestion of disapproval (12.1.9). Plutarch cites Empedocles and Heraclitus as claiming that it is "unnatural" to rear *any* offspring, although he himself
clearly disapproves of their views.[128]

In the *controversia* of the elder Seneca dealing with the crippling
of *expositi* (discussed above) one speaker says that the parents who
exposed them harmed the children more than the man who maimed
them, but given the circumstances this is probably not a blanket
condemnation: if the children had been reared in happier circumstances the same person might not have regarded the abandonment
itself as reprehensible. Another argues on the side of the crippler—
clearly with irony—that his actions may result in fewer parents exposing children, which certainly suggests regret about the extent of
the practice, but not necessarily disapproval of individual actions.
When the abandoning parent is involved in the case (9.3), there is no
suggestion of improper or immoral behavior on his part.

Some of those presenting cases in Quintilian's *Declamationes*
criticize parents who exposed children. "If it had been up to you," a
foster father chides the man who abandoned the son over whose
prize for heroism they are contending, "the state would not have
had such a hero: beasts would have torn him apart, or birds carried
him off, or—much worse—the pimp or the gladiator-trainer would
have gotten him."[129] But such comments must be understood in the
context of the quarrel at issue. The parents have not failed an absolute standard; they have simply put themselves in an awkward position as regards equity. Is it fair for them now to demand a reward if
they had previously given the child up? Although the point of the

127. "Publica detestatione communique odio dignum" (12.1.9).
128. *De sollertia animalium* 964E.
129. *Declamationes* 278 (Winterbottom, p. 87).

controversia and *declamatio* genres is to present every type of argument on either side of a case, the inherent impropriety of exposing a child is never adduced in any of the many arguments dealing with abandonment.

Even philosophical texts expressing opposition to infanticide and abortion often treat abandonment as normal and unobjectionable. Of the writers who do question its morality, only Epictetus raises the issue modern ethical systems would regard as paramount—the nature of parental responsibility for children. Other treatments are predicated on issues of procreative purpose or civic or family duty. A good citizen should neither have too many children (Plato, Aristotle) nor too few (Musonius Rufus, Hierocles), but either would allow, and the former possibly even require, abandonment. Nor is there any insistence (even in Epictetus) that having begotten a child in itself engenders a duty to support him.

Ethical writings frequently evince or urge levels of virtue which the average person would regard as idealistic and would not entirely expect of himself or his neighbors. Roman fiction may provide a better indication of the ordinary moral views of Romans. Few literary figures expressly address the propriety of abandoning children, and when they do, it is usually in passing, but this makes such remarks more rather than less valuable, since they appear not to have been at issue. Terence has the wife of a man who has exposed his daughter say that this was "severe," although nowhere else in the play is any disapproval expressed, and the mother's own feelings were not likely to reflect abstract ethical considerations.[130] The husband had, in fact, originally intended to kill the girl, and upbraids the wife for insisting on abandoning her instead, since she might thus be used as a prostitute or slave, which would be worse, in his view, than death.[131]

Callirhoe, the heroine of Chariton's romance *Chaereas and Callirhoe,* considers killing her unborn baby to prevent him from being reared as a slave, but ultimately rejects infanticide as "savage,"[132]

130. *Heautontimoroumenos,* line 665: *duro.*

131. *Ibid.,* lines 639–40.

132. ἀγριωτέρα: Chariton, *De Chaerea et Callirhoe amatoriarum narrationum libri octo,* ed. W. E. Blake (Oxford, 1938) 2, p. 32. Infanticide is also strongly rejected in the *Aethiopica* (10.12; p. 327 in Colonna): "neither the law nor nature allows the killing of children." All pagan Romans apparently agreed that it was permissible to kill deformed children (Cicero, *De legibus* 3.8; Tacitus, *Annales* 3.27; Seneca, *De ira* 1.15), but this is not, apparently, the issue here.

and decides that life affords many opportunities for abandoned children:

> How many children of gods and kings do we hear of brought up[133] in slavery who later recover the status of their parents— Zethus and Amphion and Cyrus? You also, my child, shall sail back to Sicily. . . . You, my child, shall return your parents to each other.[134]

In *Daphnis and Chloe,* Chloe's father, who exposed her because he was short of cash and could not support her, felt that the "gods mocked"[135] him for this. Daphnis's father, who left him in a field because he already had three children and wanted no more, says he was unhappy to do so, although he did it voluntarily (4.24); the foster father later recounts in completely neutral terms his inference that Daphnis's parents exposed him because they had older children (4.19). The tone of the work does not imply that either set of abandoning parents had done anything questionable, and they are able to reclaim the children without shame or embarrassment—indeed, with public fanfare and general rejoicing.

This is perhaps the most telling single point about the morality of abandonment in Roman writing: parents who exposed a child are never represented as being ashamed of having done so when they recover her or him. Many arguments might be brought to bear to discourage exposing—encouraging the noblest possible behavior, or recommending the advantages of a large family; criticism might be leveled at a parent who exposed a child and subsequently expected benefit from him. But it was not shameful simply to abandon a child, and no reclaiming parent appears abashed about it.

On the other hand, there was universal approval and admiration for those who rescued such children. The shepherd who finds Daphnis says that he could not leave the baby in the thicket because he was ashamed to be less philanthropic than the goat who had

---

133. Literally, "born," which represents her own circumstances, but is not as appropriate to the analogy.

134. Chariton, *De Chaerea et Callirhoe* 2, pp. 32–33. The date of this novel is disputed, but it is generally considered the earliest extant complete Greek novel and probably dates from the second century.

135. *Daphnis and Chloe* 4.35.

suckled him.[136] In the *Aethiopica*,[137] the Queen of Ethiopia decides
that it would be better for her daughter, whom she loves deeply, to
be exposed than to be reared as if she were illegitimate (4.8). Neither the author nor any of the characters in the novel appear to
blame her for this, but a great point is made of the virtue and integrity of the gymnosophist who rescues the girl because his philosophy required it of him (2.31).[138] Dio Chrysostom recounts with
evident admiration the tale of a slave girl who not only never (N.B.)
exposed children of her own, but picked up the children of others
and reared them.[139] Quintilian depicts a foster father who, having
severely punished the child he reared, defends himself by arguing
that the son "could not deny that I was his father."

> "You were not," he might say, "my biological father." So much
> the worthier was I then: while others were abandoning their
> own I was taking in someone else's.[140]

And he articulates the principle that society must be grateful to
those who bring up the exposed: "Thanks are owed those who
bring up abandoned children."[141]

Despite the urgings of a few philosophers that it was better to
rear many children, Roman moral and legal views of abandonment
appear to have been quite indulgent. Neither law nor public opinion
posed any barrier to parents exposing or giving children away
through the fourth century; selling them was slightly more complicated, though by no means uncommon. Those ethical writers
who opposed abandonment appealed to concerns about the parents'
sex lives, the family at large, or the state. No one urged that children had an essential right to a place in the family into which they
were born.

Does this mean that Roman parents either lacked or suppressed

136. Ibid., 1.2,3: a pun, of course, on φιλάνθρωπος.
137. There is an English translation in Moses Hadas, *Heliodorus, An Ethiopian Romance*.
138. The novel is in fact clearly in some measure propaganda for the gymnosophists.
139. *Fifteenth Discourse* 9.
140. *Declamationes* 372 (Winterbottom, p. 268).
141. "Referendam esse gratiam expositos colligentibus" (*Declamationes* 376 [Winterbottom, p. 273]).

what most modern people would assume were innate protective feelings toward their newborn children? Plutarch wrote a treatise to demonstrate that parental affection was natural, which would suggest there was doubt about this at Rome.[142] Marcus Aurelius observed that well-born Romans tended to lack affection for their children;[143] and Fronto went further:

> Indeed, in my whole life at Rome I have found nothing so wanting as men sincerely attached to their children; which leads me to believe that the reason there is no Latin word for this virtue is that in fact no one in Rome has it.[144]

Could Romans really not have cared about children, or have held attitudes toward them that were markedly different from other people's? Certainly the fact that they employed the limited means of family planning available to them does not demonstrate this: modern parents could hardly be assumed to lack affection simply because they choose to have fewer rather than more children. Many would argue that concern for children is better exhibited by family planning than by promiscuous fertility.

Complaints about the coldness of parents are, moreover, common social criticisms.[145] Moralists always tend to paint a bleak picture of the *mores* of their contemporaries, and Plutarch's standards were not typical.[146] The great majority of Roman sources do, in

142. *De amore prolis* (On the love of offspring). In it he claims that "nature" tells all creatures to love (στέργειν) and rear (τρέφειν) their children (497D–E); but elsewhere he says that devotion to offspring is one of the three cardinal virtues, along with cherishing friends and being chaste in relations with women—a peculiar triad of "natural" feeling according to modern sensibilities (φίλους ἀγαπᾶν, πρὸς γυναῖκας σωφρονεῖν, τέκνων στερκτικοὺς εἶναι [*De liberis educandis* 7E]).

143. *Meditations* 1.11: those reckoned well-born (εὐπατρίδα) tend to be ἀστοργότεροι. At 1.10 he has listed as a particularly desirable quality being φιλοστοργότατον—the opposite.

144. *Ad Verum Imp.* 2.7.6. Cf. *Ad amicos* 1.3: "Frugi probus philostorgus, cuius rei nomen apud Romanos nullum est. . . ." But in the *Clementine Recognitions* Clement's father is described (12.9 [PG 2.308]) as being φιλότεκνος, "child loving" (in the Latin version [PG 1.1359] "tenere diligeret filios").

145. "There are no more marriages, nor social friendships, there is no love of children. . . ." Apuleius, *Metamorphoses* 5.28.

146. He was, for example, scandalized that people put "useless" slaves in charge of their children, or paid tutors too little (see *De liberis educandis* 4 and 5), and even disapproved of nurses, because "they love for pay" (ibid., 3: μισθοῦ φιλοῦσαι).

fact, assume strong parental affection. The same mythology that recorded abandonment of many children records the tender sentiments of Niobe and many other parents, both divine and human.[147] Cyrus's fearful grandfather seeks his death, but he apparently cannot perform the deed himself, and both men entrusted with the task find themselves emotionally unable to harm the child. Most mythic efforts at infanticide or exposure are thwarted by tender feelings for the child, which are integral to the tales. Paris may have been exposed, but his relative Aeneas flees their burning homeland with his father on his back and his son at his side. Plautus bases an appeal to a father for humane treatment of a slave on the fact that the man's own son has been captured: "There is a god who sees and hears what we do. He will preserve your son there as you treat me here."[148] A husband in Ovid's *Metamorphoses* tells his wife to kill her baby if it is a girl, but both of them cry about it, and the gods intervene to prevent it;[149] elsewhere Ovid appeals to parental affection as a touchstone of natural human sentiment, as do many other Roman writers.[150] Juvenal even suggests (14.48–49) that a father contemplating a dishonorable act form a mental image of his infant child, which will dissuade him.

The same Seneca who discussed the crippling of *expositi* mentions one man who tried to hang himself in despair when he lost his three (N.B.) children and wife in a fire,[151] and another who stole his grandson when denied visiting rights.[152] He describes a father who sent his son to be reared in the countryside after his first wife died giving him birth, and subsequently sent the son of his second wife as well. When both returned to the household, he refused to disclose to his wife which was hers, on the grounds that only thus would the boys be loved equally: *he* would not be tempted to give more love to the one "without a mother"—an extremely subtle and sensitive paternal attitude, by any standards.[153] When he presents the case of a man who exposes twin sons, he pictures him as "weep-

147. Nor was this without impact: see, e.g., Achilles Tatius, *Clitophon and Leucippe* 3.15.

148. *The Captives* 313–14.

149. *Metamorphoses* 9.678.

150. E.g., *Heroides* Ep. 12, where Medea uses Jason's presumed fatherly affection for their children as a means to win him back; or Apuleius, *Metamorphoses* 3.7.

151. *Controversiae* 5.1.

152. *Controversiae* 9.5.

153. *Controversiae* 4.6.

ing and trembling" as he does so.[154] Quintilian's lawyers imagine that a mother who had abandoned a child would agonize over other people's children and constantly torment herself wondering what had become of her own. "Already," she imagines, "he would have a career, or would be a soldier. I would already be seeking a wife for him."[155] And Quintilian himself begins his sixth oration with an extremely sentimental lament over the death of his youngest child.

Throughout the empire the image of a "loving father" steadily gained ground as a religious image, among pagans as well as Christians, and the social reality on which this symbol drew surely had much to do with increasing limitations on such practices as selling, castrating, or prostituting children. So normal was sentimental attachment to the young, in fact, that Plutarch was shocked that hunters could take animal mothers away from their babies.[156]

As in all times and places, there were doubtless some people in the empire with relatively little emotional attachment to children, but there is no reason to suppose that Romans as a people were significantly different from any other humans in this regard. To understand how people with normal human responses to the young in general and their own children in particular could face abandonment with equanimity, one must understand the biological necessity that prompted it, the moral environment that allowed it, and the circumstances that actually surrounded it. What became of the children? Was it, in fact, a fate worse than death, as some fathers claimed, or better than death, as most mothers seem to have assumed?

154. *Controversiae* 9.3.5: "flens, tremens, tamquam cum exponerem."
155. *Declamationes* 306 (p. 134).
156. *De sollertia animalium* 965B: ἀπὸ σκύμνων καὶ νεοσσῶν ἐλεεινῶς ἀγομένοις.

2

❖   ❖   ❖

ROME:
LITERARY FLESH
AND BLOOD

He was born of my kindness.

Foster father of abandoned child he adopted;
in Quintilian(?), *Declamationes minores* 278

To answer questions about the actual practice
and reality of abandonment—who was abandoned, and why, and
how, and what become of them—the historian must supplement
legal, historical, and ethical materials with other types of sources:
private letters, satire, drama, etc. These are adduced in the following discussion to a much greater extent than in the preceding analysis of structural influences such as law and ethics, although relevant
historical documentation is considered here as well.

Writers of fiction preserved more detailed information about
Roman social and family life in general and about abandonment in
particular than those authors generally considered "historical." The
former were, moreover, often acutely aware of the issue of "realism" and "accuracy." Plautus explains to his audience in *Casina* that
although the marriage of slaves depicted in the play was impossible in
Rome, it *could* happen in Greece, Carthage, and Apulia—implying
that audiences expected some degree of realism even in plays based
on Greek models.[1] Both Juvenal and Minucius Felix score satirical

---

1. This can, of course, be a playful device: Achilles Tatius has the hero of his
romance remark that his adventures seem "almost like fiction" (τὰ γὰρ ἐμὰ μύθοις
ἔοικε [1.2])—a witty suggestion of the obverse. The reliability of the testimony of
Plautus and Terence on abandonment in particular is upheld by Radin ("Exposure," pp. 342–43); and Fossati Vanzetti, without explanation, intersperses citations from legal codes and from Plautus and Terence as if there were no difference.
The fact that they based their plays on Greek materials does introduce complica-

points from the fact that reality mimics literature—implying the obverse as well—in relation to abandonment: so many exposed children of unsavory origin, Juvenal snipes, are reared by wealthy parents that fortune thereby makes a "secret comedy" for herself.[2] And Minucius Felix jibes that Romans abandon their children with such regularity that when they have recourse to prostitutes they unwittingly "weave a tale about incest."[3] When playwrights depict aspects of abandonment regulated by law they do so with great accuracy. In Plautus's *Curculio* a man who buys a girl worries that if she turns out to be freeborn he will have to give her up (11.490–93); Terence recognizes this principle as well,[4] and in his *Heautontimoroumenos* (11.835–36) a father who recovers his abandoned daughter repays her upkeep,[5] a requirement confirmed by legal literature.

Some aspects of ancient fiction inspire skepticism not because they are inherently unlikely but because they are unfamiliar to modern readers. Children as well as adults in plays and novels are frequently stolen by pirates or abducted by thieves and sold into prostitution or slavery—which might be considered preposterous if so much legislation had not been enacted to deal with kidnapping,

---

tions into their use as indications of Roman social life, and for this reason particulars derived from them have generally been relegated here to notes. But there is no reason to believe that, except for a few legal niceties about sale or inheritance, abandonment in urban Greece at a given moment would have differed significantly from its counterpart in Rome; and both Plautus and Terence wrote to entertain Roman audiences. The conventional wisdom is that the latter imitated his Greek models much more closely, while the former "Romanized" to a considerable degree. However true this may be in general, in regard to abandonment it is Terence's situations which appear to be distinctly Roman in several ways: see, e.g., note 5, below.

2. 6.602–9: "secretum sibi mimum parat."

3. "Sic incesti fabulam nectitis, etiam quum conscientiam non habetis" 31 (PL 3.336–37). *Incestum* does not mean incest in the specific sense of sexual relations within prohibited degrees of relationship, but it includes this and is clearly the sense here.

4. *The Eunuch* 805 ff. Although, as discussed at length above, this was not made law until later, the emperors who ruled on it described it as "an evident principle of law." It is also assumed in Heliodorus's novel, the *Aethiopica* (discussed below), at 2.31. Plautus's *Curculio* includes a speech (495 ff.) claiming that pimps do not own the persons they employ, suggesting that brothels may have employed mostly abandoned children or women forced into prostitution by circumstance, rather than slaves, who would certainly have been owned.

5. There is no evidence that this was ever a requirement in Greece, and it is one of many indications that Latin drama, even when based on Greek stories, accurately reflects Roman legal and social structures.

piracy, and the restoration of freeborn persons to natal status after they had been wrongfully reduced to servitude.[6] In fact, piracy and kidnapping were very real social problems (as the latter is today), and doubtless an important aspect of the slave trade.[7] They occur, moreover, as background in stories where they do not advance the plot.[8]

The frequency with which fictional shepherds find abandoned children and rear them in Arcadian simplicity before restoring them to their natal parents may strain credulity: the inspiration for this seems so obviously the mythical archetype of Oedipus, or Romulus and Remus. Aside from the fact that the archetypes themselves may arise from some social reality, it is worth noting that there was actually legislation in the later empire prohibiting the upper classes from "handing their children over to shepherds,"[9] and many indications both that infants were regularly sent to the countryside for rearing—because this was thought to be healthier for them—and that this could give rise to separation from, or at least possible confusion about, the identity of young children.[10]

6. Many of these citations are not laws addressing the problem, which might arise from isolated instances or even theoretical considerations, but casual mentions in other contexts: e.g., Dig. 40.12.3, on parents discovering a natural son in slavery.

7. Even slave children were stolen (Dig. 47.2.68), and children were seized legally as well: the historian of the Palatine library had been taken as a boy from his home in Alexandria according to Suetonius (*De grammaticis et rhetoribus* 20: "nonnulli Alexandrinum putant et a Caesare puerum Romam adductum Alexandria capta"). Seneca the Elder mentions a grandfather who stole his grandson when the father denied him visiting rights (*Controversiae* 9.5).

8. E.g., in Longus's novel *Daphnis and Chloe* (discussed below), where the pirates have nothing to do with twists of the story line, but simply add verisimilitude, especially in 2.32, where the old men amuse themselves bragging about having escaped pirate raids.

9. "Ne pastoribus dentur filii nutriendi" (TC 9.31): "Nemo curialium plebeiorum possessorumve filios suos nutriendos pastoribus tradat. Aliis vero rusticanis, ut fieri solet, nutriendos dari non vetamus. Si vero post istius legis publicationem quisquam nutriendos pastoribus dederit, societatem latronum videbitur confiteri."

10. E.g., Dig. 32.99.3 (Paulus): "eum, qui natus est ex ancilla urbana et missus in uillam nutriendus, interim in neutris esse quidam putant . . ."; 50.16.210 (Marcianus): "is, qui natus est ex mancipiis urbanis et missus est in uillam nutriendus." In Seneca's *Controversiae* 4.6, cited above, the mother would not know her son after he returned from nursing in the countryside unless the father identified him. Even in early modern times children in Italy were sent from foundling homes (e.g., San Gallo in Florence) to the countryside specifically because this was thought to be healthier; see G. Pinto, "Il Personale, le balie e i salariati dell'Ospedale di San Gallo di Firenze negli anni 1395–1406," pp. 128–29.

Although some have dismissed the corpus of Greek novels or "romances" as historical evidence because of the seemingly far-fetched nature of the events depicted in them,[11] this is probably unwise. They were the closest ancient equivalent to "popular" literature, and they are deeply conventional, reflecting, by and large, very traditional values and points of view. To residents of the stable and peaceful democracies of the modern West, the constant and dire mishaps of heroines and heroes separated from each other by pirates, sold into slavery, threatened with execution for crimes they did not commit, subjected to the advances of lecherous bandits and unscrupulous masters—through all of which they usually remain steadfastly faithful to each other until they are ecstatically reunited at the end—may seem grotesquely exaggerated and fantastic. As literature they are doubtless caricatures to some extent, but they are far from being as unrealistic as they seem to the twentieth century.

Mediterranean society of the first centuries of the present era was turbulent; people who ventured from their towns (or who suffered the fortunes of frequent wars) were wrongfully sold into slavery, shipwrecked, attacked by pirates, separated by mishap from parents or lovers, sent to the mines for crimes they had not committed. The exaggerations of the novels are probably more comparable to those of American crime entertainment—in which crime is unrealistically prominent and the criminal is always caught, but the nature of the crimes and the social context are reasonably accurate (sometimes even based on real incidents)—than to truly fantastic genres, like science fiction.[12] The provision of the Twelve Tables freeing a son who was sold into servitude, manumitted, returned to

11. E.g., Germain, "L'Exposition," 217 (in *L'Enfant* 1). The novels have, in fact, rarely been used for any sort of historical investigation. For an introduction to them, see B. E. Perry, *The Ancient Romances,* and Graham Anderson, *Ancient Fiction: The Novel in the Graeco-Roman World* (London, 1984); for an assessment of their historicity by a classicist, see J. J. Winkler, "Lollianus and the Desperadoes," *Journal of Hellenic Studies* 100 (1980) 155–81. Winkler sagely notes that there were, for example, both bandits and a "bandit lore," which were separate but closely related.

12. Although they may in some cases be like westerns—i.e., reasonably accurate recreations of life long before. It would be unrealistic, of course, to take westerns as evocative of American life at any time or place other than their particular, limited locale; yet it would also be a mistake to attribute to the ancient or medieval world in general the rate of social, economic, and technological change which has characterized the United States in the last two centuries: a temporal disjunction as dramatic as that in California between 1850 and 1920 is comparatively rare in human history, and usually quite evident in sources.

his father, sold again, manumitted again, and sold and manumitted a third time would certainly invite disbelief if it occurred only in fiction. The jurist Ulpian soberly discusses an incident in which a kidnapped baby "was in slavery in good faith [i.e., believed he was a slave], although he had been born of free parents; then, unaware of his real status, he ran away and began to live secretly as free: his living in freedom is therefore fraudulent."[13] A court case of the first century is every bit as convoluted and entertaining as Plautus: a woman hired as nurse by a man who found an abandoned baby tries to persuade him (and the judge) that the foundling has died and the baby she has is her own, who was born at the same time.[14]

There is indeed no reason to doubt the testimony of romance or theatrical literature on either the fact or mode of abandonment, where it is probably most useful. The greatest hurdle either places in the way of credibility is a predilection for dramatic *anagnorisis*— the joyful rediscovery of long-lost parents, children, or lovers after many perils and tribulations. Recognition scenes certainly appealed greatly to the imagination of the time, but many other sources— laws, inscriptions, and other reliable evidence—leave little room for doubt that they were, in fact, a reasonably common occurrence.

Abandonment is such a regular fulcrum for plots in ancient literature, moreover, that it is somewhat difficult to imagine its effectiveness if it were not a part of the experience of much of the audience. Endless comedies can revolve around marital squabbles or adultery, because these familiar situations lend themselves to enormous variation, most of which evokes response from an audience already familiar with the basic problems and tensions of conjugal relationships. Relatively few comic plots in a given age, by contrast, can turn on the mishaps of identical twins being mistaken for each other. Almost every century and literary genre can supply a plot or two along these lines, but not whole genres; the situation,

13. Dig. 40.12.12: "Infans subreptus bona fide in seruitute fuit, cum liber esset, deinde, cum de statu ignarus esset, recessit et clam in libertate morari coepit: hic non sine dolo malo in libertate moratur."

14. OP 37 and 38, discussed in Bieżuńska-Małowist, "Expositio," pp. 132–33. Cf. Azucena in Verdi's *Il Trovatore*. Procopius recounts as historical truth an episode in the life of the general Belisarius which sounds like the plot of a modern television series: Belisarius appeals to his stepson to avenge him against the latter's natural mother (Belisarius's wife), who is having an affair with Belisarius's adopted son, arguing that the stepson should subordinate ties of blood to the gratitude he must feel for all that Belisarius, his adoptive father, has done for him (*Anecdota* 2.8–9).

funny because it involves a bizarre circumstance, does not sustain repeated use: its effect arises from its peculiarity, which diminishes with repetition. Plautus and Terence (like the Greek New Comic poets they imitated) wrote what would today be called "situation comedy": they turned the irritations, vexations, and tensions of familiar circumstances to comic relief. Clearly the abandonment of children was familiar, a part of many people's "situation," and therefore fertile ground for comic variation. This is explicitly indicated in *The Eunuch,* where Terence compares an abandoned and substituted [15] child as a likely subject for a play with a runaway slave, a goodly matron, a nasty whore, a greedy parasite, a pompous soldier, a dishonest servant, and love, hate, and suspicion—all of which were certainly familiar and realistic aspects of life in Rome. [16]

Juvenal and other satirists of the day doubtless exaggerate in their excoriation of society, and this must be factored into assessments of their claims about, for example, the frequency of abandonment. But it is most unlikely that they have chosen to pillory or make fun of situations which have no relation to the lives of their readers, which are not perceived as social problems or abuses, or which they have exaggerated to the point that their audience will not be affected by the description. All of these sources, like the clues to any mystery, must be sifted and presented in juxtaposition to arrive at a clear picture of what happened.

MOTIVES FOR ABANDONMENT

The received wisdom is that two kinds of children were particularly likely to be abandoned: girls, and those born in poverty. [17] There is little evidence for either of these beliefs, although both seem plausible. A parchment letter surviving from the last year be-

15. On substitution, see below. Plautus (*The Captives,* epilogue) also compares the substitution of a child (*suppositio pueri*) to a love affair, a swindle, or freeing a prostitute (from slavery), although his point is to contrast the former as a "nice" subject with the latter, which are "risqué."

16. In *The Captives* a father has lost two sons: one stolen by a slave at age four and another captured as a prisoner of war. Both of these are certainly believable enough in the Rome of Plautus's day; but, interestingly, he needs to justify only the second in terms of realism ("*ut fit in bello*").

17. "The exposing of children points to the very pinched circumstances of the free poor" (Ramsay MacMullen, *Roman Social Relations 50 B.C. to A.D. 284* [New Haven, 1974], p. 92); see also the works cited above, in note 2 of chapter 1; on the

fore the Christian era includes instructions from a man to his wife to expose her child if it turns out to be a girl,[18] but laws regulating the sale or abandonment of children evince no special concern with girls. Known historical instances are too few to constitute a sample, but they generally involve male children as often as female: Plutarch mentions that Lucullus found the citizens of ruined cities in Asia selling their sons *and* daughters.[19] Suetonius records various cases of abandonment; in some the gender of the child (or children) is unclear, but where it can be determined it is more often male than female.[20] The use of inclusive masculine pronouns makes it difficult to draw inferences, but it appears that most of the *expositi* in the several *controversiae* of Seneca on the subject are male, and where it is unambiguous, they are. Musonius Rufus mentions a man who had sold his son, apparently for sexual purposes, because he was beautiful,[21] and Christian complaints about the prostitution of abandoned children specifically mention that boys are used thus as well as girls.[22] Of the half-dozen cases of abandonment in Quintilian's declamations,[23] all involve male children. In one,[24] a husband setting out on a trip orders his wife to expose any child born to her while he is gone, regardless of gender. She bears a son and abandons him. Despite the letter cited above, nursing contracts and other papyrological evidence indicate that boys were often abandoned in Roman Egypt.[25]

Numerous literary and philosophical sources, however, suggest

---

higher incidence for females, see, in addition to those, Brunt, *Italian Manpower*, p. 151.

18. "If you have a boy, leave it; if you have a girl, throw her out" *Oxyrhynchus Papyri* (OP) 4.244, item 744. Cf. Ovid's account in the *Metamorphoses* (9.676–7).

19. *Lucullus* 20.1. He also describes a subordinate of Cato's buying boys from among public prisoners (*Cato* 10): were these captured or sold by their parents? Xenophon (*Agesilaos* 1.21) describes parents in war zones selling their children because they feared they would not be able to feed them.

20. Unclear instances: *Augustus* 65, *Caligula* 5; female: *Claudius* 27; male: *Claudius* 15, *De grammaticis et rhetoribus* 7 and 21. Flavia Domitilla, born of free parents but apparently brought up as a slave until reclaimed by her father (*Vespasian* 3), may also have been abandoned or sold.

21. Lutz, pp. 102–3.

22. See chapter 3, below.

23. *Institutio* 7.1 and 9.2; *Declamationes minores* 278, 306, 338, 358, 372, 376.

24. *Declamationes minores* 306.

25. These include *Berliner griechische Urkunden (Ägyptische Urkunden aus den Königlichen Museen zu Berlin)* (Berlin, 1895–) 4.1058, 1106, 1107, 1108, 1110; *Pa-*

that it was more common to abandon girls. The axiom "Everyone raises a son, including a poor man, but even a rich man will abandon a daughter" was already eight hundred years old when Stobaeus quoted it in his fifth-century compilation of philosophical wisdom.[26] Chremes in Terence's *Heautontimoroumenos*, a man of moderate means, had a son and exposed his only daughter when she was born. When he later recovers her he explains to her quite matter-of-factly that he simply had not wanted a daughter.[27] Both Ovid and Apuleius have fathers tell expectant wives to kill the child if it is a girl (but neither does).[28] A courtesan announces to her lover in Lucian's *Dialogues of the Courtesans* (2.1) that she is not going to expose their child, "especially if it is a male."

Apart from comments of this sort and some very uncertain efforts to determine the sex ratio of abandoned children in the ancient world,[29] it is impossible to be sure whether this is a "quick-

---

pyrus grecs et démotiques, ed. Théodore Reinach (Paris, 1905) 103, 104; OP 1.37, 38 (as above), and 73; *Papiri greci e latini (Pubblicazioni della Società italiana per la ricerca dei papiri greci e latini in Egitto)* (Florence, 1912–) 3.203.

26. *Florilegium* 24.40 (Wachsmuth, p. 614).

27. Lines 666–67.

28. Ovid, *Metamorphoses* 9.676–7: the girl is reared as a boy; Apuleius, *Metamorphoses* 10.23: the mother gives the child to a neighbor to bring up.

29. Leclercq, for example, found that of 66 inscriptions to *alumni* (adopted abandoned children: see below), 45 (68 percent) were to males, 21 (32 percent) to females; Teresa Nani ("ΘΡΕΠΤΟΙ," p. 66) reported 124 males (56 percent) to 97 females (44 percent); but neither of these can be taken as revealing anything even about *alumni*, much less about abandoned children in general: boys were commemorated nearly 50 percent more than girls even in the population at large (Brunt, p. 133). Of manumitted *alumni* the proportion is reversed: 33 females (59 percent) to 23 males (41 percent) (Nani, p. 66). This could be because manumission was the one instance in which there was a strong incentive to make a record of female *alumni*, and this proportion may therefore be more accurate, but it is simply impossible to tell. Many male guardians freed and married *alumnae*, and this might have been a reason to see that the manumission was legally recorded: see discussion below. Rawson ("Children in the Roman *Familia*," pp. 179–80) found that the sex ratio among *alumni* under five was very high, but more nearly equal at higher ages, and thought that this indicated that people would pick up male children of any age, but females only when they were old enough to work. Rawson also finds that the number of infant *alumni* of either gender was small compared to older ones, which is at odds with all other sources of information, and seems most likely to result from the distortions of epigraphic evidence. It is reasonable to assume that people simply did not bother with inscriptions to *alumni* who died young, because they were not members of the family by blood, nor would the family have had much chance to develop affection for the child. Rawson recognizes

sand" topos or a reflection of reality. There are virtually no abandoned female mythological figures, although both abandoned
children and women figure prominently in Greco-Roman mythology. Some sources indicate that parents were careful to see that they
had one or two boys as heirs and would abandon children after
this;[30] such a practice would presumably result in the exposing of
more girls in the population at large, but would also have affected
only those social classes for whom estates and inheritance were a
real concern—certainly not a majority of the population.

The evidence is similarly vague about whether poor children
were more commonly given up. Poverty would be a likely inspiration for abandonment, but it does not predominate over other motivations in legal, historical, moral, or other writings. Temporary
indigence due to war or famine is mentioned, but usually as applying to a group of people reduced in circumstance (e.g., the inhabitants of a region) rather than to a permanent lower class. Moralists
and satirists critical of exposing children usually consider poverty a
mitigating circumstance, but mention it predominantly in complaints about exposure by the rich.[31] Indeed, Plutarch seems quite
surprised that the poor abandon children, and speaks of it as peculiar: "When the poor do not rear children it is because they consider
poverty the greatest of evils and do not wish to share it with their
children; it is as though poverty were a contagious and dangerous
disease."[32] Juvenal specifically contrasts poor mothers, who have
children and nurse them, with wealthy women, who do not.[33] The
tendency of poorer classes (and nations) to have higher birthrates
than their wealthier counterparts often reflects deliberate choice as
much as lack of alternatives, and it may well be that the Roman

---

the possibility of this (p. 199, n. 31) but imagines that people actually did pick up
infants less often than older children. There is very little evidence about the age at
which children were sold.

30. "Two sons are not uncommon, three occur now and then, but more than
one daughter was practically never reared. . . . Of 600 families from second-
century inscriptions at Delphi, one percent raised two daughters" (Jack Lindsay,
The Ancient World [London, 1968], p. 168). But cf. Lacey, *The Family*, p. 165.
Brunt believed that there were many more male than female slaves: *Italian Manpower*, pp. 143–44.

31. E.g., Quintilian (?) 306: "alia tamen condicio est eorum, quibus obvium
patrem quaerit exponentium paupertas."

32. *De amore prolis* 497E.

33. *Satires* 6.591–97.

lower classes, like the urban poor of India and the United States, considered children an asset, no matter how difficult it was to provide for them.[34]

Opinions like Plutarch's and Juvenal's might, of course, simply reflect the fantasies of the rich about the humble poor, but if the underprivileged were particularly prone to expose their young, one might expect to see this reflected in some way in legal and historical materials. It is not. In his "Panegyric to Trajan," Pliny lauds the emperor for having created a social climate in which both the rich and the poor will want to bring up children—something which, by implication, had not existed for some time. Although both Pliny and Trajan are known to have established foundations and allowances to help the free poor in rearing their children,[35] and financial support is one of Trajan's contributions to the felicity of childrearing, Pliny did not consider it paramount for either rich or poor.

> There is a considerable incentive to a parent to bring up children
> in the hope of subsidies and doles, but more in the promise of
> freedom and security. So even if a ruler is not generous, as long
> as he does not despoil—and even if he does not support, as long
> as he does not kill—he will not lack subjects who desire to have
> children.[36]

Of the cases of exposed children mentioned by Quintilian, only one might involve a poor father. The others were parents of means, to judge by the nature of the litigation which arose subsequently (though then as now the rich were more likely to litigate than the poor, and the sample is unquestionably biased in this way). More revealing is the fact that in two of the cases, comparatively poorer

34. See, e.g., discussion of this in Flandrin, *Families in Former Times*, p. 235.

35. For Trajan's foundation at Veleia, see Brunt, pp. 150–51, E. M. Smallwood, *Documents Illustrating the Principates of Nerva, Trajan, and Hadrian* (Cambridge, Mass., 1966), no. 436, pp. 142–51; and *Inscriptiones latinae selectae,* ed. H. Dessau (Berlin, 1887–1933) 6509, 6675. The foundation supported 263 legitimate boys and 35 girls, and one illegitimate boy and one illegitimate girl. (Brunt argues that the gender disproportion arises from the fact that the foundation supported only one child per family, so families enrolled sons unless they had only daughters.) For Pliny's foundation see his *Epistles* 1.8.19, 5.7.2, 7.180. For such support generally, see Dig. 34.1.14.1; CIL 2.1602, p. 309; and A. R. Hands, *Charities and Social Aid in Greece and Rome* (London, 1968), pp. 108 ff.

36. *Panegyric* 27.

people took up children exposed by parents of greater means.[37] It is, indeed, not inconceivable that the rural poor (loosely described in literary and legal sources as "shepherds") needed or desired more children than the urban middle classes,[38] either because they were useful on farms or in shepherding, or possibly because their own rate of infant mortality was higher.[39]

In later epochs legislation declaring all abandoned children free may have been an incentive for parents of servile status to expose children, but under the early empire it is not likely that many slaves would have had the choice to make, and since abandoned children might be brought up in servitude of one sort or another, slave parents could not reasonably have anticipated any certain improvement in status. For their richer neighbors or owners, abandonment of a child might have been preferable to the alternatives of diminishing the inheritance of heirs born previously, killing it outright, or consigning it to a life of shame; but for slaves it was probably simpler to allow the master to retain his legal ownership of and responsibility for any children they bore.[40] On the other hand, Dio Chrysostom opines that if they can do so without being caught, many slave women destroy their children either before or after birth to avoid adding the burdens of motherhood to those of slavery.[41]

Many other motivations for abandonment appear in a variety of Roman sources. Augustus forced the abandonment of the child

---

37. Although poverty is a motive for exposing children in literature (e.g., Menander, *Epitrepontes, Perikeiromene,* and Terence, *Heautontimoroumenos*), it is often the poor who take in exposed children: a charcoal burner in *Epitrepontes;* a poor woman in *Perikeiromene;* a farm bailiff in *Samia.* Some of the foster parents of *alumni* recorded in inscriptions were illiterate: Nani, "ΘΡΕΠΤΟΙ," p. 83. Dio Chrysostom praises the humble servant Oeneus and his wife for rearing all the abandoned children they found: *Discourses* 15.9.

38. "By the time of Augustus a tenth or more of the people of Italy were crowded into the city of Rome . . ." (Brunt, p. 134).

39. On the other hand, Brunt (p. 140) considered that the rate of marriage—which would obviously have some effect on the birthrate—among the *proletarii* was extremely low.

40. Radin ("Exposure of Infants in Roman Law," p. 341) had argued that later imperial legislation was "more concerned with slaves than with free children that are abandoned at birth, and we can readily see that the cases of the former would be much more numerous than the latter," while Nani (p. 61) felt it necessary to point out that not all *expositi* had been born free: "ma non tutti i trovatelli esposti erano di nascita libera."

41. *Discourses* 15.8.

of his granddaughter because the mother had been banished, and Claudius, apparently in anger, ordered the exposing of his former wife's child by another man.[42] Gaius Melissus, a famous grammarian, had been abandoned when his parents had a falling out;[43] people exposed children as a sign of grief when Caligula died;[44] and Seneca mentions, as noted previously, that a father exposed a pair of twins because he could not choose between them.[45] Most moralists and satirists suggest that selfish parents were simply "disinclined" to have children,[46] or that they thus increased the inheritance they could leave to the older children (e.g., Musonius Rufus).[47] Seneca says that "many parents are accustomed to exposing unnecessary babies," which suggests family planning as a motivation;[48] some people may not have wished to be parents at all. Quintilian refers to a man who had disinherited one son and exposed another.[49]

Although Roman law and custom apparently allowed parents to kill deformed children, there is no reason to suppose that they always did. The topos of the man who crippled *expositi* could have arisen from faulty inference if, in fact, people exposed children born with some physical abnormality and someone else brought them up as beggars. There is, however, virtually no evidence about what families under the empire did with such offspring.

42. Suetonius, *Augustus* 65; *Claudius* 27: "Claudiam ex liberto suo Botere conceptam, quamvis ante quintum mensem divortii natam alique coeptam, exponi tamen ad matris ianuam et nudam iussit abici."

43. Suetonius, *De grammaticis et rhetoribus* 21: "Ob discordiam parentum expositus." He was later reclaimed by his mother, however.

44. Given the nature of Caligula's reign, it is conceivable that either the abandoning parents or Suetonius meant this as bitter irony about the extent of their "grief," but even so, it implies that exposing children would be a mode of responding to bereavement.

45. The need to choose may have been related to means, or the ancient and widespread notion that twins were the result of adultery, although the latter usually applied to the mothers rather than the fathers.

46. E.g., Clement of Alexandria, *Stromateis* 2.18 (PG 8.1033): "What cause has a man for the exposing of a child? If disinclined to have children, he ought not to have married in the first place. . . ." Cf. Musonius Rufus and Plutarch, above, and other Christian writers in chapter 3.

47. Juvenal complains that wealthy mothers use contraception or abortion to avoid the difficulties of pregnancy (6.602–9).

48. "Multos patres exponere solitos inutiles partus" (*Controversiae* 10.4.16). That *inutiles* does not refer to deformed children is clear from the additional comment that in the case of the latter, "parentes sui proiciunt magis quam exponunt."

49. *Institutio* 9.2.89. The disinherited son brought up the exposed brother and later tried to persuade the father to reclaim him.

It is likely that there was another reason for abandonment which, oddly, does not appear in classical texts, at least not where one might expect it: incest. Unless Roman society was wholly anomalous in this regard, there must have been sexual abuse of children by parents and other relatives, leading, in some cases, to pregnancy.[50] The offspring would almost certainly have been killed or exposed, but there are extremely few references to such incidents in any of the sources.[51] Incest does appear as a theme in some writings as a concern *after* abandonment, when there is worry that a child will (or horror that he did) unwittingly marry a relative (Oedipus), that an inappropriate relationship will arise between a foster parent and an adopted foundling, or that a parent or sibling will have intercourse with an abandoned child become a prostitute (especially Christian moralists: see chapter 3).[52] These may be oblique, even subconscious recognitions of an underlying motivation for abandonment itself, but they were also realistic concerns in their own right. The somewhat surprising absence in Roman writings of references to incest as a cause of abandonment could be ascribed to reticence, but this would be perhaps the sole aspect of human sexuality on which Latin sources were restrained by modesty. And it seems unlikely in a culture in which the chief deity and his wife were also brother and sister.[53] In a famous legal action an *expositus* sought (and the em-

50. Not only is this a disturbingly frequent occurrence in modern societies, but it was evidently known among the Greeks (see, e.g., Plato, above) and a great social issue in the High and later Middle Ages, as discussed below.

51. Ovid recounts the attempted abortion and subsequent exposure of one such child: see below.

52. Elizabeth Archibald is preparing a study of incest as a theme in late classical and medieval literature; see her 1986 article, "The Flight from Incest: Two Late Classical Precursors of the Constance Theme," or Otto Rank's study (1912), *Das Inzest-Motif in Dichtung und Sage*.

53. The possibility of incest is a subtle worry in the *Epidicus* of Plautus, and in the *Clementine Recognitions*, where the incestuous aspect of advances from her brother-in-law so inspires a wife with shame that she cannot even disclose to her husband why she is leaving him and one of their sons (she takes the other two with her). (The Latin text is edited in PG 1, and by Bernard Rehm, *Die Pseudoklementinen* [Berlin, 1953] [*Die Griechischen Christlichen Schriftsteller der ersten Jahrhunderte*, 41], in which the *Recognitions* occupy chapters 7 and 8; the Greek version is edited by the same author in the same series [vol. 52] under the same title [Berlin, 1965], and comprises chapters 12, 13, 14, and 20. Both probably originated in the second century. There is an English translation in the Ante-Nicene Fathers: 8.67–346.) On the other hand, in Apuleius's *Metamorphoses* (4.26) a noble girl is espoused to a *consobrinus* (relative) who had been reared in her house and slept in the same room with her. The author of the *Shepherd of Hermas* loved a woman as his sister and

peror apparently approved) marriage with the woman he believed to be his mother in order to force her to acknowledge the relationship (i.e., she would have to confess this to be excused from the marriage): the tone of declamation on the subject suggests bemusement more than horror.[54]

It is worth considering that the ready availability of sexual alternatives—prostitutes, courtesans, servants, and slaves of both sexes—made abuse of one's own children less common among Romans than it was among subsequent European peoples.[55] Some of these were themselves children, of course, and liaisons with them doubtless produced offspring who were abandoned.[56] But either exposing an illegitimate child or pretending that he was an adopted *expositus* would obviate the stigma of illegitimacy.[57] Brunt believed that the virtual nonexistence of bastards in Roman writings was

---

wished she were his wife; this is related to the selling of one of them as a child (see discussion below), and may therefore reflect apprehensions about incest arising from abandonment, although it is rather muddled.

54. Apparently a real incident elaborated on by Quintilian(?), *Declamationes minores* 306: see below, note 123.

55. Sexual abuse of children is noted in Roman literature (and generally disapproved: e.g., Cicero, *Pro Sestio* 8), but is greatly complicated by the fact that slaves, whether children or adult, had no real rights over their persons. Plautus (*Epidicus* 109–10) shows a man who has bought a well-born captive and does not compromise her, although he loves her. Martial writes movingly of Domitian's efforts to stop castration and sexual abuse of young boys: "cradles were the pimp's, to the extent that an infant boy torn from his mother's breast would solicit sordid payment with a wail. . . . Before, boys, young men and grown-ups loved you, Caesar; now infants do, too" (9.8; cf. 9.5). Contrast Petronius (*Satyricon* 140), where Philomela tries to get her male and female children (adolescents, apparently) named as heirs by offering them to the testator as sexual objects. Although this is presented as an example of the appalling lengths to which fortune-hunters would go, the children are depicted as rather enjoying themselves, which may indicate something about Petronius's own attitudes toward sexuality with minors.

56. "No doubt rich men could gratify their sexual instincts outside marriage, by taking slave-girls as mistresses; the children of these unions were slaves, and may well have constituted a notable proportion of the *vernae* [household slaves] . . ." (Brunt, p. 146).

57. A couple in Terence's *Andria* claim to have taken in an orphan as explanation for an illegitimate child (221 ff.). Dig. 34.9.16 recounts a case in which a man called the illegitimate daughter of his concubine his *alumna* and made her co-heir with his own granddaughter, which may suggest that he was the father, although this is not clear in the text (despite what Rawson [p. 178] says; she also misreads the gender of the co-heir).

strong evidence of widespread abandonment,[58] but *alumni* (see below) might be illegitimate children even in the father's home. Roman concepts of marriage and concubinage, moreover, coupled with privileged categories of descendants (e.g., *sui heredes*), probably rendered "illegitimacy" in its modern sense less of a social problem than it would be in later cultures.[59]

Literary sources also focus on reasons for abandonment other than poverty. Some are fantastic: the Queen of Ethiopia in Heliodorus's *Aethiopica* abandons her daughter because she is born discolored (white) and will be thought illegitimate; she writes to her that she thought it better to give her up to the "ambivalence of fate" than to the certainty of death or the disrepute of bastardy.[60] Most literary motives are more credible: rape is often a cause (e.g., Terence, *Hecyra;* Plautus, *Cistellaria*), and in fiction, as in philosophical and legal texts, family limitation or economic necessity also seem to be common inspirations. As noted, in *Daphnis and Chloe* both children were legitimate and abandoned by stable, upper-class families.[61]

Overall, a desire to limit the family to two or three children and the dread or reality of adverse circumstances seem to be the most common reasons for abandonment. The latter might be either individual, as in the case of rape or adultery, or, more commonly, general: there are a great many allusions in classical literature to the fact that no one wants to have children during times of social turbulence, and it is only when peace and prosperity prevail that people are encouraged to rear children.[62]

58. *Italian Manpower,* pp. 150–51; but cf. MacMullen (cited in note 17, above), who finds the "rate of illegitimacy" to have "hovered around 10 per cent" (p. 13); and A. Calderini ("ΑΠΑΤΡΕΣ," *Aegyptus* 33 [1953], 358–69), who elicited from various documents percentages of bastards ranging from 1 to 17 percent.

59. I am grateful to Diana Moses for this suggestion. For the category *sui heredes* (those subject to the *patria potestas* of the deceased at the time of his death), see, e.g., Dig. 28.5.

60. Colonna, 4.8, p. 124; Hadas, p. 95.

61. In the *Clementine Recognitions,* as noted above, Clement is "abandoned" by his mother when his uncle makes advances toward her—a situation which, like many in ancient literature, seems less fanciful when considered in light of what is known about sexual abuse in modern families—and then by his father, who goes to look for her. But neither "abandonment" is actually comparable to the other cases at issue here, since the mother leaves him in the care of the father, and the father in the care of guardians.

62. Even allowing for exaggeration and other agendas, the frequency of this theme, in all types of sources, is striking. See, in addition to Pliny's *Panegyric,* his

METHODS OF ABANDONMENT

Once the decision had been made, how did parents actually go about abandoning a child? Three methods are specifically described in various sources; others may have been employed and not recorded. (1) Legal documentation, as discussed above, makes clear that outright sale was extremely common. Sales of children are, interestingly, not frequently mentioned in literary sources, although the audience may have assumed that children being purchased were probably abandoned,[63] and "substituted" children (see below) were probably bought in some cases. But commerce in general is relatively rare in premodern literature.

(2) "Substitution" was a substantial concern of the law, and appears in literature as well, but neither offers much insight into how it was accomplished. The intricate provisions of Roman law for verifying that a child was really born of the mother strongly imply that midwives and servants had little difficulty helping a woman pass a baby off as her own: Terence depicts a woman and midwife smuggling a baby into the house at night under the wraps of a maid (*Andria*, lines 720–70).

(3) The most common form of abandonment was probably exposing in a public place. An Augustan lexicographer defined the word *lactaria* as "columns in the public market, called the 'nursing columns' because people deposit nursing infants there;"[64] and Juvenal (6.602–9) referred to places where poor women leave babies which the wealthy (or their servants) pick up. In the *Cistellaria* a girl is abandoned and found at the hippodrome. Literary sources sug-

---

Epistle 10.2.2–3; Seneca, *Controversiae* 2.5.2; the younger Seneca, *De Clementia* 1.13.5; Velleius Paterculus 2.103.5; CIL 6.1527.2.25–26 (*Laudatio Turiae*); and discussion in Eyben, pp. 79–81 and n. 243.

63. The author of Hermas's *Shepherd* says that he was purchased at Rome. Literary sources also suggest that children were worth less than adults: Plautus has a pimp buy a little girl for ten minas and sell her for thirty when she is older (*Curculio* 528; cf. *Epidicus* 53); in Terence's *The Eunuch* an old and broken-down eunuch costs nearly seven times as much as an Ethiopian girl (471, 984). But in Apuleius the youth of a girl apparently greatly enhances her value (7.9).

64. Sextus Pompeius Festus, *De verborum significatu,* ed. W. M. Lindsay (Leipzig, 1913), s.v. *lactaria,* p. 105: "Lactaria columna in foro olitorio dicta, quod ibi infantes lacte alendos deferebant." It is impossible to translate the dense layers of suggestion in these lines: *lacte alendos* could (and probably does) mean either that the children were nurselings when brought there or that they were brought there in order to be nourished with milk.

gest that it was normal to have a servant deposit the child at dawn, usually with some token or sign which would make recognition and/or reclamation possible at a later date. The privacy of child-birth, which involved only women, made it possible for women to "substitute" abandoned children, as noted above, or to claim that there had been a stillbirth if they wished to abandon the baby: in Terence's *The Mother-in-Law,* the mother of a girl who has been raped promises her husband that she will expose the daughter's child as soon as it is born and say there was a miscarriage (lines 398–400); the queen in the *Aethiopica* who wants to expose her white daughter plans to persuade her husband that it died in childbirth.[65] Doubtless opportunity and circumstance played a role in how and where such children were left. Even in literary sources there is wide variation, ranging from simply "casting the baby out," to transporting him to a particular venue, to the direct transfer from exposer to someone waiting to claim the child.[66]

WHAT HAPPENED TO THEM?

Some of the uses to which abandoned children might be put were horrifying. Plutarch describes an ancient Punic custom of sacrificing children to Kronos: wealthy people sacrificed their own or bought children from the poor.[67] Child sacrifice of this sort is mentioned in many Mediterranean cultures (see chapter 3), but cannot have been common by the time of Roman hegemony, and is usually recorded as a curiosity from a more barbaric age.

A large percentage of exposed or sold children doubtless became slaves. Most of the legislation regarding sale of children is concerned with this possibility; Brunt argued that *expositi* constituted a "high proportion" of the Italian-born servile population.[68] Some

---

65. Colonna, 4.8, pp. 123–24.

66. Casting out: Plautus, *Cistellaria* 618 (*iussit parvam proici*); transporting: *Daphnis and Chloe, Aethiopica;* direct transfer: Plautus, *Casina* 40–46, where a slave persuades the exposer to hand the child over to him.

67. Plutarch, *Superstition* 171.

68. *Italian Manpower,* p. 152. Moreover, Brunt felt that the growth in population in Italy from five to seven million at the time of Augustus could be "fully accounted for by the accretion of slaves" (p. 131). Cf. MacMullen, *Roman Social Relations,* pp. 13–14; also p. 92: "many slaves came into their conditions as the price for life itself, having been abandoned by their parents at birth and reared by their finders for later sale."

have argued that infants were not valuable as slaves,[69] and it does seem that arranging to nurse an infant might be more troublesome than simply buying someone of working age. But this would depend to a considerable extent on the market. Victory in war had been a source of servile labor under the republic, but sustained peace under the early empire and less successful military action against barbarians in later centuries gradually reduced this, and in any particular time and place demand for servile laborers might exceed supply, making it worth the investment to rear a child who would later prove valuable. There is no doubt that some people paid to nurse abandoned children they intended to keep as slaves.[70]

In Plautus's play *The Captives* a father buys a four-year-old slave as a companion for his son of the same age, but the child had been stolen, not exposed. Most references to "girls" or "boys" in servile positions cannot be taken as indicating a particular age, given the conflation of Latin terms for youth and servitude (see Introduction). Imperial rulings steadily undermined the validity of sales of the freeborn, as noted above, but it is difficult to know how great a problem this posed for the slave trade, since proving freeborn status would in many cases be difficult.[71]

Abandoned children were clearly used to a considerable extent as prostitutes. There was a holiday for boy prostitutes in Augustan Rome: although some of them may have been born to slaves or captured in war, most were probably abandoned children.[72] A father in

69. E.g., Leclercq, pp. 1289–90. H. Antoniadis-Bibicou ("Quelques notes," p. 79) considers slaves to have been valuable from age ten. Evidence is available for the price of slaves at various ages in the many works devoted to Roman slavery: see, e.g., L. Westermann, *Slave Systems of Greek and Roman Antiquity* (Philadelphia, 1955); M. Finley, *Slavery in Classical Antiquity* (Cambridge, England, 1960); Anne Hadjinicolaou-Marava, *Recherches sur la vie des esclaves dans le Monde Byzantin* (Athens, 1950). See also, I. Bieżuńska-Małowist, "Les enfants-esclaves à la lumière des papyrus," *Hommages à M. Renard* 2.91–96; G. Sacco, "Osservationi su *tropheis, trophimoi, threptoi,*" *Settima miscellanea greca e romana* (Rome, 1980) 270–86; and S. M. F. Van Lith, "Lease of Sheep and Goats. Nursing Contract with Accompanying Receipt," *Zeitschrift für Papyrologie und Epigraphik* 14 (1974) 145–62.

70. OP 37, 38; discussed in Bieżuńska-Małowist, "Expositio," pp. 132–33.

71. Maxime Lemosse notes that it was "primarily" abandoned children who occupied the shadowy legal category "liber homo bona fide serviens" (a free person in servitude in good faith)—i.e., someone whose free status is not provable, and who is therefore in legitimate servitude ("L'Enfant sans famille en droit Romain," in *L'Enfant* 1, p. 263. See also R. Reggi, *Liber homo bona fide serviens* (Milan, 1958), pp. 84 ff.

72. CIL 1.2.236 (A.D. 6–9), discussed in Jasper Griffin, "Augustan Poetry and the Life of Luxury," *Journal of Roman Studies* 66 (1976) 87–105 (p. 102), and

Terence's *Heautontimoroumenos* who believes his exposed daughter is still living does not doubt that she is now a prostitute, a common worry of fathers in classical literature; and the demand for child prostitutes was sufficient to inspire concern about theft of children for that purpose.[73] Justin Martyr adduced this as the reason that Christians should not abandon children: "We have been taught that it is wrong to expose even the newborn . . . because we have observed that nearly all such children, boys as well as girls, will be used as prostitutes."[74] Clement of Alexandria describes how boys being sold as slaves were "beautified" to attract potential buyers, and asks, "How many fathers, forgetting the children they abandoned, unknowingly have sexual relations with a son who is a prostitute or a daughter become a harlot?"[75] Such use of children was discouraged by law in the later empire.

Castrating boys to be eunuchs was a big business in the early empire, although it, too, was limited by law, and eunuchs become steadily less common in the West throughout the Christian era, except from the end of the Middle Ages through the beginning of the nineteenth century, when they were again popular as singers.[76] Employing *expositi* as beggars, possibly even crippling them to make them more pitiful, as Seneca describes, may have been common, although it is difficult to know from the extant sources.[77]

Boswell, *Christianity*, p. 70. Athenian law had not permitted prostituting citizens' sons according to Aeschines (*Against Timarchus* 13–18), and Roman law several centuries later explicitly prohibited any prostitution of males, but it is unclear whether Domitian's legislation (referred to in note 55, above) applied to prostitution or simply to castration.

73. Line 640. Two of Plautus's plays, *Rudens* and *Poenulus,* deal with the abduction of children for prostitution.

74. 1 *Apology* 27 (PG 6.639). Cf., below, chapter 3, and Boswell, *Christianity,* p. 144.

75. *Paedagogus* 3.3 (PG 5.585). Cf. Tertullian, as cited below, in chapter 3.

76. See Suetonius, *Domitian* 7; Martial as cited above, note 33; JC 4.42.1–2; Dig. 48.8; and cf. Antoniadis-Bibicou, p. 82. Even Petronius was horrified by castration (119). For later law, see chapter 4, below. A major study of eunuchs is badly needed; one treatment of later ages is Angus Heriet, *The Castrati in Opera* (London, 1956).

77. A similar practice was known in early modern China, although in this case the children had been stolen: "Evil men are constantly stealing children. They put out their eyes or cut off their feet! A thousand tricks they have to injure them so that by exciting compassion they may be the more successful in begging alms." Cited in Waltner, "The Adoption of Children in Ming and Early Ch'ing China," p. 182.

Had slavery, prostitution, or mutilation represented the only or even the major prospects for abandoned children, it is difficult to believe that many parents could have faced consigning their offspring to such fates. But in fact, there were many happier possibilities. One of the more colorful of these was substitution. The idea of substituted children might seem the product of a creative imagination if it were not attested everywhere in ancient sources, "historical" as well as "literary."[78] A considerable body of Roman legislation was designed to prevent substitution,[79] which was apparently sufficiently common that it might be used as a credible charge to disqualify an heir by jealous relatives.[80]

Dio Chrysostom's fifteenth discourse includes an exchange between two men about substitutions of this sort. One asserts that many famous Athenians turned out to be not only not their father's children, but not even their mother's. His interlocutor agrees:

> Yes, I know. Free women who are childless often substitute [other children] when they themselves cannot have babies, because they all want to hold on to their husband and home, and they do not lack the means to support them.

A prostitute in the *Cistellaria*, as noted above, has a friend on the lookout for an abandoned baby—boy or girl—she can pretend is her own.[81] Substitution took many forms in the ancient world, from institutionalized fraud to private deception.[82]

---

78. Latin words for "substitution" are *supposititio, subjectio, substitutio;* for the children, *suppositi, subiecti, subditi;* for the substitutors, *suppositores.* In Greek, ὑποβάλλω is the normal verb, and the children are ὑποβολιμαῖοι. Polybius mentions substitution of children (2.55), as does Isaeus (6.23: a man too old to produce children biologically will have no difficulty, his relatives fear, in producing one "some other way"). For an ornithological parallel which certainly affected the imagination of later writers, see notes 114 and 115 of chapter 1.

79. Discussed in note 71 of chapter 1.

80. E.g., Dig. 34.9.16, where, to get their uncle's estate, two nephews accuse their aunt of substituting (*partus subiecti*) their cousin.

81. Plautus, *Cistellaria* 133–36:
. . . huic meretrici dedi,
quae saepe mecum mentionem fecerat,
puerum aut puellam alicunde ut reperirem sibi
recens natum, eapse quod sibi supponeret.

82. Abandoned or purchased children were being substituted for the children of the nobles required in the sacrifice to Kronos, according to Diodorus (20.14)—

Since heirs were a prerequisite for certain legal benefits, there was a material incentive for Romans to adopt children if they were childless.[83] Adoption was, in fact, extremely common in the early empire—satirical literature suggests that fortune-hunters made a profession of seeking out the childless wealthy in the hopes of being adopted—but the most prominent cases involve the adoption of relatives or adults, usually for reasons of inheritance or as an expression of political loyalty or personal affection.[84] The extent to which abandoned children were formally adopted is difficult to determine, especially since some of the words for adoption in Latin, as in English, might be used loosely to mean "took under one's care."[85]

Social critics from Isaeus (fourth century B.C.) to Seneca commented on the fact that the rich could not lack heirs, since they

---

an organized form of substitution. Herodotus says that since parricide was unknown among the Persians, whenever someone had appeared to murder a parent it must have been a substituted child (ὑποβολιμαῖος; 1.137). In Euripides' *The Phoenician Women*, Oedipus is given by the shepherds who rescue him to a woman who pretends to her own husband that the baby is hers. Terence's *Andria* portrays the mistress of Pamphilus as being able to send for a baby from the midwife whenever she wants to claim a baby from him (lines 515–16). When the courtesan Cistellaria finally obtains an abandoned baby, she takes to her bed, "bears it," pretends it is her own, and claims a "foreign lover" as the father (123–51). But cf. the hilarious passage in Aristophanes' *Thesmophoriazusae* (502–19) which describes how a woman must feign childbirth for ten days while a nurse desperately seeks a child to substitute, and the panicky father runs from one doctor to another. A baby is eventually procured and brought into the house with its mouth plugged so it will not cry. The nurse then assures the unwitting father that it resembles him exactly. "Don't we do these naughty things?" the chorus of women asks. "By Artemis, we do!" Juvenal hints that substitution is very widespread (6.601–9: "Transeo suppositos . . .").

83. On this complicated subject, see the preceding chapter. As noted there, two basic forms were known: *adrogatio*, the voluntary submission of an independent (*sui iuris*) person to the *patria potestas* of another; and *adoptio*, the taking up of a *filius familias* by a new family. Only the latter, obviously, would be possible in the case of an *expositus*, although the former might be considered a form of "abandonment" if the original parents arranged it.

84. As in the case, e.g., of Aemilius Paullus's sons' adoptions and their political implications, or the use of adoption to stand for plebeian office by Clodius Pulcher, or Augustus's adoption by Julius Caesar, a relative.

85. This is especially true of *adoptare*, which has about the same range of meaning and association in Latin that its equivalent has in English; *adrogare* is a much more specific and juridical term. Glotz opined that "les enfants exposés n'entraient guère dans les familles ni par voie d'adoption ni par supposition frauduleuse" (p. 206), but offered little proof.

could buy them if they failed to beget any.[86] One of Seneca's *controversiae* deals with a rich man who disinherited his own children and then tried to obtain the son of a poor man. "That is how the nobility of the patricians has survived," he declaims when challenged, "from the founding of the city to this day. Adoption is the cure for chance."[87] A teacher of Cicero's had been abandoned by his parents as a child and was adopted by the man who reared him.[88] Children often appear to have been "adopted" in literary accounts of abandonment, in the sense that their guardian treats them as his or her own offspring,[89] but the legal aspects of Roman adoption do not appear in these stories, and the authors probably have in mind the informal category "alumnus," which appears to have been the most common position for abandoned children.

ALUMNI

Alumnus was not a legal category: although *alumni* are frequently mentioned in legal texts, the term is nowhere defined in relation to status, privilege, or obligation.[90] The *alumnus* does not

86. Isaeus, *Philoctemon* 23; Seneca, *Controversiae* 2.1.13 ("ne liberi quidem nisi alieni placent"), and 2.1.31 ("non posset diviti deesse filius"). This has been the case in other cultures as well; cf. Waltner, "Adoption . . . in China," p. 104: "When a good man has no heirs, he can easily arrange to get one."

87. *Controversiae* 2.1.17 (Winterbottom, 1.222). Cf. Shakespeare, *All's Well That Ends Well* (1.3): "Adoption strives with nature and choice breeds / A native slip to us from foreign seeds."

88. Suetonius, *De grammaticis* 7.

89. E.g., Selenium in Plautus's *Cistellaria,* or Charicleia in the *Aethiopica,* who says of her foster father (designated τὸν ταύτης τροφέα), ἐμαυτοῦ θυγατέρα καὶ ἐνόμιζον καὶ ὠνόμαζον (Colonna 2.32, p. 82; cf. 2.33, p. 84, where he wishes she would have children so he will not be without descendants). The distinction between her relation to her adoptive and natal parents is expressed in the phrases ἡ νομισθεῖσα θυγάτηρ and θυγάτηρ ἀληθὴς οὖσα. Of course, children can be found and adopted without having been abandoned, as in the case of two shipwrecked boys in the *Clementine Recognitions* (Latin: 7.32, PG 1.1368; Greek: 13.7, PG 2.333–34), or in the Acts of Paul and Thekla (in L. Vouaux, *Les Apocryphes du Nouveau Testament. Les Actes de Paul et ses lettres apocryphes* [Paris, 1913]). In *The Brothers,* by Terence, a man gives one of his two sons to his brother to rear: the word *adoptare* is used (114), but it is probably not meant to be understood as a legal arrangement.

90. Ulpian draws a distinction between natal children and *alumni* in terms of prosecution for murder of the head of the household, perhaps implying that without such a differentiation they would have been treated equally (Dig. 29.5.1). Justinian's *Institutes* 1.6.5 permits *alumni,* along with family members and others

figure explicitly in the status hierarchy *freeborn/freed/slave,* nor in the *father/wife/child/slave* structure of Roman family patriarchy. The great bulk of information about *alumni* comes from inscriptions, which are frequently terse and contextually unyielding.[91] Uncertainty has therefore attended their treatment in scholarly writings. Leclercq, the first writer to deal extensively with the many inscriptions about *alumni,* assumed that the term applied to *expositi* reared as foster children, and concerned himself little with categories of slavery or freedom or possible legal ramifications.[92] Although many followed his lead,[93] others challenged it and argued that the word had either more or less specific meanings: for example, that it implied servile status, or was used of children who had simply been given to wet nurses.[94] These studies, however, were based on comparatively small samplings of epigraphical materials, and none took thorough account of the general legal and social context of abandonment.

Two modern analyses, based on much wider inscription samples, demonstrate that, at least as regards the epigraphic evidence, Leclercq was basically right, if slightly simplistic.[95] Although *alumnus*

---

who stand *in loco parentis* (e.g., teacher, nurse, foster parent) to be manumitted: the provision is based on the *Institutes* of Gaius (1.38–39), but the latter do not mention *alumni,* so it is unclear whether Justinian's law is an innovation or simply a clarification of long practice.

91. Cf. Brunt's comments on inscriptions and longevity: "We must then regretfully conclude that the inscriptions on which scholars have laboured so pertinaciously can never furnish us with valid statistics on the expectation of life" (*Italian Manpower,* p. 133).

92. Henri Leclercq, "Alumni."

93. E.g., Lemosse, in *L'Enfant* 1, esp. p. 264; Brunt, p. 150. The translators of the Watson edition of the Digest almost unfailingly render *alumnus* as "foster child," and appear to understand the term as applying to abandoned children.

94. Most notably, A. Cameron, "Θρεπτός and Related Terms in the Inscriptions of Asia Minor," *Anatolian Studies Presented to W. H. Buckler* (Manchester, 1939) 27–62.

95. The first (and clearest) of these was Nani, "ΘΡΕΠΤΟΙ," who points out, for example, that only two of the more than twenty inscriptions Cameron cites to show that θρεπτός could refer to a free child given to a wet nurse could possibly mean this, and even they do not necessarily (pp. 63–64). Nani concludes (p. 59) that "θρεπτός è termine del linguaggio familiare, non giuridico, ed indica un bambino od un adulto che è, od è stato nutrito, allevato, da altre persone che non siano i suoi genitori."

Rawson, "Children in the Roman *Familia,*" uses 431 published inscriptions dealing with *alumni* from the first two centuries of the Christian era (one percent of extant pagan inscriptions). She also concludes that—with possible rare excep-

and its Greek equivalent, θρεπτός, were occasionally used in loose or metaphorical senses (like most words in any language), and although neither was a juridical designation, both clearly denoted in the vast majority of cases children abandoned by their parents and brought up in the home of someone else.[96] The term implies nothing specific about how the child was reared.[97] If something about the treatment of an *alumnus* placed him or her clearly in a more specific legal category—if he were regarded as a slave, for example, or legally adopted—it would be normal to use the apposite term or to specify this.[98] *Alumnus* and θρεπτός designate, basically, dependents in a relationship which does not arise from blood, law, or property.

This does not mean that one of the latter might not also be involved: a slave might be treated as an *alumnus,* or an *alumnus* as a slave; an *alumnus* might be adopted as heir; or, what appears to have been most common, he or she might be regarded as somewhere between an heir and a slave, partaking in different ways of both categories. This may seem surprising at first, but slaves at Rome varied from anonymous chattel, working fields or mines, to highly valued household members—often teachers or nurses to the master's chil-

---

tions—the term does not apply to children given to wet nurses (p. 178), to illegitimate or stepchildren (p. 196), or to adoptees (p. 184), although she conflates *vernae* (household slaves) with *alumni* in a somewhat confusing way, often assuming that *patronus* must refer to a "foster parent" when it might mean "owner," "benefactor," or "liberator." *Patronus* applied to a variety of positions in Roman society, and is by no means necessarily the correlate of *alumnus* simply because it often appears in connection with the latter.

96. Of 230 inscriptions mentioning θρεπτοί, Nani found four references to home-born slaves and several to disciples or θρεπτοί in some metaphorical sense; all the others appear to have referred to foundlings. Θρέπτω, from which θρεπτός is derived, is the verb used for bringing up abandoned children in Greek (e.g., *Aethiopica* 10.13, Colonna p. 329). *Alumnus* is used almost everywhere in Latin literature where one expects to find the word for abandoned children in someone's care; e.g., in Juvenal 6.605, 609: "fortuna . . . semper producit alumnos"; Plautus, *Cistellaria* 762: "nostra haec alumna est, tua profecto filia"; even Seneca the Elder, *Controversiae* 10.4.25, where the pun about the *expositi* requires that *alumnus* mean this.

97. This is also the conclusion of Bieżuńska-Małowist, "Expositio," p. 131: "ein aufgelesenes Kind, unabhängig davon, ob es mit dem Status eines Freien oder eines Sklaven angezogen worden ist."

98. As Trajan does in his letter to Pliny, designating that the θρεπτοί in question were born free, exposed, and reared as slaves—and thus implying that the word did not necessarily denote or connote these conditions. Commemorative inscriptions, notably terse, offer less information about the status of *alumni*.

dren; an enormous proportion were freed during their lifetime. And children, as noted above, were, in theory, the property of the father, unless he "emancipated" them. Their position was structurally not unlike that of highly valued slaves: their actual freedom—in the sense of liberty of action and lifestyle—depended less on their juridical position than on their relations with the head of the household, and even their legal status would likely affect them only to the extent to which the *paterfamilias* wished it (and to which society was willing to uphold his rights). Their position was, of course, *de facto* greatly superior to that of slaves in most cases, although Dionysius of Halicarnassus (2.26) wrote with evident disapproval about the absolute power of Roman fathers over their sons, contrasting this with more reasonable Greek laws about parent-child relations. (Dio Chrysostom compared the position of even Athenian sons with that of slaves, unfavorably.) [99]

There was, therefore, not necessarily a contradiction between "unfree status" and affection: an *alumnus* might be treated both as a beloved child and as a household servant, [100] in the same way that even in modern democracies, where there is much greater homogeneity and social regulation of the treatment of children, some are treated as adults and others subject to constant supervision; some made to work to help support the household and others only cared for and nourished.

In all of the available sources—epigraphical, legal, and literary— the same various, multi-layered picture of the position and role of *alumni* emerges. Some were servants, [101] some thought of as children, some both. Some were used as gladiators, [102] but many were manumitted or adopted. [103] Some received generous bequests from

99. *Fifteenth Discourse* 19–21. Aristotle suggests that the Greeks of his day had also viewed children as servants: *Politics* 7.5.13.

100. In Plautus's *Casina* (line 46) an abandoned child is specifically said to have been reared by a woman almost as if she were her own child ("quasi si esset ex se nata, non multo secus"), but is also referred to as *ancilla* or *conserva,* words for domestic servants. Conversely, Cato the Younger's mother suckled the infants of her slaves so that they would have fraternal feelings for her son (Plutarch, *Cato the Elder* 20.3). Or so, at least, is the tale.

101. For *alumni* who were *vernae,* see CIL 6.4412 and discussion in Rawson, p. 188. Rawson found that less than a third of *alumni* were slaves (p. 182).

102. Leclercq, p. 1294.

103. Gaius, *Institutes* 1.19; Dig. 40.2.13 (Ulpian); 40.5.38 (Paulus). Cf. Nani, p. 62.

their guardians and many were entrusted to other family members for care.[104] In several declamations, foster fathers specifically claim the legal and moral rights of natal fathers, even though they do not say they have actually adopted the *alumnus*. One, whose foster son has been reclaimed by his biological parents, refers to him as "our son," and asks the court,

> During the time when our son . . . was away at war, whose was he? Was it not I who hung from the city walls in suspense? Not I who seized everyone returning from the battlefield? Not I who, desperate, fell upon the messengers? . . . Who bandaged his wounds when he returned? Who washed away the blood? Who took him to the temple and gave thanks?[105]

Another says of his foster son: "He was born of my kindness."[106] The point is rhetorical, but clearly an indication of an ideal of foster parenting.

Many *alumni* were so designated even as adults, and although the epigraphic sample available suggests that they were a socially inferior group—"young and of comparatively low status"—in the first two centuries of the Christian era more than half were citizens.[107]

Most were probably cherished: Eutyche ("happily found") was a common name for *alumnae*.[108] Many inscriptions to *alumni*—and

104. E.g., Dig. 31.88.6; 36.1.80.12 (Scaevola).

105. Quintilian(?), *Declamationes minores* 278 (Winterbottom, p. 88).

106. Ibid.

107. Rawson, table 7.2 and p. 186.

108. See Leclercq, pp. 1293–96; Acts 20:9 records a boy named Εὔτυχος, but gives no information about his background. Treptus, presumably from θρεπτός, was also common (Leclercq, p. 1299). For other names, see ILCV (1.278, 577, etc.) and the sources cited in Nani and Rawson, above. Eutychus (occasionally Euthychus) may have been used as a name for children who were not foundlings: a Lucius Eutychus is named in Dig. 31.88.3 without any indication that he was an *alumnus*. Some authors have suggested that children abandoned on dung heaps were given copronyms (i.e., names including the root of κόπρος, "dung"), but Nani found of 230 Hellenistic inscriptions only a single one with such a name (p. 72). Cf. Bieżuńska-Małowist ("Expositio"), who finds more evidence of such names; and Pomeroy ("Copronyms"), who argues that although such names may have originally applied to abandoned children, they were ultimately common names with no specific associations. (Cf. the Italian name Esposito.) An eighth-century Byzantine emperor was nicknamed "Copronymous," allegedly because he dirtied the font during his baptism.

even laws—record very tender sentiments guardians felt for them;[109] they are frequently commemorated along with biological sons or daughters.[110] The mere fact that so many inscriptions commemorating the deaths of *alumni* survive is eloquent testimony to the affectionate bonds between them and those who found and reared them, who sometimes referred to themselves as "guardians," but also often as "mother" or "brother."[111] The relationship appealed to refined sensibilities precisely because it was voluntary, largely unregulated by law, and drew its strength and force from personal ties of love and kindness. Neither guardian nor *alumnus* owed any particular duty by law to the other (as opposed, for example, to the freed slave, who owed his former master certain services for the rest of his life). Simple devotion went into making the bonds between them, and the term *alumnus* became a symbol and expression for a particular type of selfless and loving relationship in Roman society and among its Christian heirs.[112]

109. E.g., Leclercq, p. 1294 ("to the *alumnus* whom he always loved as his son"; "whom I love as my own daughter"; "For you, Claudius, Happily-Found, our *alumnus,* your family"; "Here lies Sagittia, sweet of spirit, with her *alumnus* Eventius"); ILCV 1.577 ("Erotis, sweetest *alumnus*"), 1.761 ("for his *alumnus,* whom he loved tenderly"). For law, see, e.g., Dig. 40.5.38, where an *alumna* is described as "the one whom the father had loved." For comparable Greek inscriptions see *Corpus inscriptionum graecarum,* ed. August Boeckhius 2 (Berlin, 1843) 3318, 3358, 3385, etc.

110. E.g., ILCV 1.278, 2.3237, 2.3357.

111. E.g., Leclercq, pp. 1297–98, for "patronus" or πατρώνα; p. 1295 for *mater*; p. 1298: a statue erected by an *alumnus* and his "brother." In *Daphnis and Chloe,* Chloe's foster mother is called her "apparent mother" (ἡ δοκοῦσα μήτηρ, 3.4) but the man who brought Daphnis up says that he is not his father (4.19). Charicleia declares in the *Aethiopica* that her foster father, Charicles, is no less dear to her than her biological parents (10.38; Colonna, p. 356); and Terence has a boy in *The Brothers* refer to his foster father (who is actually his uncle) as "father." But in Plautus's *Cistellaria* a slave insists on the difference between a "guardian" and a "real mother" (lines 558 ff.), and in much fiction there is substantial concern with locating biological parents on the part of abandoned children: see below.

112. See, e.g., Fronto, *Ad Verum* 2.7.3, where he comments of his client that he put up with things "even my *alumnus* would not have stood"—i.e., the patience of an *alumnus* was the touchstone of exceptional devotion. In the Greek version of the Jewish scriptures, the Greek equivalent of *alumna,* θρεπτή, is used to describe Esther (Esther 2:7), who was reared by her uncle in the absence of father and mother, although the text also implies that Mordecai intended to marry her ἐπαίδευσεν αὐτὴν ἑαυτῷ εἰς γυναῖκα. Both the Hebrew and the Latin, however, say that she was brought up "as a daughter" (לְקָחָהּ מָרְדֳּכַי לוֹ לְבַת; "sibi eam adoptavit in filiam").

RECOVERY

The happiest but least convincing outcome of abandonment in literary treatments is the ecstatic recovery of children by natal parents (or vice versa). Beginning with Oedipus,[113] exposed children in literature set out to find their parents, and their parents to reclaim their offspring, and under the benevolent reign of kindly authors clement circumstances conspire to make this *anagnorisis,* as ancient writers called it, come to pass.

Fictional parents are usually delighted to receive back their exposed children. Sometimes this is because their circumstances have changed: Persinna did not have any more children, and after a long and faithful marriage assumes her husband would no longer be suspicious about Charicleia's odd whiteness.[114] Chremes has changed his mind about wanting a daughter. And although Daphnis's father had thought at the time he exposed him that he had enough children—most likely for reasons of inheritance, since he was rich—he reapportions his estate when Daphnis reappears, a pointed note of realism about the ramifications of exposing and recovery: many parents might be in a position later in their lives to welcome back children they had not been able to support earlier, and it was probably not uncommon for people to end up with fewer children than they expected when they abandoned an early one because of gender, spacing, or circumstance. Like Persinna, they would be pleased to recover the exposed child. Tokens are left with the baby abandoned in Plautus's *Cistellaria* so that someday "your parents may more easily identify you."[115]

In Oedipus's case the results of the reunion were hardly joyous, but Ion's mother, as noted above, was ecstatic to recover her son. In Plautus's *Casina* an exposed girl turns out to be the daughter of her next-door neighbor, and is therefore of sufficiently genteel back-

---

113. See, e.g., the prologue to Euripides' *The Phoenician Women,* where Oedipus sets off to find his real parents while his father is seeking to find the son. (Since the son was prophesied to kill the father, however, the situation is not entirely due to familial affection.)

114. *Aethiopica* 4.12. Rapture reigns on all sides when Charicleia is restored to her natal parents, the king and queen of Ethiopia, after many years' separation; she, unusually fortunate child, was being sought not only by her natal parents, but also by her second foster father, from whom she had also been separated, and who had importuned her own biological parents (without realizing it, of course) to restore his daughter to him.

115. "Parentes te ut cognoscant facilius" (lines 636–38).

ground to marry the son of her foster mother.[116] Terence's *Heauton-timoroumenos* includes a happy recognition scene in which a mother is able to identify her exposed daughter by a ring she had given her.

Are such scenes realistic? That such happy endings were useful for the writers is a moot point. They may, of course, have distorted the likelihood of parental recovery to achieve dramatic ends, or emphasized a delightful but remote possibility. If so, it is revealing that of many possible resolutions of plot available to them storytellers chose this one. Perhaps a public that included a good many parents who had exposed children yearned for such a consummation, or even expected it, in the way that modern audiences expect love affairs to end happily, not because in life they always do, but because they sometimes do, and one wishes they always would.

In fact, a great deal of imperial legal material—about repaying the cost of rearing, for example, or regaining freeborn status—deals with the real-life problems occasioned by real-life *anagnorisis*. Some of it mentions specific cases (e.g., Constantine's ruling of 313: see above). And many other laws not dealing directly with recognition (*agnitio*), mention it in passing or regulate some incidental aspect of it.[117] Pliny's correspondence with Trajan about the θρεπτοί of Bithynia turns largely on the difficulties occasioned by abandoned children at least discovering who their parents were, if not actually being reunited with them. Gaius Melissus, exposed as a child by his parents, was brought up by a man who gave him an excellent education and treated him "as a friend" (*in modum amici*). When his mother later tried to reclaim him he preferred to remain with the man who had reared him.[118] Inscriptions to *alumni* sometimes list

116. The apparent unlikelihood of this may be an illusion of modern perspective: cf. "Introduction."

117. E.g., Dig. 40.12.3 (Ulpian), about parents discovering a natural son in slavery, or 40.11.2. Fragments of litigation from Herculaneum record a case which could well have formed the plot of a comedy: a freedwoman abandoned her daughter to the care of her former master, but much later returned and reclaimed her, repaying the cost of her rearing, as required by law; still later the girl entered into a legal dispute with her foster mother about her natal mother's status at the time she was born, which would affect her inheritance from the foster father, now dead. This complicated case is presented, along with the evidence, in A. J. Boyé, "Pro Petronia Iusta," *Droits de l'antiquité et sociologie juridique: Mélanges Henri Levy-Bruhl* (Paris, 1959) 29–48; for a brief summary, see Rawson, "Children," pp. 172–73.

118. Suetonius, *De grammaticis* 21. His "friend" then manumitted him, but this is not necessarily a juridical term. *Alumni*, as noted, occupied a somewhat gray area in Roman society, and Melissus's *servitudo* may not have been actual slavery, but simply permanent obligation to his guardian and rescuer.

both the foster and natal parents.[119] In Seneca's discussion of the man who cripples *expositi* (*Controversiae* 10.4) there are numerous allusions to the likelihood of parental recovery: one speaker says that in their present condition it would be a greater sadness for the parents to recognize them than not to; another alleges that the young beggars not only wander about their parents' homes, but that their "rescuer" points these households out to them as particularly likely to offer them money. In another case (9.3, noted above) a father who exposed twins is able to locate the man who has reared them, but has difficulty regaining both, since the foster father is not anxious to give them up.

All six of Quintilian's declamations about exposed children assume the possibility or certainty of eventual parental recovery, although demonstrating the likelihood of such an event is not the concern of any of them.[120] Of course these incidents were chosen (or devised) because they posed interesting legal problems,[121] and it would be naïve to infer from them that an overwhelming percentage of exposed children were eventually recovered. Nonetheless, it is probably not unreasonable to conclude that recovery occurred often enough to attract considerable attention from legists, and therefore to constitute a not unrealistic hope on the part of parents (and a not extravagant plot device on the part of writers). In three of the cases, the father who had exposed the child eventually relocates him; in one the foster father discloses on his deathbed the identity of his foster son's natal father (in return for a promise to marry his daughter).[122] Sometimes recognition is disputed: a grown son believes he has located his mother, but she denies it—a case apparently decided by the emperor Claudius.[123] A pauper claims as his the son

119. Leclercq, p. 1303, n. 5.

120. In no. 278 a father reclaims an exposed son; in no. 306 a son claims to have located his mother, but she denies this; in no. 338 a poor man claims as his son the scion of a wealthy couple, but the mother denies it; in no. 376 a dying foster father reveals to his adopted son the whereabouts of his natal parents, who claim him (this appears to be the case referred to in *Institutio* 7.1.14, unquestionably by Quintilian).

121. In at least one case, *Declamationes minores* 358, a foster father had punished his adopted son in a way reserved to the *paterfamilias,* and the son sued him after he was recovered by his natal father; no. 372 concerns the same problem. The two may be different versions of the same dialogue.

122. In no. 306 the argument appears to assume that a foster parent would naturally know the identity of the natal father: "ille, qui te educat, sci[a]t parentes."

123. He seeks to marry her as a means, the declaimant contends, of forcing her to confess that she is his mother to prevent the marriage, which he has claimed as

of a gentleman who has divorced and remarried since the son was born; the gentleman and the stepmother are willing to concede the boy to the pauper, but the first wife claims he is really hers (by the husband).[124]

Whether or not Seneca's and Quintilian's "cases" should be understood as real incidents, they were intended as legal argumentation, and it is clear that jurists had to contend with many difficulties occasioned not only by the abandonment of children but also by their recovery, as noted previously. Nor is this in any way surprising: although imperial society was troubled and often turbulent, it was an age of limited mobility. Children might be exposed or stolen or separated from their parents, but families rarely moved across oceans and continents as they do now. Most abandoned children were probably picked up by someone who lived in the vicinity. Dio Chrysostom is amazed that the slave girl of Oeneus would adopt abandoned children "without even knowing where they came from"—as if this were unusual.[125] Even if they were sold into slavery this was not a long-distance prospect: transoceanic slave trading was a development of a later period, and the demand for slaves was certainly great enough in most of the empire to have absorbed abandoned children locally.[126]

Many parents may have known the foster parents of abandoned children, and/or vice versa, as epigraphy and legal materials suggest. In such cases recovery would follow upon a decision by one or both sides to return the child to his natal family. What happened

---

a reward for heroism in battle (no. 306). Suetonius says that Claudius forced a woman who would not recognize her son to confess by constraining her to marry him ("feminam non agnoscentem filium suum dubia utrimque argumentorum fide ad confessionem compulit indicto matrimonio iuvenis," *Claudius* 15).

124. The degree of detail in this and some of the other cases lends them pathos as well as an aura of realism. In the last (no. 338), a nurse is tortured by the father to determine whether the boy is in fact really the first wife's. At first she maintains that he is; she is tortured again, and this time says he is not. It is argued by the first wife's side that this is what the father wanted to hear, since his new wife hated the boy, so he had the nurse tortured until her resistance broke and she would say what he wished. Since she died during the second session, it is easy to credit this argument, although there are reasons to suspect fraud as well: see note 140, below.

125. *Discourse* 15.9.

126. In Plautus's *Epidicus* (565; cf. 86), a father has his servant buy a girl he believes to be his illegitimate daughter, who had been stolen from her mother; in Terence's *The Eunuch* (520 ff.), Chremes, who lost a little sister, suspects the courtesan Thais of planning to pass herself off as his sister—as if it would be likely that she were still around.

when parents and children had really lost track of each other, as would happen more often, for example, in great cities? Although historical evidence suggests that such families were sometimes reunited, it offers little insight into how this was achieved. The virtually unanimous testimony of literature is that parents left with an abandoned child a "token," "sign," or "symbol."[127] (Tokens are also often mentioned in later historical sources: as late as the nineteenth century, Milanese parents identified children in foundling homes by tokens they had left with them, sometimes twenty years previously.)[128] A token could be a ring, ribbon, painting, article of clothing, or simply the material in which a baby was wrapped, and although in some instances it may have been chiefly a sentimental gesture of leaving something from the family with the child,[129] it was also often intended to serve other purposes: (1) to alert the finder to the status of the child—i.e., expensive tokens indicated lofty birth, humble tokens (or none) signified a child of the poor;[130] (2) to make it possible for the parents to identify the child with some assurance if he should turn up later;[131] (3) to prevent someone else from claiming to be their abandoned child.[132]

127. Usually σύμβολα in Greek (e.g., Euripides, Ion 1386), or γνωρίσματα—a word directly related to anagnorisis; in Latin monumenta (e.g., Terence, The Eunuch 750–53) or, more commonly, crepundia or signa.

128. See Hunecke, "Les enfants," p. 22.

129. Terence has the mother give her daughter a ring as she exposes her in the Heautontimoroumenos (650–53), "so she would have a share in our possessions if she died." She castigates herself for this "superstitition of women," but the ring does ultimately enable her to recognize the daughter (614–15).

130. The tokens of Daphnis and Chloe play a considerable role in the action of the novel: the finders are able to tell from them that each of the children is well born (1.2, 3.26, 4.32), and each couple saves them for future use (3.30, 4.18). Daphnis's parents even hope to get rich when they locate his parents (3.26; cf. 1.8). The tokens do enable both sets of natal parents to identify the children (4.34–35), and have also been at least potentially useful to children or parents in other social contexts as ways of establishing status or lineage (e.g., 3.32, 4.18).

131. Charicleia was exposed with a silk ribbon which had her story on it, and a necklace of precious gems (2.31, 9.24, Colonna, pp. 61 and 311). In Parthenius (1.5) a father abandons his son, leaving his belt as a "token" (γνώρισμα) so that he may someday recognize him, which he does (1.6); the same motif appears in Parthenius 2, with Ulysses. In The Eunuch, a stolen girl is returned to her family with "casket and proofs" (753)—possibly a confusion of topoi on Terence's part.

132. Of course, tokens could also be fraudulently used if they fell into the wrong hands: Charicleia, an abandoned child, recognizes this in the Aethiopica (9.24, Colonna, p. 311), and says that a mother's love is the only certain proof. Valuable tokens could also endanger a child, since someone might try to steal them or the child: this, too, is mentioned in the Aethiopica 2.31 (Colonna, p. 81).

EMOTIONAL ATTACHMENTS

Literature also provides a supplement to epigraphy and law concerning the sentiments of the children, their parents, and their adopters. Abandoned children, as noted, almost invariably wish to locate their natal parents once they become aware they were abandoned, no matter how much they love their foster family. They assume that this will be an occasion of joy to all concerned—a somewhat dubious assumption, given some of the motivations for abandonment. Charicleia believes that maternal love is an unquenchable passion:

> The maternal nature is the indisputable token: from it the begetter conceives parental tenderness toward her child from their first contact, established by an inexpressible empathy.[133]

When Daphnis finds his mother and father he embraces them readily, because, as Longus says, "nature is quickly believed."[134] (But Daphnis and Chloe return to the fields where they grew up and to their foster parents for their wedding [4.37–38]). Whether these reflect in some way the fantasies of abandoned children or simply those of writers about abandoned children is impossible to determine.[135]

In literary sources no conflict arises about returning children to the natal family. Sometimes the issue is addressed: the foster mother in *Cistellaria* specifically thinks her adopted child should be returned to her natal parents;[136] Chloe's adoptive father is sure that if she finds her "true parents" it will make them all happy. In real life the many legal texts about adjudicating disputes in the matter suggest that it was not always so, and this is probably one area where writers have simplified for the sake of happy endings. Under the later empire the

---

133. *Aethiopica* 9.24, Colonna, p. 311; cf. trans. by Hadas, p. 239.

134. 4.23: οὕτω φύσις ταχέως πιστεύεται. Daphnis's parents had agreed to pretend to the outside world that he was their own (1.3), but in fact both Daphnis and Chloe knew they were adopted (1.8).

135. It was widely believed in the ancient world—as now—that children shared physical and moral characteristics of their parents, and that this would facilitate *anagnorisis*. See, e.g., Aristotle, *Politics* 2.1; Terence, *Heautontimoroumenos* 1020–24. Authors also maintained that a person's social status showed in his appearance, which might provide a further clue: see Achilles Tatius, *Clitophon and Leucippe* 5.17 (ed. and trans. S. Gaselee [London, 1969], p. 272).

136. "Ut eorum quoniam esse oportet te sis potius quam mea" (632).

previously unquestioned right of parents to reclaim was considerably abridged, and in the early Middle Ages denied completely, but feelings about blood relation may have triumphed over law even in these societies.

In few cases do writers portray children as remembering their parents.[137] Charicleia could remember the name of the man who reared her in infancy, but not his face, and had no idea about her original parents. Gellius quotes Favorinus as observing specifically that the filial sentiments of abandoned children become entirely focused on their rescuer, and they retain no attachment to the natal mother.[138] Most *expositi* in fiction do not even know they were abandoned, which suggests a general presumption that exposed children were brought up as adoptees. And, although Chloe's foster parents seem to entertain somewhat venal attitudes toward her,[139] relations between adopted children and their guardians are generally happy in fiction. This, in fact, accords well with the evidence from historical and legal sources about the treatment of *alumni*.[140]

DEATH

The one prospect for abandoned children which neither literary nor historical sources treat is death: only once in the large and varied

---

137. A stolen child in the *Menaechmi* of Plautus remembers that he was stolen at age seven, when his baby teeth were falling out (1116), and has clear recollection of his parents and childhood, although unlike most abandoned children he seems to feel no need to locate them. (But when his brother finds him, he does return to his natal family: 1153.) A girl stolen by pirates in Terence's *The Eunuch* remembers her parents' names, but no more.

138. *Attic Nights* 12.1.23.

139. They consider keeping the gifts her suitors bring her for their own natal son (3.25).

140. Stepmothers, later arrivals to the family themselves, appear, by contrast, to have been notorious for bad relations with stepchildren. Many sources suggest that stepmothers made trouble for their stepsons—even the law: parents who wrong their children in wills do so "for the most part corrupted by inducement and instigations of stepmothers" (Dig. 5.2.4). Juvenal says they plot to murder stepsons (6.628). Quintilian(?) describes the case of a stepmother who apparently tries to disinherit her stepson by hiring a pauper to claim him, in the course of which he accepts the hatred of stepmothers for their stepsons as axiomatic: "hunc iuvenem sic oderat, tamquam noverca" (*Declamationes minores* 338). Both Heliodorus (1.9) and Apuleius (*Metamorphoses* 10) have stepmothers sexually harass stepsons. Seneca relates a case in which a stepmother poisons her stepson (*Controversiae* 9.6).

corpus of legal texts covering many aspects of abandonment is the death of *expositi* alluded to;[141] nowhere in literary sources are children depicted as actually dying; no historian comments on dead *expositi* or even about concern for the safety of exposed children. No source mentions corpses of infants or assigns responsibility for burial in such cases. Only moralists and orators raise the possibility of death, and it is notable that none of them adduces an instance. One of Quintilian's declaimers paints a grave picture:

> It is rare that exposed children survive. We humans are fragile beasts at our beginning. Movement and the seeking of the breast come instantly to the infants of other animals, but among us the baby must be sustained and protected from the cold.[142]

But he also says that the poor prevent their abandoned children from dying by leaving them in very public locations, suggesting either that only the offspring of the rich die—which is a bit hard to understand—or that the dire predictions are rhetorical.[143]

Mythological babies were sometimes torn to pieces by animals or threatened with this fate,[144] but since in myths adults were also frequently mauled, torn, devoured, or carried off by animals, this is not necessarily a useful datum. The sources themselves are sometimes ambivalent: Livy's account of the abandonment of Romulus and Remus (1.19) seems to involve an effort to drown them ("the Tiber, having overflowed its banks, . . . gave those carrying the babies hope that even though it was slow they might be drowned"), but they floated ashore in the basket in which they were exposed. Leaving children in a floating basket seems an odd way to drown

141. And this is suspect: see above.

142. *Declamationes minores* 306 (Winterbottom, p. 133). In no. 278 he suggests as possible fates for an abandoned child that "beasts would maul him or birds carry him away." The former is mentioned elsewhere as well; the latter may provide a clue to the degree of rhetoric involved.

143. 306: "ille relinquitur loco celebri, hunc et libet custodire longe et expectare fortunam."

144. E.g., Ion's mother in Euripides' *Ion* (900–910) imagines that he has been killed by eagles, although her intention had been that he be rescued (965). Ovid contemplates the horror of an abandoned child being ripped to pieces by animals in *Heroides* (11) when the child of an incestuous union is ordered exposed by his grandfather in a "desert" place (83ff.). Crotopos's daughter exposed a son who *was* subsequently killed by dogs (Pausanius 1.46), but this is unique—a *hapax genomenon*.

them.[145] (Rivers, which occur frequently in accounts of abandonment, may be symbolic of the ambivalence of entrusting the children to fate: the water could either drown them or transport them to happier lives. Cf. Talmudic prescriptions about this in chapter 3.)

Parents in literature sometimes announce that in exposing a baby they are seeking "to do away with it," but there is good reason to believe that this is a misleading figure of speech, or that they are at least uncertain about the baby's survival. Infanticide was known at Rome, could certainly be effected when people wished to do so, and is clearly characterized in the sources when it occurs.[146] In Plautus's *Cistellaria* a girl who has been raped is said to have exposed her child "to die" (*ad necem*), but if she meant this,[147] certainly no one else in the story anticipated the child's death. Tokens were left with the baby expressly for later recognition, and the servant who exposed her waited specifically to see who picked her up. When the man who ravished the mother eventually returned, he undertook at once to locate the abandoned daughter, not even considering the possibility that she might have died.

Although Daphnis's father says he left him to die, he also left expensive tokens with him, and registers only delight—no surprise—when he later turns up, quite alive. Persinna considers the possibility that her daughter may die when she exposes her (4.8; Colonna, pp. 124–25), but clearly hopes she will not, and considers death and survival equally likely possibilities at the time. Later she seems to have no doubt that her daughter is still alive. Callirhoe contemplates infanticide and abandonment at length as *opposite* pos-

145. In Plutarch's account the vessel is used to carry them down to the river, but the king has only ordered the servants to "cast them away" (ῥῖψαι).

146. Tertullian alludes to drowning children in water in *Ad nationes* 1.15 (CSEL 20.85); Juvenal discusses stepmothers murdering their stepchildren and the danger of wives murdering the children of concubines (6.627–42); in Apuleius's *Metamorphoses* a mother decides to kill her daughter to obtain her inheritance (10.28); in *The Mother-in-Law* Terence has the grandfather forbid removal of a child from the house, apparently because he fears his wife will harm it (653–56); Ovid describes a husband ordering his wife to kill their baby (see above, p. 93). For a general discussion of infanticide among the Romans, consult the works cited in the introduction.

147. In the *Heautontimoroumenos* there is a similar ambiguity: at line 630 the child is merely to be exposed ("ei dedi / exponendam"), but at line 636 death seems to have been envisioned ("interemptam oportuit"). Cf. Terence, *The Mother-in-Law* 749, where the mother-in-law wishes to *extinguere* the child.

sibilities, but eventually rejects the former as "mindless" (ἀνόητος) since the latter is possible.[148]

Christian moralists, like some pagans, objected to abandonment as *tantamount* to killing a child, but both the fact that they had to make this argument and the specific objections they brought to bear argue persuasively for the contrary. "You [pagans]," Tertullian carps, "abandon your children to the kindness of strangers or to adoption by better parents."[149]

It is hardly possible, of course, that some abandoned children did not die: the infant mortality rate in industrialized nations of the West is around 1 percent, but in nonindustrial countries it often approaches 20 percent.[150] Hopkins found a mortality rate at Rome of about 33 percent among nonabandoned children under nine.[151] Even if they were picked up in every case and reared tenderly as *alumni, expositi* would run considerable risks: the normal dangers of infancy in preindustrial societies, plus the difficulties finders might have in locating a wet nurse, and any complications attendant on the circumstances that inspired the abandonment in the first place (such as poverty, the death of the mother, poor health of infant or mother, etc.).[152] It is not necessary to imagine dogs devouring or birds carrying off abandoned children to believe that exposing increased the risk of death, but the increase was incremental, quantitative rather than qualitative. The overwhelming belief in the ancient world was that abandoned children were picked up and reared by someone else. It was, indeed, because they were so certain this would be the fate of abandoned children that some fathers preferred infanticide, many legislators worried over problems of status and recovery, and most moralists and much literature raised the specter of incest.

148. Chariton (*De Chaerea et Callirhoe,* ed. Blake), p. 34.

149. Tertullian, *Ad nationes* 1.16 (CSEL 20.87). See chapter 3 for Christian arguments predicated on the likelihood of survival.

150. These figures are based on statistics for 1970–1980, the last full decade for which they are available (*Statistical Abstract of the United States,* ed. William Lerner [Washington, D.C., 1980], pp. 77–79, 901–2). The rate in Sweden is about 0.8 percent, the U.S. and the U.K. both 1.4, France 1.1. By contrast, Afghanistan has a rate of 21–23 percent, Ethiopia 15–20, Turkey 11.9, Zaire 16–17, Morocco 16.2, and Nepal 13.3.

151. Keith Hopkins, "On the Probable Age Structure of the Roman Population," *Population Studies* 20 (1966) 245–64; see tables 4 and 5.

152. See, e.g., the case discussed in note 14, above; see also translation in Appendix ("The Disputed Baby").

NUMBERS

Is there any way to know how many children were abandoned? Hardly. We do not know the absolute population of Romans, how many married and at what age, how long the marriages lasted, or how long the husband and wife continued to have conjugal relations (husbands could have recourse to slaves or prostitutes without committing adultery, although many wives objected). We know too little about Roman health and diet to guess the fertility of wives, the frequency of miscarriage, the onset of menopause; we have next to no information about what contraceptive modes of intercourse were known or practiced or how often abortions were performed. We could hardly, therefore, have an idea how many children were born to how many people or what percent of these would have been abandoned.

What we do know is this: it is rare in legal, historical, or literary sources to encounter a Roman family with many children. Moralists hold up large families as admirable—from which one infers they were rare—and even the state felt it had to offer inducements to persuade couples to bring up three children (four in the case of freedmen). If a couple remained married for a decade,[153] was fertile, engaged in chiefly procreative forms of sexuality,[154] and hired a wet nurse for the children,[155] the wife might have had six or more chil-

153. In view of the divorce rate and the age at which women apparently died, it would be unreasonable to hypothesize an average length of marriage beyond this.

154. Hopkins ("Contraception") was unable to show any widespread effective means of contraception among Romans. Most Romans had an aversion to oral sex, and Latin writers suggest that anal sex was inappropriate with wives. See discussion in Boswell, *Christianity,* p. 162, and sources cited there. It has often been assumed that one of the purposes of prostitution in the ancient world was to provide husbands a nonprocreative sexual outlet, and many Christian writers acknowledged this (see, e.g., ibid., pp. 148–49), implying that husbands would not engage in such activity with wives. Indeed, the overwhelming rhetorical stance of ancient writers was that the *purpose* of relations with one's wife was procreation: "We have mistresses for pleasure, concubines for daily intercourse, and wives to produce children legitimately and to have a faithful guardian of the home" (Athenaeus, *Deipnosophistae* 13.573B, misquoting Apollodorus).

155. Because nursing may be contraceptive: see J.-P. Habicht et al., "The Contraceptive Role of Breastfeeding," and Ula-Britt Lithell, "Breast-Feeding Habits." For wet-nursing at Rome, see Keith Bradley, "Wet-nursing at Rome: A Study in Social Relations," in Rawson, *The Family in Ancient Rome.*

dren. Even an infant mortality rate of thirty-three percent[156] would leave such a couple with more than three children. Since one finds little evidence of infanticide in Rome and constant references to abandonment, it seems reasonable to infer that the unwanted babies would be abandoned.

Indeed, abandonment is the only inference that accounts for all of the available clues. Without effective contraception or infanticide it is very difficult to explain the apparently small size of Roman families, but if Romans had practiced either of these on the scale required to explain the low number of recorded children, one would expect demographic effects not indicated by the sources (e.g., a dramatically diminishing population). Abandonment seems the obvious answer, especially since it is ubiquitous in Roman writing.[157] The exposing of children would have precisely the same impact on the recorded family size as contraception or infanticide, and would reduce overall reproductivity, since those children brought up in servitude or poverty would have less chance than others of establishing families (even *alumni* would probably be at some disadvantage in the marriage pool). But it would not have as drastic a demographic impact, either on the *expositi*'s own generation or the next, as the killing (or nonconception) of the same number of children, since some proportion of them would certainly reproduce. Abandonment is a gentler check on overall population than infanticide, as well as being "gentler" for the parents in both moral and emotional terms.[158]

In addition to familial or social problems of gross reproductive rate, exposing provided relief from difficulties posed by gender, timing, or circumstance: if the first four children were female, some

156. Among the Julio-Claudians, of ninety-four children known to have been reared, twelve died as infants or in early childhood (Étienne, "La Conscience médicale," p. 43); the father of Caligula had nine children, of whom two died in infancy (Suetonius, *Caligula* 7); but the histories of those at the very top of Roman society cannot be assumed to be typical.

157. See summary of such arguments in note 2 of chapter 1.

158. If one accepts Russell's argument (LAMPC, xii–xiii) that a replacement rate of 3.5 was needed to sustain population in ancient and medieval Europe in normal times, a rate of abandonment as low as twenty percent over several centuries among the Roman population as a whole (perhaps lower among the rich, higher among the poor) would account for the gradual decline in the Roman population observed through the fifth century, without requiring the positing of widespread infanticide or any biological or demographic disaster.

or all of them were probably abandoned. Beyond three or four children of either gender, many if not most couples would abandon. Some parents would abandon even a first-born boy if they were not ready to start a family. A prosperous husband could have children with slaves, servants, or courtesans: these might also be exposed; and if the wife had illegitimate children they were almost certainly abandoned. Of course, sterile or nonprolific couples would not have given up any children at all, but would number (along with the unmarried and those seeking laborers) among those who picked up and reared the offspring of others: this was essential to the functioning of the system.

It is beyond question that abandonment was a familiar part of Roman life, affecting every class of person and every type of extant source, from inscriptions to novels, from laws to plays, from moral advice to imperial chronicles. Romans regarded it as remarkable that other nations did not expose children.[159] Equally revealing, it was seen as exceptional that some mothers did not abandon children.[160] Musonius Rufus says that "most people" ignore ethical advice to rear all their children. A speaker in Seneca's *controversiae* claims that every parent who passes the crippled *expositi* fears that one of them is a child he or she exposed—as if every Roman parent walking through the forum would have abandoned a child at some point.[161] He is no doubt straining to make a point, but no point would be made if the claim fell too far short of credibility. In a legal debate one side argues that a boy ought to have suspected that he was an *expositus*—as if this were an obvious concern for a child—

159. E.g., Diodorus (quoting Hecateus) on the Egyptians and the Jews, who were required to rear all the children born to them (1.80.3, 40.3). (Cf. Aristotle frag. 258; Strabo, *Geography* 17.2.5; and, on the Jews, Josephus, *Against Apion* 2.202, though his claim is certainly false: the Mosaic law does not require this.) Diodorus says both peoples were able to follow this rule because it was cheap to rear children in their climate. See also Athenaeus (quoting Theopompus) on the Etruscans (12.517D), and Tacitus on the Germans (*Germania* 19), where infanticide is at issue. Tacitus's view of the superiority of German family life is usually not reliable about the Germans; it may reveal something about Roman expectations, but must be viewed as cautiously as all social criticism in efforts to assess what was common practice.

160. E.g., Dio Chrysostom on Oeneus and his wife, who "not only did not expose their own children, . . . but finding the children of others in the road, picked them up and reared them as their own. . . ." (*Discourse* 15.9).

161. *Controversiae* 10.4.10: "Everyone gives alms to each of them, since everyone is afraid he might say no to his own child."

because the man who brought him up was cruel to him.[162] Justin Martyr tries to dissuade Christians from going to prostitutes on the grounds that they are likely to commit incest with some relative who has been abandoned and brought up in prostitution—"a son, or a brother, or some other relative": implying that in every family someone had probably been exposed and ended up a prostitute.[163]

One of Terence's characters suspects he had been abandoned and adopted when his (in fact, natal) parents begin to ignore him; his servant considers this a reasonable fear, and urges him to seek his original parents.[164] Another figure imagines she can send for an abandoned baby whenever she wants, and, according to Terence, she can.[165] When Chloe's foster father notices that her beau does not resemble his parents he immediately suspects that he had been abandoned (3.32). And when Chloe herself is seeking her natal parents, "many of the wealthy women" of Mytilene pray that she will turn out to be their daughter—since, apparently, they had all abandoned a daughter who could be her age.[166]

There is no way to quantify any element of the human landscape of the ancient world. It might be reasonable to assume that since abandonment is much more prominent in the cultural muniments of Rome than it is in those of early modern cities in which the rate is known to have reached thirty percent or better of the birthrate, it must have been considerably higher than this in urban centers of antiquity. But this would be to assume an unprovable and unlikely uniformity of cultural records. What seems a reasonable (if disappointingly modest) quantitative inference is that a substantial percentage—perhaps a majority—of women who had reared more than one child had also abandoned at least one, and that the overall rate of abandonment fell near the high end of the European scale—twenty to forty percent of urban children—at Rome during the first three centuries of the Christian era.[167]

162. Quintilian(?), *Declamationes minores* 358.

163. 1 *Apology* 27 (PG 6. 372). The fathers themselves, he adds, prostitute not only their wives but their children.

164. *Heautontimoroumenos* 985 ff.

165. *Andria* 515–16 and 720 ff.

166. 4.33: literally, "many of the wealthier women prayed to the gods that they would be considered the mother of such a beautiful daughter," which could be taken to mean something less specific than my interpretation, but the context makes any other reading unlikely.

167. Russell's low estimate of an average of 4.2 children per mother in late antique and medieval Europe (LAMPC, xii–xiii), combined with an infant mortality

If the Roman data do not resolve numerical questions precisely, they do offer clues about several other mysteries of abandonment. Legal, historical, and ethical writings, assessed largely by themselves, present a picture strikingly similar to what appears in Roman literary sources: the extent of divergence between the two, in fact, is less than the variations within each. One could therefore conclude, with some reason, that abandonment in the literature is by and large reflective of reality and not a "quicksand topos," although this would not guarantee that any particulars were trustworthy. It would be more cautious to view the literature simply as a *part* of the reality, contributing to and participating in the social phenomenon through inspiration, parody, guidance, and the promulgation of attitudes of acceptance.

Moralists did not oppose it (except a few Stoics, and they not categorically), and although some parents regretted having exposed a particular child, none seems to have felt he or she had done something wicked. Nor did their contemporaries, or the law: the latter strove (with some variation) to preserve freeborn status without limiting the right or ability of Roman parents to abandon. The authority of the natal father, or the master in the case of slave children, was not even abrogated by his abandoning the child until the fourth century.

These facts do not demonstrate that Roman parents held views about children or childrearing that were fundamentally different from those of their modern counterparts. Their opinions and feelings span the same range as those of humans in any age, from utter devotion to callous indifference. They abandoned children by and large because, in their view, they had no choice: they had no knowledge of or access to the modes of prenatal family limitation employed by most modern parents in the West. If they wished to maintain quality of life for themselves and at least some of their children they had to control their family size postnatally. Abandonment was preferable, in the view of most, to killing the children.

In both a historical and a physical sense, then, Roman families,

------

rate of twenty percent, would produce families of three children among those who matched the mean exactly. But those who exceeded it—possibly as many as a third or more, to balance the twenty percent infertile plus those who had fewer children because of divorce, etc.—would have had to produce many more, and to abandon some. They alone could account for a rate of abandonment of twenty percent or more.

as recorded, are likely to be missing some of the "flesh" that would give a true picture of their shape: very many of them had once included children subsequently separated from it, still related in law, and likely, in some cases, to rejoin it. And some households comprised children they had collected from other families, who may have been permanent or temporary residents, free or servile, exploited or cherished, legally adopted or simply supported.

The empire developed no institutions to care for these children. Their fate was left to chance, which may have been one of the factors that allowed parents to abandon with few qualms: although a son or daughter might be brought up in slavery or as a prostitute, he or she might also be adopted by a kindly stranger of greater status or resources than the parents, treated as an *alumnus,* and even reunited with parents later in life, under more favorable circumstances. The "kindness of strangers" figures prominently in Roman writings on the subject, from laws to novels; embodied in the statue of a kindly wolf suckling two fatefully abandoned human infants, the metaphor stood watch over the forum and was carried with Roman culture throughout the known world, reflecting and encouraging not only the hope of anxious parents, but a real, important, and often inspiring aspect of ancient social and family life.

3

❖   ❖   ❖

FATHERS OF
THE CHURCH AND
PARENTS OF CHILDREN

Sing, O barren, thou that didst not bear; break forth into singing, and cry aloud, thou that didst not travail with child; for more are the children of the desolate than the children of the married wife, saith the Lord.

Isaiah 54:1 (cf. Galatians 4:27)

CHRISTIANITY was itself a foundling in a way: born into Judaism but rejected by it,[1] it was adopted by Rome and grew up to be much more a part of its foster than its natal family. Indeed, Roman language and culture achieved their greatest impact on the Western world chiefly through their *alumnus*, Christianity—an abandoned child reared to greatness by a loving foster parent. By the middle of the fourth century, Christianity had eclipsed the traditional religions of the empire as well as the other imports from the Middle East. It was not only established by its adoptive family as the favorite son and heir apparent, but had, to a considerable extent, taken control of the household; the "Romanizing" of Christianity resulted in the "Christianizing" of the Roman world. Emperors were more and more often Christians from the opening of the fourth century on; the ruling classes were increasingly Christian; the collapsing government of the empire was supplemented and ultimately

---

1. As illegitimate—although the metaphor cannot be pushed, and it would be equally accurate to say that Christianity rejected its parent. The first Christians were themselves mostly Jews, and directed their preaching efforts, even when they went abroad, toward other Jews, the majority of whom were apparently not persuaded. By the time the new religion was well established at Rome it was directing its message chiefly at pagans: but cf. note 61, below. Isaiah (49:23) prophesied that Gentile rulers would become "foster parents" (אמן) to the Jews—an ironic prediction, all things considered (cf. Numbers 11:12, 2 Samuel 4:4, Ruth 4:16).

replaced by the ecclesiastical structure of Christianity, which was directly modeled on it and well suited to fill in; and the intellectual life of the empire had become almost exclusively Christian by the end of the fourth century.

Like other abandoned children, Christianity had come with tokens, most notably the Jewish scriptures.[2] And although their impact, like that of Greco-Roman mythology, cannot be determined precisely, they doubtless exerted an influence on those who pored over them for inspiration and guidance. Three aspects of the Hebrew scriptures in particular may have affected attitudes among Christian cultures where they were studied as the Old Testament: (1) a startlingly matter-of-fact attitude toward parental sacrifice or execution of children;[3] (2) the definition of guidelines for the selling of children; (3) the implicit acceptance of abandonment in general.

(1) It is one of the commandments of the decalogue that children honor their parents, but there are few regulations in the Jewish scriptures about how parents must treat their offspring. The sacrifice of children to gods in general or to Moloch (Molech) or Baal in particular is prohibited, condemned, or mentioned disparagingly in a dozen places, but the exact nature of the practice (particularly,

2. The Hebrew text of the Jewish scriptures used by modern Jews and taken as the basis of the Old Testament by Protestants differs in wording, order, and content from the Greek version of the Jewish scriptures, the Septuagint (LXX), compiled by and for the Greek-speaking Jews of the Mediterranean during the centuries before the beginning of the Christian era. Partly a translation from Hebrew, but also containing some materials composed in Greek—the language of a majority of Jews by this time—the LXX was the version most used by early Christians. Jerome followed the structure and numbering of the Septuagint in making his fourth-century Latin translation, the Vulgate, the bible of the Middle Ages, although he rendered its Old Testament largely from Hebrew. Numbers in brackets in the citations that follow indicate LXX / Vulgate numberings where they differ from that of the Hebrew ("Masoretic") text and the King James Version based on it (from which all translations are taken unless otherwise noted)—i.e., 2 [4] Kings = 2 Kings in the KJV and 4 Kings in the LXX / Vulgate. I have provided the English for Septuagint or Vulgate passages not included in the KJV (e.g., from the Wisdom of Solomon).

3. Related to this, but not directly apposite here, is the theme of the killing of princes by ambitious relatives, with one special child escaping and being reared in secret: see, e.g., Judges 9:5, where Abimelech kills seventy children, but Jotham hides and survives; and 2 [4] Kings 11 and 2 Chronicles 22:10–12, where Athaliah kills all the royal children except Joash, who hides in the temple for six years (cf. Samuel, below) and ascends the throne at age seven. These motifs may have inspired similar stories common in the Middle Ages.

whether it involved killing the child), the identity of the god in question, and the relation of this sacrifice to that in Carthage mentioned above, remain unclear.[4] Quite clear is the paradoxical relationship of children to religious sacrifice: because they were valued, the gods would be pleased to receive them as offerings, but they were not so precious that parents could not bring themselves to perform the deed. The heathen are usually condemned for doing this, and the Jews prohibited,[5] suggesting that natural sentiment would

4. Moloch is given as the identity of a pagan god in 1 Kings 11:7 and associated with the sacrifice of children in Jeremiah 32:35 and possibly Leviticus 18:21 and 20:2–5 (see note 5, below), and with the sacrifice of children through fire in 2 [4] Kings 23:10, where the practice is located in the Valley of Hinnom. Sacrifice of children through fire is linked to this same valley in 2 Chronicles [Paralipomenon] 28:3 and 33:6, and although Moloch is not mentioned, it seems reasonable to infer that the same deity is involved. Jeremiah 19:5 condemns sacrificing children through fire to Baal, and 2 [4] Kings 17:31 prohibits the same sort of sacrifice to two other named deities, while Deuteronomy 12:31 and 2 [4] Kings 16:3 refer to the sacrifice of children through fire to an unnamed pagan god, which could certainly be Moloch (*m-l-ch*). The name might, in fact, be simply the word "king" with the vowels for reading (*qere*) perhaps from "shame" (בשׁת). This is clearly how the translators of the LXX often took it: although they gave Μολοχ at 2 [4] Kings 23:10 and Jeremiah 32 [39]:35, in Leviticus 18:21 and 20:2–5 they offer ἄρχων, and at 1 [3] Kings 11:7 βασιλεύς. If the word only meant "king," most of the references could be to the same deity. Ezekiel 23:37 and 39 refer to the sacrificing of children to be "eaten" by the pagan divinity involved, which may or may not be a reference to fire; the LXX took it as such and inserted ἐμπύρων, but Jerome did not. He did add to the Hebrew-Greek notion of sacrifice in general more specifically cultic expressions (e.g., *consecrare, initiare, immolare*) at 2 [4] Kings 16:3, 23:10, Jeremiah 32 [39]:35, and Ezekiel 23:37 and 39, but it is not clear that this affected subsequent readings of the text in any substantive way.

5. Leviticus 18:21, 20:2–5. The inclusion of child sacrifice in these chapters is peculiar, because both are otherwise devoted to violations of sexual purity. An obvious interpretation would be that the Hebrew word מֶזְרָע, which is translated "children," should be understood instead as "seed," or "semen," an equally common meaning and the one apparently taken by the LXX, Vulgate, and KJV—i.e., a suggestion of some sexual practice involved in worship, also common in the ancient world. But modern translators have generally preferred to understand the passage as referring to children (see, e.g., JB and *The Torah* [Jewish Publication Society, Philadelphia, 1981]), probably influenced by the Jewish exegetical tradition, which uniformly understood the prohibition to apply to offering children to idols: see, e.g., Nachmanides (Ramban, *Commentary on the Torah. Leviticus,* trans. Charles Chavel [New York, 1974], pp. 258–67 and 313–19), who registers no horror at the idea of killing children in this context, and focuses entirely on the issue of idolatry. Indeed, whatever was sacrificed, Leviticus 20:3 makes clear that the reason for punishment is the defilement of the sanctuary and God's name, not the loss of children (or seed).

not suffice to preclude it.[6] The King of Moab sacrifices his eldest
son on the city wall merely as a sign of grief in 2 [4] Kings (3:27),
and in Judges (11:30–40) the Israelite hero Jephthah kills his only
daughter to fulfill a vow he has made to the Lord.[7]

A pivotal moment in Jewish history, in fact, involves the demand by God that Abraham sacrifice his son as a test of submission,
which Abraham proves willing to do (Genesis 22).[8] In several crucial ways the incident sets Jewish religious tradition apart from
others: one person's sacrifice ultimately affects the whole people—a
recurring theme in the Jewish and subsequent Christian traditions—
and it is not the sacrifice itself that God desires, or accepts, but the
willingness to perform it. It is, nonetheless, a striking and fundamental parallel to the use of children as sacrificial offerings in other
cultures. In Exodus (13:12–13; 22:30; 34:20), the firstborn sons of
all Jews are said to belong to God, and must be redeemed.

An even more startling trope occurs in Leviticus (26:29), where
God tells the Jews, "Ye shall eat the flesh of your sons, and the flesh
of your daughters shall ye eat." The topos of eating children (or siblings) was not unique to the Jews; it occurs elsewhere in ancient
literature.[9] But it is repeated again and again in the Bible, sometimes

6. This same ambivalence is present in the famous story of Solomon's judgment on the disputed baby (1 [3] Kings 3:16–28): on the one hand it is horrifying
that he would propose to slay the child to settle a dispute; on the other, it is a sign
of the love the real mother feels for it that she would yield rather than harm it, and
an indication of Solomon's own high estimation of a mother's love that he would
count on this response.

7. Although some commentators have been sufficiently troubled by this disturbing story to argue that Jephthah did not actually kill his daughter, Rabanus
Maurus invoked it as a positive precedent for oblation in the Middle Ages (see
below).

8. Rabbinical tradition (see, e.g., *Pentateuch with Targum Onkelos, Haphtaroth,
and Rashi's Commentary*, trans. M. Rosenbaum and A. M. Silbermann [N.Y., n.d.]
1: *Genesis*, p. 114, section 20) held that Isaac was thirty-seven at the time (because a
Midrash claimed that Sarah had died of grief when Abraham returned alone from
Moriah, and since she died at one hundred twenty-seven and Isaac was born when
she was ninety, he must have been thirty-seven at Moriah), but neither the text
itself, which clearly labels Isaac a "boy" (נַעַר) nor modern scholarship support this.

9. For pagan parallels, see above, chapter 1, notes 84 and 85. In Achilles
Tatius's novel *Clitophon and Leucippe* (3.15), priests appear to devour the entrails of
a woman as part of a regular ritual; although the act disgusts those who see it, no
moral issues about cannibalism (or even murder) are raised. At the end of the extant text of the *Satyricon* the Roman troops capturing Numantia discover the
mothers cradling their half-eaten babies ("cum esset Numantia a Scipione capta,

in lurid detail:[10] a curse in Deuteronomy (28:53–56), predicting the consumption of children during a siege, expresses the depths to which humans will sink when driven by hunger. It is not simply that parents will devour their children, but that "tender and delicate" men and women will begrudge their relatives the flesh of the children they themselves eat.

During a famine in Samaria a starving mother complains to the King of Israel:

> This woman said unto me, Give thy son, that we may eat him to-day, and we will eat my son to-morrow.
>
> So we boiled my son, and did eat him: and I said unto her on the next day, Give thy son, that we may eat him: and she hath hid her son. (2 [4] Kings 6:28–29)

These and other references[11] to the slaughter of innocents are clearly intended to shock, and represent extremes of behavior. They may reflect willingness to deal with children—under the duress of divine command or extreme necessity—in ways later ages would find repugnant; and later Jewish commentary would accuse the "ancient inhabitants" of Israel of both cannibalism and murdering their own children,[12] but there is no reason to suppose that they are indications of real behavior.

(2) By contrast, the sale of children appears not as a bizarre or horrifying occurrence, but as a normal matter subject to regulation.

---

inventae sunt matres quae liberorum suorum tenerent semesa in sinu corpora" 141.11). A study of cannibalism in the West is much needed.

10. The Qur'an also refers to cannibalizing of relatives, although in this case a brother (49:12: "and would one of you love to eat the flesh of his dead brother?"). On cannibalism in later ages, see chapters 9 and 11.

11. Jeremiah 19:9: "I will cause them to eat the flesh of their sons and the flesh of their daughters"; Ezekiel 5:10: "Therefore the fathers shall eat the sons in the midst of thee"; Lamentations 2:20: "Shall the women eat their fruit, and children of a span long?"; cf. 4:10. For more general but equally brutal forms of infanticide, see 2 [4] Kings 8:12: "[thou] wilt dash their children, and rip up their women with child"; Psalm 137:9: "Happy shall he be, that taketh and dasheth thy little ones against the stones"; Hosea 13:16 [14:1]: "their infants shall be dashed in pieces"; cf. 9:16. The most famous such instance, of course, was Pharaoh's effort to kill all of the male children of the Israelites in Exodus 1:22, which profoundly influenced many particulars of Jewish and Christian religious practice: see below, on parallels to Romulus and Remus.

12. Wisdom of Solomon [only LXX and Vulgate] 12:1–6.

And if a man sell his daughter to be a maidservant, she shall not go out as the menservants do.

If she pleases not her master, who hath betrothed her to himself, then shall he let her be redeemed: to sell her unto a strange nation he shall have no power, seeing he hath dealt deceitfully with her.[13]

This provision is strikingly like pre-Christian Roman attitudes toward the sale of children: their labor may be sold by parents, but they may not be permanently reduced to servitude.[14] It occurs immediately after rules regarding male slaves, who are automatically freed in the seventh year of service, and it may not have struck Christian readers as a question of genuine slavery, although it is clear authorization for fathers to sell female children.[15] Whether it applied to male children as well is ambiguous in the text: the preceding regulations about male slaves refer to "buying" them, and one might understand the rule about daughters to be a refinement of this, although it would also be possible to understand that only female children can be sold in this way.[16] The case of Joseph's brothers selling him into slavery (Genesis 37) is not a clear parallel, but in 2 [4] Kings 4:1 a widow fears that her creditors will take her sons as slaves, and in Nehemiah there is an unambiguous reference to the selling of children by poor Jewish parents to richer ones:

The ordinary people and their wives began complaining loudly against their brother Jews. Some said, "We are having to barter our sons and daughters to get enough corn to eat and keep us

13. Exodus 21:7 [21:7–8 in Vulgate]. The word here translated as "menservants" (עֲבָדִים) usually means "slave"; the word for the daughter (אָמָה) more commonly applies to a servant who is not a slave, but, as the preceding verses suggest, any Jewish "slave" occupied a position more like that of an indentured servant than a Roman slave. The Greek appears to contrast the sold daughter as οἰκέτιν with δοῦλαι (*sic,* though the Hebrew here is masculine), whereas the Latin uses *famulam* for her and *ancillae* for the more general category; these normally imply the reverse.

14. A similar provision occurs in the Code of Hammurabi (section 117), according to which a man in debt may sell his wife, son, or daughter, but they are only indentured thereby for three years, after which they are free.

15. It also affected Christian legislation of the early Middle Ages: see below, chapter 4.

16. The Mishnah (*Kethuboth* 3.8) allows fathers to sell daughters up to the age of twelve (mothers may not: Sotah 3.8; cf. Hullin 1.7), but makes no comparable provision about sons.

alive." . . . Still others said, ". . . Though we are of the same
flesh as our brothers, and our children as good as theirs, we are
having to sell our sons and our daughters into slavery. . . ."[17]

This passage was cited by jurists in the Middle Ages as scriptural
authorization for the sale of children by impoverished parents.[18] In
Isaiah (50:1) Israel's interlocutor adduces as one of his mercies that
he did not sell her to his creditors ("To which of my creditors have I
sold you?"), but the selling of the poor to the rich is cited in Amos
(2:6, 8:6) as a sign of Israel's wickedness.

Lot's offering his daughters to an angry crowd as appeasement
(Genesis 19) is a surprising act from the one virtuous inhabitant of
Sodom, and seems to fall somewhere between sacrifice of children
and sale. Although other aspects of the famous incident overshadowed this for most subsequent commentators, some later writers
did note it.[19]

(3) Two instances of child abandonment in the Jewish scriptures
were central to Western religious consciousness at least from the triumph of Christianity on. The case of Ishmael, the son of Abraham

17. Nehemiah [2 Esdras] 5:1, 2, 5; translation from JB. The Hebrew for 5:2
says, ambiguously: "Our sons and daughters and we are many; let us take grain
and eat and live," which is reflected in both the LXX and some modern translations (e.g., KJV: "We, our sons, and our daughters, are many: therefore we take up
corn for them, that we may eat, and live"). But Jerome's translation inserts the notion of bartering ("Filii nostri et filiae nostrae multae sunt nimis: accipiamus pro
pretio eorum frumentum, et comedamus et vivamus"), possibly because 5:5 is an
unambiguous reference to selling children into slavery. It was obviously common
to mortgage children if not to sell them: in the appealing and popular story of
Elisha (2 [4] Kings 4:1 ff.) a creditor comes to claim two children as his slaves for
their parents' debt ("the creditor is come to take unto him my two sons to be
bondmen" [Hebrew עֲבָדִים]).
18. E.g., the gloss on the section of the *Siete Partidas* dealing with the sale of
children: see *Las Siete Partidas,* ed. Andrea de Portonariis (Salamanca, 1555), with
gloss by Gregorio Lopez, 1.48.
19. Nachmanides, for example, was shocked at Lot's making prostitutes of his
daughters, and characterized it as the one evil act of an otherwise virtuous man
(Ramban [cited in note 5, above], *Genesis,* p. 251). Their subsequent behavior
(19:31–38) could be interpreted as confirmation of his attitude toward them.
Jerome's translation of 2 Maccabees 4:12 also implied the forced prostitution of
Jewish boys, although not by their parents ("et optimos quosque epheborum in
lupanaribus ponere"). St. Thomas, among others, noted this: *Super epistolam
ad Romanos lectura,* 1.8.151; but the original Greek did not contain this idea (τοὺς
κρατίστους τῶν ἐφήβων ὑποτάσσων ὑπὸ πέτασον ἤγαγεν).

and an Egyptian slave woman, Hagar,[20] is unlike nearly all other instances of abandonment at the order of a parent, because it is the
wife who forces the father to dispose of a child he wishes to keep.[21]
Jealous of Hagar's son, Sarah tells Abraham to cast out both mother
and child, which, with great regret, he does. Out of water in the
desert, Hagar, herself unable to watch the boy die, leaves him under
a bush and waits in the distance for his death. But God tells her
to reclaim him (*tolle puerum* in the Vulgate, "pick up the child"—
a Latin expression with explicit overtones in relation to abandonment)[22] and provides water for them. Ishmael is brought up in the
desert (like exposed children reared in rural settings), but God has
promised that (also like other famous *expositi*) he will one day rise
to greatness. Jewish, Islamic, and Christian traditions all eventually
associate Ishmael with the origins of Islam—the abandoned child
made good, founder of a dynasty. It is, strikingly, immediately after
this abandonment of Ishmael that Abraham is called upon by God
to sacrifice Isaac, although commentary has rarely suggested a connection between the two.

The case of Moses, even more fundamental to Western religious
thought, is also a subtle blend of familiar and novel aspects of abandonment. His mother's aim, of course, was not to dispose of an unwanted child, but to preserve him from death. The evil ruler has
commanded that all male Israelite children be cast[23] into the river,

20. Who is, ironically, characterized in the Hebrew as אָמָה, the term for a
daughter sold into service by a Jew in Leviticus 21:7. LXX has παιδίσκη; Vulgate
ancilla.

21. A case could be made that Ishmael is hardly a child at this juncture, since
Abraham was eighty-six when he was born (Genesis 16:16) and 100 at Isaac's birth
(Genesis 21:5), so that even if Ishmael was ejected immediately he would have had
to be fourteen, but all of the texts refer to him as a "child" (Hebrew: יֶלֶד; Greek:
παιδίον; Latin: *puerum*—none of which would normally be applied to a fourteen-
year-old), and it is extremely difficult to imagine Hagar "depositing" (Greek:
ἔρριψεν τὸ παιδίον; Latin: *abiecit puerum subter unam arborum*) a fourteen-year-old
boy under a bush (21:15). The chronologies of Abraham and Sarah's lives in Genesis are manifestly difficult: in Genesis 12:11 and 12:14–15 Sarah's beauty causes
concern for Abraham and action by the pharaoh, although according to Genesis
12:4 and 17:17 she is sixty-five at the time.

22. See the discussion of *tolle* in note 34 of chapter 1. Several words in the
LXX and Vulgate versions are associated with abandonment: e.g., Sarah tells
Abraham to ἔκβαλε Hagar and Ishmael, the most common Greek word for "ex-
pose" after ἐκτίθηναι; ῥίψω, at 21:15, is also a common word for "expose."

23. Greek has ῥίψατε, one of the most common words for "expose"; Latin has
proiicite.

and Moses is left in a basket along its banks, only to be found by
Pharaoh's daughter, who hires the child's own mother to nurse him
(Exodus 2). Although there are significant differences, and certainly
no need to hypothesize any common origin, the parallels with other
cases of great dynastic leaders abandoned to avoid murder by an in-
secure autocrat, found in a basket by a kindly stranger, and reared
to greatness, must have been resonant coincidences to Christians of
Roman culture.[24] The Latin translation even reads adoption into the
Hebrew, perhaps thinking of *alumni*.[25]

More suggestive of the quotidian reality of abandonment among
biblical Jews[26] is the extended metaphor in Ezekiel of Israel herself
as an abandoned child:

> And as for thy nativity, in the day thou wast born thy navel was
> not cut, neither wast thou washed in water to supple thee; thou
> wast not salted at all,[27] nor swaddled at all . . . but thou wast
> cast out in the open field, to the loathing of thy person, in the
> day that thou wast born. (16:4–5)

God rescues the child (16:9ff.), takes her as wife,[28] and has children
by her (16:20). The image would seem to lack force if abandoned
children were not a familiar part of life among those to whom it was
directed, particularly with its graphic details about the postnatal
treatment of a child to be abandoned. It must certainly have had impact on Roman readers.[29]

24. The colorful detail of his mother's being hired to nurse him found parallels
in the Middle Ages: see below, chapter 7.

25. Exodus 2:10: "quem illa adoptavit in locum filii." Hebrew: וַיְהִי־לָהּ לְבֵן;
Greek: καὶ ἐγενήθη αὐτῇ εἰς υἱόν. Cf. the Muslim treatment in chapter 4, below.

26. Other incidents are worth noting: in 1 Esdras 9:36 [LXX] Israelites who
have married "foreign women," dismiss them (like Abraham) "with their children." In the Hebrew and Vulgate versions [Ezra 10:44] the matter is put more
delicately, each noting that among the dismissed wives there were women who had
borne sons. Jephthah the Gileadite, the son of a harlot, was thrown out of the house
by legitimate sons, a case of "abandonment" of a sort, but more reminiscent of
Joseph: Judges 11:1–2; cf. Numbers 26:29–34 and 1 Chronicles 7:14–19.

27. Both Galen (1.1.7) and Soranus (*Gynaecia* 2.12) refer to salting newborn
infants. R. Étienne ("La Conscience médicale antique," p. 32) believes that this was
to eliminate mucus.

28. Or at least in some erotic relationship: cf. the very similar arrangement in
Esther 2, where Mordecai raises his orphaned niece as an *alumna* but also to be his
wife, according to the Greek text and subsequent Jewish exegesis.

29. Psalm 27:10 ("When my father and my mother forsake me, then the Lord
will take me up") may also have suggested child abandonment to later readers, al-

The biblical story which had the greatest practical impact on the children of subsequent ages, however, was the account of Hanna's "lending" her son Samuel as a child to the service of the Lord "as long as he liveth."[30] Although it is arguable whether consigning him as a child to priestly service constituted abandonment in the sense at issue here—Hanna continued to see him regularly—her action inspired a medieval form of abandonment common in Europe for nearly a millennium.[31]

The circumstances which produced and are reflected in these writings fall outside the present study. They are of interest here because of their impact on subsequent Jewish and Christian traditions, which would add their own meanings to them. Philo, an Alexandrian Jewish philosopher of the first century, was strongly opposed to abandonment, and in constructing his arguments against it he had to ignore these passages and appeal to others, sometimes rather distantly apposite. He claimed, for example, that the rules in Exodus (21:22) about miscarriage resulting from injury during a brawl also prohibited the exposing of children, which, he noted, was "customary" among many other nations. He equated exposing with infanticide (he describes the methods of the latter: strangulation or drowning) and alleged that they were not only "unholy" and "unnatural"—a proof that the conjugal relations that produced the child were sinful because not directed toward procreation—but also murder. He admitted that in the case of abandonment the parents themselves say they hope the child will be saved, but

> all the beasts that feed on human flesh visit the spot and feast unhindered on the infants, a fine banquet provided by their sole guardians, those who above all others should keep them safe, their fathers and mothers. Carnivorous birds, too, come flying down and gobble up the fragments, that is, if they have not discovered them earlier, for, if they have, they get ready to fight the beasts of the field for the whole carcase.[32]

This grisly picture could reflect conditions in and around Alexandria, which may have been different from those elsewhere in the

---

though the language used both in the Hebrew and in the Greek and Latin translations is vague and not obviously related to the disposing of unwanted offspring.

30. 1 Samuel 1–2.
31. Oblation: see chapter 5.
32. Philo, *The Special Laws,* trans. F. H. Colson (Cambridge, Mass., 1929) 3.116, pp. 547–49.

Roman world: Philo says that parents abandon children in "desert places" (ἐπ' ἐρημίαν). But historical and legal evidence suggests that Egyptians usually exposed children on garbage heaps,[33] the point of which was certainly that they were constantly frequented rather than deserted.

Philo's warning about the possibility of death is similar to Quintilian's, and perhaps, like his, more a rhetorical device than a realistic apprehension.[34] His insistence that the killing of infants is murder (ἀνδροφόνον εἶναι τὸν βρέφος ἀναιροῦντα) and possibly more reprehensible than the killing of adults because of their innocence (ἀκακωτάτοις), is an unusually clear-cut position on infanticide by the standards of the ancient world. But it is surprising that he should have subsumed exposing under this rubric without qualification, since it was not condemned even obliquely by the Jewish scriptures, and one might suppose that a highly developed ethical system would take into account whether the exposed child in fact died or not, at least in leveling a charge of murder. The *intention* of the parents, as he himself admitted, was that the child be saved. And Philo was clearly aware of the real possibility of rescue:

> But suppose some passing travellers, stirred by humane feeling, take pity and compassion on the castaways and in consequence raise them up, give them food and drink, and do not shrink from paying all the other attentions which they need, what do we think of such highly charitable actions? Do we not consider that those who brought them into the world stand condemned when strangers play the part of parents, and parents do not behave with even the kindness of strangers?[35]

It is possible that for Jews living in a predominantly Gentile environment the probability of rescue for Jewish children by non-Jews added to, rather than diminished, apprehensions about exposing, as the possibility of servitude had for freeborn Romans. The issue was addressed specifically by later Jewish writers.

In discussing the abandonment of Moses (who was brought up by Gentiles), Philo even depicts the parents as reproaching them-

33. See discussion, above, in note 108 of chapter 2.

34. Golden ("Demography," pp. 330–31) argues specifically that the use of words for infanticide in relation to exposure by Hellenistic writers is "tendentious" and for "shock value."

35. Philo, *The Special Laws* 3.116 (cited above, note 32).

selves for being "child-murderers" (τεκνοκτονοί), although the baby
would have been killed if they had not exposed him, and was saved
as a consequence of their doing so. This is particularly striking because he repeats the biblical detail that Moses' sister waits out of
sight to see "how it would turn out"—a clear acknowledgment that
she, at least, did not expect that exposed children necessarily died.[36]

His contemporary, Josephus, also a Hellenized Jew, also claimed
that Jewish law required the rearing of all children and prohibited
aborting or destroying a fetus.[37] Although no scriptural or rabbinic
text in fact required this, it is possible that it was a cultural expectation among Hellenized Jews, and that Jewish writers of the time
regarded it as a part of oral tradition. The fact that it is so closely associated with Alexandrian sexual ethics, however, may be reason to
conclude that it was more a Hellenistic tradition than a Jewish one.
Alexandrian moral philosophy—pagan, Jewish, and Christian—
was characterized by a particularly ascetic and rigid adherence to
principles of procreative purpose in sexual matters.[38] This was easily
invoked in ethical writings as support of particular injunctions—

36. Philo, *Moses* 1.12: τὸ ἀποβησόμενον. This detail is biblical, of course, at
least by implication (cf. Exodus 2:7). Behind Philo's rather shrill condemnations
one can read subtler and more revealing views. He composes a conversation between Moses' parents, who blame themselves for having waited for three months
(cf. Exodus 2:2) before the abandonment, because this made it harder for all concerned. In the course of this poignant scene he adduces the "general belief"—
presumably of Jews—that "a child who has not survived long enough to partake of
a day's nourishment is not a person" (*Moses* 11; this was a folk belief among other
ancient peoples as well: see chapter 4). Although this "general belief" contradicts
the teachings of the law as he has described them, it was certainly closer to biblical
prescriptions (in Numbers 4:15, 34, 40 and elsewhere the Jews are instructed to
count male children only after they are one month old), and probably nearer to the
common view than his own position in *The Special Laws*, a propagandistic effort to
harmonize Jewish ethics with Hellenistic philosophy. Philo's philosophy and its
particular Hellenistic context is examined in great detail in H. A. Wolfson, *Philo:
Foundations of Religious Philosophy in Judaism, Christianity, and Islam* (Cambridge,
Mass., 1947).

37. *Against Apion* 2.24.

38. To this same milieu belongs the terse negative comment on abandoning
children in the *Oracula Sibyllina* 2.282 (ὅσοι τε τόκους ῥίπτουσιν ἀθέσμως; cf. prohibition of infanticide at 3.765: τὴν δ' ἰδίαν γένναν παίδων τρέφε μηδὲ φόνευε). These
texts are a complex intercalation of pagan, Jewish, and Christian apothegms and
injunctions, and in the current state of scholarship it is not possible to assign a precise context to most of them. The use of the feminine in the commandment against
infanticide is revealing.

against contraception, abortion, homosexuality—but probably rarely adhered to by married couples, and certainly not an outgrowth of traditional Jewish teachings.[39]

The Mishnah, the part of the Talmud compiled toward the end of the second century of the Christian era, was the foundation of postscriptural law among the Jews, and articulated the principle that a father is not required to maintain a daughter.[40] The Talmud's subsequent commentary on this evinces substantial uneasiness on the part of the rabbis: most agreed that there was no legal obligation to feed and care for either sons or daughters, but a clear moral duty to do so.[41] "The raven cares for its young," Rabbi Hisda noted, "but [a bad] man[42] does not care for his children."[43]

Even the legal exemption, the Talmud concluded, extends only to the poor: the rich can be required to support their offspring. This approach is strikingly like that of earlier Roman and contemporary Christian ethicists (see below), who blamed the rich for abandoning children but were more understanding of the poor. Even the ornithological examples occur in all three traditions.[44]

The Talmud takes for granted the presence of a considerable number of abandoned children within the Jewish community. They constitute one of the ten genealogical classes returning to Israel from Babylonia,[45] and were obviously a familiar part of Jewish life. "All the peoples of the world," according to the Talmud, made fun

39. See discussion of this in Boswell, *Christianity,* pp. 128–29.

40. *Kethuboth* 4.6. Danby translates: "The father is not liable for his daughter's maintenance. R. Eleazar b. Azariah thus expounded it . . . : 'The sons inherit and the daughters receive maintenance'—but like as the sons inherit only after the death of their father so the daughters receive maintenance only after the death of their father" (*The Mishnah,* trans. Hebert Danby [Oxford, 1933], p. 250).

41. *Kethuboth* 49a–51a: for English trans., see I. Slotki, in *The Babylonian Talmud,* ed. I. Epstein, *Nashim* 2 (London, 1936).

42. Literally, "that man": see commentary in the English translation by Slotki, p. 284.

43. Slotki trans., p. 284.

44. Although some Christian writers found birds to be a negative example: see below. A difference between Jewish and Christian attitudes toward family size, however, is evident in attitudes toward contraception, which the Talmud allows to minors, pregnant women, and nursing mothers: *Niddah* 45a. Cf. *Kethuboth* 37a; *Yemaboth* 34b and 35a; *Nedarim* 20b. These texts and their implications are discussed in Étienne ("La Conscience médicale antique," pp. 24–25). Étienne does not discuss the passage under consideration here.

45. *Kiddushin* 4.1 (69a).

of Abraham and Sarah when they gave a banquet for the weaning of Isaac: "Have you seen that old man and woman, who brought a foundling [אֲסוּפִי] from the street, and now claim him as their son! And what is more, they make a great banquet to establish their claim." [46]

Talmudic regulations on this (as on most matters) are complicated, but not harsh or arbitrary, and at bottom quite similar to concerns in the rest of the Mediterranean world during this period. Foundlings have limited marriage rights—i.e., cannot marry into the highest four genealogical classes (priests, Levites, Israelites, חֲלָלִים)—because their parents cannot be known and there is some danger of incest. The rabbis acknowledge that anyone marrying a foundling, including another foundling, might commit incest, but considered the chance slight enough not to pose a barrier to marriage except in the groups where genealogical purity was of particular importance. [47]

Yet a foundling was exempted from these restrictions if the mode of his or her abandonment offered evidence of parental concern, suggesting that a good family had given him or her up under duress: if he was found circumcised; with limbs set; massaged with oil and powdered; wearing beads, a tablet, or an amulet; suspended from a tree out of reach of animals; left in a synagogue near a town where many congregate, in moving water, [48] or near a public thoroughfare. The absence of such attentions would be indication that the child's parents did not care about him, or possibly that he was of undesirable ancestry, and he would then be liable to marriage restrictions, although in other ways regarded as a normal person. In times of famine, no exposed child was subject to the restrictions—a

46. *Baba Mezia* 87a: for English trans., see E. W. Kirzner, in *The Babylonian Talmud*, ed. I. Epstein, *Nezikin* 2 (London, 1935). Abraham confounds them by having Sarah provide milk for the children of the guests.

47. *Kiddushin* 4.1 (73a): "Why then did they [the Rabbis] rule that a foundling is unfit [sc., to marry]? Lest he marry his paternal sister. If so, one foundling should not marry another, lest he marry his sister by his father or and [*sic*] his mother?—Do all these go throwing [their children away]! Let him not marry the daughter of a foundling, lest he marry his sister? But . . . it is rare: then here too it is rare!—But . . . a higher standard was set up in respect to genealogy [sc., for the higher classes]." Trans., I. Epstein, *Nashim* 4 (London, 1936).

48. Probably because a child could only be "found" on moving water if the parents had gone to some trouble to place him in a sturdy conveyance, whereas in shallow or still water it would be difficult to tell if he had been just cast away there or left to drown.

clear indication of what the rabbis thought might inspire abandonment.[49] Illegitimacy is also mentioned as a cause (73a), though less often than poverty or hunger. Parents could reclaim abandoned children, and their word was sufficient to establish paternity, but only if they did so before the child had been picked up by someone else, at which point they lost their rights, except in times of famine; then they might reclaim at any time.[50]

In contrast to the scriptures of the Jews, those of the Christians included little specific material about children. Jesus praises those who would leave either parents or children for his sake (Matthew 19:29; Luke 14:26), and asserts that his followers are his family (Matthew 12:49; Mark 3:34; Luke 8:21), but attends to his mother as one of his last acts (John 19:25–27), insists that everyone must be as a little child to enter the kingdom of heaven (Mark 10:15; Luke 18:17), and warns against "despising" little children, each of whom has a guardian angel in heaven.[51] Curses involving infanticide or at least infants occur, as in the Jewish scriptures, although less often and less graphically (Matthew 24:15; Mark 13:17; Luke 19:44, 21:23). The author of Galatians recalls, with apparent acceptance, Abraham's abandoning (ἔκβαλε) Hagar and their son—"What saith the scripture? Cast out the bondwoman and her son; for the son of the bondwoman shall not be heir with the son of the free woman"[52]—

49. *Kiddushin* 4.1 (73a–b). The Mishnah offers a further suggestion of economic duress in *Gittin* 4.9: "If a man sold himself and his children to a Gentile, they may not redeem him, but they may redeem his children after the death of their father" (trans. Danby, p. 312).

50. *Kiddushin* 4.1 (73b): this distinction utilizes a pun on the Hebrew אָסַף, which means "to gather," or "collect": the rabbis say that once a child has been "gathered" in from the street he is necessarily an אֲסוּפִי—i.e., one "gathered," and therefore his position is established. Before that, the parents can reclaim him, because he has not yet been "gathered." Given the humane provisions regarding famine, this technical distinction is probably not the inspiration for the difference.

51. Matthew 18:10: "Take heed that ye despise not [μὴ καταφρονήσητε] one of these little ones; for I say unto you, That in heaven their angels do always behold the face of my Father which is in heaven." This gave rise to both a general belief in "guardian angels" among Catholics and to particular notions about abandoned children, discussed below, notes 72 and 73.

52. Galatians 4:30: a new level of meaning is present in this passage, where, somewhat ironically, the Jews would be understood by Christians as the sons of the bondwoman (because bound by the old law), and the Christians the sons of the free woman (because free under the new covenant). This greatly convolutes the rela-

and Acts refers to Moses' parents' "exposing" him.[53] The killing of the male children of Israel by the Egyptians is slightly altered, so that it is the Jews themselves who are forced to "expose" their children, and it is not clear that it is only the males.[54] This change could indicate a greater familiarity with abandonment as a social phenomenon by early Christian times, and a conflation of this with the more specific aim of the Egyptians' infanticide, but it is hard to be sure that it is not simply a loose quotation.

The New Testament also reiterates the commandment of the Old that children honor their parents (e.g., Ephesians 6:4), but it adds to this in several places obligations of parents to children,[55] and it might be argued that the emphasis on caring for widows and orphans—a term that probably included abandoned children[56]— is more pronounced in the New Testament as a whole than in the Hebrew scriptures as a whole, although it would not be accurate to imagine either as existing during late antiquity in the canonical forms in which they were later known.

Some of the most potent imagery of the New Testament bearing on attitudes toward abandonment is also the subtlest, and its influence must be viewed cautiously. Jesus' metaphor of God as father and his followers as brothers, not unique to Christians but more

---

tionship to the "Ishmaelites," although relatively few Christians were ever aware of these complexities.

53. Acts 7:21: ἐκτεθέντος (Vulgate: *exposito*).

54. Acts 7:18: οὗτος κατασοφισάμενος τὸ γένος ἡμῶν ἐκάκωσεν τοὺς πατέρας τοῦ ποιεῖν τὰ βρέφη ἔκθετα αὐτῶν εἰς τὸ μὴ ζῳογονεῖσθαι. Cf. Vulgate: "Hic circumveniens genus nostrum afflixit patres nostros, ut exponerent infantes suos, ne vivificarentur."

55. E.g., "Children ought not to lay up [treasure] for the parents, but the parents for the children" (2 Corinthians 12:14), or the command in Titus 2:4 that the older women teach the younger ones to love their children. One of the aspects of the "last days," when evil will predominate in the world, will be that people will lack affection for their relatives: Romans 1:30–31, 2 Timothy 3:2. The word used for "lacking affection," ἄστοργοι, usually referred to a parental lack in relation to children, rather than the reverse (see note 143 of chapter 1), but it could also mean a more general lack of affection (Suidas gives τοὺς ἀπηνεῖς καὶ ἀφίλους).

56. E.g., James 1:27. The Greek, ὀρφανός, refers to children without parents (for whatever reason) or parents without children, or anyone deprived of anything necessary or dear: cf. Latin *orbus*. Comparable Islamic injunctions sometimes specify abandoned children as well as "orphans" in the English sense: see below, on Islam. Clement of Alexandria uses ὀρφανός specifically of abandoned children (*Paedagogus* 3.4 [PG 8.597], cited below), and Armenian law uses the Armenian equivalent for *exposti* (also cited below).

prominent in Christianity than in other contemporary religions, took on a more legal cast in the epistles, where the salvation of the Gentiles is characterized as their "adoption" by God through Christ, using, in both the Greek and Latin, a term used for adoption of abandoned children.[57] The author of Galatians contrasts the position of a natural heir, which is no better than that of a slave, with the superior position of the adopted son.[58]

On the other hand, the recurrence in the New Testament of the common religious theme of the sacrifice of children is not subtle at all, and could hardly have escaped the attention of anyone familiar with the young religion. In a startling reversal of the familiar antique patterns of giving up a child to a deity, Christians believed that the deity had given up a child to them, and although it did not involve "exposing" in a traditional sense, the sending of the child to be born of human parents in a stable, far not only from the glories of heaven but even from the comforts of a normal human home, is certainly redolent, in a starkly ironic way, of the abandonments that gave rise to the great houses of the Ionians and Romans, and to the religions of Moses and Muhammad. Jesus had a foster father and was in a sense both abandoned and sacrificed by his "natal" father—his final words in Matthew ask God why he has abandoned him. And although he was sacrificed as an adult, he continuously referred to himself as the "son of man,"[59] an expression emphasizing not only filial subordination and dependency, but also the reciprocity of foster relationships in the New Testament: Jesus has "adopted" humankind both as his parents and as his children.[60]

Even of literate Christians in the early church—themselves a tiny minority of the population—relatively few would have had ac-

57. Υἱοθεσία, adoptio: Romans 8:15 and 23, 9:4; Galatians 4:5; Ephesians 1:5.

58. Galatians 4:1–7: οὐδὲν διαφέρει δούλου. Several Greek and Roman writers had also compared children to slaves. The comparison is subtly strengthened in Galatians by the use of the word παιδαγωγός, normally "teacher," to mean "custodian," as of prisoners, at 3:24–25.

59. I repeat this expression from the KJV; in the Greek it is not gender-specific.

60. It is perhaps not straining the point too far to note that there may have been some subliminal relationship between the eating of Jesus in communion and ancient notions of eating children in religious contexts, in mythology, or through sacrifice. Visions of Christ in communion were frequently of him as a baby, and Christians may have betrayed their own subconscious anxieties in the High Middle Ages when they frequently accused Jews—almost certainly falsely—of "sacrificing" Christian children. On this complicated subject, see Caroline Bynum, *Holy Feast and Holy Fast: The Religious Significance of Food to Medieval Women*.

cess to complete "Bibles." The canon of the scriptures was fairly well established by the time of Jerome's Latin translation, but it was the invention of printing a millennium later, not the triumph of Christianity in the fourth century, that filled the Western world with copies of the two testaments. Most Christians before the Renaissance would have known the contents of the Bible through liturgy, sermons, Christian instruction, art, or echoes in popular culture, which absorbed and incorporated both the general tenor of the New Testament and the colorful phrases and stories from both the Old Testament and the New. The impact the text of the scriptures had on scholars and clerics must be distinguished from the influence the scriptures had on the vast majority of the faithful, largely by osmosis of Christian culture.

Stories from the Hebrew scriptures such as the rescue of Moses through abandonment, the sacrifice of Isaac, the casting out of Ishmael, and the willingness of the mother to give up her child rather than have Solomon divide him probably stuck in the popular imagination. They would convey, perhaps, the complementary notions that parental love is a great good, but not inherently incompatible with relinquishing a child. Human parents cannot necessarily provide for all the children born to them, or love them perfectly; only God can do this.

> Can a woman forget her sucking child, that she should not have compassion on the son of her womb? yea, they may forget, yet will I not forget thee. (Isaiah 49:15)

Christians discounted the importance of lineage and descent, which had been prominent in Jewish religious identity. The Christian scriptures begin with the genealogy of Jesus, but, significantly, his immediate male forebear is a foster father, not biological. Christians claimed that they had been "substituted"—not unlike an abandoned child—for the posterity of Abraham. They were all *alumni:* in the broadest sense because they had been adopted by God as heirs to his kingdom, in replacement, they would say, of the original natal heirs, the Jews. In a more individual sense, unlike Jews, who were usually Jews by virtue of the fact that their parents were Jews,[61]

---

61. Although proselytes were extremely common in Hellenistic Judaism, and Christianity may even have derived some of its inspiration from the kind of "ethical Judaism" apparently preached to the Gentiles. Jewish proselytes were *alumni* in the sense that through circumcision, ritual immersion, or simple adherence to Jew-

Christians were all "adopted" into Christianity, provided with a "birth" through baptism—a kind of rescue of abandoned children. "Christians are made, not born," St. Jerome opined, specifically in the context of advice to parents.[62] "Spiritual parents" were even provided in time, who "took up" the child much as adopting finders had done in Roman cities.[63] And rather than being asked, like pagans or their adopted forefather Abraham, to sacrifice their own children, they worshiped a God they believed to have sacrificed his: "For God so loved the world that he gave his only begotten Son . . ." (John 3:16).

---

ish belief and practice they were incorporated into the "family" of Abraham and his posterity, with whom God had established his covenant. It is very likely that this concept affected early Christian preachers and was in part the inspiration for the Christian theology of "adoption." Moreover, there were many parallels in Jewish thought to Christian disregard for biological ancestry: e.g., Rachel's regarding the children of her maid as her own (Genesis 30:1–13).

62. Epistle 107.1 (CSEL 55.291). This was truer in the early centuries of Christian history than subsequently. In Jerome's day a high percentage of Christians were still converts, and the ideology of "choosing" Christianity had social meaning. By the time most of Europe was officially Catholic, most Christians were Christian because their parents had been, a situation not significantly different from that among the Jews, although Christian rhetoric continued to portray being Christian as volitional. Neither Christians nor Jews really had a "choice" in Catholic Europe: it was a sin (and usually a crime) for Christians to abandon the faith they had been born into; and even if Jews converted to Christianity, they continued to be perceived, and at times persecuted, as Jews.

63. The "raising up" of newborns is charged with significance about responsibility for rearing in many cultures (see Nicole Belmont, "Levana") and a crucial act of godparents was "lifting" the child wet from the water. (On this and other aspects of godparenting, see the excellent study of Joseph Lynch, *Godparents and Kinship in Early Medieval Europe*.) This may be partly inspired by the special sense of *tollere* among Romans in relation to the decision of the *paterfamilias* about whether or not to rear a child born to him (see, e.g., Terence, *Heautontimoroumenos* 627: "nolle tolli"). *Tollere* was not generally used for the action of the godparents (*suscipere, excipere, levare* are more common), but this may be less significant than the structural parallels with a father—natural or foster—"picking up" a newborn (the same idea, for example, was conveyed in Icelandic with the expression *borit at föður*). During the Middle Ages, *tollere* itself could be applied to "rearing" children (*Fragment Gaudenzianus* 20 [MGH LL 1.1]) in a general sense, or even to "thinking about having" a child, as in Godfrey of Winchester (d. 1107, in Thomas Wright, *The Anglo-Latin Satirical Poets and Epigrammatists* [London, 1872] 2.136, no. 203).

EARLY OBJECTIONS:
THE THREAT OF INCEST

Given both Roman and Judeo-Christian traditions about abandonment, it would be surprising if Roman Christians had evinced
horror or shock at the practice, and indeed, most did not, although
it was manifestly familiar to the "fathers" of the church and their
"spiritual children." A few Christian moralists, cited below, condemned it, as a few pagan ethical writers had, but they were a minority and almost certainly urging their followers to a higher
standard of conduct than the norm. More interesting, their objections were never predicated on inherent obligations of parent to
child, but always on less specific ethical considerations relating either to the possibility of death (in which case the exposer would be a
murderer),[64] the disreputable behavior of pagans or their deities, or
sexual anxieties. Most such critics were literate members of prosperous classes, writing to or for other well-to-do, literate persons.
Through the time of Augustine, in fact, although the majority of
Christians were certainly not upper-class, the majority of Christian
writers were, and their view of abandonment would necessarily
emerge from a perspective rather different from that of the poor.
Among their privileged acquaintances abandonment functioned
chiefly as a means of regulating inheritance or avoiding the nuisance
of childrearing, and they tended to regard it as a selfish indulgence
of the rich. Only relatively late did the desperate plight of the urban
poor begin to appear in Christian ethical considerations on the
subject.

Athenagoras was the first of the "fathers of the church" to offer a
substantive comment on the topic. In the second half of the second
century he reported that Christians were forbidden to expose children because doing so was the equivalent of killing them.[65] His contemporary, Justin Martyr, did not imagine, however, that many
abandoned children died, since he believed (as noted previously)
that "practically all such children are used as prostitutes. . . . Even
as the ancients were said to keep flocks of cattle and goats and sheep,
or grazing horses, now children are kept for wicked purposes."[66]

---

64. Herlihy's statement in "Medieval Children" (p. 117) that "Christianity,
like Judaism before it, unequivocally condemned infanticide or the exposure of infants" is a considerable oversimplification.

65. *Legatio pro Christianis* 35 (PG 6.969).

66. 1 *Apology* 27 (PG 6.369–72).

Clement of Alexandria, a third-century heir to the purely pro-creative sexual ethic for which Philo spoke, contrasted Pythagorean and Mosaic ethics, which, he claimed, enjoined against separating even a small animal from its mother,[67] with the pagan practice of exposing human children, and referred to those who did so as "child killers"[68]—as Philo had in the case of Moses' parents. But he apparently believed, like Justin Martyr, that most such children would survive, since the possibility of committing incest with an exposed relative constituted a major objection to prostitution in his *Paedagogus*, a manual of childrearing.[69] He envisioned abandonment as an indulgence of the wealthy, exclusively for convenience.

> What cause has a man for the exposing of a child? If disinclined to have children, he ought not to have married in the first place. . . .
>
> They will not take up an abandoned child,[70] but they support parrots and curlews: children conceived in their own households they abandon, while they take up the young of birds. . . .[71]

On the other hand, Clement assured Christians that all abandoned children had a special guardian angel (cf. Jesus' words in Matthew 18:10, cited above),[72] to whom they were entrusted for rearing and education,[73] an idea also emphasized by Methodius, who contrasted God's tender regard for newborn children in this respect with the callousness of parents who expose them "to death."[74] He warned

67. Cf. Plutarch, discussed in preceding chapter.

68. *Stromateis* 2.18 (PG 8.1033–37).

69. Cited above, in preceding chapter.

70. Ὀρφανός.

71. *Paedagogus* 3.4 (PG 8.597).

72. The idea that each person has a guardian angel, although a widespread ele-ment of popular Catholic piety, especially in regard to children, has never been defined as dogma, and theologians have failed to agree on whether in fact angels care for humans individually or in groups.

73. *Eclogae ex scriptures propheticis* 41 (PG 9.717, or *Die griechischen Christlichen Schriftsteller der ersten drei Jahrhunderte* 3, ed. Otto Stählin [Leipzig, 1909], p. 149): "The scripture says that abandoned babies will be given to a guardian angel, by whom they will be taught and reared." Cf. 48, where ἄγγελος τημελούχος also oc-curs in relation to abortion. It is possible that the Eclogues were not written by Clement, but they clearly reflect opinion in his time and from his intellectual circle.

74. Εἰς θάνατον; see Methodius of Olympus, *Symposium* 2.6.45 (ed. Herbert Musurillo, *Méthode d'Olympe, Le Banquet* [Paris, 1963], p. 82).

that the children themselves would call their parents before the seat of judgment, although the crime of which they would accuse them was not actually abandonment, but the improper sexual union which had produced a child they did not wish to rear.[75]

Through the third century this rather rigid attitude of Christian moralists appears to have prevailed, taking no account of parental motivations other than shame or selfishness, and relating abandonment solely to issues of procreative purpose, subsequent incest, or technical infanticide, although the assumption of rescue was virtually ubiquitous. Minucius Felix (*Octavius* 31) sniped at the pagans:

> Since you pursue Venus promiscuously, since you engender children *passim,* since you often expose even those born at home to the kindness of strangers, you necessarily end up having relations with your relatives and children. . . . Whereas we bind ourselves with the chains of one marriage, and know one woman for the sake of procreation, or none.[76]

Tertullian strikes a similar note: although he twice compares abandoning children ("to hunger or dogs") to infanticide,[77] he recognizes that the children are not actually likely to die, and even acknowledges as parental motivation the hope of a better life for the child, which one might have thought would temper his opposition. But the threat of sexual impurity was paramount:

> You expose your children, in the first place, to be rescued by the kindness of passing strangers, or abandon them to be adopted by better parents. Naturally the memory of the cast-off relation dissipates in time, and . . . in some place—at home, abroad, in a foreign land—with lust, whose realms are universal, as companion, you easily fix unknowingly somewhere upon a child or some other relation . . . and do not realize the encounter was incestuous. We are preserved from this sort of thing by the most diligent and faithful chastity; and by avoiding all promiscuous

---

75. Ibid. By the end of the fourth century, Gregory of Nyssa was taking a somewhat less sanguine view of the prospects for deceased infants: see Περὶ νηπίων πρὸ ὥρας ἀφαρπαζομένων (PG 46.161–92, especially 46.177).

76. PL 3.336–37 (CSEL 2.44–45).

77. *Ad nationes* 1.15 (PL 1.651, CSEL 20.85), where he says it is worse (*asperius*); and *Apology* 9.7 (PL 1.318–19, CSEL 69.24), where he wonders whether strangulation or exposing to the elements is crueler.

or extramarital indiscretion we also avoid any possibility of incest.[78]

None of these comments had as its major target the prohibiting of abandonment: each is actually directed against something else, usually something sexual, and uses the dangers posed by abandonment to weight the argument. More important, from the third century on, the conclusion drawn is not that Christians should not abandon, but that they should avoid extramarital intercourse.

It is impossible to judge the likelihood of these dangers. The death of *expositi* does not appear to have been common at any time under the empire, and particularly as other sources of slaves dried up it seems extremely unlikely that laborers of any sort would remain unclaimed. This increased the likelihood of servitude for abandoned children. It is easy to see why well-born Romans might feel horror at the prospect of the enslavement of free children, but difficult to articulate a case against it based on any New Testament principles, especially since the latter appears to have accepted slavery with equanimity.

It is not surprising that incest should evoke disapproval or disgust (although it is scarcely mentioned in the New Testament), but its invocation by ascetic moralists can hardly be considered a reliable indication of its occurrence, since one of their central contentions is that, given the number of children exposed and the extent of prostitution in ancient cities, one simply could not know one's own child in a brothel. How, then, do they gauge the magnitude of this problem? Their appeal to it is probably rhetorically effective because of the visceral revulsion it inspires, and although it may well be a good index of how widespread abandonment was, it is no clue to the frequency of accidental incest.

THE PLIGHT OF THE POOR

Lactantius, the last of the fathers to make this argument, cites Oedipus as his sole case in point, and, perhaps not coincidentally, his approach seems to mark a dividing line between early rigidity and the development of a more complex and realistic view of the situation of parents, due both to the maturing of Christian thought

78. *Apology* 9.

and to the times in which he wrote—the early fourth century, when the social structure of the empire was increasingly chaotic and more and more parents were forced by circumstances to sell or abandon their children. Although he tries to make a case that abandonment is as "wicked" (*nefarius*) as infanticide, he acknowledges that there are two crucial differences: parents expose children when they do *not* wish to kill them,[79] and the really horrible possibilities for such children are not wild animals (though these are mentioned in passing), but slavery or prostitution, the latter leading, of course, to incest.[80]

These arguments are familiar enough; what is new is that Lactantius does recognize that parents might have motivations other than lust or selfishness for exposing children, although his response could not be characterized as sympathetic.

> The child-murderers either complain of difficult circumstances or pretend that they simply cannot support more children—as if resources were actually under the control of those possessing them and God did not daily make paupers of rich men and rich men of paupers.
>
> If someone really cannot support children because of poverty, better he should abstain from relations with his wife than undo the work of God with guilty hands. (*Institutes* 6.20)

This approach acknowledges, for the first time, the dilemma forced on Christian parents by Christian moral philosophy's increasing insistence on exclusively procreative sexuality, even within marriage, and the reduced circumstances in which many persons found themselves in the famine-ridden and war-torn empire of the fourth century. Since nonprocreative forms of sexuality were disapproved, couples were under moral pressure to see that every act of marital love might result in a child. If they could not afford another child, they should abstain from conjugal relations.

Some Christians doubtless did so: Nilus of Ancyra's autobiogra-

79. This point is made twice: pagan parents either kill their children, or, if they are too ethical for this, abandon them (*Institutes* 5.9 [PL 6.578, CSEL 19.427] and 6.20 [PL 6.708, CSEL 19.559]).

80. "Who can doubt that it is wrong to surrender [a child] to the kindness of strangers? Even if what the exposer hopes for happens, and the child is reared, he has condemned his own flesh and blood to slavery or prostitution. And who does not know, who could be ignorant of what things can and usually do happen by mistake to either gender?" (*Institutes* 6.20.)

phy represents him as choosing to refrain after two sons. "After these I ceased to have conjugal relations, considering [the sons] to suffice both as regards the propagation of the species and as consolation in old age."[81] When St. Melanie the Younger (d. 439) was married at fourteen, she and her husband made an agreement, according to her biographer, that after producing two children "to be heirs to our property," they would both renounce the world.[82] Other Christians, perhaps inspired by Christ's challenge to leave all to follow him, were apparently renouncing their children along with the world: a synod held at Gangra (on the edge of Armenia) in 340 anathematized parents who "abandon their own children and neglect to feed them . . . on the pretext of religious observance."[83]

The Christian emperor Valentinian (ruled 364–75) decided in 374 that all parents must support their children, and that those who abandoned them should be subject to the penalty "prescribed by law."[84] This was the first and only official Roman juridical requirement that citizens rear all children born to them, but since there had never been a penalty for abandonment in Roman law, it is difficult to know exactly what it meant.[85] Even if earlier rulings invalidating the sale of children were interpreted as prohibiting abandonment, they did not specify a punishment, and there is no subsequent reference in Roman law to any prohibition of abandonment, although a

81. Nilus, *Narratio* II (PG 79.600–1). The *narrationes* are not the work of Nilus himself (though apparently taken to be so by Evelyne Patlagean, "Birth Control in the Early Byzantine Empire," p. 13), but they do probably reflect the outlines of his life and contemporary opinion.

82. *Vie de Sainte Mélanie,* ed. Denys Gorce (Paris, 1962), Sources Chrétiennes, 90, p. 132.

83. Canon 15 (Mansi 2.110). This became one of the nomocanons of Photius: PG 104.864.

84. "Unusquisque subolem suam nutriat. Quod si exponendam putaverit animadversioni quae constituta est, subiacebit" (JC 8.52.2). Valentinian, in A.D. 366, had already required that any person who had been sold to or captured by barbarians—i.e., one of the Germanic or Asian tribes ravaging the northern and eastern portions of the empire—be returned to his home without being held responsible for any costs incurred by the rescuer except the purchase price, if her or his freedom had been purchased: TC 5.7.1–3. Although the edict did not specifically mention children, there is no reason to assume that they would not have comprised a proportion of those sold to barbarians.

85. Bennet (p. 351) says that exposure of infants became a capital crime in 374; Eyben (p. 77) more cautiously remarks that "exposure" was "probably" banned in 374.

great many laws deal with the subject in some way and assume its legality.[86] Valentinian's legislation may have been unknown outside legal circles, or reinterpreted, or simply disregarded as unworkable. Christian rulers, moreover, were scarcely consistent in safeguarding parent-child relations: Valentinian's co-ruler decreed that the children of free women married to slaves were to be confiscated, as slaves, for the imperial treasury.[87]

All of the available evidence suggests that very widespread abandonment and sale of children persisted, and perhaps increased, throughout the fourth century. Jordanes described the effects of war on desperate parents of the time:

> Once they have no more slaves or furniture, the greedy merchant demands, as the cost of food,[88] their children. Unable to provide for them otherwise, the parents [thus] ensure the survival of their offspring, thinking it better that they lose their

86. An edict of the same year preserved in a separate collection makes infanticide, apparently in the context of a pagan ritual, a capital offense (TC 9.14.1): one might deduce that it was to this penalty that the emperor referred, except that (1) there is no reason he should not have so specified, particularly since the latter was a novel law; and (2) no previous or—more significantly—subsequent Roman law equated infanticide with abandonment. The law in the Theodosian Code is sometimes thought to be a restatement of the earlier law against parricide, but, as noted above, the earlier law dealt with children killing parents as well as parents killing children, and does not appear to have addressed itself to infants, as this one does: "necandi infantis piaculum." The use of the word *piaculum* (sin offering) is striking and suggests that the practice in question had to do with a religious rite. Sacrifice of children was widely discussed in the Mediterranean world, as has been noted. Tertullian claims to have heard about child sacrifice in North Africa from eyewitnesses, and says that although it has been outlawed, it persists "in secret" (1 *Apology* 9; see discussion in Aline Rousselle, *Porneia: On Desire and the Body in Antiquity,* trans. Felicia Pheasant [New York, 1988], pp. 107–28). Pagan rituals were common in Roman provinces long after the triumph of Christianity: see, e.g., S. McKenna, *Paganism and Pagan Survivals in Spain up to the Fall of the Visigothic Kingdom* (Washington, D.C., 1938); J. N. Hillgarth, *Christianity and Paganism, 350–750: The Conversion of Western Europe* (Philadelphia, 1986). Cf. C. Pharr, p. 236, n. 3. But even if originally inspired by such practices, this law would have been interpreted subsequently as constituting a blanket condemnation of infanticide.

87. TC Novel 1.3 of Anthemius Augustus (467–72).

88. "Overcome by necessity" is a possible translation of this (*victus necessitate*), but not likely, given the rest of the sentence. Cf. the similar phrase (*dum victum requirit*) in the law cited in note 97, below.

free status than their lives; since the child who will die if kept is mercifully fed once sold.[89]

As a consequence, Christian writers like St. Basil of Caesarea (himself one of ten children of very wealthy parents), were forced to contemplate the role of circumstance in inducing parents to abandon their offspring.

Although he never compares them explicitly, Basil describes separately three categories of parents who abandon, and assigns a different ethical status to each. Women who "despise the child they have born and abandon it in the road when it could have been saved, or who hope thus to hide sin, or who are motivated by bestial and inhuman thoughts," are to be given the punishment for murder.[90] "The punishment for murder" refers to an ecclesiastical penalty, and should be understood in context: most serious crimes (adultery, fornication, harming a priest) received this sanction, which is often adduced to indicate that the penalty involved is to be the maximum, not necessarily that the offense is actually the moral equivalent of murder.[91]

In his *Hexaemeron,* adducing the oft-cited eagle as a negative zoological example, Basil deals with the middle classes and their concern with inheritance:

> The eagle is particularly unfair in the rearing of her young. For after hatching two eaglets, she throws one out on the ground, driving him off by beating him with her wings, and taking up[92]

89. Jordanes, *Getica* 26.135 (MGH AA 5.1, p. 93). Jordanes was writing in the mid-sixth century, and this sounds almost like a paraphrase of some legal enactments, but the account is corroborated by Ammianus Marcellinus (31.4.11).

90. Epistle 217.52 (PG 32.796). Cf. Epistle 199.33 (PG 32.728): "A woman who gives birth on the road and neglects the baby is to be given the punishment for murder." The word Basil uses for "neglect" (κατεφρόνησεν) is the same one Jesus uses in Matthew 18:10, where Christians are forbidden to "despise" little children; this may be the inspiration for this rule, apparently condemning both selfish maternal neglect and abandonment as consequence (and proof) of sexual license. The same expression, somewhat oddly, occurs in an erotic context in the Hellenistic romance *Daphnis and Chloe* (1.15: ὡς παιδὸς καταφρονήσας), and it seems possible that it connotes cruelty or abuse rather than simple neglect or contempt.

91. See note 117, below.

92. Ἀναλαβών, perhaps meant as reminiscent of the juridical term *tollere:* see note 63, above.

the other one, rears him alone, rejecting [one of] her offspring because of the difficulty of obtaining food. But they say that the vulture does not leave it to perish: she takes it up and rears it with her own little ones. This is like those parents who expose their infants pleading poverty, or even make unequal distribution among their children in arranging their estate. It would be just, since they have given each equally a share of life, also to give each equally and uniformly a share in the means of living.[93]

The poor are mentioned here, but Basil seems to conflate their motivations with what he regards as willful parental neglect by the bourgeoisie, doubtless more familiar to him personally. He disapproves of abandonment of this sort but does not represent it as particularly heinous, and suggests no penalty.

In another, very moving passage, he does, however, expressly acknowledge the desperate plight of the urban poor.

How can I bring before your eyes the suffering of the poor man? He considers his finances: he has no gold and never will. He has some clothes and the sort of possessions the poor have, all worth only a few coins. What can he do? He turns his glance at length on his children: by selling them he might put off death. Imagine the struggle between the desperation of hunger and the bonds of parenthood. The former threatens him with a horrible death; nature pulls him back, persuading him to die with his children. Often he starts to do it; each time he stops himself; finally he is overcome, conquered by necessity and inexorable need.

Then what are his thoughts? Which one shall I sell first? Which one will the grain auctioneer favor the most? Should I start with the oldest? But I am reluctant to do so because of his age. The youngest? I pity his youth and inexperience of life. That one is the spitting image of his parents. This one is so quick to learn. What horrible misery! What is to become of me? Which one of them shall I afflict? What sort of animal am I turning into? How can I ignore my natural feelings? If I hold on to them all, I will see all of them die of hunger, but if I sell one,

---

93. *Homilia VIII in Hexaemeron* 6 (PG 29.177–80): "Do not," he adds, "imitate the cruelty of the birds with crooked talons, who, when they see their young developing the courage to fly, cast them out of the nest, striking them with their wings and driving them off, and never again concern themselves about them."

how will I face the rest, having become suspect of treachery in their eyes? How will I live in a household which I myself have deprived of a child? How will I come to the table when its contents were obtained in this way?[94]

This description, probably of a real incident,[95] occurs in a treatise dealing not with parental obligations but with the avarice of the wealthy, and it is a sobering indication of the social reality of the time that the subject of Basil's moral indignation is actually the *sangfroid* of the auctioneer who will handle the sale:

After a thousand tears [the father] comes to sell a beloved child, but no pity moves you; you do not defer to nature. Hunger has made him desperate; you delay and dissemble, prolonging his agony. He asks for the price of food in return for his own heart, but you—not only does your hand not shrink from wringing profit from his misery, but you dicker with him for more, bargaining eagerly to get a better deal, piling further suffering on the desperate.

This social context helps explain why Christian writers steadily expanded their view of abandonment through the third and fourth centuries: their initial opposition to exposing for purely selfish reasons or in consequence of disapproved sexual relations gradually abated, and was supplemented by moderate misgivings about parents limiting the number of legitimate heirs and sympathetic views of the circumstances of the poor. Basil explicitly addressed all three, and his position not only reflected but determined the moral views of Greek-speaking Christians through the early Middle Ages, since his opinions were taken as "canonical" and formed the basis of ecclesiastical law in the East.[96]

94. Basil, *Homilia in Illud Lucae, Destruam* 4 (PG 31.268–69).
95. In his *Homilia II in Psalmum XIV* 4 (PG 29.277), Basil says explicitly that he saw a freeborn man selling his children in the marketplace because of debt. It was a pitiable sight, he writes, and he cites it to urge parents not to deprive their children of liberty simply because they cannot leave them wealth. This seems a slight distortion of the scene he apparently witnessed—there is a substantial difference between leaving no inheritance and being in debt—but it is revealing that he felt a need to offer such advice to his hearers.
96. And into the present: the provisions from Epistle 217.52 are included in the *Pedalion,* or manual of ecclesiastical law employed by most Greek Orthodox Christians (see *The Rudder,* trans. D. Cummings [Chicago, 1957], pp. 817 and 826).

IN THE WEST

In the West, where conditions were probably worse, increasing sympathy for parents appears both in theology and in the legal enactments of Christian rulers. Valentinian II took measures in 391 to rescue free children sold into slavery by their parents, but—in contrast to Constantine—he did not allow the persons who reared the children to demand any payment. Far from regarding the parents as criminals (as had his predecessor and namesake; see above), he evinced considerable sympathy toward them:

> All those whom the pitiful circumstances of their parents, lacking sustenance, have relegated to slavery should be restored to their original free status. Nor may any repayment be demanded, since the service of a free person for a considerable length of time should suffice.[97]

By contrast, anyone who found a slave child exposed with his *master's* knowledge and consent could retain him—presumably because he would be more valued by the finder. At first Christian law denied the owner any right of reclamation,[98] but later it allowed that he could recover the child if he repaid both what the collector had spent for support and twice any purchase cost.[99]

St. Ambrose, Bishop of Milan from 374 to 397, exemplified, if he did not effect, the transition in Latin moral theology from early disapproval of abandonment to the resignation that would characterize Christian writings for the next millennium. He was himself one of three children of a rich and powerful father. Urging parents to love and care for their children, he contrasted the tender parental devotion of birds (other than eagles; see below) with the indifference of humans, but he also drew subtler distinctions about abandonment than any previous Christian writer, and was clearly affected by the plight of the poor. The rich he castigated as "parricides" for

97. TC 3.3. This law seems to be phrased in specific rejoinder to Constantine's law on the selling of children, and this plus the title ("De patribus, qui filios distraxerunt") and the interpretation ("Si quemcumque ingenuum pater faciente egestate vendiderit") all make it apparent that it deals with selling, although the text of the statute itself does not mention how the children are reduced to servitude. It could also be applied to those abandoned anonymously.

98. TC 5.9.2 (A.D. 412).

99. TC, *Sirmondian Constitutions* 5 (A.D. 419).

failing to nurse their children, for performing abortions, and for disinheriting some to favor others. Of the poor, however, he simply noted that "poorer mothers abandon their children and expose them, and if they are recovered deny that they are theirs."[100]

Ambrose knew that Basil had maintained that the king of birds, the eagle, abandoned some of its young. This was a troubling datum for an ethical system inclined to cite animal behavior as a model of "natural" morality—and it undermined his appeal to aviary parental devotion.[101] The eagle did so, Ambrose argued, not simply to make providing for the other offspring easier, but only on satisfying herself that a particular eaglet was in some way defective and "not worthy of rearing": "she rejects him therefore not because of a hard heart but a sound judgement; she does not abandon her own but refuses something alien."[102] Moreover, Ambrose notes, the abandoned eaglet is rescued by the kindness of a stranger:

> The mercy of a more common bird excuses, in the view of some, the severity of the regal one. A bird called the *fulica* . . . takes up the baby rejected—or not recognized—by the eagle, places him in the nest with her own and feeds and cares for him with the very same maternal devotion and provision of nourishment she offers her own.[103]

Ambrose thus distinguishes between the eagle's "failure to recognize" her offspring and the disinheriting by humans of children they have already recognized—using terms with unmistakable legal and social significance for Roman parents. Whether he would have regarded birth defects or even bad character as justification for abandonment is unclear; later ages would find such allowances in the example.[104]

Ambrose did view poverty—temporary or permanent—as justification for abandonment. In his commentary on Tobias he says

100. *Hexaemeron* 18.58 (PL 14.231).

101. Animal behavior was a major source of argumentation in sexual matters: see discussion in Boswell, *Christianity,* pp. 137–43.

102. *Hexaemeron* 18.60 (PL 14.232).

103. Ibid. Traditionally the φήνη and so designated by Basil, but *fulica* usually refers to waterfowl, so I have left the Latin. Ambrose explicitly equates *fulica* with φήνη (*quae graece dicitur* φήνη), but it is not possible to know how he understood the latter.

104. See, e.g., the Irish tale justifying the struggle between Red Hugh and Rury with this story: *Catalogue of Irish Manuscripts in the British Museum* 1 (London, 1926), p. 481.

that he himself saw children being sold at public auction to pay off their parents' debts. The creditor haggles over the price of each under the spear which is the auctioneer's symbol. "Such is the inhumanity of the creditor, such the stupidity of the debtor, that from children to whom he can leave no money he takes even their freedom, in place of a will he pays a debt [with them], for their inheritance he leaves a contract of servitude."[105] Ambrose regards the father as stupid, even insensitive, but does not suggest that his behavior is either wrong or illegal, and in fact strongly implies that he has no choice:

> Suppose someone approaches who might help. Who could appease Charybdis? Who understands the motivations of moneylenders? Who can satisfy avarice? How far will he inflate his prices when he sees a rescuer? He is as interested in emptying everyone else's as in filling his own pockets. (Ibid.)

This seems to be a description of middle-class financial disaster: to be indebted in this way would probably require some assets to begin with, and Ambrose's attitude appears to be in some measure a disapproval of bad stewardship.

In treating the truly poor he implies no disapproval at all: in the *De Nabuthae,* recalling another case he had personally witnessed, he expanded and elaborated Basil's account of the desperate father deciding which child to sell, dwelling with almost maudlin sympathy on the man's pitiful deliberations, and directing moral indignation entirely at the wealthy who refuse to help.[106]

---

105. *De Tobia* 1.8.29 (PL 14.769–70). Note that Semichon (*Histoire des enfants,* pp. 295–96) has completely misread this passage, and attributes the anguish to the mother.

106. *De Nabuthae* 5.19–25 (CSEL 32, 2.477–81). The proximate complaint about the wealthy is of a rich man who rewards a dancing girl by providing her the head of a "poor prophet"—Salome and John the Baptist. This juxtaposition and the fact that it is a reworking of Basil's example could both be urged against any correspondence to real life here: even if Ambrose believed that biblical stories were true, he would not necessarily imagine that they could take place in his own society. But, in fact, a great deal of Ambrose's writings involved reworking materials from other authors (especially Origen and Basil), usually contemporary, and certainly applicable, in his mind, to his own flock, and he introduces Basil's material in the context of having seen with his own eyes a father bringing his sons to auction. His readers would certainly have found it a weak example if it were inherently unlikely, and Ambrose, a master orator, was not likely to have misjudged what would convince or move his audience.

Augustine, too, evinces a kind of ambivalent resignation in the matter, unusual for him. (He was one of three children of middle-class parents, and himself the loving father of an illegitimate child.) Although he twice refers to the "cruelty" of parents who abandon children,[107] he does not state that it is sinful except to the extent that it reflects a lack of procreative purpose in the sexual acts that produced the children. He did not characterize even abortion, much less contraceptive sexual practices, as murder,[108] and he seems fairly clearly to have regarded the latter two as much more serious than abandonment, which he adduces as the ordinary recourse of parents who have unwanted children. His position thus shares more with Roman moralists than with Philo or the early Christian ethicists who had attempted to show that exposing a child was the moral equivalent of infanticide. That he focused his ethical scrutiny on procreative purpose in marriage rather than on the well-being of the child probably does not mean that he lacked concern for children: he simply recognized, like Ambrose, that most parents had little choice about abandoning, and he directed his disapproval at those cases where he assumed there was choice.

Both the new Christian consensus[109] on the matter and the social difficulties underlying it are eloquently expressed in a law regarding the sale of children, issued in 451 by the Western emperor Valentinian III.

It is well known that a very terrible famine recently devastated all of Italy, and that people have been reduced to selling their children and relatives to escape the danger of imminent death. Pitiful emaciation and the deathly pallor of the starving so un-

---

107. Epistle 98 [23] *ad Bonifacium* (PL 33.362): "aliquando etiam quos crudeliter parentes exposuerunt"; *De nuptiis et concupiscentia* 1.15.17 (CSEL 42.229–30): "ut exponant filios, qui nascuntur inuitis . . . occulta turpitudo manifesta crudelitate coniuncitur."

108. See Noonan's discussion in *Contraception* (p. 136), and his essay "An Almost Absolute Value in History," in *The Morality of Abortion. Legal and Historical Perspectives,* ed. Noonan (Cambridge, Mass., 1970), pp. 1–59 (esp. p. 16); and Eyben, pp. 73–74 and n. 221.

109. "Consensus" in the Christian community is a comparative designation. In the fifth century, for example, Orosius was still assailing the pagans with the misdeeds of mythic parents, Oedipal incest, and the sacrifice of youths to the minotaur (*Historiarum aduersum paganos* 1.12–14 [CSEL 5.60–63]). It may be revealing that despite this, he did not explicitly condemn abandonment.

nerved everyone that people forgot all of the affection nature bestowed on them and regarded it as a kind of parental duty to get rid of their children. For despair of his life will drive a man to anything: nothing is wicked, nothing forbidden to someone starving [*esuriens*]. His sole concern is that he should somehow survive. But I consider it wrong that freedom should perish because life did not, or should be so overcome by the horror of degrading servitude that it is ashamed to have escaped death. What free person would not rather die than bear the yoke of a slave?[110]

While he wished to restore to freedom any children who had thus been condemned to slavery, it is striking that, in the desperate circumstances of the age, he strove with extraordinary delicacy to avoid discouraging future purchasers of children—no doubt realizing that such sales might save the lives of children and parents. He therefore required that although the sales be considered "annulled" in terms of the child's status, buyers be reimbursed at a rate of twenty percent above what they paid,

> so that neither will the buyer—who gets back more than he paid as the price—be sorry to have bought [the child] under such wretched and desperate circumstances, nor will freedom succumb to the weight of misfortune.

It is unlikely that the state actually played a large role in such matters at the end of the fourth century. Custom, necessity, and the church would have had more effect on both thought and behavior regarding most family issues. Theodosius made bishops the arbiters in his ruling of 412 about masters reclaiming,[111] and when he threatened (in 428) to send to the mines parents who forced daughters

---

110. TC, Novels of Valentinian 33. A subtle and perhaps considerate distinction is obscured by Pharr's translation of this line (p. 544). He renders "Cui non ingenuo mori satius est quam iugum servile perferre?" as "To whom is it not preferable to die a free man rather than to bear the yoke of slavery?"—a question to which a slave could scarcely provide an answer, since even emancipation would not make him a "free man" (a natal category; emancipated slaves were "freedmen," a lower status). The Latin, however, asks a question that turns on a *change* in status from free to slave. Both Basil and Ambrose also raise this point in regard to selling children, as had imperial legists.

111. TC 5.9.2.

into prostitution, he directed that girls abused in this way appeal to the bishop, not to a civil authority.[112]

PRACTICAL MEASURES

The institutional church, into whose hands such matters were increasingly entrusted, itself adopted an entirely realistic attitude toward abandonment. No councils or ecclesiastical authorities prohibited it or lent their support to ascetic condemnations of parents who exposed their children, although conciliar legislation of the period does condemn a wide range of other activities relating to sexuality and family life.[113] On the contrary, canons of the early church concern themselves solely with means to ensure that the children themselves are properly cared for. An African canon from the opening of the fifth century insisted that infants whose baptismal status could not be determined should be baptized, and explains that this is necessary because of the many babies "redeemed" from the barbarians.[114] A council of 442 in Vaison (in southern Gaul) seeks to encourage the faithful to pick up *expositi* without fear of subsequent complications.

> Concerning abandoned children: there is general complaint that they are nowadays exposed more to dogs than to kindness, because even those disposed by the precepts of mercy to rescue

112. Briefly in JC 1.4.12; quoted at greater length in both JC 11.40.6 and TC 15.8.2; on the motivation of the punishment, in the latter two: "quae minor poena est, quam si praecepto lenonis cogatur quispiam coitionis sordes ferre, quas nolit."

113. The Council of Elvira in 305 had condemned "mothers or parents" who prostituted "someone else's body or their own," but this is clearly a separate issue (Canon 12, in *Concilios visigóticos e hispano-romanos* [hereafter, *Concilios*], p. 4).

114. These were probably children sold by parents, although they could have been captured, or might even have been barbarian children Christians purchased specifically to bring up as Christian (though "many" such seems unlikely). The text is: "De infantibus, quoties non inveniuntur certissimi testes, qui eos baptizatos esse sine dubitatione testentur, neque ipsi sunt per aetatem de traditis sibi sacramentis idonei respondere, absque ullo scrupulo eos esse baptizandos, ne ista trepidatio eos faciat sacramentorum purgatione privari. Hinc enim legati Maurorum fratres nostri consuluerunt, quia multos tales a barbaris redimunt" Mansi 4.491–92 (see also introduction, ibid., 477–78); *La Colección canónica hispana* 3.381, where it is quoted from the medieval *Collectio hispana* and identified as the sixth canon of the Fifth Council of Carthage, A.D. 401. It was quoted later in Greek ecclesiastical legislation: see below, chapter 4, note 55.

them are restrained by fear of legal action. It has seemed best to require, therefore, in accordance with the enactments of the most devout, pious, and august emperors,[115] that anyone who picks up an abandoned child should notify a church and obtain a statement from it [saying that he has done so]. The pastor, furthermore, should announce from the altar on Sunday that the church has received notice of the finding of an abandoned child and will hear the claim of anyone who wishes to acknowledge the child, for up to ten days from the exposing. The finder[116] may, as he prefers, be repaid for the ten days of care in the present by humans or with God's grace in the hereafter.

And if, after this very careful disposition, anyone who exposed a child should try to reclaim or bring any charge against a finder who observed its provisions, he is to be punished with the ecclesiastical sanctions for murder.[117]

This ruling, about one-fifth of the council's proceedings, does not attempt to prevent parents from abandoning children: they will suffer no penalty if they reclaim within ten days or do not reclaim at all. Its aim is, like that of Constantine's legislation a century earlier, to preserve the status quo, particularly as a means of encouraging people to pick up and rear abandoned children without fear of unpleasant consequences or of losing the child in whom they invest time and money. That abandonment was a substantial social problem is apparent; the edict was repeated, provision by provision, about a decade later at a council in Arles, in Provence.[118]

Both a tendency on the part of Christians to regard abandonment as irrevocable—despite legislation before and after Constantine that privileged freeborn status above rights of finders or foster

115. Leclercq, annotating Hefele (see note 117, below), identifies this as the decree of Honorius and Theodosius of 412 (TC 5.9.2), discussed above, but fails to take note that this enactment (1) made reference only to owners and patrons, not parents, and (2) was effectively repealed by Sirmondian Constitution 5, of 419, by the same emperors. The reference to bishops in the earlier decree does not argue for equating it with this canon; the church was clearly involved in a number of family issues throughout the empire.

116. That is, if the child is reclaimed.

117. Text in PL 84.262, Mansi 6.451, Charles Hefele, *Histoire des conciles d'après les documents originaux* 2.459–60, and *Concilia Galliae A.314–A.506,* pp. 100–1.

118. Second Council of Arles, Canon 51, in Mansi 7.884; *Concilia Galliae,* p. 124. Emil Friedberg (CIC) placed this council between 443 and 506; Mansi places it "around" 452.

parents—and the increasing role churches played in the "distribution" of abandoned children are also evident in the version of Constantine's ruling preserved in epitomes of Roman law specifically for Christians of the East. The Armenian version, dealing with children "of unknown parentage or resulting from fornication," left "at the doors of churches or elsewhere," grants anyone who gives the child milk the right to rear him or her [both sexes are specified] as child or slave at his discretion.[119] The Arabic version also applies to both genders, envisions that such a child, found in the street,[120] would be either "the offspring of fornication [*zanā'i*] or of the poor," and also grants the finder complete license to bring up any and all such children in whatever status he prefers.[121] If the finder dies without specifying, the child is presumed a slave[122]—an indication, perhaps, of the most common choice made by finders?

Leaving children at the doors of a church may be a Christian continuation of exposing them in public places, since churches were often converted Roman public buildings, or an adaptation of the Jewish practice of employing synagogues for this purpose—another "token" Christianity retained from its natal parent—although it is possible that both these customs developed simultaneously. Since churches were, by the fifth century, vastly more numerous than synagogues, they doubtless played a much greater role in the abandonment of children in the Mediterranean than the latter, and likely even more of a role than public buildings did, for reasons which will become evident.

CONCLUSIONS

The Christians of the first five centuries were also denizens of the empire, and it would be a mistake to view their family patterns as inherently different from those of their contemporaries, or unaffected by the aspects of Roman culture bearing on abandonment

---

119. *Syrisch-Römisches Rechtsbuch aus dem fünften Jahrhundert*, Armenian version, section 129 (1.134).

120. N.B.: *tarīq*, not *sabīl*, as in the Qur'anic expression "children of the way."

121. *Syrisch-Römisches Rechtsbuch*, Arabic version, section 130 (1.94). This provision does not occur in the Syriac versions. The German translation (2.114) is inaccurate.

122. "And if he dies, and made no disposition concerning them, they are slaves."

discussed previously. Most of the solutions proposed for the mysteries of abandonment at Rome apply also to early Christianity, although there is so little evidence of a purely literary nature for Christians that the relationship of fictional to historical abandonment is not a problem.[123]

Less can be said about the demographics of abandonment among Christians than among Romans in general. The former were strongly discouraged from engaging in sexual acts, including those between husband and wife, for any reason other than to produce a child, but it cannot be known whether such advice was followed, or what effect it would have had if it were. Even if the overall result of Christian ethics was to reduce the level of conjugal activity, the demographic impact of this might be entirely offset by the vehement hostility of Christianity to nonprocreative *modes* of intercourse: while it was a venial sin for parents to engage in a procreative form of sexuality if they did not desire another child, it was a grave sin to engage in a nonprocreative one.[124] St. Augustine advised Christian wives to insist that their husbands visit a prostitute if they wished to indulge in such acts: this would be less sinful for all concerned than sullying the marriage bed.[125] Especially as the subtleties of Christian ethics were reduced to a legalistic system of negative injunctions in canons and sermons, it seems very likely that the overall effect might be to produce more children.[126] Sheer increase in numbers

123. In the *Clementine Recognitions,* a kind of Christian romance, a woman buys two children who had been stolen by pirates and rears them as her own (text PG 2, GCS 42; for discussion, see Archibald, "The Flight from Incest," and Perry, *The Ancient Romances,* pp. 285–93). *The Pastor of Hermas* begins with the *nutritor* himself selling the author to someone else without any indication of disapproval on anyone's part (Greek text GCS 48, or in LCL *Apostolic Fathers* 2 [New York, 1930]; in the Latin text, PG 2, the sale [891–92] is less clear). Many years later the author was joyfully reunited with the woman who bought him, from whom he had been separated in the meantime: an unusual twist on *anagnorisis.*

124. Contraception is regularly condemned through the sixth century, with an insistence suggesting that preachers, at least, suspected their flocks of practicing it, although no sure methods are known to have been in use. See discussion in Hopkins, "Contraception," esp. p. 139.

125. *De bono conjugali* 1.1.

126. Most historians have assumed that the population of Europe declined steadily from the fourth century, although the diminution would not necessarily be even: the fifteenth canon of the Council of Elvira (A.D. 305) prohibited marriages between Christian girls and pagans, which might occur "because of the great number of girls" (*Concilios,* p. 4), suggesting a serious disproportion in Christian society in Spain at the time. Patlagean, *Pauvreté économique et pauvreté sociale à Byz-*

was not an official theological objective of Christianity, but it was often adduced as a positive good. A fifth-century homilist warned wealthy women against the hypocrisy of expecting their servants to produce children without being willing to do so themselves, but he clearly envisioned the possibility that they might, if they bore off-spring, give them to someone else to rear.[127]

Neither the Jewish scriptures, which Christianity brought with it to its foster home in Rome, nor its own sacred writings opposed abandonment. On the contrary, both included archetypal examples of God requiring or accepting the sacrifice of a child (including his own), or of abandonment leading to a greater destiny, as in the case of Moses or Ishmael. Some early ascetics regarded exposing children as sinful,[128] but their condemnations were based on the claim that it was tantamount to infanticide—despite the overwhelming expectation that the child would survive—or that it was certain to lead to incest. Others objected to selfishness or sexual impropriety which might be manifested in abandonment, but no Christian writer articulated the position that engendering a child necessarily created an obligation to support him. By the fourth century a broader consensus had emerged, in which reservations about abandonment—when practiced for selfish reasons by the rich or libidi-

---

ance. 4e–7e siècles (chap. 4, "Affirmations et négations des structures familiales"), argues that in the East during this period there was great pressure against procreation, in the form of diminishing opportunities for the wealthy and resources for the poor, but she includes abandonment as one of the means used to "limit birth," which is a misleading conceptualization; and elsewhere (ibid., pp. 150–51) she concludes that Christian families of the fourth century, at least in Asia Minor, generally had six children, which is substantially higher than the size of earlier Roman families. On the other hand, she is undoubtedly correct in suggesting that one effect of Christianity was to discourage marriage, which would certainly lower the birthrate ("Birth Control," pp. 20 ff.).

127. "Et ideo sicut unaquaeque vult ut sibi mancipia nascantur quae illi serviant; ita illa quantoscumque conceperit, aut ipsa nutriat, aut nutriendos aliis tradat" (PL 39.2298; formerly attributed to Augustine, but now thought to have been written by Caesarius of Arles).

128. Eyben (p. 67) says that the *Didache* condemns exposing children, but it does not. The passage in question (5.2) condemns the killing of children (φονεῖς τέκνων), and it is only Eyben's own conflation of abandonment with infanticide that makes this seem a reference to the former. Even Christian writers who argued that abandonment was the *moral* equivalent of infanticide distinguished the two as separate categories.

nous ones by anyone—coexisted with equanimity and compassion for parents driven by necessity to expose or sell their children.

Did Christians abandon children? No mystery remains here: they did. Even if one discounted injunctions against abandonment as evidence of its occurrence, prohibitions of other activities such as promiscuity and recourse to prostitutes are predicated on the consequences of Christian parents having exposed children, and by the fourth century, theology, Christian law, and conciliar canons all provide abundant testimony that abandonment was widespread among Christians, apparently as familiar as it had been among pagan Romans. Nor should this surprise, since the people who had been the pagan Romans were now the Roman Catholics, and their ethical tradition not only accommodated but in some ways institutionalized forms of abandonment.

None of this, however, indicates a lack of parental sentiment among Christians. All earthly attachments were discouraged by ascetics, and this included parental sentiment;[129] but rhetorical appeals to loving parenthood were more common among Christians than among any contemporary religious group. Children were idealized, and parental attachment to them assumed: there was a vast homiletic literature on the "Holy Innocents," for example, including sermons by Basil's friend Gregory Nazianzen and his own younger brother, Gregory of Nyssa.[130] In the latter there are long, heart-rending descriptions of babies torn from the mother's breast and a passage in which a mother cannot decide whether to attend to her one-year-old, crying inarticulately, or her two-year-old, who can form words.[131] (One wonders if this was perhaps inspired by some real-life situation, like Basil's seeing the father selling his children?)

129. There was also a widespread feeling that childhood was necessarily a time of horror and suffering; even Augustine, who could hardly have had more devoted parental care, articulates this view: *City of God* 21.14. Cf. his Epistle 107 (PL 22.877), where he recommends to Laeta that she give her daughter to someone else to rear.

130. The festival of the Holy Innocents was probably known in both East and West at least by the fifth century (see Francesco Scorza Barcellona, "La Celebrazione dei Santi Innocenti nell'omiletica greca," *Bollettino della Badia greca di Grottaferrata*, NS 29 [1975] 105–35).

131. PG 46.1144–46. For other sermons on the Innocents, see Nazianzen (PG 36.311–34), Chrysostom (PG 57.175–84), Basil of Seleucia (PG 85.387–98), John of Eubea (PG 96.1501–8), and the unknown or falsely attributed PG 61.697–700, 61.705–10.

In some ways the position of the abandoned grew worse under Christian influence. Whether or not parents produced more children as a result of a sexual morality that focused on procreation, the systematization of abandonment under the aegis of the church—which provided in most cities and towns a safe location and a kind of clearinghouse for them—almost certainly made the prospect a little more palatable for parents. Moreover, under Christian influence abandonment had become largely irrevocable by the end of the fifth century: despite imperial efforts to restore freedom to large numbers of children sold by their parents into slavery, at the local level parents were not allowed by the church to reclaim after ten days, under threat of severe penalty, and finders could rear foundlings however they wished—even as slaves. The change may be less the consequence of Christian principles than of the increasingly complicated social and economic dynamics of abandonment itself: if children would die unless rescued or bought, and if would-be rescuers or buyers were discouraged by the prospect of losing the child in whom they had invested precious resources, it was better for all concerned to limit the rights of parents to reclaim.

No doubt some were inspired by Christian principles of compassion or respect for life to rear abandoned children,[132] but, as has been seen, there was no lack of foster parents (or new owners) in Roman society before the advent of Christianity, and this probably changed little in areas under Christian control or influence. Christianity probably made some difference in the treatment of abandoned children. Although some stigma attached to children whose parents had not had procreation in mind when they were conceived, it was counterbalanced as the status of *alumnus,* already a symbol of selfless love in pagan writings, was further elevated in Christian culture. Christians saw themselves as God's *alumni,* and, directly or by implication, Christian literature was filled with positive and idealized images of adoption and of transference from natal families to happier and more loving adopted kin groups, including such influential metaphors as the "adoption" of the Gentiles, adoption into a monastic "family," or baptism itself, the foundation of Christian

132. The *Apostolic Constitutions* (probably fourth century) enjoin Christians to rear as their own Christian orphans (4.1 [PG 1.808]), but these were largely rejected as spurious by later Christian legislation, and the requirement is specifically sectarian.

experience.[133] These ideas could exert a considerable influence on the willingness of parents to adopt, on how people viewed and reacted to abandoned children, and on how the children viewed themselves. Though subtle, they were widespread: unlike any previous ethical system, Christianity strove to be both universal and exclusive. In the centuries following the fifth it would encourage "the kindness of strangers," both explicitly and implicitly, to a degree and on a scale unprecedented in Europe, carrying its ideas about and rules for abandonment into every town and village in most regions of the continent. One of those ideas—ironically, a token from its natal parent Judaism, about the sacrificing of children to the service of God—would have profound and surprising consequences for the lives of many European children.

133. E.g., Salvian, *Epistula 4 ad socerum et socrum* (PL 53.162): "Osculare quia absens labiis non vales, saltem obsecratione pedes parentum tuorum quasi ancilla, manus quasi alumna, ora quasi filia." Note the juxtaposition of the categories *ancilla, alumna, filia* (maidservant, *alumna,* daughter). See also Salvian's Epistle 5 (PL 53.165), Prudentius, *Peristephanon* 2.569 (PL 60.337), Venantius Fortunatus, *Carmina* 5.3.11, and discussion in Leclercq, pp. 1299–1300.

PART II

THE EARLY MIDDLE AGES

4

❖   ❖   ❖

VARIATIONS
ON FAMILIAR
PATTERNS

THE SOCIAL TOPOGRAPHY of the Mediterranean be-
came much more complex around the year 500, as the institutional
and cultural unity provided by Roman government and Greco-
Roman culture collapsed, both from its own internal weaknesses
and the pressure of the non-Roman peoples attacking it. Much that
was Roman survived among the upper classes in most of Europe
and the Near East, and among all social classes in some areas of
Italy, Spain, and Gaul—language, literature, religion (i.e., Roman
Catholicism), legal texts, and customs. But elsewhere the Semitic
cultures of the Near East, the Greek cultures of the northeastern
Mediterranean, and the Germanic and Celtic societies of Western
Europe either undermined Roman culture and social structures or
were gradually blended with them, creating complex hybrids of
custom, law, language, and religion.

Abandonment was a common aspect of life in all of these areas,
as it had been at Rome, and in many of them the same methods persisted. Because there were fewer cities, its forms were somewhat
less organized, at least in the West, than they had been in antiquity.
There were fewer standard locations for abandoning children, and
no uniform government to supervise the treatment of the servile;
the traditional status of exposed children reared in new homes
(*alumnus*) was less clearly defined among the inchoate societies of
most of Europe during this period than it had been in antiquity.
Laws were still enacted and invoked in defense of *expositi*, but most

aspects of their lives, from their juridical status to the ability of their parents to reclaim them, depended more on circumstance than on institutions or statutes. In the chaos following Rome's demise, only her own foster child, Christianity, wielded enough power and influence in Europe to offset the increasingly haphazard and uncontrolled character of abandonment. It was she who composed and disseminated new rules for exposing, selling, and rearing children, she who undertook to facilitate the finding of new homes for *expositi* through churches and parish organization, and she who created—for the first and only time in European history—a system of caring for them (oblation, discussed below) in which they were at no social, legal, or moral disadvantage because of their abandonment.

The interaction of surviving Roman custom and law with Christian ideals, pagan cultures, and an increasingly rural and subsistence economy accounts for much of the history of abandonment in the Mediterranean and European lands once linked, politically and culturally, by the state that traced its origins to the foundling twins Romulus and Remus. But in two formerly Romanized areas somewhat different factors prevailed: in the Middle East, Christianity was overshadowed by Islam, which developed its own traditions regarding abandonment; and in Byzantium, Roman government survived—officially, at least—throughout most of the Middle Ages.

ROMAN RUINS: THE MIDDLE EAST

Because the subsequent cultural disjunction came to seem so profound, it is easy to forget that large areas of the Middle East had been part of the Roman Empire in the same way that parts of northern Europe and the British Isles had been. Here, however, the remnants of Roman civilization were picked up and refashioned not by Christianity, but by Islam.[1] Islam, unlike Christianity, could not be

---

1. Medieval Christians often referred to Muslims as "Ishmaelites" (*Ismaeliti*, spelled in a variety of ways) or *Agareni*, from Hagar, and these terms may have subtly influenced views of abandonment as well as of Islam, but it is unlikely that ordinary Christians gave much thought to the derivation or connotations of such terms. Jerome (*Commentary on Ezekiel* 25) and Sozomen (6.18) both related the Greco-Latin word "Saracen" (actually probably from the Arabic root *sh-r-q*, "East") to Sarah, and even St. John Damascene, who lived among Muslims, explained it as derived from "those sent away empty by Sarah" (Σαρρα κενούς) (*De haeresibus liber* 101 [PG 94.764]).

said to have been born of Judaism, since it arose in a milieu as pagan and Christian as Jewish. Indeed, it seems in many ways to have re-acted particularly against Judaism, although Muslims did stand in a peculiar familial relationship to the Jews:[2] they shared many Semitic customs which they incorporated into their religious life (e.g., cir-cumcision, dietary regulations); they adopted much of Jewish the-ology, and claimed that they were its rightful heirs (the Jews having distorted it and become unworthy); and they traced the descent of the "House of Islam" to Ishmael, whom they regarded as the legiti-mate heir of Abraham.[3] According to Muslim tradition, Abraham went with Hagar and Ishmael to Arabia and then abandoned them in the desert, giving rise, in one view, to a part of the ritual all Muslims perform at Mecca.[4]

The Qur'an repeats the Jewish scriptures' account of the expos-ing of Moses, adding explicit reassurance from God to his mother that all will turn out well if she abandons him.[5] It is the pharaoh's wife who finds the child, not his daughter, and she contemplates two uses for the foundling: "He may be of use to us, or we might

2. One could use the metaphor of a rebellious child in the case of Islam's rela-tion to Judaism, as opposed to a foundling in the case of Christianity, although the respective histories of Jesus and Ishmael make this somewhat ahistorical.

3. In contrast to the Jewish and Christian view that he was the son of a servile concubine. For Muslim opinions see, e.g., al-Bukhari, *Sahih, Anbiya'* ["Prophets"] (ed. L. Krehl [Leiden, 1862–68]), 9. According to some Muslim authorities, he was the progenitor only of the tribes known as *musta'riba,* "arabicized," but the more common belief was that the Arab peoples were all descended from him. An eleventh-century Muslim polemic against Christianity, for example, says that Muhammad was sent "from the best of peoples, the children of Ishmael—peace upon him—and from the best of the children of Ishmael, the Quraysh [Muham-mad's tribe]" (D. M. Dunlop, "A Christian Mission to Muslim Spain in the Elev-enth Century," *Al-Andalus* 17, 2 [1952], 259–310, sec. 29). Some authorities claim that it was Ishmael rather than Isaac whom Abraham was ordered to sacrifice. On the controversy among Christians, Muslims, and Jews over his status, see, e.g., Moshe Perlmann, "Medieval Polemics between Islam and Judaism," in *Religion in a Religious Age,* ed. S. Goitein (Cambridge, Mass., 1974), 103–29, or S. Baron, "Socioreligious Controversies," in *A Social and Religious History of the Jews,* vol. 5 (New York, 1957), pp. 82–138.

4. The *sa'y:* see, e.g., Ahmad ibn Hanbal, *Musnad* (Cairo, 1895) 1.347 ff.

5. Surah 28:7: "Nourish him; and when you fear for him, throw him in the river. But do not be afraid or sad: we will restore him to you." The verb used in the Qur'anic account for "slaying" the male Israelite babies, *dhabah,* has connotations of "sacrifice," but the sacrifice of children is not mentioned elsewhere in the Qur'an.

adopt him as a son."[6] Strikingly, the very same expression (which is not in the Jewish account)[7] is used in the Qur'an by the Egyptian who buys Joseph from his brothers: "Perhaps he will be of use to us, or we will adopt him as a son."[8] This strongly suggests a conceptualization of abandoned children in early medieval Arabia comparable to that of *alumni* under the empire: they might be taken in as children, or used as household servants.[9]

Although the Qur'an frequently makes reference to the undesirability of female children—a motif familiar from the ancient world[10]—it also unambiguously labels as evil the killing of daughters.[11] In the apocalyptic vision of surah 81 (verses 8 and 9) there is a haunting reference to the burying alive of unwanted girls: ". . . when she who was buried is asked / For what was she killed?" No children were in fact to be killed: "Do not kill your children in fear of poverty. We will support them and you. Killing them is a great evil."[12] These and other allusions suggest that infanticide was familiar to the pre-Islamic Arabians, and possibly associated with paganism (though not necessarily sacrifice).[13] But Muhammad also says explicitly (e.g., at 19:77) that children are a blessing *when coupled with wealth*—leaving open the possibility that abandonment might be a legitimate option for poorer parents, a parallel to the position of Christian theologians of his day.

If his prohibition of infanticide had effect, children who would once have been killed may have been abandoned under Islam and become the "children of the way" or "brethren" frequently men-

6. "'Asa an yanfa'ana au nattakhidhahu waladan" (28:9). "Ittakhadha" is not necessarily a technical term for adoption, although it might be. What she actually does with him is characterized by the verb *k-f-l*—to nourish, or foster—at 28:12.

7. For the Hebrew and Greek, see chapter 3, note 25. The Qur'an's version is closer to the Latin, which was probably influenced by Christian views of "adoption." Some scholars believe that Muhammad's knowledge of Judaism was largely filtered through Christians.

8. Surah 12:21.

9. Roman law as known to Arabian Christians explicitly allowed foundlings to be reared as slaves or adopted children.

10. E.g., 37:149: "Hath God daughters, while they have sons?" Cf. 2:223, 4:31 and 117, 16:59 (see next note), 43:19, etc.

11. See 16:59: "And he conceals from the people the misfortune announced to him [sc., the birth of a daughter]; does he accept it in shame or bury it in the ground?" Scandinavians also buried unwanted children; see below, chapter 7.

12. 17:31—interestingly, from the surah called "The Children of Israel"—and 6:151.

13. 6:137 and 140.

tioned in the Qur'an.[14] The "women's pledge"[15] for female Muslims includes a promise not to kill children and, interestingly, not to substitute babies—a problem one would expect only in a society with a good supply of abandoned children.[16] An early version of the "changeling" idea (see below) may be present in surah 18 (verses 74 and 80–81), where a mysterious stranger kills a youth because he is troublesome to his parents, "so that their Lord might replace him with a better one."

Oddly, however, Muhammad specifically prohibited to his followers the legal adoption of children, including foundlings.[17] Interpretations of the reasons for this vary. It was not simply indifference: in at least three places he expresses concern for the "children of the way," and requires that a fifth of the booty taken in war be spent on the needy, among whom such children are numbered.[18]

14. See note 17, below. At 2:220 Muhammad notes that those who become involved with orphans have them as "brothers" (*ikhwān*), but, oddly, considers that it is more difficult to feed orphans who are actually related to one: 90:15.

15. 60:12: not to worship any god but God, not to steal, not to commit fornication.

16. The Arabic is obscure: "not to give falsehood feigning it between their hands and their feet." Both Abdullah Yusuf Ali (*The Holy Qur'an* [Lahore, 1938] 2:1536) and Mohammed Pickthall (*The Meaning of the Glorious Koran* [New York, n.d.], p. 397) take the reference to falsehood in a general way—i.e., lying or slander. But George Sale's more learned translation (*The Koran* [London, n.d.], p. 409 and note b) and John Penrice (*Dictionary and Glossary of the Koran* [London, 1970], p. 110, s.v. *iftara*) cite Muslim commentators as interpreting it as a reference to the substitution of children, which the Arabic does suggest.

17. 33:4–5: "God has not made those you call such your sons. Call them after their fathers . . . , and if you do not know their fathers, then they are your brothers in faith or clients [*mu'ālī*]." Cf. 33:37, where a special category is mentioned for "adopted sons": *ad'iya'ī*. Robert Roberts, *The Social Laws of the Qoran* (London, 1925), p. 50, understands "if ye know not their fathers" to apply to foundlings, which is probably right. The category "foundling" would include many illegitimate children, but the reverse is not necessarily true, and illegitimate children as such are not mentioned elsewhere in the Qur'an, while abandoned children are. The traditional understanding of this prohibition is that it enabled the prophet to marry the wife of his own adopted son, Zaid, which would have been incestuous if he had actually been counted as a son: see, e.g., Roberts, ibid., and Toufy Fahd and Muhammad Hammoudi, "L'Enfant dans le droit Islamique," in *L'Enfant* 1, pp. 334–36; cf. W. R. Smith, *Kinship and Marriage in Early Arabia* (London, 1903), p. 52, and Syeed Ali, *The Personal Law of the Mohammedans* (London, 1880), pp. 166 ff.

18. "'Ibn as-sabīl": 2:177, 2:215, and 8:41 (requirement of one-fifth the booty).

Abandonment seems to have been at least well known in the Middle East at the time of Muhammad, although the evidence does not permit inferences about how widespread or common it was.[19] He did not oppose it, although he did condemn infanticide, and he made provision for the care of exposed children. Poverty may have been the most common motivation,[20] although the negative view of daughters might also have prompted their abandonment. (It was probably offset to some degree by polygamy—Muslims were permitted concubines in addition to four wives—which allowed wealthy households to absorb women who might have had no prospects in a monogamous society.[21])

Like all of the heirs of Rome, early Islamic society enshrined abandonment in its mythology and discourse: Moses and Ishmael had both been abandoned, as in Judaism, and Abraham had been asked to sacrifice his son. All Muslims were *alumni* in a sense: the prophet told them that they were nearer to him "in relation" than to anyone else, and that his wives were "their mothers" (33:6). In

---

19. For abandoned children later in Islam, see Fahd and Hammoudi, as cited above, note 17. Although later Muslim law lies outside the scope of this study, two of its provisions (ibid., p. 337) are particularly interesting. One is that foster parents of abandoned children *with money* must be responsible with the child's resources—strongly suggesting that in later times even wealthy people abandoned children as a means of family planning, as they had in Rome. The other is the rule that children found by Muslims in Muslim territory may be presumed Muslim; those found in non-Muslim territory by non-Muslims are the religion of the finder—a provision strikingly like Maimonides' rule for Jews.

20. In the *Synaxarion* (liturgical lesson book) of the Jacobite Christians, however, there is an Arabic parable about a woman who bore an illegitimate child and "threw him to the dogs, who ate him": René Basset, "Le Synaxaire arabe Jacobite (rédaction Copte) 2," *Patrologia Orientalis* 3 (Paris, 1909), pp. 398–99. She was buried alive as a divine punishment at the prayers of a saint, although it is not clear that destroying the child had been her chief sin; she had also slept with two brothers, a serious breach of chastity under early Christian sexual restrictions. Arab Christian mores may have been substantially different from those of their Muslim neighbors, however.

21. As Islam spread and developed, local practice diverged from early ideals just as it did in Christian and Jewish communities. In the eleventh century, for example, a Muslim Turk, Yusuf Khass Hajib, counseled his royal patron concerning daughters, "The best is if they are not born at all, or else do not survive. And if one is born, better for her the bosom of mother earth"—precisely what Muhammad had prohibited in the Qur'an (trans. Robert Dankoss, *Wisdom of Royal Glory (Kutadgu Bilig): A Turko-Islamic Mirror for Princes* [Chicago, 1983], 63, p. 187). A study of abandonment in medieval Islam is beyond the scope of this investigation but would be extremely valuable.

much of the Islamic world outside Arabia, converts to Islam were designated as "adoptees" or *alumni* of Arabian tribes,[22] perpetuating the Judeo-Christian analogy between God's benevolence and the kindness of adoptive parents, and subtly fostering the idea that a happy fate awaits abandoned children.[23]

EASTERN CHRISTIANITY

In Constantinople and the lands under its hegemony, Roman government officially persisted, and although indigenous cultures slowly transformed the heritage of Rome, they were constrained in large measure by Roman administrative structures and models.[24] The most thorough compilation of Roman law ever made, for example, was drawn up in the Greek-speaking East at the behest of the emperor Justinian in the sixth century; it included almost all of the legislation regarding abandonment and sale of children enacted under imperial rule during the previous five centuries.[25]

Many of these decrees contradicted each other, as has been noted previously. Either to resolve the confusion this occasioned, or in response to contemporary social ferment (or both), the emperor issued a new policy in 529, ruling that

22. E.g., the *muwalladūn* of North Africa and Spain: the term means "reborn," and suggests that by allying themselves with one of the original Arabian tribes (or sometimes just with the "House of Islam") the convert becomes a part of this genealogical group, as an adopted child. As in the Roman world, however, the status of such persons was usually *de facto* lower than that of biological descendants.

23. Less directly, Muslim writers propounded the idea that great persons might rise from humble circumstances of birth generally: see, e.g., ibn Hawqal's comments that "many sultans" were born of mulatto slaves (Abu'l Qasim Muhammad ibn Hawqal, "Ibn Haucal, Description de l'Afrique," trans. M. G. de Slane, *Journal Asiatique* 3, 13 [1842] 249–53). Ibn Rustah admires the custom he attributes, possibly falsely, to the Rus (Abu 'Ali Ahmad ibn Umar Ibn Rustah, *Kitāb al-A'laq an-Nafīsah,* ed. M. J. de Goeje [*Bibliotheca Geographorum Arabicorum*] [Leiden, 1892], p. 145: "and when a child is born to one of the men, he places before the child a drawn sword and puts it between his hands and says to him, 'I leave you no inheritance and you will have nothing but what you earn for yourself with this sword'").

24. On the family in early medieval Byzantium, see, in addition to the sources cited above, Evelyne Patlagean, "L'Enfant et son avenir," and *eadem,* "Birth Control," largely repeated in *Pauvreté,* pp. 128–43.

25. In the West its effect was negligible before the beginning of the second millennium, after which it gradually became an influence on almost all Western jurisprudence, though it was never "in force" anywhere in the West. Even in the East, it probably affected the emperor's subjects less than his own rulings.

no one may claim as his own[26]—under the rubric of lordship, legal obligation or servile tenure—an exposed infant, whether he is of free or freed parents, or is marked with servile status. Nor do we concede to those who bring up such children, whether male or female, any license or under any pretext to pick them up and educate them as freedpersons or slaves or serfs [*colonorum*] or dependents [*adscriptitiorum*]. But without distinction those who are reared in this way by such persons are to be regarded as free and freeborn persons, and they may acquire and dispose of property as they wish, to their own heirs or others, untouched by any taint of servitude or legal subordination or condition of serfdom.

Nor is it right that those who abandoned the children in the first place, possibly hoping they would die, and having rendered their status uncertain even if someone picks them up, should try to reclaim them and reduce them to servitude,[27] any more than those who have brought them up, motivated by piety, should later be able to change their minds and relegate them to servile status, even if they were moved to act in the first place with this in mind. . . .

This is to be enforced not only by the authorities of the provinces, but also by the bishops, by all officials, by civic leaders and officeholders, and by every governmental agency.[28]

This decree has given rise to a number of misinterpretations, including the claim that it outlawed abandonment,[29] which it clearly did not. Its intent was to resolve long-standing controversies over two issues: the personal status of foundlings, and rights of reclamation. It does not in fact make a very clear case about the latter, as it only prohibits reclaiming for servitude, and leaves unclear whether parents might reclaim freeborn children as their own. On the first

26. It is unclear in the Latin ("in suum dominium vindicare") whether this refers to the person who exposed the child or the one who reared him, but in view of the following sentence and the general use of *vindicare* for parental reclaiming, the former seems more likely.

27. "Hos iterum ad se revocare conari, et servili necessitati subiugare." Scott takes this phrase as referring to the rescuers, but this interpretation seems incorrect to me. (Samuel Parsons Scott, trans., *The Civil Code* [Cincinnati, 1932], 17 vols.)

28. JC 18.52(51).3; cf. briefer version at 1.4.24, where the prohibition of reclaiming is omitted.

29. So, e.g., Lemosse, "L'Enfant sans Famille en Droit Romain," in *L'Enfant* 1, p. 267.

issue, however, it offers a resounding and unprecedented resolution: *all* abandoned children are free, not just those born free and reduced to unfree condition by finders. No foundlings can be raised in any form of servitude.

While this seems an extraordinarily generous provision—much of the population of the empire was of servile status, and their children could now become free simply through abandonment—it is extremely unlikely that it could have been enforced. It lays claim to jurisdiction throughout the empire, but Justinian exercized juridical control only over the Byzantine East.[30] And even there, who was going to prove that the servants in a household were *expositi*? Prior to this, natal parents and masters had been able to reclaim children they had exposed, which was probably the chief means by which these children regained their natal status (for good or ill). The edict certainly prohibited masters from doing so; and possibly also parents. If the ruling was, in fact, understood to preclude the latter from reclaiming, it probably did away with the only regular avenue of escape for exposed children reared in unfavorable circumstance.[31]

That the edict had little, if any, effect is indicated by a subsequent imperial rescript of 541. Justinian was horrified to learn from an official of the church in Thessalonica that people were abandoning newborn children in churches and then, after they had been brought up by someone else, reclaiming them *as slaves,* "so that those whom at the very outset of life they consigned to death, they now, as adults, would deprive of freedom." All such children, the emperor ruled, were to be treated as free—even if someone could prove that they were his property—and those who tried to return them to servitude were liable to "the most severe penalties."[32] If

30. Roughly, the northern Mediterranean littoral from Asia Minor up to the coast of Italy; he controlled Gothic Italy briefly through military conquest from 535–55.

31. The children themselves might, when they grew older, sue for freedom under the terms of the law if they could prove that they were abandoned, and in this sense the statute materially improved their position at law, but there are no known instances of this, and it seems unlikely, given the relative social positions and resources of abandoned children and those who reared them, that many such suits would arise. Possibly the church, with whom *expositi* were sometimes deposited, would follow the imperial will in seeing that children it placed in foster homes were not relegated to servitude, which they might have been otherwise, but this was certainly not the case elsewhere in the Christian world, as noted in the previous chapter.

32. Scott (17.180) renders "extremis poenis subici" as "they should also undergo the penalty of death," which is a possible construction of the Latin itself but

masters were forbidden to abandon aged or ill slaves (as they had been since the time of Claudius), should they not also be prevented from attempting to enslave children they had committed "to the kindness of strangers"?[33]

This law did not prohibit abandonment by parents but by owners, and strongly suggests that many slaveholders of the late empire did not find it profitable to rear slaves born to their households,[34] although there might have been motivations for exposure other than economic ones (e.g., shame, if the child had been fathered by the master). It substantially undermined the apparent liberality of the previous statute by requiring masters to retain infant slaves, thereby preventing the children from obtaining freedom through abandonment, although it could not have been necessary unless the previous law was being ignored. Part of the reason for this may have been the mildness of the sanctions: the previous ruling had imposed no penalty for violation, and in the second one, although he twice compared the offense to homicide, the emperor in the end proposed a penalty of five pounds of gold for violators—an extremely lenient punishment compared, for example, to that established for castration during the same year.[35] It is not obvious, moreover, whether "violating the law" meant abandoning infant slaves or attempting to reclaim them, or both; only the latter would seem to be easily provable.

Although the emperor evinced disgust at this practice and described it as a crime so revolting that even barbarians would not perpetrate it, his reaction may stem from the particular circumstance involved rather than from feelings about abandonment as a more general phenomenon: it was callous, to say the least, for slaveholders to reclaim as slaves children they had cast off and left to someone else to rear—not only an abuse of earlier civil measures to make reclamation possible for parents (under which it was difficult

---

not a credible interpretation here, since at the end of the law the penalty is prescribed as a fine. "Should be punished severely" is what is meant.

33. Novel 153 (Greek and Latin). The Latin title is "De infantibus expositis"; the Greek, ΠΕΡΙ ΤΩΝ ΧΑΜΕΥΡΕΤΩΝ ΒΡΕΦΩΝ, not the usual Greek expression for abandoned children, may reflect the rather particular nature of the ruling.

34. Patlagean (*Pauvreté*, pp. 392–96) found that prices for young slaves (e.g., below ten) were only about thirty percent of those of older slaves, although her figures are quite uncertain: the highest prices all come from a single document.

35. Novel 142: those who castrate lose their property and are exiled.

for foster parents to refuse to return a child),[36] but a contravention of the more recent ruling of church councils, which had prohibited reclamation after ten days even by parents.[37] Under Justinian's rule foster parents could not only say no to someone laying claim to a child they were rearing, they could prosecute him for asking.

Whether this was any help to non-slave children or had an impact on the rate of abandonment is very difficult to assess. Prohibiting and severely penalizing castration may actually have done more to improve the lot of abandoned children than either of these statutes, since it declared eunuchs automatically free, and it would not be difficult for a eunuch to demonstrate that he fell into this category.[38] Several other measures taken by Justinian may also have indirectly helped children. In 530 he legalized the marriage of guardians and *alumnae,*[39] which could result in a considerable improvement in status for abandoned girls, although it might also license sexual exploitation. The next year he simplified the process of emancipating children, so that artificial "sales" were no longer needed;[40] this may have discouraged real sales as well. And at least by 533, children could no longer be given up to an injured party in redress of a grievance ("noxal actions").[41] For middle-class children Justinian's rules about who was liable for child support in the case of divorce, his prohibition of disinheriting, and his stipulations about estate distribution when a parent entered a monastery may have reduced the chances of being abandoned, but they probably had little impact on the poor.[42] These, however, may have been helped somewhat by the liberalization of laws about "natural children."[43]

36. See pp. 167 and 171, 77B and 79.

37. I.e., Vaison and II Arles, discussed in chapter 3. Although it is not certain that Christians of the East would have access to the records of either one of these councils, other Western synods were often quoted in Byzantine church legislation, and Roman law among other Eastern Christians had come to the same conclusion (also in chapter 3).

38. Novel 142.

39. JC 5.4.26.

40. JC 8.48(49).6.

41. *Institutes* 4.8.7. Concern for the chastity of the daughter, an increasing preoccupation of Christians, appears to have motivated this ("cum in filiabus etiam pudicitiae favor hoc bene excludit").

42. Novels 5.5, 115.3–4, 117.7, 123.38.

43. Novel 89, but note that sec. 15 explicitly prohibits the rearing ("neque alendus est"; οὐδὲ ἀποτραφήσεται) of children born of forbidden unions; cf. Justinian's restrictions on what a mother could give to illegitimate children born before her

Shocked to find that pimps were combing the cities of the empire and enticing into their service girls younger than ten, the emperor took strong measures in 529 to curb child prostitution, levying penalties on all those involved in the trade, including landlords of brothels.[44] His law is not directed at parents who sell their children into such situations, possibly because prostituting one's children was already illegal, but more likely because parents did so under the pressure of need, and one more law would hardly help. The chronicler John Malalas specifically describes panderers as buying poor girls from their parents and forcing them into prostitution, and says that Justinian's wife, Theodora, would repay the panderers the price of the girls to set them free—suggesting that, as far as he knew, the parents' action was not considered punishable (or worth punishing).[45]

Unfortunately, little other historical material survives from this period to flesh out the skeleton provided by the laws. We are informed about the lives of the wealthy and powerful, but cannot take them as representative. Theodora, according to one very hostile biographer (Procopius), often had abortions, but on one occasion waited too long and had to bear an illegitimate child. The father, fearing she would kill it, claimed it "because it was male," Procopius reports, patently implying that it would have been killed or abandoned if it had been female.[46] Infanticide is mentioned so casually in some Byzantine sources that abandonment could hardly have been a major moral issue. Moschus reports a case in which a widow kills her two sons because her new husband was ill-disposed toward them.[47] Apart from prostitution, as noted above, sale of children

---

marriage: JC 5.5.6, 6.57.5, and limitations on the inheritance rights of illegitimates in JC 5.27.2, Novels 18.5 and 89.12.4–6.

44. Novel 3.1.14. This measure was not, however, directed against parents' prostituting their daughters, as the earlier edict of Theodosius and Valentinian of 428 had been.

45. *Chronographia* 173 (PG 97.649). Measures of Justinian and Theodora against prostitution, mentioning poverty but not children, are described in Procopius, *Buildings* 1.9; measures of Theodora alone, in *Anecdota* 17.5–6.

46. *Anecdota* 17.17. The word used for the father's "claiming" it is ἀνείλετο, which is the Greek equivalent of Latin *tollere*, although not necessarily with juridical connotations: it is also used in canons to describe simply "picking up" an abandoned child.

47. *Pratum Spirituale* (PG 87.2851–3112), discussed in Patlagean, *Pauvreté*, p. 76. Cf. *Apocalypsis Mariae Virginis*, ed. M. R. James, in *Apocryphae anecdota* (*Texts and Studies* 2.3) (Cambridge, 1893), p. 123.

does not figure prominently in sources from the sixth century, although a seventh-century papyrus shows that a man had indentured his son to a creditor.[48]

In an account of the life of St. Symeon Stylite a man is rescued from punishment because he has performed three kind acts during an otherwise wicked life: providing a monk with clothing, giving money to a stranger, and rescuing an abandoned child. The man seeks to hire a nurse for the child from among the monks, and succeeds (i.e., he suspected there would be women present and there were; this bit of humor eludes the modern editor).[49] The hagiographer states specifically that the child had been exposed (ῥιφὲν) by its mother.[50]

Parallels to the earlier position of *alumni* are visible: Belisarius and his wife adopt a boy from Thrace in an elaborate ceremony (adoption having taken on religious significance in the Christian East).[51] A man who is bankrupted by a fire leaves his daughters to Justinian in his will, and Theodora takes them up as *alumnae*.[52] There are rules against incest with a foster sibling.[53]

The mention of ecclesiastics as plaintiffs and enforcing agents in some laws about exposed infants, as well as the fact that the children were being deposited mostly in churches[54] suggests that Christian institutions were clearinghouses for abandoned children in the East as they were in the West. A council of 691 stipulates that when no witnesses can be found to verify whether an infant has been bap-

48. *Non-Literary Papyri,* ed. C. J. Kraemer (Princeton, 1958) [*Excavations at Nessana,* ed. H. Dunscombe Colt III], item 56, pp. 156–60.

49. Who remarks that "on se perd en conjectures pour expliquer cette recherche d'une nourrice dans les cellules des moines!" and concludes that the monks must simply have been a good source of information on such subjects (!). *Vie ancienne de Saint Syméon Stylite le jeune* 2, ed. P. Van den Ven (Brussels, 1970), pp. 171–72, n. 2.

50. Ibid., 1 (Brussels, 1962), pp. 146–47 (sec. 165).

51. Procopius, *Anecdota* 1.16. This causes great difficulty: Belisarius's stepson becomes jealous of the adopted boy, and his wife falls in love with him. Later Belisarius appeals to the stepson to avenge him against his wife (the boy's own mother) for carrying on with the adopted son, and claims that it is not by ties of blood that men gauge their devotion (στοργή) to each other, but by deeds, and since he has acted as father to the stepson, enriching and advancing him, he should be treated as father (2.8–9).

52. PG 97.618–19. On the other hand, Justinian sometimes claimed to have been "adopted" by wealthy persons simply to get their estates, at least according to Procopius (*Anecdota* 19.11).

53. In the penitential attributed to John the Faster: PG 88.1893–96.

54. The text mentions only churches initially, but subsequently says "abandoned in churches or streets or other places."

tized or not the sacrament must be administered.[55] This provision
was almost certainly intended to deal with abandoned children, either those left in churches in particular or *expositi* in general.[56] The
council says nothing about the morality of such abandonment, although it had much to say about many other ethical issues in its
102 canons.[57] Perhaps the fathers felt that the extant legal and patristic traditions (e.g., the provisions of Basil and the legislation of
Justinian) provided sufficient ethical guidance, or maybe they were
simply realistic.[58] Life was becoming more difficult in the seventh
century, and the prelates probably understood that hard-pressed
parents in a world without effective contraception had very few
options.

On the other hand, a somewhat later canon quite explicitly
equates abandonment with murder:

> The issue arose in this council of those who abandon their
> household [οἰκεῖα] infants at the doors of churches, and it was
> decided that they should be punished as murderers, even if some-
> one else picks the child up and undertakes to nourish him.[59]

This peculiar provision appears to involve a conflation of the ruling
of Vaison ("arises in the synod")[60] with Justinian's legislation about

55. Canon 84; the text of the council is in Mansi 11.930–1106; this canon with
commentary by Balsamon can also be found at PG 137.796. The canon begins with
an acknowledgment that the council is "following the canonical sanctions of the
fathers" (τοῖς κανονικοῖς τῶν πατέρων θεσμοῖς) and is, in fact, almost identical to an
early African canon identified in the *Collectio hispana* as V Carthage (A.D. 401),
canon 6 (cited above, chapter 3, note 114).

56. Although Balsamon was aware that the fathers at Carthage had in mind
children who had been captured by barbarians and ransomed: PG 137.796.

57. Canon 66 prohibited bonfires, apparently in the context of a pagan ritual,
but citing 2 Kings 23:4–6. At 23:10, passing children through fire is mentioned
(see previous chapter), and Balsamon in his twelfth-century commentary on this
canon cites Cyril as saying that it refers to the burnt offering of children to demons
(PG 137.741), but the canon itself makes no mention of children, and no subsequent legislation cites it in reference to infanticide, despite misleading citations in
Schmitz and Wasserschleben.

58. The later medieval canonical collection of Constantine Harmenopulus included both of Basil's comments on women losing children they bore in transit, the
canon attributed (by him) to John the Faster, and the odd provision that a woman
who "throws her baby away unwillingly [ἀκουσίως]" must do penance for a year:
PG 150.164.

59. PG 88.1933.

60. I.e., that those who attempt to *reclaim* children abandoned at churches
should be viewed as murderers, perhaps confused with Justinian's similar com-

abandoning slaves (hence, the adjective οἰκεῖα). Although its provenance is unclear (it has been falsely attributed to John the Faster), it may reflect attitudes at the time it was composed.[61]

Ninth- and tenth-century Byzantine legal texts also took an increasingly dim view of abandonment, twisting, paraphrasing, recasting, or simply mistranslating earlier regulatory laws into statutes prohibiting it.[62] It is impossible to know whether the attitudes of the lawyers were widespread, or even had a real impact as law on the general populace. As in the case of early Christian ascetics, Byzantine social critics from prosperous families may have assumed that abandonment resulted from purely selfish motives. The less fortunate in the same society could entertain quite different views.

But the clues are too few to be certain. There is already in the eighth century a great stillness about social structures in the historical records of the East: centuries will pass before they are again full enough to allow reconstruction of details of real life.[63]

---

parison because of the reference to "murderers," although "murder" was a very common benchmark of moral gravity.

61. The canons attributed to John the Faster are generally agreed to postdate him considerably, and this provision is not even included in them: it occurs in *scholia* on Basil.

62. The opinion of Paulus, for example, that failure to support children was tantamount to killing them (Dig. 25.3.4) appears in the *Basilika* as law (31.6.4). A minor point in a third-century ruling regarding the invalidity of the sale of a free child by a father to his son-in-law (JC 7.16.37) is completely transformed in the *Basilika* (48.20.36) into grounds for prosecution for "kidnapping" (ἀνδραποδισταί: a term with biblical overtones from 1 Timothy 1:10). In the ninth century the very abbreviated summary called the *Epanagoge* reduced many earlier enactments regulating specific forms or aspects of abandonment (e.g., by owners of slaves) to a series of simple statements that all parents must support all children (in C. E. Zachariae von Lingenthal and J. P. Zepos, eds., *Jus Graecoromanum* [Athens, 1931], 6.192–93). The tenth-century *Synopsis Basilicorum* (in Zepos, *Jus* 5.441–42) groups together Paulus's opinions, a conflation of Ulpian's rules about parental support (see note 33 of chapter 1) with opposition to exposing, and a paraphrase of Justinian's Novel making abandoned children free. But the trend was not unidirectional: under Leo the Wise penalties against castration were relaxed somewhat (Novel 60), and the position of infant slaves regulated with greater concern for the rights of owners (Novel 29).

63. Both Patlagean ("L'Enfant et son avenir," p. 85) and Timothy Miller (*The Birth of the Hospital in the Byzantine Empire* [Baltimore, 1985], p. 24; cf. also *Dictionnaire d'Archéologie chrétienne et de Liturgie* 1, ed. Cabral-Leclercq-Marrou [Paris, 1903], p. 2034) refer to institutions that may have cared for abandoned children in the East: the βρεφοτροφεῖα, or "baby homes." None, however, is able to supply any historical details about these beyond their existence and the obvious inference

WESTERN EUROPE IN
THE EARLY MIDDLE AGES

Few voices survive from Western Europe in the early Middle Ages; they are widely scattered in time and place, and therefore very difficult to assess as typical or idiosyncratic. Although it would be more convenient to organize—and read—the surviving indications of abandonment from the early Middle Ages under thematic headings (motives, methods, etc.), this might lead to misunderstanding of both the period and the subject. Early medieval Europe was a congeries of dozens of cultures, ethnicities, languages, and social structures, all undergoing profound transformations for half a millennium. Even when ostensibly similar laws are enacted by sixth-century Visigothic rulers and ninth-century Carolingian churchmen, they have profoundly different social, political, and religious significances. It is more accurate and revealing to present the data from this period in roughly chronological order, loosely grouped according to cultural traditions (Roman, Germanic, Celtic, etc.), and to introduce analytical topics within these specific settings. A more general overview is provided in chapter 6, but it would be misleading if offered first or in isolation from the temporal and geographical variegations it necessarily obscures.

For the West as for the East from the fifth century to the tenth, there are comparatively few sources on any aspect of social life. Literacy is rare and of less value to most Europeans during this period than martial or agricultural skill. Government is unstable, records few. A subsistence (or less than subsistence) economy prevails in Western Europe, characterized in many areas by less commerce, less mobility, and less production than there had been in antiquity. Traditional urban centers decline; new population concentrations, smaller than their predecessors, form around strategic defensive points or episcopal seats. The great majority of people are servile agricultural laborers.

Plague sweeps across the continent in the sixth century, and if its effects are less drastic than they would be in the fourteenth, this is chiefly because the population is already much reduced by war,

---

from the name about their function. *Brephotrophia* (and *orphanotrophia*) also sometimes occur in Western sources, also without context, and the names could in fact refer to something other than foundling homes: they could be for "orphans" in the modern sense, or maternity hospitals, or both.

poverty, and social chaos, and because commerce and communication are so restricted that even disease has difficulty traveling.[64] The West reaches its lowest demographic point in the seventh and eighth centuries, and throughout the early Middle Ages the population of most areas is much less than it had been under the empire. Even the church, which comes closest to creating a European cultural bond, has yet to achieve the uniformity and organization that will later characterize medieval Roman Catholicism.

Given the difficulty of documenting abandonment under the best of conditions, it is striking how frequently it occurs, in a variety of contexts, in the records of these centuries.[65] This may be an

64. See J.-N. Miraben and Jacques LeGoff, "The Plague in the Early Middle Ages," *Biology of Man in History: Selections from the Annales, Economies, Sociétés, Civilisations* (Baltimore, 1975), pp. 48–80.

65. By contrast, there is virtually no modern writing on abandonment during the period, aside from summary treatment in the nineteenth-century surveys (and scattered brief remarks, e.g. by George Payne, *The Child in Human Progress*, p. 289). Even detailed treatments of population control or infanticide have ignored the possibility of abandonment, despite the considerable body of evidence about it. Flandrin (*Families in Former Times*, pp. 180–81) argued that the "prominence of bastards in medieval history, compared with their almost total absence from ancient history, suggests that they owed their survival to Christian morality," but went on to say that parents generally reared them personally, which is not evident in the sources. Elsewhere he notes that "negligence" constituted the major form of family regulation during the Middle Ages, but mentions abandonment only in passing, having concluded that Christianity prohibited exposing children ("L'Attitude à l'égard du petit enfant et les conduites sexuelles dans la civilisation occidentale. Structures anciennes et évolution," ADH [1973] 143–210, esp. pp. 204–5). Duby believed that the settling of slaves on *mansi* by owners in the seventh and eighth centuries, "increased slave productivity and placed on the slaves the burden of bringing up their own children" (Georges Duby, *The Early Growth of the European Economy*, trans. Howard Clarke [London, 1974], p. 33). Richard Lyman ("Barbarism and Religion," p. 76) opined that "it may have been less necessary, and even counterproductive to expose or dispose of children [sc., during the early Middle Ages] . . . in times of precarious life expectancy and short labor supply." Pierre Riché ("Problèmes de Démographie," p. 43) specifically acknowledges the importance of abandonment, although he devotes only a single paragraph to it. Robert Lopez recognized that Balkan parents often sold their children into slavery during this period (*Medieval Trade in the Mediterranean World*, ed. Robert S. Lopez and I. W. Raymond [New York, 1955], p. 115), and cited documents (e.g., ibid., pp. 45–46) showing that Western Europeans did so as well. There is very little other secondary material of relevance to this chapter. Beyond the general surveys of childhood cited in the introduction (Herlihy et al.), one might note the essays dealing with the early Middle Ages in *Medieval Women*, ed. Derek Baker (Oxford, 1978), esp. Pauline Stafford, "Sons and Mothers: Family Politics in the Early

indication that the practice was especially common, which would hardly be surprising in an age when many people found themselves in such reduced circumstances that they sold or gave themselves into slavery or serfdom.[66]

Some of what survives is recapitulation of Roman provisions and must be viewed cautiously, because the elements of early medieval European population conscious of Roman heritage strove to conserve its traditions, and were not necessarily adapting them to their present circumstances or even keeping them alive except symbolically. A code made for the Romans who lived under the rule of the Visigoths in sixth-century Spain, for example, repeats many of the enactments of the emperors on the subject of abandoning children.[67] This could mean that it was a pressing issue at the time, but it could also indicate only that Roman jurists in Spain were trying to preserve what they saw as their legal heritage.

Much more revealing is the local council held in the city of Agde in southern France in 506, which is typical of conciliar legislation of the period. Of its seventy-one canons, all but three involve matters of ecclesiastical discipline (the marriage of clergy, the arrangement of prayers and hymns, church property, ordination, the exclusion of sinners from communion) and all but one are contemporary. That one exception deals with exposed children: the bishops decreed tersely that "in regard to exposed children the enactment of the re-

Middle Ages" (pp. 79–101); Ilene Forsyth, "Children in Early Medieval Art: Ninth through Twelfth Centuries," *Journal of Psychohistory* 4 (1976) 31–70; Mary McLaughlin, "Survivors and Surrogates," in deMause, *History* (as above), pp. 101–81; B. Bachrach and J. Kroll, "Child Care and Child Abuse in the Early Middle Ages," *Journal of the American Academy of Child Psychiatry* 24, 4 (1986) 562–68; and specialized studies by region, such as Christine Fell, *Women in Anglo-Saxon England* (Oxford, 1984), esp. chap. 4, "Family and Kinship."

66. See, for example, the seventh-century formula whereby a man commends himself for life to the service of a lord who is to provide him food and clothing, in L. Rozière, *Recueil générale des formules usitées dans l'empire des Francs du Ve au Xe siècle* 1 (Paris, 1859), no. 43, p. 69, trans. in James Robinson, *Readings in European History* (Boston, 1905), pp. 175–76.

67. *Lex romana Visigothorum,* ed. Gustav Haenel (Berlin, 1849): 3.3 = TC 3.3 (law of 391 restoring sold children to freedom); 4.8.2 = TC 4.8.6 (law of 323 on same); 5.7.1 = TC 5.10.1 (329 ruling that buyer has right to child's service); 5.7.2 = TC 5.9.2 (ruling of 412 that owners and patrons cannot reclaim if bishop has witnessed collection of child); Novel of Valentinian 3.11 (pp. 290–92) = TC Novel of Valentinian 33 (ruling of 451 that buyer recovers price of child plus one-fifth if parents wish to reclaim); *Pauli sententiarum* 5.1.

cent synod must be observed."[68] Both of the two possible synods referred to had taken place half a century before, and it is notable that such a provision should have been so prominent in the clerics' minds: no other previous legislation is referred to in the council, nor do the bishops find it necessary to restate the cited decree; its provisions were apparently quite familiar in Gaul.[69]

At about this same time the ruler of the Ostrogothic population that had settled in Italy issued a brief code of some 154 laws, of which one specifically authorized parents to sell children in case of need, but stipulated that such sales did not alter the status of freeborn children.[70] Parents could also sell the labor of their children, but not pawn them: anyone who accepted a child from a parent in payment of a debt was subject to exile.[71]

These provisions are not quoted from Roman law, though they do approximate the import of those earlier imperial enactments that allowed the sale of children while guaranteeing them the right to reclaim their freedom subsequently. Such sales were apparently commonplace in sixth-century Italy, and not limited to cases of need on the part of parents. In a letter from the second decade of the century, Cassiodorus, who had been governor of the area, describes the richness and bounty of Lucania in southern Italy, where, at a great fair, the peasants sell their children in the market:

> There are boys and girls on display, distinguished by age and sex, put on sale not as a result of captivity but freedom: their parents naturally [*merito*] sell them because they profit from their servitude. And, indeed, they [the children] are doubtless

---

68. Canon 24: "De expositis id observandum quod jam dudum synodus sancta constituit," CCSL 100.204, Mansi 8.319, also PL 84.267; cf. *La Colección canónica hispana* 4.130, sec. 275.

69. On the other hand, ancient canonical traditions were also repeated as part of canonical collections, without necessarily reflecting persistent conditions: this is the case, for example, with the *Excerpta canonum,* a Hispanic collection compiled and copied from the seventh to the tenth century, and incorporating most of the conciliar edicts cited above as relating to abandonment (e.g., Book 4, Title 30, on rebaptizing infants in cases of doubt; Book 5, Title 11, "De expositis infantibus," citing the councils of Vaison and Agde: see the new critical edition by Gonzalo Martínez Díez, *La Colección canónica hispana* 2, pp. 163–64, 175–76).

70. *Edictum Theodorici,* ed. F. Bluhme (Hannover, 1875–79) MGH LL (Folio) 5, p. 162, sec. 94.

71. Ibid.

better off as slaves if they are thus transferred from labor in the fields to household work in the city.[72]

There is no indication of particular duress here: no poverty or famine or war; the rural population simply divests itself of surplus children by selling them to buyers—from the city, Cassiodorus assumes. Even selling their children to each other could be a help to farmers in areas where custom or Roman law enforced partible inheritance:[73] within a few generations a family estate could be subdivided beyond utility if each generation produced a large number of children, each with a legal claim on the patrimony. Selling some to city-dwellers or even to other farmers would alleviate the burden on the estate, and if the other residents of the area bought the children to work on their own farms, a general expectation of considerate treatment would probably have prevailed: many families would have, in effect, traded children, retaining a large enough number to work the land, while limiting the cohort of heirs. It is unclear whether such children would have been able to reclaim free status in adulthood; circumstances probably varied. This mode of creating a servile class by depriving offspring of their patrimony is reminiscent of the law regarding three-fold sale among Romans, and emphasizes the general similarities between the status of children and slaves in ancient and medieval Europe.

Sale could also take place in the case of anonymous abandonment. In a contemporary collection of form letters from Anjou there is a witness-form for the finder of a child abandoned at a church, written in broken and colloquial Latin:

In the name of God. Whereas, I, brother _____, one of the dependents of the parish of St. _____, whom Almighty God sus-

72. Cassiodorus Senator, *Variarum liber* 8.33 (ed. Theodor Mommsen [Berlin, 1894], in MGH AA 12, pp. 261–63; or PL 69.763–65).

73. "Most early medieval societies, especially those influenced by Germanic customs, practiced some form of partible inheritance. For Italy, the Lombard laws make it clear that division of the patrimony among male heirs, usually after the father's death, was the norm." Richard Ring, "Early Medieval Peasant Households in Central Italy," *Journal of Family History* 4, 1 (1979) 2–25, p. 16. Ring perhaps overestimates the role of law codes as either determinants or accurate reflections of early medieval custom: see Patrick Wormald, "*Lex scripta* and *Verbum regis*: Legislation and Germanic Kingship, from Euric to Cnut," in P. Sawyer and I. N. Woods, eds., *Early Medieval Kingship* (Leeds, 1977) 105–38, p. 123. But partible inheritance does seem to have been common in much of southern Europe during the early Middle Ages.

tains there through the offerings of Christians, found there a newborn infant, not yet named, and was unable to find relatives of his among any of the populace, it was agreed to and permitted by the priest [*marterario*] [74] _____, that I could sell the child to _____, which I have done.

And I received for him, as is our [my?] [75] custom, a third [76] plus food. [77]

And I wish to make clear that if the owner or parent of the child should try to take action counter to this document, in the first place Christ the Son of the Living God [should cause this to redound] not to his benefit but to his loss, and should strike him with an eternal penalty, terrible and terrifying, and that he should not be able to reclaim what he seeks, and that this deed should remain in force for all time. [78]

This document, whose language, form, content, and context all suggest popular usage, offers a rare glimpse into the everyday operations of abandonment in the sixth century. The infant was left at a church and sold by the finder, himself a poor man, at a profit—as is "our custom." The church is involved as witness: it would probably issue the document, which must have constituted the "testi-

74. *Marterario*: for *matriculario*?

75. Since the whole letter is written in the first person plural it is impossible to tell whether the "our" here indicates that the person in question is in the habit (or business?) of disposing of children in this way, or has followed local custom.

76. Probably of a sum of money, although possibly of a commodity such as wine or beer.

77. "Uno cum nostro pasto" could mean nourishment (or one meal) for the finder, or repayment of what he had spent on the child. Since he is characterized as poor, the former seems more likely.

78. *Formulae Andecavenses* 49, MGH LL 5.1: *Formulae,* ed. Karl Zeumer (Hannover, 1886), pp. 21–22: "Incipit carta de sanguinolento, quem de matricola suscipi. Cum in Dei nomen nos vero fratris, qui ad matricola sancti illius resedire videmur, quos nobis ibidem omnipotens Deus de conlata christiannorum pascere videtur, invenimus ibidem infantolo sanguinolento, qui adhuc vocabulum non habetur, et de cumpto populo parentes eius invenire non potuemus: ideo convenit nobis unianimiter consencientes et per voluntate marterario nomen illo presbitero ut ipso infantolo ad homine nomen illo venumdare deberemus; quod ita et fecimus. Et accipimus pro ipso, sicut aput nos consuetudo est, treanto uno cum nostro pasto. Et intimare rogavimus, si nus [*sic*] ipsi aut domenus vel parentis eius, qui contra carta ista venire voluerit, inprimitus Christus filius Dei vivi terribilem et meduendam, ut non sit ad gaudium, sed ad eius detrimentum, quod ei incuciat sempiternam pena, et quod repetit vindicare non valeat, et hec facta nostra omni tempore firma permaneat."

mony" called for in fifth-century civil and church legislation.[79] In accord with Roman law—but apparently not confident of it—the finder includes provisions condemning any efforts on the part of parents or owners to reclaim.

That his apprehensions about reclamation were justified is indicated by another document, issued in 516 by Sigismund, king of the Burgundians (a Germanic people settled among the Roman population of the fertile valleys of eastern Gaul):

> Since we have learned from the worthy and laudable suggestion of Bishop Gimellus[80] that the rescue of exposed children used to be inspired by a compassion which is now wanting, because potential rescuers fear that claimants will subsequently take their *alumni* away from them, and that now without their kindness the souls of the children may perish, . . . we herewith decree . . . that among the Roman portion of the population the provisions of Roman law should be observed in this matter. If a case arises between Romans and Burgundians, it shall be settled by a ruling from us.[81]

It is difficult to know what provisions of Roman law Sigismund has in mind. His aim, clearly, is to prevent claims by natal parents or owners, but the tradition of Roman law was confused on the subject, and the last imperial rescript (of 451) had permitted reclamation. He could have been citing Constantine's ruling—which had more influence on Christians than other imperial rescripts. Or since the Catholic hierarchy of the region was predominantly composed of Roman aristocrats, and because their rulings, written in Latin, took on the force of "Roman law" in much of early medieval society, he may have meant the decree of the council of Vaison, which stipulated that parents or masters who tried to reclaim should be regarded as homicides.[82]

The ruling refers to *alumni,* which evokes an image rather different from the instances of sale mentioned above (although the buyer

---

79. TC 5.9.2 (A.D. 412: see above, pp. 167, 171); Council of Vaison (A.D. 442: see chapter 3, pp. 172–73).

80. Bishop of Vaison, A.D. 508–526.

81. *Leges Burgundionum,* ed. L. R. de Salis (Hannover, 1892), MGH LL 1.2.1, Constitutiones extravagantes, xx, p. 119.

82. On the other hand, the summaries of Roman law for Eastern Christians also took the position that the finder could do as he wished with abandoned children, without any conciliar ruling.

in that case could have reared the infant as an *alumnus*). This may reflect an idealized view from the top of society, or the range and variety of circumstances in which abandoned children found themselves, as at Rome.

In the mid-seventh century, the Germanic tribes that had settled in what is now Spain drafted their own law code, drawn partly from Roman legal tradition and partly from legislation by their own rulers. It included a number of provisions regarding abandoned children. Most of them bear some relation to Roman legal principles, but nearly all include subtle changes which reveal much about the society and the role of child abandonment within it. Visigothic legislators appear to have considered abandonment wrong in the case of freeborn children, and came closer than any previous jurists to punishing the parents for it. If an abandoned freeborn child was later recognized by his parents, they not only could but must repay the *nutritor*[83] his value or provide a substitute; if they declined to do so, a judge could redeem the child using their property, and exile the parents (cf. the Edict of Theodoric, above, where the buyer might be exiled, but not the parents). If their property was not sufficient to redeem the child, they themselves could be made to serve. The statute accords to judges the right to prosecute for this "crime," but it is unclear whether "crime" refers to abandonment or the failure to redeem; the latter seems more likely.[84]

On the other hand, although the sale or gift or pawning of children was invalid, the burden here seems to have fallen on the purchaser, who lost his interest if it was discovered that he bought a child from its parents. No penalty for the parents is suggested.[85] That there was a substantial supply of children for sale, nonetheless, is suggested by restrictions on dowries, which list ten boys and ten girls as a proper accompaniment to twenty horses and certain sums of money: few estates would be likely to have twenty child slaves on hand for a wedding. Such a gift would certainly be purchased, and would require a considerable market.[86]

---

83. I have used the Latin word because it could refer to either a foster parent or someone who merely employed the child as a laborer, and there is no English equivalent.

84. LV 4.4.1: "Ut pro exposito infantulo ingenuo serviat qui proiecit."

85. LV 5.4.12.

86. LV 3.1.5: cf. *Formulae visigothicae* 20 (in MGH *Formulae,* as above), p. 584, where a long nuptial poem also mentions this ("Ecce decem inprimis pueros totidemque puellas . . ."). *Puella* is not common as a synonym for "slave," and probably justifies understanding *pueri* as "boys," although it could mean "slaves."

The position of servile children was significantly different from that of free ones. If slaves or servants abandoned a child without the master's knowledge, he could reclaim by paying only one-third the "price."[87] If the master had been aware of the exposing, he could not reclaim, but also suffered no penalty.

Perhaps the most interesting provision of Visigothic law is one dealing with a gray area of abandonment that appears to have been common among both Roman and Germanic populations throughout the early Middle Ages. The third entry under the general rubric "abandoned children" concerns infants given to someone for "rearing" or "nourishing":[88]

> If someone accepts a child from his parents for rearing, he may demand for this the price of one *solidus* per year each year until the child is ten. After that, nothing further is to be paid, since the child himself can work off his support through his own labor. If he [the child] declines to pay the sum required, he remains in servitude to the person who supported him.[89]

This curious provision provides an escape for parents, in contravention of the provisions restricting abandonment, by allowing them to entrust a child to someone else for rearing, at a small fee set by law, and to take no further responsibility for him: the child himself will have to repay his upkeep after he is ten. Even parents of modest means could probably raise the sum required up to that age—a total of ten *solidi*—which might be compared, for example, to the suggested figure of one thousand *solidi* for a dowry in the same code. It is a private system of "foster parenting" in a sense analogous to what modern states do: farming children out to persons who, for a set fee, rear them in their homes. Even the text recognizes it as a legal form of abandonment.

The same code was extraordinarily concerned with protecting

---

87. "Tertium partem pretii": probably of the child's upkeep, although possibly a sale is envisioned by the legislators.

88. The Latin (see note 89, below) is ambiguous and could even mean "nursing" in some contexts, though not here, as the text makes clear.

89. LV 4.4.3: "Si quis a parentibus acceperit infantulum nutriendum, usque ad decem annos per singulos annos singulos solidos pretii pro nutrito infante percipiat. Si vero decimum annum etatis excesserit, nihil postea mercedis addatur; quia ipse, qui nutritus est, mercedem suam suo potest conpensare servitio. Quod si hanc summam qui repetit dare noluerit, mancipium in nutrientis potestate permaneat."

the inheritance rights of children of the prosperous, whose share in parental resources was minutely regulated by law, and who could not be disinherited.[90] Kidnappers were handed over to the relatives of the child, who could kill them or sell them into slavery.[91] But, as in the case of Roman law, these measures were actually designed to protect status more than children: parents could farm their children out at a very low fee and forget them, so long as they were not made slaves; slave children became the property of those who found them (as opposed, for example, to the rule in the East by this time that all abandoned children were free); only natural children could inherit;[92] and several church councils of the period actually prescribed enslavement or separation from parents for certain classes of children.[93]

The provisions of the Visigothic Code about paying someone else to rear children may be a vestige or reflection of a widespread Germanic custom of "fostering" children, which ranged in practice from actual abandonment to merely educating children away from home. Germanic and Celtic literature makes frequent reference to the placing of offspring in the household of a friend or relative to be trained or reared until adulthood (usually somewhere between fourteen and seventeen).[94] In some cases the parents remained in close

90. Except for violence against parents or grandparents. See LV 4.5.1–7. Many provisions of Visigothic law ostensibly designed to protect children (e.g., parents and grandparents were forbidden to dispose of property without consideration of natural heirs; the wife's ability to bequeath her dowry was circumscribed; no more than one-third of an estate could go to one child) may, ironically, have contributed to abandonment, since estates were inevitably greatly reduced by a system of shared inheritance. Even though one-third of the estate could be set aside for a preferred child, for instance, his total share would be considerably enhanced by having fewer rather than more siblings, since he would also get an equal share of the remaining two-thirds. Female children were allotted equal shares with males.

91. 7.3.3: "De ingenuorum filiis plagiatis."

92. 4.5.4: "De filiis de diversis parentibus . . ." This law was clearly aimed at stepchildren, not adoptees, but affected the latter as well.

93. E.g., IV Toledo (A.D. 633), canon 60, which instructed that Jewish children be taken away from their parents and given to Christians, or IX Toledo, canon 10 (A.D. 655) (both in *Concilios*, pp. 212, 302–3, respectively), which prescribed enslavement for the children of priests—a common way of punishing the father through the child.

94. "Fostering" often involved sending children to live in wealthier or more powerful households—a means of cementing alliances with superiors for the parents and of keeping watch over potential enemies for the fosterer: Bathilde, the

touch, even visiting the child; in others the foster household was far away and the parents never saw their offspring again.[95] In either case, "abandonment" is itself too strong a word, since the arrangement of fostering was understood to be the proper way to discharge parental duties, and the child was brought up in a household specifically appointed by his natal family. The extant codes of the Germanic peoples and others who practiced "fostering" do not afford a clear enough view of its details to judge whether it might have obviated the need for abandonment, in limiting, for example, the number of heirs who might lay claim to a patrimony.[96] (For fostering in the High Middle Ages, see below.)

Of the early medieval codes independent of Roman law, only one makes reference to abandoned children.[97] The seventh-century laws of the Anglo-Saxon king Ine specify who gets the *wergild* of an

-----

wife of Clovis II, was nurse to a cohort of young aristocrats being reared at court (see Janet Nelson, "Queens as Jezebels: The Careers of Brunhild and Balthild in Merovingian History," in Baker, *Medieval Women*, pp. 31–78, esp. pp. 46–52). On the general issue of fostering, see M. W. Stein-Wilkeshuis, "The Juridical Position of Children in Old Icelandic Society"; Detlef Illmer, "Zum Problem der Emanzipationsgewohnheiten im Merowingischen Frankenreich"; Werner Ogris, "Das Erlöschen der väterlichen Gewalt nach deutschen Rechten des Mittelalters und der Neuzeit," in *L'Enfant* 2, pp. 417–52; Fell, *Women in Anglo-Saxon England,* pp. 81–83 (correctly concluding that too little is known on the subject to write with authority about it). See also discussion below, in chapter 9. On the age of fosterage among the Irish, see Robin Chapman Stacey, "Lawbooks and Legal Enforcement in Medieval Ireland and Wales," Ph.D. diss., Yale, 1986, pp. 43 ff. "Emancipation" of children—i.e., releasing them from the authority of the father in societies where this is of juridical importance—exhibits characteristics of abandonment (e.g., the triple "sale" of Roman sons), but is often motivated by concern for rather than neglect of the child in question.

95. See, e.g., Gregory of Tours, *History of the Franks* 5.46, 8.22, 9.38; MGH SSRRMM 4.607 (*Vita Sigiramni,* chap. 2), 5.16 (*Vita Wandregiseli,* chap. 7).

96. These laws are often a complex overlay of later Christian elements on pagan foundations, virtually impossible to distinguish at this distance; some, e.g., the Irish laws, reflect much later poetic reconstructions or commentary rather than early medieval custom. Provisions about fostering in *Ancient Laws of Ireland* [ALI], *3: Senchus Mor or Customary Law and the Book of Aicill* (Dublin, 1873), pp. 310–12, 402, 502–4, for example, are much later than the period in question.

97. Irish codes as published appear to mandate sale of children under some circumstances (e.g., Aicill, ALI 3.402–3, 540–42), but elsewhere to impose a fine for neglecting to care for a child (Senchus Mor, ibid., p. 136). However, these passages are later commentary and not necessarily reflective of early medieval legal practice or custom.

illegitimate child abandoned by his father,[98] and set fees for the maintenance of foundlings for the first three years of life (after which the rate varies according to their "prospects").[99] It is unclear who pays the fee: this may be an arrangement comparable to that of the Visigothic Code, with the child who is put out to "rear" designated conventionally as a "foundling."[100] The code also prohibits the selling of free or slave countrymen "over the sea,"[101] which might have been invoked to prevent parents from selling children into slavery.[102]

Given that all of the major Roman codes make abundant mention of abandonment and regulate it in a variety of ways, it seems odd that it appears so rarely in the contemporary law codes of the Germanic and Celtic peoples.[103] Possibly abandonment was less common among them, but if so, not necessarily because they reared

98. *The Laws of the Earliest English Kings,* sec. 27, p. 44. *Wergild* refers to fines or compensation for personal injury owed to relatives or guardians of the injured: it was the basis of conflict resolution in many Germanic and Celtic societies.

99. Ibid., sec. 26: "Be fundenes cildes fostre." "Wlite," which I have interpreted as "prospects," normally means "beauty"; Attenborough renders it "appearance" but seems to understand it as I do: see his note, p. 186.

100. Sec. 38 prescribes support for a widow, the obligation for which clearly falls on the husband's relatives, but this would not seem to apply in the case of a genuine "foundling." The ninth-century Laws of Alfred appear to regulate charges which might be brought against someone fostering a child for someone else: sec. 17 (in Attenborough, p. 75), but the context is unclear.

101. Ibid., sec. 11, p. 41.

102. Or even so intended, if children constituted a major portion of the slave trade; but this is not determinable. The Laws of Ine also prescribe the support to be given by the family of the husband when a widow is left with children: sec. 38. The tenth-century Laws of Edmund II make provision for "abandonment" of malefactors by their kin group, who thereby avoid responsibility for their actions, but this would seem to apply to adults (*The Laws of the Kings of England from Edmund to Henry I,* 1.1.1, p. 8). A tenth-century Welsh law (Haddan and Stubbs, *Councils* 1.276–77) limits the ability of an illegitimate child "born in grove and bush" to inherit when there are other heirs: the phrase might be related to the frequent abandonment of such children, but could also refer simply to clandestine birth, as it does in Scandinavian materials: see discussion of this in Ruth Mazo Karras, "Concubinage and Slavery in the Viking Age," forthcoming in *Scandinavian Studies.*

103. This is not due to any lack of attention to children or family issues, or to a low estimation of the value of offspring. The Salic Law of the sixth century imposed a much greater penalty for killing a child under twelve than over (45 *solidi* for the latter, but 600 for the former), and prescribed a special penalty for killing a baby not born or not yet named: "infra nouem noctibus" (less than that for an infant, but more than for an adult); clearly children were valuable (Texts C, H, K, and A; ed. A. Boretius [Hannover, 1962], MGH LL 1.4.1, sec. 24, pp. 89–92, and

all their children; they may have tolerated outright infanticide. The mother of St. Germain of Paris (d. 576) wanted to abort him because he was conceived too soon after the birth of another child.[104] According to Paul the Deacon, a future king of the Lombards (Lamissio) and his siblings had been tossed in a fish pond to die by their mother, a prostitute, and was rescued when King Agelmund stopped to look at the children and the baby grabbed the king's spear.[105] A more credible source is the complaint of the eighth-century English missionary to Germanic lands, Boniface, who complained that even nuns murdered illegitimate children:

> And it should be noted that another terrible wrong is implicit in that one [fornication], namely, homicide. For when these harlots, whether in the world or in convents, bear in sinfulness their ill-conceived offspring, they also for the most part kill them, not filling the churches of Christ with adopted children, but rather filling tombs with their bodies and hell with their pitiful souls.[106]

Texts D, K8, and E, ed. K. A. Eckhardt [Hannover, 1969], MGH LL 1.4.2, sec. 31, pp. 70–73, and Text S, ibid., sec. 33, p. 213). The penalty for killing a woman who can no longer bear children is one-third that for a childbearing woman: Text D, secs. 32–33, p. 72. The laws of the Alamans legislate minutely on causing a woman to have an abortion (MGH LL 1.5.1, ed. K. Lehmann [Hannover, 1885], chap. 91, p. 150), and the Lombard Laws (Liutprand 13, 129, ed. F. Bluhme [Hannover, 1869], MGH LL 4) even reprove older women who marry underage boys (probably to obtain their inheritances). The Irish code *Cáin Adamnain* (ed. and trans. Kuno Meyer, in *Anecdota Oxoniensia: Medieval and Modern Series* 12 [Oxford, 1905]) is entirely devoted to issues regarding women and children, but contains not a word about abandonment, which was clearly familiar in Irish society (see below).

104. "Pro eo quod hunc post alterum inter breve spatium concepisset in utero. . . ." Venantius Fortunatus, *Vita Germani episcopi Parisiaci,* in *Passiones vitaeque sanctorum aevi Meovingici,* ed. B. Krusch and W. Levison (Hannover, 1913–29), (MGH SSRRMM 6–7) 2.372. Also cited in Herlihy, *Medieval Households,* p. 53. K. J. Leyser (*Rule and Conflict in an Early Medieval Society: Ottonian Saxony* [London, 1979]) comments tersely: "Infanticide was not unknown even among the aristocracy" (p. 64).

105. *Historia Langobardorum,* ed. G. Waitz (Hannover, 1878), MGH SSRRLL, chap. 15, pp. 54–55. "Lamissio" is derived, Paul says, from the Lombard word "lama," which means pond. This story has fantastic elements: the mother had had seven children at once, which Paul insists is entirely possible. But "Laiamicho" is listed as the successor to Agilmund in the *Origo gentis Langobardorum,* Waitz, sec. 2, p. 3, and was doubtless a real monarch, possibly abandoned as a child, if not under these precise circumstances.

106. Haddan and Stubbs, *Councils* 3.354.

Clearly Boniface would have preferred that the women give up the children to "adoption" by abandoning them at churches, as canon law of the period required.[107]

The law of the Frisians, promulgated under Charlemagne in the ninth century (but reflecting older customs) specifically exempted mothers who killed their newborn children from the normal fines for murder,[108] and contemporary (Christian) texts state explicitly that pagan Germans did commit infanticide. The birth of yet another girl in the person of Liafburg (the mother of St. Ludger) so enraged her pagan grandmother that she sent servants to kill the child before she could take milk from her mother's breast, "because it was the custom of the pagans, that if they wished to kill a son or daughter, they would be killed before they had been given any food."[109] When the servants tried to drown her in a bucket of water, the infant clung to the side and was rescued by a woman who took her home and rubbed honey on her mouth, after which she could

---

107. An echo of such practices may also be preserved in a later, anonymous, and much less credible account of Gregory the Great's horror when the heads of more than 6,000 (probably best understood to mean "a great number of") infants were withdrawn from a fishpond, inspiring the pope to regret his decree insisting on clerical continence, which (according to the account) was the cause of the massive infanticide: *Pseudo-Udalrici epistola de continentia clericorum,* ed. L. de Heinemann (Hannover, 1891), MGH, Libelli de lite, 1, p. 257 ("cum vice quadam in vivarium suum propter pisces misisset et allata inde plus quam sex milia infantum capita videret; . . . suoque decreto prorsus dampnato. . . ."). This text is polemical and late (probably eleventh-century), but the likelihood of drowning unwanted infants is assumed, and it would hardly make its point if this were inherently improbable to its (German) readers. On the other hand, German readers would perhaps believe the Roman clergy capable of this even if it could not occur elsewhere.

108. *Lex Frisionum,* ed. Karl Freiherrn von Richthofen (Hannover, 1863), MGH LL 3, title 5, p. 663: "De hominibus qui sine compositione occidi possunt: . . . infans ab utero sublatus et enecatus a matre"; or in Karl August Eckhardt and Albrect Eckhardt, *Lex Frisionum,* MGH Fontes Iuris Germanici Antiqui (Hannover, 1982), 5.1, pp. 46–47.

109. ". . . quia sic mos erat paganorum, ut si filium aut filiam necare voluissent, absque cibo terreno necarentur": *Altfridi vita Sancti Liudgeri episcopi Mimigardefordensis,* ed. G. Pertz (Hannover, 1829), MGH SS 2, sec. 6–7, p. 406; or, better, *Altfridi vita sancti Liudgeri,* ed. W. Dickamp (Münster, 1881), vol. 4 in *Die Geschichtsquellen des Bistums Münster,* pp. 10–11. Note that Philo had described a similar attitude among Hellenized Jews. Among the Alamans the crucial determinant of whether a child was ever a legal person was whether he or she had been "alive for a while or for one hour, so that he can open his eyes and see the roof of the house and the four walls" (*Laws of the Alamans and Bavarians,* trans. Theodore Rivers [Philadelphia, 1977] 89, p. 98), but this provision appears to have been intended to resolve questions of inheritance rather than infanticide.

212 · *The Kindness of Strangers*

not be killed. The foster mother nursed the baby with milk through a horn, and the natal mother secretly supported her until the grandmother died, after which she reclaimed her daughter.[110]

The fabulous and polemical elements in these stories inspire skepticism, and even taken at face value they would only indicate that some of the Germanic peoples tolerated infanticide, a practice known in some degree in most premodern cultures. The evidence, however, does not support broader inference. Gregory of Tours, in an earlier description of the Frankish mother of a severely deformed child, indicated that it was inconceivable that mothers should kill even deformed children.[111]

There is, moreover, much evidence of abandonment among the Germanic and Celtic peoples from literary and biographical sources. Irish annals, folktales, and saints' lives[112] include almost the same

110. It is presumably on the basis of this story that Stein-Wilkeshuis ("Juridical Position," cited above, note 94) concludes that "the Frisian law . . . permitted the mothers to expose their newborn babies before they were given the first suck, but it was the grandmother who took the final decision about the child's fate" (p. 367). The law itself, cited above at note 108, makes no such reference. The story in fact only indicates that this particular grandmother was sufficiently powerful to intervene in her daughter-in-law's life, something that could happen in many societies. Moreover, *necare* is not a normal word for "expose," and it seems likely that the Frisian custom involved infanticide, as by drowning.

111. *De virtutibus Sancti Martini* 23 (ed. Bruno Krusch [Hannover, 1885], MGH SSRRMM 1.617).

112. This body of literature is extraordinarily difficult to treat chronologically because material that is clearly ancient is overlaid with accretions from later hands. Often it is impossible to separate pagan from Christian elements, or to be sure what is truly old and what is the result of archaizing. The main corpus of Irish saints' lives, for example, was composed in Latin in the eleventh and twelfth centuries, and although it clearly incorporates older material, it is almost impossible to be sure what represents ancient tales and what is the invention of the compiler. For suggestions, see Pádraig Riain, "Towards a Methodology in Early Irish Hagiography," and Charles Doherty, "Some Aspects of Hagiography as a Source for Irish Economic History," both in *Peritia* 1 (1982); and the older but still useful work of Kathleen Hughes, especially *Early Christian Ireland: Introduction to the Sources* (Ithaca, 1972), "Hagiography," pp. 217–48. Herlihy (*Medieval Households,* esp. chap. 2) treats such sources as evidence about pre-Christian Celtic society, creating for it the category "Late Barbarian Antiquity." I am less confident than he about the reliability of these sources: a text he refers to as a "biography" (p. 37) includes suckling by a wolf, and I would call it a legend, although the distinction is admittedly not easy to maintain. In the examples which follow I have tried to rely on sources whose *content* can be attributed with considerable likelihood to the period between A.D. 600 and 900, although even in these cases the possibility of later interpolation, even of important elements, cannot be ruled out, so I have used them chiefly to supplement other sources of information rather than to establish points.

range of forms and motivations for abandonment as Roman literature: children are exposed as the result of prophecy,[113] adultery,[114] incest,[115] illegitimacy,[116] and jealousy;[117] they are left in fields, in bas-

113. *Fragmentary Annals,* A.D. 615–710 (entry for 649), in S. H. O'Grady, trans. and ed., *Silva Gadelica* 2 (London, 1892) 430–31: the king of Connacht's wife abandons their daughter in response to a prophecy; a swineherd is told to kill her but cannot; he leaves her hanging on a cross outside a church, where she is found by a pious woman who rears and loves her; the king later has an affair with her. Although there are echoes of Oedipus in the story, it is unlikely that the author was familiar with that legend, and in any event parent-child incest is a common enough occurrence in life not to require specific literary inspiration.

114. "Alio tempore quidam infantulus, qui in adulterio natus est, allatus est occulte ad civitatem Rathen, et dimissus est ibi iuxta ecclesiam" (VSH 1.183). The "infantulus" grew up to be Bishop Dimma. Compare Cináet ua h'Artacáin's (tenth-century) poem on Brugh na Bóinneg, in which an adulterous child born to the king and a woman he slept with is abandoned "on the cold plain" when the woman's brother returns home and would punish her; the child is brought up by a foster father without knowing about his natal ancestry, but is eventually told, first by a soldier in the foster father's employ and then by the latter himself, in consequence of which he tries to claim an inheritance from the king: in Lucius Gwynn, "Cináed ná Hartacáin's Poem on Brugh na Bóinne," *Ériu* 7 (1914) 210–38, p. 210; translation in Françoise Le Roux, "La Courtise d'Étain. Commentaire du texte," *Celticum* 15 (Actes du Ve Colloque International d'Études Gauloises, Celtiques et Protoceltiques) (1965) 328–75.

115. Ca. 800: *The Martyrology of Oengus the Culdee,* ed. Whitley Stokes (London, 1905), p. 243. Fiachna begets Cuimmin, who is eventually king of Westminster, with his own daughter when drunk; the child is abandoned in a basket (hence, his name, which means "little basket") on a cross. The father of St. Barr begets a child by his own daughter and exposes it: VSH 1.65. Although the child is suckled by a wolf, the writer draws a biblical analogy with Lot ("similitudine Loth, cum sua filia concubuit"). The story of Rome's founding was, however, clearly known in Ireland by this time; the "Annals of Tigernach" (before 1088) include an account of the founding of Rome: see Whitley Stokes, "The Annals of Tigernach," *Revue Celtique* 16 (1895) 374–410, p. 396.

116. *Annales of Ireland. Three Fragments Copied from Ancient Sources by Dubhaltach Mac Firbisigh,* ed. John O'Donovan (Dublin, 1860), pp. 25 ff.: a woman given to a convent has an illegitimate baby (Acdh Allan) and gives him to two women to drown; one rears him instead; the mother later recognizes him and conveys him to the father, Ferghal.

117. Myles Dillon, *Early Irish Literature* (Chicago, 1948), pp. 25 ff.; or T. P. Cross and C. H. Slover, *Ancient Irish Tales* (New York, 1936), pp. 93–126: a child by a former wife is ordered killed by a new one, but the baby laughs and the men ordered to do it cannot bring themselves to perform the deed; in another version (see Whitley Stokes, "The Destruction of Dá Derga's Hostel," *Revue Celtique* 22 [1901], pp. 9–61, esp. pp. 19 ff.) the father orders the daughter killed and slaves who prove unable to do so then bring her up; she is therefore called "Mess Buachalla" ("cowherd's foster child"). The great fifth-century hero Niall of the

kets, hung on crosses, or "thrown at churches";[118] fathers abandon, as do mothers and servants; the wealthy and powerful abandon,[119] as well as the ordinary and poor. In the *Life of Senán,* St. Patrick predicts that in times of famine fathers will sell their sons and daughters to see that they will be fed;[120] but St. Brigit's father sold her simply because he was displeased with her,[121] and the *Annals of Ulster* record sales of children to save the parents.[122]

The English author of *Beowulf* believed that Scyld, the founder of the Danish royal line, had been exposed in a boat as a child—the ubiquitous founding foundling—and an eighth-century Anglo-Saxon riddle poignantly describes the rescue of an exposed child:[123]

Nine Hostages was alleged by the opening of the eleventh century to have been exposed under circumstances somewhat reminiscent of Hagar and Ishmael: his mother was a secondary wife of an Irish king, and the king's first wife was intensely jealous of her, so when she bore a son neither she nor anyone else dared to rear it. Finally Torna the great poet took the child home. All written versions of the legend are eleventh-century or later (e.g., in Cross and Slover, "The Adventures of the Sons of Eochaid Mugmedon," pp. 508–13), but it is possible that the story had existed in oral form long before this, even though it is not historically "accurate."

118. "Qui iectant infantes super aecclessiam . . ." *The Book of the Angel,* ed. Whitley Stokes, in *The Tripartite Life of Patrick with Other Documents Relating to that Saint* (London, 1887), p. 355; other modes in material cited in preceding and following notes.

119. In the "Vita sancti Albei episcopi" (*Vitae sanctorum Hiberniae ex codice olim salmanticensi nunc brusellensi,* ed. W. W. Heist [Brussels, 1966] [Subsidia Hagiographica, 28], p. 119), for example, a king exposes a baby. Herlihy, oddly, cites this passage (*Medieval Households,* p. 37), but claims on the same page that only the "fallen" expose their children.

120. *Anecdota Oxoniensia: Lives of Saints from the Book of Lismore,* ed. and trans. Whitley Stokes (Oxford, 1890), pp. 56, 203.

121. Ibid., pp. 187–88.

122. Ed. and trans. Seán Mac Airt and Gearóid Mac Niocaill, 1 (Dublin, 1983), pp. 404–5, *sub anno* 965.

123. *Beowulf,* lines 6–7 and 45–46:

. . . syððan ærest wearð
feasceaft funden;

þe hine æt frumsceafte forð onsendon
æenne ofer yðe umborwesende.

In Edwin Morgan's translation: ". . . he who had been found long since as a waif" and "the men who cast him at his life's beginning / A child out over the waves alone" (Berkeley, 1962), pp. 1 and 2. For the riddle, see *A Choice of Anglo-Saxon Verse,* ed. and trans. Richard Hamer (London, 1970), pp. 98–99 (from which the following lines are quoted), or *The Exeter Book,* ed. G. P. Krapp and E. V. K. Dobbie (New York, 1936), no. 9.

Me in those days my father and my mother
Gave up as dead. . . .
. . . Then a loyal kinswoman
Wrapped me in clothes and kept and cherished me,
. . . As kindly as she did for her own children,
Until . . . in her care
I became mighty-hearted among those
Who were no kin of mine.

(The answer to the riddle is the cuckoo: an indication that not only
the abandoning of children but the related zoological lore was
known among early medieval denizens of England.)

St. Bathilde was sold as a child in the mid-seventh century
and purchased (at about age eleven) by the mayor of the palace of
Neustria. Nonetheless, she married a king, Clovis II.[124] She subsequently persuaded her husband to take measures to prevent the
Frankish people from "desiring the death of their children,"[125] and
also prohibited the sale of Franks to non-Christians or foreigners of
any sort. Significantly, when she actually rescued some of those
sold, they were children, whom she then gave to monasteries to
rear.[126] But in the next century Frankish children were still being sold
in Italy;[127] and still later, Bede considered it likely that English chil-

---

124. *Vita Balthildis,* chap. 2, ed. in MGH SSRRMM, 2 (ed. B. Krusch, Hannover, 1888) 475–508. The "A" version is believed by the editor to be contemporary; the "B" version is a much later reworking. For modern commentary, see
Nelson, "Queens as Jezebels," pp. 46–52. Nelson's view of Bathilde's success is
rather odd: she argues that the mayor of the palace would not have married
her because she was a commoner (pp. 46–47), but does not account for Clovis's
doing so.

125. "Ordinavit etiam . . . ut et alia pessima consuetudo cessaret, pro qua
multo plures homines filios suos magis mori quam nutrire optabant." The phrase
could mean that the parents actually killed their children, but it suggests that they
allowed them to die, i.e., exposed them. The reason for this was a burdensome tax,
which Bathilde moderated or abolished.

126. Ibid., chap. 9: "Dato etiam justae remunerationis pretio plurimos cap-
tivos redimi praecepit, et quosdam liberos relaxavit, quosdam vero cum religionis
habitu sub regula in monasteria transmisit. Praecipue autem de gente sua viros et
puellas, quas ipsa nutrierat, . . . coenobialem vitam ducere instituit."

127. Ermedruda sells "a boy named Satrelano," "natzonem Gallia," in Milan
in 725 for 12 *solidi* (L. Schiaparelli, *Codice diplomatico longobardo* 1 [Rome, 1929],
pp. 126–28). She appears to have inherited the boy from her father ("professa est
quod ei de paterna successione aduenessit"); the provision regarding any claim
which might arise against the sale is not unusual, but could be particularly appropriate in the case of children, to prevent reclaiming by parents.

dren were sold in the markets of Rome, at least in the time of Pope Gregory: according to Bede, Gregory's seeing beautiful English boys for sale and learning from the dealers that they were pagan inspired him to dispatch St. Augustine to convert their people.[128] Whether or not the story is true, it is striking that Bede (himself given to religious life at age seven by his relatives) thought the Roman pontiff's chief concern on finding boys for sale in the markets of Rome would be the religious status of their homeland rather than their plight as slaves.[129] Slavers, of course, might have captured them,[130] but parental sales were also often involved. Pope Hadrian I wrote to Charlemagne in 776 in an effort to stop Italians from selling "servants" (*mancipia*) to the "unspeakable" Greeks. Although the pontiff seems reticent about saying so directly, his wording strongly implies that many if not all of those sold were Italian children.[131]

128. *Historia ecclesiastica* 2.1. The anonymous *Vita antiquissima* of Whitby (chap. 9) has full-grown men visiting Rome as the inspiration for Augustine's mission.

129. In a later German retelling of this incident Gregory is depicted as disturbed by the sale ("des was sin leit manicvalt, daz man sie verdoufte also"), although even here he neither says nor does anything to prevent it (*Das Passional: Eine Legenden-Sammlung des dreizehnten Jahrhunderts,* ed. Karl Köpke [Bibliothek der gesammten deutschen National-Literatur, 32], [Amsterdam, 1966], p. 194).

130. Saints Willibrord, Anskar, and Rimbert are mentioned as ransoming boys from the Danes: see Ruth Mazo Karras, *Slavery and Society in Medieval Scandinavia;* also David Pelteret, "Slave Raiding and Slave Trading in Early England," *Anglo-Saxon England* 9 (1981) 99–114. Agobard mentions infant slaves brought to Spain by Jews, but claims they had been stolen: Epistle 7 (MGH, *Epistulae Karolini aevi* 3.185).

131. "Sed in litoraria Langobardorum semper navigaverunt necdicendi Greci et exinde emebant ipsa familia et amicitia cum ipsis Langobardis fecerunt et per eosdem Langobardos ipsa suscipiebant mancipia. . . . Sed a Langobardis, ut praefati sumus, plura familia venundata sunt, dum famis inopia eos constringebat" (*Epistolae Merowingici et Karolini aevi* 1 [Berlin, 1892] [MGH, Epp. 3], 59, pp. 584–85). *Familia* did not, of course, mean "family" in the modern sense, and could refer to household slaves, but it could also mean "relatives," and seems almost certain to have this sense here. Although it is possible that Hadrian's antipathy to the "unspeakable Greeks" was so great that he would have objected even to selling them slaves of foreign origin, it is much more likely that he objects to the selling of Lombards, and it is difficult to imagine whom persons "driven by the force of hunger" would have sold except their children: they could hardly have been wealthy slaveholders. The 33rd Novel of Valentinian (and Novel 3.11 in the *Lex romana Visigothorum;* see above) allowing the sale of children by parents motivated by "necessity" specifically prohibits sale to "barbarians" or for export (*ad transmarina*). The Pactum Sicardi of 836 between Naples and the Lombard prince Sicardo prohibited the buying of any Lombards or selling them overseas, presumably allowing

Ninth-century chronicles of Languedoc imply no disapproval in relating that Spanish Christians and Jews sold their offspring into slavery after the economic disruptions of the Muslim invasion.[132]

A form-letter from the eighth century, written near Tours in much better Latin than its earlier Angevin counterpart (above), records the finding of a newborn infant in a church by the *matricularii*—officials in charge of the poor—and their effort to locate his parents "for three days or more,"[133] after which they name him and give him to someone "to bring up . . . so that he might retain him according to the law in his service and for his comfort."[134] For this they receive a price.[135] They close the letter citing, by name, the Theodosian Code as requiring that a parent or owner who wishes to reclaim an abandoned child must repay the *nutritor* the price or provide a servant in his place. While this may have constituted a guarantee of some sort to the purchaser that he would not lose his investment altogether, it is a considerable retreat from the guarantees offered in the sixth century to the rescuers of such children; it also suggests the presumption that abandoned children would be reared as servants.[136]

More or less the same practice, recognized in the fifth century by the councils of Vaison and Arles, must have been known in many areas of continental Europe. Carolingian legislation included the provisions of the latter synod,[137] and the ninth-century life of

---

sale of Lombards within the peninsula, as is indicated in other sources (e.g., Cassiodorus, above): G. Padelletti, *Fontes iuris italici medii aevi* (Turin, 1877), pp. 318–24, trans. in Lopez, *Medieval Trade*, no. 7, p. 34.

132. "Christianos in Ispania et Judeos in tantum tributa exigendo oppressit, ut filios et filias suas venderent. . . ." *Annales Anianenses,* ed. C. DeVic and J. Vaissete, *Histoire générale de Languedoc* (Toulouse, 1875), 2, Chronique 1, p. 9; cf. *Annals of Uzès,* ibid., Chronique 7, p. 27: "Christianos & Judeos tantis tributis oppressit ut liberos suos, ut mancipia venderent." The second is probably dependent on the first, and neither may be factual, but it is the attitude which is of most interest here.

133. A substantial reduction from the ten days required by Vaison.

134. "Ad nutriendum dedimus, . . . ipsum in suis servitiis ac solatiis iuxta legis ordinem retineat."

135. "Pro quo pretium accepimus, in quod nobis bene conplacuit, valentem soledos tantos."

136. *Formulae Turonenses* 11 (*Formulae,* p. 141). The last portion is a paraphrase of TC 5.10.1 and the *Lex romana Visigothorum* 5.8.1.

137. Sec. 144 of Book 6 of the "Capitula legis divinae" by Étienne Baluze (*Capitularia regum Francorum* 1 [Paris, 1677], p. 947, and better edited by George Pertz in MGH LL 2 [Hannover, 1837], 2.80 [2.6.144]). Note that sec. 4 of the same collection repeats Exodus 21 on selling a daughter into servitude.

St. Goar describes almost the exact same circumstances in Trier, in northern Germany:

> For it was then the custom at Trier that when a woman bore a child whose parents did not wish to be known, or whom they [she?] could not afford to rear because of poverty, she would expose the newborn infant in a certain marble basin designated for this . . . and when the exposed child was found, there would be someone who, moved by pity, would take him and rear him. If, as sometimes happens, the wardens or *matricularii* of the church took the child, they would ask among the people if someone wished to bring him up and have him for his or her own, and when someone would come forward for this, the abandoned child would be taken to the bishop, and by his authority the right to bring up and retain the infant would be assigned to the person who had accepted him from the *matricularii*.[138]

This description provides a useful example of one of the investigative difficulties presented by early medieval sources. It is thoroughly credible: it matches almost perfectly a variety of evidence from other times and places (with which the author was probably not familiar);[139] only the element of money changing hands is missing, and this could be either a local variation or a pious suppression on the part of the biographer of St. Goar. But it is introduced as background to an incident which is much less easy to believe: to test St. Goar, the bishop of Trier has a three-day-old exposed child brought before him and asks him if he can cause the child to indicate who his parents were. The saint is embarrassed, but at length does so, and the child reveals that the bishop himself is his father. The humorous and miraculous aspects of the story raise some doubts about the author's reliability, but it is probably wisest to judge each element of his report on its own merits: that he wished to believe and repeat something wonderful about St. Goar does not necessarily mean he could not accurately describe the quotidian reality of abandonment.

The less credible portions of the account do at least underline a probable cause of abandonment not mentioned elsewhere: the bishop of Trier, himself thus exposed, promises to do penance for

---

138. *De vita et miraculis sancti Goaris* 20 (PL 121.649).

139. On the *matricularii*, for example, see the contemporary testimony of Hincmar of Reims, PL 125.779, 797, 802.

seven years. This is presumably for episcopal fornication, not for child abandonment itself. The church played a major role in receiving and distributing exposed children, but in none of the conciliar edicts or clerical statements on the subject is there any indication that abandonment was itself morally wrong.[140] This is not surprising in view of patristic attitudes, although there was variation in Christian morality from place to place and time to time. By the sixth and seventh centuries, handbooks of punishment for sins, called penitentials, were circulating in Europe and provided guidance to confessors on what was sinful and how severely it should be punished. Scholars disagree substantially on the extent to which these manuals, whose textual histories are unusually convoluted and uncertain, represent accurately the moral views of the clergy or their parishioners. They often contradict each other and sometimes themselves; they vary extravagantly in their assessment of moral gravity of the same offense; and they were repeatedly condemned by councils for errors and unreliability.[141]

But they supply, at the least, some indication of the moral viewpoint of their compilers, Christian clerics of education and possibly some influence. One of the earliest of the penitentials states explic-

140. Isidore of Seville in his *Etymologies* (5.28.33) says that the "cruelest" ways to kill are drowning, burning, freezing, starving, and exposing to dogs or wild animals. The last could be a reference to abandonment in the spirit of the early fathers, but it seems more likely that it refers to execution of adults, which had sometimes been accomplished in the Roman world by throwing victims to dogs or wild animals. The next section of his work, for example, describes the legendary Roman punishment for parricide: sewing the criminal into a sack with a monkey, a rooster, and a snake and throwing the sack into the sea. (Cf. TC 9.15.1.)

141. See Raoul Manselli, "Vie familiale et éthique sexuelle dans les pénitentiels," in *Famille et parenté dans l'occident médiévale,* ed. G. Duby and J. LeGoff (Rome, 1977), pp. 363–78; Boswell, *Christianity,* pp. 180–83; Allen Frantzen, "The Tradition of Penitentials in Anglo-Saxon England," in *Anglo-Saxon England* 11 (1983) 23–56; idem, *The Literature of Penance in Anglo-Saxon England* (New Brunswick, N.J., 1983); Pierre Payer, *Sex and the Penitentials;* and James Brundage, *Law, Sex, and Christian Society in Medieval Europe* (Chicago, 1987), each with bibliography. Payer acknowledges the institutional church's hostility to and deprecation of penitentials (pp. 58–59), but believes nonetheless that they are a useful guide to early medieval popular morality. Brundage also views them somewhat uncritically, although his account of their import and contents is extremely detailed and learned. Frantzen tends to avoid the hard question of their historical impact and to focus on the texts themselves, whose difficulties remain substantial. For the most recent technical information about penitentials, see, in fact, Allen Frantzen, *Mise à Jour du C. Vogel, Les "Libri Paenitentiales."*

itly that a father "driven by necessity" may without sin sell his son into slavery, although the age up to which this is permitted and the length of servitude are muddled in the textual tradition.[142] An eighth-century collection declares that "a woman who exposes [*projicit*] her unwanted child because she has been raped by an enemy or is unable to nourish and sustain [him], is not to be blamed, but she should nevertheless do penance for three weeks."[143] This is a strikingly understanding attitude, considering that the same penitential imposes a penance of five years on women who place babies on roofs merely "to cure them"—apparently a folk remedy—and that in contemporary collections the penance for infanticide is fifteen years.[144] An "Irish canon" stipulates that children abandoned in a church—the usual mode in most of Christendom[145]—become its slaves, but also prescribes a seven-year penance (for whom?) if the child is "fostered" (for money) by the church and is allowed to die through negligence. It adds that "some people believe" that this

---

142. *Penitential of Theodore* (seventh century) 2.13.1: "Pater filium suum necessitate coactus potestaem habet tradere in servitium XIV annos; deinde sine voluntate filii licentiam non habet." H. J. Schmitz, *Die Bussbücher und die Bussdisciplin der Kirche* 1.548; cf. 2.579: "Pater filium (suum) necessitate coactus potestatem habet tradere in (servitium VII) servitio (XIV) septem annos (nam). Deinde sine voluntate filii licentiam tradendi non habet" (parens. in Schmitz). Cf. also Haddan and Stubbs 3.202: "Pater filium suum necessitate coactus potestatem habet tradere in servitutem VII annorum . . ."; and the English translation in McNeill and Gamer, *Medieval Handbooks*, p. 211.

143. *Poenitentiale Valicellanum* 1.40, in Schmitz, 1.285; cf. *Poenitentiale Casinense* (ibid. 1.429): "Si quae mulier ab hoste rapta infantem invito projicit, III ebdomandibus poeniteat." The textual history of *Valicellanum* is complex; in addition to the discussion in Payer, now see Günter Hägele, *Das Paenitentiale Vallicellianum, 1: Ein oberitalienischer Zweig der frühmittelalterlichen kontinentalen Bussbücher: Überlieferung, Verbreitung, und Quellen* (Sigmaringen, 1984).

144. *Valicellanum* 1.92: "Si quae mulier infantem suum super tectum aut in fornacem ponit et vult sanare eum, V annos peniteat" (Schmitz, 1.316); *Casinense* (57) prescribes ten years: "Si quae mulier filium suum aut filiam suam supra tectum aut in fornacem aut supra puteum vel ad parietem aut ubiqunque pro sanitate transposuerit, X annos peniteat" (Schmitz, 1.412). Note that this provision is more common than rulings on abandonment, and also occurs in the Penitential of Egbert (Schmitz, 1.581). Schmitz equates it with the sixty-fifth canon of the council held in the palace of Trull (discussed above, chapter 3), but the connection seems dubious. For infanticide, see, e.g., *Penitential of Theodore* 1.14.25 (McNeill and Gamer, p. 197), which prescribes a penance of fifteen years; 1.14.26, a penance of seven years for a "poor woman"; and 1.14.29, a penance of one year if a child dies of neglect before baptism up to age one, three years up to age three.

145. And mentioned in the Irish *Book of the Angel:* see note 118, above.

penalty ought to apply to persons who abandon children, but this remark refers to the harm they do the church by burdening it with children—not to their dereliction of parental duty.[146] Another collection punishes those who abandon infants in a church where bishops are buried or present: again, the issue appears to be the dignity of episcopal churches rather than the ethics of parenting.[147] Only a late Spanish penitential of little influence castigates abandonment

146. Hermann Wasserschleben, *Die Irische Kanonensammlung* (Leipzig, 1885), 42.24. This section deals not with family morality, but with sacred places, and the issue is apparently more the respect owed churches than proper relations between parents and children. Cf. following note, and, on "fostering" in this sense see above for secular parallels, and below for similar ecclesiastical practices. Kathleen Hughes (*Early Christian Ireland,* p. 78) interprets these passages together: "The canons lay down penalties for those who abandon children on the Church without the knowledge of the abbot—if the parents give a fee for fostering the child he is to be brought up as their son, if not he is to be a slave of the church." I do not find this much information in the text, which is her only source. The collection has as much connection with Brittany as Ireland, and Bieler (*The Irish Penitentials, passim,* but esp. p. 23) does not consider it an Irish penitential, although it clearly incorporates much Irish material, and both these canons are introduced as originating from an "Irish synod" (*Synodus Hibernensis*). See further in Hughes, as cited, and Frantzen, *Mise à Jour,* p. 41, notes.

147. "Quicumque infantes in ecclesia Dei projiciunt ignorante abbate, si in ea episcopi sunt sepulti, aut praesentes sint, III annis et dimidio peniteant. Si vero homicidium in ea fecerint, VII annis peniteant. Unde hoc sumptum est, quod episcopus VII gradus habet et ecclesia septiformis est, si vero non habuerint episcopos, sed parva sit ecclesia, anno et dimidio peniteant" (Wasserschleben, 42.22, p. 168; cf. McNeill and Gamer, p. 141). Genuine Irish canons often confuse issues of purity with ethical issues: the Penitential of Cummean prescribes abstinence, presumably from conjugal relations, for thirty-three days after the birth of a son and sixty-six after the birth of a daughter (2.31; McNeill and Gamer, p. 105). The numbers are derived from Leviticus 12:4–5, but in Jewish law they applied to the woman's purification, not the husband's abstinence. The same penitential (2.32–33; McNeill and Gamer, p. 105) prescribes a penance of three years for a man who allows his child to die through neglect without baptism, but, especially in view of sec. 33 (about clerics who do not accept the child, presumably for baptism), the moral issue appears to be the failure to baptize rather than the neglect itself—although being directly responsible for the death of a child was always wrong in the eyes of the church. Provisions against neglecting to baptize children are common in ecclesiastical legislation (see, e.g., J. Pérez de Urbel and L. Vázqez de Parga, "Un nuevo penitencial español," *Anuario de historia del derecho español* 14 [1942] 5–32, p. 31, 13.162—"Si quis christianus abuerit filium et sine baptismare mortuus fuerit. Parentes eius agant penitentiam annos III"), but do not necessarily reflect attitudes toward abandonment in general. By the High Middle Ages a sort of folk code had been established about placing salt on exposed children to indicate whether they had been baptized or not.

per se, and it is simply a reiteration of the Synod of Gangra's ruling about deserting children in the name of religious service.[148]

The first of the authoritative collections of canonical decrees to influence the whole Western church was compiled by Regino of Prüm around 906. It imposes severe penalties for infanticide, for accidental suffocation of infants by parents, and even for the possibility of negligence when a child dies and the parents may not have done everything possible to prevent it.[149] It also includes four canons regarding abandonment.[150] Three of these are paraphrases of Roman legal principles, and stipulate that (1) those who pick up abandoned children may rear them as free or slave, as they wish; (2) lords or owners may not reclaim children abandoned with their knowledge; but (3) a parent or lord may reclaim if he replaces the child with "a servant of comparable value" or pays the finder the value of the child.[151] The first of these, like provisions of Christian Roman law in the Middle East (discussed above), ignores later imperial legislation denying finders the right to keep freeborn children as slaves

148. "Si quis dereliquerit [laiscaret] proprios filios, et non eos alat [pasceret gobernaret], vel filii parentes deseruerint in occasione [algodre] cultus [collitura de dio], hoc iustum esse [sedere] iudicantes, anathema sint" (*Penitential of Silos* 11, ed. R. Menendez Pidal, *Glosas silenses,* in *Orígenes del español: Estado lingüístico de la Península Iberica hasta el siglo XI* [Madrid, 1964], p. 20; or in Francisco de Berganza, *Antiguedades de España* [Madrid, 1721] 2.670; cf. trans. McNeill and Gamer, pp. 288–89). This penitential is probably ninth-century (see Frantzen, *Mise à Jour,* p. 33; cf. McNeill and Gamer, pp. 285–86). The wording is only a slight variation on the decree of Gangra (noted above) and *anathema* is used in the collection only in quotations from ancient councils.

149. *De synodalibus causes et disciplinis ecclesiasticis,* ed. F. Wasserschleben (Leipzig, 1840) 2.60–67 (pp. 237–41).

150. Possibly five: the provision of 2.5.6 (p. 209) is ambiguous, and may apply to either infanticide or abandonment: "Est aliqua femina, quae in fornicatione concipiens, times, ne manifestaretur, infantem proprium aut in aquam proiecerit, aut in terra occultaverit, quod morth dicunt?" Tossing in water or "hiding" an infant could be modes of abandonment rather than infanticide, or the question of whether the child survived or not might be irrelevant. Surrounding canons deal with killing or murder.

151. Ibid. 69, 70, 71, respectively, all cited as being from the Theodosian Code, although each is a paraphrase. Note that (2), prohibiting lords (*domini*) and owners from reclaiming, seems to contradict (3), allowing lords and parents to do so. This may be the result of haphazard selection—most of the canonical collections include inconsistencies and contradictions—although Regino may have understood (3) to apply to lords when the children had been abandoned without their knowledge.

and invokes the earlier ruling of Constantine. This may be because its principles suited the needs of the time, or because Constantine was seen as the archetypal Christian lawgiver. But all three of the canons seem consistent with the picture of early medieval practice presented in other sources: widespread abandonment, probably motivated chiefly by poverty, was regarded as morally neutral, and there was general acknowledgment throughout Christian society of the superior claim of the finder.

The remaining entry on the subject is an exhortation to the mothers of illegitimate children to leave them at the doors of churches.

> We advise all priests to announce publicly to their congregations that if any woman should conceive and give birth as the result of a clandestine affair, she must not kill her son or daughter . . . but should have the baby carried to the doors of the church and left there, so that it can be brought to the priest in the morning and taken in and brought up by some one of the faithful. She will thus avoid being guilty of murder and, even worse, of parricide.[152]

Concerning the fact and mode of abandonment in the early Middle Ages, and of official civil and ecclesiastical attitudes toward it, there is thus abundant information. What happened to the children after they were sold or picked up or placed by church officials is less clear. In Germanic lore, as in pagan mythology and Christian scripture, all usually turns out happily: Lamissio is reared as the *alumnus* of King Agelmund and becomes his heir, succeeding to the throne of the Lombards.[153] Scyld becomes a great king, and is returned at his death to the sea on which he was cast as a child. But reality is much harder to judge. Bathilde becomes a queen through marriage, and herself watches out for the children in her realm.[154] Some proportion of children may have been adopted, formally

152. Ibid., 68. Regino identifies this as "Ex concilio Rotomagensi," but no such canon is known from any council at Rouen (or elsewhere). Aside from the concentration on adultery, however, it is similar to most early medieval ecclesiastical legislation on the subject.

153. Paul refers to him as *alumnus suus* at 1.17 (ed. Waitz, p. 56), and the *Origo gentis* describes him as "ex genere Gugingus," just as it does Agelmund (2.3).

154. "Viduis, orphanis et pupillis subsidia vitae ministrabat . . ." (*Vita Balthildis* 1.4).

among the upper classes and informally by the poor. Evidence of
such adoption survives in law, in specific records and in general *formulae.*[155] Some may have been reared by friends;[156] some survived on

155. Three adopted children, for example, are made heirs in a charter of 737
from Lucca (Schiaparelli, *Codice* 62, 1.194–96). No particulars are provided about
the circumstances, although it seems clear that the father is known but no longer
involved with the children. A ninth-century formula for adopting unrelated persons as heirs ("Si quis extranio homine in loco filiorum adoptaverit") is preserved
among the *Formulae Turonenses* (MGH *Formulae*) 13, pp. 83–84; it details obligations for the "son" to care for the "father" in his old age, strongly suggesting an
alumnus-guardian relationship. Cf. "Epistula qualiter extraneis in loco filiis adob-
tetur," in *Collectio Flaviniacensis* 23, ibid., p. 478; and 21 in *Formularum codicis S.
Emmeranii fragmenta,* pp. 466–67, also adoption. Although it is not certain that
such adoptions involved abandoned children, this seems the most likely interpretation: when relatives are involved this is usually specified, even in form letters (e.g.,
a grandfather adopting grandchildren as heirs: *Marculfi formularum* 2.10, ibid.,
pp. 81–82; *Formulae Turonenses* 22, p. 147; *Formulae salicae Lindenbrogianae* 12,
pp. 274–75; and *Collectio Flaviniacensis* 29, p. 478; or by a stranger but through arrangement with the natural father: 23, pp. 147–48; or for orphans: 24, pp. 148–49).
Although the distinctions in imperial law between *adrogatio* and *adoptio* were preserved in areas of medieval Europe with a strong tradition of Roman law (they are
repeated, e.g., in the *Lex romana Visigothorum* [ed. Haenel, p. 320]), they were
modified or misunderstood in many places, and terminology devoid of context
cannot be pressed. Early medieval rulers sometimes adopted presumptive successors to strengthen their claim on the throne or lands associated with it (especially Visigothic rulers: see, e.g., Roger Collins, "Julian of Toledo and the Royal
Succession in Late Seventh-Century Spain"). On Merovingian adoption, see Karl
Eckhardt, "Adoption," *Studia merovingica: Bibliotheca rerum historicarum* 11 (Aalen,
1975) 240–61. At the end of the tenth century Duke Henry the Great of Burgundy
adopted Otto William when he married his mother: see Maurice Chaume, *Les origines du Duché de Bourgogne* (Dijon, 1925–27) 1.464–65, 472–73, and Neithard
Bulst, *Untersuchungen zu den Klosterreformen Wilhelms von Dijon (962–1031)* (Bonn,
1973), pp. 23–24. (I am grateful to Patrick Geary for bringing this to my notice.)

156. In the early medieval tale of Apollonius of Tyre (possibly based on late
antique models), a father who has lost his wife gives his infant daughter to friends,
even though the girl's grandfather is a king. The child is reared in ignorance of her
true identity, and thinks her foster parents are her natal parents until she is fourteen, when her nurse tells her the truth (chap. 29). This is not exactly abandonment, since the father declares that he will not cut his beard or fingernails until she
has married (chap. 28), and obviously intends to remain involved with her upbringing. Elements of classic abandonment stories predominate, however: jealousy
involving natural children, a brothel scene, incest. Recent editions are Franz
Waiblinger, *Historia Apollonii regis Tyri* (Munich, 1978), and G. A. A. Kortekaas,
*Historia Apollonii Regis Tyri: Prolegomena, Text Edition of the Two Principal Latin Re-
censions, Bibliography, Indices and Appendices* (Groningen, 1984); for a critical study,
see Elizabeth Frances Archibald, "Apollonius of Tyre in the Middle Ages and the
Renaissance," Ph.D. diss., Yale, 1984. In lieu of an English translation, Perry (*Ancient Romances*) provides an extended summary in an appendix.

their own.[157] Some may have been maintained in hostels for the poor or ill, although this appears to be primarily a development of a later epoch.[158] But most likely the majority were brought up as servants: in the severely depressed economy of the early Middle Ages, having few children was a blessing for the poor, even in the countryside, since partible inheritance prevailed in most of Europe and made many heirs a threat to family lands. The childless rich may have adopted foundlings, but fertile couples of all classes employed them as domestics, and the church itself regarded them as slaves in many areas. This makes them extremely difficult to locate in documents of the period after the abandonment itself, because most of the population of Europe at the time was servile, and because the terms for "children," "servant," and "slave" are interchangeable.[159] This semantic uncertainty reflects real social fluidity and confusion: there

157. The tenth-century abbot John of Saint Arnulf in Metz was abandoned by his mother when his father died and she remarried: he took charge of his younger siblings and maintained the household (PL 137.247–48).

158. Almost all previous writers (e.g., Leclercq [1306]; Semichon, p. 69; Riché, "Problèmes," p. 41; Antonio Pertile, *Storia del diritto italiano* 5 [Torino, 1892], pp. 586–87; Luigi Passerini, *Storia degli stabilimenti di beneficenza e d'istru-zione elementare gratuita della città di Firenze* [Florence, 1853], p. 659; Isaac Abt and Arthur Garrison, *A History of Pediatrics* [Philadelphia, 1965], p. 58; Trexler, "Infanticide in Florence," p. 99) have accepted as genuine a foundation charter of 787 for a foundling home in Milan published in L. Muratori, *Antiquitates italicae medii aevi* (Milan, 1740) 3.587, in which the archpriest Datheus, to prevent children conceived of adultery and fornication from perishing without baptism, establishes a home where they will be supported until age seven, after which they should be free to leave. The charter says the infants are currently being left in sewers and thrown in rivers. The document seems bogus to me: its Latin is manifestly of a much later date than its purported composition, and there is no other evidence of a foundling home in Milan for centuries after this. It was probably devised during the later Middle Ages to justify a claim of antiquity.

159. This general problem is discussed in the introduction. The particular difficulty of interpreting early medieval documents, even when some context is available, is well illustrated by an eighth-century letter of introduction from Boniface to Denhard for Athalhere (MGH Epp. 3: *Merowingici et Karolini aevi* 1 [Berlin, 1892] 6.99, p. 387). Athalhere is a *puer*, which might mean either "boy" or "slave," but two other facts made clear in the letter seem to militate against either interpretation: he is to be treated with every consideration and as a free man ("sicut ingenuum hominem: . . . non quasi pro servo"); and he is engaged to be married. Children were sometimes engaged, and a letter of introduction for a slave is not inconceivable, although a letter of commendation to a priest for an engaged slave would certainly be an oddity. The editor assumes he is a slave, nonetheless, apparently on the basis of *puer*. This seems especially questionable, given the last line ("ut non timeat, quod servus sit": the grammar in the letter is far from strict, but the use of the subjunctive here suggests that he is in fact not a slave). Cf. ibid.,

were few strictly defined social "systems" in Europe between the end of effective Roman government and the rise of corporate states during the High Middle Ages, and in most areas both dependence and control were established more by particular circumstance than by general rule of law.

"Servile condition" could be permanent or temporary: in early medieval law codes, being "enslaved" was a common penalty even for simple debt. It could be limited or absolute, onerous and degrading, a kind of protective custody, or largely a technicality. All of society was interrelated through personal dependency of some sort, through which almost every social class was both subordinate to and dominant over others. The idealized "feudal pyramid" of textbooks is vastly neater and better oganized than the social reality it strives to describe, but it does convey a sense of the way in which most of society would be "servile" in one sense, owing service to those above, and *served by* those below. Few people in such a society would have understood "freedom" in any sense other than being excused from particular obligations: one might be "free" of a certain tax, or from a particular military or agricultural duty, but social identity in early medieval Europe depended on interlocking personal dependencies, and "freedom" in the modern sense of personal autonomy and general social equality was not only impossible, but unsafe. Many adults who found themselves unconnected—and therefore unprotected—voluntarily "commended" themselves to the service of someone more powerful, usually accepting servitude for life in return for economic security or simple personal safety.[160]

Understanding this helps to place in perspective the fact that most abandoned children became "servile": their condition may have been in some particular way different from that of the parents who abandoned them, but it was not worse in kind or in concept, and almost no parents in early medieval Europe would have felt the horror of servitude for their offspring that freeborn Romans did. For the latter, all of the human race was divided by kind into those born free and those born unfree. For medieval Europeans there were almost infinite gradations of servitude and authority, in ordinary experience scarcely ever independent of each other, and all me-

5.11.2 (p. 204): "de pueros etiam, quos ad opera dominica per vestra ordinatione direximus. . . ."

160. See note 66, above.

diated by the more important reality of another world, in which every human is equally "free" and equally a servant: of God.[161]

161. 1 Corinthians 7:22 and Galatians 3. This is not to suggest that the concepts "free" and "unfree" had no semantic or political import. On the contrary, some basic social divisions in early medieval societies hinged on this distinction (participation in courts, liability for military service, etc.), but the facts that (1) even the free classes were obligated to "serve" those above them, and (2) the servile classes occupied varying degrees of servitude (serf, servant, slave, etc.) greatly blurred and diffused the polarity which had been so pronounced and extreme at Rome.

5

❖   ❖   ❖

A CHRISTIAN
INNOVATION:
OBLATION

THERE WAS ONE WAY of abandoning children that
dramatically altered the terms of "servitude" affecting them, and it
constitutes the most striking evolution in the history of abandonment in the West during the early Middle Ages. Religious institutions of early medieval Europe received children in a great variety of
ways, many involving abandonment in some form by parents; one
of these was called "oblation," and through it the symbolism of
abandoning childen at the doors of churches was incarnated in a
startling reality. Oblation was the donation (in Latin, *oblatio*, "offering")[1] of a child as a permanent gift to a monastery.[2] No previous
modern author has considered oblation as a form of abandonment,
although a number of medieval writers did.[3] It was unquestionably

1. *Oblatio* also occurs in monastic charters to describe gifts of land, money, or
property. (See, e.g., *Formulae visigothicae*, in MGH *Formulae*, pp. 578–80.)
2. It is thus distinguished from the schooling of children in a monastery, also
common in the Middle Ages, although initially, as noted below, the two were not
always distinguishable. For education, see Pierre Riché, *Les Écoles*, and his "L'Enfant dans la société monastique du XIIe siècle," in *Pierre Abelard, Pierre le Vénérable:
Les Courants philosophiques, littéraires et artistiques en Occident au milieu du XIIe siècle*,
Actes et mémoires du colloque international, Abbaye de Cluny, 2 au 9 juillet, 1972:
Colloques internationaux du Centre National de la Recherche Scientifique, no. 546
(Paris, 1975).
3. For medieval comments, see below; Riché ("Problèmes," p. 43) mentions
that many abandoned children ended up in monasteries, but it is not clear whether
he is thinking of oblation or some less formal circumstance. I have made the com-

much else besides, and served important purposes—both spiritual and practical—unrelated to issues of family size. These are not inherently incompatible with its utility as a means of family regulation, but they lie outside the limitations of a study of the latter. The emphasis in what follows is laid on oblation as a mode of abandonment, not because this was necessarily its primary social function, but because the relationship between the two is preeminently apposite to this study. Oblation as a purely religious phenomenon has been treated at greater length elsewhere.

The precise origins of oblation are somewhat obscure: like both Christianity and monasticism, it was apparently born in the East, but was adopted by the West and rose to greatness in its new home.[4] The putative social utility of oblation must be viewed apart from its religious function and intent, although these aspects are not mutually exclusive, and may not even be clearly distinguishable at this remove. It is not possible to know whether its relation to abandonment played some role in the origins of oblation, or whether a cus-

---

parison previously in my "*Expositio* and *Oblatio*." The standard treatment of oblation in the West has been that of M. P. Deroux, "Les Origines de l'oblature bénédictine," but it should now be supplemented by Patricia Quinn, "Benedictine Oblation" and "Benedictine Child Rearing"; and by Majke de Jong, *Kind en Klooster in de Vroege Middeleeuwen: Aspecten van de Schenking van Kinderen an Kloosters in het Frankische Rijk (500–900)* (Amsterdam, 1986) (Amsterdamse Historische Reeks, 8), to appear in English as *In Samuel's Image: Child Oblation in the Early Middle Ages (500–900)* in 1988. (Only a summary of this work was available to me as I completed the present study, and although I am aware that de Jong disagrees with my argument that oblation served social and economic purposes as well as religious ones, I cannot provide a detailed response to her criticisms without first studying her book in its final form.) For other, less comprehensive studies, see Artur Steinwenter, "Zum Problem der Kontinuität zwischen antiken und mittelalterlichen Rechtsordnungen," *Iura* 2 (1951) 15–43, pp. 36–38; D. Lentini, "Note sull' oblazione dei fanciulli nella regola di S. Benedetto," *Studia Anselmiana* 18–19 (1947) 195–225; Giles Constable, *Medieval Monasticism: A Select Bibliography* (Toronto, 1976), items 760–67; José Orlandís, "La Oblación de niños," pp. 53–70; René Metz, "L'Enfant dans le droit canonique médiévale," in *L'Enfant* 2.9–96, pp. 50–59; and Joseph Lynch, *Simoniacal Entry into Religious Life from 1000 to 1260,* p. 55, nn. 47–48. Lynch is preparing a major study of oblation, of greater chronological scope than that of either Quinn or de Jong; it has not been my aim to present here a detailed analysis of it as a religious phenomenon.

4. Quinn, "Benedictine Oblation," pp. 19–21, relates it to the inclusion of boys in the religious communities of the Therapeutae described by Philo (in *De vita contemplativa* 9).

tom that began in a purely religious context was adopted for more practical ends.

The story of Samuel, given to priestly service shortly after birth by his grateful mother, may have provided inspiration for oblation, although the idea of "giving" children "to the service of God" may be so obvious as to require no specific precedent or warrant.[5] By the turn of the fifth century it was already common to place children in monasteries, although it is not clear that these were irrevocable donations, in the classic sense of oblation, as opposed to education or a kind of holy "fostering." A work attributed to Rufinus recounts how John the Hermit instructed a man whose pregnant wife had been cured of a serious illness to rear his son to age seven, and then "give" [*tradere*] him to monks to be instructed in "holy and heavenly matters."[6] Basil discusses at some length the proper handling of children in the monastery—clearly a common feature of monastic life in his day—but recommends that their commitment to religious life not be considered permanent until they are old enough to understand virginity, which he reckons to be "beyond the age of sixteen or seventeen."[7] There were clearly large numbers of children in monasteries·in the West as well by the last decades of the fifth century, since rules of the time evince substantial concern about dealing with them.[8] Such children were not necessarily oblates: they

5. 1 Samuel [Kings] 2:11ff. Jerome invokes Samuel as precedent in his Epistle 107, and it is adduced as justification for the Bishop of Mérida's taking control of his nephew, as well as in Rabanus's long treatise on oblation, all mentioned below. Note also figure 9, in which the offering of Samuel is associated with religious sacrifice of children in general, and the sacrifice of Christ in particular. The image of the child on the altar probably evoked associations of the ceremony of oblation itself, at least among those familiar with it.

6. *Historia monachorum* 1.1.122–23 (PL 21.393): "hic nutriatur in domo tua absque ulla contaminatione Gentili septem annis; quibus peractis, trade eum monachis erudiendum sanctis et caelestibus disciplinis." This work was not composed by Rufinus: it is apparently a translation from Greek and may even postdate him.

7. *Regulae fusius tractatae* 15 (PG 31.952–57) and Letter 199 (PG 32.719). The Rule of Pachomius included references to infractions of the rule by boys living in monasteries (10.2, 46.3, 47.20, 48.5, 58.6), but it is not clear that they were oblates: they could have been present for educational purposes or have entered with parents and been allowed to leave when grown. The Rule was written in Coptic; only a Latin translation by Jerome survives: PL 23.

8. See, e.g., chaps. 17 and 18 (pp. 68–70) of the *Regula orientalis,* in Carmela Franklin et al., *Early Monastic Rules: the Rules of the Fathers and the Regula Orientalis* (Collegeville, Minn., 1982).

might have been present temporarily for educational purposes.[9] Salic
law, originally redacted during this period, contains a rather curious
prohibition of tonsuring children without the permission of their
parents, which may have been intended to forestall the professing of
children placed in monasteries for such reasons.[10]

The Rule of the Master, written in the late fifth or early sixth
century, describes the "taking up" of children of nobles[11]—apparently
in a permanent arrangement[12]—in terms much like technical
oblation, although it seems to be assumed that it is the child's decision to enter, which does not suggest donation by parents. The
Rule of St. Benedict, compiled sometime in the first half of the sixth
century, established the most widespread and detailed pattern of
monasticism in the West, and explicitly included oblation. Benedict's fifty-ninth chapter deals with "children of nobles or poor
people who are donated":

> If a noble should donate his child to God in the monastery, and
> the child should be very young, the parents themselves should
> make the formal request [sc., to become a member of the com-
> munity] we have previously described; and with the offering
> they should wrap the child's hand and the petition itself in the
> altar cloth, and thus offer him. . . .

9. Although provisions of chap. 23 (ibid., pp. 72–73) forbidding relatives
who appear at the gate to see or speak to those within might apply to parents or
relatives of oblates.

10. E.g., E Text 34.1 ("Si quis puerum sine consilio parentum suorum tonsorauerit, soledos LXII semis culpabilis iudicetur"), 34.2 ("Si uero puella sine
uoluntate parentum suorum tonsorauerit, soledos XLV culpabilis iudicetur");
D Text 35.1–2. The textual tradition of the *Lex salica* is unusually complex; it survives in many redactions of different lengths and age. All the major versions are
edited in the MGH LL; none show any significant discrepancies in this provision.
Hair was of political significance to the Franks (Gregory of Tours, *Historia Francorum* 2.41, 3.18, etc.), and it is possible that this measure is entirely secular in
import.

11. Chap. 91: "Quomodo suscipi debeat filius nobilis in monasterio." The
Regula magistri is edited in PL 88.943–1052, but the edition of A. de Vogüé, *La
règle du maître* (Paris, 1964) is preferable. On the relationship between the Rule of
the Master and that of Benedict the literature is vast; for an introduction, see David
Knowles, "The *Regula magistri*," in *Great Historical Enterprises* (New York, 1964).

12. The child's inheritance is to be given away at the time he enters, so that he
will not be tempted to return to the world: it is suggested that one-third be given to
the abbot for the poor; one-third given to the monastery itself; and one-third retained by the family.

Poorer parents should do likewise.

Those who have absolutely nothing can make a simple request and offer their child before witnesses.[13]

This chapter follows immediately a section establishing that no one who has taken monastic vows can ever leave the monastery. Whether Benedict understood the two to be related is not clear: the same word (*suscipere*) is used for entering the monastery of one's own choice and being given by parents;[14] but other contemporary Western rules follow Basil's advice that children should not be considered formally committed, or "professed," to religious life until they are old enough to choose for themselves.[15]

By the end of the century any ambiguity had been resolved: Western society decided that oblates—like abandoned children—should remain in their new homes. A council in Orléans decided this for women as early as 549, declaring excommunication for women who left monasteries "which they joined of their own accord, or to which they were given by their parents."[16] This was re-

13. There are hundreds of editions of the Rule: it can be most easily found in PL 66 and CSEL 75.

14. Ibid.: "Et si, habita secum deliberatione, promiserit se omnia custodire et cuncta sibi imperata servare, tunc suscipiatur in congregatione, sciens et lege regulae constitutum, quod ei ex illa die non liceat egredi de monasterio, nec collum excutere de sub iugo regulae, quem sub tam morosa deliberatione licuit aut excusare aut suscipere." (But *suscipere* is also a common Latin word.) J. R. Riepenhoff (*Zur Frage des Ursprungs der Verbindlichkeit des Oblateninstituts: Ein Beitrag zur Geschichte des mittelalterlichen Bildungswesen* [Münster, 1939]) believed that Benedict had not envisioned oblation as irrevocable, but this was challenged by A. Lentini, "Note sull'oblazione dei fanciulli nella Regola di S. Benedetto" (cited above, note 3), 220–25. The rule is so terse, and so little is known about Benedict, that this controversy probably cannot be settled. Cf. the summary in Lynch, *Simoniacal Entry*, p. 55 (and n. 47).

15. E.g., the rules of Cesarius, which recommend that children not even be accepted before six or seven (canon 5) and that profession be made at age of reason (canon 4; both PL 67.1108); and the rule of Aurelian, which recommends ten or twelve, apparently, as the age of profession (canon 17, PL 68.390; cf. canon 22). Other early medieval rules mentioning oblation are, e.g., that of Donatus (32, PL 87.284), of Fructuarius of Braga (6, PL 97.1115–16), and of Waldebert (24, PL 88.1070).

16. "Seu propria voluntate monasterium expetunt, seu a parentibus offeruntur. . . ." (Mansi 9.133; also in MGH *Concilia* 1.107). Here and elsewhere I translate *parentes* as "parents," because I believe this is what the writers had in mind. But the word could also mean "relatives," and the drafters may not have intended to limit the right of donating children to biological parents; compare note 54,

iterated at Mâcon in 583, where it was added that if such women married, the relationship was "fornication" (*stuprum*) and they should be denied communion up to the hour of death.[17]

In 633 the Fourth Council of Toledo applied these principles to boys as well, devoting not one but two canons to the question:

(49) Either parental desire or personal devotion can make a monk; both are binding. We deny henceforth any possibility of returning to the world for either category, and we forbid any resumption of secular life.

(55) . . . Those who have been dedicated to religious life[18] by their parents or who have devoted themselves in the absence of their parents, and who have subsequently resumed a secular existence,[19] . . . if they cannot be recalled, are to receive a sentence of excommunication as if they were apostates.[20]

Though enacted in Visigothic Spain, these measures were known and accepted in much of Europe; they became part of the great canonical collections of the High Middle Ages.[21] A contemporary monastic code, attributed to Isidore of Seville, adopted the same principle (citing the example of Samuel), and was repeated in discussions of the issue for half a millennium.[22] Moreover, they were

---

below. This canon could have been inspired by an earlier (527) provision about irrevocability in the case of boys "given over" (*manciparit*) to careers as diocesan clergy: see below, p. 252.

17. Mansi 9.935; MGH *Concilia* 1.158, canon 12: "up to the hour of death" is ambiguous in Latin ("usque ad exitum") as in English, and could mean that they can communicate at the end, or that *even* at the end they cannot. Although the wording of canon 12 is not definitively applicable to oblates ("aut parentibus suis rogantibus"), canon 19 specifically clarifies that it does apply to oblates ("Et licet priori titulo legatur definitum, quod de puellis quae se divinis cultibus, aut parentum aut voluntate sua dicaverint, debeat observari").

18. Literally, "tonsured."

19. Literally, "clothing."

20. Mansi 10.631; better edited in *Concilios,* pp. 208, 210.

21. Burchard of Worms (PL 140.793); Anselm of Lucca (PL 149.517); Ivo of Chartres (PL 161.553); cf. Peter Damian (PL 145.374).

22. *Regula monachorum* 4 (PL 103.558–59): "Anyone who has been relegated [*delegatus*] to a monastery by his parents should know that he will remain there forever. Hanna, through love of God, donated her newborn son as soon as he was weaned, and he remained in the service of the temple to which his mother con-

models for civil law: the Laws of the Visigoths shortly made it a civil crime to leave the monastery for anyone who had chosen monastic life "from the devotion of his own desire" or "who merited oblation by virtue of the piety of his parents." Anyone who did so was to be returned by force, held forever in the same monastery, and subjected to a more rigorous discipline than before.[23] The same subject came before the Tenth Council of Toledo in 656, with the same result: donated children who left were to be returned and kept. This council did, however, set one limitation on the rights of parents: they could donate children only until the age of ten, after which the child could choose for himself.[24] (Note that ten was also the age at which "fostered" children became responsible for themselves according to contemporary Iberian laws.)

By the opening of the seventh century, oblation was well established and defined.[25] Parents of any social status could donate a child of either sex, at least up to the age of ten.[26] According to both civil and ecclesiastical law, the child could never leave the monastery, and the parents took a vow never to endow the child with any property or inheritance (although they were free to make gifts to the monas-

---

signed him, and served where he was placed." This is cited not only by later monastic commentators on oblation (e.g., Smaragdus, at the opening of the ninth century, *Expositio in regulam Sancti Benedicti,* ed. A. Spannagel and P. Engelbert [Siegburg, 1974] [Corpus Consuetudinum Monasticarum, 8], p. 300), but also in canon law.

23. *Leges Visigothorum* 3.5.3, p. 161.

24. "Parentibus sane filios suos religioni contrahere non amplius quam usque ad decimum eorum aetatis annum licentia poterit esse" (Mansi 11.36–37; *Concilios,* p. 313).

25. At least in the West: although oblation was original to and common in the East, as is clear from materials cited below, it was less regulated there. The Code of Justinian had ruled (4.43.1) that children could not be transferred to the authority of anyone else by any means, including "titulo donationis," which would seem to rule out oblation, but it does not mention religious life. The council held in the palace of Trull (canon 40) prohibited monastic profession before the age of ten, which probably only affected the age of solemn vows for children in monasteries, not the ability of parents to place them there. See commentary by Balsamon and Zonaras, PG 138.652–57.

26. Western monastic rules themselves rarely set either a maximum or minimum age for oblation, but most children were apparently donated after weaning, to judge from the absence of concern in contemporary documents about obtaining wet nurses. And after puberty they would be regarded as capable of taking their own vows, so "oblation" would not be involved.

tic community).[27] The practice was common enough to elicit comment and regulation from civil codes, church councils, and most monastic rules. Was it really abandonment?

It may seem unduly cynical to assume that it was, especially since most contemporaries regarded it as a religious act; and it is certainly important to bear in mind that, whatever its relationship to abandonment, oblation served many functions in early medieval Europe. But the meaning of "religious" must be viewed subtly and in context. Safeguarding the well-being of siblings or the family unit as a whole through more traditional means of abandonment— e.g., by exposing or selling a child—might also be considered "religious" in some senses,[28] and some parents apparently regarded exposing as "religious" even in the most conventional sense of the word.[29] Indeed, by the early Middle Ages both religious and secular mythology were so imbued with the moral and religious significance of famous instances of abandonment that it would have been difficult for a parent not to associate it with religion. There is no reason why oblation could not have been a religious act on the part of the parents and still have functioned socially as a means of divesting the family of children.

One might argue that oblation is more comparable to Germanic "fostering" than to abandonment in the sense under consideration here, since it was usually not anonymous,[30] the monastery might be

27. Rule of Benedict, chap. 59; *Pauli Warnefridi diaconi Casinensis in sanctam regulam commentarium* (Monte Casino, 1880), pp. 449–50; Hildemar, *Expositio regulae ab Hildemaro tradita,* in *Vita et regula SS. P. Benedicti una cum expositione regulae a Hildemaro tradita,* ed. R. Mittermüller (Regensburg, 1880), p. 550; both discussed in M. A. Schroll, *Benedictine Monasticism as Reflected in the Warnefrid-Hildemar Commentaries on the Rule* (New York, 1941), p. 77. Smaragdus insists on this pointedly in the early ninth century, suggesting that parents divide the oblate's inheritance into three parts, of which one should go to the monastery at the time of oblation, one to the poor, and one to his siblings; there must be no temptation to return to the world to claim any worldly portion, "like a dog returning to his vomit": Hildemar, *Expositio,* pp. 300–302.

28. The word "piety," for example, now associated chiefly with devotion to the Deity or his service, originally denoted fidelity to relatives or the family unit, and during the Middle Ages *pietas* could mean either.

29. Glotz, "L'Exposition," pp. 200–201, argues that even in the ancient world parents thought of abandoned children as religious offerings, and that some of the accoutrements of exposing (vessels, clothing, etc.) had religious significance. This was certainly true in Rome (see above) and among some of the Germanic peoples.

30. In the early Middle Ages it was almost always expected to take place *coram testibus,* although the frequency of legislation against oblation "without the consent

located near the child's natal family, and the parents might retain some link to the child through the monastery. Abandonment and "fostering" cannot, in fact, be distinguished absolutely: parents sometimes maintained some connection with children they had exposed, and often managed to reclaim them; Visigothic legislators regulated "fostering" under a section of their law code devoted expressly to "abandonment." There were, nonetheless, important differences. While a child might have been *de facto* abandoned to a fostering household, he was not legally or even culturally constrained to remain there once he had grown up, and his parents could at any time reclaim him. They had not given up their legal authority over him, under either Roman or Germanic law and custom, by entrusting him to the fostering family, whereas oblation, like exposing, transferred the child permanently out of parental control and authority, under both civil and ecclesiastical law.[31]

A further difference might subsist in the fact that parents who exposed or sold children made no investment in them and possibly even reaped a profit, whereas the parents of an oblate received nothing in return and often had to make a substantial contribution to the monastery for accepting her or him.[32] But the contrast is not as sharp as it appears. Parents exposing children often left expensive tokens with them to make sure they would be treated well,[33] and paying someone ten *solidi* to take permanent charge of a child was a form of abandonment common enough to be regulated by law in early medieval Spain: it is hardly different from making a financial offering to a monastery to perform a similar function. In both cases, moreover, the parents profited in the sense of conserving resources they would otherwise have spent to rear the child. Taking into account the value systems of the period, moreover, parents of oblates

---

of the parents" (discussed below) very strongly suggests that this was not always the case. By the High Middle Ages it often took place privately, without the parents.

31. It was sometimes conceived of as "emancipation": see Illmer, "Zum Problem der Emanzipationsgewohnheiten," pp. 141–43.

32. A gift to the monastery of land or money was expected from parents who could afford it at the time of oblation, to offset the cost to the monastery of rearing the child: see, e.g., Rule of Benedict, 59; Rule of the Master, 91.48–51. Most documents of oblation are designed to record the transfer of such property, and those of the prosperous are, hence, enormously overrepresented.

33. This was true in the Middle Ages as well as in antiquity, apparently: see the discussion of "Fresne" in chapter 10, below.

benefited even more than those of exposed children, since the latter hoped only for temporal benefits while the former anticipated eternal rewards. Instruments of oblation emphasize—with striking consistency—the spiritual rewards accruing not to the oblate but to the parents or relatives:

> Since both the Old and the New Testaments authorize the offering of children to God, as Abraham did . . . , I herewith offer this my son to Almighty God and Holy Mary his mother, according to the Rule of Benedict, for the good of my soul and those of my parents. . . .[34]

> Whereas: The law of God ordains and prescribes for all that each man shall do what seems good to him with his property,

---

34. PL 66.842. "Sancitum est in Veteri et Novo Testamento pueros Deo offerre, ut Abraham . . . fecisse . . . , ego ille, pro remedio animae meae et parentum meorum, nunc offero hunc filium meum illum Deo omnipotenti, et S. Mariae genitrici ejus, secundum Regulam B. Benedicti in monasterio. . . ." The editor does not mention the date of the manuscript from which this is taken, but it corresponds to many ninth-century documents of this nature: see, e.g., Smaragdus, *Expositio*, p. 302; MGH *Formulae, Extravagantes* 2.32, p. 570, "Traditio infantum"; or the many documents of oblation of the same period for St. Germain preserved in Bibliothèque Nationale ms. lat. 13090, folios 72r–77Av. The tenor and form of documents of oblation are conservative and remain basically unchanged throughout the Middle Ages—most retaining, e.g., phrases such as the opening *sancitum*, above, quotations from the Rule of Benedict, and stipulations that the child may never leave, often quoting early canonical legislation ("ut ab hac die non liceat illi collum excutere de sub jugo regulae" [from an instrument of oblation of 1063, published in Jaime Villanueva, *Viage literario a las iglesias de España* 15 (Madrid, 1851), doc. 16, p. 241], which is almost identical to the ninth-century form for "Traditio infantum," cited above). But many more instruments survive from after 1000 than before: from San Cugat, for example, several dozen are preserved from after 1000 and none from before, although it is certain that the monastery accepted oblates before that time. This probably results from two factors: (1) the amount of documentation of every sort increases dramatically after 1000—most monastic cartularies double or triple the number of entries in the eleventh and twelfth centuries; (2) one point of such documents was to record property given the monastery along with the child, and as Europe became more prosperous, people apparently had more property to give. But many monasteries never kept records of oblation: see, e.g., Chartularium Sithiense, doc. 49 bis, p. 118, in *Cartulaire de l'Abbaye de Saint-Bertin,* ed. M. Guérard, in *Collection des Cartulaires de France* 3 (Paris, 1840) (Collection de Documents inédits sur l'histoire de France), where a man who wishes to divide his estate among his children gives one *mansus* to the monastery in which he had put a son ("quem inibi ante monachum fecerat"), although the monastery's cartulary contains no references to oblation at all.

and no official in office at the time is to hinder him in seeing to the welfare of his own soul. When according to the will of the merciful God my son Peter was born, I thought of the great number of my sins. I made provision that if he lived I would give him to the holy [place] of Apa Phoibammon in the mountain of Jeme for the salvation of my soul.[35]

This does not mean that parental sentiment was wanting. In the second example, above, Peter's father grew quite attached to his son before he actually gave him to the monastery[36] (". . . as I watched the boy grow up, I wanted to break the promise that I had made to God and His saint"), and would have reneged on his promise if his son's illness had not prompted him to fulfill it in the hopes that God would heal him.[37]

Oblation was in many ways the most humane form of abandon-

35. W. E. Crum and G. Steindorff, *Koptische Rechtsurkunden des achten Jahrhunderts aus Djême (Theben)* (Leipzig, 1912), nos. 100–103, pp. 314–20, translated by L. S. B. MacCoull, "Child Donations and Child Saints in Coptic Egypt," *East European Quarterly* 13, 4 (1979) 409–15; see also discussion in A. Steinwenter, "Kinderschenkungen an koptische Klöster," *Zeitschrift der Savigny-Stiftung, Kanonistische Abteilung* 11 (1921) 175–207, and Steinwenter, "Zum Problem der Kontinuität," pp. 37–38. Crum and Steindorff publish twenty-six documents of oblation involving twenty-seven oblates. However, some children given to Coptic monasteries were clearly intended as servants, not monks: see discussion in Quinn, "Benedictine Oblation," pp. 34–35.

36. In the East, children were often not given until they were seven to ten years old, even if they had been promised at birth, although there was no absolute uniformity. Bibliothèque Nationale, ms. Coislin 257 (s. xi), folio 76v, records an anecdote in Greek about a child "given" to a monastery by parents (παῖς τις ἐδόθη εἰς κοινόβιον ὑπὸ τῶν γόνεων αὐτοῦ) who come to see him and are surprised—but delighted—that he has become a monk, which they had apparently not intended or authorized.

37. In a contemporary Coptic story the father's motivations are more complex: rather than surrender this three-year-old son, promised to a monastery by the previously infertile mother, he has him "appraised" by Saracen slave traders and offers the abbot the child's price in gold: E. Amélineau, "Monuments pour servir à l'histoire de l'Égypte chrétienne aux IVe, Ve, VIe, et VIIe siècles," *Mémoires publiés par les membres de la Mission archéologique française au Caire* 4, 2 (1895), pp. 719–25. The abbot is offended, and the child dies a short time later. This story was apparently quite popular: it appears in the later Arabic Synaxarion of the Jacobites (René Basset, "Le Synaxaire arabe Jacobite [rédaction Copte] 2," *Patrologia Orientalis* 3 [Paris, 1909], pp. 399–400). In the Arabic, however, the father makes his own estimate of the child's worth and offers it as a "substitute" (*wafad*).

ment ever devised in the West.[38] Both the ideal of nonbiological, fostering love and the possibility of success despite humble beginnings were built into oblation and virtually never left to chance, as they were in the case of other forms of abandonment. The very idea of monasticism entailed the creation of a voluntary family, the application of familial affections and relationships by and to persons whose responsibility for each other was voluntarily assumed rather than inherited. This provided, in a sense, an ideal climate for foster children, since they suffered no disadvantage whatever either in regard to natural siblings, or the attitude of the public. The monastery or convent consisted of a father ("abbot" comes from the Aramaic for "father") or mother chosen rather than inherited, and siblings chosen rather than given (nuns called each other "sister," monks "brother"); so it was quite natural, in one sense, that abbeys also included "sons" or "daughters" chosen along with siblings and parents. Oblates were *alumni* in a family in which *all* the children were adopted: ecclesiastical legislation even referred to them as the church's *alumni*.[39]

From the point of view of the abandoning parents, oblation was not merely morally neutral, but laudable, and its superiority to other forms of abandonment at the practical level was enormous. Parents who sold or exposed might *hope* that the child would find more to eat or a better home subsequently, but parents of oblates could be quite sure that the child was fed and clothed and secure. Justinian might claim that abandoned children were free and could not be brought up as slaves, but he could hardly make it so. Parents of oblates knew exactly what status their child would have.[40] Oblation

38. The donation of children to monasteries was known in other cultures as well: many children of seven or eight were deposited in monasteries by poor parents in Ming and early Ch'ing China: see, e.g., Ann Waltner, "The Adoption of Children in Ming and Early Ch'ing China," Ph.D. diss., U. C. Berkeley, 1981, pp. 55–56, 83.

39. E.g., *Irische Kanonensammlung* 42.14 (Wasserschleben, pp. 165–66): "De alumnis ecclesiae," about oblates who leave the monastery; also 42.15 and 16 ("Quidam episcopus ait de quodam alumno desertore sui monasterii: Non maledices ei in quantum alumnus est, nec benedices ei, in quantum desertor").

40. Not necessarily "free": there were distinctions of status in many monasteries which doubtless affected oblates. In some only the children of the upper classes could become priests or even fully professed religious; offspring of the lower classes were laborers who took lesser vows. But even so, their position was probably materially better than it would have been outside the community.

absolutely precluded the more horrifying possibilities of other forms of abandonment: the child could not be harmed by wild animals, enslaved, or unwittingly drawn into an incestuous relationship.[41]

The only cost to the parents was the emotional sacrifice, which would obviously vary from case to case, and the initial offering—waived in the case of the poor.[42] In the case of the wealthy, even a very large gift to the monastery was doubtless worthwhile if it freed an entire share of the patrimony: since they could not own property,[43] oblates could lay no claim to an estate, and whatever the parents offered to give the monastery at the time of donation was the last material obligation they would ever have to the child. In return they received the spiritual benefits of the sacrifice itself and the oblate's lifelong prayers, and—if the oblate rose to a position of prominence and was so inclined—potential political and ecclesiastical benefits. Indeed, placing children in the church was a regular stratagem for social advancement among aristocratic families in medieval Europe; oblation was simply the most extreme form of a common practice.

It does not require a particularly cynical view to see that nonspiritual motivations might prompt oblation: from the very outset monastic leaders themselves complained about this. "Many are those," Basil lamented as early as the fourth century, "whom parents or siblings or some relatives bring before the proper age, not having undertaken celibacy of their own accord, but disposed of for some material advantage to those who brought them."[44] Jerome complains that parents dedicate to virginity those daughters who

41. He might be sexually abused (see note 46, below) but this was probably relatively rare: monastic rules went to great lengths to separate children and adolescents from older monks and even from each other.

42. Both according to the Rule of Benedict and subsequent legislation: the Council of Frankfurt in 794, having "heard that some abbots, inspired by avarice, require gifts from those entering monasteries," prohibited this and demanded that the Rule of Benedict be observed in regard to those "being taken up" by the order (Mansi 17.266; MGH *Concilia* 2.168, canon 16). Compare MGH *Capitularia* 1, no. 170, p. 348, canon 75: "Ut nullus pro munere recipiatur in monasterio, nisi quem bona voluntas et morum commendat probitas."

43. At least according to most monastic rules: the civil status of monks was much debated. See the bibliography cited in Constable, nos. 784 f.

44. Epistle 199.18 (PG 32.720). Διοικούμενοι here is a pun, meaning both "disposed of," in a general sense, and "dwelling apart" or "put out of the house," literally.

are deformed or defective in some way, although he did not refer exclusively to oblation.[45]

From society's point of view oblation was also a considerable improvement over other forms of abandonment. Children offered to monasteries became part of an effective, well-organized work force, often contributing significantly to the economic, political, and cultural well-being of the area. Their lifestyle limited their consumption, and they were strongly discouraged from producing offspring, thus reducing demands on the ecology of the region. Much of Europe during the early Middle Ages was underpopulated, and no society would wish too many of its members to forgo reproduction, but it seems reasonable to assume that where children were abandoned in large numbers, rates of reproductivity were disproportionate to the means of support for many families, if not for the region as a whole. Moreover, the practice itself was not, like infanticide, objectionable on moral grounds. Far from constituting antisocial behavior, it ostensibly involved altruism, sacrifice, and devotion to the major benevolent institution of the day. It was a way of "returning fruits to the Lord," and in Christian society the giving up of a child for a greater good could hardly have had greater subliminal religious significance.

It was the child, obviously, who bore the cost of these benefits to family and community, as, of course, children always paid the price for parental decisions regarding abandonment. Confined irrevocably to a life of religious discipline, the child could never legally own property, leave the community, or marry. His diet, drink, education, labor, and occupation were determined by his superiors in the community. He could not even question their decisions without wrongdoing. His loss of personal freedom thus equalled, in some ways, that of exposed children reared as slaves; but even they could enjoy intimate physical relations,[46] and had hope in many cir-

45. Epistle 130, PL 24.1111.

46. Oblates might have sexual relations with other members of the monastic community or even with lay persons under some circumstances, but they were necessarily illicit: although there was controversy about imposing celibacy on the diocesan clergy, members of religious communities had always been expected to take vows of celibacy. For sexual relations with oblates or other monks or nuns, see McLaughlin, "Survivors," pp. 130–31; Ilene Forsyth, "The Ganymede Capital at Vézelay," *Gesta: International Center of Medieval Art,* 15 (1976) 241–44, nn. 14–18; Boswell, *Christianity,* pp. 81, 137, 143–44, 188–89; Quinn, "Benedic-

cumstances of recovering freeborn natal status or earning emancipation from benevolent masters. The oblate, by universal social
consensus, was consigned irrevocably to a life of poverty, obedience, and celibacy.

These were Christian virtues, of course: not just the misfortunes
of the servile. They set apart those in religious communities and
conferred a special status on them, a status with enormous influence
and power even in the secular world. Many oblates achieved through
monastic life positions they could not have attained otherwise, and
most of them gained opportunities—e.g., for education—that they
would not have had under other circumstances. An extraordinary
number of influential churchmen of the early Middle Ages, in both
East and West, had been given to the church (though not in every
case as technical "oblates") at an early age and rose through it to
become figures of considerable cultural importance: the theologian
Paphnutius, Gregory Nazianzen, Daniel the Stylite, Symeon the
Stylite, Euthymios the Great, Sabas the Great, Cyril of Skythopolis,
Nicolas of Sion, Theodore of Sykeon, Willibald, Bede, Boniface,
Rabanus Maurus, Notker Balbulus—to name but a few. Parents
could hardly hope to rear children more "successful" than these by
the standards of piety, which, while not universal, were certainly
widespread.

Nor, during an epoch when few individuals chose their own
patterns of life, did either parent or child necessarily regard the sacrifices required as undue or unfair. Many serfs might well have
willingly traded places with oblates. The loss of economic and
erotic opportunity, perhaps the most striking deprivation of religious life from a modern point of view, probably seemed much less
oppressive in regions and times where, for the first, economic au-

---

tine Oblation," chap. 6; see also the discussion of the Nun of Watton in chapter 8,
below, and the translation in the Appendix. If oblates were sometimes the object of
erotic attention from older monks, this was not unlike a major hazard of abandonment in the ancient world, and in a monastic community the child had the advantage that the person responsible would certainly be punished if it came to light,
whereas Romans could abuse *expositi* or even *alumni* with impunity. Herlihy suggests that even youthful brides, handed over to their future husband's family, were
often sexually exploited (*Medieval Households,* p. 76). Child abuse occurred at
home as well: see, e.g., the "Penitential of the German Churches," canon 157
(Schmitz, 2.444). Cf. Claude Roussel, "Aspects du père incestueux dans la littérature médiévale," in *Amour, mariage et transgressions au moyen âge,* ed. Danielle
Buschinger and André Crépin (Göppingen, 1984).

tonomy was not a realistic possibility for most people, and, for the second, few people would expect to arrange their sexual lives to suit their inclinations. Sexuality, moreover, appeared fraught with dangers to the soul and, especially for females, even to the body. Nor did official sanctions necessarily preclude affection in monasteries: it is striking that almost all of the love poetry of the age was, in fact, written by members of religious communities, usually to each other, rather than by lay persons free to indulge in amorous pursuits.[47] (But this can be ascribed, to some extent, to the literacy of the monasteries.)

The advantages of oblation over other forms of abandonment did not render it satisfactory for all concerned. Some authorities felt considerable ambivalence about it, and the problem of oblates who, as adults, felt no vocation for religious life and wished to leave the monastery was raised again and again throughout the early Middle Ages. In reply to questions about it in the eighth century the papacy asserted that it was "wicked for a gift from the parents to God to be undone by the whims of the children,"[48] but throughout the ninth century vehement controversy about aspects of oblation persisted.[49] Charlemagne found it necessary to prevent parents from using convents as nurseries, and decreed that girls could be placed in them

47. See Boswell, *Christianity,* chap. 7; Quinn, "Benedictine Oblation," chap. 6.

48. "Nefas est ut oblatio a parentibus Deo filiis voluptatis froena laxentur" (Mansi 12.245). Deroux, pp. 88–89 and n. 4, presents this as the reply of Gregory II to an inquiry from Boniface (an oblate at age seven, according to Deroux) about the possibility of oblates leaving. This makes a poignant picture, but rather a misleading one. Too little is known of Boniface's early years to be sure that he did not enter religious life voluntarily; and it is not clear whether the letter was written by Gregory II or Gregory III, or, indeed, someone yet later. It does, however, conform to ecclesiastical opinion of the time.

49. Interestingly, there was similar agitation in the East at about the same time. The sixth novel of the Emperor Leo, in response to controversy about estates of children who became monks, addressed the apparent conflict between the ruling at Trull that boys could be professed at ten and Basil's opinion that this could not properly take place until they were sixteen or seventeen. Leo compromised: if the heir entered after seventeen, he could dispose of his property at will; if he entered as a child, he could not. If an oblate died in the monastery before reaching sixteen or seventeen, the monastery got two-thirds of his property, and his relatives the rest. (See the commentary on this by Balsamon, PG 138.656.) This was a considerable gain for monastic communities, since under Justinian (Novel 123.38) they had received only half. On the larger issue the East agreed with the West: anyone professed, under whatever circumstance, was permanently bound to monastic life (Novels 7 and 8).

only if the parents were actually offering them as oblates; boys
could not be entrusted to female communities at all—presumably
because in such cases they were clearly not oblates.[50] Both measures
suggest that, despite canonical legislation, parents were able to reclaim children given to monasteries and convents with relative ease
(and that many parents wished to avoid the burden of rearing infants without irrevocably donating their children).[51]

Early in the ninth century, rulers and councils urged that children be given an opportunity to ratify personally the choice of
religious life, but left ambiguous whether they should be able to
withdraw if they had not done so.[52] This issue yielded subse-

50. Capitulary of 804, canon 6, MGH *Capitularia* 1.42, p. 119: "Quicumque
filiam suam aut neptam aut parentem, Deo omnipotenti offerre voluit, licentiam
habet; sin autem, domui infantes suos nutriat et non aliam infra monasteria mittere
nutriendi gratia presumat, nisi quae in ipso loco firmiter in Dei servitio perseverare
voluerit, vel secundum instituta sanctorum patrum seu canonicam auctoritatem."
Canon 7: "Omnino prohibemus ut nullus masculum filium nepotem aut parentum
suum in monasterio puellarum ad nutriendum commendare praesumat nec quispiam ullum suscipere audeat."
51. A canon of 817 prohibits having schools in monasteries except for oblates:
"Ut scola in monasterio non habeatur, nisi eorum qui oblati sunt" (canon 45, Capitulary of 817, MGH *Capitularia* 170, p. 346), but it is clear that this was ignored
at St. Gall, for example: see Patricia Quinn, "Benedictine Child Rearing," p. 41.
52. Charlemagne decided (805) that girls could not be bound to monastic life
until they were old enough to choose for themselves (no specific age is mentioned).
He seemed to recognize that this might conflict with earlier canonical rulings: Capitulary of 805, canon 14 (MGH *Capitularia* 1.43, p. 122). A canon of Louis the
Pious (817) requires that boys also personally ratify the donation of their parents
"at the age of discretion": Capitulary of 817, canon 36 (ibid. 170, p. 346). A council
in Mainz, presumably in response to some agitation on the issue, decided in 813
that anyone tonsured "without his consent" must remain in orders, but that caution should be exercised in future to see that no one is tonsured unless "of legitimate age and of his own accord or with the permission of his lord" (MGH *Concilia*
2.1.36, canon 23, p. 267: "De clericis iniuste tonsoratis. De clericis vero hoc statui-
mus, ut hi, qui hactenus inventi sunt, sive in canonico sive in monachico ordine,
tonsorati sine eorum voluntate, si liberi sunt, ut ita permaneant, et deinceps caven-
dum, ut nullus tondeatur nisi legitima aetate et spontanea voluntate vel cum licentia domini sui"). This text poses several semantic difficulties: "si liberi sunt," for
example, could mean either "if they are children," or "if they are free," which
would have rather different implications, although "ut ita permaneant" strongly
implies the latter; but the phrase about the lord is the most puzzling—does it mean
that a feudal superior could authorize oblation while a parent could not, or does
"lord" apply to parents, taking the traditional authority of the *paterfamilias* as a
kind of *dominium*? Either is possible; the latter seems considerably more likely, in

quently to deliberations about the problem of children tonsured without even their parents' consent;[53] a difficulty probably occasioned when guardians committed children to monasteries either to evade responsibility or to obtain their estates.[54]

By far the most celebrated dispute was provoked by Gottschalk of Orbais (d. ca. 868), the son of a Saxon noble, who had been

---

which case the council's ruling does not actually limit the right of parents to donate children, but restricts this authority to them or those standing legally in loco parentis.

53. Two capitularies of Louis the Pious explicitly prohibit the tonsuring of children without the permission of their parents (or relatives: the Latin is ambiguous) and subject violators to civil penalties; the child in such cases is free to remain in religious life or not, as he chooses: Capitulare ecclesiasticum, canon 20, MGH Capitularia 138, p. 278; Capitula legibus addenda, canon 21, ibid., p. 285.

54. So little evidence survives on the subject that it is difficult even to guess what persons or circumstances such decrees were directed against. Tonsuring was an ancient method of preventing accession to Germanic thrones (see, e.g., Gregory of Tours, Historia Francorum 2.41, 3.18, etc.), but clearly more than that is involved here, since many children of no particular social standing appear to have been involved. Were monks tonsuring children who had been entrusted to them only for education? Did monks or nuns tonsure children being "fostered" with them? The ambiguity of the Latin parentes complicates the matter. Although Smaragdus specifically glossed it as "father or mother" (citing the example of Hanna and Samuel: Expositio, p. 300), the ninth-century oblation records of St. Germain, for example, include a very large number of oblations by relatives other than parents: grandparents, uncles, cousins, brothers, even apparently unrelated persons (Bibliothèque Nationale, ms. lat. 13090: e.g., folio 72r, "nepos"; folio 73v, "sobrinum meum affectu uero et effectu filium adoptiuum Stephanum"; folio 74v, "nepos," "vice patris sui"; folio 76r, "fratrem meum nomine Rodericum," "hunc puerum nomine Eurardum"; etc.). These may have become guardians of the children when relatives, friends, or even feudal dependents died, and they preferred to donate them to monastic life rather than bring them up personally. Possibly this is what Carolingian churchmen and legislators were attempting to forestall. Lynch, Simoniacal Entry, pp. 45–47, cites nearly a dozen cases of orphaned children being placed in monasteries by unwilling guardians. If tonsure were absolutely irrevocable, it might even be worth kidnapping and forcibly tonsuring an inconvenient heir, which could be the origin of the law cited above. There were also persons desirous of heirs who adopted relatives or even strangers specifically as children, as noted previously. See also MGH Formulae, pp. 81–82, 83–84, 147–48. Rabanus Maurus mentions (PL 107.431, translated in Appendix) that in his day there was controversy about proper "witnesses" to oblation, but so much of his tract consists of attacks on "opponents of oblation" generalized from the particular case of Gottschalk (discussed below) that it is not a reliable source of information about the general phenomenon.

given as a child to the Benedictine monastery of Fulda.[55] When he came of age, he felt no inclination to religious life and asked to leave. His abbot, Rabanus Maurus (who had also been an oblate), refused, asserting that oblation was irrevocable. Gottschalk appealed to higher authorities, and the Council of Mainz of 829 freed him, on the grounds that "no one should be made a monk against his will."[56] Rabanus appealed the decision to the Carolingian emperor.

The dispute produced a number of fundamental texts and precedents, including decrees of the Council of Mainz in favor of freedom for oblates and Rabanus's treatise *On the Oblation of Children,* which presented the contrary and prevailing view, and represents the only substantive justification of oblation offered by any medieval theologian. (Portions of it are translated in the Appendix.)

Rabanus based his defense chiefly on biblical examples: Abraham's sacrifice of Isaac, God's claiming the firstborn children of Israel as his due and consigning the tribe of the Levites to priestly service in fulfillment of this debt, Jephthah's slaying of his only daughter to keep his vow to the Lord (Judges 11:30–39), Hanna's dedication of Samuel to priestly service in consequence of her vow (1 Samuel [Kings] 1), the "offering" of Jesus in the temple as a boy, and his rebuking, as an adult, his disciples for trying to prevent little children from coming to him. In addition, Rabanus argued that it was an honor to be a "slave" to God, that parents unquestionably had the right to dispose of minor children as they saw fit, that it was a grave sin to fail to observe any solemn vow,[57] and that mo-

---

55. For the details of Gottschalk's life see K. Vielhaber, *Gottschalk der Sachse* (Bonn, 1956). His own writings survive only in fragments (PL 121.347–68), because they were condemned by his contemporaries, but his story and some of his feelings can be traced in materials by or about his abbot, Rabanus Maurus, and Hincmar of Reims (on whom see Jean Devisse, *Hincmar, archévêque de Reims, 845–82,* 3 vols. [Geneva, 1975–76]).

56. "Neminem debere invitum fieri monachum" (MGH *Concilia* 2.2.50, p. 602). The records of the council itself were lost in the seventeenth century, and its deliberations can only be reconstructed through contemporary correspondence referring to it: see ibid., pp. 602–5.

57. This point is the least developed of the three, and a number of questions are left unanswered. Are vows binding, for example, if made for one Christian by another, as was the case with oblation? Rabanus notes that parents are allowed by the church to make vows for their children at baptism. He does not point out that these are considered irrevocable and binding, but this would presumably have been his line of argument had he developed it more fully. He also ridicules the argument by "opponents of oblation" that only countrymen may be admitted as witnesses to

nasticism had been established by divine authority, not by human invention.

The emperor ruled that Gottschalk must remain a monk for the rest of his life. Resigned, he tried to interest himself in theology, but Rabanus and others condemned his writings as heretical, and he was finally imprisoned for life in the monastery of Hautvilliers, where he died insane after a confinement of nearly twenty years. His pitiful case not only highlighted but to some extent determined the most poignant aspects of oblation, by prompting civil and ecclesiastical authorities of the day to rule on its irrevocability.

Gottschalk himself composed a touching poem to a little boy in another monastery, possibly also an oblate, who had written to him in prison—apparently out of sympathy for his plight.

Why do you order, little lad,
Why do you command, little son,
That I sing a sweet song,
When I am far away in exile
In the middle of the sea?
O why do you bid me to sing?
More likely, sad little one,
Should I weep, little boy,
And lament rather than sing
A song such as you demand.[58]

Gottschalk was clearly not the only oblate unhappy with his position.[59] Others took private action: a form-letter survives from

---

religious profession, since "the law of his own people could not suffer a person of another to be called as witness for limiting someone's legal freedom" (PL 107.431; see translation in Appendix). This suggests that even if parental vows were considered binding, some question might arise subsequently as to their form or authenticity, or about the witnesses sought to confirm these.

58. Text published in *Oxford Book of Medieval Latin Verse,* ed. F. J. E. Raby (Oxford, 1959), pp. 126–28 (no. 92); cf. Bernhard Bischoff, "Gottschalks Lied für den Reichenauer Freund," *Medium aevum vivum: Festschrift W. Bulst* (Heidelberg, 1960), pp. 61–68, where three additional stanzas are edited. A translation is available in P. S. Allen, *The Romanesque Lyric* (Chapel Hill, N.C., 1928), pp. 150–51. I have argued elsewhere that this is a love poem (see *Christianity,* pp. 192–93, where opposing arguments are also cited).

59. Dissatisfaction might focus on the particular order or monastery to which a child had been committed rather than on religious life in general: see, e.g., the

the ninth century for writing to a bishop about an oblate ("qui in monasterio nobiscum fuit notritus [sic] tonsuratusque est") who has fled the monastery.[60] After a Roman synod of 853 ruled that no one should be held against his will in a monastery,[61] Pope Nicholas I freed from monastic life a man whose father had forced him to take the habit as a boy ("between eight and eleven"), arguing that to be virtuous an act must be voluntary.[62] The boy was, however, not to be free to return to the world: "rather, until such time as divine inspiration should move him of his own free will to submit to monastic life, let him live in canonical life among churchmen, apart from worldly and secular pursuits and concerns."

The view that oblation was permanent prevailed for at least a century more in most of Europe. Ninth-century oblation formulae include provisions for what to do—e.g., with the parents' gift to the monastery—if the child should eventually be found unworthy of acceptance, but no mention is made of the possibility that he or she might not want to stay (though, by contrast, such reservations are common in later periods).[63] The year after Nicholas's death (868) the Council of Worms declared that children given to monasteries could never leave, and could be retained by force if necessary.[64] This

---

enormous problems generated by the donation to St. Radegund in Poitiers of Chlothild, the daughter of Charibert, resulting in an armed attack on the convent led by Chlothild herself and culminating in a bitter trial (Gregory of Tours, *Historia Francorum* 9.39, 10.15).

60. *Additamenta collectionis Flaviniacensis* 5, in MGH *Formulae*, p. 491. This was almost certainly composed before the decrees of Worms of 868, because it cites only much earlier canons dealing with the subject.

61. Mansi 14.1008, canon 32: "Sicut enim qui monasteria elegerunt, a monasteriis egredi non permittuntur; ita hi qui inviti sine justae ostensionis crimine monasteriis sunt intromissi, nisi volentes non teneantur, quia quod non petunt, non observant."

62. Quoted in Ivo of Chartres, *Decretum* 6.356 (PL 161.519–20); Gratian, *Decretum* 2.20.3.4 (ed. Friedberg, 1.849–50), translated in Appendix. It is striking that this letter was ignored by ecclesiastical legislation shortly after it was drafted, although it was influential centuries later: perhaps contemporaries took as particularly significant the fact that the boy had expressed opposition to his profession, in contrast to cases in which the child put up no objection but later regretted it.

63. See, e.g., *Collectio Sangallensis* 6b (A.D. 870) in MGH *Formulae*, p. 400.

64. Canon 22: "Si pater vel mater filium filiamque intra septa monasterii in infantiae annis sub regulari tradiderint disciplina, non liceat eis, postquam ad pubertatis pervenerint annos, egredi et matrimonio copulari. . . . Non liceat eis susceptum habitum unquam deferre: sed convicti quod tonsuram vel religiosam vestem aliquando habuerint, nolint, permanere cogantur" (Mansi 14.873).

was reiterated at Tribur (near Mainz) in 895, when the prelates added that "if [the oblate] leaves, he is to be returned; if he has let his hair grow, he is to be tonsured again; if he has taken a wife, he is to be forced to dismiss her."[65]

As a formal system, oblation bore striking resemblances to other forms of abandonment, in terms of its social utility (e.g., in limiting the number of heirs), the conflicts it raised about irrevocability (much like imperial Roman struggles over the permanence of servile status) and even some very technical details: the setting of ten, for example, as the ultimate age for such donations in some locales matches age distinctions for other forms of parental divestment, such as fostering or sale. There is even a striking parallel in the actual process, in that abandonment at churches appears to have been the most common form of exposing in the Middle Ages, and oblation involved "leaving" the child at a religious institution.

Given the enormous variations in patterns of life for children (and adults) in Europe at the time, it is difficult to generalize about the extent to which the daily experience of oblates was different from that of other abandoned children or even of siblings retained at home. They were brought up by strangers, like *expositi,* but also communally, as were (and are) most children sent away to school. That they would never again live at home might have made a considerable difference in their outlook on life, but this would obviously vary greatly according to individual circumstance and personality. Those offered as infants could hardly have "missed" their parents, and evidence from later ages suggests that many oblates prided themselves on their complete isolation from mundane experience, although this does not mean that their childhoods were not missing essential emotional elements.

Their daily life was not greatly different from that of children in strict religious boarding schools in many ages, except that in addition to school and work, they had long and exacting liturgical duties throughout the day.[66] By and large, the monastic daily regimen

65. Canon 16, Mansi 18.144; cf. canon 4 (ibid.), which specifies that girls below the age of twelve who take the veil *of their own free will* ("non coacta sed propria voluntate") and remain in religious life for a year and a day may never leave the convent (this becomes part of the *Decretum* of Gratian: 2.20.2.2 [Friedberg 1.847–48]).

66. On the life of oblates, the best sources are the Rule of Benedict itself, which describes the ideal of monastic life to which they were committed; commentaries (e.g., of Warnefrid and Hildemar, both discussed in this context in Schroll); and the memoirs of Walafrid Strabo about his schooldays as an oblate, translated

involved about four hours of liturgy, four of reading, six of work, six to eight hours of sleep (from about 5 P.M. to about 2 A.M.), and two to four hours for eating, hygiene, and other physical needs.[67] Most oblates would have spent more time in school than at work. Children were required to eat standing, but were usually given more meat and fed more frequently than the adult monks (although the amounts and variety were still ascetic); in influential Carolingian commentaries a special diet is prescribed for each year of childhood.[68]

Commentaries on the Rule of Benedict suggest three or four masters for every ten boys.[69] The children's dormitory in the plan of St. Gall seems to have accommodated about twenty-five children and five adults.[70] It appears to have been carefully placed near a warming room—as opposed to the much colder adult dormitories—and the children's quarters were all located in the innermost recesses of the monastery, presumably for protection.[71] Once a week or once a month the oblates were to be taken to a meadow or a similar location and allowed to play, but apart from this no amusement was permitted.[72] Constant supervision, severe discipline, and

---

by James Butler, "The School Life of Walafrid Strabo," *Bibliotheca Sacra: A Theological Quarterly* 40 (1883) 152 –72. Of the few secondary studies, the most complete are Quinn, "Benedictine Oblation"; McLaughlin, "Survivors"; Deroux, "Les Origines"; Berlière, "Les Écoles"; and the works of Riché.

67. The classic description of monastic life is that of Cuthbert Butler, *Benedictine Monachism* (London, 1927); for the divisions of the day, see pp. 280, 287. For a fuller treatment, see Quinn, "Benedictine Oblation," chap. 5.

68. About standing, see Hildemar, p. 427, Schroll, p. 130; about diet, see Warnefrid, pp. 346–47, Hildemar, p. 419, Schroll, pp. 142–43. Even penitentials acknowledged a special diet for oblates: "Children brought up in a monastery shall eat flesh for fourteen years"; in Haddan and Stubbs 3.209–12 (attributed to Theodore [668–690], but probably later); discussed and translated by McNeill and Gamer, pp. 215–16.

69. See, e.g., Warnefrid, pp. 271, 345; Hildemar, pp. 331–32, 418; Schroll, p. 65.

70. See Quinn, "Benedictine Oblation," pp. 89–92. Walter Horn and Ernest Born estimate twenty children as the number at St. Gall (*The Plan of St. Gall: A Study of the Architecture and Economy of and Life in a Paradigmatic Carolingian Monastery* [Berkeley, 1979] 1.313). Adalhard of Corbie suggested twelve as the ideal number of oblates (*Consuetudines Corbiensis* 1, in Joseph Semmler, ed., *Corpus consuetudinum monasticarum* [Siegburg, 1963] 1.366).

71. Quinn, "Benedictine Oblation," pp. 93–95.

72. Warnefrid, p. 346, Hildemar, p. 419, Schroll, p. 143. See also Quinn, "Benedictine Oblation," pp. 171–72.

corporal punishment are prescribed in the Rule and its contemporary commentaries. The last was to be employed in moderation, however, and both custody and correction were to be motivated by concern for the well-being of the oblates. Praise and even rewards of better food are also encouraged in some commentaries as means of inspiring good behavior.[73] If they seemed mature enough, oblates became regular members of the community in their teens.[74]

It would be a mistake to attribute to early medieval Catholicism the degree of systematization and homogeneity that would later characterize it. The Rule of Benedict and its variants competed with many other monastic programs, some far less systematic, and it was itself adapted, modified, altered, and observed selectively or desultorily throughout Europe. Oblation, like many aspects of monastic life, took many forms and should not be envisioned as a uniform and rigid entity. Early councils and Carolingian legislation formally regulating its particulars would eventually influence international legal compilations, both civil and ecclesiastical, but even these were of arguable efficacy, and in their own day they may have affected only the areas in which they were enacted.

Even at the official level there were ways to give up children to the church which were neither clearly oblation nor clearly not, and a great many children throughout the whole of the Middle Ages were granted or abandoned to the church under informal or individual arrangements not regulated in any systematic way. From very early there are mentions in Christian literature of "devoting" children to God, to the church, or to virginity. In some cases this may have amounted to oblation; in some it may have been closer to "fostering," with the hope that the child would eventually choose to remain in religious life. St. Jerome praised parents for "consecrating" daughters to virginity even before birth, and thought infants not too young to be given to monasteries.[75] The father of a girl

73. Warnefrid, p. 347, Hildemar, pp. 419–20, Schroll, pp. 144–46.

74. See, e.g., Warnefrid, p. 471, Hildemar, p. 581, Schroll, p. 80.

75. In Epistle 107 (PL 22.877; CSEL 55.293) Laeta's daughter Paula is said to have been "consecrated to God before she was born" ("quae prius Christo est consecrata quam genita"), and Jerome recommends that she either be reared at home according to strict monastic discipline or sent to a monastery as an infant. He cites Samuel frequently as an example. Cf. Epistle 128 (PL 22.1098; CSEL 56.156–62), about the daughter of Gaudentius, also sworn to virginity as an infant, and also to be brought up under strict discipline. Cf. the *Vie de Sainte-Mélanie*

cured by St. Martin "was so moved that he immediately promised the child to God and dedicated her to perpetual virginity," "donating" her to St. Martin himself.[76]

The first canon of the Second Council of Toledo in 527 addressed the issue of parents dedicating their sons in infancy not to monastic life but to the priesthood, for which they were trained in a parish church under the supervision of a bishop. At the end of their eighteenth year they were to be asked publicly whether they wished to undertake a life of chastity or not, and if they declined, they were allowed to marry as laymen.[77] Although the ultimate consequences for the child were less drastic, this sounds like a variation on oblation, in which parents give up a baby to a "better" life in the church and play no further role in his childhood.[78] In the next century the Fourth Council of Toledo (633), acknowledging that prevailing custom allowed the ordination of "infants" as priests, set the minimum age of ordination in the future at twenty-five.[79] This did

---

(cited above, note 82, chapter 3), sections 1–6. Observations about children being "consecrated" to God by their parents, could, of course simply express the parents' intention to bring them up as good Christians; but in general such a purpose is assumed, and phrasing of this sort implies a more specific vow about religious life. In one of the lives of St. Bavo of Ghent, a father "devotes" an infant son to monastic life ("infantulum Sancto devovit Monachum") but then retains him at home and the child dies in a tragic accident during a birthday party—clearly a lesson in the eyes of the narrator (*Miracula sancti Bavonis* 3, in ASOB 2 [Paris, 1935], p. 415). This story is quite distorted by Quinn, "Benedictine Child Rearing," p. 52, n. 20: the child had never been in the monastery; there is no indication that it was his birthday; he was serving the guests at the party.

76. "In tantum valuit ut statim puellam Deo voverit et perpetuae virginitati dicavit; profectusque ad Martinum puellam ei praesens virtutum ejus testimonium obtulit" (Sulpitius Severus, *Life of St. Martin* 19 [ed. in PL 20, CSEL 1]). Note that *obtulit* (from *offero*) is the verb most closely related to *oblatio*. On Sulpicius and St. Martin, see Clare Stancliffe, *St. Martin and His Hagiographer: History and Miracle in Sulpicius Severus* (New York, 1983).

77. Canon 1: "De his quos parentes ab infantia in clericatus officio manciparunt. . . ." (*Concilios*, p. 42); *La Colección canónica hispana* 4, pp. 347–49: "De his quos uoluntas parentum a primis infantiae annis clericatus officio manciparit. . . ."

78. Cf. the second canon of this council, which prohibits the children from even transferring to another cleric for education: "quia durum est ut eum quem alius rurali sensu ac squalore infantiae exuit, alius suscipere aut uindicare praesumat" (ibid., p. 350)—a concern rather like arguments over the fate of *expositi* under the empire.

79. Canon 20, *Concilios*, p. 200. This was taken up in most subsequent canonical collections: Burchard, 2.12; Ivo, *Decretum* 6.32, *Panormia* 3.31; Gratian, *Decretum* 1.77.7 (Friedberg 1.274).

not, obviously, limit the age at which boys could be accepted for training.

Some early medieval canons, as noted above, describe "fostering" by the church itself, which may have involved apprenticeship for clerical office, or simply a charitable function of local parishes for parents who could not bring up their children themselves.[80] Gregory of Tours mentions various prominent clerics who had been given as children to the church under circumstances not precisely equaling oblation,[81] and the author of the *Vita Trudonis* relates a conversation between a bishop and a boy he is taking into his "service," which suggests an arrangement somewhere between oblation and a traditional *alumnus*–foster-parent relationship: "Know, my son, that from this hour you will be my son by inviolable law, and I will take the place of your father in spiritual law forever."[82] Irish saints' lives include a great many examples of this hybrid between oblation and "fostering" by holy persons, and although the dating of this material is unusually complex, some of the instances doubtless reflect early medieval practice.[83]

Gregory the Great (d. 604) tells a story about St. Eleutherius visiting a convent where a small child in residence is tormented by an evil spirit; the saint simply takes the child away to his own monastery.[84] When a seventh-century bishop of Mérida discovers his own nephew traveling in the entourage of a group of merchants, he constrains them to leave the boy with him—which they agree to do with much reluctance and only after a long argument—and then immediately tonsures him and dedicates him to the priesthood. The

80. See above, p. 220.

81. In the *Vitae patrum* (MGH SSRRMM 1): Germanus, Abbot of Grandivall, 5.33; Ribobert, 7.61; Lupus, Bishop of Sens, 4.179; Landibert, Bishop of Utrecht, 6.353. Note that in the *De virtutibus sancti Martini* 2.4, he cites the case of a master who forces his servant to enter a monastery.

82. *Vita Trudonis* 7 (MGH SSRRMM 6.280).

83. See note 112 of chapter 4, above, on problems of dating. For instances, "Vita sancti Berachi," VSH 1.78; "Vita sancti Mochoemog," VSH 2.180–81 (note the strong affect in this case: "Sanctus episcopus Furseus, et beatissimus abbas Mochoemog iuuenem vnum multum diligebant, qui dicebatur alumpnus eorum, quia frequenter vitam suam a puericia apud eos ducebat"); "Vita prima sancti Brendani," VSH 2.99, where a virgin is foster to a male child. Cf. "Vita sancti Fintani," 2.100.

84. *Dialogues* 3.32. Wilfrid of Ripon "seized" a seven-year-old boy dedicated to a monastery when his parents had second thoughts: Eddius Stephanus, *Vita Wilfridi episcopi*, ed. and trans. B. Colgrave (Cambridge, 1927), pp. 38, 40.

clerical author of the story cites Samuel as a suitable precedent.[85] The same author mentions a number of "boys" serving as "ministers" of Spanish churches.[86] The Council of Mainz in the next century seems to understand oblation to apply to boys in diocesan as well as monastic institutions.[87] Altfrid mentions in his life of St. Ludger that the saint's maternal grandmother had "commended" her two sons to Willibrord "for rearing": one became a priest, the other died in childhood.[88] Bathilde also "commended" to monastic life children she rescued from slavery or whom she had taken on as wards. Such commendations may have been oblation, or less formal arrangements.[89]

Girls, too, entered religious life in less formal arrangements. The Penitential of Theodore allowed a girl who refused to marry a man to whom her parents had betrothed her to enter a convent;[90] and the Laws of the Lombards made provision for female slaves placed in monasteries by their owners as "offerings" (*oblationem*).[91]

Some children entered religious institutions along with their parents: it was usually supposed that they, like oblates, would become members of the order, and it appears that they were generally treated as oblates, separated from their parents and cared for by monastic personnel appointed for the purpose.[92]

It is tempting to view the rationalization and institutionalization of abandonment made possible by oblation (and other modes of yielding offspring to the church) as representing a decline in the

85. Paul the Deacon (of Mérida), *De vita et miraculis patrum emeritensium,* ed. Henrique Florez, in *España sagrada* 13 (Madrid, 1782), chap. 5, pp. 348–49. Note that Paul uses *offero* in the phrase "Deo omnipotenti serviturum obtulit," recalling *oblatio* (see note 76, above).

86. Ibid., chap. 1, pp. 336–39.

87. "Sive in canonico sive monachico ordine," cited above, note 52.

88. *Altfridi vita sancti Liudgeri* (ut supra) 1.5: "Adelburg pridem suos duos germanos fratres sancto commendavit episcopo Willibrordo. . . . Horum prior in levitarum obiit gradu, iunior non pervenit ad gradum, sed ita in iuventute de hac luce migrabat."

89. "Quosdam liberos relaxavit quosdam vero cum religionis habitu sub regula in monasteria transmisit. Praecipue autem de gente sua viros et puellas, quas ipsa nutrierat, sicut semetipsam Deo commendavit, et coenobialiem vitam ducere instituit" (*Vita sanctae Balthildis* 2.12 [AASS 3.359]).

90. 2.12.34, trans. in McNeill and Gamer, p. 211.

status of, or concern with, children in the early Middle Ages—an indication of increased social acceptance of a practice treated with embarrassed silence or benign neglect in the ancient world. This view would coincide with generally low estimates of medieval sentimental attachments to children. But it does not agree with the evidence. Employing oblation as a means of family limitation— whether in addition to, in congruence with, or despite its religious functions—placed a major form of abandonment not merely under public scrutiny, but under the control of the most admired, conscientious, orderly, and public-spirited institution of the Middle Ages, an entity represented nearly everywhere in Catholic Europe and more likely than almost any other social body to discharge its responsibilities in good faith. Oblation foreclosed certain possibilities (such as marriage) open to other abandoned children, but it facilitated access to many others, including the ecclesiastical power structure, and, in the view of contemporaries, eternal salvation: the major goal of life. Its ease and superiority in some respects to sale or exposing probably allowed parents to evade responsibilities of child care with fewer misgivings; but if so, it also rescued many children who would have passed into slavery or worse through traditional modes of abandonment.

91. *Edictus Langobardorum* 95.12 (MGH *Legum* 4, ed. George Pertz [Hannover, 1868], p. 146): "Si quiscumque liber homo ancillam suam pro religionis et munditiae causa vestem religiosam induerit, ut ei, sicut consuitudo terrae istius est, inferendam aut oblationem per loga sanctorum deveat deportare. . . ."

92. See, for example, the seventh-century *Regula Communis* of St. Fructuosus, chap. 6 ("Qualiter debeant viri cum uxoribus ac filiis absque periculo vivere in monasterio" [PL 87.1115–16]), which directs that children who enter with parents should be subject to monastic discipline and remain permanently in the monastery, and that parents and children should not converse unless specifically authorized by the abbot, but which allows very young children to see and speak with parents when they wish. For instances, see, *inter alia*, the case settled by Pope Nicholas, and that of Sadalberga in the seventh century, who entered monastic life with her husband and children: MGH SSRRMM 5.8 and 12 (pp. 54, 56). See also Quinn, "Benedictine Oblation," p. 39.

6

❖   ❖   ❖

DEMOGRAPHIC
OVERVIEW

TO THE EXTENT that they can be determined—the
documentation for the early Middle Ages is comparatively far less
diverse and less abundant than that for Roman antiquity—the motives for abandonment, whether secular or religious, appear to have
been similar to those in the ancient world. Poverty was viewed in
nearly all quarters as justification for exposing a child, and the
church met the needs of poor parents by providing a safe location to
leave children and a system for placing them. In a Europe where
much of the adult population could barely sustain itself, many parents could not support children at all. Periodic famines and plagues
aggravated the plight of the poor and increased their numbers, and
under such circumstances many children were sold (although sales
also took place under normal conditions), apparently both to maintain a manageable family size and to produce extra income. If they
lived near a monastery and it would accept children of the lower
classes, poor parents could donate their offspring to monastic life.

Among the middle and upper classes (probably less than ten percent of the population), issues of property and inheritance were
doubtless the primary economic motivation for abandonment, and
oblation the preferred method, because of its obvious superiority in
many respects to sale and exposing. Fragmentary evidence suggests
that despite the occurrence of some very large families, a great
many prosperous Europeans of the time drew the line at about
where Romans had in regard to the desirable number of heirs: noble

German families seem to have had about two children per couple during Carolingian times, and acts of donation to German religious houses in the eighth and ninth centuries reveal families with an average of 2.6 children per couple among the donors.[1] Clearly the aim in many cases was to prevent fragmentation of an estate or to maximize the inheritance of older children. Monastic chroniclers themselves[2] complain that this is a principal motivation for oblation. As early as the fifth century, Salvian had written a long and bitter treatise about parents keeping estates for the other heirs rather than granting their portion to those in religious life, and property arrangements between parents and monasteries became increasingly complex and acrimonious throughout the Middle Ages.[3] In the High Middle Ages, when documentation is somewhat more detailed, it can be shown that it is usually younger sons who are donated to monasteries, and there is no reason to suppose this was not also the case in earlier centuries.[4]

Dynastic considerations might render children not only unwanted but dangerous: younger sons or siblings regularly challenged succession to the thrones of early medieval Europe, and children of second and third marriages represented threats to those of the first, and vice versa. The motif of the child destined to injure his parents, his family, or his kingdom, ubiquitous in ancient and medieval mythology and folklore, must to some extent reflect anxieties of this sort: "The fewer full-grown male relatives a king had around him, the easier he slept at night."[5] Abandoning such per-

---

1. See Jean-Pierre Cuvillier, "L'Enfant dans la tradition féodale germanique," in *L'Enfant au Moyen-Age,* p. 50. Like most demographic figures, these could easily be misunderstood: although Cuvillier based his study on a fairly wide sample (580 acts of oblation), they are all from a single area, which may have been atypical. More important, 40 to 50 percent of the parents had no heirs at all, so his figure of 2.6 is a statistical mean somewhat removed from the most common number of children per household. It does, however, match other evidence, such as that from the monastic inventories discussed below.

2. Basil in the early Middle Ages, as noted above. In the High and later Middle Ages this was a common lament: see note 3, below.

3. Salvian, *Ad ecclesiam adversus avaritiam* (CSEL 8.224–326). See esp. 5.3 (CSEL 8.276): "Why, I ask, oh most inhuman of parents, do you impose on them [your children in religious life] the necessity of humiliating poverty? Leave this to the religion to which you have relinquished your children—better that they should become paupers on their own."

4. See chapter 8.

5. Stafford, "Sons and Mothers," p. 95.

sons as children—through exposing, fosterage, or oblation—was certainly more humane than murdering them, sometimes resorted to in later ages.[6]

The death of one or both parents, common even among the wealthy in an age of plague and erratic nutrition, also seems to have prompted oblation in many cases.[7]

Although the sources provide no numerical data, there is some indication that gender disproportion led to abandonment in all social classes. The number of regulations about oblation that apply specifically to female oblates is striking considering that the documents in which they occur otherwise direct far more attention to males.[8] Although brides and mothers were valued in much of early medieval Europe, and this might indicate a shortage of women,[9] females below and above childbearing years usually were not highly prized, and it is entirely possible that the low supply of marriageable women was in some measure a consequence of abandonment of female children to religious communities or to servile status (in which case they might become concubines, but generally not wives).[10] It is apparent that large numbers of women in the early

6. On this, see esp. Stafford, "Sons and Mothers." The internecine violence and bloodshed that characterized transitions of power even within families among the ruling Visigoths of early medieval Spain was dubbed the "sickness of the Goths" (morbus gothorum) by Fredegar (Chronicae [ed. B. Krusch] 4.82, MGH SSRRMM 2 [Hannover, 1888], p. 163) and detestabilis consuetudo by Gregory of Tours (Historia Francorum 3.30), but it was, in fact, typical of all early medieval monarchies, and had been common under the later Roman empire as well. For the Visigoths, see Collins, "Julian of Toledo," and P. D. King, Law and Society in the Visigothic Kingdom (New York, 1972). For a more general view, see P. Grierson, "Election and Inheritance in Early Germanic Kingship," Cambridge Historical Journal 7 (1941) 1–22.

7. Euthymios the Great entered religious life at three when his father died and his mother became a deaconess (Cyril of Scythopolis, Life of Euthymios 3); St. Sabas lost his parents at age five, and at eight was put into a monastery when his uncles could not agree about responsibility for him (Cyril, Life of Sabas 1–2). Cf. the ninth-century cases cited above, in note 54 of chapter 5.

8. Not only is it striking how frequently girls are mentioned along with boys, but in many cases they alone are mentioned in regulations about oblation which might have affected boys as well: see above, e.g., Councils of Orléans (549) and Mâcon (583), and Capitularies of 804, 805.

9. See Herlihy, "Medieval Children," p. 116, where he estimates that among the Franks a childbearing woman was valued at three times the worth of a free male; cf. Herlihy, Medieval Households, pp. 73–78.

10. See, e.g., Leyser, Rule and Conflict, chap. 6, esp. pp. 63–65, and the useful

Middle Ages did not marry, and that religious life was widely employed as a decorous means of accommodating them: "Nunneries were emphatically the favoured way of disposing of surplus daughters." [11]

Shame, which also affected all social classes, involved factors familiar from earlier centuries—illegitimacy, adultery, incest—but also new ones: although clerical celibacy would not be a firm rule until the eleventh century, sporadic pressure was exerted against clerical marriage throughout the early Middle Ages, and it was always scandalous for bishops or those in monastic communities to have children. The Ninth Council of Toledo declared all children of clerical unions slaves of the church—removing from the parents the decision about whether to abandon them or not.[12] (It is somewhat poignant that at the Council of Nicea the major opponent of obligatory clerical celibacy had been Paphnutius, himself given to the church as a child.)[13]

In addition, folk beliefs regarding the causes of birth defects, which may always have inspired some abandonment, became incorporated into the official ethical system. Christian couples could not

---

observations on the position of women in the review by Lawrence Duggan, *Speculum* 56 (Jan. 1981), p. 169. Most specific cases are known because of something remarkable about them and do not justify extrapolation. Wrssingus and Adalgarda had two sons and nine daughters; six of the daughters died unmarried, but the family had moved, and this might have been the result of lack of connections in the community (*Altfridi vita sancti Liudgeri* 1.5). Charlemagne would not allow any of his daughters to marry—for dynastic reasons, according to Stafford, "Sons and Mothers," p. 96. C. N. L. Brooke argues that monks "vastly outnumbered" nuns before 1200 (e.g., in *The Monastic World* [London, 1974], pp. 167, 177–78, 254; or in "St. Clare," with Rosalind Brooke; or in Baker, *Medieval Women,* 275–88, p. 276), but the evidence does not seem to me to justify such certainty. In the modern world there are approximately three women in religious orders to every man, as Brooke himself notes, and medieval population figures of all sorts for women are infamously inaccurate. There were certainly more monasteries than convents prior to 1200, and they were larger, but this does not necessarily mean that there were "vastly" more monks than nuns, since nuns occupied smaller quarters.

11. Stafford, "Sons and Mothers," p. 97. Pretenders to thrones, as Stafford notes, often raided nunneries for well-connected brides.

12. "The offspring produced by such pollution, moreover, shall not only have no share in their parents' estate, but shall remain in perpetual servitude to that church of whose priest or minister they were ignominiously born" (*Concilios,* p. 303). The status of clerical offspring became a major problem in the High Middle Ages, and is discussed below, in chapter 9.

13. Socrates, *Historia ecclesiastica* 1.11, cf. 1.23 (PG 67.104, 925).

engage in conjugal relations during menstruation, lactation, Lent, or on Sundays, and it was apparently widely believed that violating these rules would produce deformed offspring.[14] Gregory of Tours describes a child with severe birth defects and notes that "he was viewed by most people with derision, and the mother, who was blamed for having produced such a child, tearfully confessed that he had been conceived on a Sunday night." Infractions of this sort, Gregory warns, will produce crippled, deformed, or leprous offspring, and Christians should beware lest the deed of one night should haunt them for many years thereafter.[15] The child in this particular case was reared by his mother and then exhibited as a freak by traveling merchants, but many parents would doubtless have abandoned children with visible abnormalities lest moral censure add to the inherent difficulties of bringing up such a child. Whether the kindness of strangers would extend to the point of rescuing and rearing these *expositi* is hard to know. Oblation provided a home for them in the High Middle Ages, as is evident from monastic complaints on the subject; but no such references survive from early medieval monastic writers.

How many children were abandoned? Given the paucity of figures for all periods in regard to abandonment, it would certainly be jejune to hope for statistical indications from the least documented centuries of European history. The aggregate population of Europe during the period is not known, nor the sex ratio, nor rates of birth and mortality. The number of monasteries cannot even be determined with certainty, much less their population or the percentage of oblates.[16]

14. See Payer, "Sex and the Penitentials," pp. 127–28, for periods of restraint required in penitential literature. For deformities resulting from sex during menstruation in particular, see also Sermon 292 in PL 39.2300 (spuriously attributed to Augustine; possibly by Caesarius of Arles, though this is by no means certain); and Caesarius's genuine Sermon 44 (ed. G. Morin in CC 103 [Turnhout, 1953], pp. 187–91); cf. Charles Wood, "The Doctors' Dilemma: Sin, Salvation, and the Menstrual Cycle in Medieval Thought," *Speculum* 56, 4 (1981) 710–27, and Noonan, *Contraception*, p. 282 and *passim*.

15. *De virtutibus sancti Martini* 2.24 (in *Miraculorum libri viii*, ed. Krusch, MGH SSRRMM 1.2, p. 617). I have rendered *ephilentici* as "diseased." Flandrin ("L'Attitude à l'égard," p. 155) thinks it means "epileptic," but this seems unlikely to me. (Medieval medical terms are extremely uncertain.) Caesarius of Arles (Sermon 44.7 [cited above, note 14], p. 199) also inveighs against making love on Sunday.

16. Quinn ("Benedictine Oblation," p. 89) estimates that twenty-five percent

If one were to make the simplifying assumptions that everyone in the West knew all of the Christian sexual restrictions, respected them, and tried to live by them, he would still not have a clear idea whether this would result in an increase or a decrease in abandonment as compared to Roman society. Though there would be fewer extramarital sexual encounters, sex within marriage would be exclusively procreative. Some would believe it their duty to "increase and multiply"—which few Romans did—while others would espouse celibacy, or even abstinence within marriage, lauded by moralists. The presence of a large element of the population called to celibacy is, indeed, a significant change in the social demography of Europe, but available evidence suggests that it was generally disregarded by diocesan clergy before the eleventh century, and probably affected the population only through monasticism, a small percentage of the clergy. Oblation may have lowered the rate of reproductivity by placing many abandoned children in a situation where they could not marry—but as a class abandoned children were probably always at some disadvantage in the marriage market.

Three tantalizing fragments of demographic evidence survive from the opening of the ninth century: inventories of monastic lands (including lay households) from St. Germain in northern France, St. Victor of Marseilles, and Farfa, near Rome.[17] Previous scholarship, not taking into account the possibility of abandonment, has been much vexed by the peculiar populations suggested by this data, and many theories have been proposed (and criticized) to account for them.[18] To be sure, the data are peculiar and not en-

---

of the Carolingian monastic population was composed of oblates, on the basis of structural considerations. The reliability of this guess depends to a large extent on how "paradigmatic" the plan of St. Gall actually is, a question not determinable in the present state of the evidence.

17. All three were published in the nineteenth century: *Polyptych de l'abbé Irminon,* ed. B. Guérard (Paris, 1844) and *Polyptych de l'abbaye de Saint-Germain-des-Prés,* ed. A. Longnon (Paris, 1886–95); *Cartulaire de Saint-Victor de Marseilles,* ed. B. Guérard (Paris, 1857), 2 vols.; *Il regesto di Farfa compilato da Gregorio da Catino,* ed. I. Giorgi and U. Balzani (Rome, 1879–88), 5 vols. These pose considerable analytical difficulty; other *polyptiques* pose even greater questions, and are barely usable in demographic contexts: see, e.g., the new edition of the *polyptique* of St. Remi of Reims by Jean-Pierre Devroey (*Le polyptyque et les listes de cens de l'Abbaye de Saint-Remi de Reims [IXe–XIe siècles],* ed. Devroey [Reims, 1984]) and discussion therein of the many troublesome aspects of the collection.

18. E.g., Emily Coleman, "Infanticide in the Early Middle Ages"; Richard

tirely trustworthy,[19] but their most troubling aspects are substantially explained by the evidence of abandonment presented above. In all of the communities there are far fewer children than scholars would have predicted[20]—indeed, far fewer than would be necessary to sustain the population[21]—and in at least two of them the sex ratio among the children is remarkably skewed in favor of the males.[22]

Ring, "Early Medieval Peasant Households," pp. 2–25; Herlihy, "Medieval Children," and idem, *Medieval Households,* esp. pp. 62–77. On the general difficulties of using such sources, see J.-P. Devroey, "Les méthodes d'analyse démographique des polyptyques du Haut Moyen Age," in *Histoire et Méthode,* ed. M.-A. Arnould et al. (Brussels, 1981), pp. 71–88 (*Acta Historica Bruxellensia* 4).

19. This is discussed at length by both Ring and Devroey. It is essential in assessing statistical tabulations to consider carefully how each demographer has resolved the ambiguities of the sources. Herlihy, for example, in tabulating the peasants of St. Victor, takes a reference to *filii* as indicating "two children of uncertain sex" (*Medieval Households,* p. 77, note a to table 3.3), although contemporary households show great variation in the number of children (at Farfa, for example, Ring finds that twenty-eight percent of the households have four or more children, some as many as seven).

20. At Farfa, according to Ring, 2.3 per nuclear household, 3.2 per multiple household, and 2.1 per extended household (p. 12). At St. Victor, as calculated by Herlihy (*Medieval Households,* p. 77), 360 children to 667 adults. At St. Germain (ibid., pp. 69–71) 1.11 boys per man, and 0.79 girls per woman; or (Herlihy, "Medieval Children," pp. 116–17) 85 to 116 children (depending on how one reads the documents) per 100 adults.

21. In all three the number of children per household is far below the 3.5 Russell postulated as necessary for replacement in ancient and medieval Europe; at St. Germain and St. Victor the number is even below the 2.2 children needed in modern Western societies and thought to be the absolute minimum replacement number under any circumstances (see, e.g., Keyfitz, "The Population of China," p. 44). Herlihy comments: "In the great ninth-century survey of St. Germain-des-Prés, the paucity of children attributed to the households makes it hard to see how the community was even maintaining its numbers" (*Medieval Households,* p. 142).

22. See following discussion and note 24, below, for figures, although each of the secondary studies cited above must be consulted to have an idea how sex ratio can be estimated for each population, and what variations might be produced depending on the methods used. The biological ratio of male to female births is 1.05 (or 105, if expressed as the number of males per 100 females), according to A. Coale, "The History of Human Population," *Scientific American* 231 (1974), p. 43. (Thus a "high" sex ratio is many men to few women; a "low" sex ratio the reverse. I apologize to readers for employing this convention, but it seems too well established to revise through individual action.) Russell (LAMPC, p. 21) estimated that the sex ratio "in much of the Middle Ages" was high (between 110 and 130), using evidence under consideration here, as well as other materials. His data usually indicate

Infanticide has been proposed as an explanation,[23] but since the ratio is not skewed comparably among the adults, it does not solve the demographic problem, and is, in any event, unlikely in these regions in the ninth century, since ecclesiastical law, which would have been influential on monastic lands, punished it severely. (And there are extremely few references to it in contemporary sources.)

Where it can be determined, moreover, the number of children in the households of the wealthy is greater than would be expected, and shows an obverse sex ratio: at St. Germain the wealthiest ten percent of the households have twenty percent of the community's children, many of them unnamed and apparently not biologically related to the householder; at Farfa the sex ratio among the general population (122) is four times higher than that at the manor house (32).[24] There is, moreover, a marked difference of birth order in the sex ratios at Farfa and St. Germain, which has often been noted but rarely discussed and never explained. The ratio among the firstborn is staggeringly high (500 at Farfa; 270 at St. Germain) and falls to much less than half this (108 and 54, respectively) for the second child.[25]

The explanation for this seems obvious when abandonment is

---

higher sex ratios for adults than for children, however (see remarks on this in Ring, p. 5, n. 10).

23. By Coleman, "Infanticide"; this is challenged on methodological grounds by Ring. Herlihy proposed in "Medieval Children" (p. 117) that the disproportion was due to lack of interest in recording female children, but in *Medieval Households* (pp. 68–70) he suggests that the figures be corrected by removing "male solitaries" and assuming that many females "were temporary transfers into the [wealthier] household and not the natural offspring of the head"—a solution much like the one proposed here.

24. At St. Germain the overall ratio is even higher (135), and higher still in the ranks of children and slaves on individual plots, but the servants of the manor house are not listed, and most are presumably female. At St. Victor the sex ratio among children whose gender is given appears to be slightly low (99 males to 106 females), but the gender of nearly half the children (155) is not indicated, which makes any inference highly dubious.

25. See figures in Ring (p. 6). Ring accounts for this by proposing that firstborn females were often recorded as males, but I find this unpersuasive, especially since a probable explanation, supported by many other data, is available in the practice of abandonment, particularly in monastic communities, which could not only absorb boys as oblates (or girls in convents, but these are not at issue here), but children of either sex as workers.

264 · *The Kindness of Strangers*

taken into account: peasants wanted at least one son and made sure that their first child was male by abandoning daughters to the service of the wealthy or to nearby monastic communities. After they had a boy, they were much more willing to have a girl, and the sex ratio fell to normal or below. Many of the poorer couples, though not all, abandoned children of either sex if they had more than three or four. Most of these were picked up and recorded in the great households, where many more children, especially girls, appear. In addition, some were probably not recorded, some probably died, and some may have been sold or given away outside the community. Abandonment of this sort entailed no sin, and requires no supposition of parental cruelty, biological abnormality, demographic disruption, or even faulty record-keeping. Like countless Europeans before and after them, a proportion of the parents in these regions abandoned children, especially girls, to monastic communities or the kindness of strangers. The children may have been formally offered as oblates or officially indentured or "fostered"; the arrangement may have been impersonal through sale or exposing; or it may have fallen somewhere in between.

It is hardly surprising that abandonment persisted and underwent elaboration and refinement in Catholic Europe. If the continent was underpopulated during most of the period, it was also desperately poor, and balancing the number of mouths to feed against the number of hands to feed them is as difficult in a sparsely populated subsistence economy as it is in a crowded urban setting. By insisting that sexuality be directed always and only to the production of children, and by prohibiting every means of contraception or terminating pregnancy, the prevailing moral and legal systems of Catholic Europe all but forced Christian parents into coping with an abundance of offspring, and many responded to this by abandoning some of them.

Whether in acknowledgment of some responsibility for the situation or simply from Christian concern, the church intervened in several ways to ameliorate the one means of family regulation available. Most notably, it offered some parents the option of oblation, which, though not without cost, was more humane than traditional modes of abandonment in many ways—perhaps in all ways in the view of contemporaries.

Apart from this innovation, most early medieval forms of abandonment were variations on themes familiar from the ancient world: churches replaced civic buildings or columns in the forum as preferred locations for leaving infants (many of the churches were themselves Roman buildings or based on Roman models); laws about abandonment and reclamation were selected and adapted from Roman precedents to meet new circumstances and exigencies; the position of *alumni* retained the sentimental appeal it had held in the Roman world, but was both enhanced and blunted by its use as a general Christian metaphor.[26] Even among peoples little influenced by Roman culture and government, the same general patterns of abandonment emerge from the sources: children are exposed in public places, sold outright, donated to religious houses or to the wealthy as servants; and parents are prompted by the same range of motivations—from poverty to shame to selfishness to dynastic or gender considerations—discernible in Roman sources. Resignation and acceptance of most forms of abandonment appear to prevail among most of the population, even moral writers, as they had at Rome. If individual and social determination to preserve freeborn status ceases to benefit children, the rise of religious communities that were prepared to welcome them without stigma provides a new safeguard, the one major departure from the traditions of the ancient world. Like many medieval institutions, oblation constituted a compromise between a highly developed moral system and primitive social structures. Christian society entertained small hope

26. Another form of spiritual guardianship that developed during the early Middle Ages, although it did not involve abandonment, both reflected and influenced popular attitudes toward nonbiological parenting: by the ninth century, children were presented for baptism by "godparents," who were not members of their immediate family. The relationship between the child and the godparent was called "spiritual affinity," and it affected other relatives as well. In some areas of Europe elaborate social structures evolved around the "co-parenting" of godparents and natal kin, and in all Christian states persons closely related through "spiritual affinity" were prohibited from marrying. On this, see Lynch, *Godparents and Kinship in Early Medieval Europe*. Godparents sometimes "fostered" their godchildren and were expected to oversee spiritual development or act as guardians in case of the death of parents, but this did not involve any abrogation of responsibility by the parents, so godparenting is apposite to abandonment only when other aspects of the relationship make it so. Its importance did, however, enhance the position of "affective" kinship in Christian cultures.

of eliminating the ills of a world corrupted by sin, among which numbered the problem of unwanted or unsupportable children, but it held out to its members the hope of alleviating suffering on an individual basis and facilitating transition to a happier life in another world, ends to which oblation doubtless seemed better suited than ancient forms of abandonment.

PART III

THE HIGH MIDDLE AGES

7

❖   ❖   ❖

NEW DEMOGRAPHICS:
1000–1200

BY THE YEAR 1000 the population of Western Europe had approximately doubled over its seventh-century low, and had surpassed even the numbers achieved under the empire, its previous high point. During the next two centuries what had been a gradual expansion became an explosion: by the end of the thirteenth century the population had doubled again—not merely once but perhaps twice.[1]

Many factors were responsible for the increase from the sixth century to the tenth: the gradual cessation of violent incursions by barbarian peoples; the steady increase in domestic tranquility as local and regional governments coalesced and began to reestablish the social order lost after the decline of Rome; and the introduction or invention of more productive methods of agriculture capable of

1. Russell (LAMPC, p. 36) estimates that the population of Western (including Central) Europe was 5.5 million in A.D. 650; 12 million in 1000; and 35.5 million in 1340. For other estimates, see general works on demography cited in the Introduction, note 18. The absolute numbers are much disputed, but the general trends are not, and many researchers have argued that Russell underestimated the rate of increase in the High Middle Ages: e.g., M. Postan, in *Cambridge Economic History* 1 (Cambridge, 1964), p. 562, who thought that the pre-plague population of England might have been double what Russell had posited; cf. Herlihy, *Medieval Households,* pp. 80 and 144, where he notes that much of Europe did not regain until 1850 the population levels it had reached by 1300. For an overview of some of the demographic difficulties of the period, see R. Fossier, "La Démographie médiévale: Problèmes de méthode (XI–XIIIe siècles)," ADH (1975) 143–65.

sustaining much greater human and livestock populations. Whether these same factors account for the sudden growth in the High Middle Ages is less clear. Momentum would play some role, but could not entirely account for the dramatic change in the rate of increase. Whatever else was involved, it was closely related to the tremendous increases in economic prosperity at the time. Europe as a whole remained predominantly agricultural, but the revival of city life was a major factor in all the changes—economic, demographic, political, and cultural—of the High Middle Ages. London, Paris, Barcelona, Venice, Rome, Bologna, and a great many other cities had by this point far outgrown the walls to which they had been confined during the turbulent centuries of the early Middle Ages and were spilling out into the countrysides around them, as merchants, students, lawyers, clerics, administrators, wealthy nobles, and even runaway serfs flocked to them. Large areas of Europe (e.g., northern Italy, Flanders) were increasingly characterized by predominantly urban economies, based on commerce and manufacturing rather than agriculture alone. Even so, the urban centers extant at the opening of the eleventh century proved inadequate to the pressure of increasing populations, and throughout the eleventh and twelfth centuries new towns and cities sprang up everywhere on the continent and in England, either through the expansion of small villages or the planting of settlements in what had been rural or even desert areas.

The end of this period of expansion is even more mysterious than its beginning. Historians and demographers have debated for decades whether it was sudden or gradual, the natural tapering off of the bulge or a catastrophic discontinuity, the cause or the result of the great plagues of the mid-fourteenth century—and these questions still await definitive resolution. What is clear is that already by the second half of the thirteenth century the demographic expansion had stalled, and after the Black Death of 1348–50 the population of Europe fell to lows from which it would not fully recover for centuries. Not until the eighteenth century did areas of Italy, for example, regain their thirteenth-century populations. Less certain, though probable, is that economic prosperity was also declining in the later thirteenth century, possibly under the pressure of unprecedented and unsustainable population density and increasing national and international violence in Europe, and that most of the continent suffered drastic economic shifts and dislocations throughout the fourteenth century.

1. She-wolf suckling the foundlings Romulus and Remus, legendary founders of Rome. Date disputed; probably Etruscan, sixth century B.C. This statue, the "Capitoline wolf," or a similar one stood on the Capitoline Hill over the forum at Rome at least as early as the third century B.C., conveying to Romans who passed under it, for many subsequent centuries, the potentially happy prospects for abandoned children. A similar image appeared on imperial coins, altars, murals, and mosaics. Many ancient and medieval dynasties included abandoned children in their founding legends. (*Courtesy of the Capitoline Museum, Rome*)

2. Oedipus, in a thirteenth-century illumination. In the upper left, Oedipus is exposed at the order of his father, King Laios; in the upper right, he fights with Laios, unaware of his identity; in the lower left, he slays the Sphinx; in the lower right, he rules as king. The exposing of children at the command of the father, consequent misfortune for the parents, and great accomplishment by the foundling himself are common themes of the literature of abandonment. The peculiar mode of exposing depicted here (hanging the child by his feet) is probably a conflation of the Greek story, in which the baby's ankles were pierced, with the medieval custom of hanging children in trees to protect them from animals. Contemporary written descriptions, however, suggest that such infants were carefully wrapped and left with tokens. Cf. plates 3 and 13. (*Courtesy of the Schlossbibliothek, Pommersfelden: Cod. 295, fol. 52v—Bildarchiv Foto Marburg*)

3. In this slightly later (fourteenth-century) illustration of
the Oedipus legend, the exposing, the fight, and the
marriage of Oedipus to his mother are all presented in the
same frame. The abandonment itself is probably somewhat
more realistic than in the previous illustration: a servant
hangs the baby in a tree rather than on a post, although he is
still naked, a detail doubtless designed to provoke pity.
(*Courtesy of the Staatsbibliothek, Munich: Cod. gall. 6, fol. 21—
Bildarchiv Foto Marburg*)

4. Abraham preparing to sacrifice his son Isaac (Genesis 22). Chartres Cathedral, North Portal, thirteenth century. After abandoning Ishmael at the insistence of Sarah, Abraham was then asked by God to sacrifice his other son, Isaac, who is shown here with his feet bound, ready for the altar, standing on the ram that eventually replaced him. Abraham's tender gesture and wistful gaze toward heaven may reflect the poignant dilemma of ancient and medieval parents who felt called to part with children for religious reasons. (*Bildarchiv Foto Marburg*)

5. The abandonment of Moses. Thirteenth century. The most famous abandoned child in the Western tradition, Moses was exposed in a basket on a river not because his parents did not want him, but because he would otherwise have been killed by the Egyptians (Exodus 2). (Note the grief-stricken expression on his mother's face here.) That he was promptly found, was reared with great tenderness, and subsequently rose to be the central figure in Jewish history probably offered comfort to parents who felt constrained to abandon their children. The curious detail that his own mother was hired to nurse him found parallels in real life. In this high medieval picture Bible, the exposing of Moses is juxtaposed with the birth of Christ, of which it is seen to be a prefiguring. (*Courtesy of the Bodleian Library, Oxford: Ms. Bodl. 270b, fol. 37*)

6. Solomon proposing to divide the disputed infant with his sword (1 Kings 3:16–28). Thirteenth century. The "false mother," the *Bible Moralisée* explains, would allow the child to be cut in two, while the "true mother" would give up her child rather than see him harmed. The claiming of someone else's child as one's own, the killing of infants at the command of a higher authority, and the ambivalence of giving up a child to save him were all staples of the literature—moral, fictional, and historical—of abandonment. (*Courtesy of the Bodleian Library, Oxford: Ms. Bodl. 270b, fol. 163v*)

7. The surrendering of children to creditors (based here on the story of 2 [4] Kings 4:1–7). Thirteenth century. Selling, pawning, or giving children to creditors to satisfy a debt was an extremely common practice in antiquity; it was known, but less common, in the Middle Ages, because the lending of money was severely discouraged in medieval Europe. (*Courtesy of the Bodleian Library, Oxford: Ms. Bodl. 270b, fol. 176*)

8. Two starving mothers fight over whose child they will eat (2 [4] Kings 6:30). Thirteenth century. The king, observing the pitiful scene, rends his garments in horror. This shocking topos occurs with surprising frequency in biblical and medieval literature, and indicates, at the least, concern about the fate of children during periods of social distress. (*Courtesy of the Bodleian Library, Oxford: Ms. Bodl. 270b, fol. 181*)

9. The offering of children to the service of God in the Judeo-
Christian tradition. This tableau from a fifteenth-century picture
bible (*Biblia pauperum*) ties together many strands of Christian
tradition regarding the offering of children to religious service. The
left panel treats the obligation of Israelites to present their first-born
to the Lord, and is taken to prefigure the offering of Christ in the
temple by his mother (center). On the right, Hanna offers Samuel as
an infant to the service of God—the precedent, medieval authorities
claimed, for oblation. The word *oblatum* occurs in the legend below
the drawing, which says that the offering of Samuel denotes Christ's
offering himself. (*Courtesy of the Morgan Library, New York: 19328,
Biblia pauperum, fol. 4*)

10. Grammar is depicted as a teacher holding a switch over
oblate schoolchildren (note that the boy on the right is
wearing a cowl). Chartres Cathedral, Royal Portal, twelfth
century. This was probably a familiar incident in the lives of
many medieval churchmen: donated to monastic life as
children and educated under strict discipline. A manuscript
illustration of the same theme is reproduced in the following
plate (no. 11), more realistically portraying the teacher as
a monk. Women were oblates as well, but had less opportunity to commemorate their childhoods in art. (*Bildarchiv
Foto Marburg*)

11. Oblates in school. Fourteenth century. A monk in the upper-left-hand corner uses a rod on a schoolchild, while the other oblates look on (note tonsures and cowls). (*Courtesy of the Beinecke Library, Yale University: Ms 404 ["Rothschild Canticles"], fol. 6*)

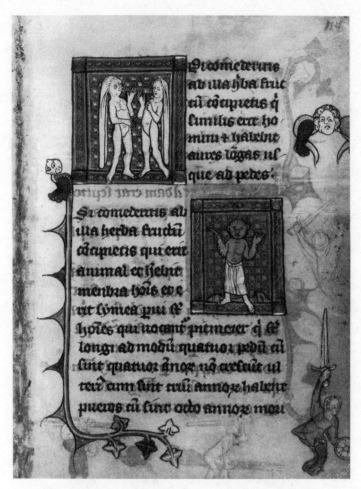

12. Deformed children. Fourteenth century. In the upper drawing the children have long ears, hanging to their feet. In the lower drawing the child is simian. Both of these birth defects occur, the text warns, as a result of eating the wrong foods, but parents were also admonished that intercourse in the wrong season or position would result in defective offspring. The implication of parental culpability for the child's condition doubtless provided an incentive for parents to abandon abnormal children or donate them to monasteries. (*Courtesy of the Beinecke Library, Yale University: Ms. 404 ["Rothschild Canticles"], fol. 114*)

13. Illustrations from an article on "abandoned children" in a fourteenth-century encyclopedia, the *Omne bonum*. The upper miniature shows a nurse depositing a child, carefully wrapped in swaddling clothes, in a doorway, which might represent a foundling home of some sort or merely a public location. The mother looks on while the father appears to direct the abandonment—a common pattern in literature. A third party appears to be admonishing the parents.

The lower miniature is an abandoned child, carefully wrapped (enlarged in next plate). In the lower margin there are two line drawings of babies hung in sacks —a method of exposing children in the Middle Ages. Cf. the illustrations of Oedipus, above. (*Courtesy of the British Library, London: Royal 6E VII, fol. 104*)

14. An exposed child, wrapped in swaddling clothes, from the *Omne bonum*. (*Courtesy of the British Library, London: Royal 6E VII, fol. 104*)

Cōmēt les dolorouses peheresses aptes leur ensantement auōant euiter la honte du monde sans penser en dieu en leur ames par la monetement des dyables ietoiēt leurs ensans sans baptesme en la rmere du tymbre a rōme.

15. Mothers tossing unwanted children into a river. This is the first in a sequence of fifteenth-century manuscript illustrations describing the founding of the Hospital of the Holy Spirit in Rome in the late twelfth century (two others follow). The woman approaching from the left looks furtively about, and the child being dropped from the bridge, though carefully wrapped, has a weight attached to ensure that he will drown. Abandonment is frequently associated with rivers or water in ancient and medieval texts, but the childen were usually rescued. The caption reads: "How the pitiful sinners after childbirth undertake to avoid the contempt of the world, without a thought for God or their souls; at the suggestion of the devil they throw their babies, without baptizing them, into the Tiber in Rome." (*Courtesy of the Hôpital du Saint-Esprit: Manuscrit sur la fondation, miniature 3*)

Coment les pescheurs et seruiteurs du pape peschoient en la Riuere
du tymbre et ne prindrent que petis enfans que on auoit gettes
en la dicte Riuere dont ilz furent moult esbahis en disant quilz
nauoyent peu prendre nultre poisson.

16. Fishermen find the babies thrown in the Tiber. The
caption reads: "How fishermen and servants of the pope
fished in the Tiber and drew out nothing but babies tossed
into the river, at which they were dumbfounded. . . ."
(*Courtesy of the Hôpital du Saint-Esprit: Manuscrit sur la
fondation, miniature 6*)

Comment toute lordre du Saint espent en leur chapitre general
A Romie au Jour de penthecouste se presenta par deuant pape nicolas
v.° lan Jubile · mil · quatrecens cinquante · aux quelz se dit pape
reconforma tous leurs priuileges et indulgences · et les receupt
Joieusement ·

17. "How they took the babies they fished from the Tiber to
the pope, who was deeply disturbed and set himself to pray, asking
God to disclose to him what should be done about these babies."
According to the story, the pope then established in Rome and
France the Hospital of the Holy Spirit, which took in abandoned
children. Ironically, the children were probably more likely to die
in such foundling homes than they had been when they were
abandoned surreptitiously. (*Courtesy of the Hôpital du Saint-Esprit:
Manuscrit sur la fondation, miniature 7*)

One would not expect that population control of any sort would be as widespread in Europe during the period of expansion (roughly, 1000 to 1200) as it had been during the many earlier centuries of low and declining population. Indeed, if an average of 3.5 children per family is necessary simply to maintain the population in preindustrial societies, a 300-percent increase in population over less than three centuries would require most families to produce nearly as many children as biologically possible. At the very least it is necessary to postulate a sharp increase in the birthrate in many segments of the population.

But elevation of the level of prosperity of a whole society does not necessarily alleviate burdens or constraints on individual families. Abandonment in previous centuries had been occasioned by such factors as individual poverty, shame, and the desire to safeguard the integrity of estates. Would general increases in prosperity alleviate these problems?

In fact, whether it was the accumulation of wealth that provoked such changes or not, at least two and probably all three of these factors were substantially mitigated for much of the population during the High Middle Ages. In most of Western Europe between about 1000 and 1200, legal, social, and cultural structures began to incorporate mechanisms to allow the maintenance of estates in the hands of a single heir, thereby greatly reducing the need to limit the number of legitimate children, as had been the case under previous systems of partible inheritance. In some areas (e.g., England) this was achieved by the gradual establishment, in law, of systems of primogeniture, whereby the eldest son automatically inherited the majority of the estate and titles; in some (e.g., Castile) by entailment, through which the testator (or the crown) designated particular estates or portions thereof as indivisible; in some (especially Italy) by family strategies, such as confraternal arrangements whereby heirs worked lands or properties together; in many areas (e.g. France) by combinations of all these.[2] The result was that almost nowhere in

2. This is a particularly difficult topic to survey because inheritance practices vary enormously from region to region, even within the same political-linguistic structures. Michel Parisse, *Noblesse et chevalerie en Lorraine médiévale: Les familles nobles du XIe au XIIIe siècle,* is useful as an introduction to the problem in France and the Low Countries (*passim,* but esp. pp. 86–87 and 170), or Jacques Yver, *Égalité entre Héritiers et exclusion des enfants dotés: Essai de géographie coutumière* (Paris, 1966). Georges Duby argued that primogeniture was already established among the highest nobility in northwestern France by the beginning of the eleventh cen-

Europe by the fourteenth century were the wealthy required to divide their estates among their heirs to the point of endangering family interests. One would expect that this would occasion a considerable increase in the number of children in wealthy households, and the evidence suggests that it did.[3]

An additional factor in relation to the upper classes may have

---

tury, and was universal in the area by the end of the twelfth ("The 'Youth' in Twelfth-Century Aristocratic Society," p. 202). For legal cases involving primogeniture in France in the thirteenth century, see *Les Olim ou registres des arrêts par la cour du roi,* ed. Arthur Beugnot (Paris, 1839–48), 3 vols., 1.4, 376, 527. Karl Leyser ("The German Aristocracy from the Ninth to the Early Twelfth Century: A Historical and Cultural Sketch," *Past and Present* 41 [1968] [reprinted in idem, *Medieval Germany and Its Neighbors, 900–1250* (London, 1982)], especially pp. 50–51) addresses the issue in Germany; cf. John Freed, *The Counts of Falkenstein: Noble Self-Consciousness in Twelfth-Century Germany* (Philadelphia, 1984), pp. 45–49 and 63–67, and idem, "Reflections on the Medieval German Nobility," AHR 91, 3 (1986) 553–75, esp. pp. 562–63. For Spain, see the old but reliable survey in Juan Sempere y Guarinos, *Historia de los vinculos y mayorazgos* (Madrid, 1847), esp. chap. 19, or the massive study of the legal complexities involved in particular cases in Andrew Villalon, "The Law's Delay: The Anatomy of an Aristocratic Property Dispute (1350–1577)," Ph.D. diss., Yale University, 1984. Villalon uses many unpublished documents demonstrating that *mayorazgo* (entailment) was in widespread use as early as the mid-thirteenth century (e.g., pp. 201–5). For England also, old studies remain the standard: Courtney Kenny, *The History of the Law of Primogeniture in England* (Cambridge, 1878); F. Pollock and F. Maitland, *A History of English Law* (Cambridge, 1898), vol. 2, pp. 262–78, 292–94. Herlihy (*Medieval Households,* pp. 93–96) provides a more recent brief overview of the development of primogeniture in England and Germany, and of *consorterie* in Italy.

3. Michel Parisse (*Noblesse et chevalerie,* p. 227) argues specifically that cadet children were better off as a result of widespread primogeniture since it was no longer necessary for the family to take measures to prevent sibling rivalry or internecine struggles over the property; parents were even more willing to invest energy in marrying off younger children once they were no longer a threat to the family. And he finds that the number of children among the noble families in his study increased by about thirty percent between the twelfth and thirteenth centuries alone (p. 275). Although they vary in specifics, most studies indicate an average number of children per household among nobles of the High Middle Ages which is significantly higher than that among their ancestors: see, e.g., Georges Duby, "Lignage, noblesse et chevalerie au XIIe siècle dans la région mâconnaise," *Annales* 27 (1972) 803–23; Michel Parisse, *La Noblesse lorraine, XI–XIIIe siècles* (Paris, 1976); T. H. Hollingsworth, "A Demographic Study of the British Ducal Families," *Population Studies* 11 (1957) 4–26; M.-T. Lorcin, "Retraite des veuves et villes au couvent," ADH (1975) 187–204. Some had extremely large families (ten to fifteen children) which Duby argues ("The 'Youth'") was not unusual. On the other hand, Jean-Pierre Cuvillier ("L'Enfant dans la tradition féodale germanique,"

been the concept of "nobility." In the Roman world the great divide among humans was between "free" and "slave"—a distinction created by social arrangements, invested with enormous emotional significance, and imagined to be related to the essential character of a person. Although it happened commonly, the reduction of freeborn persons to servile status was nonetheless deeply troubling to Romans. Within and among the free classes themselves differences of status were both *de facto* and conceptually fluid, and status was frequently determined as much by effort and opportunity as by blood relationship. Adoption, for example, was often "the cure for chance"—that is, what one lacked in birth could be made up for by adoption, or by the accumulation of wealth, or by being in the right place at the right time. During the early Middle Ages numerous systems of social stratification competed in Western Europe, none of which is yet fully understood. Germanic peoples had aristocracies that were based, apparently, on both heritable privilege and personal qualities—usually martial skill—while Europeans of Roman heritage added to the traditional senatorial aristocracy new bases of status related to high standing in the structures (some of them ecclesiastical) that replaced Roman bureaucracy.

Sometime in the High Middle Ages—social historians have been much exercized about exactly how and when—these systems crystallized into the notions of "nobility" now associated with aristocratic social structures. "Nobility" came to be seen as an inherited, personal characteristic conferring both privilege and obligation, possessed in varying degrees by all classes from knights up, and wholly wanting in everyone else, even in prosperous, freeborn peasants and merchants.[4] The development and dissemination of this concept, which cannot be precisely traced, must have discour-

---

in *L'Enfant au Moyen Age,* p. 50) argues that the *Zweikindersystem*—the preference for having only two children—persisted in Germany through the eleventh century.

4. The category "burgher," or "bourgeois," initially characterized where one lived, not whether he was noble or not. Nobles often had residences in cities, especially in Italy, Spain, and southern France, and might even engage in commerce; but simply being a wealthy burgher would not convey any degree of nobility, no matter how much power it afforded. By the fourteenth century, nobles could not officially engage in commerce in many areas of Europe, although there were many ways to circumvent the prohibition: see, e.g., Archives Nationales, Register JJ 112, no. 325, fol. 163 (June 1378), in which the French crown upholds the nobility of Hilairet de Bournezeau, accused of marrying a *bourgeoise* and engaging in commerce (published in *Recueil* 5: 1376–1390, no. 621, pp. 72–79).

aged abandonment among medieval European "nobles" in much the way that concerns about free status would have restrained Romans: the idea that a noble child would be brought up "ignobly" would have horrified most aristocratic parents, although, like their Roman predecessors, they might have found it the lesser of evils in some cases.[5] But such sentiment would not likely have had a comparable effect on the other classes—about ninety percent of the population. This is a further reason to anticipate increasingly large families among the most powerful (and most frequently recorded) elements of the population, and, likewise, to be wary of extrapolating from this to their less privileged contemporaries.[6]

Social ethics regarding sexuality also underwent profound changes in eleventh- and twelfth-century Europe, as they often do under the pressure of unprecedented wealth.[7] If not more common, extramarital sexuality was certainly much more on the minds of Europeans of the period, and illegitimacy, which had occasioned se-

5. By the thirteenth century, for example, there was a general belief that nobility was innate and visually discernible. When a soldier comes across St. Alban and his family dressed in classless penitents' garb, he nonetheless recognizes them immediately as noble: "video . . . quod paenitentiales estís, sed ut mihi videtur effigie quadam nobilioris sanguinis praefulgetis" (Karin Morvay, *Die Albanuslegende: Deutsche Fassungen und ihre Beziehungen zur lateinischen Überlieferung* [Munich, 1977] [Medium Aevum: Philologische Studien, 32], p. 30). Compare Wolfram von Eschenbach, *Parzival,* line 3658. In *Hrólfs saga Kraka* (ed. D. Slay [Copenhagen, 1960] [Editiones Arnamagnaeanae, Series B, 1], p. 23) a man observes that another has "not thrall's eyes"—suggesting that the difference between lofty and ignoble ancestry was evident in the eyes.

6. On the other hand, fear of having to marry a daughter to a social inferior might be a motive for either oblation or abandonment, since such a marriage could tarnish the standing of the entire family. But according to Constance Bouchard ("Consanguinity and Noble Marriages in the Tenth and Eleventh Centuries," *Speculum* 56, 2 [April 1981] 268–87), nobles did marry their daughters to inferiors.

7. Guibert of Nogent constantly decries the falling off of morals in his day, particularly among married women, calling God as his witness that his observations are accurate: *De vita sua sive monodiarum suarum libri tres,* especially 1.12 (the translation by John Benton, *Self and Society in Medieval France* [Toronto, 1984]), is based on the edition of Georges Bourgin, *Guibert de Nogent: Histoire de sa vie* [Paris, 1907] [Collection de textes pour servir à l'étude et à l'enseignement de l'histoire], but there is now a better edition: Guibert de Nogent, *Autobiographie,* ed. and trans. Edmond-René Labande [Paris, 1981]). On social and cultural change in the twelfth century, see the classic study of C. H. Haskins, *The Renaissance of the Twelfth Century* (Cambridge, Mass., 1927), or more recent essays in R. Benson and Giles Constable, *Renaissance and Renewal in the Twelfth Century* (Cambridge, Mass., 1982) and Sidney Packard, *Twelfth-Century Europe: An Interpretive Essay* (Amherst, 1976).

rious difficulty for women in the newly Christian societies of the early Middle Ages, appears to have become considerably less scandalous.[8] The ability of mothers—whether single, widowed, or divorced—to support children was probably greater in the urban centers of these centuries than it had been at any previous period in European history: in addition to the economic security afforded by social stability, inherited wealth, and commercial opportunity, they also enjoyed more legal independence (though by no means equality with men) than they had even at Rome.[9]

General prosperity does not usually eradicate individual poverty. There were doubtless poor people in Europe in the wealthiest communities in the best of times. But it is very likely that two aspects of the condition of the poor would have reduced their need to abandon children during the High Middle Ages:[10]

(1) Even desperately impoverished people in a relatively rich society are much more likely to find help than those in a society with fewer resources: in the early Middle Ages the number of people to whom one could turn for aid was vastly smaller than in the eleventh or twelfth century, when the proportion of well-to-do persons was much greater. Few general famines or widespread domestic wars

8. Good examples of this can be found in Andreas Capellanus's treatise of courtly love or the erotic poetry called "Goliardic," which celebrates adulterous liaisons. On "courtly love," which may or may not have been primarily adulterous, the literature is too vast for even a sampling: useful recent introductions are Roger Boase, *The Origin and Meaning of Courtly Love: A Critical Study of European Scholarship* (Manchester, 1977), and Douglas Kelly, *Medieval Imagination: Rhetoric and the Poetry of Courtly Love* (Madison, 1978).

9. A flawed survey of the position of women during the period is provided in Shulamith Shahar, *The Fourth Estate: A History of Women in the Middle Ages*. More careful but also more limited material can be found in Derek Baker, ed., *Medieval Women*, and *Women of the Medieval World*, ed. Kirshner and Wemple.

10. There is no adequate study of the poor during this period. The general treatment by Michel Mollat, *Études sur l'histoire de la pauvreté* (Paris, 1974) (Publications de la Sorbonne, Études, no. 8), 2 vols. (trans. Arthur Goldhammer, *The Poor in the Middle Ages: An Essay in Social History* [New Haven, 1986]), will be of some help, and can be supplemented by specialized studies (e.g., *Assistance et charité;* Jean-Marc Bienvenu, "Pauvreté, misères et charité en Anjou aux xi et xii siècles," *Le Moyen Age* 72 [1966] 389–424, 73 [1967] 5–34, 189–216; or Jacqueline Caille, *Hôpitaux et charité publique à Narbonne au Moyen Age de la fin du XIe à la fin du XVe siècle* [Toulouse, 1978]). On the conceptual relationship of social to idealized poverty, see Lester Little, *Religious Poverty and the Profit Economy in Medieval Europe* (Ithaca, 1979); cf. Brian Tierney, *Medieval Poor Law: A Sketch of Canonical Theory and Its Application in England* (Berkeley, 1959).

afflicted whole areas between 1000 and 1200, as they had regularly in much of Europe during most of the previous millennium. Money was much more available, making poor-relief more practical: charity became much easier to organize. Indeed, the stunning increase of wealth among the upper classes in the eleventh century occasioned such an ethical crisis among the followers of the indigent Jesus that there was a general rush to divert money and possessions into the hands of the worthy poor.

(2) There were also many more opportunities for the offspring of the disadvantaged. Parents could hardly have felt, as they must have centuries before, that their children would be no better off than they. Opportunities for making one's fortune abounded during the High Middle Ages, whether as a soldier, farmer, merchant, clerk, monk, or servant to the wealthy. Just the fact that there were many more households that could afford to hire or support servants would make a considerable difference in the ability of the poor to bring children into the world without fear of the consequences.[11] Whether strictly factual or not, it is revealing that a biography of the twelfth-century troubador Marcabrus would allege that he "was abandoned at the door of a rich man."[12]

Considering these trends, one might anticipate that abandonment would be less common from about 1000 to about 1200 than it had been previously, and would reappear as a social problem during the thirteenth century, when conditions took a turn for the worse. And the evidence suggests that this was almost precisely the case. Evidence about secular abandonment is strikingly lacking for the eleventh century, and there is only a little more for the twelfth. Such a silence is the more surprising because the amount of written data on almost every other subject—from royal finances and papal politics to clandestine marriage and personal hygiene—increases geometrically from the opening of the eleventh century to the close of the twelfth.

At the opening of the eleventh century, when Burchard of Worms compiled his *Decretum* (a collection of canons intended to serve as a basis of ecclesiastical law), he found no more recent enact-

11. Note that this would not be the case in societies like those of the modern West in which being a servant is itself considered an undesirable fate.

12. "Marcabrus si fo gitatz a la porta d'un ric home . . ." (Jean Boutière and A.-H. Schutz, *Biographies des Troubadours: Textes provençaux des XIIIe et XIVe siècles* [Paris, 1964], p. 12). The rich man (Aldric d'Auvillars) brought him up, and Marcabrus later engaged in a poetic dialogue with him (ibid., pp. 12–13, n. 1).

ments on the abandonment of children than the sixth-century decrees of the councils of Vaison and Arles, which specified how
children abandoned at churches were to be handled, and the edict
(of uncertain origin) quoted by Regino of Prüm instructing priests
to exhort women to deposit illegitimate children at church doors.[13]
Burchard even introduced these into a section dealing with proper
behavior in church, rather than in the context of family morality. It
is not particularly revealing that he should cite ancient precedent—
all the great canonical collections relied on early rulings to a large
degree—but it is significant that two sixth-century councils had
found it necessary to pronounce on the issue, and dozens would do
so in the thirteenth; but there was absolutely no apposite legislation
from Burchard's own lifetime, or a century before or after. Ivo of
Chartres, compiling more than four thousand previous canons in
his *Decretum* at the end of the century, found no more than Burchard had, and simply reiterated the latter's material.[14] The *Decretum*
of Gratian—the foundation and largest portion of canon law from
the beginning of the twelfth century until the twentieth—repeated
the early medieval prescriptions of the second council of Arles, ostensibly authorizing the exposing of children at churches so long as
no subsequent attempt was made to reclaim.[15] Apart from Scandinavia (a special case: see below), and apart from English laws that

13. *Decretorum libri xx,* 3.200–202 (PL 140.712–13). Burchard attributes his
canon 200, "De illis qui clam concipiunt," to a council of Mâcon; it is a paraphrase
of Regino of Prüm's 2.68, which Regino attributes to a council at Rouen (as he did,
also erroneously, his canon 67, on infanticide). No canon to this effect is to be
found in any extant council held in Mâcon.

14. *Decretum* 3.252–54 (PL 161.256–57); also in a section dealing with proper
behavior in church.

15. "Expositos defendat ecclesia, si quis eorum calumpniator extiterit" (1.87.9;
ed. Emil Friedberg [Leipzig, 1879], 1.306); for the text see discussion of Arles II, in
note 118 of chapter 3, above. (Gratian mistakenly attributes the canon to a council
of Toledo.) "Ut homicida" might be taken to imply sanctions against exposing
parents, even though that was not what Arles had intended, but both the rubric
(added by Gratian) and the placement of the canon, in a section on the protection of
widows and orphans by the church, strongly suggest otherwise. Gratian also cites
the ruling of Gangra (1.30.14), but clearly understands it to apply to the problem
of persons with children entering religious life, not as a general prohibition of
abandonment. His point in adducing it, in fact, is to argue that it is not to be taken
seriously as an argument against clerical celibacy, because it was enacted under specific and no longer applicable conditions—"Illud autem, quod in canone apos-
tolorum, et in Gangrensi concilio, et in VI. sinodo legitur, ex causa consideratur et
ex tempore" (ibid.). Cf. Ivo, *Decretum* 8.318 (PL 161.655).

denied to parents who abandoned children the right to compensation for their deaths,[16] no civil codes of the eleventh or twelfth century address the subject.[17] Nor did the revival of Roman law result even in the reiteration of passages from the Code which Eastern legists had taken to prohibit abandonment.[18]

Arguments from silence are risky, but after so many previous centuries had witnessed extensive ecclesiastical preoccupation with the issue, it is arresting that during two hundred years of unprecedented legislative output, when European Catholicism regulated in minute detail every other aspect of family morality, from the degrees of relationship within which one could marry to the circumstances under which parents could baptize their own children, there was not a single canonical comment on the abandonment of children. Infanticide, by contrast, was regularly prohibited throughout

16. *Leges Henrici primi,* ed. and trans. L. J. Downer (Oxford, 1972), 78.4 (p. 244), compiled in the early twelfth century, deny wergild explicitly to parents who have refused to acknowledge illegitimate children, and (78.5) generally extend the principle to foundlings (*inventis*). Abandoned children may also be intended in 10.3 (p. 108), making the king the "kinsman"—i.e., responsible for protection and avenging—of clerics, strangers, the poor, and the "cast out" (*abiectis*), although *abiectis* occurs in 78.5 as a separate category, and seems more likely to mean those disowned by their families in general. The connection between clerics and abandoned children may be circumstantial, but could also reflect recognition (conscious or subliminal) of the extent to which children were abandoned to churches or monasteries. Royal protection of clerics, however, was an ancient principle, at least as old as the laws of Edward and Guthrum (*Laws of the Earliest English Kings,* p. 108, no. 12).

17. But it should also be noted that there are relatively few civil codes of the period. The eleventh-century laws of Canute include an odd provision extending royal protection to infants against an injury of a somewhat unclear nature (II Canute 76.2–3, in *The Laws of the Kings of England from Edmund to Henry I,* ed. and trans. A. J. Robertson [Cambridge, 1925], pp. 214–15); and a charter of William I requires fathers to regard all children as heirs (ibid., pp. 230–31), but it is not likely that either of these was addressed to abandonment.

18. Glanvill's *De Legibus et Consuetudinibus Regni Angliae* (ed. George Woodbine [New Haven, 1932]), for example, is heavily influenced by Roman law, and might certainly have invoked either the principles equating abandonment with murder cited by Eastern Christians or the more common Constantinian rules about the rights of finders, but does not. It is worth noting, however, that Glanvill's treatise was intended to explain the workings of the king's courts rather than provide a comprehensive legal code. The odd phrase "si . . . habuerit filium vel filiam clamantem et auditum infra quatuor parietes" (7.17, p. 115) may be a reference to ancient or contemporary modes of precluding substitution of infants.

the period—three papal rulings were issued on the subject during the twelfth century[19]—and there was almost obsessive concern with the baptism of children.[20] Guibert of Nogent's father appeared to his mother in a vision, bloody and wounded and holding a piteously wailing baby, his illegitimate child who had died before being baptized, for which he was being tormented throughout eternity.[21]

It would be extreme and, in fact, erroneous, to infer from this silence that abandonment was unknown in Europe during this period, but it was apparently much rarer than it had been during the early Middle Ages or would be subsequently. The very few instances that do occur in sources of the period generally take the form of sales or direct transfer rather than exposing. When the infant son of a wealthy citizen of Bayeux died, his wife arranged, without his knowledge, to obtain a child of comparable age from a woman in a nearby village.[22] The arrangement was more a rental than a sale: she paid the mother ten sous per year, and when she and her husband died the mother brought suit against the relatives to regain her child, since she was no longer receiving her annual fee. The relatives denied the mother's claim, the matter became a *cause*

19. Alexander III, Lucius III (two rulings): in CIC, *Decretalium Greg. IX,* 5.10.1–3 (Friedberg, 2.792–93). See, in addition, Schmitz, 2.444, or the sermons against female infanticide among twelfth-century Germans by Otto, Bishop of Bamberg (Ebo, *Vita Ottonis,* ed. G. H. Pertz, in MGH SS 12 [Hannover, 1856] 850–51; cf. Herbord, *Dialogus de vita Ottonis episcopi Bambergensis,* ed. Rudolfo Köpke in MGH SS 20 [Hannover, 1868] 733, 741). But the laws of Henry I of England rather ambiguously state that there is no penalty for a parent who kills a child "voluntarie non" (88.8, p. 272). This may refer only to accidents, but it is difficult to tell; abortion is punished severely in the same code, although not as murder (70.16–16a, p. 222), and unrelated persons who kill even unborn infants must pay the full wergild (70.14, 14a, 15; p. 222).

20. "Neglexisti infantem tuum, ut per culpam tuam sine baptismo moreretur? Si fecisti, unum annum per legitimas ferias poenitere debes, et nunquam sis sine poenitentia" (Schmitz, *Bussbücher* 2.445). *Neglego* in this context is distinctly ambiguous, but probably does not refer to overt abandonment.

21. Guibert of Nogent, *De vita sua* 1.18. On the other hand, Adam of Eynsham, *Magna vita sancti Hugonis,* ed. and trans. D. L. Douie and H. Farmer, 5.14 (2.164), mentions, without comment, the baptism of a seven-year-old boy, the nephew of a knight.

22. P. le Cacheux, "Une charte de Jumièges concernant l'épreuve par la fer chaud (fin du XI siècle)," *Société de l'histoire de Normandie: Mélanges* (Rouen, 1927) 205–16; translated herein as "Complications Regarding a Rented Child" (see Appendix).

célèbre and was adjudicated, at the behest of William of Normandy, by subjecting the mother to an ordeal of hot iron to determine if she was telling the truth. When the ordeal indicated that she was, the child was returned to her. There was no question, apparently, about the mother's right to reclaim the child, and no one evinced disapproval of her behavior, including the clerical chronicler of the story, who wrote it down not as a moral example (or even as a colorful tale), but simply to record and establish the disposition of the property, which reverted to the crown when it could not pass to the substituted boy. The privileging of the rights of the natal mother, in contravention of the apparent tenor of prevailing ecclesiastical and Roman law, is striking. Normans of the time might not have known or considered themselves bound by the latter; possibly they were also ignorant of the former, or considered it inapplicable to cases of "renting." On the other hand, careful reading of the surviving documentation discloses that three of the witnesses to the "judgment of hot iron" ultimately came into possession of the estate under dispute, and it is entirely possible that property interests determined the outcome rather than any beliefs about parent-child relations.[23]

A similar case occurred in England in the following century, and also required the intervention of authorities. The wife of a knight without heirs feigned pregnancy (with a pillow), had her maid procure a baby girl, and produced it as her own. She then hired the natal mother as the girl's nurse. Her brother-in-law, who would have inherited her husband's considerable estate, suspected the substitution (because his brother was old and sickly), and appealed, unsuccessfully, to both ecclesiastical and civic authorities to reinstitute him as rightful heir. The substituted heiress was married to three nobles in succession, but ironically produced no children herself, and the estate did finally revert to the brother-in-law.[24] The clerical narrator of the events evinces horror that a noble male (the first of the husbands of the substituted heiress) would marry a woman of presumably servile origin, but the groom's relatives, apprised of

23. See Appendix of Translations, esp. note 36.

24. The outlines of this incident are narrated in Adam of Eynsham, *Magna vita sancti Hugonis* 4.5 (2.20–27). Legal documents supply the names of those involved and the subsequent fates of the principals: *Abbreviatio placitorum*, p. 3; *Rotuli Hundredorum*, 3d Edward I, 1, p. 294; *Rotuli Curiae Regis* (London, 1835) 1.78; *Rotuli de Oblatis et finibus in Turri Londinensi asservati, tempore regis Johannis,* ed. Thomas Hardy (London, 1834), entry for 1199 (p. 20); all cited in Douie and Farmer.

this, were unmoved and argued that "according to the laws of England, a child is considered legitimate if the husband of the wife regarded him as legitimate during his lifetime."[25]

The villains of the story are the avaricious wife who attempts to defraud her brother-in-law and the weak-willed husband who will not oppose her; the sole moral issue is fraud. There is no implication that the mother who sold the baby had done wrong, nor any interest in locating or punishing her.

Most of the incidents of abandonment which have left traces in the records of this period were sales.[26] During a famine in Ireland at the opening of the twelfth century, desperate parents sold their children, according to contemporary chroniclers.[27] An Irish council at Armagh in the second half of the century,[28] noting that it had been "a common vice" among the English, "[even] before they suffered any want or need, to sell their own children and relatives to Ireland,"[29] freed all the English slaves in the country. The council considered that both buyers and sellers had been involved in "a great crime," but this was presumably the reduction of freeborn children to servitude, and not simply parental dereliction, as both the word-

25. Adam of Eynsham, 4.5 (2.25): "iuxta leges Anglie cuiusque sobolem legitimam discerni, quam uxoris maritus legitime quoad uiueret legitimam habuisset." This principle, couched in similar terms, occurs in both ancient and medieval codes, but, significantly, it is usually phrased in terms of the "mother's husband," not the "wife's husband." Few societies regard a substituted child unrelated to either parent as a legitimate heir, though English law of the thirteenth century did (Bracton 69b ff, discussed below), so the narrator may be accurate in adducing the principle.

26. John of Salisbury complains in his *Policraticus* (3.13) that husbands prostitute their wives and daughters (PL 199.503–6), but the accusation is part of a jeremiad against the mores of the times, pasted together from classical sources (e.g., Juvenal), and not a likely source of accurate social information (for an English translation, see Joseph Pike, *Frivolities of Courtiers and Footprints of Philosophers* [London, 1938], pp. 199–201).

27. *Chronicum Scotorum: A Chronicale of Irish Affairs from the Earliest Times to A.D. 1135,* ed. William Hennessy (London, 1866), p. 318.

28. This may simply be a calumny against the English: Gerald is the sole authority for the details of this council, but both Mansi (21.862) and Hefele (7.359) accept it as genuine. The latter places it in 1158. English slaves in Ireland appear in Gottfried's *Tristan.*

29. Gerald of Wales (*Expugnatio Hibernica,* ed. James Dimock [London, 1867] 18, p. 258): "Anglorum namque populus, adhuc integro eorundem regno, communi gentis vitio liberos suos venales exponere, et priusquam inopiam ullam aut inediam sustinerent, filios proprios et cognatos in Hiberniam vendere consueverant."

ing of the report and the remedy suggest.[30] Adam of Eynsham mentions that the Archbishop of Canterbury bought a five-year-old boy "for a small sum" during this same period, and "found" another boy at Caen. Both were apparently brought up in religious life.[31]

The familiarity of the sale of children underlies a wry literary joke of the eleventh century. A Swiss merchant returns from a business trip of two years and his wife meets him with a baby in tow. She explains with a Latin pun that she conceived the child as a result of eating snow in the Alps,[32] and he purports to accept her explanation. But when he must subsequently travel again he takes their son, now six years old, with him, and sells him for a large sum. He returns childless and wealthy.

> "I'm so sorry, darling,
> so sorry, dear,
> I have lost your child,
> whom you yourself
> could not have loved
> more than I.
>
> "A storm came up,
> and the fury of the winds drove us,
> utterly exhausted,
> onto the sand banks of North Africa.
> The sun beat down heavily[33] on us all,
> and the snow child
> melted."[34]

The central motifs here are ancient: the cuckold has vengeance on his wife, a lie is turned against the teller. The sale of the child is a

30. "Decretum est itaque praedicto concilio, et cum universitatis assensu publice statutum, ut Angli ubique per insulam servitutis vinculo mancipati, in pristinam revocentur libertatem" (ibid.).

31. Adam of Eynsham 3.14 (1.132–33): "a Cantuariense archiepiscopo Huberto aere comparatus exiguo . . ."; "Benedictum, si memoria non fallit, apud Cadomum prius ipse inuenit."

32. Having satisfied her thirst with snow, she became *gravida,* which means both "full" and "pregnant."

33. "Nos omnes graviter torret sol"—maliciously expanding the pun of *gravida.*

34. *Die Cambridger Lieder,* ed. Karl Strecker (3rd ed.: Berlin, 1966), 14, pp. 41–44; also in F. J. E. Raby, ed., *The Oxford Book of Medieval Latin Verse* (Oxford, 1959) 120, pp. 167–70; translated herein (see Appendix).

minor detail: the poet might have chosen many ways to dispose of him, and it is probably a sign of the times that sale seemed the most obvious.[35] If merchants did not often sell their own children, there was certainly a thriving slave trade for children in general, and contemporary accounts suggest that traveling merchants might abandon their families when they went away on business, as some of those who took the cross also did during the various crusades of the twelfth century.[36]

There are some instances of abandonment in other contexts: parents who abandoned offspring when they entered religious life,[37] or who "exposed" seriously ill children in desperation or as part of a ritual to cure them.[38] Evidence survives from the eleventh and twelfth centuries of the cult of St. Guinefort, the "holy greyhound" who healed sick children in southern Europe and whose cult some-

35. The tale enjoyed wide popularity in subsequent ages: it appears as "De mercatore," in *Commedie latine del XII e XIII secolo* 3, ed. Ferrucio Bertini, P. Budraghi, et al. (Genoa, 1980); as a fabliau (Anatole de Montaiglon and Gaston Raynaud, *Recueil général et complet des fabliaux des XIIIe et XIVe siècles* [Paris, 1872–90] 1.162–67 [trans. by Robert Hellman in *Fabliaux: Ribald Tales from the Old French* (New York, 1965) 17–21]); as tale 90 in Giovanni Sercambi's fourteenth-century *Novelle;* tale 19 of the fifteenth-century *Cent Nouvelles Nouvelles;* tale 47 in vol. 2 of Von der Hagen's *Gesammtabenteuer* (cf. Franz Pfeiffer, "Altdeutsche Beispiele," 40: "Das Schneekind," *Zeitschrift für deutsches Alterthum* 7 [1849] 377–80); and in numerous other collections ranging from Sansovino to Hans Sachs.

36. There is probably a grain of truth, for example, embedded in the somewhat fanciful tale of Bona of Pisa, whose father, a merchant, abandoned her and her mother and married a woman in the Levant: see discussion in Rudolph Bell and Donald Weinstein, *Saints and Society: The Two Worlds of Western Christendom, 1000–1700* (Chicago, 1982), p. 31. One of the exemplary tales in British Library MS Additional 32678, S. XIII, folios 5–8, is about a merchant who becomes a Carthusian monk and, sent to the market on monastery business, buys back the son of a knight (description in J. A. Herbert, *Catalogue of Romances in the Department of Manuscripts in the British Museum* 3 [London, 1910], pp. 336–39).

37. See, e.g., Adam of Eynsham, 4.12 (Douie and Farmer, 2.55). Abelard and Heloise's child Astrolabe was left with Abelard's sister in Brittany when both parents entered religious life (under duress), but he was not exactly "abandoned"; Abelard was still concerned enough to address poetry to him late in life: Peter Dronke, *Abelard and Heloise in Medieval Testimonies: The Twenty-Sixth W. P. Ker Memorial Lecture Delivered in the University of Glasgow, 29th October, 1976* (Glasgow, 1976), 14–15, 43–45. (There is controversy about this poetry, which Dronke discusses.)

38. AASS, Aug. 2, 650–56 ("Circumvectio et miracula sancti Taurini," 3.25): "Cumque membra infantilia vitalis calor dereliquisset, vix spiritus tenuissimus in ejus pectore sentiri poterat. Parentes illius infantis de[sperantes] eum tanquam [mortuum] exposuerant."

times involved "exposing" children at least temporarily; but the details are murky before the thirteenth century.[39] Both heretics and "foreigners" are accused by contemporaries of stealing, killing, abusing, and even eating children: Anna Comnena said that the Normans roasted babies on spits.[40] Some charges of this sort may be related to abandonment by parents who then accused someone else of harming the children. Ecclesiastical law of the period required that the offspring of priests be confiscated as slaves of the church,[41] which could be viewed as the clerical class abandoning its children in concerted effort, but the measures were chiefly an effort to enforce clerical celibacy through a severe threat, and it is unlikely that the children were actually enslaved. The ruling may, however, have been an incentive for priests to place children in monasteries to avoid controversy about them.

At the opening of the eleventh century St. Peter Damian was "abandoned" in his own home: he was born into a family prosperous enough to have servants but burdened with too many children, and when an older brother reproached his mother for adding yet another claimant to the already impoverished patrimony, she, in a rage, refused to nurse the child. Although the mother was ultimately persuaded to accept and nourish him, after her death he was "adopted" by the same brother and treated as a slave in his household.[42] Guibert of Nogent felt "abandoned" as an adolescent when

---

39. See Jean-Claude Schmitt, *The Holy Greyhound: Guinefort, Healer of Children since the Thirteenth Century,* and discussion below.

40. *Alexiad* 10.6. This seems too outrageous a calumny to believe, although Foucher of Chartres admits that Christians in the Holy Land were reduced to eating the bodies of their enemies, which they roasted, but "insufficiently" (pp. 112–13 in the translation by Frances Ryan, *A History of the Expedition to Jerusalem* [New York, 1969]). Christian writers often complained about Muslim abuse of Christian children (see Boswell, *Christianity,* pp. 279–83), but do not always make clear how the children came into the hands of their sellers or tormenters. For heresy, see, e.g., Walter Wakefield and A. Evans, eds., *Heresies of the High Middle Ages* (New York, 1969), pp. 74–81.

41. Ruling of Benedict VIII in 1022, repeated by Synod of Goslar (Mansi 19.343–56) and by Henry II as imperial law (MGH Const. 1.70–78, no. 34; cf. Bernhard Schimmelpfennig, "*Ex fornicatione nati:* Studies on the Position of Priests' Sons from the Twelfth to the Fourteenth Century," pp. 14–16).

42. Peter's early life is told, not without exaggeration, by John of Lodi, who claims to have heard it all from Peter himself: PL 144.114–17. The accuracy of the account has been much discussed; perhaps most apposite to the present study are McLaughlin, "Survivors," pp. 108–9, and Lester Little, "The Personal Develop-

his mother entered religious life, although she certainly continued to exercize parental concern about him.

> She knew that I should be utterly an orphan with no one at all on whom to depend, for great as was my wealth of kinsfolk and connections, yet there was no one to give me that loving care a little child needs at such an age. . . . Although she knew that I would be condemned to such neglect, yet Thy love and fear, O God, hardened her heart. . . . She knew for certain that she was a cruel and unnatural mother. Indeed, she heard this said aloud, as she had in this way cut off from her heart and left bereft of succor such a fine child.[43]

Many children of the period were abandoned by parents entering religious life, which was undergoing an immense resurgence throughout the eleventh and twelfth centuries and attracted many young adults.[44] Others, of all social classes, were probably sent away from home as soon as they were old enough to be apprenticed, to work as servants, or to train as knights in a court.

On the edges of Europe, where the increase in prosperity was felt late or not at all, and where subsistence farming or even more precarious modes of support remained general means of livelihood, the anonymous exposing of infants remained common throughout the High Middle Ages. When the Icelanders agreed to accept Christianity around 1000,

> it was made law that everyone should be Christian, and that those in the country who had not been baptized should now accept baptism. But in regard to the abandoning of children and the eating of horsemeat the old law should remain in force.[45]

---

ment of Peter Damian," in *Order and Innovation in the Middle Ages* (Princeton, 1976); cf. Jean Leclercq, *Saint Pierre Damien, ermite et homme de l'église* (Rome, 1960).

43. 1.14, trans. Benton, p. 74.

44. E.g., Ivetta of Huy (1157–1228), who left her three sons in the care of their grandfather so she could run a hostel for pilgrims: Hugh of Floreffe, *Vita Ivettae reclusae Huyi*, ed. G. Henschenius, ASOB, January 1 (Antwerp, 1643), pp. 865–66; commentary in Brenda Bolton, "*Vitae matrum:* A further aspect of the *Frauenfrage,*" in Baker, *Medieval Women*, 253–74, p. 258.

45. "Þá var þat mælt í lögum, at allir menn skyldi kristnir vera ok skírn taka, þeir er áðr váru óskírðir á landi hér; en of barna útburð skyldu standa in fornu lög

Although this is one of the most direct narrative statements about abandonment from the period (it was composed more than a century after the event it describes), it embodies several mysteries. The most obvious is why the Icelanders thought that abandoning children and eating horsemeat were contrary to Christian law. After some ascetic hostility in the very early church, Christianity had not, in fact, been opposed to abandonment at any time during the early Middle Ages, nor had the eating of horsemeat ever been a substantial moral concern among Christians.[46]

One solution to the mystery is to view it as a mistake, on the part of the author, or the Icelandic converts, or both. Horsemeat was sacred to northern European deities (Odin and Frey) and eaten at great rituals, and there is some reason to believe that abandonment was sometimes a religious ritual. In one of the sagas, the population of a pagan city debates at length whether, as a sacrifice for better weather, they should expose children and kill the elderly, or expend their resources to preserve both. Each alternative is defended, although the "right" decision is ultimately made: to save the children and elderly.[47] If they associated such practices with paganism, as the story implies, the Icelanders or the author of the account of their conversion (Ari Thorgilsson)—or all of them—

---

ok of hrossakjöts át" (Ari Thorgilsson, *Islendingabók,* ed. Halldór Hermannsson [Ithaca, 1930] [*Islandica* 20], p. 53). Hermannsson's translation of this passage, p. 66, renders *barna útburð* as "infanticide," which is unlikely: its literal meaning is "the carrying out of children," and it is the phrase used everywhere in Norse-Icelandic literature for exposing. *Utsláto barns* is the expression for infanticide. But cf. Introduction, note 107.

46. Kiersten Hastrup, *Culture and History in Medieval Iceland* (Oxford, 1985), maintains that horsemeat was a major foodstuff for the poor (p. 174), probably relying on the comment in *Heimskringla* cited below. Her account of the conversion (pp. 179–89) does not shed light on its more curious aspects.

47. *Saga af Vermundi ok Vígaskútú eptir gömlum handritum útgefnar at tilhlutun Hins Konúngliga Norræna Fornfræða Félags* [*Reykdæla saga*] (Copenhagen, 1830), chap. 7, p. 20. Note that although the setting is pagan, the chieftain thinks it "outrageous" (*ómælilegt*) that the townsfolk should contemplate these acts, suggesting a substantial conflation of pagan and later Christian values: although it contains older material, the saga was certainly written down long after the introduction of Christianity. Cf. the incident in *Saga Heiðreks Konungs ins Vitra* ([*Hervarar saga*], ed. and trans. Christopher Tolkien, chap. 6, p. 25), where an augury suggests that the "highest-born child" (*svein:* possibly "youth") should be sacrificed. This also is set in the past by a Christian author.

may have believed that Christianity would prohibit them,[48] and since they persisted after the introduction of Christianity, subsequent generations might conclude that the first converts had refused to accept them.

The same details are provided in several later histories of the conversion of the Icelanders, but none of them is clearly independent of Ari Thorgilsson's work, and all could have been repeating his misprision.[49] On the other hand, even sources not concerned with the incident suggest or state explicitly that abandonment had been common in the region *before* the arrival of Christianity,[50] and it does seem likely that, for whatever reason, the arrival of Christianity made exposing children a moral issue. Moreover, the fullest of the later versions offers supplementary details which suggest that there was more than pagan connotation involved in the practices in question:

> However, since those who have most opposed the preaching of Christianity scarcely understand that it would entail the bringing up of all children that are born, whether of poor or rich, or

48. Christians were, indeed, forbidden from apostolic times to eat meat sacrificed to idols (Acts 15:20, 29; and 1 Corinthians 10:14–30), but the passage in Corinthians would make clear that it was not the particular kind of meat that mattered.

49. E.g., the account in *Saga Ólafs Tryggvasonar*, translated below (reference in note 52, below), and in the *Kristni saga* 11, where Thorgeir proclaims that "all should be baptized in Iceland and believe in one God, but as regards the abandonment of children and the eating of horsemeat they should be held by the old law" (ed. Guðni Jónsson in *Íslendinga Sögur* 1 [Reykjavik, 1946], p. 272). In *Njáls saga* 105 (many editions, e.g., ed. Einar Sveinsson in IF 12 [Reykjavik, 1954], Thorgeir says on this occasion that all men are to become Christian and worship the Trinity, and that they are no longer to worship idols, to expose children, or to eat horsemeat. Although outlawry is the punishment, no one will be prosecuted for doing any of them in secret. This is clearly related to the other versions, but disagrees with all of them in claiming that abandonment was proscribed at the outset.

50. "It was customary then, when the country was entirely pagan, that those who were less wealthy and less able to support dependents had their children exposed, although they always thought this was undesirable [literally, 'ill done'—*illa gǫrt*]," *Gunnlaugs saga Ormstungu*, ed. Sigurður Nordal and Guðni Jónsson, in IF 3 (Reykjavik, 1938), 3, p. 56. Cf. *Þáttr Þorsteins uxafots:* "For it was legal at that time for poor people [*úríkra manna*] to expose children [*út bera börn*] if they wanted to, although they did not think it was exactly right [literally, 'not well done': *eigi vel gert*]," *Fornmanna sögur* 3 (Copenhagen, 1827), p. 111; this "tale" is also edited in *Flateyjarbók: En Samling af Norske Konge-Sagar* (Christiania, 1860), pp. 249–63.

the prohibition and banning for human consumption of that food which is most important to the common people, they should have their say[51] on this, that [what was] law until now should stand regarding the abandonment of children [*barna útburð*] and the eating of horsemeat, and that it should not be punishable when people worship in private, so long as there are no witnesses.[52]

As will be seen, much of Catholic Europe became concerned about exposing children during the thirteenth century—just when most of these sources were composed—and one might assume that they have conflated contemporary attitudes with earlier ones. But the earliest and most authoritative version is from the twelfth century, when there was no widespread opposition to abandonment anywhere else in Christian Europe; and the thirteenth-century sources either follow or agree precisely with it, so this explanation does not seem sufficient. Moreover, both Icelandic and Norwegian law codes of the twelfth century do prohibit the eating of horsemeat, and the latter also forbids the abandoning of children in some circumstances (see below). Possibly the Icelanders were imitating the Norwegians, although if Ari Thorgilsson's account is to be trusted, they had the idea that abandonment and horsemeat were forbidden more than a century before the extant versions of the Norwegian laws were written down. In any event, positing Norwegian models only displaces the mystery eastward: where did the Norwegians, themselves converted at about the same time, get the idea that abandonment and horsemeat were forbidden to Christians?

Irish penitential sanctions against abandonment in particular cases (discussed above) may have been known to and misconstrued by Norwegians or Icelanders[53] as generic condemnations. St. Olaf,

51. Literally, "opinion": *mál*.
52. Oddr the Monk, *Saga Ólafs Konúngs Tryggvasonar* 229, in *Fornmanna sögur*, ed. C. C. Rafn (Copenhagen, 1825), 2.242.
53. There are few recent studies of the family in medieval Scandinavia. The most helpful are William Miller, "Some Aspects of Householding in the Medieval Icelandic Commonwealth," forthcoming in *Continuity and Change;* Jenny Jochens, "En Islande Médiévale: À la Recherche de la famille nucléaire," *Annales* 40, 1 (1985) 95–112; Jochens, "The Church and Sexuality in Medieval Iceland"; and Roberta Frank, "Marriage in Twelfth- and Thirteenth-Century Iceland," *Viator* 4 (1973) 473–84. The last believes there was little abandonment in medieval Iceland, although she presents no arguments to prove this. In an article forthcoming in

an influential figure in the Christianizing of Norway, often pat-
terned ecclesiastical legislation on English models, and could conceivably have known the Irish canons. The influence of Irish and
English canons on penitential literature in general, the particular
cultural, mercantile, military and demographic interactions of the
British Isles and Scandinavia,[54] and the fact that Irish canons do
contain prohibitions of eating horseflesh,[55] all provide reason to sus-

---

Scandinavian Studies, Carol Clover argues that abandonment in medieval Scandinavia was, in fact, infanticide. She adduces as evidence (1) the use of *bera út* in
cases where infanticide is apparently involved; (2) "documentary" and archaeological indications of the death of infants; (3) the Scandinavian "dead-child" literary
tradition; and (4) the severity of the Nordic winter. Both the "dead-child" tradition (for which she relies on Pentikäinen, discussed above, in the Introduction,
note 107) and the Nordic climate might be reasons to suspect that some exposed
children died, but not that the object of abandonment was to kill them. (In *Harðar
saga* 8, for example, a man exposes a baby at the gate of a farm specifically so it will
be found, *instead of* killing it, as he was instructed.) Moreover, Scandinavian literature specifically depicts the survival of infants left in the open for days (see, e.g.,
below, chapter 10, note 82), which the authors obviously anticipated their audiences would find credible. (In one case the baby is found "nearly dead"—so it is
not that the question simply did not occur to them.) The archaeological evidence,
as Clover makes clear, is highly controvertible and of dubious value, and it seems
obvious enough that the expression "to carry out" (*bera út*) might be used in connection with the killing of children without *denoting* such an act, just as it might in
English. For the "documentary" evidence, Clover herself notes, surprisingly, that
"every description [sc., of abandonment] we have ends with the infant's being
found and saved."

54. I use "Scandinavia" to describe the geographical area now so designated,
plus Iceland. Although this would not be correct for later periods, the cultural
unity of the area in the High Middle Ages seems to me to warrant such usage. For
specialists in either Icelandic or Norwegian history this collapse will be madden-
ing, and I can only apologize. Moreover, I have focused within "Scandinavia" on
Icelandic and Norwegian laws because the surviving corpus of Norse-Icelandic
sagas makes it possible to compare legal with literary and narrative materials for
these regions in a way one could not for the areas to the south and east. The picture
evinced by the roughly contemporary Swedish (*Corpus Iuris Sueo-Gotorum Antiqui,*
ed. H. S. Dollin and C. J. Schlyter, vols. 1–3) and Danish (*Danmarks gamle land-
skabslove,* ed. J. Brondum-Nielsen [Copenhagen, 1945–48] vols. 1, 5, and 8) codes
is somewhat different, but to assess this carefully, taking into account the complexities of the textual traditions and the contextual differences between these and the
Norse-Icelandic tradition, would require a separate study.

55. A penance of four years for eating horseflesh in *Canones Hibernenses* 1.13,
in *The Irish Penitentials,* ed. Bieler, p. 160; three years in "The Old-Irish Penitential," 1.2, ibid., p. 259. The former is probably from the early seventh century, the

pect that these might be a source for northern misunderstanding. Against this, one might point out that abandonment was common among the Irish and the English at the time, and not considered sinful until the thirteenth century—if then—and that tracing the equine culinary prohibition to Ireland again only displaces the mystery.[56]

The most likely explanation is a circumstantial one. In the rest of Europe churches served as the major depositories of abandoned children, which meant both that the infants would certainly be baptized and that there was little chance of their meeting accidental death. In Iceland and Norway there were few churches at whose doors children could be abandoned; it was an intensely rural setting just receiving Christianity. Even after "conversion" it was several centuries before the countryside of Scandinavia was dotted with churches. Since the Norsemen tyrannized the northern seas and lands, there were no slave traders—apart from the abandoning Scandinavian population itself—in search of human merchandise. What has often been falsely assumed of exposed children generally might actually have occurred in Scandinavia: they might die, and die unbaptized. Either of these reasons alone might have been sufficient to cause concern: together they meant that children would perish for eternity. Nearly all Scandinavian law codes[57] of the High Middle Ages, civil and ecclesiastical, begin with very elaborate rules about baptizing, and sometimes require the forcible baptism of foreign adults, so it is easy to see why substantial concern might be attached to the possibility that children would die without receiving the sacrament. The penalty in Norwegian law for leaving a child unbaptized for a year was exile.[58]

---

latter from the eighth, but both continued to influence some canonical collections much later.

56. I have, in fact, discovered no answer to the question of the ultimate origins of the prejudice against eating horsemeat.

57. See note 54, above.

58. The same penalty as for abandonment resulting in death, and prescribed in the same place, Gulathing Law, 21: see note 63, below. Part of the preoccupation with baptism may, however, be itself a pagan remnant: much evidence suggests that, even before conversion, the northern peoples sprinkled their children with water. This may be connected to awareness of Christianity, but it could also be a birth ritual comparable to the ancient use of salt or Frisian honey. For an example, see *Saga Heiðreks Konungs ins Vitra,* ed. and trans. Tolkien, chap. 3.

Ari Thorgilsson's account says that "a few winters later these heathen customs were done away with like the others,"[59] but this may represent wishful thinking. St. Olaf of Norway (d. 1030) is depicted in a later biography as taking a dim view of the state of Christianity in Iceland because the Icelanders were allowed by their laws to eat horsemeat and abandon children "like heathens."[60] Icelandic law of the twelfth century does include a prohibition of eating horsemeat and begins, at least in its thirteenth-century redaction, with the requirement that every child be brought to church for baptism, even if severely deformed; it also includes very elaborate provisions for the maintenance of and responsibility for dependent persons, including children, although it does not expressly forbid abandonment.[61]

59. "En síðar fám vetrum var sú heiðni af numin sem önnur" (as in note 45, above, p. 54). So also *Saga Ólafs Tryggvasonar,* as cited above (note 52), where the account is again somewhat fuller: "It happened by the kindness and mercy of our Lord that a few years later this remainder of heathendom was also removed with the approval of all the nobility [*höfðingya*] and the consent of the common people as regards what was mentioned above, i.e., private worship, eating horsemeat, and abandoning children" (ibid., p. 243). *Kristni saga* 11 repeats *Islendingabók.*

60. "Þá þótti honum mikilla muna ó vant, at vel væri, því at þeir sǫgðu frá kristnihaldinu, at þat var lofat í lǫgum at eta hross ok bera út bǫrn sem heiðnir menn . . ." (*Oláfs saga helga* 58, in Sturluson, *Heimskringla* 2.74).

61. These laws are unusually clumsy to utilize and cite, because they survive in two related but distinct redactions, published separately: the older and fuller Konungsbók or Codex Regius (*Grágás: Islændernes lovbog i fristatens Tid udgivet efter det kongelige Bibliotheks Haandskrift,* ed. Vilhjálmur Finsen, 2 vols. [Copenhagen, 1852]; or Páll Ólason, ed., *The Codex Regius of Grágás* [Copenhagen, 1932] [Corpus codicum Islandicorum medii aevi, 3]), hereafter "K," and the later but more scholarly Arnamagnean Legate, ed. Vilhjálmur Finsen, *Grágás efter det Arnamagnæanske Haandskrift Nr 334* [Copenhagen, 1879/Odense, 1974]), hereafter "Staðarhólsbók." The second does not contain all of the material comprised in the first, but the prohibitions of eating horsemeat and requirement of baptism are contained in both, in "Kristinrettr hinn gamli." In the unfinished English translation of "K" by Andrew Dennis, Peter Foote, and Richard Perkins (*Laws of Early Iceland: Grágás* [Winnipeg, 1980]) these are rendered, "People must not eat horses, dogs, foxes, and cats. . . . If a man eats these animals which are excluded, he is liable to a penalty of lesser outlawry" (1.49); "Every child that is born is to be brought for baptism at the first opportunity, however deformed it may be" (1.23). The regulations regarding helpless persons also occur in both ("Omaga-balkr"), but not in Dennis. In Section 128 of "K," for example, it is decreed that everyone must support his mother, and if he has sufficient means ("en ef hann orcar betr") father, children, brothers, sisters, etc., down to freedmen ("leysing sinn") (ed. Finsen, 2, pp. 3-4).

Norwegian law contains such a prohibition, and was probably the first European code to do so.[62] St. Olaf himself imposed a fine of three marks for abandoning a healthy child—though he allowed the exposing, to death, of severely deformed children once they had been brought to church and baptized.[63] (Three marks is also the fine for eating horseflesh, or eating any kind of meat on Friday; by contrast, confiscation of all property and permanent outlawry is prescribed for offering pagan sacrifice.)[64] His successor, Magnus, apparently amended this, decreeing that if an exposed child died the parent was guilty of murder and should suffer outlawry,[65] but the Frostathing Law reinstated the penalty of three marks and reduced it by more than two-thirds for the poor.[66] Supervision and punishment of such cases lay with the bishop. Included in the Frostathing Law is a provision that orphaned children of the indigent may be given to anyone who will have them as slaves, and if no one wants them, they become the financial responsibility of the district and the personal charge of the nearest householder. This suggests that superfluous children were a problem, and that the potential labor

---

But these rulings almost certainly were not intended to prevent abandonment on the part of the poor, since (1) they are predicated on the possession of sufficient wealth to sustain each level of obligation; and (2) the same section of the code expressly permits parents to hand over children in payment of a debt: "it is a man's choice whether to go into debt-slavery for his children or to hand them over instead" (ibid., pp. 4–5). But the latter is, confusingly, followed by a restatement of the obligation to care for children ("Sit barn scal hver maðr fram fora alanðe her"). The expression *a cost* ("at choice") may be a clue to the apparent contradiction, since *kost* frequently connotes a difficult choice, or dilemma. Compare the apparent conflict between "K" 134 (Finsen, 2.17), that a man may confiscate as debt slaves any children of a freedman who has become a burden on him, and "K" 112 (Finsen, 1.191–92), that a man who frees a slave must maintain his children.

62. Like the Icelandic codes, Norwegian written law was compiled in the mid-thirteenth century, incorporating both earlier and contemporary material.

63. Gulathing Law, 21 (*Den ældre Gulathings-Lov,* in NGL 1.12–13; cf. L. M. Larson, trans., *The Earliest Norwegian Laws: Being the Gulathing Law and the Frostathing Law* [New York, 1935], pp. 49–51).

64. Horseflesh: Gulathing Law, 20; meat on Fridays: ibid.; pagan sacrifice: Frostathing Law, 3.15.

65. Gulathing Law, 21 and rubric to 22, as cited above.

66. Frostathing Law, 2.2, in *Den ældre Frostathings-Lov,* NGL 1.131 (Larson, p. 226). Note that the issue in this provision may also be the death of the child. The section is introduced under the rubric "Um utslato barns," and the verb used is *slær út,* which may mean "throw out" in this context, but *slá* normally means "to

value of a child often failed to outweigh the cost or nuisance of his rearing.[67]

These apparent prohibitions appear yet more mysterious when one considers that elsewhere in the same code abandonment is specifically authorized, for profit or as the result of penury.

> When a freedman marries a freedwoman . . . their children are the heirs of both. But if they are reduced to poverty, [the children] become grave people: a grave should be dug in the churchyard and they placed in it and left to die. The lawful master may take the one that lives longest and support him thereafter.[68]

One could suppose that this was a pagan remnant inadvertently retained in the code, but freeborn Norsemen were also permitted to abandon their children, in payment of debts up to three marks, so long as this was done in a public setting—at a feast or a church gathering—which could hardly be a residue of heathen practice.[69]

---

strike" or "to kill," and it is entirely possible that the ruling is intended only to apply to exposings that result in death. *Bera út* ("carry out") is the normal expression for abandonment almost everywhere else in Icelandic and Norse literature. Section 2.1 appears to recognize the continued liceity of abandoning deformed infants ("ef mannz er hafuð a"), and *Den ældre Borgarthings- eller Vikens-Christenret* 1 (ibid., p. 339), also twelfth-century, explicitly does so. Cf. *Nyere Borgarthings Christenret* 2, 3 (NGL 2.293–94).

67. Arni Pálsson, "Um Lok Þrældóms á Íslandi," *Skirnir* 106 (1932) 191–203, argues that large-scale slavery could not have been viable in Iceland, and that the prohibition of abandoning children in the eleventh century made it impossible for masters to support the families of their slaves. The vexed issue of slavery in Scandinavia is surveyed incisively in Ruth Mazo Karras, *Slavery and Society in Medieval Scandinavia;* see esp. chap. 3. For other indications that superfluous children were a problem, see, e.g., *Grágás* (K) 2, sec. 148, pp. 38–39 and *Staðarhólsbók,* sec. 132, p. 167, both efforts at controlling the fertility of the poor.

68. Gulathing Law, 63 (NGL 1.33; cf. Larson, p. 83).

69. "Ættboren maðr ma gera barn sitt i skulld. ef hann gefr a thingi. æða at kirkiu sokn. þa ma hann geva i þriggia marca skulld oc eigi meiri . . ." Gulathing Law, 71 (NGL 1.36–37; Larson, p. 87). One could argue that this is a replacement for a pagan practice, structurally similar, but given the high relief with which the issue of child abandonment was treated during the conversion of the Scandinavians, it seems very unlikely that such vestiges of paganism would remain in a Christian code if they were thought inimical to Christian praxis. Note also that under the Frostathing Law, 9.11, only one-third of the children of a free woman and a freedman follow the status of the mother (NGL 1.212), a likely incentive for the parents to abandon or enslave the rest.

It seems likely, on balance, that restrictions on abandonment were aimed at couples who might practice ordinary family limitation through abandonment, not at those driven by some necessity to expose children. Even illegitimate children were often reckoned lawful heirs under Norwegian law,[70] and the formulations regarding this suggest that children of extramarital unions were common in Scandinavian households.[71] Prosperous folk may have wished to maximize the inheritance of legitimate, firstborn, or favorite heirs by abandoning others, and Christian lawgivers, like early ascetics, probably regarded this as unjustified, but felt greater sympathy for the plight of the bottom levels of society, such as the "freedman" allowed to dispose of his children.

The fact that something is prohibited is hardly indication that it did not take place. Quite the contrary: Snorri Sturluson comments drily that although Earls Eric and Svein allowed themselves to be baptized and adopted the true faith, "while they ruled Norway they let everyone do as he wished regarding adherence to Christianity; they respected the old law and all the customs of the land."[72] The same may well have been true of subsequent leaders in a land where custom was the foundation of social cohesion. Abandonment of children is extremely common in Icelandic and Norse sagas of all types,[73] more than in any other genre of medieval literature. Most of these were "composed" in the thirteenth century, but it is generally supposed (and overwhelmingly likely) that they drew on older materials, both written and oral, and they are probably a good indication that exposing was common throughout Scandinavian his-

70. Although this issue was complicated by questions of status: see discussion in Karras, "Concubinage and Slavery," and in Jenny Jochens, "The Politics of Reproduction: Medieval Norwegian Kingship," AHR 92 (1987) 327–49.

71. But in practice things may have been quite different: in *Jómsvíkinga saga* (a semihistorical saga written in the thirteenth century but set in the tenth, ed. N. F. Blake [London, 1962], chap. 7) a man's two legitimate sons exclude a third, illegitimate, son from his inheritance although he is the eldest. He takes revenge by killing one of them, which the "foster brother" of the other two then avenges in turn: see below, chapter 9, on foster brotherhood during this period.

72. *Oláfs saga Tryggvasonar*, 113 (ed. Aðalbjarnarson, 1.372).

73. See discussion in chapter 9, below, and Juha Pentikäinen, *The Nordic Dead-Child Tradition* (Helsinki, 1968) p. 74. Unaccounted-for children are also common: see, e.g., the "dependent children" Geirumund and Guðríd (brother and sister) in *Gísli saga*, chap. 10, who are divided as if property, although no indication is given of their provenance: discussed in William Miller, "Some Aspects of Householding in the Medieval Icelandic Commonwealth."

tory. (They are treated more fully below as a literary genre, because they are later reconstructions of events long past.) Overpopulation and harsh conditions, moreover, had driven the northern peoples south, again and again, throughout the Middle Ages, often in great migrations. All in all, it seems probable that abandonment of children was prevalent in much of Scandinavia and persisted there and in other poorer regions of Europe even during the centuries when it had abated in the newly prosperous areas of Europe, like England and the central continent.

8

❖ ❖ ❖

OBLATION
AT ITS
ZENITH

There is no good that is not voluntary.

Pope Nicholas I (d. 867) on the involuntary religious profession of minors

ALTHOUGH the eleventh and twelfth centuries mark a low point in abandonment of children in Europe (outside Scandinavia), they were also witness to the fullest flowering of oblation; and it is likely that these developments are more than coincidentally related. For the upper classes, at least, oblation may have become such a convenient way of divesting the family of supernumerary or awkward children that it simply obviated the need for "secular" abandonment.[1] And it was the upper classes, during the period of transition from partible inheritance to systems allowing concentration of estates, that had the greatest need for a decorous means of limiting family size. The poor, as noted, quite likely found it easier to cope with many children in this period of unprecedented economic expansion than they had for many centuries before or after.

It is simply impossible in the present state of the documentation to reconstruct the population of most monastic communities, but

---

1. In the middle of the twelfth century, the bishop of Bamberg, in a sermon against infanticide, presents holy orders as the obvious alternative: "et partus . . . femineos, audio, quia vos, o mulieres, necare consuevistis. Quod quantum abominationis habeat, exprimi sermone non potest. . . . Sive igitur sit masculus sive femina, diligenter enutrite partus vestros; Dei enim est et marem procreare et feminam. Septimum itaque sacramentum est ordinatio sive consecratio clericorum. . . . Unde adhortor vos et invito, quia cogere non debeo, ut de liberis vestris ad clericatum tradatis liberalibus studiis prius diligenter instructos. . . ." (Herbord, *Vita Ottonis* 2.17, MGH SS 12, p. 785 [in some printings: 2.19, p. 733]).

the few data available strongly suggest that oblation accounted for a high proportion of monks from the tenth through the end of the eleventh century, and only began to decline in the twelfth.[2] The Register of New Minster, at Winchester, contains unusually detailed lists of monks for the eleventh century. Between about 1030 and 1070, of forty-one new monks, thirty-five (85 percent) are oblates. Even when the tide began to turn against oblation in the following century there were three boys to every five adult recruits.[3] There is no reason to suppose these figures extraordinary.[4] Guibert

2. Part of the difficulty is the opacity, at least at this remove, of monastic terminology: see the very sensible remarks on this by Giles Constable, "Aelred of Rievaulx and the Nun of Watton," in Baker (ed.), *Medieval Women*, p. 218. Cf. Duane Osheim, "Conversion, *conversi*, and the Christian Life in Late Medieval Tuscany," *Speculum* 58, 2 (April 1983) 368–91, p. 373: "*Conversi* regularly would refer to themselves as *conversi, commisi, oblati, Deo devoti, servitialis fratres*, or *sorores*, most often using a combination of these terms. . . . Even a careful reading of the early-fourteenth-century statutes of the Sienese hospital of Santa Maria dell Scala fails to yield a clear distinction between the *fratres, conversi*, and *oblati*." Thus when Osheim notes (p. 378) that *conversi* were forty-five percent of extant "oblations" in monasteries in Tuscany in the later Middle Ages, it is almost impossible to be sure what he means. And since *oblatus* is simply the past participle of the verb "to offer," *offero*, which naturally occurs in a majority of surviving monastic charters (nearly all of which record gifts or donations), it is hard to be sure when it is used in relation to technical oblation and when to the "offering" of a person in some more general sense. Any Christian might "offer" himself or someone else to the service of God, even temporarily, and use this word. Children might be "offered" to monasteries in a sense analogous to being "enrolled" in school, and references to them as *oblati* could mean this or real "oblation." Or, by contrast, children may be clearly oblates when no technical term is employed, as when Caesar of Heisterbach refers to a young child "joining" the order (*Dialogus miraculorum* 12.37, ed. Strange, 2.346–47). On education without oblation during this period see Riché, *Les Écoles*, and Berlière, "Les Écoles"; on girls brought up in convents not as oblates, see F. Rapp, "Les abbayes, hospices de la noblesse: L'Influence de l'aristocratie sur les couvents bénédictins dans l'Empire à la fin du Moyen Age," in P. Contamine, ed., *La Noblesse du Moyen Age* (Paris, 1976), pp. 315–38.

3. British Library, Stowe ms 944, folios 21–22; published as *Liber vitae: register and martyrology of new Minster and Hyde Abbey, Winchester,* ed. Walter de Gray Birch (London, 1892); the statistics it yields are discussed in Christopher Brooke, *The Monastic World 1000–1300* (New York, 1974), p. 88.

4. Giles Constable repeats the estimate of J. Hourlier that boys constituted between a third and a fifth of the whole community at Cluny in the first half of the eleventh century, although they were not necessarily all oblates: *Statuta Petri Venerabilis Abbatis Cluniacensis IX,* in *Consuetudines benedictinae variae (saec. XI–saec. XIV)* (Siegburg, 1975) (*Corpus consuetudinum monasticarum* 6), p. 86, note. Pierre Riché ("L'Enfant dans la société monastique du XIIe siècle," *Pierre Abelard / Pierre*

of Nogent recalled that during his youth "the churches were . . . in the hands of those who had been placed in them by the piety of their kinsmen early in life."[5]

Nor is it unreasonable to view this as more than the blossoming of piety. There are constant complaints in monastic literature about parents simply abandoning to monasteries children they do not wish to keep at home. Ulrich of Cluny observed in the second half of the eleventh century that

> after they have a houseful, so to speak, of sons and daughters, or if they have any who are lame or crippled, deaf and dumb or blind, hump-backed or leprous, or who have any defect which would make them less desirable in the secular world, [the parents] offer them as monks with the most pious of vows . . . so that they themselves are spared having to educate and support them, or because this redounds to the advantage of their other children. Anything born of honest and pious motivations can, indeed, be turned to bad use, and this holy institution has been corrupted by the greed of parents, who, for the benefit of the [rest of the] family, commit to monasteries any hump-backed, deformed, dull or unpromising children they have. . . .[6]

---

le Vénérable [Paris, 1974], p. 693) opines that by the eleventh century there were already no oblates at Monte Cassino or Hirschau, that in the twelfth century Cluny accepted only six oblates, and that in 1132 Peter the Venerable set twenty as the minimum age of profession, but all of these statements give a misleading picture, and some are untrue. If there were no oblates at Monte Cassino in the eleventh century, there certainly were in the thirteenth, when St. Thomas was there. The minimum age of profession has little to do with oblates, who can be given to monasteries in infancy and allowed to make their profession at any subsequent point, as they were at Cluny: the regulations that specify profession at twenty (chap. 36) also make provision for oblation of boys (chaps. 56, 66; cited below at note 34). The idea that there were only six oblates (at a time) at Cluny is based on Ulrich's statement "Pueri autem qui sunt in conventu nostro, non ultra senarium protendunt" (*Antiquiores consuetudines Cluniacensis monasterii* 3.8 [PL 149.742]; cf. Berlière's similar interpretation in "Les Écoles," p. 568). But this a doubtful inference. Constable (as above) takes "ultra senarium protendunt" to apply to a particular group of boys separated for liturgical purposes, but it also seems possible that it refers to the age of the oblates, not their number; "plusquam senarium" would seem a more likely expression for number than "ultra."

5. 1.8, trans. Benton, p. 54.
6. PL 149.635–36.

Half a century later, Peter the Venerable, himself an oblate, forbade further reception at Cluny without express permission of the abbot, because of the great number—practically a majority, he felt—of peasants, infants, old men, and mental defectives the monastery had been receiving; and later in the twelfth century the abbot of Andres "was horrified and shocked at the crowd of deformities"[7] in his monastery, "among whom were the lame, the malformed, the one-eyed, the squinting, the blind, the crippled. . . ."[8] Guibert of Nogent's father had promised him as an oblate during a difficult birth, but "no one doubted," according to Guibert, that his father (if he had lived) would have broken the promise once he saw how clever Guibert was and "fit for worldly pursuits." Extra or undesirable children were sent to the monastery; clever ones were kept at home.[9]

Physical defects stand out in these accounts, but probably because they were conspicuous in life. Estate division was in all likelihood a more common nonspiritual motivation for oblation among the prosperous, as it had been since the time of Basil. The Bishop of Paris noted in the early thirteenth century that children were

> cast into the cloister by parents and relatives just as if they were kittens or piglets whom their mother could not nourish; so that they may die to the world not spiritually but . . . civilly, that is, so that they may be deprived of their hereditary portion and that it may devolve on those who remain in the world.[10]

Numerous specific instances are known in which oblation was employed to exclude someone from an inheritance; the gift of money

7. Literally, "deformity of the crowd": see following note.

8. *Statuta,* chap. 35, p. 70; cf. Peter's bitter letter on this in PL 149.636–37, and the later restatements of his rule cited in Constable, *Statuta,* as above, note 4; *Chronica Willelmi Andrensis,* ed. J. Heller (Hannover, 1879), p. 705 (MGH SS 24): "abhorruit et expavit deformitatem gregis. Quidam enim claudi, quidam contracti, quidam monoculi, quidam strabones, quidam ceci, quidam vero manci inter eos apparebant. . . ." Both are mentioned in Lynch, *Simoniacal Entry,* pp. 44–45, and the latter is discussed in Riché, "L'Enfant dans la société monastique," pp. 692–93, citing the earlier edition of Acherius. As late as 1303, when rules for oblation had been much tightened, a blind child of ten was given to the Benedictine house at Domène along with a gift of cash: see Deroux, p. 110.

9. 1.3–4, Benton, pp. 43–44.

10. William of Auvergne, trans. Lynch, *Simoniacal Entry,* p. 42.

or land which had to accompany an oblate (an incentive for the monastery to accept even a defective child) was doubtless well worth preserving the estate or saving the cost of a dowry.[11] Lynch found that among sixty-one cases of high medieval oblation forty-two involved families with three or more sons, and twenty-nine with four or more: in all of them, in other words, oblation (or some form of abandonment) was needed to bring the number of heirs close to the three typical of propertied classes in many times and places.[12] Other studies have indicated that twenty to twenty-five percent of children of the prosperous were placed in religious life (or orders), and in many specific cases the percentage was higher.[13] A fourteenth-century marriage contract specifies that the eldest daughter will be married with an annual income of thirty pounds;

11. See, e.g., Lynch, p. 58; Deroux, pp. 106–7; Rolf of St. Trond, Epistle 2 (PL 173.195–208). In the last case, although the abbot argues that monasteries were founded to help the pious poor, not to release wealthy families from duties to children, one suspects that the fact that the offending parent refused to make any gift to the monastery, specifically mentioned in the sources, played some role in the subsequent quarrel. In fact the monastery's position was not that the child should not have been made an oblate, but that he should receive his lawful inheritance, which would then pass to the monastery.

12. *Simoniacal Entry*, p. 42, utilizing data for 1050–1200 from C. Blanc, "Les pratiques de piété des laïcs dans les pays du Bas-Rhône aux XIe et XIIe siècles," *Annales du Midi* 72 (1960) 137–47.

13. Parisse (*Noblesse et chevalerie*) found that twenty percent of the sons of families of the higher nobility in Lorraine in the twelfth and thirteenth centuries were placed in religious life (see pp. 278–79), but cites many cases of higher figures, such as Agnes of Bar, who placed two of four sons in religious life precisely, in Parisse's estimation, because she considered that two were sufficient as heirs (p. 240), or Ferri de Brixey, who had three of four sons in orders (p. 243). M.-T. Lorcin ("Retraite des veuves") found that twenty-five percent of daughters of testators in Lyons from 1301 to 1510, long after the classical period of oblation, were "destinée au couvent." Alexander Murray (*Reason and Society in the Middle Ages* [Oxford, 1978]), summarizing a number of studies of the High Middle Ages, concluded that noble families placed about twenty-five percent of their members in the clergy (pp. 341–45), but not all through oblation. Goodich (*Vita Perfecta*, p. 93) found that "of those saints whose age of profession is known, twenty-five percent were clearly oblates or made profession immediately upon reaching puberty, which suggests that they were already residing in the monastery." Cf. the observations of Nicolas Huyghebaert, "Les femmes laïques," p. 373: "De prime abord, ces abbayes semblent avoir été créées pour recueillir des cadettes de familles nobles. . . ." Or Berlière, "Recrutement," p. 6: "Des parents trouvèrent dans l'oblature un excellent moyen de se débarrasser d'enfants nombreux ou atteints d'infirmités, ou encore, de rétablir l'équilibre dans leur état de fortune."

all the other daughters will be religious, with an annual income of a hundred sous.[14]

Parents also donated their children to monasteries when they entered themselves, or went on pilgrimage or crusade.[15] In a statement strikingly reminiscent of other parting paternal instructions to ancient and medieval pregnant wives, Petrus of Tornamira wrote as he set off on a pilgrimage to the Holy Land:

> If my wife, who now appears to be pregnant, gives birth to a child, I relinquish him to become a monk in the said place, with a villa called Pomairol. If she does not have a child and she herself wishes to become a nun or to place another of her children in monastic life, the same agreement should be made, viz., with the same villa.[16]

St. Rectrude offered all three of her children as oblates so she could enter monastic life.[17] When Peter Waldo undertook a life of poverty he gave both of his daughters to Fontevrault, a wealthy convent, along with a large gift of money—without even consulting their

14. From the *Nobiliaire du Limousin,* published in *Bulletin de la Société scientifique, historique et archéologique de la Corrèze* (Brive) 14 (1892), p. 188. Cf. ibid., a contract stipulating that a man's daughter be *monachisée,* in return for which he will give the convent one hundred sous a year for her maintenance until she dies; then it will be reduced to ten.

15. See *Cartulaire de l'abbaye de Saint-Père de Chartres,* ed. B. Guérard (Paris, 1840) 2.3.21; *Cartulaire du prieuré de Saint-Hippolyte de Vivoin,* ed. L.-J. Denis (Paris, 1894), p. 138; and *Cartulaire d'Affligem,* ed. E. de Marneffe, in *Analectes pour servir à l'histoire ecclésiastique de la Belgique* 2: *Cartulaires et documents étendus* (Louvain, 1910), 11, no. 5; Adam of Eynsham, 1.5; and the model letter written by a man trying to dissuade a friend from going on pilgrimage precisely because it would constitute abandonment of his wife and children: Léopold Delisle, "Notice sur une 'Summa dictaminis' jadis conservée à Beauvais," *Notices et extraits des manuscrits de la Bibliothèque Nationale et autres bibliothèques* 36 (1899), p. 199. The reception of illegitimate children in monasteries along with parents was explicitly prohibited in Spain in the fourteenth century: *Synodicon Hispanum,* Synod of Santiago de Compostela, 6 (1320), canon 4 (p. 294), and Synod of Santiago de Compostela, 8 (1320), canon 5.

16. *Cartulaire de l'Abbaye bénédictine Saint-Martin de Tulle en Limousin,* ed. Jean-Baptiste Champeval, in *Bulletin de la Société scientifique* 15 (1893) 171–76, 319–33, 493–512, 653–68, no. 465, p. 325 (A.D. 1109).

17. "Tres filias candidas veluti columbas gratissimas illi fieri hostias" ("Vita sanctae Retrudae," 2, in ASOB 2 [Paris, 1701] 944).

mother.[18] Hildegard of Bingen (d. 1179), the tenth child of a noble family, was given to a convent at eight as a "tithe."[19]

By the High Middle Ages parents did not always need to be present for oblation—at Cluny, for example, they did not—which made it much simpler for great numbers of children of awkward parentage to find their way into religious life.[20] Many of the children abandoned for reasons of shame in medieval literature (Gregorius, Alban, Laurence—all discussed below) were either reared in a monastery or became monks at some point in their lives.[21] By the fourteenth century the influx of illegitimates, primarily the children of priests, was staggering.[22]

There was also the traditional concern for the parents' spiritual well-being:

> I, Bemond, fearing that for the stain of my many sins and that without the grace of God I may not be among the elect, . . . hand over, give, and offer my son William with the will and advice of Richildi, his mother . . . so that with him living henceforth under regular discipline, aided by his intercession I may be worthy to be a co-heir in the election of the servants of Jesus Christ.[23]

18. *Chronicon universale anonymi Laudunensis,* ed. Georg Waitz (Hannover, 1882), MGH SS 26, p. 447: "Ille vero de mobilibus his a quibus iniuste habuerat reddidit, magnam vero partem pecunie sue duabus parvulis filiabus contulit, quas matre earum ignorante ordini Fontis-Evrardi mancipavit." Lynch (pp. 48–49) cites the mother of Guibert as an example of a parent offering a child so as to enter monastic life, but these were not actually the precise circumstances: see above, pp. 284–85.

19. "Hildegardis vita, auctore Guiberto," 1, ed. J.-B. Pitra, in *Analecta sacra* 8: *Analecta sanctae Hildegardis* (Montecassino, 1882), p. 408; cf. *Vita Sanctae Hildegardis auctoribus Godefrido et Theodorico monachis* (PL 172) 1.1.2.

20. On this, see Berlière, "Recrutement," pp. 26–31; for oblation without parents present, see Customs of Cluny, 3 (PL 149.941).

21. On the abandonment of illegitimate children, see Lynch, *Simoniacal Entry,* pp. 42–43, 58. Caesar of Heisterbach tells a story of a monk who begot two illegitimate sons during a wild youth; both became monks (*Dialogus miraculorum* 7.16, 2.17–23).

22. The master-general of the Dominicans applied in 1346 for dispensation from illegitimacy for 200 Dominicans, many of them children of priests; during his first year as pope, Benedict XII granted 374 dispensations for illegitimacy, 148 of them to priests' sons desiring to enter religious orders; Clement VI granted 484 during his first year: see Berlière, "Recrutement," pp. 26–27.

23. Lynch, *Simoniacal Entry,* pp. 41, 57. Note that this is one of the most disinterested parental statements cited by Lynch. Similar emphasis on the benefits for

I offer my son . . . to be a monk according to the rule of St. Benedict in the aforesaid monastery, so that he may implore the mercy of God for me and his mother and all his relatives.[24]

As in the early Middle Ages, children were also donated to the church in arrangements similar to monastic oblation but with important variations. Icelandic law recognized the making of oblates for the diocesan clergy—as Spanish law had earlier.

It is lawful for a man to have a priestling [*prestling*] taught for his church. He is to make an agreement with the boy himself if he is sixteen winters old, but if he is younger, he is to make it with his legal administrator. The whole agreement they make between them is to be binding. If they make no special agreement and a man takes the priestling for his church, . . . then he is to provide him with instruction and fostering; and have him chastised only in such a way that it brings no shame on the boy or his kin; and treat him as if he were his own child.[25]

Such boys could never leave the churches for which they were trained, except by training someone else to serve in their stead: if they fled, those harboring them suffered full outlawry.

There seems to have been a personal aspect to this relationship, a kind of hybrid of oblation and "fostering." The boys bought and "found" by the Archbishop of Canterbury (see above), who were brought up in the church, appear to have had such a personal relationship, and other evidence suggests this kind of "oblation" into the care of a particular religious person was widespread.[26] Monastic

---

parents occurs in charters of oblation all over Europe. For Spain, for example, see the *Cartulario de Sant Cugat del Vallés,* ed. José Ríus Serra, 3 (Barcelona, 1947), 187 (". . . donamus Domino Deo et s. Cucuphate cenobio . . . nostrum filium . . . faciendum propter remedium nostrarum animarum sive parentum nostrorum") and following note. These examples are from later centuries, but they are not different from earlier documents, as the eighth-century example above shows (p. 237).

24. José Lacarra, "Documentos para el estudio de la reconquista y repoblación del Valle del Ebro," *Estudios de Edad Media de la Corona de Aragón* 2 (1946), 474.

25. *Laws of Early Iceland,* trans. Dennis, vol. 1, p. 34.

26. See, e.g., the letters referring to a monk as the "adopted father" of a boy killed by a bear in "Epistolae ad Amicum and Three Poems," in *Analecta Dublinensia: Three Medieval Latin Texts,* ed. Marvin Colker (Cambridge, Mass., 1975), letters 7 and 8. This was a long-standing tradition in Ireland, although it is difficult to date precisely because the materials describing early medieval incidents are

304 · The Kindness of Strangers

communities also trained children for the diocesan clergy at the behest of parents.[27]

During a famine in the region of Vendôme in the middle of the
twelfth century, mothers "would throw their babies at the doors of
monasteries."[28] Whether the children were then reared as oblates or
simply supported by the monastery until they grew old enough to
choose a lifestyle for themselves is not clear, but the incident high-
lights the role of monasteries in high medieval society as safety nets
for hard-pressed parents. (This was true even in literature: see discussion of Marie de France's *Fresne* in chapter 10, below.)

Contemporary sources rarely indicate the ages of children at the
time of oblation. The minimum age at which they could be offered
to religious life or bound by profession (two separate questions)
was debated throughout the High Middle Ages by canonists and
governing bodies of religious orders, but custom and parental motivations appear to have played a greater role in determining practice
than official pronouncements. Some were given in infancy; many at
about six or seven;[29] some even older. Many monasteries would not
be able to nurse infants, and parents were sometimes reluctant to
give up very young children, out of affection or concern. Ordericus
Vitalis was sent away at ten, and although Guibert of Nogent's father intended at the time of his birth to offer him as an oblate, this
was apparently not to take place for some years. St. Thomas was
given to Monte Cassino at six;[30] Innocent V to the Dominicans at
eleven;[31] but Engelbert of Cologne was already a *praepositus* of regu-

---

themselves mostly from the High Middle Ages. See, e.g., the account of St.
Mochoemog, who was brought up for twenty years by St. Yta ("Vita sancti
Mochoemog," 8, in VSH 2.167), or the blind child of the Neill clan who is "fostered" with St. Colman after being rescued from infanticide ("Vita sancti col-
mani," 26, VSH 1.268–69).

27. See, e.g., the instance of a woman making a gift to the priory of St. Augustine to have them educate and raise her son, who becomes a deacon: T. Grasi-
lier, *Cartulaires inédits de la Saintonge: I: Cartulaire de l'abbaye de Saint-Étienne de
Vaux* (Niort, 1871), p. 71.

28. "Tanta autem postea fames exorta est, ut matres projicerent infantulos ad
portas monasteriorum. . . ." *Annales de Vendôme,* p. 72, cited in Penelope Johnson,
Prayer, Patronage & Power: The Abbey of La Trinité, Vendôme, 1032–1187 (New
York, 1981), p. 159; cf. J. Bienvenue, "Pauvreté, misères et charité en Anjou aux
XIe et XIIe siècles," *Moyen Age* 72 (1966), p. 399.

29. In literature children are usually abandoned at monasteries in infancy, but
Gregorius was given at age six (lines 1158–60): see discussion below.

30. According to Riché, "L'Enfant," p. 693; some authorities say five.

31. See his life: AASS, Aug. 3, 1.283–310.

lar canons at age twelve.[32] Of the nine female saints of the thirteenth
century whose age of entry to convents is known, four were donated at seven, one at ten, and one at twelve.[33]

Surviving monastic provisions for the care and governance of
oblates during the period suggest a life of considerable austerity,
little different from the regime of the early Middle Ages.[34] Cluny's
regulations were influential and (partly for that reason) typical:[35] the
boys slept in a dormitory, where their beds were separate from each
other and from those of the masters (of which there were at least
two). They took part in the rigorous daily liturgical life of the monastery, sitting on tree trunks, stools, or the ground; their posture
and decorum were minutely regulated, and they were beaten with a
"light, polished cane" if they "committed an offense in chanting the
psalms," or in any other way. They were required to inform on
each other, and anyone who concealed an infraction was to be
whipped along with the perpetrator. They could speak only with
permission. Although the rule took cognizance of their frailty in
some ways, modifying fasting rules for them in regard to breakfast
and allowing them milk once a week, in a few particulars it seems
gratuitously harsh: they were not permitted to go to the bathroom
in the morning until after liturgy, and every morning the master
was to hold the whipping cane over their heads as they arose. (Caesar of Heisterbach depicts a boy in a monastic school as being terrified almost literally to death by the master of the school.)[36]

32. AASS, Nov. 7, 2.623; cf. Gabriel le Bras, *Institutions écclésiastiques de la
Chrétienté médiévale* 2 (Paris, 1964), p. 384.
33. Goodich, *Vita Perfecta,* p. 93. The "Nun of Watton" was taken into the
Gilbertines as a four-year-old: see remarks in Constable, "Aelred of Rievaulx,"
p. 219, and Appendix of Translations. Cf. Caesar of Heisterbach, cited in note 41,
below.
34. For monastic regulations on oblation see, in addition to the following
note, Deroux ("Les Origines") and Berlière ("Les Écoles"), and the *Corpus consuetudinum monasticarum,* ed. Kassio Hallinger (e.g., 10: *Liber tramitis aevi Odilonis
abbatis,* ed. Peter Dinter [Siegburg, 1980], chap. 22; 6: *Consuetudines Benedictinae
variae* (Saec. XI–XIV), ed. Constable [Siegburg, 1975], chaps. 56 and 66; 3: *Decreta
Lanfranci monachis Cantuariensibus transmissa,* ed. David Knowles [Siegburg, 1967],
chap. 105).
35. Ulrich of Cluny, *Antiquiores consuetudines Cluniacensis monasterii* 8, PL
149.741–47. Cf. the rules for oblates from St. Bénigne at Dijon, translated (with
some evident bias) by G. G. Coulton, *Life in the Middle Ages* (New York, 1930),
pp. 99–101.
36. 8.74. On the other hand, he also tells of a nine-year-old girl who defied
her parents to become a nun. They abducted her, but she managed to regain the
convent, and was eventually elected its abbess (1.43).

The most poignant aspect of their lives was the concerted effort of monastic authorities to prevent any expression of affection or warmth toward them by the older monks, or even among themselves. This was, in a way, inevitable in communities of celibates in a society increasingly troubled about homosexuality, but it nonetheless suggests an emotional life of pitiable aridity. The boys were never to touch each other, and no monk was ever to touch them (or even their garments). They were never to be left alone with each other or with a single master. If a boy needed to go out at night "for necessaries," both a master and another boy had to accompany him, with a lantern. Even the kiss of peace during the liturgy—the one physical contact permitted adult monks—was explicitly forbidden to oblates.[37]

A clue to the paranoia felt by monastic authorities on this subject—and perhaps a justification for it—is provided in Walter Map's cynical story about St. Bernard's failed attempt to restore to life the son of a Burgundian noble.

> Bernard ordered the body to be taken to a private room, ejected all the bystanders, and lay down on top of the boy. After saying a prayer, he got up. The boy, however, did not get up: he lay there quite dead. I then said, "This is surely the most unfortunate of monks, for never have I heard of a monk's lying down on a boy without the boy's immediately rising up after him." The abbot turned red and everyone else slipped out to have a laugh.[38]

Ulrich of Cluny concludes his description of the spartan life of the monastery's oblates with the somewhat surprising observation

37. Aelred, abbot of the Cistercian abbey of Rievaulx in northern England, allowed his monks to hold hands and express physical affection (Walter Daniel, *The Life of Aelred, Abbot of Rievaulx*, trans. F. Powicke [London, 1969], p. 40), but this was highly unusual, as his biographer notes, ibid.

38. *De Nugis curialium*, ed. M. R. James, revised C. N. L. Brooke, R. A. B. Mynors (Oxford, 1983), 1.24, p. 80 (my translation; James provides one, as does John Mundy, *Europe in the High Middle Ages* [New York, 1973], p. 302). In addition to the obvious tenor of the story, the Latin contains several ribald puns: *incumbere*, for example, is used for Bernard's lying on the boy, and although it was an appropriate verb (evoking Mark 5:40), it also had distinctly sexual connotations (e.g., *incubus*). For further discussion see Boswell, *Christianity,* chaps. 8 and 9, and bibliography cited there.

that "it would be difficult for any king's son in a palace to be brought up with more care than the lowliest child at Cluny."[39] This seems less ironic if viewed in the context of an ethical system which valued (officially, at least) asceticism, self-denial, and spiritual struggle more than material prosperity, comfort, or even human affection. The life of the Irish saint Munnu describes a duke who has placed two sons in two different monasteries and goes to visit each. One son is treated with honor and respect; the other dressed as a servant and forced to labor like the rest of the monks. The duke, St. Munnu, and the narrator all agree that it is the latter who has received the better portion.[40]

Despite these rigors, many oblates retained pleasant memories of their childhoods.[41] Toward the end of the eleventh century Ordericus Vitalis was sent away at age ten from his home in England to a monastery in a foreign country; although the parting was agonizing, he remembered his reception at the monastery as a mitigating circumstance, not a terrible fate.

> So, weeping, he gave me, a weeping child, into the care of the monk Reginald, and sent me away into exile for the love of Thee and never saw me again. And I, a mere boy, obeyed him willingly in all things. . . . I abandoned my country and my kinsfolk, my friends and all with whom I was acquainted. . . . And so, a boy of ten, I crossed the English Channel and came into Normandy as an exile, unknown to all, knowing no one. Like Joseph in Egypt, I heard a language which I did not understand. Thou didst suffer me through Thy grace to find nothing but kindness and fellowship among strangers. . . .[42]

39. ". . . difficile fieri posse ut ullus regis filius majore diligentia nutriatur in palatio quam puer quilibet minimus in Cluniaco" (PL 149.747; cf. note 35, above).

40. "Vita sancti Munnu," 21, VSH 2.233–34.

41. See, for example, the cases cited in Orlandís, "Notas sobre la 'Oblatio puerorum' en los siglos XI y XII," p. 207, nn. 6, 7, and 8. Caesar of Heisterbach (1.20) tells a story of a monk who regrets leaving in the world a younger brother too young to enter the monastery, but a vision persuades the abbot to admit him. It is unclear what canonical impediment is understood here: the reception of children at any age was permitted by ecclesiastical law so long as they were not professed. Particular monasteries, however, might have rules that set higher ages even for reception.

42. Ordericus Vitalis, *Ecclesiastical History,* ed. and trans. Marjorie Chibnall (Oxford, 1980), 6.555.

Some adult churchmen who had been donated (e.g., Thomas Aquinas) articulated justifications for oblation. The oblates in at least one monastery created a conflict with the older recruits by claiming that their innocence of the world guaranteed them a moral superiority: "Oblates are like angels; adult recruits like holy men."[43] And some ecclesiastics were much more paternal and sympathetic toward monastic children than the common rule suggested. Citing Christ's comment about truth from the mouths of babes, Bishop Herman in Verdun asked—and followed—the advice of the children of the community of St. Vanne about who should be the next abbot.[44]

One of the most appealing and influential figures of the eleventh century, Anselm, abbot of the monastery of Bec and later Archbishop of Canterbury, had wished to become a monk as a teenager, but his father opposed it, and the abbot to whom Anselm applied would not accept him without his father's permission. After his mother died he left home and finally succeeded in becoming a monk. He took a special interest, as prior, in the oblate boys and young men of the monastery, because, he said, they were the "soft wax" on which God's image could most successfully be printed.[45] His relations with some of them were intensely personal.[46] To the oblate Osbern (1.10) he was the father neither of them had had: he oversaw his development with great care, indulging him sometimes as a child, but as the boy grew older he gradually insisted on greater austerity to forge a mature character; he sat by him day and night when he was ill, and said mass for him every single day for a year after his untimely death—just as the boy's natal father might have

43. "Angeli enim sunt quasi nutriti, sancti vero homines quasi conversi." (*Liber Anselmi de humanis moribus per similitudines* 78, in *Memorials of St. Anselm,* ed. R. W. Southern and F. S. Schmitt [London, 1968], pp. 68–69 [or PL 158.649]; discussed in Deroux, "Les Origines," pp. 105–6).

44. ASOB, "Vita B. Richardi," 6.1, p. 521; cf. Deroux, "Les Origines," p. 15.

45. Eadmer, *Life of St. Anselm, Archbishop of Canterbury,* ed. and trans. R. W. Southern (London, 1962), 1.11. Subsequent quotations are also taken from this edition, but the translations are mine.

46. Although I have argued elsewhere that there might be an erotic aspect to Anselm's relations with some other monks (*Christianity,* pp. 218–20), I see no indication of sexuality in his interactions with oblates or novices. The vast majority of human adults appear to have tender and protective feelings for the young, while only a tiny minority experience paedophilia. (Nor is there any evidence that homosexuality is more frequently associated with paedophilia than is heterosexuality.) In the absence of other indications it is more reasonable to assume that Anselm's attachments to the young were paternal.

honored his memory. When Anselm and Osbern called each other "father" and "son," respectively, according to monastic custom, one imagines that the words had an emotional force, and a reality, beyond their communal implications. Anselm's biographer, Eadmer, himself an oblate from infancy, records with great admiration the saint's stern rebuke of an abbot who complained of the rowdiness of oblates in his own monastery:

> "Pray tell me, my lord abbot, if you were to plant a little sapling in your garden and then immediately enclose it so tightly on all sides that it could not branch out in any direction, what sort of tree do you suppose it would be when you freed it after some years?"
>
> "Perfectly worthless, with twisted and knotted branches."
>
> "And who would be to blame for this except you, who so severely constrained it? This is just what you are doing to your boys. They are planted by oblation in the garden of the church, to grow and bear fruit for God. You, however, so hem them in on all sides with intimidation, threats, and blows that they are hardly given a chance to master any degree of freedom,[47] and they, having been so badly oppressed, form and harbor and nurse within themselves perverse and distorted feelings, like thorns. . . . If you want your boys to behave decorously you yourself must provide, along with the restraint of blows, the encouragement and support of fatherly love and tenderness." (2.22)

The abbot found himself so well rebuked that he fell on the ground at Anselm's feet.

It was, nonetheless, at best an austere life, one for which even the theology of the church recognized not everyone was likely to have a vocation. Matilda, the daughter of Malcolm and Margaret of Scotland—later the wife of Henry I of England—was taken into religious life as a child with her aunt, but so despised it that she would take off her veil, throw it on the ground, and stamp on it; her father eventually took her away.[48]

---

47. "Ut nulla penitus sibi liceat libertate potiri": Southern's translation, "that they are utterly deprived of their liberty" does not quite convey the sense of *potiri*. Anselm (or Eadmer) seems to be emphasizing that freedom cannot be enjoyed without having first been mastered.

48. Eadmer, *Historia Novorum in Anglia,* trans. G. Bosanquet (London, 1964), p. 127; R. W. Southern, *St. Anselm and His Biographer* (Cambridge, 1963), pp. 182–

Aelred, abbot of the Cistercian monastery of Rievaulx, high-lights, probably unintentionally, the tragic side of oblation in his account of the Nun of Watton.[49] A girl donated to a convent at age four[50] felt no inclination to religious life as she approached adulthood, but was constrained to remain a nun for life. She fell in love with a young man (probably a monk) working for the convent and had an affair with him. When the nuns discovered the romance, they punished her severely: she was flogged, chained in a cell, and fed only bread and water; she escaped worse only because she was pregnant. The young man, whose whereabouts the girl disclosed in the hopes of being married to him, was captured and castrated by the nuns in a scene of stupefying horror: the sisters forced the pregnant girl to perform the operation with her own hands, and one of the bystanders placed the severed organs in her mouth. Even this failed to appease their fury; they returned the girl to her cell and chained her again while she awaited the birth of her child. The tale ends in a miracle: the pitiful girl curses the Archbishop of York, who had inspired her donation to the monastery in the first place, and he appears to her in a vision and takes away her newborn child, leaving her with no signs of pregnancy or childbirth. Whether one accepts this at face value or understands it as camouflage for some means of disposing of the baby, it is not least among the touching ironies of the story that the girl whose life was made so unhappy by her abandonment to a monastery must then save herself by abandoning her own child.

Ecclesiastical authorities of the period recognized, as had their predecessors in Carolingian Europe, the problem posed by oblates who wished to withdraw from an onerous, confining, and permanent commitment made for them by others, but they had difficulty effecting a resolution of the issue. In the *Decretum* Gratian treated it under four rubrics:

93; and Derek Baker, "'A Nursery of Saints': St. Margaret of Scotland Reconsidered," in Baker, ed., *Medieval Women*, pp. 122–24.

49. PL 195.789–96. Translated in Appendix.

50. The donation, by a bishop who seems to have been the girl's guardian, may have been an extraordinary event rather than ordinary oblation, since there is no other indication of oblates in the convent. Ellen Barrett, in a paper delivered before the seventh annual Berkshire Women's History Conference, argued that oblation was unknown among the Gilbertines and that the whole episode derives its character from the anxiety of the nuns to safeguard their reputation, since theirs was a double monastic community (i.e., for men and women).

Two boys were donated to a monastery by their parents; one accepted the habit[51] unwillingly, the other willingly. When they reached puberty, the unwilling one returned to secular life; the willing one petitioned to enter a stricter community. (1) It is therefore asked, in the first place, whether those donated during childhood can be forced to persevere in religious life? (2) Second, if someone accepted tonsure or monastic habit as a child without the consent of parents,[52] can he be withdrawn from it or not? (3) If someone put on the habit without giving his own consent, can he be compelled to retain it, or not? (4) Is it permitted to transfer from one monastery to another, stricter, one?[53]

Of these, only question four, of no direct relation to oblation, receives a conclusive answer (to wit: not without the permission of the abbot). For the other three Gratian adduces earlier precedents— some erroneously—which as a whole are somewhat inconclusive, in some cases even contradictory. The answer to question two appears to be that parents can, under limited circumstances, withdraw a child whose profession they did not authorize, and that proper oblation requires the consent of the parents. The rulings cited for point three imply that someone who openly and explicitly resisted a profession forced on him would not be bound by it, but it is clouded by the addition of a final text which stipulates that in at least some cases such persons might be constrained to remain in religious life.[54]

Neither of these addresses the real problems of oblation, since there is no evidence that parents often changed their minds, and most children donated to monasteries were not in a position to resist profession overtly, or to prove later that they had done so even if they did.[55] Question one was the crux. Gratian quotes five canons which, he says, indicate that "parental decision does obligate chil-

---

51. Monastic garb, and therefore, by metonymy and church law, monastic life.

52. Or, possibly, "relatives": *parentum*.

53. *Decretum* 2.20 (Friedberg, 1.843).

54. "Hii vero, qui illecti comam deposuerunt, in eo, quod ceperunt, perseuerare cogantur, res uero eorum heredibus reddantur" (*Decretum* 2.20.3.5 [Friedberg, 1.854–55]).

55. The case Gratian cites in support of the principle of absolving someone who had been expressly unwilling (2.20.3.5) involved a father who was a monk and forced his son to take the habit of his own order: both could therefore later be interrogated, and the father confessed his actions; this cannot have happpened often.

dren,"[56] and then subjoins two later papal rulings which imply the contrary,[57] without suggesting how the conflict should be resolved. (The degree to which near contemporaries perceived the inconclusiveness of this treatment is revealed by the fact that a century later another hand inserted, apparently as a compromise, a spurious papal rescript allowing the tonsuring and professing of children but requiring that they be asked to confirm their vows at age fifteen.[58] This entered canon law as part of Gratian's treatment.)

It was a hard question, and perhaps not surprising that Gratian should have avoided it: to have ruled that parents could not bind their children to religious life might release a flood of oblates on the world, greatly reducing monastic populations, and would bring into question a well-established tradition regarding oblation and even baptism, which parents also undertook on behalf of children. On the other hand, how could a vow be binding if not consented to by the person required to discharge it? An anonymous canonical treatment of a decade or so later (inspired perhaps by Gratian's distinction between those who actually resisted and those who did not) settled the problem by distinguishing between children given before reaching the age of reason and those given after. The former must be excused if, on reaching the age of discretion (not specified here, but generally assumed to be between seven and fourteen), they do not wish to be in religious life. The latter are assumed to have consented if they did not actively resist.[59]

In several squabbles with Bernard of Clairvaux over specific

56. (Canon 1) Basil, cited above in chapter 5, note 7, but misidentified by Gratian as "Ninth Synod"; (canon 2) Gregory to Boniface, cited in chapter 5, note 48, but misidentified by Gratian as Gregory to Augustine; (canon 3) IV Toledo, 48, cited in chapter 5, note 20; (canon 4) a statement from the rule attributed to Isidore, citing Hanna's gift of Samuel as precedent for irrevocable oblation; and (canon 6) Tribur, 27, cited in chapter 5, note 65. Glossators added quotations from Gregory to Anthemius and a canon attributed to Theodore allowing the substitution of one child for another (canons 5 and 7).

57. Canon 8, Leo IX, Epistle 90 to Rusticus, chaps. 13 and 14, forbidding the marriage of girls who had taken the veil "not coerced by their parents," from which Gratian infers that if they had been coerced their profession would not be binding; and canon 9, from a synod of 826 (Mansi 14.1008), arguing that no one should be retained in a monastery against his will.

58. Canon 10, Palea: "Unde Marcellus Papa."

59. *Incerti auctoris quaestiones* 5, ed. F. Thaner, in *Summa Magistri Rolandi* (Innsbruck, 1874), pp. 242–43. Cf. Anselm of Lucca, *Collectio canonum una cum collectione minore,* ed. idem (Innsbruck, 1915), 7.1, p. 362, which, however, is less helpful.

monks, twelfth-century popes upheld the irrevocability of parental oblation,[60] but at the end of the century Pope Celestine III (reigned 1191–98) issued a landmark ruling resolving a dispute between a monastery and a boy whose father had taken him with him into religious life and "forced him to assume the habit."[61] The boy disliked and left the monastery, and sued to recover his estate, which the father had donated to the community. Celestine ruled that since the boy had not attained the age of reason when he was professed, he was not bound to religious life, and could reclaim both his lay status and his inheritance.[62] His successor, Innocent III, wrote to the Archbishop of Lyons that oblates should be asked to reconfirm their vows at fifteen and allowed to leave if they did not wish to remain.[63]

As a result of these and other papal, episcopal, conciliar, and monastic decrees,[64] the issue had been substantially relegislated by

60. St. Bernard's cousin, Robert, who was given to Cluny as a child, went to Clairvaux at fourteen but then cited his oblation to Cluny as grounds for returning there when he found Clairvaux too strict; Bernard disagreed, and argued that Robert's own profession at Clairvaux should have more force than his parents' donation to Cluny; but Pope Calixtus II agreed with Robert that the parents' oblation was paramount: Bernard, Letters 1, 324, 325, all in PL 182. Cf. the case of Thomas of Saint-Omer: ibid., letters 382, 395.

61. ". . . filium suum fecit habitum suscipere monachalem."

62. CIC, *Decretalium Greg. IX* 3.31.14 (Friedberg 2.573–74).

63. "Cum igitur reperiatur in canone ut minoris aetatis filiis qui oblati fuerint, suscipientes habitum vel tonsuram, si a praelatis suis anno quinto decimo requisiti, se in assumptae religionis proposito consenserit permansuros, poenitendi licentia praecludatur, alioquin eis non adimatur ad soeculum redeundi facultas, ne coacta praestare Deo servitia videantur." PL 216.627; cf. the Palea in the *Decretum,* which Friedberg cites as "incertum" (1.845).

64. Robert of Flamborough, in his influential *Liber poenitentialis,* attempts to reconcile all the preceding legislation by stating that children donated by parents when they were of discretionary age ("doli capax") and who themselves consented, can never leave the monastery; those who did not consent may choose to stay or not—at fifteen for males, twelve for females; but he then acknowledges that "others say" that parental vows are irrevocable, and at a later point repeats only this point of view (2.3.54, p. 87). Bernard of Pavia (*Summa decretalium,* ed. E. Laspeyres [Regensburg, 1860], 3.27 [pp. 108–11]) opined that oblation was only binding on children who were "doli capax" at the time; otherwise they should reconfirm or leave at age fourteen. Cf. *Quinque compilationes antiquae,* ed. Emil Friedberg (Leipzig, 1882), 1.3.27 (p. 38). In 1134 the Cistercians required novices to be fifteen, but by 1196 had raised it to eighteen (*Instituta capitula,* PL 181.76). A council at Paris in 1212 prohibited any order from accepting anyone below eighteen, but this must certainly have applied to profession, not reception into the monastery (or else it was simply universally ignored; Mansi 22.1164, canon 2: "Juxta aetatem re-

the mid-thirteenth century. In the *Decretales* of Pope Gregory IX, the first major addition to canon law after Gratian, the tenor of the texts adduced is clearly that children should not be professed before twelve (for girls) or fourteen (for boys), and that those consigned to monastic life before this could leave if they wanted.[65] Innocent IV confirmed this, and included in canon law an authentic papal provision for reconfirmation of vows at age fifteen.[66]

Theologians by and large concurred.[67] St. Thomas Aquinas, himself an oblate at six, held that no one could be bound by a vow made before the age of reason, which, he said, "is usually around

---

cipiendorum ad religionem, cujuscumque fuerint ordinis, districte prohibemus, ne aliquis recipiatur infra octavum decimum annum"). A similar measure passed the Council of Oxford in 1222 (Mansi 22.826, canon 43: "Monachus non recipiatur minor octo decem annis, nisi evidens utilitas seu necessitas aliud inducat"; cf. Louis Thomassin, *Vetus et nova ecclesiae disciplina* 1 [Mainz, 1787] 417). Another London council in 1247–48 raised the age to twenty, clearly for profession, although even novices had to be nineteen: Powicke and Cheney, *Councils and Synods* 2.253–54; cf. Matthew Paris, *Chronica majora* 3.499–500. For Franciscan efforts to come into conformity with this trend, which ultimately resulted in a rule setting their age of admission at eighteen except in special cases, see *Bullarium franciscanum* (ed. J. B. Constantius and J. H. Sbaralea [Rome, 1759]), 1.6, 14, 190; Armand Carlini, ed., "Constitutiones ordinis fratrum minorum anno 1316 Assisi conditae," *Archivum franciscanum historicum* 4 (1911) 277, and 34 (1941) 38–42; Franz Ehrle, "Die ältesten Redactionen der General-constitutionen des Franziskanerordens," *Archiv für Literatur- und Kirchengeschichte des Mittelalters* 6 (1890), p. 88. For the Dominicans, see Heinrich Denifle, "Die Constitutionen des Predigerordens vom Jahr 1228," *Archiv für Literatur- und Kirchengeschichte des Mittelalters* 1 (1885) 165–227. Clare's rules on oblation are ambiguous, referring only to "legitimate age," without specifying what that should be: "Juvenculae in monasterio receptae infra tempus aetatis legitimae tondeantur in rotundum; et deposito habitu seculari, induantur panno religioso, sicut visum fuerit Abbatissae. Cum vero ad aetatem legitimam venerint indutae juxta formam aliarum faciant professionem suam." *Bullarium franciscanum* 1, item 496 ("Regula et Vita Sororum pauperum inclusarum"), canon 2, p. 672.

65. *Decretales Greg. IX* 3.31 (Friedberg 2.569–78). This eventually became secular law in much of Europe as well: see, e.g., *Siete Partidas* (second half of the thirteenth century), 1.7.4, prescribing twelve and fourteen, respectively, as the ages at which girls and boys could enter holy orders.

66. *Sexti Decretales* 3.14.1 (Friedberg 2.1050–51).

67. Aquinas's view, in accord with ecclesiastical law, would triumph, but his contemporary, John Pecham, Archbishop of Canterbury, appears to uphold the irrevocability of oblation ("Quaestio Johannis Pecham," ed. Livario Oliger, "De pueris oblatis in ordine minorum," *Archivum franciscanum historicum* 8 [1915] 414–39), chiefly on the grounds that a father has greater authority over a son than a master has over a slave (or: "than a lord has over a serf"; the Latin is ambiguous: "maiorem potestatem habet pater in filio, quam dominus in servo" [p. 419]).

fourteen for males and twelve for females, . . . although in some it is earlier and some later, according to the varied dispositions of nature."[68] But after puberty, oblates' vows were binding. This did not mean that parents could not commit children to monasteries: simply that they could not be considered professed, and therefore unable to leave, until after puberty. (On the other hand, "donating" children to diocesan clergy was expressly forbidden, at least in Spain, from the mid-thirteenth century, under pain of excommunication for the clergy—not the parents.)[69]

The implicit consequence that oblates could as teenagers reject religious life and return to their families, at least in theory, may be the reason that no theologian of the High Middle Ages considered whether oblation might constitute a dereliction of parental duty, despite the constant complaints of monastic authorities that it was too often precisely this. The inherent obligation of all parents to rear all their children is explicitly posited elsewhere in the *Summa:* it forms the crux of Aquinas's argument against promiscuity (which is sinful because it produces an unwanted and uncared-for child, and is therefore not a "victimless" sin),[70] but it is not even considered in the case of oblation.[71]

Aquinas does consider whether it is desirable to have unlearned children in monasteries (he concludes it is); and he notes that monastic life is a state of penitence, and that children, as innocents, are exempt from penitential discipline. This difficulty he resolves, somewhat obliquely, by replying that although religious life is a state of penitence, it is also a school of perfection, and "innocent children may therefore be taken into religious life just as they would into any school, so that they may preserve their innocence more perfectly."[72]

68. *Summa theologica* 2-2, q. 189 a. 5.

69. *Synodicon Hispanum,* Synod of Santiago de Compostela, 2 (1259?–1267), canon 4: "Si clerici filios laycorum nutriendo acceperint ut ami fiant, sint excommunicati ipso facto" (p. 270). This was repeated in the fourteenth century, which would suggest that it was not wholly efficacious.

70. *Summa theologica* 2-2 q. 154 a. 2 *ad* 6.

71. In addition to the extended discussion of oblation in 2-2 q. 189, as cited above (note 68), there is discussion at 2-2 q. 89 a. 9, and in the *Quaestiones quodlibetales,* ed. R. P. Mandonnet (Paris, 1926), 3.4.11.12, 4.12.23. St. Thomas himself had had to struggle to join the Dominicans against the wishes of his parents, who had second thoughts about religious life after initially donating him; this may have influenced his views.

72. *Quaestiones quodlibetales* 4.12.23 (pp. 160–73), "Utrum pueri non exercitati in praeceptis debeant recipi in religione": "Praeterea, status religionis est status

It would be naïve to imagine that either law or theology would necessarily be the determining factor in deciding the fate of most oblates. The rereading of vows at fifteen may well have been *pro forma,* and children could hardly have returned to families that did not want them in the first place. The children themselves would in many cases have known no other life. Deroux maintains that at Cluny oblates were considered professed from the time of entry, despite the ceremonial reconfirmation at fifteen.[73] On the other hand, there is evidence that oblation did become less permanent as the High Middle Ages wore on. St. Stephen Harding's biographer, William of Malmesbury, himself a monk, notes casually that although given to a monastery as a child in the late eleventh century, St. Stephen became interested in secular pursuits and simply left to study in Paris.[74] Most eleventh-century charters assume or state irrevocability, specifying that the child is to remain until death, or employ the traditional, chilling clause that "from this day forward he may never take from his neck the yoke of the rule."[75] But there are also eleventh-century examples of donations that allow the child to leave if he chooses, and such arrangements become quite common in the twelfth and thirteenth centuries as ecclesiastical legislation begins to insist on this right.[76] Both parent and child doubtless found this a more satisfactory approach to oblation. The former

---

poenitentiae. Sed pueri excipiuntur ab omni paenitentiae [sic] coercitione, ut habetur in Decretis de poenitentia, distinct.iv. Ergo non sunt ad religionem inducendi" (no. 7, p. 161). "Ad septimum dicendum, quod status religionis, et est status poenitentiae, et est exercitium sive schola perfectionis: unde ad religionem recipiendi sunt pueri innocentes quasi in schola quadam perfectionis, ut perfectius innocentiam conservent" (p. 170).

73. "Les Origines," p. 96.

74. *Gesta regum Anglorum,* ed. W. Stubbs, 2 (London, 1889) 380–85. Stephen returned to monastic life as an adult.

75. "Ut ab hac die non liceat illi collum excutere de sub jugo regulae," in oblation charters from all over Europe and in every century: for an example from 1063, see Villanueva, *Viage literario* 14.241, no. 14, or Orlandís, "Notas," pp. 209–10; cf. ibid., pp. 212–13 and n. 19; ibid., pp. 78–79 (1092) "ibidem omnibus diebus uite sue permansurum."

76. A document of 1060 from Pont-Château (dependency of Marmoutier) allows a noble child to choose whether to become a monk when grown or be supported, as a layman, by the monastery: see discussion in Berlière, "Les Écoles," p. 556. For twelfth-century cases see, e.g., Ríus Serra, *Cartulario de Sant Cugat del Vallés* 3.191, no. 1022 (1158); C. Chevalier, *Cartulaire de l'abbaye de Noyers* (Tours, 1872), p. 449, no. 413; for the thirteenth century, Berlière, p. 564; Osheim, "Con-

still did not have to rear the child, who was brought up and educated by monks, and the latter, whatever the rigors he endured in the cloister, could at least now live his adult life in the world if he so chose.

It probably did not seem so desirable to the monastic communities themselves, which might invest time, energy, and resources in oblates from childhood to adolescence only to have them leave the monastery just when they would have been able to assume their own share of work and responsibility. This may, indeed, be the reason one finds increasing opposition to oblation in the High Middle Ages not from parents or oblates but from monastic authorities.[77] The decline of enthusiasm for oblation on the part of the religious is almost exactly coeval with the steady rise in the age of profession[78] and the development of legislation allowing adolescents to withdraw from religious life.

Between the twelfth and fourteenth centuries, in fact, oblation waned markedly. The reasons for this have not been carefully analyzed, and a detailed treatment of them would require a separate study.[79] The great monastic orders were suffering material and spiritual decline after their extraordinary efflorescence from the tenth century through the twelfth, and were being displaced to a large ex-

---

version," p. 278 and n. 29; John Mundy, "Charity and Social Work in Toulouse 1100–1250," *Traditio* 22 (1966) 203–87, p. 266, n. 204 (note that the child is to choose at age ten—before the traditional "age of discretion").

77. See, e.g., Peter the Venerable's complaints (in the first half of the twelfth century) in *Statuta,* ed. Constable, chap. 36, pp. 70–71; Innocent III, Epistle 10 (PL 215.1113); or the Abbot of Trond and others cited in Berlière, "Les Écoles," p. 567, and discussion in Lynch, *Simoniacal Entry,* p. 39.

78. Much of this legislation, it should be noted, was enacted by the orders themselves.

79. Deroux, "Les Origines," pp. 102–10, discusses as causes the dissatisfaction of monastic communities with the tendency of parents to dispose of unwanted or undesirable children through oblation, the decline in family atmosphere in increasingly large and impersonal monastic communities, and difficulties with simony. Berlière suggests abuse by parents, the rise of episcopal schools as alternatives, the increasingly urban character of European life, and the intellectual decline of the monasteries (pp. 567–68). The last seems rather strained to me: the intellectual brilliance of monastic orders certainly contributed to their overall appeal, but probably had relatively little to do with parental decisions to offer children, much less reluctance to accept them on the part of the monasteries. Cf. also his observations in "Recrutement."

80. Except as the recipients of charity: see chapter 11, below.

tent by friars, mendicants, and other noncloistered religious groups, whose structures less easily accommodated children,[80] and whose recruits were mostly adult. Perhaps even more important, the sudden expansion all over Europe of diocesan educational structures from the elementary to the university level meant that by the thirteenth century prosperous parents could educate their children, without cloistering them in monasteries, in subjects and skills (such as law or theology, the former not offered by monasteries) that would enable them to achieve success in life without abandoning the world. As noted previously, the rise of inheritance systems that obviated the fragmentation of estates also meant that they could retain in the family as many children as they could afford, without fear of their claim on the patrimony.

During the thirteenth century the danger that sons would be attracted to and enter one of the new religious orders, especially while they were away at school, so worried parents that they began to accuse some orders of "stealing" and "brainwashing" their children—rather like the worries of American parents about radical religious groups in the 1970s. A poem of the period complains:

> They procure adolescents for their communities,
> And entice them with various promises.
> With their eloquence they harden their hearts [sc., against their
>   families],
> And care not about the sighs of the parents.[81]

The order's response to these charges is, interestingly, not to deny them, but simply to point out to the parents, as Rabanus had to Gottschalk and his supporters, that it was a privilege to be bound to a life of virtue.[82]

But many parents of children wealthy enough to be educated no longer considered the cloister the best outlet for their sons. Ideally,

---

81. "Iam suis cenobiis iuvenes procurant / Et promissis uariis illos assecurant, / Suis nam eloquiis illos sic indurant, / Et iam de suspiriis parentum non curant." Cited in Oliger, "De pueris oblatis," p. 442.

82. Ibid. Cf. Similar complaints from subsequent centuries cited on pp. 443–47. A character in a poem of the twelfth or thirteenth century about a young man contemplating entering a monastery says that his parents will mourn him as dead if he does so: for text, see Otto Schumann, "Über einige *Carmina Burana*," *Zeitschrift für deutsches Altertums* 63 (1926) 81–99; translation in Boswell, *Christianity*, pp. 378–80.

the eldest was brought up to be heir and the others educated to support themselves and to assist the family through law or the church. In practice, younger sons were a considerable problem in the High and later Middle Ages, but not specifically for the parents. By swelling the ranks of the knighthood, landless younger sons aggravated one of its most troubling aspects: How could an increasingly peaceful and prosperous society support, or even occupy, the members of a social class whose position rested on a tradition of military prowess? With no land to inherit and little left to win in battle, the growing throng of cadet nobles in a Europe implementing rules of primogeniture and entailment found themselves restless and redundant, reduced to fighting mock battles in tournaments or joining foreign crusades for land and glory overseas.[83] But this was a problem for society as a whole, and does not seem to have persuaded noble parents of the High and later Middle Ages to limit the number of their sons as severely as their Roman predecessors or bourgeois successors would.[84]

Daughters were another matter: a character in the *Divine Comedy* recalls an earlier time (i.e., before the early fourteenth century) when "the birth of a daughter did not yet strike terror in her father's heart."[85] While oblation of sons decreased markedly from the thirteenth century,[86] oblation of daughters remained an important demographic factor in prosperous households throughout the Middle Ages.[87] Indeed, as monastic institutions became less prosperous and

83. The classic study of this is Duby, "The 'Youth' in Twelfth-Century Aristocratic Society"; Herlihy raises similar issues for a later period in "The Tuscan Town in the Quattrocento," *Medievalia et Humanistica. Studies in Medieval and Renaissance Culture*, new series 1 (1970) 81–110.

84. As Herlihy rather cynically notes, "Great wealth conveys many advantages, and wealthy couples apparently found it easier to respect the Church's hard prohibition of contraception within marriage" (*Medieval Households*, p. 149).

85. "Non faceva, nascendo, ancor paura / la figlia al padre . . ." (*Paradiso* 15.103–4).

86. Even so, the influx of children was still so great at Schuttern in 1269 that the monastery had to declare a five-year moratorium on accepting children: Deroux, "Les Origines," p. 108; cf. Lynch, *Simoniacal Entry*, pp. 39–40 and 57, and idem, "The Cistercians and Underage Novices," *Citeaux-Commentarii Cistercienses* 24 (1973) 283–97.

87. On this see sources cited in notes 13–15, above, as well as Huyghebaert, "Les femmes laïques," pp. 366–71, and M. Parisse, "Les chanoinesses séculières dans l'Empire germanique," *Francia* 6 (1978) 107–26; and Eileen Power, *Medieval English Nunneries* (Cambridge, England, 1922), esp. chap. 1. On the general diffi-

daughters more problematic, "letters of expectation" (guarantees of a place in a convent when someone died) became valuable and coveted prizes in much of Europe, obtained through political pressure, bribery, and sometimes outright force.[88]

Probably none of these trends—the great extent of oblation from the tenth through the twelfth centuries, or its decline, for males, thereafter—affected the poor very much. The High Middle Ages were the great age of the nobility, and those religious orders dedicated to stability became, for a variety of reasons, more and more noble in composition, direction, and outlook throughout the period.[89] Few of the great monasteries would accept poor children as genuine oblates after the twelfth century, although they might have agreed to rear them to be laborers.[90] Fortunately for them, during the classic period of oblation the poor had less need of outlets for their children than ever before or long after. When the need returned along with the straitened circumstances of the thirteenth century, they apparently had recourse to more traditional modes of abandonment.

For the rich and powerful, increasingly reluctant to cast noble children into the arms of vulgar and classless fate, oblation remained a major means of dealing with unwanted daughters, and

---

culty of the surplus of women among the upper classes in the High and later Middle Ages and family strategies for coping with this, see, for example, Diane Hughes, "From Brideprice to Dowry in Mediterranean Europe," JFH 3 (1978) 262–96; countered to some extent by Herlihy, "Alienation in Medieval Culture and Society," in *The Social History of Italy and Western Europe, 700–1500: Collected Studies* (London, 1978); idem, "The Making of the Medieval Family: Symmetry, Structure and Sentiment," JFH 8, 2 (1983) 116–30, and idem, *Medieval Households*, pp. 98–111.

88. Berlière, "Recrutement," pp. 31–45. Such letters were obtained for males as well, and for adults as well as children, but the preponderance were to assure places for noble daughters.

89. The abbot of Andrès in his complaint about the poor physical state of oblates notes specifically that they were almost all scions of noble families ("et hi fere omnes genere nobiles existebant," *Chronica Willelmi Andrensis*, p. 705), and Peter the Venerable compared reception of peasants to that of mental defectives or others "not useful for anything" (*Statuts* 35, as cited in note 4, above). The "exclusivisme de la noblesse" among monasteries of the thirteenth and fourteenth centuries is thoroughly discussed in Berlière, "Recrutement," pp. 14–26.

90. Berlière, "Recrutement," pp. 16–21, lists the very many monastic institutions that accepted only noble applicants by the thirteenth and fourteenth centuries, including St. Gall, Reichenau, Fulda, Corbie, and dozens of others.

although boys were donated in decreasing numbers after the thirteenth century, both practical and religious considerations kept the practice alive until well into early modern times. One of Luther's allies against the Catholic religious orders, Ulrich von Hutten, had reason to be bitter about them: being so frail that his father had no hopes for his future, he had been consigned as an eleven-year-old to Fulda.[91]

91. Berlière, "Recrutement," p. 48.

9

❖　　❖　　❖

THE THIRTEENTH
CENTURY:
ABANDONMENT
RESUMES

In addition, the child is the more obliged to love and honor his
father because the latter was willing to take the trouble to rear him
rather than give him to someone else . . .
   Las Siete Partidas 4.19.1

IF, AS THE thirteenth century wore on, Europeans
gave up fewer children to the service of God, they surrendered
more and more of them to the kindness of strangers. After a conciliar silence on the subject of more than five centuries, between 1195
and 1295 at least thirteen different councils in England alone passed
legislation directly or indirectly bearing on the abandonment of
children, some addressing it more than once in separate contexts.
Their dispositions were not simply prohibitions, which might have
resulted from abstract moral interest, but were much more practical regulations concerned with quotidian reality—particularly,
whether or not to baptize abandoned children found without any
indication of their baptismal status.

Salt had become, it seems, the "token" of that most crucial aspect of an abandoned child's ancestry in Catholic Europe: whether
he was baptized or not.[1] And its significance seems to have been attended by some confusion.

According to the Council of York:

1. Salt had been part of birth ritual at least since the time of Ezekiel (see above,
chapter 3, note 27, and accompanying text—"But thou wast cast out . . ."), was
used in the rite of baptism, at least in England, by the ninth century, and was required for proper administration of the sacrament in most areas by the thirteenth:
see, e.g., Synodal de l'Ouest, 4, in *Les Statuts synodaux français du XIIIe siècle* 1, ed.

When an exposed child is found whose baptismal status is unknown, whether he is found with salt or without, he should be baptized. . . .[2]

According to London:

Where there is doubt concerning baptism and confirmation we decree, in accord with the decisions of the holy canons, that they should be conferred, because something cannot be said to be repeated which is not known to have been conferred. Exposed children [N.B. plural] whose baptismal status is unknown are therefore to be baptized, whether they are found with or without salt. . . .[3]

According to Canterbury:

If it happens that exposed children are found with salt, they should be baptized; if exposed children are found without salt, and there is doubt about whether they have been baptized or not, let them be baptized [conditionally]. . . .[4]

According to Wells:

We decree that abandoned children and others whose baptism might reasonably be doubted should be baptized [conditionally], whether they are found with salt or not. . . .[5]

According to Exeter:

---

and trans. Odette Pontal, p. 140: "ablato puero ad fores ecclesie, suppleatur quod deest, scilicet pabulum salis et aurium linitio cum saliva. . . ." The symbolism in the case of unbaptized *expositi* is apparently that the salt is to be used for the baptism, although in France the presence of salt indicated that the child *had* been baptized.

2. Canon 4 of the Council of York, 1195 (Mansi 22.653).
3. Mansi 22.714 (Council of 1200, according to Mansi).
4. Statutes of Canterbury, 32 (1213–14), *Councils and Synods with Other Documents Relating to the English Church,* ed. F. M. Powicke and C. R. Cheney, 2.31; cf. p. 33: "Similiter de confirmatione, si dubitetur, conferatur quia dici non debet iteratum quod nescitur fuisse collatum." The provision regarding baptism is repeated verbatim in the Statutes of Salisbury (1217–19), 27 (*Councils and Synods* 2.70); the Statutes of Exeter I (1225–37), 21 (ibid., 2.234); and the Statutes of London II (1245–59), 8 (ibid., 2.635).
5. Statutes of Wells (1252), 2 (ibid., 2.590).

Lest anyone be left unbaptized on the pretext of some doubt, which might easily happen in the case of exposed children or others baptized at home not following the formula cited above, we dispose that in this sort of doubt they should be baptized. . . .[6]

A council in Bordeaux in 1234 instructed parents and nurses to place infants in cribs for their safety, and added that "since some wicked women are accustomed to abandoning their own children, they should be told that if, God forbid, they are going to do this, they should use salt as a sign that the child has already been baptized."[7] The Synod of Nîmes of 1252 provided that "if an infant is found exposed next to a church or elsewhere, and there is neither evidence nor sign as to whether he was baptized or not, in such cases the priest should . . . baptize him with these words: 'If you are already baptized . . .'"[8] The same synod offers, in two canons,

6. Statutes of Exeter II (1287), 3 (ibid., 2.988). Two other synods address the same problem in their own words: *Constitutiones cuiusdam episcopi* (1225–30?), 11 ("Ideoque baptizantur expositi, de quorum baptismo dubitatur probabiliter, sive inveniantur cum sale sive sine sale" [ibid., 2.183]); and Statutes of Chichester I (1245–52), 3 (ibid., 2.452), with a formula for conditional baptism. In addition, four councils during the same period condemned the substitution of children, which requires abandonment by natal parents. Statutes of Norwich (1240–43), Additional Statutes, 57: "qui falso supponunt partum vel dolose vel fraudulenter supponi procurant ad alicuius exhereditationem . . ." (ibid., 1.357); Statutes of London, II, 6: ". . . vel super falso testimonio, vel de partu supposito vel exposito" (ibid., 2.632); Statutes of Chichester I (1245–52), 19: ". . . partus suppositionem, et testamenti mutationem, et similia . . ." (ibid., 2.455); Statutes of Exeter II, summula of Bishop Peter (1287), 32: "Item, supponens partum, id est faciens alienum partum suum ut alii exheredentur" (ibid., 2.1073). The text in all cases specifies or indicates by context that the nature of the sin involved was the defrauding of other heirs, but note that London (above) and Winchester (note 40, below) did seem to condemn abandonment itself.

7. Although the general sense is quite clear, the text of this canon is uncertain. Odette Pontal (*Les Statuts synodaux français du XIIIe siècle* 2, p. 48) gives "Et ne parvuli a parentibus vel nutrice in lectis aliquatenus collocentur sed diligenter in cunabulis ponantur et quia quedam nephande mulieres consueverunt proprios filios prohicere conjuratus, instruantur ut si, quandoque istud quod absit contigerit, in signum babtismi jam suscepti. . . ." But she notes that after *suscepti, sal apponitur* can be read where the manuscript is damaged. This does not solve the problem of *conjuratus*.

8. "Vel forte infans expositus inventus est juxta ecclesiam vel alibi ne[c] habetur certitudo vel aliud signum utrum sit baptizatus vel non, in his casibus . . . sacerdos . . . baptizet ipsum sub hiis verbis: si baptizatus es . . ." (*Statuts* 2, canon 9,

a rare indication that abandoned children were sometimes found dead: in cases of uncertainty about the baptismal status of deceased infants, burial in hallowed ground was to be allowed, "which," the council added, "we think is also permissible when exposed infants are found dead next to churches or elsewhere and there is no sure indication about their baptismal status."[9] But

> if written evidence or some other sign should indicate that an abandoned child found dead had not been baptized, [the child] should not be buried in a church cemetery.[10]

Canon law also suddenly took cognizance of abandonment. Pope Gregory IX, during the third decade of the century, obviously inspired by Roman law, ruled that children abandoned with the knowledge or consent of their fathers were automatically freed from his legal control (*patria potestas*). He suggested no other consequences for the parent—a leniency which is particularly striking in the collection of his *Decretales* that was added to Gratian's *Decretum* as part of canon law. Here his ruling on abandonment, without penalty other than loss of control, stands in stark contrast to surrounding provisions requiring penances from life in a monastery to a year on bread and water for unpremeditated or even accidental cases of infanticide, and a section on voluntary and accidental homicide which, *inter alia,* holds anyone causing sterility in someone else to be guilty of murder.[11]

A number of civil codes of the period expressly permit abandonment. A German code, the *Schwabenspiegel,* authorizes it in the form of sale:

---

p. 274). Bibliothèque Nationale, ms. Coislin 363, folio 23v, preserves a twelfth-century Greek formula for the conditional baptism of an abandoned child (ἐὰν παῖς εὑρέθη ἐν τίνι τόπῳ . . .).

9. *Statuts* 2, canon 10, p. 276.

10. "De infante exposito invento mortuo. Si autem in baptismo infantis a layco baptizati et mortui antequam presbytero presentetur, inventum fuerit formam debitam non fuisse servatam vel infantem expositum et mortuum inventum constiterit per scripturam vel per alia signa baptizatum non esse, non debet in cimiterio ecclesiastico sepeliri" (ibid., canon, 11, p. 276).

11. *Decretales Greg. IX* 5.10.1–3 and 5.12.5 (Friedberg 2.792–93, 794). Section 13.1 denies Christian burial to persons who die fighting in tournaments. Some commentators on this passage, however, took a severer view: see Hostiensis, p. 334, below.

If a man sells his child for a reason that is legally binding, he acts properly. But he should not sell him to someone who might kill him, or into prostitution. He should sell[12] him rather to a lord.[13]

Some recensions mention exposing:

If any father or mother abandons [literally, "throws from her"] a child, and someone else picks it up and rears it and feeds it until it is old enough to serve, it should serve the one who saved its life. And if the father or mother should wish to reclaim, or a lord desires to claim the child as his, they must first repay whatever cost [the finder] incurred. . . .[14]

A contemporary legal compilation by German rulers of Sicily forbids selling daughters into prostitution and prescribes slitting the nose as a penalty for mothers who do so, but adds that this punishment would be cruel in the case of the poor, who have no other recourse.[15]

12. Or possibly, "gives him to a lord to be his": see text and the contemporary French translation in note following, and, for *aigen*, cf. note 14, below.

13. *Urschwabenspiegel*, ed. Karl Eckhardt (Aalen, 1975) (Studia Iuris Suevici, 1), Dritter Landrechtsteil, sec. 357 (p. 543): "Und ist das ain man sin kind verkoft durch ehaft not das tuot er wol mit recht. er sol es aber nit verkoffen das man es toet oder in das huorhuss. er git es ainem herren wol fur aigen etc." Several redactions of this code are extant; the wording of this provision varies somewhat. Cf., for example, the contemporary French version, where the final stipulation appears to relate to service or "fostering" rather than sale: "Se il avient que .i. hons vande son anfant por sa necessitee il le puet bient faire per droit. for que por occire et por metre au bordel. et lo peut doner a .i. seigniour por home liege se il vuet" (*Le miroir de Souabe*, ed. George Matilde and K. Eckhardt [Aalen, 1973], sec. 125, p. 160).

14. *Urschwabenspiegel*, sec. 363, p. 154: "Von funtkinden. Swelh vater oder muoter ir kint von ir werfent. und swer ez uf hebt und ez zivht. und der fuoret ez unz ez zesinen tagen kvmt daz ez dienen mac. ez sol den dienen der im sins libes geholfen hat. vnd ist daz ez vater vnd mvoter heimen wil oder sin herre ob ez eigen ist. die svln im zen ersten sine koste gelten swaz er bereit daz er sin schaden genomen hab." This is reminiscent of provisions in Roman law, which might have been known to the compiler.

15. *The Liber Augustalis or Constitutions of Melfi Promulgated by the Emperor Frederick II for the Kingdom of Sicily in 1231,* trans. James Powell (Syracuse, 1971) 80 (57), p. 146; and 85 (62), p. 148. Although the sale of a girl into prostitution would not necessarily result in abandonment by the mother, most legal treatments equate the two. This law is immediately followed by one against selling free persons, but despite the juxtaposition it is unlikely that the latter would include children, who

The laws of Teruel, influential in eastern Spain,[16] also forbade selling daughters, and imposed a draconian penalty—burning. But strategic considerations motivated this: it was to prevent Christian women or children from falling into the hands of Muslims.[17] The code does recognize, however, a basic responsibility for child care, at least on the part of mothers: "Any woman who is proven to have abandoned [literally, thrown away] her child shall be punished and constrained to care for the child, according to the law."[18]

The Castilian *Fuero Real* of the mid-thirteenth century drew on earlier Roman and Visigothic legal traditions, in some cases melding them, but its three titles dealing with abandonment were not simply reiterations; their innovations and wording suggest that the matter was a live issue. It decreed, first, that a father, a mother, or lord lost all authority over a child she or he abandoned or wittingly allowed to be abandoned. Finders might assume this authority if they reared the children as servants, but if they brought them up "as a kindness" they did not acquire such a right, and in these cases, presumably as compensation, local authorities might reimburse the foster parent his expenses from the property of the abandoning parent or lord.[19] But a parent or lord could reclaim a child abandoned without his knowledge, repaying the cost of the child's upkeep to

---

were not in fact "free persons" under Roman, German, or ecclesiastical law *unless* their parents sold or alienated them in some way.

16. The family of legal texts called "Cuenca-Teruel," of which this is one of the foundation documents, influenced the content of many other codes, such as Baeza, Plasencia, Behar, Albarracín, etc. Its influence on family legislation in particular is discussed in Enrique Gacto Fernández, "La situación jurídica de los hijos naturales e ilegítimos menores de edad en el derecho histórico español: Alimentos y tutela" (*L'Enfant* 2, pp. 169–82).

17. *El Fuero de Teruel,* ed. Max Gorosch (Stockholm, 1950) (Leges Hispanicae Medii Aevii, I) 454, p. 287: "Del que su fija enpennare." The *Fuero* dates from the second half of the thirteenth century.

18. "Toda muger que su fijo en algún lugar echará et provado'l será, sea fostigada et sea sobr'esto costreynnyda que su fijo críe, segunt la ley" (485, pp. 297–98).

19. "Si algun niño, ò otro de mayor edad fuere desechado por su padre, ò por otro, sabiendolo él, è consintiendolo su padre, no haya mas poder en él, ni en sus bienes, ni en vida, ni en muerte: y esto mesmo sea de madre, ò de otro qualquier que lo habie en poder: è si fuere siervo, sea forro, y el señor pierda todo el derecho que en él habie si lo desechó, ò lo mandó, ò lo consintió, è hayalo aquel que lo crió; pero si fizo merced en lo criar, no haya ningun poder sobre él de ninguna servidumbre, y el Alcalde fagale dar las costas de los bienes de su padre, ò de aquel que lo habie en poder" (*Fuero Real* 4.23.1 [in *Los Códigos Españoles* 1.423]).

age ten, after which the child's service was expected to have discharged any obligation—even though not all children could be reduced to servitude.[20] The *Fuero* takes a stern view of parental responsibility for death as the result of exposing:

> Anyone who exposes an infant who then dies because there is no one to take care of him will himself be liable to death for this: causing a death to take place is the same as killing someone.[21]

This principle is unprecedented in codes influenced by Roman law, although its concern about the death of *expositi* is paralleled in other parts of Europe during the thirteenth century. Apart from it, the *Fuero's* provisions suggest a familiar pattern: exposed children brought up either in servitude or as *alumni*, parents losing rights over them if they gave them up voluntarily, repayment required to reclaim, a change in status at age ten, etc.

The successor code and eventual supplanter of the *Fuero Real*, the *Siete Partidas*, a huge and generally enlightened compilation of Roman, Germanic, and new law effected for Alfonso the Wise of Castile, often repeats or embellishes provisions of the *Fuero*, but includes none of these regarding abandonment. On the subject of children it adopts some traditional and some startling stipulations. The right of parents to sell children is upheld on the basis of the increasingly dire circumstances in which some families found themselves:

> A father who is oppressed with great hunger or such utter poverty that he has no other recourse can sell or pawn his children in order to obtain food. And the reason he can do so is this: since he has no other means to rescue himself or his child from death, it is proper that he should sell the child and make use of the proceeds so that neither dies.[22]

---

20. 4.23.2: ". . . pero quando lo demandáre à aquel que lo cria, dele las costas que fizo en lo criar, fasta diez años . . . ; è si lo mas tuvo de diez años, no sea tenudo de le dar las costas de alli en adelante, por el servicio que del rescibió. . . ."

21. 4.23.3: "Todo home que desecháre niño alguno, è no hobiere quien lo tome para criar, è muriere, el que lo echa muera por ello: ca pues que él fizo cosa porque muriese, tanto es como si lo matase."

22. 4.17.8.

This passage (which is consonant with but not a repetition of Roman legal tradition) occurs in a section of the *Partidas* otherwise characterized by rather ordinary family concerns regarding parental authority (emancipation, wills, etc.). But it is followed by an astounding concession to parental authority:

> And there is another reason that a father can do this: according to the true law of Spain[23] a father who is besieged in a castle he holds from his lord, may, if so beset with hunger that he has nothing to eat, eat his child with impunity rather than surrender the castle without permission of the lord. If he can do this for his lord, it is appropriate that he be able to do it for himself as well.[24]

(The mother did not enjoy the authority either to sell or eat her child.)[25] It is difficult, in the twentieth century, to take this law seriously, either as a principle or as an indication of circumstance. To sell a child to forestall starvation is one thing: it even obviates, to a considerable extent, the possibility of accidental death through exposure, a concern in some discussions of abandonment at the time. But to eat a child is to kill to save one's own life, something most Christian moral and legal systems have allowed only in cases of self-defense. (Many Catholic moralists still, for example, prohibit killing a fetus to save the mother.)

There was, on the other hand, a biblical tradition in which God predicted again and again that starving parents would devour their children, and the theme is clearly one of disaster rather than atrocity. It would hardly be surprising if Christians felt that starvation

23. The gloss of Gregorio Lopez from the Salamanca edition of the *Partidas* of 1555 provides a Latin text, possibly the origin of the "fuero leal" cited here: "Pater famis necessitate confectus, potest filium vendere; vel pignorare si eum habet in potestate; mater vero non potest. Item si pater est in castro obsessus potest ob dictam necessitatem filium comedere."

24. "E aun ay otra razon por que el padre podria esto fazer: ca segund el fuero leal de España, seyendo el padre cercado en algun Castillo que touiesse de Señor, si fuesse tan cuytado de fambre que non ouiesse al que comer, puede comer al fijo, sin mala estança, ante que diesse el Castillo sin mandado de su Señor. Onde, si esto puede fazer por el Señor, guisada cosa es, que lo puede fazer por si mismo" (ibid.).

25. ". . . [el] poder que ha el padre sobre sus fijos, que son en su poder, el qual non ha la madre" (ibid.). But note that the *Fuero Real* specifically suggests that mothers do have *potestas* over their children, since they lose it if they abandon them.

placed them, without sin, in the position foretold in the scriptures, but it is startling that a law would suggest that such an act was justified simply to avoid surrendering the lord's castle.

It is impossible to know how realistic the law was. The siege of castles worked, of course, precisely because it cut off the food supplies of those within, who eventually had to surrender or starve. Ancient and medieval literature of many sorts includes references to cannibalism (e.g., see the charge of Anna Comnena, cited above, p. 284), but one is inclined to dismiss them as exaggerated or hypothetical. St. Thomas, writing at the time the *Partidas* were composed, adduces cannibalism as an example of an immoral act, comparing it in gravity to homosexual behavior.[26] The latter was hardly unknown in his society, but one normally supposes that the former did not occur in Catholic Europe. Why does Aquinas cite it—just because it makes a logical point? An Italian chronicler of the thirteenth century, himself a bishop, notes matter-of-factly that in 1212 in Sicily "there was a famine so severe, especially in Apulia and Sicily, that mothers even ate their children."[27] A Hebrew chronicle from Spain maintains that in the following century during a terrible siege in Toledo, Jews ate the flesh of their children.[28] But these could, of course, be *topoi* of horror and gravity rather than historical descriptions.

Whether or not parents actually did eat their children, it is no-

26. *Summa theologica* 2-2.142.4 *ad* 3.

27. "Eodem anno fuit fames adeo valida, praecipue in Apulia, & Sicilia, ut matres etiam pueros devorarent" (*Sicardi Episcopi Cremonensis Chronicon,* SSRRII 7.624).

28. אכלו בשר בניהם: Abraham ben Samuel Zacuto, *Sefer Yuhasin,* ed. Herschell Filipowski (Frankfurt, 1925), p. 224. Of course this does not necessarily mean that they killed the children to eat them: the children may have died of hunger beforehand. The incident is supposed to have taken place in 1370, during the terrible internecine warfare between Peter the Cruel of Castile and Peter the Ceremonious of Aragon. Jews and Muslims were often taken as hostages or oppressed in other ways during this conflict, and it does not defy credulity that they would have been reduced to desperate measures: see discussion of the text in F. Fernández González, "Ordenamiento formado por los procuradores de las aljamas hebreas, pertenecientes al territorio de los Estados de Castilla, en la Asamblea celebrada en Valladolid el año 1432," *Boletín de la Real Academia de la Historia* 7 (1885) 145–88, 275–305, 395–413; on the war and its effects on non-Christians, see John Boswell, *The Royal Treasure: Muslim Communities under the Crown of Aragon in the Fourteenth Century,* pp. 9–11, 178–93, 385–93; on the general situation of the Jews during the period, see Yitzhak Baer, *A History of the Jews in Christian Spain* (Philadelphia, 1961).

table that a medieval legal tradition would regard the *patria potestas* as including not only the right to sell children but to sacrifice their lives to meet feudal obligations. In this, the *Partidas* may reflect a strand of popular morality. A popular tale of the twelfth and thirteenth centuries idealizes a knight's sacrifice of his children for a friend, when he slays them with his own hands and uses their blood as a cure for the friend's leprosy.[29] On the other hand, in the twelfth-century romance *Guillaume d'Angleterre* an extremely pious and devout woman who has given birth to twins in a forest is so hungry that she tells her husband she is going to eat one of them if he cannot find any other food. He opposes her doing so on the grounds that it would be a mortal sin and proposes that she eat him instead.[30] It is unclear why this would be less sinful; it appears to be an emotional appeal to parental sentiment.

French legal compilations of this period ignore abandonment altogether. Even a known instance of the outright killing of a child incurs no civil penalty in the *Établissements* of St. Louis—it is to be handled by the church—so it hardly seems likely that abandoning children would be severely punished.[31] In the *Coutumes de Beauvaisis* a long inquest about an abandoned baby is concerned solely with whether the child is still alive: the court is not at all interested in the abandonment or even with who should ultimately be responsible for its upbringing.[32]

29. Edited in its classic form by MacEdward Leach, *Amis and Amiloun* (London, 1937), recently translated by Samuel Danon and S. Rosenberg, *Ami and Amile* (York, S.C., 1981); for discussion see Gédéon Huet, "Ami et Amile: Les origines de la légende," *Moyen Age* 30 (1919) 162–86; Ralph Hexter, *Equivocal Oaths and Ordeals in Medieval Literature* (Cambridge, Mass., 1975) 27–37, and Boswell, *Christianity*, pp. 239–40.

30. "Quant vos enfans mangeriiés, / Don pechié mortel feriiés" (Chrétien de Troyes, *Guillaume d'Angleterre*, ed. Maurice Wilmotte [Paris, 1927], lines 551–52).

31. A second offense is punishable at law: "Se il meschiet à famme qu'ele tue son anfant, ou estrangle, ou de jorz ou de nuiz, ele ne sera pas arse dou premier; ainz la doit on randre à sainte Eglise; mais s'ele en tuoit un autre, ele en seroit arse por ce que ce seroit acoustumance, *selonc droit escrit ou Code, De episcopali audientia, l. Nemo, in fine, cum suis concordanciis*" (*Les Établissements de Saint Louis*, ed. Paul Viollet [Paris, 1883] 1.39, 2.55). The penalty (death), derived from the Code of Justinian (1.4.3), is not aimed at infanticide in the original, but happens to mention *parricida*: "homicida et parricida quod fecit semper expectet." The provision of the *Établissements* is borrowed from the earlier *Coutume de Touraine-Anjou* 29 (2.16–17).

32. Philippe de Beaumanoir, *Coutumes de Beauvaisis* 2.417–18, sections 1813–14.

The English jurist Bracton has nothing to say about the legality of parents' abandoning their children, although he seems to have written in a society in which many parents were willing to part with their progeny, judging by the extent of his interest in the issue of substitution and the minutely detailed procedures he recommends for preventing women in many different situations and circumstances from passing off someone else's child as their own.[33] Some of these concerns and recommendations are influenced by Roman law,[34] but they are also clearly related to and probably inspired to some extent by actual cases of such substitution, which created serious difficulties regarding inheritance and property. Bracton approved the received principle that any child reared and acknowledged by both parents must be considered a legitimate heir, no matter how uncertain his or her origins, unless "the husband's avowal and admission cannot be reconciled with nature, that is, if he has been absent for a year or two . . . or . . . has been castrated or is so infirm that he cannot beget. . . ."[35] This disposition, if widely accepted, would render substitution easier, and perhaps enhance the possibility of "adoption" of abandoned children, at least in the homes of the childless wealthy.[36] It was paraphrased later in the century in *Fleta* and *Britton*:[37] the latter proposed a penalty for women feigning pregnancy, but neither suggested any action, civil or criminal, against mothers who abandoned.[38]

33. Bracton, *De Legibus et consuetudinibus Angliae*, ed. and trans. S. E. Thorne, *Bracton on the Laws and Customs of England* (Cambridge, Mass., 1968), 1.186–87 (folio 63b), 201–7 (folios 69–71). On the other hand, of the five instances of substitution actually cited in Bracton's "notebook" of cases, none involves a child unrelated to both parents—all are fairly clearly children of the mother whose status as heirs of the father is questioned: *Bracton's Note Book. A Collection of Cases Decided in the King's Courts during the Reign of Henry the Third*, ed. F. W. Maitland (London, 1887), no. 247, 2.200–202 (1227), and no. 1761, 3.589–90 (1226) (= *Curia Regis Rolls of the Reign of Henry III* [hereafter CRR], 12 [London, 1957] no. 2243, p. 451; and CRR 13, no. 24, pp. 4–5); no. 303, 2.251–53 (1220); no. 1229, 3.243–44 (1237); no. 1503, 3.417–18 (1221) (= CRR 10.36–37; cf. further discussion in H. G. Richardson and G. Sayles, eds., *Select Cases of Procedure Without Writ under Henry III* [London, 1941] [Selden Society, 60], pp. cliii–clv); no. 1605, 3.473–74 (1223) (= CRR 11, no. 602, pp. 115–16).

34. E.g., Dig. 25.4.1 (discussed in chapter 1, above), and 37.9.1.14.

35. Bracton (Thorne trans.), 3.311, folio 278a.

36. Ibid., esp. 1.186–87 and 204.

37. *Fleta* 1.15, pp. 31–34; *Britton* 3.2.13–19 (2.14–19), 3.23.5 (2.157–58).

38. "Soit ele punie par prison et par fin" (3.2.14, pp. 15–16). Note that *Fleta* treats abortion by the mother as homicide (1.23, 2.61), whereas Bracton had re-

The moral status of abandonment as evinced in the considerable body of thirteenth-century legislation is thus not uniform. Most statutes, ecclesiastical or civil, assume or imply its general legality, or at least give no indication of penalties in effect against it. Since canon law appears to have accepted it,[39] it would have been difficult to erect an absolute case against it on moral grounds, although, as has been seen, some Scandinavians understood it to be prohibited, and even the council of Bordeaux characterized mothers who abandoned as "wicked" (*nephande*), though without recommending any penalty for their actions.

Two English councils did impose or imply the existence of such penalties. The Statutes of Winchester (1224) prohibited priests from excommunicating or condemning their parishioners without the permission of their superiors, except in cases of failure to pay tithes, theft, witchcraft, arson, or exposing children.[40] A council in London authorizing inquisitions for certain crimes listed "substituting or exposing children" after usury, witchcraft, perjury, and false testimony.[41] Possibly the English clergy held their flocks to a higher standard than the rest of Catholic Europe, although given the number of conciliar decrees on abandonment in England, the vast majority of which mention no punishment, this seems somewhat unlikely.[42] The *Liber poenitentialis* of Robert of Flamborough, a

---

ferred only to the provider of the abortifacient (folio 121, p. 341). None of the English codes treat infanticide on the part of the parents, and their statements about deformed children suggest that killing or at least exposing them might have been accepted: Bracton, folio 70, pp. 203–4; *Britton* 3.2.19, 2.19. On the other hand, the death of infants clearly provoked legal action in many cases: see, e.g., *Close Rolls 1247–51* (London, 1922), p. 249, regarding prosecution for an abortion; and *Close Rolls 1259–61* (London, 1934), p. 44, regarding inquiry into what was apparently a miscarriage.

39. In addition to the passages cited above, see, e.g., the "Quaestio Johannis Pecham," ed. Oliger, which expressly invokes Roman law to authorize the sale of children by parents "under some circumstances" (p. 438): "in casu tantum licet uendere filium, seruum semper. Amplius refert in filio uenditio, ut patet ff. *de patribus qui filios distraxerunt*."

40. "Prohibemus ne sacerdotes sine auctoritate superioris aliquando nominatim excommunicent vel denuntient, nisi pro retentione decimarum et consuetarum obventionum. Sed nec generalem faciant excommunicationem vel denuntiationem sine superioris auctoritate, nisi pro furto, sortilegio, et incendio, et puerorum expositione" (73, *Councils and Synods,* 2.137).

41. See note 6, above.

42. Exposing, it might be noted, is a more specific phenomenon than abandonment, and might be considered to entail elements of risk that sale, for example, did not.

334 · *The Kindness of Strangers*

highly detailed English penitential manual of the same period, includes under its rubric on abortion the statement: "If by your authority or with your counsel or aid any infant was abandoned and then died of hunger or mishap or was not found, in my opinion you should not be ordained."[43] This is perhaps the most refined moral statement to appear in the Western tradition to this point, since it explicitly takes into account what actually becomes of the abandoned child and therefore, implicitly, the range of motivations, intentions, and circumstances involved in abandonment. It does not, however, suggest a penalty that would apply to parents generally (as the *Fuero Real* did), but only cites this as a possible disqualification for ordination. (Note the implication that the ordinand might have counseled someone to abandon a child.) In the section of the work on infanticide, clearly intended to affect parental behavior, abandonment is not mentioned.[44] Aquinas, as noted above, bases his argument against promiscuity on the assumption that an illegitimate child will be abandoned, but does not articulate any objections to the abandonment itself.

In his commentary on the passage in canon law about abandoned children (above) Hostiensis says that "it would seem" (*videretur*) that exposing a child was a capital crime, and he carefully limits his discussion of parental rights of reclamation to cases where the child was exposed without the father's knowledge; but his suspicion about its criminality derives from a misreading of Roman law,[45] and at the end of his treatment he concludes that although exposing a child "might be [*fore*] a great sin," it is not on the basis of parental dereliction or risk of the child's dying, but, on the contrary, because of the danger of accidental incest—that ancient bugbear, newly revived as a result of the church's recent vigor in developing and prosecuting its rules on the subject.

In sum, it should be noted that the exposing of infants might be a great sin because, the [child's] relatives being in many cases unknown, he could have relations with a sister or some other relative, and marry her. The exposing parent would be held re-

43. Robert of Flamborough, *Liber poenitentialis* 3.3.104, p. 120.
44. Ibid., 5.4–6, p. 222.
45. Henricus de Sugusio, Cardinalis Hostiensis, *Summa* (Lyons, 1537) 5 ("De infantibus et languidis expositis"): "Videretur tamen quod pater capitalem penam pati deberet, unde dicuntur filii sanguinolenti in rub. C. eo de patribus qui filios distraxerunt l.ii. quare hoc crimen sanguine expiandum est . . ." (241).

sponsible and punished for this sin as would the abandoned child if he did so knowingly.[46]

Perhaps more fundamental ethical objections to abandonment were so obvious that ecclesiastical authorities felt no need to belabor them, but it was the nature of works like penitentials and summas to encompass and comment on all matters, from overeating to cannibalism; frequency or obviousness do not usually determine their structure. Lists of cases reserved to bishops, like the English one that does mention exposing, survive from all over Europe; most, although they are otherwise similar to it in content, do not include abandonment, often mention infanticide or other parental derelictions, and originate in areas where children are known to have been exposed.[47] But perhaps most important, canonical traditions clearly took cognizance of and tolerated abandonment in various forms. Occasional categorical objections or derogations probably reflect, therefore, both an inevitable human ambivalence about a troubling but widespread part of family life in societies without contraception, and the multiplicity and variegation of Christian moral teaching. As noted previously, penitential writings comprised a wide range of opinions, frequently conflicting. By and large, Christian morality continued to view abandonment, like slavery or poverty or the economic forces that affected all three, as a part of the world to be regulated and coped with rather than opposed absolutely.

Information about the motives for abandonment in the thirteenth century is as spare as for any other. Although poverty probably constituted a major cause, it is rarely recorded. This is not surprising; the poor are grossly underreported in all contexts during most of history. A couple in Bristol who had abandoned their two

46. Ibid. In "popular" literature of the time—e.g., the Gregorius legend, treated below—foundlings were apparently held morally accountable even if they married relatives *unknowingly*.

47. The Synod of Nîmes, for example, which specifically addresses other issues about exposed children, does not include abandonment in its own list of cases reserved to the bishop, although it does mention deliberate or accidental infanticide, passing off illegitimate children as legitimate, or supplying abortifacients (canon 63, p. 318). The fact that in all times and places both civic and religious legislators have had to argue specifically that abandonment might be the moral equivalent of infanticide is reason enough not to assume that the first of these implicitly covers exposing. Cf. the slightly later *"Liber de excommunicacione" du Cardinal Bérenger Frédol,* ed. Eugène Vernay (Paris, 1912).

children and then brought charges of kidnapping against a relative who took them in were pardoned—for the false charges, not the abandonment, which was not at issue—"because they were poor."[48] In 1296 in Banbury

> perverse manufacturers and sellers of adulterated and false seed managed to obtain a child recently born in that city and publicly christened through holy baptism in the parish church by his parents, who were poor, by giving the parents hope of reward and relief of their poverty and a better life [*ditationis*] for their offspring; when he was only two days old, the child, a boy, was handed over to them in evil transaction and flagrant fraud, bought still tender and wrongly removed from the arms of his parents through who knows what deception and trickery. . . . And they had the child, already properly and publicly christened, rebaptized, against canonical rules. . . .[49]

The major crime here seems to be the repetition of baptism, a sacrament conferring an indelible mark and therefore not repeatable, but some scandal probably attaches to the sale as well. The baby's parents and another woman involved confessed and did penance. Interestingly, the other parties, including the purchasing parents, declined to repent and were excommunicated.[50]

The possibility of freeing them from servitude might have inspired serf or slave parents to expose children. Even where it was not specified by statute, abandonment would *de facto* cut ties to the owners or masters of the parents, but would, of course, then also leave the child at the mercy of whoever found him, and in most of Europe servile status was determined more by economic reality than juridical nicety. Still, parents with little to offer their offspring

48. "Perdonatur quia pauperes": *Select Cases in the Court of King's Bench under Edward I (Placita Coram Rege)*, ed. G. O. Sayles (London, 1936) (Selden Society, 55), 90 (Coram Rege Roll, no. 88 [Hilary 1285], m. 5), 1.135–36. Earlier in the century provisions had been necessary in Bristol to deal with orphans whom relatives would not agree to care for: see M. Bateson, ed., *Borough Customs* 2 (London, 1906), p. 146.

49. *The Rolls and Register of Bishop Oliver Sutton, 1280–1299*, ed. Rosalind Hill, 5 (Hereford, 1965) (Lincoln Record Society, 60), pp. 126–28.

50. Note that this case took place long after the conciliar edicts on substitution cited above, which could not therefore have been in response to this particular celebrated instance.

may have been more inclined to accept at face value widespread cultural myths about the bright prospects that awaited foundlings. The gradual disappearance of clearly defined slave populations from the north of Europe during the twelfth and thirteenth centuries could be one of the causes of the great increase in legislation about abandonment.[51] Few societies bother to regulate what slave parents do with their children, either because they do not care or prefer to leave this to owners. As the formerly servile population of England and Scandinavia became, in the eyes of the law, full persons, their parental responsibilities and duties (e.g., to baptize) doubtless came to seem more urgent moral concerns to governing institutions.[52]

Other familiar motives for abandonment were deformity or ill health of the child. As part of the cult of St. Guinefort, a greyhound believed to heal children in some regions of France, mothers would make offerings of salt and hang swaddling clothes on bushes—customs strongly evocative of abandonment—toss the baby through tree trunks, leave him alone in the dark, plunge him in water, and ask the fauns to take away the sick child and return a fat and healthy one. It was expected, apparently, that children might die in the process, which would be considered the will of God or St. Guinefort. Although the evidence is sketchy, it seems possible that the cult involved or disguised abandonment in several forms: at the least, children could be left in the forest to die and said not to have survived the ritual; at the most, it may have facilitated the exchange and sub-

51. For example, David Pelteret ("Late Anglo-Saxon Slavery: An Interdisciplinary Approach to the Various Forms of Evidence," Ph.D. diss., University of Toronto, 1976) found that nine percent of the population of England were slaves at the time of the Domesday survey in the eleventh century, but that within a century slavery had died out entirely. Cf. Karras, *Slavery and Society,* on Scandinavian slavery. In the south of Europe slavery persisted, and affected abandonment: see below.

52. The issue of servile status and children, legitimate and illegitimate, is so complex and varies so much by time and place that it would be impossible to treat it even summarily here. Gratian opined that the child always followed the lower status when parents were of different background, except in cases of illegitimacy, where the mother's status prevailed (*Decretum* 2.32.4.15 [Friedberg, 1.1131–32]), and this principle prevailed widely in Europe (see, e.g., for Germany, M. Lintzel, *Die Stände der deutschen Volksrechte hauptsächlich der lex Saxonum* [Halle, 1933], p. 370), but local variation was immense. See, for Scandinavia, the very detailed discussion in Karras, *Slavery and Society,* and "Concubinage." On the disappearance of the slave class in England, the brief and lucid observations of Warren Hollister (*The Making of England* [Lexington, Mass., 1976], esp. p. 93) are also helpful.

stitution of healthy babies unwanted by some mothers for sickly children then left to perish in the woods.[53]

The elaboration of moral notions about the origins of defective children must have increased reluctance to raise such progeny. Gratian added to this tradition by citing in the *Decretum* a letter of Boniface suggesting that corrupt unions would produce corrupt children,[54] and in Marie de France's *Fresne* (discussed in chapter 10) a woman who has claimed that twins are the result of adultery subsequently gives birth to twins herself and must expose one: that there was a popular association of twins with sexual misconduct is further suggested by the suspicion in the case of the Nun of Watton that the pregnant nun was carrying twins.[55] (Of course, multiple births might well be an occasion for abandonment simply because they put an extra strain on parents and family.) The persistence of limitations on conjugal intercourse, forbidden during Lent, menstruation, and while the mother was nursing, offered even married couples many opportunities to conceive children sinfully, and thirteenth-century writers hastened to keep alive fears of the dire consequences of ill-timed passions. Robert of Flamborough warned that children conceived during pregnancy, menstruation, or before weaning would be lame, leprous, given to seizures, deformed, or short-lived;[56] Berthold von Regensburg added to this list the dangers of deafness, meanspiritedness, and demonic possession;[57] and a contemporary French synod proclaimed that the offspring of untimely

53. The basic rituals are described in Schmitt, *The Holy Greyhound,* pp. 5–6. Schmitt does not raise the possibility that the cult afforded opportunities for abandonment.

54. *Decretum* 1.56.10 (Friedberg, 1.222); on this letter (published in Haddan and Stubbs, 3.354; translation in Ephraim Emerton, *Letters of Saint Boniface* [New York, 1976], pp. 124–30), see Boswell, *Christianity,* pp. 202–3.

55. This idea is at least as old as the story of Castor and Pollux, the father of one mortal, the other immortal, but the idea that a double birth is the consequence of double conception may be obvious enough not to require a cultural tradition to explain it. Cf. the story of Tamar in Genesis 38:27.

56. *Liber poenitentialis* 4.8.226 (pp. 197–98): "in menstruo et puerperio multi generantur leprosi, epileptici et aliter male se habentes"; 5.6.288 (p. 238): "ita ut leprosi et elephantici ex hac conceptione nascantur, et foeda in utroque corpora pravitate vel enormitate membrorum sanitas corrupta degeneret" (cf. 5.14.296 [p. 243]; App. B, p. 297): "quia in menstruo et ante purificationem leprosi et caduci et alii male se habentes nasci solent."

57. *Vollständige Ausgabe Seiner Predigten,* ed. Franz Pfeiffer (Vienna, 1862), 2 vols., 1.322–24.

couplings would be humpbacked, crippled, or deformed in some way.[58] Parents of children suffering any of these misfortunes would, one supposes, feel considerable incentive to abandon them discreetly, or, if they could afford it, place them in a monastery.[59]

Prohibitions of intercourse before weaning,[60] in fact, may have affected abandonment doubly. Since children were often nursed for up to three years,[61] they could have a great impact on a couple's conjugal life, and many parents who could afford it would hire a wet nurse.[62] In a thirteenth-century romance, a well-to-do father even sells children born in awkward circumstances because the mother is too weak to nurse them.[63] And if prosperous parents did sometimes abandon children to avoid the problems occasioned by nursing, it is likely that the poor would have more incentive to do so, since they not only could not afford a wet nurse for their own infants, but might ameliorate their circumstances by hiring themselves out—in

58. Synodal de l'Ouest, 96: ". . . si in puerperio, quod prohibetur in lege, sive menstruis . . . ubi est etiam periculum corporale et patris pariter propter periculum elephantie et prolis, quia ex corrupto semine nascitur corruptus fetus et fere semper, ut asserunt fisici, vel gibbosus vel contractus vel hujusmodi" (Pontal, *Statuts* 1.204–6).

59. Caesar of Heisterbach records (*Dialogues* 10.42) the baptism of a deformed child, who obviously had not been abandoned, but children might be abandoned later, when their defects became more manifest or more obviously incurable: Margaret of Metola, born dwarfed, blind, hunchbacked, and lame, was abandoned by her parents at age sixteen after she was not cured at the miraculous shrine of Città-di-Castello: see AASS (May 19) 3.67–71, and Michael Goodich, *Vita Perfecta*, p. 156, n. 42.

60. Prohibited in many Christian communities from the early Middle Ages (Bede, *Historia ecclesiastica* 1.27 [ed. Plummer, 1.55]), and by ecclesiastical law from the twelfth century: Ivo of Chartres, *Decretum* 8.88 (PL 161.601–2); compare Robert of Flamborough, *Liber poenitentialis* 5.7.289 (Firth, pp. 238–39).

61. See, e.g, *Grágás,* trans. Dennis, p. 49, which allows nursing for three Lents, but excuses the mother from fasting only during the first. Weaning customs vary widely both individually and culturally.

62. James Schultz will include in a forthcoming work on childhood in Middle High German literature a detailed analysis of literary attitudes toward nursing. He will report, in brief, that the data from Middle High German narratives "corresponds roughly to what historians believe was the situation among the medieval aristocracy: maternal nursing was the ideal and was advocated by doctors, but wet-nursing was common."

63. Ulrich von Etzenbach, *Wilhelm von Wenden,* ed. Hans-Friedrich Rosenfeld (Berlin, 1957), discussed below, in chapter 10. Patlagean (*Pauvreté,* p. 151) mentions the possibility of inability to nurse as a cause of abandonment in the early Middle Ages in Byzantium.

which case, depending on their health and situation, they might need to dispose of their own.[64] On the other hand, since nursing has a contraceptive effect in many women, and this might be perceived even subconsciously, some mothers may have welcomed the respite from any possibility of childbearing.[65]

Despite improvements in the means of maintaining the integrity of estates, children may still have been abandoned to limit the number of heirs, particularly in Spain and Italy, where laws often retained Roman requirements for partible inheritance.[66] Parents no doubt continued to "abandon" children when they entered religious life, although perhaps most often into the care of relatives or friends. The biographer of Adelaide of Rheinfeld considered it particularly "excellent and magnificent" that when she entered the convent she "abandoned [*deseruit*] her husband, a young knight who was quite outstanding in secular affairs, along with their two little children."[67] One of the children died in the cradle, but the husband then joined an order himself and "committed" the daughter back into the mother's care in her community, along with a substantial sum of money.

And there were, as always, people who simply did not care: a dying widower in Caesar of Heisterbach's *Dialogues* (1.40) commends his daughter to a servant who promptly abandons her. The story need not be factual to reflect a real social problem.

But there were also new reasons for abandonment, occasioned

64. This occurs as a literary motif in a high medieval German romance, *Der Trojanische Krieg:* see note 7 of chapter 10.
65. See discussion in Flandrin, *Families in Former Times,* pp. 201–2, and Meyer, "Illegitimates and Foundlings," p. 260.
66. The *Fuero Real,* for example, repeated later Roman law in severely limiting the ability of parents to apportion their estates: at least seven-fifteenths had to be divided equally among the progeny, since no more than one-fifth could be given away and no more than one-third given to a favorite child. The *Furs de València* required division of property equally among sons and daughters when there was no will (". . . sens testament, que sien partits entre·ls fils e les filles per equals parts," 33.18.3, p. 258), although it allowed greater flexibility in parental disposition.
67. Jeanne Ancelet-Hustache, "Les 'Vitae sororum' d'Unterlinden: Édition critique du manuscrit 508 de la Bibliothèque de Colmar," *Archives d'Histoire doctrinale et littéraire du Moyen Age* 5 (1930) 23, p. 394: "Quodque excellencius magnificenciusque fuit, maritum suum, iuuenem militem ac in rebus seculi ualde preclarum, cum duobus paruulis liberis suis deseruit. . . ." That this was a sacrifice on her part rather than an escape is suggested by the particular ecstasy afforded her by a vision of Jesus as a baby (pp. 403–4).

by the rapid evolution of Europe during the preceding two centuries. One of these was doubtless simple overpopulation: the thirteenth century inherited the cumulative effects of growth of the preceding two hundred years, and Europe was more densely populated than it would be again for half a millennium.[68] Related to this was a great increase in the number and variety of illegitimate children, caused partly by the rise of urban centers, in which prostitution, concubinage, and casual sexuality were possible on a larger scale than they had been in the small rural communities of the earlier Middle Ages.

Another less obvious but far-reaching cause was the creation of new categories of illegitimacy through church legislation on marriage and clerical celibacy. The children of priests, for example, were increasingly regarded as necessarily illegitimate, since marriage was prohibited to priests everywhere in Europe by the thirteenth century.[69] It proved difficult to dissuade the clergy from producing offspring, so the church adopted the expedient of making life difficult for the children themselves, either in the hopes that this would in the end discourage their fathers, or simply as punishment of the parents through the children. Technically such children were slaves, but this penalty was probably not applied. Clerical progeny could not, however, enter religious orders or communities, could not contract valid marriages, and could not legally inherit.[70] The injustice of punishing the children for the sins of the parents passed unremarked at the time, perhaps because one tendency of

68. For population figures see chapter 11, notes 33–39, and discussion there. P. P. A. Biller ("Birth-Control in the West in the Thirteenth and Early Fourteenth Centuries," *Past and Present* 94 [Feb. 1982] 3–26), argues contrary to the received wisdom that Europeans of the period may have practiced *coitus interruptus* and other means of contraception in reaction to this unprecedented population growth. His evidence is highly speculative, but perhaps no better materials will present themselves in this area.

69. Through the twelfth century it remained controversial. For a useful introduction, see Anne L. Barstow, *Married Priests and the Reforming Papacy,* and R. I. Moore, "Family, Community, and Cult on the Eve of the Gregorian Reform," *Transactions of the Royal Historical Society* 30 (1980) 49–69.

70. See Bernhard Schimmelpfenning, "*Ex fornicatione nati,*" pp. 18–19, 24. As he notes, this places such children in the same position as traitors, although they themselves are innocent of wrongdoing. There were institutions specifically devoted to the care of clerical offspring (e.g., the chapter of St. Lambert in Liège, Schimmelpfenning, p. 33), but "probably in many cases the members of the parish themselves contributed to the support of the children of priests" (p. 32).

popular morality, as noted, tolerated sacrifice of children for higher causes, or perhaps because the draconian penalties could not actually be enforced. Already in the early twelfth century, Paschall II dispensed the children of priests in England and parts of Spain because "almost the larger and better part of the clergy" were themselves the sons of priests.[71] Schimmelpfennig found that from ten to fifteen percent of the clergy in the thirteenth and fourteenth century were still scions of priests, and in the second half of the thirteenth century the Bishop of Liège boasted of having produced fourteen sons in twenty-two months.[72] Many such children were doubtless given up to monasteries, and some exposed, although it is also clear that many clerical fathers did rear their children, sometimes even in monasteries.[73] They may in such cases have been treated as oblates and therefore, in one sense, abandoned even if a parent was present.

Ironically, the efforts of the church to regularize marriage—the primary purpose of which, according to Scholastics, was the production of legitimate children[74]—rendered more and more children illegitimate throughout the High and later Middle Ages, although often in technical ways which would not necessarily inspire abandonment. The rules regarding consanguinity (degrees of relationship permissible between marriage partners), for example, were greatly streamlined at the opening of the thirteenth century by the Fourth Lateran Council, but they were also much more vigorously enforced, and created enormous difficulties for some spouses and their children.[75] Children of relationships of twenty years or more

71. Ibid., pp. 38–39.

72. Ibid., pp. 33 and 40–41.

73. See, e.g., Eudes Rigaud, *The Register of Eudes Rigaud*, p. 127: a monk of St. Wandrille is raising his child in the priory; p. 376: the priest of Notre-Dame at Sauchay is ordered to send away the children he has at home; p. 377: the priest of Rousmesnil is living with his daughter in his home; p. 470: Brother Richard of the priory of St-Laurent-en-Lyons is censured for secretly giving his daughter in marriage; p. 544: the priest Walter is censured for living with his concubine and their daughter; pp. 587–88: Gervaise, the priest of Ste-Croix, has his daughter living near him. Nuns also appear in this context—p. 48: Joan of l'Aillerie leaves the convent of Villarceaux to visit her child; p. 384: Nicola has had two children (the second, born in the convent, is given to her sister in Rouen; both children were fathered by the parish priest). Penelope Johnson is preparing a detailed analysis of monastic infractions based on this register.

74. E.g., Thomas Aquinas, *Summa contra gentiles* 3.124: "Certitudo prolis est principale bonum quod ex matrimonio quaeritur."

75. Much of the second part of the *Decretum* is devoted to canonical issues of

might be declared illegitimate if the parents found they were related within prohibited degrees, which would mean that the marriage had been invalid from the beginning. And the system of prohibitions was so complex, involving as it did relationships of blood, marriage, and "spiritual affinity" (created chiefly through godparenting), that couples might well contract marriages in ignorance of such a relationship, or disguise it at the time of the marriage and later use it to apply for an annulment.[76] To prevent this, the banns of marriage were required (again by the Fourth Lateran Council) for the first time everywhere in Catholic Europe: pending marriages had to be announced publicly in church on successive occasions so

---

marriage, and charts of consanguinity and affinity are appended in most editions (e.g., Friedberg, 1.1425–36). The issue of the new rules and their purpose and import has been widely discussed in the past decade; see, *inter alia*, Georges Duby, *Medieval Marriage: Two Models from Twelfth-Century France* (Baltimore, 1978); *idem, The Knight, the Lady and the Priest: The Making of Modern Marriage in Medieval France* (New York, 1983); the reply to the former by Constance Bouchard, "Consanguinity and Noble Marriages in the Tenth and Eleventh Centuries," *Speculum* 56, 2 (April 1981) 268–87; C. Brooke, "Aspects of Marriage Law in the Eleventh and Twelfth Centuries," in *Proceedings of the Fifth International Congress of Medieval Canon Law, Salamanca, 21–25 September 1976,* ed. S. Kuttner et al. (Vatican City, 1980) (Monumenta Iuris Canonici, Series C: Subsidia, 6) 333–44; Josef Ziegler, *Die Ehelehre der Pönitentialsummen von 1200–1350* (Regensburg, 1956). The standard treatments are Jean Dauvillier, *Le mariage dans le droit classique de l'église: Depuis le Decret de Gratien (1140) jusqu'à la mort de Clement V (1314)* (Paris, 1933), and A. Esmein, *Le Mariage en droit canonique* (New York, 1968), to which should now be added the collection of basic studies in Henri Crouzel, *Mariage et Divorce, célibat et caractère sacerdotaux dans l'église ancienne* (Torino, 1982) (Études d'histoire du culte et des institutions chrétiennes, 11), and Brundage, *Law, Sex, and Christian Society.*

76. Although this was by no means limited to the High Middle Ages: in a celebrated variation from the eighth century a queen (Audovera) acts as godmother to her own child at the urging of a wily maidservant (Fredegund), who then points out to the king that he and the queen are now related within prohibited degrees. The king puts the queen and the daughter in a convent and marries the maid: *Liber historiae Francorum,* ed. Bruno Krusch (Hannover, 1888), MGH SSRRMM 2.292–93. Doubtless apocryphal, the story nonetheless reflects the cynicism felt in many quarters about spiritual affinity and its impact on marriages. By the ninth century the laity so frequently employed the rules about spiritual affinity to escape unhappy marriages that the Frankish bishops in 813 reversed the previous canonical tradition and declared that co-parenthood did not dissolve marriages, although those who had established co-parental relations with spouses would have to do penance for it: Council of Châlons, canon 31, in MGH *Concilia* 2.1, p. 279. See also discussion in Lynch, *Godparents,* pp. 278–80. Nonetheless, it was used throughout the Middle Ages as grounds for dissolution.

344 · *The Kindness of Strangers*

the whole community could bring its collective knowledge about the couple's relatives to bear in precluding any irregularities.[77]

Part of the point of the banns may also have been to elicit information from those in a position to know that the intended of someone who had been abandoned as a child was too closely related to constitute a suitable partner—perhaps even a sibling. The system of proclaiming banns was promulgated at the same time, and often in the same synods, which evinced such concern about baptizing, burying, and otherwise attending to exposed children, and the problem of accidental incest was a major issue for canon lawyers like Hostiensis.

Under the new rules, there were, indeed, many more opportunities for children to become illegitimate, even late in life, than just the possibility that a parent might suddenly be discovered to have married a prohibited relative. Marriage had become, ironically, more fragile as a result of regulations designed to strengthen it. Unions that would have passed for marriages in common law or even in the eyes of the church in the tenth century were nullified by the High Middle Ages. Although Augustine had considered that any woman who intended to be faithful to the man she lived with was married to him, much more than this was needed under the new rules. In a famous case submitted to Celestine III at the end of the twelfth century, a man who had returned to his former mistress after the death of his wife and lived with her for ten years asked the pope to recognize them as a couple. By this point they had ten children, but this only made their illicit liaison worse, the pope responded, rejecting the request. The ten children were bastards, though the widower and their mother considered themselves married and wished to be recognized as such. Nonetheless, the pontiff added, it was the parents' responsibility to take care of their ten illegitimate children.[78]

77. The banns were made a universal requirement at IV Lateran, Canons 51 and 52 (many editions; most recently by Antonio García y García, *Constitutiones Concilii quarti Lateranensis una cum commentariis glossatorum* [Vatican City, 1981] [Monumenta Iuris Canonici, A: Corpus glossatorum, 2]). For local implementation, see, e.g., Council of Angers (1216–19), canons 63, 65, 67, and 68 (in Pontal, *Statuts* 1.180). That the point of them was to obviate problems of consanguinity is clearly articulated therein and in canons 65 and 67 of Angers; these also state quite forcefully the consequences for the children of prohibited unions (e.g., in the latter, "soboles de tali conjunctione suscepta prorsus illegitima censeatur . . ."). See also the Synod of Paris (ca. 1216), *Statuts* 1.66–68, canons 40–45.

78. "Solicitudinis tamen tuae intererit, ut uterque liberis suis . . . , secundum

Church and civil law were unanimous in requiring one or both parents to take responsibility for illegitimate offspring. In most cases the responsibility for actual care fell on the mother for the first years of the child's life (usually to age three), during which time the father, if known, was obligated to support them financially. After this the duty devolved on the father.[79] Such laws could not have pre-

---

quod eis suppetunt facultates, . . . necessaria subministret" (*Decretales Greg. IX* 4.7.5 [Friedberg 2.689]).

79. Illegitimate children in the Middle Ages constitute a complicated and rich issue, deserving their own study. The many legal compilations of the Cuenca-Teruel family in Spain all require that the mother care for an illegitimate child during its first three years, with the father paying her what he would pay a nurse; if he refused she could abandon the child to him; after three, he passed entirely into the care of the father until majority: *Fuero de Cuenca* 290 (11, 38), *Fuero de Baeza* 260, *Fuero de Plasencia* 101, etc., all discussed in Enrique Gacto Fernandez, "La situación" (as above, note 16), pp. 172–73 and n. 4. (On the *Fuero of Cuenca* and its influence, see further in *Fuero de Cuenca: Formas primitivas y sistemática*, ed. R. Ureña y Smenjaud [Madrid, 1935]). The *Fuero Real* concurred (3.8.3), but allowed local authority to intervene to keep the child with the mother beyond age three if this seemed appropriate, in which case the father must offer financial support. (If the mother was Jewish or Muslim, however, the father retained the child and she paid financial support.) But the roughly contemporary *Siete Partidas* draw a distinction between the children of a mistress and those of "adultery, incest or fornication": the mother and her family are obligated to care for the latter, but not the father (4.19.5). The *Fuero de Jacca*, also contemporary, disagrees even between redactions, the A version requiring the father to recognize and support any child ("es tengut lo paire de tener-lo per fill & de nodrir-lo") the mother can prove to be his, although he does not have to bequeath him anything (ed. Mauricio Molho [Zaragoza, 1964], p. 181), whereas the B version (ibid., sec. 164) simply describes an ordeal of linen to determine whether a mother is telling the truth about the father: if she passes, he rears the child; if she fails, she does. (For similar provisions see *Fueros de Aragon* 234; *Costumbres de Lérida* 3, and *Fuero General de Navarra* 5.3.16, 4.4.1.) For a summary treatment of English law on the subject, see F. Pollock and F. Maitland, *A History of English Law*, 2.397–98, and for actual incidence in England and elsewhere, Peter Laslett et al., eds., *Bastardy and Its Comparative History;* for French law, H. Regnault, *La Condition juridique du Bâtard au Moyen-Age* (Pont-Audemer, 1922) or the more recent article by Anne LeFebvre-Teillard, "L'Enfant naturel dans l'ancien Droit français," in *L'Enfant* 2. 251–69, and for incidents, Shahar, *Fourth Estate*, pp. 113–16; for German law, "Die Rechtsstellung des unehelichen Kindes in Österreich vom Mittelalter bis zur Gegenwart," *L'Enfant* 2. 493–515; for Hungary, Andor Csizmadia, "L'Enfant dans le Droit hongrois depuis le Moyen Age jusqu'au milieu du XIXe siècle," *L'Enfant* 2.517–41, p. 529; for Norwegian practice, Larson, *Earliest Norwegian Laws*, pp. 77–78, and Karras, "Concubinage"; and for Iceland, Stein-Wilkeshuis, "Juridical Position of Children," p. 370. In some societies illegitimate children could be legitimized by the parents (e.g., Iceland: see *Járnsída eðr Hákonarbók*, ed. T. Sveinbjörnsson [Copen-

cluded abandonment by either or both parents, and, indeed, often occur in codes which specifically allow abandonment.[80] They were probably designed to regulate situations in which ample resources were available to support a child but responsibility was disputed.[81] Genuine poverty apparently excused both parents.

The pressure to conform to increasingly rigid rules about sexual conduct also rendered the children of premarital cohabitation more embarrassing than they had been earlier, before strict requirements of public solemnization made it so painfully clear that some children were born too early to have been conceived in wedlock. Many cases of "substitution" in English law of the thirteenth century appear to involve an effort to legitimize the offspring of premarital relations.[82]

A form of abandonment familiar to many modern parents but rare in Christian Europe before the High Middle Ages was dereliction by divorced spouses who "abandoned" their children along with their partner. Despite theological traditions opposing it, divorce was permitted under both civil and ecclesiastical law in many parts of Catholic Europe during the Middle Ages,[83] although it was

---

hagen, 1847], p. 73, title 16), and popes could declare children legitimate, which they often did when marriages were dissolved or annulled.

80. Note, for example, that the *Siete Partidas* imply that it is a kindness for parents to rear their children, as if it were quite likely that they would not: 4.19.1, cited at head of this chapter.

81. The extent of shame involved in bearing illegitimate children would obviously vary widely according to circumstance and personal attitude. Shahar's observation (*Fourth Estate,* p. 113) that the "illegitimate son of a married woman was usually accepted by the family and considered legitimate" is too broad, and single mothers often faced severe difficulties: Caesar of Heisterbach depicts a girl as hanging herself after the birth of her illegitimate child (4.43), although this may be only a didactic warning.

82. See cases cited from *Bracton's Note Book,* above, note 33. The most likely explanation in my view for the decision of John of Monte Acuto and his wife Lucia (case 247) to abandon their daughter Katherine is that she was born too soon after their marriage and would have caused scandal: both father and mother subsequently acknowledge her existence and, implicitly, relation to them—e.g., at the time of her marriage—but continue to try to keep it secret even from their own collateral relatives. In addition to the texts cited above, see brief commentary in C. Meekings, "A Roll of Judicial Writs," *Bulletin of the Institute of Historical Research* 32 (1959) 209–21, p. 213.

83. The received wisdom that divorce was not allowed to Catholics from early times was promulgated as propaganda for a stricter stance on the issue from the twelfth century on. There is surprisingly little secondary material challenging this tradition; for an excellent introduction to what is available the reader may consult

generally limited to the prosperous. Poorer persons, who could not afford the niceties of legal divorce, simply left their spouses.[84] Both civil and ecclesiastical legislators established rules to prevent divorced parents from shedding parental duties along with spouses. That this would constitute juridical abandonment is evidenced not only by the provisions themselves, but also by the fact that they are frequently introduced under the rubric of "exposed infants," and in at least one case are even accompanied by illustrations of children being exposed (see figures 13 and 14).

Hostiensis begins his commentary on abandoned children in canon law by considering who should care for the children in cases of divorce, and in a later encyclopedia divorce custody forms a major part of the entry for "exposed infants."[85] The general rule,

---

Jo-Ann McNamara and Suzanne Wemple, "Marriage and Divorce in the Frankish Kingdom," in Susan Mosher Stuard, *Women in Medieval Society* (Philadelphia, 1976), pp. 94–124. Christian civil law allowed divorce throughout the early Middle Ages (e.g., *Lex Romana Visigothorum* 3.16, following the Theodosian Code, ibid., although Valentinian's Novel 35.1.11 had modified this; Justinian, Novel 140 [by mutual consent: "Nam si mutua affectio matrimonia contrahit, merito eadem contraria sententia ex consensu solvit, repudiis missis quae eam declarent"]), and many extant formulae of divorce leave no doubt that it was common and countenanced by church and state: see, e.g., MGH *Formulae,* pp. 94, 248, and 478. Even the ruthlessly orthodox laws of the crusader Kingdom of Jerusalem drafted in the thirteenth century allowed divorce, explicitly overseen by the church, for such causes as bad breath or urinary incontinence ("li put trop durement la bouche ou le nes, ou pisse toutes les nuits au lit" [Victor Foucher, ed., *Assises du Royaume de Jérusalem* (Paris, 1839), pp. 322–24]). Note that as late as Boccaccio there was a popular equation of annulment (the only official ecclesiastical dissolution of marriage by this point) with divorce: *Decameron* 10.10.

84. Again, paradoxically, the high medieval church both affirmed its prohibition of divorce and greatly expanded the grounds on which marriages could be dissolved—through annulment, a declaration that the marriage had never been valid—for a host of reasons ranging from impotence to fraud. Annulment rendered the offspring of the marriage, no matter how many or how old, illegitimate, since the marriage had now never taken place, although it lay within the pope's power to declare them legitimate.

85. *Omne bonum,* British Library ms Royal 6E VII, folio 104v (source of the illustrations cited above). The entry begins: "Nunc sequitur videre de expositis infantibus et languidis per diversos"; it treats first the freedom from *potestas* of children or servants abandoned by parents or masters, respectively; second, the obligation of an abbot to receive back an expelled monk; third, repeating twice the rubric "expositus," it quotes Hostiensis's discussion of custody in divorce cases, including his final observation that the danger of incest might make exposing a grave sin. For this manuscript and its author, see Lucy Freeman Sandler, *Gothic Manuscripts*

inspired by Roman law and established as early as the twelfth century, was similar to that for children of unmarried mothers: the mother was to have custody until age three, after which the child would be the responsibility of the father until coming of age, unless some overriding consideration, such as great disparity in means or inappropriate religious faith (usually of the mother), should require an adjustment.[86]

The historical record yields relatively little information about modes of abandonment or the precise fate of the children thereafter, aside from issues of baptism or burial. Literature, assessed in the following chapter, is more generous. Caesar of Heisterbach tells two stories involving abandonment: in one, a wealthy matron finds and rears a "destitute" child "as her own," and he is eventually ordained a priest (3.42). In another, a wealthy woman has her daughter reared in a neighboring town.[87] Sale, however, is more common: Caesar also mentions that his mother bought a ten-year-old pagan

---

1285–1385, 2 (London, 1986) (A Survey of Manuscripts Illuminated in the British Isles, 5), pp. 136–38, and further commentary in *eadem*, "Face to Face with God: A Pictorial Image of the Beatific Vision," in *England in the Fourteenth Century. Proceedings of the 1985 Harlaxton Symposium*, ed. W. Ormrod (Suffolk, 1986), pp. 224–39.

86. The twelfth-century *Summa* of Piacentino gives the rule quite concisely: "It is often a matter of contention in cases of divorce whether the children should remain with the mother or the father, and we take note of this. Clearly as a matter of course those older than three ought to remain with the father and those younger with the mother. A judge can decide whether it would be better for them to reside and be supported by one or the other, but after age three they should in any case be supported at the father's expense and be his responsibility" (*Placentini summa codicis* [Mainz, 1536], reedited by Francesco Calasso [Torino, 1962], 5.24, p. 217). These provisions are repeated and elaborated in both ecclesiastical and civil legislation affected by Roman law and jurists throughout the Middle Ages: see, e.g., Hostiensis, as cited above, and the *Omne bonum*, likewise; *Fuero Real* 3.8.3; *Siete Partidas* 4.19.3. The issue of "fault" is sometimes introduced, as in the *Omne bonum*, or the *Siete Partidas*, as cited. Three years was often considered the end of infancy: see, e.g., the provisions for orphans, who no longer require a nurse after three, in *Fuero de Béjar* 270, ed. Juan Gutierrez Cuadrado (Salamanca, 1974), and similar provisions in *fueros* of Alcaraz (title III) and Alarcón (p. 109) (ed. Jean Recouil [Paris, 1968]).

87. 7.45. Whether the *Dialogues* are any less fictional than the materials addressed below as "literature" is certainly arguable; I have, with some reservations, discussed them here because I believe that both Caesar and his readers would have understood them to be in a category different from, e.g., the writings of Marie de France. There is certainly no reason to doubt the account of his mother buying a girl.

girl while he was a schoolboy, and had her baptized (10.44). There was, in fact, a thriving slave trade in southern Europe, involving many children,[88] and although some of them may have been captured, many were doubtless sold by impoverished parents, as the law in many states allowed.[89]

Infants continued to be left in churches, as the profusion of conciliar decrees mentioning this (cited above) makes clear. In settling a dispute in 1275 between two parish churches in Rheims over responsibility for a child abandoned in one of them, the cardinal archdeacon refers to officials in charge of such matters (*carcerarii*) and testifies that he has "examined the witnesses on both sides regarding the points usually investigated there in cases of exposed infants."[90] Other sources also indicate that the primary obligation for the care of abandoned infants fell on parish churches, as it apparently had for centuries.[91]

The Children's Crusade invites speculation about the role abandonment might have played in it: this mysterious event took place around 1212 when, according to scattered comments in chronicles, thousands of children undertook to free the Holy Land and marched from areas of France and Germany to points in Italy (and France), where the movement dissipated. The chroniclers do not suggest that parents encouraged their children to go, merely that adults, in awe of the holy motivation inspiring persons so young, allowed them to leave. It does not appear to have been a camouflage for abandonment, although the fact that the movement began (appar-

88. Thoroughly discussed in Charles Verlinden, *L'Esclavage dans l'Europe médiévale* 1 and 2, and in many shorter studies, e.g., *idem,* "L'Enfant esclave," esp. pp. 116–18. For the north, see Karras, *Slavery and Society,* and Marlis Wilde-Stockmeyer, *Sklaverei auf Island: Untersuchungen zu rechtlich-sozialen Situation und literarische Darstellung der Sklaven im skandinavischen Mittelalter* (Heidelberg, 1978). None of these studies addresses abandonment or sale by parents at any length.

89. That parents feared their children might be stolen is, nonetheless, implied by literature of the High and later Middle Ages: *Richards li Biaus* (ed. W. Foerster [Vienna, 1874]), for example, is about a king who walls up his daughter because he is terrified that she will be stolen.

90. "Nos, testibus quos ad requisitionem partium examinari fecimus super eo quod de expositis ibi fieri solet inspectis . . ." (published in Gaston Robert, "Les Chartreries paroissiales et l'assistance publique à Reims jusqu'en 1633," *Travaux de l'Académie nationale de Reims* 141 [1926–27] 127–264, "Pièces justificatives," 2, pp. 165–66).

91. See, e.g., note 127, below.

ently) among shepherds may mean that the children involved were already on their own in some sense. If, as several accounts maintain, some of them were actually sold into slavery at the ports they reached, it was not by parents or relatives, and was little different from other instances of slave trading involving children, apart from the peculiar ugliness of the circumstance.[92]

Another ugly circumstance more clearly related to abandonment is suggested by the church's legislation removing children of mixed unions from custody of Jewish mothers lest they "drag the child into the error of disbelief."[93] There is little indication that Jews abandoned their own offspring in the High Middle Ages[94]—

92. The first conscientious effort to separate fact from fancy in this sensational matter was Reinhold Röhricht's "Der Kinderkreuzzug," *Historische Zeitschrift* 36 (1876) 1–9; more thorough treatments may be found in D. C. Munro, "The Children's Crusade," AHR 19 (1913–14) 516–24; J. E. Hansbery, "The Children's Crusade," *Catholic Historical Review* 24 (1938) 30–38; and Norman Zacour, "The Children's Crusade," in *A History of the Crusades,* ed. Kenneth Setton, 2: *The Later Crusades, 1189–1311,* ed. Robert Wolff (Philadelphia, 1962). The latter in particular provides a very judicious assessment of the credibility of the sources for each item of the received wisdom about the crusade.

93. "Ne mater que in iudaismo remanet ad infidelitatis errorem ipsum trahat" (*Omne bonum,* folio 104r). This is similar to provisions in divorce and illegitimacy regulations cited above, from Hostiensis and, e.g., *Siete Partidas.* On mixed marriages, see Boswell, "Conversions to Judaism in the Later Middle Ages," forthcoming. In some cases, children of mixed unions were killed: see, e.g., Jean Régné, *History of the Jews in Aragon, Regesta and Documents, 1213–1327,* ed. Yom Tov Assis (Jerusalem, 1978) (Hispania Judaica, 1), no. 1316, pp. 238–39 and 428–30, for a case involving a Jew and a Muslim. A Jewish synod in Crete in 1238 prohibited cohabitation precisely to prevent infanticide: see Louis Finkelstein, *Jewish Self-Government in the Middle Ages* (New York, 1924), pp. 82–85, 271–72, and 279. Cf. Boswell, *Royal Treasure,* p. 353; but I now wonder whether *ahorco,* "hung," is not a mistake for *ahorro,* "free," i.e., not a slave: it was also common in the thirteenth century for children of mixed parentage of one sort or another to follow the higher (or freer) status. Contemporary law in Sweden, for example, held that "children go to the better half" ("gangin æ barn a bætri alf"): Gipta balkær 39.1, in *Ostgötalagen,* in *Corpus Iuris Sueo-Gotorum Antiqui* 2.111. But these were not marriages involving different faiths. For Jewish family life during this period, see Kenneth R. Stow, "The Jewish Family in the Rhineland in the High Middle Ages: Form and Function," AHR 92, 5 (1987) 1085–1110.

94. My computer search of responsa for the key words in Hebrew that might refer to abandoned children turned up no original medieval material on abandonment, only citations from Talmudic materials on אֲסוּפִי and שְׁתוּקִי (see above, pp. 151ff.) as parallels to other issues (e.g., Ibn Adret 2.16 and 3.369). The twelfth-century "Elegia giudeo-italiana" (ed. Gianfranco Contini, *Poeti del duecento* [Milan, 1960] 1.35–42) is about a Jewish brother and sister sold separately into slavery who

although there are famous instances in which Jews killed their children to prevent their being baptized during pogroms.[95] In his thirteenth-century codification of Jewish law, the *Mishneh Torah*, Maimonides elaborates on Talmudic principles about abandonment and adds some provisions that appear to be original, but it is impossible to know whether these reflect real situations or simply the comprehensiveness of his imagination. The most revealing aspect of his discussion may be that it occurs in a section dealing with prohibited intercourse, reflecting the ancient fear of incest as the result (or possibly the cause) of abandonment.[96]

---

recognize each other when their masters try to arrange for them to produce children. It is difficult to feel confident that the poem corresponds to any historical reality, although the fact that its central themes are incest and *anagnorisis* is in itself revealing: see below.

95. Especially during the massacres of Jews by Crusaders in the Rhineland at the time of the First Crusade: an account of this by a Jewish writer, Solomon Bar Simpson, is published in A. Neubauer and M. Stern, *Hebräische Berichte über die Judenverfolgungen während der Kreuzzüge* (Berlin, 1892), pp. 6–8, 9–10; in Jacob Marcus, *The Jew in the Medieval World: A Source Book: 315–1791* (New York, 1972), pp. 115–20; and, more fully, in Shlomo Eidelberg, *The Jews and the Crusaders: The Hebrew Chronicles of the First and Second Crusades* (Madison, 1977). This was clearly not abandonment in the sense under consideration here, since the parents also killed themselves, and their aim was to save rather than lose the children, but it provoked considerable controversy among contemporary and subsequent Jewish communities.

96. Maimonides, *Mishneh Torah*, Sefer Kedushah (in English: *Code of Maimonides*, 5: *The Book of Holiness*, trans. Louis Rabinowitz and Philip Grossman [New Haven, 1965]), 15.13, 21–33. The provisions of sections 30 and 31 dealing with the form and locations for abandonment are taken directly from the Talmud, but sections 21, 25, 28, 29, and 32 appear to be original. Notable are his suggestion (25) for dealing with the fact that in the societies in which Jews of his day would find exposed children they would be unlikely to be Jewish; his interpretation (29) of Leviticus 19:29 as a reference to abandonment; the suggestion in his treatment of the midwife's testimony (32) that prosperous Jews might abandon children; and the lengths (28) to which he would go to preclude accidental incest: a foundling may not marry any woman whose father or brothers were living at the time his mother became pregnant. Cf. note 94, above. There are scattered hints that Christians sometimes obtained Jewish children (as in cases of mixed parentage), but these do not imply abandonment by Jews. See, e.g., the story by Caesar of Heisterbach (2.26) about a Jewish girl brought up by an unmarried Christian knight. A later Jewish story (*Ma'aseh Book*, trans. Moses Gaster [Philadelphia, 1981], pp. 410–17) tells of a rabbi's son who is stolen and reared by priests and eventually becomes pope. He prohibits Jewish observances so that the Jews will come to him to complain; when they do, he is able to locate his father and return to his own family as a

By contrast, the charge that Jews stole, bought, and killed Christian children, which became very widespread in the later twelfth century and did incalculable harm to Jewish communities for centuries thereafter, may be a further indication of abandonment among Christians. Even in the first instance of the libel a skeptical investigator might suspect a connection between such accusations and abandonment by Christian parents. According to his official biography, William of Norwich, a Christian child, had been sent away from his home to be an apprentice at age eight. Although an aunt lived nearby, he was lodging with a stranger at the time of his disappearance, which was ultimately blamed on the Jews of the community, who were alleged to have murdered him in 1144.[97] The entire account may be fictitious, but if the libel was based on any incident at all, it is easy to believe that it involved a child separated from his parents without any malevolence on the part of strangers.[98]

The idea that Jews were responsible for any mysterious harm to Christian children captivated the imagination of the English public, and there were plenty of missing or dead children to fan the flames of paranoia and hostility. When the body of a Christian child missing for twenty-two days was found in the Severn (near Gloucester) in 1168, Jews were accused of torturing and crucifying him,[99] and similar charges were leveled in Winchester in 1192 and 1232, at Lincoln in 1202, and in London in 1244 and 1255.[100]

In France, a similar accusation led to the creation of a shrine in

---

Jew, leaving the Christians wondering what has become of the pope. This recalls the biblical story of Joseph.

97. The text of the story, by Thomas of Monmouth, was published with a translation by Augustus Jessopp and Montague James, *The Life and Miracles of St. William of Norwich* (Cambridge, 1896).

98. For a recent assessment of the incident and Thomas's account, see Gavin Langmuir, "Thomas of Monmouth: Detector of Ritual Murder," *Speculum* 59, 4 (1984) 820–46. On the ritual murder libel in general, see Cecil Roth, *The Ritual Murder Libel and the Jew* (London, 1935).

99. *Historia et Cartularium monasterii sancti Petri Gloucestriae,* ed. W. H. Hart (London, 1863–65) 1.20–22; discussed in Gavin Langmuir, "The Knight's Tale of Young Hugh of Lincoln," *Speculum* 47, 3 (1972) 459–82, p. 462.

100. See discussion in Langmuir, "The Knight's Tale," pp. 462–63. The case of Hugh of Lincoln, also allegedly slain at eight or nine years old by Jews in 1255 (Matthew Paris, *Chronica Majora* 5.516–19, 546, 552; AASS, July 6, 494, etc.) became the most celebrated of all these. It was, for example, commemorated in Chaucer's *Canterbury Tales,* "The Prioress's Tale," and many other English popular ballads and stories.

Paris before 1171,[101] and in that year thirty-one Jews were burned at Blois on the charge that a Jew had thrown a Christian child into the river.[102] That unwanted children were thrown into rivers during the period is certain.[103] It is conceivable that a Jew was seen disposing of a baby in this way (if so, almost certainly his own); or that an infant was found or seen in the river and the Jews blamed; or that the story was pure fable concocted from association of rivers with infanticide and hostility toward Jews.[104] In 1271 the Bishop of Augsburg promised the Jews of the city immunity from charges brought against them when people deposited corpses in their gardens,[105] and in the following year Pope Gregory X was even more specific:

> It happens occasionally that [when] some Christians lose their Christian children, the Jews are accused by their enemies of secretly carrying off and killing these same Christian children and of making sacrifices of the heart and blood of these very children. It happens, too, that the parents of these children, or some other Christian enemies of these Jews, secretly hide these very

101. *Lamberti Waterlos Annales Cameracenses,* ed. G. H. Pertz, MGH SS 16, (Hannover, 1859), *sub anno* 1163, p. 536; *Oeuvres de Rigord et Guillaume le Breton,* ed. H. F. Delaborde (Paris, 1882–85), 1.15; discussed in Langmuir, "The Knight's Tale," p. 462.

102. See Robert Chazan, "The Blois Incident of 1171," *Proceedings of the American Academy for Jewish Research* 36 (1968) 13–31.

103. See, e.g., the legend of the origin of the Hospital of the Holy Spirit in Rome, discussed in chapter 11; note 56, and illustrated in figures 15–17; cf. Tubach, *Index,* nos. 4107 and 4476.

104. For the Jewish account of the accusation and burning at Blois, see Neubauer and Stern, *Hebräische Berichte,* in Marcus, *The Jew in the Medieval World,* pp. 127–30.

105. "Weiter wo yemand vielleicht, das verre sei, aus teufelischen eingeben oder sunst bestochen in ire höf oder heuser todten körper, dadurch sie unbillig verunreinigt würden, werfen würden, wollen wir wider si kein klag achten oder glauben . . ." (Julius Aronius, *Regesten zur Geschichte der Juden im Fränkischen und Deutschen Reiche bis zum Jahre 1273* [Berlin, 1902], no. 751, p. 317). The text as cited does not mention children, despite the implication by Joshua Trachtenberg (*The Devil and the Jews: The Medieval Conception of the Jew and its Relation to Modern Antisemitism* [New Haven, 1943], p. 126) and James Parkes (*The Jew in the Medieval Community* [London, 1938], p. 177, n. 1). On the other hand, it is likely that this is what the prelate had in mind. As late as 1374, Philip the Good of Burgundy found it necessary to repeat, in essence, the guarantee that Jews would not be held liable for items Christians planted in their homes and then claimed to have been stolen: Jules Simmonet, "Juifs et Lombards," *Mémoires de l'Académie impériale des sciences, arts et belles-lettres de Dijon* 13 (1865) 245–72, Appendix, 9, p. 267.

children in order that they may be able to injure these Jews, and in order that they may be able to extort from them a certain amount of money by redeeming them from their straits.[106]

It is not very difficult to imagine the role abandonment might play in this scenario: "lose their children" is fairly transparent.

In 1294 the disappearance of Christian children in two Spanish cities led to accusations of murder against the Jews.[107] When, late on a Saturday night in 1301, the dead body of a two- or three-month-old baby boy was found beneath a stall in the Jewish meat market of Barcelona by a Muslim slave girl and her Jewish master, the Jewish community immediately buried the child in their own cemetery.[108] This was not because they believed that the child was Jewish, but to prevent accusations that Jews had killed a Christian infant. At an inquest into the matter many witnesses suggested that the baby had been deposited in the Jewish quarter by a Christian woman, called Rumia, precisely to foment difficulties for the Jews. The identity of the child was never discovered[109] and their own quick action saved the Jewish community of Barcelona from violence, but it also evinces eloquently the threat posed to all Jewish communities, even in the relatively tolerant states of the Mediterranean, by children abandoned or lost by Christians.

It is not clear whether Christians blamed the Jews simply to have a scapegoat, or whether Jewish families did sometimes take in exposed Christian children and were then accused of stealing and kill-

---

106. Marcus, *The Jew in the Medieval World*, p. 153, from Moritz Stern, *Urkundliche Beiträge über die Stellung der Päpste zu den Juden* (Kiel, 1893) 5–7; also in Roth, *The Ritual Murder Libel*, pp. 21–22. Cf. Innocent IV in 1247, ibid., p. 97: "Moreover, if the body of a dead man is by chance found anywhere, they maliciously ascribe the cause of death to the action of the Jews."

107. F. Baer, *Die Juden im Christlichen Spanien* (Berlin, 1929), 1, doc. 138; *idem, A History of the Jews in Christian Spain* 2.7.

108. Archive of the Crown of Aragon, Real Audiencia, Procesos, Legajo 513/10, folios 1–23, published with thorough analysis in Elena Lourie, "A Plot Which Failed? The Case of the Corpse Found in the Jewish *Call* of Barcelona (1301)," *Mediterranean Historical Review* 1, 2 (December 1986) 187–220.

109. It is not credible that a Jew would have left a corpse under a meat stall; the child was certainly Christian. As Lourie correctly notes (pp. 193–94), it would have been a simple matter for the Jewish witnesses to swear that the boy was circumcised, which they all failed to do. On the other hand, association of the slaughter of children with Jewish butchers was commonplace: see W. C. Jordan, "Problems of the Meat-Market of Beziers," *Revue des Études juives* 135 (1976) 37–39.

ing them if they died. In some areas of Europe Christians and Jews may have been sufficiently distinguishable ethnically for it to be obvious if Christian children were reared, for example, as servants in Jewish households.[110] It was common for Jews to circumcise and proselytize their household servants, to avoid ritual contamination by them,[111] and this, if Christians were aware of it, might have given rise to the lurid charges of murder and sacrifice.[112] On the other hand, it may have been pure fancy, related to the basic rallying cries of European anti-Semitism. Latin and vernacular literature had for centuries included grotesque stories connecting Jews and children, such as the legend that a Jew who came to watch communion saw in the hands of St. Basil an infant torn limb from limb,[113] or the Span-

110. This difficult but important point has not been systematically addressed in any of the literature on Jewish-Christian relations. The *Nizzahon Vetus,* a thirteenth-century compilation of Jewish anti-Christian writings, strongly suggests that some Jews, at least, perceived a noticeable difference between them and the surrounding Christian population ("Why are most Gentiles fair-skinned and handsome while most Jews are dark and ugly?" 238, pp. 224, 159 (Hebrew), in the edition of David Berger, *The Jewish-Christian Debate in the High Middle Ages: A Critical Edition of the Nizzahon Vetus, with an Introduction, Translation, and Commentary* [Philadelphia, 1979]). On the other hand, Christian efforts during the thirteenth century to force Jews to wear distinctive badges (begun at IV Lateran) imply the contrary. Christian art often stereotypes Jews iconographically, but many Jewish artists of the thirteenth century (especially manuscript illuminators) depict Jews as indistinguishable from Christian figures in contemporary art. The reality was probably as varied as the historical record.

111. Maimonides, *Mishneh Torah,* Sefer Kedushah 1.13, 14; Solomon Grayzel, *The Church and the Jews in the Thirteenth Century* (Philadelphia, 1933), pp. 23–26, 198–201; Boswell, "Conversions to Judaism."

112. The Jews of the time were themselves baffled by this preposterous calumny: "The heretics anger us by charging that we murder their children and consume the blood. Answer by telling him that no nation was as thoroughly warned against murder as we, and this warning includes the murder of Gentiles. . . . The fact is that you are concocting allegations against us in order to permit our murder. . . ." In Berger, *Nizzahon,* 244, pp. 229, 163 (Hebrew).

113. *Vita sancti Basilii, Caesareae Cappadociae archiepiscopi* 6 (PL 73.301–2). The theme of the transformation of the host into a child was, however, not necessarily related to anti-Semitism: see other instances in *Verba seniorum* (*De vitis Patrum* 5) 3 (PL 73.979), where a man who doubted transubstantiation sees a child being dismembered on the altar, and similar stories in Caesar of Heisterbach, 9.2–3, 28, 41, 42, 50; *Das Viaticum Narrationum des Heumannus Bononiensis,* ed. A. Hilka (Berlin, 1935), no. 72; Tubach, *Index,* 2685, 2689c. Herbert (*Catalogue,* p. 576, no. 33) summarizes a tale in which a duchess leaves a host in a tree, which blooms out of season; a bleeding child is later found where she left the host.

ish tale that a Jewish boy who was inspired by a vision of the Blessed Virgin was thrown into an oven by his father.[114] Whatever its origins, the Christian slander took on a grisly pseudo-reality in later ages, when some Christian parents reportedly offered to sell their children to Jews for sacrifice.[115]

High medieval forms of "fostering," like those in earlier periods, could involve abandonment, although often they did not. The term itself and its equivalents in other languages were applied to a wide variety of relationships, on which no tidy order can be imposed without doing violence to what was apparently a considerable fluidity.[116] "Foster" is the term used for rearing foundlings,[117] but also for relationships more like apprenticeship, oblation, or even godparenting.[118] Some "foster parents" were clearly supplements to natal parents, and therefore increased rather than dimin-

---

114. E.g., in Gonzalo de Berceo, *Milagros de Nuestra Señora,* ed. and trans. Amancio Bolaño e Isla (Mexico City, 1976), "El Niño judío," no. 16, pp. 70–74. Notice, however, the generally tolerant tone of this poem: the Jewish boy loves to play with Christian children, and they with him ("Acogienlo los otros, no li fazien pesar, / Avien con él todos savor de deportar"); his mother is horrified at the father's actions (stanza 364). A similar incident occurs in contemporary German literature: "Das Jüdel," *Gedichte des XII und XIII Jahrhunderts,* ed. K. A. Hahn (Quedlinburg, 1840) (Bibliothek der gesammten deutschen National-Literatur, 20), pp. 129–34; "Der Judenknabe," *Marienlegenden aus dem Alten Passional,* ed. Hans-Georg Richert (Tübingen, 1964) (Altdeutsche Textbibliothek, 64), pp. 187–205.

115. See Trachtenberg, *The Devil and the Jews,* p. 125.

116. The word is of Scandinavian origin, and seems in all medieval languages to relate to "nourish" or "sustain," but within this encompasses broadly different meanings, and often includes metaphorical extensions. In Norse-Icelandic it normally has the most direct meaning of "foster" (discussed below), although the saga *Fóstbrœðra* is actually about "sworn brothers," who were not brought up together but took an oath to defend each other (ed. Björn Þórolfsson and Guðni Jónsson [Reykjavik, 1943] [IF, 6]); cf. Welsh *cyfaill* and Irish *comalta,* both used to mean "friend" and "foster brother." In Old Swedish, by contrast, *fostre* refers to a class of domestic slaves: see, e.g., *Ostgötalagen,* "Eghna salu" 23 and "Drapa balkær" 16.1–2 (in *Corpus Iuris Sueo-Gotorum Antiqui* 2.61, 152); discussion in G. Hasselberg, "Den S. K. Skarastadgan och Träldomens Upphörande i Sverige," *Västergötlands Fornminnesförenings Tidskrift* 5, 3 (1944) 86–90. In Old English "fostr-" appears to have as its most basic meaning "nurse": see, e.g., Laws of Ine 38 ("to fostre") and 63 ("cildfestran"; as cited above, p. 209), although in Middle English it clearly has a more general sense of "rear" or "bring up" ("Fleshli fadir and modir that getes and fosters us forthe in this world").

117. E.g., in *Jómsvíkinga saga:* see discussion of this in note 127, below, and in chapter 10, notes 84 ff.

118. On the development of customs relating to this and their social and cultural importance, see Lynch, *Godparents.*

ished the care extended to children,[119] but a more common pattern in the High Middle Ages appears to have just skirted the edge of genuine abandonment. The wealthy of Scandinavia, Ireland, and Wales, in particular, placed both sons and daughters[120] with relatives, feudal subordinates, other rulers, or other householders,[121] to be reared from early childhood through adolescence (usually sixteen or seventeen).[122] Such arrangements were known but less common in southern Europe.[123] "Foster parents" could be of either

119. Especially in later sagas, "foster" seems to be more or less the equivalent of "godfather," and this may reflect increasing influence of Christian customs on Scandinavian society: see, e.g., *Vilhjálms saga Sjóðs,* ed. Agnete Loth (Copenhagen, 1964) (LMIR, 4) chap. 2, p. 5, where being "foster father" is clearly an honorific position, and the child remains with the natal family. This appears to be the case, even earlier, in *Hænsi-Þóris saga* (ed. Sigurður Nordal [Reykjavik, 1938] IF 3, chap. 9), but it is difficult to date the development (or many of the sagas) more precisely.

120. Ursula Dronke observes that only one woman (Hallgerðr in *Njál's saga*) is fostered by a man outside the *fornaldarsögur* (*The Role of Sexual Themes in Njál's Saga* [London, 1981], pp. 17–18), but I am slightly puzzled by this, since Thurid in *Hænsi-Þóris saga* seems to be fostered by Thord Gellir (chap. 11). For other examples of fostering of daughters, see, for example, *Saga Heiðreks Konungs ins Vitra* [*Hervarar saga*], chap. 3, pp. 10–11, *Víglundar saga* (Reykjavik, 1931) 7, or *Vilmundar saga Viðutan,* ed. Agnete Loth (Copenhagen, 1964) (LMIR, 4), chap. 1, p. 142 (where a woman does the fostering).

121. Gerald of Wales, who disapproved of the custom, gives nonetheless a precise and succinct eyewitness description: "principes filios suos generosis de terra sua viris diversis diversos alendos tradunt" (*Descriptio Kambriae* 2.4, ed. Dimock, pp. 211–12). Of countless examples in sagas: King Höfund sends the younger of his two sons to be fostered with a wise man, although he loves him better, and King Heidrek of Sweden asks to foster the son of King Gardar (*Hervarar saga,* ed. Tolkien, pp. 21, 28); Harald Harfagra's legitimate children are fostered by Duke Gerthorm (*Haralds saga ins Hárfagra,* in Snorri Sturluson, *Heimskringla* 1, chap. 21, p. 120); in Snorri Sturluson's *Ólafs saga Tryggvasonar* (ibid., chaps. 7–8) Astrid's foster father, Torolv Louse-Beard, follows her into exile after her husband's downfall and becomes, apparently automatically, the foster father of her child, who avenges his murder.

122. See, e.g., *Grágás* (K), ed. Finsen, 89, p. 161, trans. Dennis, p. 151 ("Legal fostering is when a man takes a child of eight winters or younger and brings him up until he is sixteen"); and p. 141, Ómaga-Bálkr, 2.22, "Vm barn fostr" (not translated in Dennis). For Ireland, see the Irish tract on fosterage, *Cáin Íarraith* 1768.32 (1341.8) and 1769.1–2; and *Bretha Crólige,* ed. D. A. Binchy, *Ériu* 12, 1 (1934), 8, both discussed in Stacey. On the continent, Tristan and other knights in romances are entrusted to nurses while infants and then to a male till around sixteen (discussed in Daniell Buschinger in "L'Enfant dans les romans de *Tristan* en France et en Allemagne," *L'Enfant au Moyen Age,* 255–60; cf. the peculiar inversion of such a relationship described in Wailes, "The Romance of Kudrun," pp. 358–59).

gender, and were not necessarily a couple. Parents usually fostered only some of their children.[124]

Sometimes the "fosterer" accepted the position as an honor, although among the Scandinavians there was a general understanding that inferiors "fostered" the children of superiors, indebting the latter to them in return.[125] It was also purely mercenary in some instances, as it had been in the early Middle Ages: parents simply disposed of children by paying someone else to look after them, full-time and permanently.[126] The major difference between "fostering" of these kinds and abandonment was that official relationship to the natal parents was not terminated or obscured, and the child would retain whatever claim he might have on his inheritance.[127]

123. E.g., in the *Gesta Romanorum*, ed. Hermann Oesterley, tales 189 (pp. 592–94) and 282 (pp. 686–88).

124. The elder of King Gormr's two sons is fostered by his maternal grandmother in *Jómsvíkinga saga* (chap. 3), while the younger one remains at home. In *Sigurðar saga þögla*, ed. Agnete Loth (Copenhagen, 1963) (LMIR, 2) a child who has not yet spoken at age seven troubles his royal parents very much, and Count Lafranz of Lixion takes him as his foster child, leaving his two brothers at home.

125. "For it was a saying of men that he who fosters the child of another is inferior" ("því at þat er mál manna, at sá væri tígnari, er ǫðrum fóstraði barn") *Haralds saga ins Hárfagra*, chap. 39, p. 145. In *Hervarar saga* a son leaving his father's household is advised "never to foster the son of a man more powerful than he" (ed. Tolkien, p. 20).

126. *Grágás* (K), 141, as cited above, in note 61 of chapter 7, where a mercenary arrangement is described (not translated in Dennis); *Staðarhólsbók*, sec. 103, ed. Finsen, pp. 133–34, and secs. 106–7, pp. 136–38, on the repaying of what the foster parent spent ("fostr laun") in various ways, including taking property from the child if he came into an inheritance. In *Hænsi-Þóris saga*, chap. 2, Þorir wishes to foster the son of Arngrim (a priest), but Arngrim does not think this fosterage will bring credit to him and declines until Þorir agrees to give half his money to the boy. The evidence of the sagas suggests a moral obligation to repay the kindness or expense of fostering, but, as William Miller points out in "Some Aspects of Householding," it provides no evidence of legal battles over it. In *Laxdæla saga* 51, Bolli's foster mother, Þorgerd, accuses Bolli of making a "sorry repayment" for his fostering when he kills Þorgerd's natural child, Kjartan. For other examples, see *Njáals saga* 93, *Þorsteins saga hvíta* 7 (all discussed in Miller: see chapter 7, note 53).

127. Although the child might also become the heir of the "foster" parent, as in the case of Gorm's son in *Jómsvikinga saga*, who inherits his foster father's lands (chap. 5, as above, note 124). Cf. *Hænsi-Þóris saga*, above, note 126. In cases of illegitimacy very complicated relations could arise: in *Jómsvíkinga saga*, chaps. 10–11, a king has an illegitimate child by a servant girl whose master then acts as foster father to the boy but sends him at fifteen to demand a retinue from the king. Hlöd, the illegitimate child of King Heidrek of Sweden, is brought up in the home of his maternal grandfather, according to *Hervarar saga*, ed. Tolkien, pp. 26, 46.

Both of these were possible, at least on occasion, in the case of exposed children who relocated their parents, so the distinction is not absolute, and "foster" arrangements bear striking resemblances to the *alumnus-nutritor* relationship of the ancient world. Not the least of these is the semantic parallel of the terms: "foster" comes from a Norse root (*fóð*) meaning "food," or "support," as does *alumnus* (from *alere,* "to feed"), and its most basic sense appears to be a child "supported" in the household who had no legal relation to the householder (such as heir, slave, etc.).[128] Latin texts use *alumnus* for children in "foster" relationships.[129]

The extent to which "fostering" could fall somewhere between abandonment and extramural childrearing is evident in the saga of Harald Hárfagra, where Athelstan of England tricks Harald into accepting a sword, a symbol of subordination. In revenge, Harald sends his illegitimate infant son Hakon to be fostered by Athelstan—thus placing the latter in a position of inferiority. As it happens, Athelstan grows to love the boy "more than his own kin,"[130] but his father evidently felt no such attachment and simply sacrificed him for political ends; his messenger even says specifically to Athelstan that he might slay the child if he wishes.

"Fostering" of various sorts appears to have had an intricately ambivalent effect on the position of children, somewhat like that of oblation: while it might establish a powerful bond between the foster family and the child,[131] making up in many ways for the distance

128. *Grágás* equates "foster" relations with members of the family in ways highly reminiscent of provisions of Roman law about *alumni:* see, e.g., *Laws of Early Iceland,* pp. 154–55, where "wife, daughter, mother, sister, foster daughter, foster mother" and "foster-father or father" occur as integral units. Cf. p. 151, where four categories of household dweller are established as capable of answering for an unfit man: son, stepson, son-in-law, and "legal foster-son" (for the definition of the last, see above, note 122).

129. In the VSH, for example, which are Latin retellings of older accounts, *alumpnus* (*sic*) is used for the child in precisely the kind of "fostering" described below (e.g., "Vita prima sancti Brendani," 3, 8 [2.99, 102]; "Vita sancti Mochoemog," 31 [2.180–81]; and many others).

130. "Meira en ǫllum frændum sínum" *Haralds saga ins Hárfagra,* chaps. 39–40, pp. 144–45.

131. Gerald of Wales complains bitterly about the Celtic tendency to privilege foster relationships over consanguinity, claiming that the Irish and Welsh love their foster kin exclusively and wage war on their blood relatives (*Topographia Hibernica* 3.23, ed. Dimock, pp. 167–68; *Descriptio Kambriae* 2.4, as above, note 121, p. 212: "Unde et inter fratres collactaneos quam naturales longe veriores invenies amicitias"). High medieval Latin lives of earlier Irish saints reflect or retain this privi-

or absence of natal parents, this very fact probably encouraged parents to resign children to foster care more casually, more completely, and on a wider scale than they would have otherwise, just as oblation, by removing the more troubling aspects of anonymous abandonment, subtly promoted its more structured form. But, also like oblation, "fostering" contributed to an atmosphere in which "foster" relationships were idealized as great and ennobling rather than makeshift or second-rate, thereby greatly offsetting disadvantages "foster children" of any sort—abandoned or not—might have suffered.[132]

Another shift in patterns of abandonment during the High Middle Ages—also ambivalent in effect—was occasioned by the rise of ecclesiastical and civic organizations to assist the poor and suffering. The ebullient struggle of the twelfth century to reconcile rapidly increasing material prosperity with ideals of apostolic poverty yielded in the thirteenth to a more conventional social preoccupation—the establishment of orderly systems and institutions of charity. Traditional welfare functions of parish churches and monasteries—feeding the poor, nursing the sick, sheltering the homeless, receiving abandoned children—were increasingly assumed by religious orders founded specifically for such purposes, and hospices

---

leging: St. Cain loved the *alumpnus* of his sister so much that he raised him from the dead ("Vita sancti Cainnici," 26, VSH 2.162); cf. *Annals of the Kingdom of Ireland by the Four Masters,* ed. John O'Donovan (Dublin, 1856), 2.976, where Amalgaid is slain by his own father and brother for killing their foster child, Conchobar. Plummer (VSH 1.cvii, n. 8) cites from *The Battle of Magh Rath* the saying that two-thirds of a child's character depends on its fostering. Scandinavian literature is less consistent on this: in *Hervarar saga,* for example, a man intercedes with his natal father to spare his foster father (chap. 7, ed. Tolkien, p. 29), but in *Jómsvíkinga saga* (chap. 14) Sveinn seeks to kill his foster father for slaying his real father, even though the latter had refused to recognize him—suggesting a strong privilege of blood relation. Compare the interesting case of the Veisusynir: second cousins so called because they had been fostered on the same farm (Veisa): cited from *Ljósvetninga saga* 22, by William Miller, "Some Aspects of Householding," n. 35.

132. By the later Middle Ages, for example, "foster brother" is a general Icelandic and Norse expression for a true and loyal friend: see *Nitida saga,* ed. Loth (LMIR, 5), p. 35; *Sigrgarðs saga froekna,* ibid., pp. 70, 100; *Valdimars saga,* ed. Loth (LMIR, 1), p. 72; *Victors saga ok Blávus,* ibid., pp. 27, 48; *Adonias saga,* ed. Loth (LMIR, 3), p. 250; also for godparents (*Sigrgarðs saga ok Valbrands,* ed. Loth [LMIR, 5], p. 120). Men, however, still become "foster brothers" in traditional ways—e.g., when one is brought up by the father of the other: *Jarlmanns saga ok Hermanns,* ed. Loth (LMIR, 3), pp. 3–5.

or "hospitals" became common in many areas of Europe.[133] Some of these accepted abandoned children. The Hospital of St. John in Jerusalem, organized and staffed by Western Europeans, officially cared for exposed children as early as the twelfth century.[134] But others would not: the hospice for the sick at Troyes included in its official regulations of 1263 a statement that

> abandoned children[135] are not accepted at this institution, because if we did accept them there would be such a host of children that our resources would not be sufficient, and because this is not our responsibility, but that of the parish churches.[136]

Records of such institutions for the thirteenth century are few and incomplete, and it is impossible to derive any clear impression of

133. For a survey of this change see, e.g., the essays in *Assistance et charité;* Mollat, *The Poor in the Middle Ages;* for a more interesting conceptual approach to some of the same issues, see Little, *Religious Poverty* (all cited above, in note 10 of chapter 7). More detailed material can be traced through local studies, e.g., *La Carità cristiana in Roma,* ed. Vincenzo Monachino, Mariano da Alatri, et al.; *Les Ordres mendiant et la ville en italie centrale (v.1220–v.1350),* in *Mélanges de l'École française de Rome; Moyen Age—Temps Modernes* 89, 2 (Rome, 1977); Jacqueline Caille, *Hôpitaux de charité publique à Narbonne au Moyen Age de la fin du XIe à la fin du XVe siècle* (Toulouse, 1978); F. Barreda y Ferrer de la Vega, *Los hospitales de Puente San Miguel y de Cóbreces en la primitiva ruta Jacobea de Cantabria* (Santander, 1973).

134. "Et tous les enfans getez de pères et de mères soilot l'Ospital ressevoir et faire norrir" ("Statuts promulgués par Roger de Molins," 2.3, in Léon le Grand, *Statuts d'Hôtels-Dieu et de Léproseries: Recueil de Textes du XIIe au XIVe siècle,* p. 14). This same rubric includes persons requiring assistance to get married, but it is unclear whether this is specifically aimed at foundlings who have grown to marriageable age in the hospital.

135. *Pueri inventi:* a literal translation, apparently, of *enfants trouvés,* and the earliest occurrence of such a phrase known to me.

136. "Pueri inventi non recipientur in Domo nostra. Quos si reciperemus, tanta afflueret copia puerorum, quod ad hoc non sufficerent bona Domus; et quod ad nos non pertinet sed ad parrochiales ecclesias": "Les anciens statuts de l'Hôtel-Dieu-le-Comte de Troyes," ed. Philippe Guignard, in *Mémoires de la Société académique d'agriculture, des sciences, arts et belles-lettres du Département de l'Aube* 17, 4 (1853), lxxxix, p. 78, and in le Grand, *Statuts,* p. 115. The Hôtel-Dieu of Angers also refused exposed children: le Grand, *Statuts,* p. 25, n. 13. The Hôtel-Dieu of Saint-Pol (near Châtillons) would maintain the abandoned children of poor mothers until age seven if they were actually born in the hospital; after that their fate would be up to the discretion of the administrator: "Quod si pueros dimiserint clam sive furtim, ne patres inveniantur ipsorum, in hospitali maneant donec sep-

how many of them received foundlings, or the numbers of infants involved where they did.[137]

That the numbers were large, and that being received at such an institution was not an unmitigated blessing, are both indicated in Salimbene de Adam's account of the punishment in hell of the administrator of an early thirteenth-century Milanese hospital: he had "allowed children born of clandestine relationships and deposited at the hospital to die without baptism out of indignation when he saw the labor and expense the hospital would incur from such abandonments."[138] He had, moreover, either "forgotten" to confess this or "not considered it necessary to confess," which suggests startling indifference to the fate of infants on the part of one of those charged to look after them.[139]

At the close of the thirteenth century the German poet Hugo of Trimberg bitterly reproached those "mothers of so little devotion that they leave their children alone in front of hospitals or

---

tennio peracto, et tunc, nos, aut heredes nostri, residuo nutrimento consulemus discretos quid agere debeamus" (*Statuts,* p. 124; statutes of 1265).

137. E.g., Umberto Rubbi and Cesare Zucchini ("L'Ospizio esposti e l'asilo de maternità," *Sette secoli di vita ospitaliera in Bologna* [Bologna, 1960], pp. 401–17) find that exposed infants were "probably" received at the Ospedale di S. Procolo in Bologna in the thirteenth century, but the evidence is unclear (pp. 402–3). For other examples see chapter 11, notes 54 and 55.

138. "Eo quod pueros ex occulto concubitu genitos et ad hospitale proiectos ex quadam indignatione sine baptismo mori permiserit, quia videbat hospitale ex tali expositione in labores et expensas incurrere" (*Cronica,* ed. G. Scalia, 1 [Bari, 1966], p. 105). Salimbene does not name the hospital. Bonvesin della Riva asserts that in 1288 the Hospital of the Brolo had 350 babies "and more" placed with nurses after their birth, but it is not clear whether this is simply a neonatal nursing service or care for foundlings ("De magnalibus urbis Mediolani," ed. Francesco Novati, *Bullettino dell'Istituto Storico Italiano* 20 [1898] 67–114, p. 80). The editor seems to assume the latter, and notes that in 1168 the different foundations already existing for the poor and foundlings were grouped into a unit by Archbishop Galdino (n. 67). Della Riva gives the whole population of Milan as 700,000 (p. 84); 350 would be a very low rate of abandonment for such a population and may indicate either that this was not, in fact, a reference to foundlings or that the hospital accommodated only a small number of the children abandoned in Milan at the time. The second is very likely: foundling hospitals only gradually became major repositories for exposed children, and during this period informal abandonment prevailed in most of Europe.

139. "Vel quia tradidit oblivioni, vel quia confitendum non credidit" (*Cronica,* p. 105).

churches," and juxtaposed this with abandoning them to animals or even killing them outright.[140] The conjunction of hospitals and churches is probably a realistic indication of a gradual change in modes of dealing with abandoned children during the later Middle Ages, and Hugo's horror may have been well grounded if Salimbene's administrator was typical. There is no reason to believe that children abandoned in other ways in the thirteenth century died in greater numbers than they had previously. Other writers of the High Middle Ages, in fact, evince a much more sanguine view of abandonment in all of its forms.

140. Hugo von Trimberg, *Der Renner,* ed. Gustav Ehrismann (Tübingen, 1909), 3.18519–18530: "Ouch ist der muoter triuwe vil kleine, / diu ir kint let alterseine / vor spitaln oder vor kirchen liegen, / vor swinen, vor hunden . . ." The poem was finished in 1300.

10

❖ ❖ ❖

LITERARY
WITNESSES

LITERATURE of the High Middle Ages had as one of
its expressed aims the holding of a mirror to life, and to the extent
that the images caught in the mirror are still recognizable they provide fleeting glimpses of the skin and flesh that adorned the skeleton
reconstructed from legal and historical sources.[1] To say that there
was an explosion of literary materials dealing with abandonment in
the High Middle Ages would be accurate, and yet misleading, because there was an explosion of literature of all sorts during the period, and an increase in a particular theme must therefore be viewed
in context. The immense variety, distribution, and range of treatments do, nonetheless, seem to indicate that it was a subject familiar
to writers throughout Europe, that it was viewed as a normal practice,[2] and that many different circumstances were thought to occasion it.

These materials cannot be presented in a strictly chronological

1. For a recent consideration of the complex and oft-discussed metaphor of
the mirror, with bibliography, see Herbert Grabes, *The Mutable Glass: Mirror Imagery in Titles and Texts of the Middle Ages and the English Renaissance,* trans. Gordon
Collier (Cambridge, 1983).
2. The fact that something is frequently mentioned hardly indicates that it was
regarded as "normal": see comments in the Introduction on murder as a literary
convention. In contrast to murder in modern fiction, however, abandonment in
high medieval literature is not depicted as shocking, criminal, or disturbing. It is
incidental to plots set in contemporary contexts as well as in the past, and, as noted
below, many admirable characters in these stories abandon children.

format, since only approximate dates can be assigned to many of them, and the same story is often told at different times by different authors. All writing draws on conventions and tradition, of course; the recurrence of a topos or even the repetition of narrative details cannot be taken as meaningless or ahistorical simply because they may be derivative. Marriage, murder, and the birth of children do not occur in twentieth-century literature simply in "imitation" of classical antecedents. Familiar *topoi* must, of course, be handled with caution: it makes a difference whether a storyteller has, insofar as can be determined, devised a new tale involving abandonment or repeated (and invariably added to) an old one; just as it matters whether he places the events in a contemporary setting as credible background, or in a remote time or foreign land for exotic detail. But to say that these choices "matter" should encourage more exacting analysis of recurring themes rather than disregard for them.[3]

That the twelfth-century *Roman de Thèbes,* for example, recounts the abandonment of a child (Oedipus) is hardly a clue to anything, since the ancient tale could not be retold without this incident.[4] But it is interesting that the baby is hung in a tree (lines 119–28) rather than left on a hillside,[5] since the former is a mode of exposing characteristic of medieval literature; and that "Edyppus" is taunted by his childhood companions as an *enfant trouvé* (lines 129ff.), possibly a clue to the status of foundlings in the author's social milieu.[6] The exposing of Paris in Konrad von Würzburg's *Der*

3. Cf. Ralph Hexter's observation that "a good author (at least) 'intends' those themes of an original that he or she maintains just as much as those which he or she alters or adds" (*Ovid and Medieval Schooling,* p. 217). (The question remains: Who is "a good author"? And even Homer nods.)

4. *Roman de Thèbes,* ed. Guy Raynaud de Lage (Paris, 1966–67). The declamation on the evils of infanticide by Oedipus's mother at lines 53–80 is also notable. (Cf. the lines on abortion, apparently influenced by Ovid, in Étienne de Fougères [d. 1178], *Le Livre des Manières,* ed. R. A. Lodge [Geneva, 1979], pp. 95–96, and the similar diatribe in *Pseudo-Ovidius De Vetula,* ed. Paul Klopsch, in *Untersuchungen und Texte* [*Mittellateinische Studien und Texte* 2] [Leiden, 1967], pp. 200–201, lines 159–90.) For a brief discussion of childhood in the *Roman de Thèbes,* see Daniel Poirion, "Edyppus et l'enigme du romain médiéval," in *L'Enfant au Moyen Age,* pp. 287–98.

5. Cf. *Gesta Romanorum* 20, where parents are forced by the emperor to abandon a child because of an evil portent—a purely classical motif; but the child is left in a tree, and reared by a childless noble couple, both medieval themes. For a medieval illustration of abandoning a child in a tree, see figure 3.

6. On the medieval Oedipus legend there are numerous studies subsequent to L. Constans, *La Légende d'Oedipe* (Paris, 1881). See Lowell Edmunds, *Oedipus: The*

Trojanische Krieg and in *Der Göttweiger Trojanerkrieg* is an inherited part of the plot, but the reactions of the narrators and their characters are original, and both of these works include scenes and aspects that reflect thirteenth-century attitudes as much as, or more than, classical ones.[7]

By contrast, some stories composed during the Middle Ages evince in structure and detail fascination with the ancient rather than a realistic portrayal of the contemporary. Although it (probably) originated at the opening of the Middle Ages and was embellished for a millennium after, the story of Apollonius of Tyre in its several versions usually includes abandonment-related motifs (brothel scenes, pirates, etc.), which are more classical than medieval.[8] (Even so, an eleventh-century chronicler adduces "the deeds of Apol-

---

Ancient Legend and Its Later Analogues (Baltimore, 1985), with extensive bibliographies (pp. 225–34). As a sampling of bibliography relating to materials discussed on the following pages, see: Redford, "The Literary Motif of the Exposed Child"; Lowell Edmunds and Alan Dundes, eds., *Oedipus: A Folklore Casebook* (New York, 1983); P. F. Baum, "The Medieval Legend of Judas Iscariot," PMLA 31 (n.s. 24) (1916) 481–632; and Paul Lehmann, "Judas Iscariot in der lateinischer Legendenüberlieferung des Mittelalters," *Studi Medievali* NS 3 (1930) 289–346 (reprinted in *Erforschung des Mittelalters* 2 [Stuttgart, 1959] 229–85). The Oedipus-Gregorius connections have been the object of frequent scholarly investigation, from Adolf Seelisch, "Die Gregoriuslegende," *Zeitschrift für deutsche Philologie* 19 (1887) 385–421, to the classic article of Günther Zuntz, "Oedipus und Gregorius," *Antike und Abendland* 4 (1949) 191–203 (reprinted in two of the *Wege der Forschung* series: *Sophokles* [no. 95; Darmstadt, 1967] and *Hartmann von Aue* [no. 359; 1973]). The industry of scholars interested in the Oedipus cycle is helpful for bringing to light the myriad studies that touch directly and indirectly on exposure, and Edmonds's bibliography will be invaluable for those who wish to pursue aspects of it in more depth or in cultures earlier than those considered in this study; for example, Gerhard Binder, *Die Aussetzung des Königkindes: Kyros und Romulus;* P. Jensen, "Aussetzungsgeschichten," in E. Ebeling and B. Meissner, eds., *Reallexikon der Assyriologie* 1 (Berlin and Leipzig, 1932) 322–24.

7. Konrad von Würzburg, *Der Trojanische Krieg,* ed. Adelbert von Keller (Stuttgart, 1858) (Bibliothek des litterarischen Vereins in Stuttgart, 44): lines 435–514 (abandonment), 455–61 (unhappiness at court, although without overt disapproval); *Der Göttweiger Trojanerkrieg,* ed. Alfred Koppitz (Berlin, 1926) (Deutsche Texte des Mittelalters, 29): lines 1328–67 (abandonment); 1319–21, 1414–18, 11193, 11210–14, etc. (disapproval). Note that in Konrad's version the foster mother gives her own child to a nurse so that she can care for Paris, because of his great beauty—a singular motif (lines 546–75).

8. A comparatively brief version occurs in the *Gesta Romanorum* 153; for others, see Archibald. Incest and *anagnorisis* are common to both medieval and classical abandonment stories.

lonius" as precedent in relating the incestuous behavior of a historical character.)[9] In medieval legend Judas Iscariot had been exposed
by his parents as the result of a prophecy, and married his mother.[10]
The story is an invention of the twelfth or thirteenth century, and
some elements in the extant versions are original and lifelike—for
example, Judas's adoptive mother coming to resent him after she
has a son of her own, or his attitude toward the foster brother who
taunts him as a foundling[11]—but there is no evidence (nor much
likelihood) that children were exposed in the Middle Ages as the
result of prophecy, and it seems reasonable to conclude that abandonment literature of this sort represents a "quicksand" motif, at
least as literal narrative detail. At a subtler level, however, it may be
revealing: the motif of the child destined to bring tragedy on parents or homeland could be a thinly disguised or even unconscious
metaphor for the urgent medieval social problem of younger sons
who often posed or created a threat to the security of older heirs to
throne or property. In this sense, the commonness of abandonment
themes related to predicted generational conflict (or misfortunes to
come) may be a clue to what medieval authors thought their contemporaries were doing with surplus heirs.

The retelling of numerous other classical tales in which abandonment occurs could indicate a particular interest in the subject,

9. "Pater vero . . . succensus face [*sic*] luxuriae, nurum viciat, antequam ad
filii perveniat thalamum. O nefas! libido sodomita inrepit patres, ut stuprum exer-
ceant in nurus et etiam in filias, ut in acta legitur Apollonii." In *Chronicon Novali-
ciense,* ed. G. H. Pertz (Hannover, 1846) MGH SSRRGG 9, 5.3, p. 64.

10. The best-known telling of this occurs in Jacopo da Voragine's *Legenda Au-
rea,* ed. T. Graesse (Dresden, 1846), chap. 45, pp. 183–85, where the author himself identifies it as "historia apocrypha" and says (somewhat disingenuously) that it
is better "forgotten than repeated" (p. 185). Judas is born of Ruben and Cyborea;
his mother has a dream indicating he will bring great harm to his *gens;* unwilling to
kill the child (N.B.), she exposes him in a basket on the sea and he floats to the
island of Scarioth (whence his name), where a childless queen finds him, feigns
pregnancy, and produces him as her own. When he learns from his younger
brother, later born to his adoptive mother, that he was adopted, he kills the
brother, returns to Jerusalem, marries his natal mother, subsequently discovers
this, and goes to Jesus for forgiveness. The legend was not widely known, but did
have some influence: see, e.g., *Das alte Passional,* ed. K. A. Hahn (Frankfurt, 1857),
pp. 312–18 (ca. 1300).

11. "Original" at least in the sense that this was not a common motif in abandonment literature before the High Middle Ages: a similar triangle of foundling,
foster mother, and natural child occurs in both *Wilhelm von Wenden* and in Hartmann's *Gregorius,* both discussed below.

but is more likely a reflection of the general hunger for classical literature in the High Middle Ages.[12] A series of witty and creative variations on the traditional theme of the abandoned child reared by a she-wolf, for example, occurs in the twelfth-century *Guillaume de Palerne,* in which a child is stolen by a wolf who turns out to be a Spanish prince: he had been turned into a werewolf by a wicked stepmother who desired his inheritance for her own son.[13] The overall structure of the tale is an ingenious inversion of older literary *topoi,* and does not seem to relate to the social reality of abandonment in the High Middle Ages, although it is filled with original and explicitly medieval detail, and aspects of the plot (e.g., the envious stepmother) may be quite realistic even if derivative.[14]

On the other hand, the vast majority of literary abandonments of the period are not classical in structure or theme, and as a body they not only corroborate and confirm each other but, like Roman literature, are consistent with legal and historical materials in many particulars, ranging from motivation to method. Two of Marie de France's (twelfth-century) *lais* deal with abandonment: in *Fresne* (The Ash Tree)[15] a married woman has maliciously spread the tale

---

12. The *Gesta Romanorum,* for instance, contain numerous reworked classical abandonment themes, including a tale that appears to be based on the *Controversia* of the elder Seneca about a father sending his sons to be nursed in the countryside (Tale 116: see above, p. 93)—a surprising influence, not noted, to my knowledge, by any other scholars; and Tale 6, about a father who will not redeem a son stolen by pirates (also possibly from the *Controversiae,* although the theme is a common classical one). The motif of children reared by wolves is presumably an echo of ancient lore: *Gesta* 110; VSH, "Vita sancti Albei," 1, 1.46; and "Vita sancti Barri episcopi Corcagie," 1, 1.65 (in this story note also the similarity to Lot and his daughters in Genesis 19), although Caesar of Heisterbach tells two stories involving attacks on children by wolves which seem original (10.65, 66; in the latter the boy becomes a feral child and runs about on his hands and feet, howling).

13. *Guillaume de Palerne,* ed. Henri Michelant (Paris, 1876) (Société des Anciens Textes Français). For a detailed plot summary and a thorough study of influences and parallels, see Dunn, *The Foundling and the Werwolf.* An English version is Walter Skeat, ed., *The Romance of William of Palerne* (London, 1867).

14. For other high medieval instances of stepmothers scheming to defraud heirs, not adduced in Dunn, see Tubach, *Index,* no. 4618.

15. There are many editions of *Fresne* and *Milon:* Jean Rychner, *Lais* (Paris, 1966), often considered standard, or A. Ewert, *Lais* (Oxford, 1978)—numbers in subsequent citations are to line numbers, which can be employed for any edition. For a brief discussion of these two *lais,* see Jeanne Wathelet-Willem, "L'Enfant dans les *Lais* de Marie de France," in *L'Enfant au Moyen Age,* pp. 301–13, esp. pp. 306–9. Rychner provides detailed bibliography.

that the birth of twins means that the mother slept with two men,[16] and when she herself then bears twins, she must face an opprobrium of her own creation. She contemplates killing one, but—significantly—her companions dissuade her from this, arguing that it would be a sin.[17] Abandonment, however, was not: her maid promises to expose the baby in a church, where some gentleman will, she assures her mistress, find and bring her up;[18] the mother wraps the infant in expensive cloth and ties a gold ring to her, so that whoever discovers her will know she is of "noble birth" (*nee de bone gent;* line 134), and the maid then places her in an ash tree outside a convent.

The convent's porter takes the child home to his widowed daughter for nursing (lines 193ff.), but the abbess subsequently brings her up in the cloister—not as an oblate, apparently—pretending she is her niece (lines 225–26). Feigned biological relationship is a common aspect of high medieval abandonment stories, suggesting that shame attached to being a foundling. (In this case, however, the abbess may simply have wished to obviate suspicion that Fresne was her own child.) The abbess does tell Fresne about her background and gives her the tokens left with her.

A nobleman who visits the abbey loves Fresne and persuades her to leave with him (a happier fate than that of the Nun of Watton), but in time his vassals insist that she is not good enough to be his wife, presumably because she has neither heritage nor inheritance.[19] A suitable bride is found: Fresne's twin sister, a fact which is exposed on the night of the wedding, when Fresne, who has humbly accepted the pending nuptials, offers her birth-token cloth as a bedcovering for the couple, and her mother recognizes it. The marriage to her sister is then annulled and she and her beloved are married.

Marriage to two sisters in succession was incestuous in eccle-

16. See note 55 of chapter 9.

17. "De humme ocire n'est pas gas" (98). On the other hand, infanticide is certainly not unknown in high medieval literature: see, e.g., Tubach, *Index,* nos. 973, 2730.

18. "Aucun produm la trovera / Si Deu plest, nurir la f[e]ra" (115–16).

19. In the fourteenth-century Latin story of St. Bartholomew, a prince who sees an abandoned girl in a convent wishes to marry her, but his parents object that it is "not appropriate, since we do not know her status or background . . . no matter how beautiful or charming she is." (Baudouin de Gaiffier, "Le diable voleur d'enfants: A propos de la naissance des saints Étienne, Laurent et Barthélemy," *Études critiques d'hagiographie et d'iconologie* [Brussels, 1967] [Studia Hagiographica, 43] 169–93, p. 191).

siastical law; with its addition the tale displays almost every motif of classical abandonment lore, from exposing by the maid to *anagnorisis* through tokens. Only a brothel is wanting. There is, however, no indication that the story is based on any ancient model: the particulars of abandonment simply inspired similar stories in different ages. Most of the tale is characteristically medieval.

In *Milon* an unwed mother sends her child to be reared by her sister in a distant land, with tokens of silk and a gold ring to facilitate later recognition of his father (which eventually happens at a tournament). The concern evinced on all parts for the illegitimate child is striking: for example, the messengers taking him to the sister stop seven times a day to nurse him. His aunt tells him about his ancestry, and he, like most literary foundlings, imagines that his father will be ecstatic to find him again (*m'amerat e tendrat chier;* line 466). This turns out to be true; and in a joyful final scene the son gives the father to his mother in marriage (lines 525–28).

Difficulties of medieval childhood intrude even on the court of King Arthur. In an early (probably twelfth-century) account of Gawain's life, Uther Pendragon, Arthur's father, holds captive at his court the sons of all the neighboring rulers, "partly as hostages, partly to train them in courtly manners and knightly discipline."[20] They are not all children: Arthur's sister, Anna, becomes pregnant as a result of her relationship with one of them. She feigns illness to disguise the birth, and with the help of her maid entrusts the child to merchants, providing him with gold, silver, clothes, a signet ring, and a document explaining his identity, "so that if he should someday return he would not be rejected, unrecognized by his relatives."[21] The baby is so richly accoutred, in fact, that he is subsequently stolen from the merchant by a fisherman, who is "poor but of good birth and breeding":[22] it would hardly do for even adoptive

20. "Eorum filios partim loco obsidum, partim honestate morum militarique erudiendos disciplina, sua in curia detinebat" (*De ortu Waluuanii nepotis Arturi,* ed. Mildred Leake Day [New York, 1984] [Garland Library of Medieval Literature, Ser. A, 15], p. 2). This edition includes English on facing pages, but passages quoted herein are my own translation. For discussion, see Elizabeth Archibald, "Arthur and Mordred: Variations on an Incest Theme," forthcoming, and Raymond Thompson, "Gawain against Arthur: The Impact of a Mythological Pattern upon Arthurian Tradition in Accounts of the Birth of Gawain," *Folklore* 85 (1974) 113–21.

21. Possibly, "his parents": "ut si forte quandoque rediens a parentibus non agnitus refutaretur" (*De ortu,* p. 4).

22. "Pauper sed genere et moribus honestus" (ibid., p. 6).

parents of a knight to be ignoble.[23] Apart from the questionable circumstances of their obtaining him and the fact that they call him "the boy with no name" until he is twelve, the fisherman and his wife love Gawain—whom the narrator terms their "adopted child" (*filius adoptivus*)—and make a good home for him. Eventually he is reunited with his natal parents, whose irregular liaison is justified, at least in the storyteller's eyes, by the nobility of their offspring.[24]

All these details cannot be taken seriously, although judging from known cases (like Abelard and Heloise) it does seem that the illegitimate children of the prosperous often received careful consideration, even when abandoned in some way.[25] And not all unwed mothers abandon their children, even in the *lais*: in Marie's *Yonec* a woman keeps her illegitimate child.

A more common pattern of unwed mother is the pregnant abbess or nun, a theme treated by Aelred (as noted above) in a story which appears to be based on fact. Pregnant nuns were an ancient source of scandal, amusement, or inspiration, depending on the aims of the storyteller: as early as the seventh century, the women who found a dead baby near the convent of Bischofsheim immediately blamed the sisters,[26] and such stories persisted throughout the Middle Ages.[27] Nor were they simply malicious tales: despite vigorous reform in the

23. Gregorius's foster parents are poor, but he leaves them as a child and enters a monastery.

24. Gawain's father was Loth, a prince of Norway, who subsequently marries Anna and rules Orkney with her, at least in the vulgate cycle. Although the *De ortu* gives no overt indication of incest, it is possible that the name Loth reflects subliminal association of exposing and incest: see comments in Archibald, "Arthur and Mordred." Incest occurred at the court, according to some authors, as discussed below.

25. In *Wolfdietrich* B (ca. 1225; ed. Arthur Amelung and Oskar Jänicke, *Ortnit und die Wolfdietriche* [Berlin, 1871–73] in *Deutsches Heldenbuch* 3, 1.165–301) the illegitimate child of Princess Hildburg and Prince Hugdietrich is temporarily hidden under a hedge beside the town wall, is found and carried off by a she-wolf, and is ultimately recognized by his father, who marries his mother. Cf. *Wolfdietrich* A, in which the same child is exposed for a completely different reason.

26. *Vita Leobae abbatissae Biscofesheimansis auctore Rudolfo,* ed. G. Waitz (Hannover, 1887), MGH SS 15.1, p. 123.

27. For high medieval stories about nuns killing illegitimate children see, e.g., Caesar of Heisterbach, 12.2; *An Alphabet of Tales: An English 15th-Century Translation of the Alphabetum narrationum of Etienne de Besançon,* ed. M. M. Banks (London, 1904–5 [Early English Text Society, 126–27]), no. 455; *Recull de eximplis e miracles, gestes et faules e altres ligendes ordenades per A.B.C. tretes de un manuscrit en pergami del començament del segle XV,* ed. A. Verdaguer (Barcelona, 1881), no. 397.

High Middle Ages, irregularities continued to occur in convents. Eudes Rigaud cites the case of a thirteenth-century nun whose second child, born in the abbey of St. Saens, must be sent to be reared by her sister; the same nun is later accused of procuring an abortion.[28]

In the twelfth and thirteenth centuries there were accounts all over Europe[29] of the miraculous delivery—in two senses—of pregnant nuns, usually involving the intervention of the Virgin Mary. As one who had herself been suspected of bearing a child out of wedlock, the Virgin would presumably have special understanding for the plight of unwed mothers. In the earliest known version of this story the embarrassed abbess becomes, through malicious gossip, the object of general scorn and derision in the community before the birth of her child, and the bishop decides to investigate.[30] But the ministrations of the Virgin have already placed the newborn with a nurse, and removed all physical signs of the birth. The bishop is on the point of executing the nun's accusers for calumny when she reveals all, including the whereabouts of the child himself in his new foster home.[31]

It is hard to imagine a more convenient popular fable to explain the sudden disappearance of an illegitimate child from a convent. "The miracle served the double end both of disposing of an unwanted child in an acceptable way . . . and of providing a basis for reconciliation in a religious community after a shattering challenge to its most cherished norms."[32] The fable occurs again and again, with variations, in Latin and vernacular poetry and prose, and although the number of versions can hardly be taken as an index of the frequency of the event it describes, it may be some indica-

28. *Regestrum visitationum,* ed. Bonnin, pp. 338, 491.

29. Hilding Kjellman (*La deuxième Collection Anglo-Normande des Miracles de la Sainte Vierge et son original latin* [Paris, 1922] [Arbeten utgifna med understöd af Vilhelm Ekmans Universitetsfond, Uppsala, 27], p. xli) notes that this was one of the "miracles les plus populaires du moyen âge"; cf. Constable, "Aelred of Rievaulx," pp. 213–14, especially n. 25.

30. See translation (from Kjellman's text), "The Abbess Who Bore a Child . . . ," in Appendix.

31. Placing the child with a trusted lay person or another religious might constitute the underlying reality in many such stories; an Irish saint's life discusses quite frankly the "fostering" of a nun's child with St. Samthanna ("Vita sancte Samthanne virginis," 18, VSH 2.258).

32. Constable, "Aelred of Rievaulx," p. 214. Eudes de Rigaud cites a case of abortion among nuns: p. 255. There was no moral ambiguity about abortion: it was strictly prohibited.

tion of the extent of public and private concern about the matter.[33] Sometimes the child is taken to a hermit for rearing, sometimes brought up by a hind, sometimes he just disappears.[34] In one disturbing variant a young girl, abused by her uncle, becomes pregnant three times. The first two times she kills the baby; the third time she tries to kill herself in desperation, but the Virgin Mary intervenes to save her life, after which the girl joins an order.[35]

Although the incestuous aspect of this troubling story was relatively minor, it points to a considerable preoccupation among medieval authors with incest in relation to abandonment.[36] The most celebrated exposed child of the Middle Ages (apart from Oedipus)

33. The best-known version is probably that of Gauthier de Coincy, "De l'abeese que Nostre Dame delivra de grant angoisse" (*Les Miracles de Nostre Dame,* ed. Koenig, 2.181–96; cf. 2.205–23, discussed below). For others, see Kjellman, as cited in note 29, above, and A. Mussafia, *Studien zu den mittelalterlichen Marienlegenden* (Vienna, 1886–98); José Canal, *El libro 'De laudibus et miraculis sanctae Mariae' de Guillermo de Malmesbury, OSB (d.c.1143)* (Rome, 1968), 154–56; and R. W. Southern, "The English Origins of the 'Miracles of the Virgin,'" *Mediaeval and Renaissance Studies* 4 (1958) 200–201; and further discussion of this point in Constable, "Aelred of Rievaulx," pp. 213–14.

34. E.g., in the seventh of the *Cántigas* of Alfonso el Sabio, the Virgin has angels carry the baby to a holy hermit for rearing; the standard edition is that of Walter Mettman, *Cántigas de Alfonso el Sabio* (Coimbra, 1959–72). In the version of Gonzalo de Berceo (second half of the thirteenth century), the abbess has the bishop send to the hermit to verify that the child is alive and well, and the bishop then instructs the hermit to keep the boy only until he is seven, after which he is to come to the bishop to be trained as his successor: a pattern of oblation not unlike that of the Nun of Watton (Gonzalo de Berceo, *Milagros de Nuestra Señora* 21: "La abadesa encinta," pp. 98–114). For other versions, see works cited in note 33, above, and Tubach, *Index,* nos. 2 and 4.

35. "Commant notre dame seva .i. feme qui occierre se voiloit" (Bibliothèque Nationale, fr. 988, folios 175v–76r [thirteenth century]); unpublished, and not mentioned in Kjellman. Paul Meyer took note of the manuscript in "Notice sur un légendier français du XIIIe siècle classé selon l'ordre de l'année liturgique," *Notices et extraits des manuscripts de la Bibliothèque Nationale et autres bibliothèques* 36 (1899), pp. 50–51. The girl was the ward of one uncle, and another one took advantage of her. See comparable stories in *Catalogue of Romances in the Department of Manuscripts in the British Museum,* ed. J. A. Herbert, 3 (London, 1910), p. 549, no. 119; p. 677, no. 15.

36. I have not attempted a survey of the high medieval incest literature, for which readers should see general treatments, e.g., Archibald, "The Flight from Incest"; the old but still useful Rank, *Das Inzest-Motiv;* Erhard Dorn, *Der sündige Heilige in der Legende des Mittelalters* (Munich, 1967) (Medium Aevum. Philologische Studien, 10), 2.2, pp. 80–89; Lowell Edmunds, *Oedipus: The Ancient Legend and Its Later Analogues* (Baltimore, 1985); Jean-Charles Payen, *Le motif du*

was Gregorius, whose tale is doubly incestuous: born of the union of brother and sister, he was exposed with tokens of silk and gold by his mother, found by an abbot, and entrusted to a poor family to rear until he was old enough to be educated in the monastery. Learning that he was abandoned, he determined to find his parents, but eventually married his mother unwittingly.[37] After long penance for this, he was elected pope.

Like the abbess saved by the Virgin, the story of Gregorius survives in different languages and forms from all over Europe in the twelfth and thirteenth centuries,[38] and like *Fresne* it weaves together many aspects of high medieval abandonment. It includes oblation of a sort, a quest to locate natal parents, triumph over adversity, great attainment, and incest as both the cause *and* effect of exposing a child—the latter an ancient and oft-articulated apprehension, the former a subject not often publicly broached before or after the period. In spite of—perhaps to some degree because of—all this, Gregorius not only reaches the loftiest post in Christendom, but also becomes genuinely holy.

Many of the versions, though drawing on a set plot, embellish the abandonment with details evocative of historical detail: Gregorius's mother is afraid to have him baptized because she would have to reveal her shame to the priest, but she also fears that he will die unbaptized, so she includes a note informing the finder that he has not

---

repentir dans la littérature française médiévale (Geneva, 1967); as well as the sources cited above and Tubach, *Index*, nos. 2729–39.

37. Which was in itself trebly incestuous, because in addition to the obvious prohibition of relations with one's mother, it violated ecclesiastical rules against carnal relations with a woman with whom either a father or uncle had previously been intimate, and in Gregory's case his father was also his uncle. On the other hand, none of this was deliberate, and Gregory's performing penance for an unwilled sin is an interesting moral issue, suggesting that sexual rules were more a purity code than a system of ethics: see comments below on this in relation to St. Alban.

38. It is widely held that two Old French redactions (A and B) gave rise to (A) Latin, Middle English, Spanish, Italian, and German prose versions, and (B) Hartmann von Aue's 4,000-line poem, *Gregorius* (ca. 1195), the longest and probably most influential form of the story, except possibly the Latin version contained in the *Gesta Romanorum* 81 (related to A). (Arnold of Lübeck's longer Latin version is based on Hartmann.) For discussion of sources, see A. van der Lee, "*De mirabili divina dispensatione et ortu beati Gregorii pape:* Einige Bemerkungen zur Gregorsage," *Neophilologus* 53 (1969) 30–147, 120–37, 250–56. Thomas Mann's *Der Erwählte* (Frankfurt, 1951) is a twentieth-century retelling.

been baptized and should be—as required in conciliar edicts cited above. In the fullest version, by Hartmann von Aue, the fisherman's wife who rears him until he is old enough to enter the nearby monastery (at seven: cf. discussion of oblation, above) mentions that she and her husband would have made him a servant[39] if the abbot had not intervened. Historical sources do suggest that servitude was a common fate for exposed children, but give little indication of abbots appearing to rescue them; monastic life would be, nonetheless, the most accessible alternative for such a child.

In all of the versions Gregorius is ashamed to discover he is a foundling, and in some his foster siblings or other children taunt him about it. But in none of the variants—all deeply moralistic—is the mother's abandoning him itself an ethical issue of any sort.[40]

The idea that children abandoned even under the least auspicious circumstances could rise to great heights is more subtly (but less optimistically) developed in the contemporary legend of St. Alban, the child of an incestuous relationship between a father and daughter (probably a more frequent occurrence),[41] exposed by the latter to prevent the father from killing him (also a likely detail). Left beside a road so he will be promptly found, he is reared by a childless king as his son, and eventually marries his own mother. In this case, however, when the tragic circumstance is discovered through tokens, husband-son and wife-mother go together to confront their father, and all do penance for seven years—an interesting conflation of guilt for a real sin (the original union) and violations of a purity code (the later, accidental coupling).[42]

<hr/>

39. "Slave" might not be too strong a translation: ". . . dienen sam durch allez reht / tæte sîn schalc und sîn kneht" (1357–58, in *Gregorius,* ed. Hermann Paul and Ludwig Wolff [Tübingen, 1973], p. 36).

40. Nor does secondary literature raise this point: K. C. King, "The Mother's Guilt in Hartmann's *Gregorius,*" *Medieval German Studies Presented to Frederick Norman* (London, 1965), pp. 84–93, for example, assesses the mother's guilt about incest, breaking a vow, etc., but never even considers whether abandoning him might have been a source of moral conflict.

41. In Matthew Paris's "Life of Offa the First" (ed. F. J. Furnivall, *Originals and Analogues of Chaucer's Canterbury Tales* [London, 1888], pp. 73–84), a Duke of York orders his daughter slain when she will not succumb to his desire for her. In *Mai und Beaflor* (ed. Alois Vollmer [Leipzig, 1848]) the Emperor of Rome makes incestuous advances to his daughter, who flees, and the father finally renounces his crown as penance. See also the story of *Sir Degare,* below.

42. One of the interesting aspects of this incest theme as it occurs in the Middle Ages is the fact that "marriage" to one's mother was being rendered nomi-

In a further striking twist, when the three are reunited, the father and daughter are overcome by passion and repeat their offense during the night. In a fury, Alban kills them, does penance for another seven years, and is himself subsequently slain by bandits. The water of the river into which his body is thrown (an echo of the ancient association of exposed children with rivers?) cures leprosy.[43]

In its longest Latin version the story contains several interesting touches: Alban's mother places expensive tokens with him (cloth and a gold ring) not so that he might later be recognized (probably not a desirable turn of events under the circumstances), but to inspire someone to care for him (*ut nutrieretur ornavi*). Presumably there would be more incentive to care for a noble child (cf. *Fresne,* above).[44] In another redaction, her purpose is to make certain that the finder has the resources to support him.[45] When she dispatches a servant to expose him she sends along a wet nurse, an unusually realistic detail in such stories; and there is a fascinating scene in which Alban, as an adult, discovers that he was abandoned and adopted. At first he is crushed because he fears that his wife, now his queen,[46] will be unhappy when she hears of his uncertain heritage—as, indeed, she is. "It is as I said; I suffer just what I thought I would," he laments, and puns darkly on his origins: "Now that the truth has been exposed I shall be contemptible to you."[47] He points out to her that he might have been abandoned by royalty (as he was, although he does not yet know this), and also delivers himself of a ringing declaration of the superiority of personal accomplishment and character over biological heritage, a kind of abandoned child's manifesto:

---

nally impossible by canonists of the period, since it involved an *error in personam* and was therefore grounds for automatic annulment: the marriage could not have taken place. This did not, of course, justify any sexual acts the couple might have performed.

43. Edited in Karin Morvay, *Die Albanuslegende: Deutsche Fassungen und ihre Beziehungen zur lateinischen überlieferung* (Munich, 1977) (Medium Aevum: Philologische Studien, 32), 25–32, superseding the thirteenth-century Vatican manuscript version edited by M. Haupt in *Monatsberichte der Königlichen Preussischen Akademie der Wissenschaften zu Berlin* (1860) sec. 24, pp. 241–56; the Paris manuscript versions are collated and published in "Passio vel vita S. Albani martyris," *Catalogus codicum hagiographicorum bibliothecae regiae Bruxellensis* (Brussels, 1886), 2.444–55. The legend is at least as old as the twelfth century.

44. Morvay, p. 29.

45. "Ut nutriendi fortuitu repertus haberet expensam" (ibid., p. 42).

46. His mother, of course, but this is unknown to him at this point.

47. Morvay, p. 28.

I see that what you loved about me was not the flower of youth,
the ornament of manners, or the elegance of style; but that to all
the gifts of the spirit you prefer the prerogatives of birth. How
much can birth really matter if we can rise above it? The beauty
of good character in the humble is more glorious than pride of
origin in the lofty.

This speech is knotted with irony: Alban's ancestry is, in fact, lofty
in social terms, but the overlay of Oedipal mythology makes it
seem that it was his birth that destined him to marry his mother—
something he regards as heinously sinful.

By the late thirteenth or early fourteenth century,[48] incest is even
said to be occurring at Camelot: Mordred is the son of Arthur and
his sister Anna (who had previously borne and exposed the illegitimate Gawain). Arthur and Anna were, perhaps significantly, unaware of their relationship at the time of their liaison—a hint of
the scattering of children in noble families?[49] When it is prophesied
that the incestuous child will wreak great harm in England, Arthur
considers it worth the good of the realm to kill one baby, but is
persuaded by Merlin to immure all noble children born at the appropriate time instead. Although the lords are displeased at having
to give up their sons, they do so.[50]

Incest so weighs on the consciousness of the age, in fact, that in

48. For the dating and text of the "vulgate" versions of the Arthurian legends,
in which these events occur, see H. O. Sommer, *The Vulgate Version of the Arthurian Romances* (Washington, D.C., 1909–13); Archibald, "Arthur and Mordred," as cited above; J. D. Bruce, "Mordred's Incestuous Birth," *Medieval Studies
in Honor of Gertrude Schoepperle Loomis* (New York, 1927) 197–205; and bibliography noted in each. Cf. also the following note.

49. Anna is by this time the Queen of Orkney, since Loth, the Prince of Norway with whom she conceived Gawain, has become its king. The versions of the
Mordred story are varied and their relationship complex: for a clear and helpful
discussion, see Archibald, "Arthur and Mordred." The details summarized here
are taken from the *Suite du Merlin,* ed. G. Paris and J. Ulrich (Paris, 1886), especially 1.147–60 and 203–12.

50. Mordred is, in fact, lost at sea on his way to Arthur's court (alone in a
vessel); he is found by a fisherman and given to a lord to rear. These aspects of the
story, reminiscent of both the legend of his half-brother Gawain (above) and of
Gregorius, are probably too formulaic to be accorded weight as "likely" details.
Indeed, the immuring of the children of the realm and the importance of the sea as
the vehicle for transporting them are all suspiciously like ancient *topoi* of abandonment of the innocents, and probably not indications of contemporary practice.

the later[51] story *Sir Degare* an unmarried woman who has been
raped fears that people will inevitably suspect her father—as if
he were the obvious candidate. She abandons the child with four
pounds of gold and ten of silver, with gloves as tokens, and with a
letter asking that the finder baptize him and give him the tokens at
age ten.[52] By contrast, in *Richars li Biaus* the incest motif is inverted:
the foster parents of a (royal) foundling wish him to marry their
natal daughter, but he refuses, thinking her to be his sister.[53]

Another inversion involves the stealing of children from happily
married couples by the devil: his mischief is almost symmetrically
opposed to the Virgin Mary's intervention in the lives of unwed
mothers.[54] In its simplest form this motif involves parents wishing
their children to the devil, who then actually carries them off.[55] In
more complex versions the reason for the curse entails some moral
subtlety: both Vincent of Beauvais and Gauthier de Coincy link it to
broken vows of abstinence on the part of married couples.[56] (This

51. Probably fourteenth-century: see following note.
52. For discussion of the sources of the story and its relation to *Richars li Biaus*
and other abandonment tales, see George Faust, *Sir Degare: A Study of the Texts and
Narrative Structure* (Princeton, 1935) (Princeton Studies in English, 11).
53. Ed. W. Foerster (Vienna, 1874), lines 750ff. A fourteenth-century (?)
Middle High German poem based on an earlier Flemish story tells of an illegitimate noble baby abandoned and reared by the Roman emperor along with the
latter's natal daughter of exactly the same age. The two fall in love only after it has
been made clear to all concerned (against the emperor's wishes) that the boy is a
foundling, and they eventually marry (*Johan ûz dem Virgiere: Eine spätmittelhoch-
deutsche Ritterdichtung nach flämischer Quelle nebst dem Faksimileabdruck des flämischen
Volksbuches,* ed. Robert Priebsch [Heidelberg, 1931] [Germanische Bibliothek,
2.32]). In the Serbian ballad of the "Foundling Momir" the Serbian Tsar Stefan of
Prizren finds an abandoned child wrapped in leaves on a mountainside, which he
and his wife adopt because they have only one daughter. When the boy is older,
jealous nobles drug him and place him in bed with his adopted sister. The tsar regards this as incest and hangs the boy, after which the sister hangs herself. A vine
grows from her grave over the tree above his. See M. E. Durham, *Some Tribal Origins, Laws, and Customs of the Balkans,* pp. 189–90.
54. On the general role of the devil in the Middle Ages, see Jeffrey Burton
Russell, *Lucifer: The Devil in the Middle Ages,* and on his relation to children in
particular, de Gaiffier, as cited above, and Carl Haffter, "The Changeling: History
and Psycho-dynamics of Attitudes to Handicapped Children in European Folklore," *Journal of the History of the Behavioral Sciences* 4 (1968) 55–61, and J. A. Macculloch, "Changeling," in *Encyclopedia of Religion and Ethics,* ed. James Hastings, 3
(Edinburgh, 1911) 358–63.
55. Caesar of Heisterbach 5.12; *Gesta Romanorum* 162.
56. In the former, the couple had resolved to have no children, and the issue is
further complicated by their breaking their vow on Easter Eve (Vincent of Beau-

could be read cynically as a circumlocution for a failure in family planning.) In both stories the mother then loves the child very much and bitterly regrets the curse: in the former the boy flees to the pope at age twelve, when the devil comes to make good his claim; in the latter, the Virgin herself intervenes against her evil counterpart.[57]

In medieval legends about the Apostle Bartholomew the saint's formerly childless parents vow to give him to the God of Israel in thanksgiving, but the devil replaces the beautiful infant with an ugly, black baby, who, in one version, causes the death of four nurses.[58] A more medieval setting is provided for St. Laurence, whose father, a "pagan king" in Spain, converted to Christianity in the hopes of begetting an heir, but when Laurence was born the devil stole him and replaced him with an evil child, causing his parents to abandon their new faith. The real baby was then left in a tree by the devil, recovered by a pope, and entrusted to a baron; he learned from taunting playmates that he was a foundling, and set out to find his natal parents. He did locate them, they recognized him instantly when they beheld him, and he even managed to reconvert them.[59]

At a structural level these are reversals of the topos of the Virgin's removing a child from a convent, since an evil being conveys a child *to* a religious setting. In one story the bishop[60] pronounces himself delighted to be able to have a child without sin: an intricate mirroring of the abbess who was horrified to have begotten a child

---

vais, *Bibliotheca mundi seu speculum majoris Vincenti Burgundi* 4 [Graz, 1965], *Speculum historialie* 7.115, pp. 263–64). In the latter, the pair had already reared enough children, and wished to have no more: "De l'enfant que le Déable vouloit emporter" (*Les Miracles,* 2.205–23).

57. For other versions, see Tubach, *Index,* nos. 975, 1582.

58. "Dit is die geboerte des heilighien gloriosen apostels sinte Bertholomeus gheboren van coninclijken gheslechte" (ed. de Gaiffier, app. 2, 185–88, from a fifteenth-century Flemish manuscript). The story is set in the past, of course, as is the life of St. Stephen, the first Christian martyr, also stolen by the devil, and left at the door of a monastery, a bishop's door, or in the desert, according to various versions: all seem to be associations with oblation, despite the ancient (and largely Jewish) milieu of the tale ("Ystoria nativitatis et educationis beati Stephani prothomartyris," ed. de Gaiffier, app. 1, 181–84). In one version, he leaves the monastery when older, but a painting shows him tonsured at this time (ibid., fig. 4).

59. *Gesta Romanorum* 201 (Oesterly, app. 5, pp. 612–14); discussion in de Gaiffier, pp. 175–76.

60. Characterized as *pontifex,* although he brings Stephen up as a Jew: see "Ystoria," p. 182.

immorally.[61] More significantly, stories like these and related folk-lore about "changelings" encouraged the belief that the devil might replace a good child with a bad one, for whom parents need feel no moral responsibility. Such notions might easily excuse or even inspire the abandonment of a troublesome child, whom parents could take to be a dangerous "changeling." It is striking that the motif almost exclusively involves legitimate children of married couples, among whom this might be one of the most common inspirations for exposing.[62] In *Wolfdietrich* a father orders the death of a son born in his absence because the child's extraordinary strength suggests that he was begotten of the devil. The retainer charged with this duty is unable to comply, however, and gives the child to a woodsman and his wife to bring up as their own.[63]

Most of the many known folk remedies for forcing restoration of the original child involved abandonment of some sort,[64] and although in stories they always work, in realms not ruled by authors they undoubtedly had less happy results much of the time. When they failed in real life the child was lost,[65] though the family was probably nonetheless relieved to be rid of the evil "replacement." Guibert of Nogent assumed that the devil was causing the disrup-

61. "Deus meus, gratias tibi ago, quia dedisti mihi unum filium sine peccato" (ibid.).

62. In at least two of the fourteenth-century tellings of the life of Constance (an inspiration for Chaucer's "Man of Law's Tale") the heroine is alleged by her mother-in-law to have given birth to a monstrous and "inhuman" child and is therefore exiled with the child (see Trivet's *Life of Constance*, ed. Margaret Schlauch, in *The Man of Law's Tale: Sources and Analogues of Chaucer's Canterbury Tales*, ed. W. F. Bryan and Germain Dempster [New York, 1958] 165–81; John Gower, *Confessio amantis*, 587–1080, ed. Schlauch, 181–93).

63. The idea of killing the child originated, however, with courtiers, and there are narrative reasons for the fate of the child other than parental discomfort. For the text, see either *Wolfdietrich* A, ed. Hermann Schneider (Halle, 1931) (Altdeutsche Textbibliothek, 28), part 1, or *Ortnit und die Wolfdietriche*, cited in note 25, above.

64. "Sweeping it out of the house, laying it on a manure-heap, throwing it into a stream, and placing it in a grave" are all methods of dealing with a changeling described by Macculloch (cited above, note 54), p. 359: all highly suggestive of abandonment. Cf. Haffter, "The Changeling," p. 57: "[The changeling] must be exposed at a crossroads at midnight or on the beach of the water whence it came." Replacement of a good child with a sickly or evil infant was one of the misfortunes St. Guinefort, the holy greyhound, was expected to cure: Schmitt, *The Holy Greyhound*.

65. Macculloch (*Encyclopedia of Religion and Ethics*) cites cases of children being placed in ovens and severely burned as late as the nineteenth century.

tive behavior of a child his mother took in, and admired her for not "shutting him out of the house"—as if this would have been the standard reaction.[66]

Literature also mirrors the sort of abandonment that Guibert himself suffered when his mother entered religious life: in Gautier d'Arras's *Ille et Galeron* a noble lady leaves two boys and a girl to enter a convent in fulfillment of a vow made while she was gravely ill (a likely circumstance), but the children are subsequently cared for by their father and a loving stepmother.[67] (Cf. the real incident, cited above, where the father also entered religious life.) Bernier, on the other hand, a bastard child in *Raoul de Cambrai,* is truly abandoned by his mother when she enters a convent.[68]

The sale of children receives literary attention, although less frequently than other forms of abandonment because it is relatively difficult to portray sympathetically. It nearly always affects legitimate children, and although it is not depicted as wrong, the lengths to which some writers go to justify it suggest a profound ambivalence. In Gautier d'Arras's *Éracle* a widow sells her son along with her other possessions to ensure her husband's entry into paradise, but later bitterly regrets having done so (lines 579ff.).[69] Gautier's tale

66. "Numquam tamen proinde puerum domo exclusit" (1.18, Labande, p. 156). But note that changeling stories might also allow parents of defective children to retain them without incurring opprobrium for illicit sexual activity: they could claim that the devil had brought the child. Haffter ("The Changeling," p. 57) notes that "This mishap was no fault of the parents, provided they at least took the necessary precautions. . . ."

67. Ed. E. Löseth (Paris, 1890) in *Oeuvres de Gautier d'Arras* 2. In Marie de France's *Eliduc* a spouse also enters religious life, and the husband contracts a second marriage, as in *Ille et Galeron,* but there are no children involved, and the motivations are dissimilar. Other literary depictions of stepmothers are less benign: in addition to *Guillaume de Palerne,* see Irish saints' lives (VSH 1.78–79 ["Vita sancti Berachi," 10]), the *Gesta Romanorum* (tale 112, and Apollonius), and Saxo Grammaticus (*The History of the Danes,* trans. Peter Fisher [Totowa, N.J., 1979], p. 43), all of which recount the machinations against their stepchildren of wicked stepmothers. In Marie de France's *Yonec* a man kills his stepfather.

68. Ed. P. Meyer and A. Longnon (Paris, 1882), lines 384–85, 1873–78; on being a bastard: 1688–92. He is tormented for this: 1655, 1661, 1699, 3618, etc. See discussion in Régine Colliot, "Enfants et enfance dans Raoul de Cambrai," *L'Enfant au Moyen Age,* pp. 233–52. In *Mai und Beaflor* (see note 41, above) a father places his only daughter with an unrelated couple after her mother dies, but this is not really abandonment, since he visits her constantly. Indeed, the point of the story is that he pays too much attention to her.

69. Ed. Guy Raynaud de Lage (Paris, 1976). The sale of Éracle is a small part of the story: his miraculous gift—to recognize the true value of horses, gems, and

is set in seventh-century Italy, and in the German retelling (*Eraclius*) this fact is exploited as explanation of the sale, which, according to the author, was customary among Romans (655–74).[70] Even so, the mother first obtains permission from the son himself (675–706), who was between five and ten at the time.

A thirteenth-century fabliau, however, makes no pretense of setting its events in distant climes or ages. It deals with a contemporary problem: the desperate plight of an old knight who has pawned his son to a moneylender. The son is ultimately rescued by a monk, with money entrusted to him to buy provisions for his monastery. The only moral issue is whether the monk ought to have used the money for this purpose (a miracle upholds his decision); the action of the knight in pawning his own child is depicted simply as an aspect of outrageous misfortune.[71] In the contemporary *Cántigas* of Alfonso X of Castile, a mother pawns her son to a moneylender, but the Virgin Mary intervenes to rescue him: again there is no indication of moral failing—indeed, the widow's fiscal plight is the consequence of her having spent too much on "good works."[72]

In the late-thirteenth-century *Wilhelm von Wenden*, the hero sells his two infant children to Christian merchants because they are a burden to his wife: the twins have been born in a meadow while the parents are on their way to the Holy Land. Although he lies to his

---

women (*sic*)—is the major focus. For discussion of the sources of the fable and Gautier's use of them, see Anthime Fourrier, *Le Courant réaliste dans le roman en France au Moyen Age* 1: *Les Débuts (XII siècle)* (Paris, 1960), pp. 210–75, 510–11. A similar story is known in many other languages: see, e.g., for Russian, A. Wesselofsky, "Eracles und die russischen Lieder von Ivan dem Kaufmannssohne," in "Beiträge zur Erklärung des russischen Heldenepos," *Archiv für slavische Philologie* 3 (1879) 549–93, pp. 561–87; or in Italian, L. Francia, *Novellistica* 1 (Milan, 1924) 26–52. In an Arabic version, the son sells his father (cited in Fourrier, p. 217, n. 156).

70. *Eraclius,* ed. Harald Graef, in *Quellen und Forschungen* 50 (Strassburg, 1883); a work of the early thirteenth century.

71. British Library ms Additional 32678 (S. XIII), folios 5–8; for a published version of this story, see Legrand D'Aussy, *Fabliaux ou contes, fables et romans du XIIe et du XIIIe siècle* (Paris, 1829) 5.159–64. Note that the monk who redeemed the boy had himself been a merchant before entering the order. Debt slavery was permitted under many Roman and Germanic law codes: see, e.g., above, p. 293.

72. *Cántigas* 62 and 63. Literary dependence is possible, since the widow is specifically identified as a "woman of France," although many other characters in the *Cántigas* are also French.

wife about it and tells her that he has sent them to the country to nurse (lines 2355–58), there is no implication that his action was immoral; on the contrary, the parents are praised throughout the poem.[73]

Most of these same themes occur in Scandinavian literature, but for several reasons this body of clues needs to be assessed separately. The Scandinavians had traditions, customs, attitudes, and even laws about abandonment somewhat different from other Europeans, partly because of differences in social structure and geography, partly because they joined the religious mainstream half a millennium after most of Europe. Their literature, moreover, affords the modern investigator particularly scant opportunity to perform conventional triage to separate the "historical" cases from the "fictional" ones, or "original" from "derivative" themes: the corpus of sagas interweaves invented and commemorative, contemporary and traditional materials so organically that the enterprise of distinguishing them is to a large extent counterproductive. Distinctions in reliability can be made among the sagas according to genre (family, kings', heroic, etc.), but most of the best known and most important sagas were composed in the thirteenth century to celebrate events of the distant past, and generally incorporated an extensive oral tradition.[74] The fact of abandonment in a particular narrative

73. Ulrich von Etzenbach, *Wilhelm von Wenden,* ed. Hans-Friedrich Rosenfeld (Berlin, 1957) (Deutsche Texte Mittelalters, 49). This story may be related to Chrétien de Troyes's *Guillaume d'Angleterre,* in which an exiled royal couple give birth in the forest. There are parallels (e.g., the role of merchants in both) but also significant differences: only one child is lost in the former, and accidentally (although the mother has threatened to eat them). R. Colliot ("Un Thème de la littérature médiévale: 'L'Enfant de la forêt,'" *Annales de la Faculté des Lettres et Sciences humaines d'Aix* 31, 1 [1964] 137–59) discusses the topos of the child in the forest, although the "littérature médiévale" of the title should be understood to apply exclusively to French texts; relevant works in other languages (e.g., *Wilhelm*) are ignored.

74. For translations of sagas, the reader may consult Donald Fry, *Norse Sagas Translated into English: A Bibliography* (New York, 1980) (AMS Studies in the Middle Ages, 3); wherever possible I have listed chapter numbers as well as pages to facilitate reference to translations. The sagas are traditionally understood to constitute four genres: kings', family (*Islendingasögur*), heroic (*Fornaldarsögur*), and romantic (*Riddarasögur*), of which the last two, in the view of most scholars, are less factual than the first two, although they may provide clues about attitudes. This is not to say that kings' and family sagas are necessarily trustworthy on all details. For a particularly lucid discussion of these issues, see Karras, *Slavery and Society,* pp. 178–83. For more detail, see *Old Norse-Icelandic Literature: A Critical Guide,* ed. Carol Clover and John Lindow (Ithaca, 1985) (Islandica, 45); Paul Schach, *Icelandic*

384 · The Kindness of Strangers

may therefore reflect historical or mythological lore, whereas the particulars of method and social attitude often seem to arise from the composer's own social milieu. By happy coincidence, the need to treat this literature separately makes it possible to control continental sources with a body of clues independent of both European and of antique literary traditions;[75] and the comparison reveals an impressive consistency.

Both historical[76] and literary sagas include nearly all of the same motifs about abandonment that occur in high medieval literature from the rest of Europe.[77] The pregnant abbess and the theft by the devil comprise the notable exceptions (although there is a mundane analogy of the "changeling" story: see below, p. 389). In *Vatnsdœla saga*[78] (an early family saga) a man's wife insists that his illegitimate child be exposed; the baby is, in fact, "hidden" (*fólgit*), as if the aim were to prevent rather than facilitate his rescue, but a relative considers this "ill done" (*illa gert*), rescues the child, and brings him up as a gesture of thanks to God ("He who made the sun") for curing his brother of fits (chap. 37, pp. 59–60). Thorkel is three when his "foster father" (*fostri hans*) dies, and is then cared for by his great-uncle, who assumes the same designation.[79] What is perhaps most interesting in this story is that although Thorkel is informally adopted by relatives, and everyone knows who his parents are, his father refuses to acknowledge paternity, and the child is brought up as someone else's until age twelve, when the father agrees to accept him as his son if he will slay a rival (42, pp. 67–69). Thorkel does

Sagas (Boston, 1984); or Glauser, *Isländische Märchensagas* (about the *Riddarasögur* in particular, which are not treated in Schach). On their utility for social history see the sage comments of Jenny Jochens, "The Church and Sexuality in Medieval Iceland"; cf. Jesse Byock, *Feud in the Icelandic Saga* (Berkeley, 1982).

75. Classical influences can be noted in the later genres, e.g., *Riddarasögur,* but not generally before this, and I have used the later materials sparingly, trying to avoid questions of borrowing.

76. By which I mean, generally, family and kings' sagas: see discussion in the works cited above.

77. Including ambiguous cases: in *Bandamanna saga* (ed. Guðni Jónsson [Reykjavik, 1936] [IF 7] chap. 1) Odd leaves home at twelve because he and his father cannot get along; though the story is not really about abandonment, it shares aspects of it (e.g., a child on his own who becomes a great figure).

78. Ed. Guðbrandr Vigfússon and Theodor Möbius in *Fornsögur* (Leipzig, 1860) (or Einar Sveinsson [Reykjavik, 1939] [IF 8]). References below are to the former; chapter designations are common.

79. Chaps. 38 (p. 61), 43 (p. 70), and 44 (p. 71).

so, and returns to his natal home, but when his father dies his legitimate brothers divide the inheritance and Thorkel gets nothing (43,
p. 70). His own loyalties also seem to rank natal ancestry low: when
Christianity is presented to him he declines it on the grounds that he
would not wish to have a faith different from that of his foster father
(Thorir, who first saved him; 46, p. 77). Yet when he is mocked for
his background by another family, his own kin support him, and he
becomes a great chieftain among his people (44–45, pp. 71–75): another foundling who rose to greatness, with some distinctly Scandinavian touches.

An illegitimate child in a later, more literary work, the *þáttr*
(short story) of Thorstein Oxfoot, is exposed at the order of his
uncle, Thorkel (not to be confused with the one above), in whose
household his mother, a mute, was living when she became pregnant by a visiting warrior (who denied responsibility and abandoned her). When the uncle

> was informed of the news that his sister was delivered of the
> child . . . he was violently angry and said that they should ex-
> pose [*út bera*] the child, for it was legal at that time for poor
> people [*úríkra manna*] to expose children if they wanted to, al-
> though they did not think it was a good thing to do. Thorkel
> summoned Freystein the slave and commanded him to do away
> with the boy, but he professed himself unwilling until Thorkel
> spoke angrily to him.[80]

The slave places the baby, with pork in his mouth,[81] in a small covered shelter at the base of a tree in the woods. He is retrieved four
days later and reared by a neighbor well aware of his origins, who

80. *Þáttr Þorsteins Uxafóts,* in *Flateyjarbók* 204, p. 252. Resistance to abandonment is more likely a characteristic of the author's own time (probably the thirteenth century) and imagination than of the tenth century, in which the story is set,
although Thorstein himself later refers to Freystein's part in his abandonment as a
"worthy deed" (*launa verdr,* p. 254).

81. Obviously to nourish and / or quiet the infant; not, I think, to prevent his
being found. Procopius reported in the sixth century that the women of Scandinavia left their newborn infants in skins with marrow in their mouths as they
went hunting, where the aim was clearly not to keep them from being found but to
placate and feed them: *History of the Wars,* ed. H. B. Dewing (London, 1968),
6.15.22, p. 420. Moreover, exposed children were known for their wailing: "to cry
like an exposed child" (*útburðr*) is an old Icelandic saying.

nonetheless specifically pretends that the child is his own.[82] Although his foster parents love him very much, when Thorstein learns of his origins, he goes to live in his natal household,[83] and, like so many literary foundlings, subsequently becomes famous and successful.

As in its continental counterpart, incest figures in Scandinavian literature ("historical" and "fictional") as both the cause and effect of abandonment. In Jómsvíkinga saga,[84] a fairly early king's saga, a German earl who has begotten a child with his sister orders the baby exposed, but also commands the servants to wait to see what becomes of the infant, who is left in a forest with tokens of silk and gold and a cloth knotted in the branches of the tree above it, presumably to attract attention. The baby is brought to the childless king of Denmark, a friend of the father's, who names him Knut ("knot"), and, not knowing his background, brings him up as his own son.[85] He even bequeaths to him the kingdom, establishing the royal house of Denmark through an abandoned child, a fact apparently known to his subjects.[86] Since these events predate the first Danish monarch for whom there is independent documentation,[87] it is impossible to verify or discount the story, but it is certainly inter-

82. Note the realistic detail, unrelated to the plot, that when Krum finds the baby the pork has fallen out of his mouth: Flateyjarbók 204, p. 252. Note also that the storyteller expects the reader to believe that the baby has survived for four days. The baby in Vatnsdæla saga had also survived for a number of days (chap. 37). This seems to argue against Clover's claim (see reference, above, in Introduction, note 107) that the Nordic winter would preclude the survival of infants in Scandinavia.

83. Flateyjarbók 204, p. 252.

84. Jómsvíkinga saga, Blake (also in Fornmanna Sögur 11 [Copenhagen, 1828]), chap. 1.

85. Blake's translation (p. 2) is misleading: "Konungr fekk honum fóstr" in this case surely means the king brought him up ("fostered him"), not "found foster parents for him": in the very next sentence the boy is referred to as fóstra sinum. (On the other hand, MS 291 does seem to suggest fostering by someone else [see Jómsvíkinga saga efter AM. 291, 40, ed. C. af Petersens (Copenhagen, 1882), chap. 1], and Blake may be conflating the two. In any event, "adopted him" for "ok kallaði sinn son" ("called him son") suggests a formality the text does not express.

86. The manuscript traditions vary: in one, Gorm simply gives the kingdom to his foster son; in another he asks his counselors and relatives for approval; they must have known Knut's origins (see Fornmanna edition, pp. 2–3).

87. Gorm ruled from approximately 940 to 950. Gorm is Knut's foster father's name in the saga, and Knut passes it on to his his own son, as if the descent were biological (Blake, chap. 2, p. 2).

esting as an expression of attitudes about incest and abandonment, and the prospects for foundlings.

An even more arresting instance is related in *Hrólfs saga Kraka*.[88] Queen Olof of Germany feels a profound lack of affection toward the daughter she bears after being raped; she manages to conceal the birth, names the child after a dog (Yrsa), and abandons her to a shepherd family, who force her to work from age twelve (p. 22). Her father encounters her unknowingly in a forest when she is thirteen, falls in love with her, marries her, and the two live quite happily together with great respect and love (pp. 23, 29, 34–35). When Olof apprises them of the truth, Yrsa is appalled, says their situation is "unexampled" (*ödæmi*), and immediately returns to Germany with her mother. Her father, however, would prefer to continue the relationship, and in fact tries to recover her. The author of the tale implicitly suggests that theirs was a happier relationship than Yrsa's subsequent marriage to King Athils of Sweden, who ultimately kills the father and is reproached by Yrsa for slaying her "husband" (p. 98). The son of Yrsa and her father, Hrólf, is the hero of the tale, and the circumstances of his birth have no effect on the remainder of his life or story; no stigma of any sort seems to pursue him.

Legitimate children are also abandoned in Norse writings, for a variety of reasons from gender to marital discord. In *Gunnlaugs saga ormstungu* a husband instructs his wife to abandon the child she is expecting if it turns out to be a girl, and the writer repeats the cliché that it was the custom "when the land was pagan" for men with few possessions and many dependents to expose children. But this is irrelevant in the case at issue, because, as the wife herself objects, her husband is wealthy.[89] The mother cannot bring herself to comply once the baby is born—"For I turn such loving eyes toward this child that I am quite unwilling to have it exposed"[90]—and sends the baby to her sister-in-law in another settlement, who arranges to have her brought up by a poor family. A joyful *anagnorisis* eventually ensues, in which the father professes himself delighted that his wife and sister have rectified his "thoughtlessness" (*vanhyggju*), and the parents bring the daughter home and rear her with "great honor and love."

88. Ed. D. Slay (Copenhagen, 1960) (Editiones Arnamagnæanae, Series B, 1).

89. *Gunnlaugs saga ormstungu,* ed. Sigurður Nordal and Guðni Jónsson (Reykjavik, 1938) (IF 3), chap. 3, pp. 55–56.

90. "Þeim ástaraugum renni ek til barns þessa, at víst eigi nenni ek, at þat sé út borit" (ibid., p. 56).

The richness and credibility of detail in Norse treatments of abandonment are particularly striking in *Finnboga saga,* a late (probably fourteenth-century) composition drawing on earlier materials. Asbjorn tells his wife to expose the child she will bear during his planned absence, whatever its gender, because he is angry at her for giving their daughter Thorny away in marriage while he was absent before. She responds with the familiar topos that "a man as wise and rich as you are should not do this. For this would be an unheard-of thing even if a poor man were to do it, but all the more so since you do not lack goods."[91] But the credibility of her claim that this is "unheard-of" is considerably undermined by the author's statement that when she complied with her husband's order, she had the baby prepared for abandonment "as was the custom," in a stone shelter with pork in his mouth.[92]

On the other hand, when the baby is found and brought home to its "foster mother," the latter herself has trouble believing that it is the child Thorgerd was expecting, since it would be "unheard-of" for so prosperous a couple to abandon a child. She and her husband pretend the boy, Urðarkauttr, is theirs, although people wonder about this, both because they are elderly and because the child does not resemble them.[93] The foster mother tries to prevent his playing with the servants in the household of his natal parents, but he does so anyway, and this ultimately leads to questions about his origins. Asked to send for his parents to clear the matter up, he touchingly refuses: "I know that you propose to get me another mother and father. They will give you no thanks for that. Moreover, I do not know that I could have a better mother or father than they."[94] The foster parents also resist coming, fearing to lose the child they love.

It is easily established that Urðarkauttr is an adopted foundling,

91. *Finnboga saga hins Ramma,* ed. Hugo Gering, 2, p. 4: "Hann mundi þat [eigi] gera sva vitr ok rikr sem þu ert. þviat þetta væri it vheyriligsta bragð þo at fatækr maðr gíorði. en nu allra hellzt er yðr skortir eck goz."

92. "Ok bua um sem vandi var á" (ibid., p. 5). The coffin is evocative of the provisions of Norwegian law cited above (see p. 293), and the detail of pork matches many other accounts of Scandinavian abandonment..

93. The child's name, Urðarkauttr, is a triple pun: it means "wild cat" (literally, "cat of the stone heap," because he was found in a pile of stones), but *urðr* also means "fate," and *köttr* has connotations of "bastard" (e.g., in *Helgakviða Hundingsbana* 1.18), so that the name also suggests "bastard of fate," although he was legitimate.

94. *Finnboga saga* 6, p. 11.

and that Asbjorn's wife abandoned her child at about the time he was found, but this is not accepted as proof that he is Asbjorn's— suggesting a general assumption that other parents might have exposed children around the same time—and in the end the two most likely paternal candidates jointly contribute to setting up Urðarkauttr with livestock, which are entrusted to his foster parents. The boy goes to live with his natal family and is apparently regarded as belonging to their (higher) social status thereafter (*upp dubbaðr*; 6, p. 13).

Married couples in other literary sagas also abandon children. A queen abandons twins who are so dark and ugly that she is ashamed of them, by forcing a servant to exchange for them her own beautiful son (a motif reminiscent of both *Fresne* and changeling stories, although not likely to have been influenced by either); ironically, the handsome child turns out to be cowardly, and the ugly twins to be brave and noble, a twist of fate which subtly draws attention to the optimistic prospects of foundlings, and—somewhat paradoxically—to the importance of lineage and blood.[95] A maternal uncle forces the exposing of a girl after the mother died in childbirth because he objected to the marriage. One king throws the children of his wife's previous marriage into the sea; another (Richard of England) warns his wife to expose any child born during his absence.[96]

A father in the late romance *Sigrgarðs saga ok Valbrands* sells his cherished firstborn son to strangers for a magical harp;[97] but, although sales of freeborn persons are otherwise common in Scandinavian literature, the sale of children by parents is rare.[98]

Like most eyewitness accounts, literary testimony has to be both privileged and carefully scrutinized. Not only the witness's general credibility, but where he happened to be standing, what his views

95. *Þáttr af Geirmundi Heljar-skinni*, ed. Gudbrand Vigfusson, in *Sturlunga saga* (Oxford, 1871) 1.1–2.

96. *Harðar saga ok Holmverja*, ed. Guðni Jónsson (Reykjavik, 1945); *Sigrgarðs saga ok Valbrands*, ed. Agnete Loth (Copenhagen, 1965), in LMIR 5; *Ala flekks saga*, ed. Bjarni Vilhjálmsson, in *Riddarasögur* 5 (Reykjavik, 1954).

97. Ed. Loth, pp. 127–28. Cf. tale 85 in the *Gesta Romanorum*, which could conceivably be an influence on such a late romantic saga.

98. Olaf Tryggvason, for example, was captured by Vikings while his widowed mother was trying to reach her brother Sigurð; he was sold, at age three, for a "good cloak" to a man who already had a son. Olaf was "well looked after" and "greatly loved," but his uncle subsequently recognized him and bought him back

on the subject are, how long before the testimony was recorded the event took place—all such factors must be assessed before the evidence is admitted. Some high medieval literary statements about abandonment are improbable. The fact that so many foundlings are of noble ancestry, for example, is almost certainly the result of the fact that the writings in which they occur were composed by or for nobles; even the lower classes in the High Middle Ages were probably more interested in hearing about the doings of nobles than of peasants. It would not be unreasonable to infer from fiction that aristocrats sometimes exposed children, since otherwise such behavior would either be omitted from their literature or condemned as vulgar; but neither is it unreasonable to withhold such a conclusion: knights also fight dragons in high medieval literature. It is possible that some of the particulars expressed are related to real class behavior—for example, leaving silk or gold with a child to encourage better care. But it is not at all likely that nobles exposed children disproportionately or particularly.

Legitimate children probably appear in fiction as foundlings somewhat less frequently than they did in reality,[99] for the same reasons that extended treatments of love between husband and wife are rare when compared to the great number of stories about adultery. Neither disproportion discloses a historical fact, although the weight of the evidence, historical as well as literary, does support an inference that extramarital sexuality was more common during this period than it had been before, and doubtless produced unwanted children. But the preponderance in imaginative literature of relationships and births that contravene traditional norms doubtless simply reflects their greater dramatic interest. There is no reason to assume that adulterous affairs were, in absolute numbers, more common than conjugal happiness, or that abandoned children were more often illegitimate than legitimate. The poor, moreover, are rarely protagonists in this literature, and since they were one of the groups most likely to expose legitimate children, this alone could account for the comparative infrequence of the latter.

(Ólafs saga Tryggvasonar, in Snorri Sturluson, Heimskringla 1, chaps. 6 and 7). In Laxdæla saga an Irish princess is stolen and sold as a slave (ed. Sveinsson, pp. 22–28).

99. If one discounts theft by the devil, which is related to abandonment but not, strictly speaking, a form of it. However, all instances of sale involve married couples or widows.

Although in absolute numbers more boys are abandoned than girls, once one corrects (roughly, at best) for the general preponderance of males in literature, the sources do not suggest a disproportion by gender: both boys and girls are abandoned, both are recovered, both loved, and both succeed in later life.[100]

Sometimes a witness's testimony may be useful for establishing a correlation even when crucial particulars remain unclear: several bystanders could identify positively, for example, the two men involved in a brawl, even if they disagreed completely about who started it. High medieval literature establishes or corroborates the broad relationship of abandonment to its social context in various ways, while leaving details of the relationship somewhat vague.

In a great proportion of writing on the subject a connection is made with religious life: the child becomes a cleric, or is born in a convent, or is abandoned at a monastery. This may be an echo of oblation, or part of an ancient and enduring juxtaposition in the popular imagination of piety and altruism—the kindness of strangers—with parental abandonment. The notion that an evil spirit might either remove a good child from a family and replace him with a bad one, or inhabit a baby who must then be abused in some way to be restored to normal, strongly suggests a cultural circumlocution for (or subliminal recognition of) the destructive effect on family life of serious personality disorder or physical defect in children. And incest is clearly associated with abandonment in a great many literary traditions of the period, as it had been in the ancient world, and almost certainly was in real life. Medieval authors were more candid on the subject than most of their predecessors or even successors, often depicting it frankly as the cause rather than merely the accidental consequence of abandonment.

The testimony of literature is particularly eloquent on the senti-

---

100. This can only be done intuitively, since the extant documentation is no reliable indication of what was written. Sigal, "Le vocabulaire de l'enfance," pp. 141–60, found that boys constituted seventy-one percent of the total number of references to children in miracle stories of the eleventh and twelfth centuries (644 mentions of children; 462 male: p. 143), but even if this is revealing for this particular genre and time it cannot safely be extrapolated to others. Also interesting, but unsound as a basis of wider inference, is the fact that very few families in high medieval literature have many children: in the *Gesta Romanorum,* for example, hardly any parents have more than three children, and only children are very common (e.g., tales 249, 251). But these facts may all have more to do with narrative requirements than social reality.

ments involved. Legal principles, such as the termination of parental authority over abandoned children, long established in Roman law, bear lightly on the behavior and motivations of medieval parents and children in countries created by the pen, all of whom seem to acknowledge biological relationship as indissoluble and of great importance even when the kindness of strangers has created powerful and happy alternative bonds. It is not necessary to imagine that authors knew foundlings or parents who had abandoned children to accord importance to this kind of data: the fact that the writers themselves, with almost unanimous consistency, ranked juridical principles lower than traditional family structures conveys useful clues to the attitudes of their compatriots who might have exposed or adopted children.

The moral ambiguities of the relationship between abandonment and incest are pointedly drawn in much of this literature, and expose a gap between the official scholastic moral theology of the church and the ethical feelings of ordinary European Catholics. Marrying even one's own mother unintentionally should not have been a sin according to Christian ethicists of the thirteenth century, but in literature it continued long after this to constitute a heinous act, for which holy protagonists performed long and excruciating penances. This is to some extent the result of the persistence in the High and later Middle Ages of narrative structures from earlier centuries, when Christian morality drew more heavily on moral codes that ignored intention, but it is also evidence of the disjunction between the philosophically tidy morality of the Scholastics and the more direct and personal beliefs of the majority of the population, according to whom marrying a close relative was a sin (and probably a crime), no matter what the circumstances. The frequent repetition of incest as a major concern of literary witnesses also suggests an overwhelming, almost universal assumption that exposed children survived: what worried the bystanders was not that the child would perish—in which case moral and literary treatments would presumably have been significantly different—but that it would live, and come to moral harm in the course of an adulthood whose likelihood is never questioned.[101]

___

101. Important fictional characters, of course, do not die in infancy; this would deprive the story of interest. But neither do incidental children—e.g., the abandoned, illegitimate offspring of adulterous liaisons—ever die in medieval fiction, although this would make a useful plot device for characterizing the wicked-

The consistent pretense in Scandinavian literature that exposing was a practice of earlier, pagan times, or that it was confined to the poor—the second directly contradicted by actual circumstance in all of the sagas cited—could not have deceived contemporaries any more than it does the modern reader. It was a cultural myth which justified the existence of abandoned children in a society struggling to become what it was not. Hearing it precisely as they said it to each other affords the modern eavesdropper an acutely realistic view of their ambivalence about something they regretted, could not avoid, and tried to explain away.

Inventive writing is usually at its most helpful in treating modes and motives of abandonment, as has been noted in previous sections. It is like visual art in this regard: though the modern investigator may be reasonably sure that a miracle depicted in a painting never took place, he is often equally confident that the clothing and architecture used to set the stage for the drama are highly revealing of actual circumstance. Such analysis is particularly apt for medieval paintings—and stories—about the ancient world, where events of antiquity or early Christian history are often set, clothed, housed, colored, decorated, understood, and expressed in characteristically medieval ways. It seems overwhelmingly likely, for example, that the actual methods of exposure related in high medieval literature are accurate: in continental Europe, children were left in churches, hung in trees (obviously both to obviate danger from animals and to attract attention), and placed with ecclesiastical authorities or in public locations (e.g., beside well-traveled roads). Tokens were probably left with children of the prosperous, as an incentive to treat them well, and in a great many cases some indication of baptismal status was included. In the north, babies were well wrapped, sheltered, and left with pork in their mouths. The absence of tokens in Scandinavian literature is striking, and probably related to the fact that in the sagas smaller communities and closer ties are involved: exposed children are usually brought up by someone who already knows or suspects who the natal family is, frequently a relative. This occurs in southern literature and in historical sources as well (e.g., in *Milon,* and in the case in Bristol) but less often. Hostiensis says that the relatives of exposed children are "often" unknown.

---

ness of the parents. Moreover, literary assumptions about survival agree with moral writings in presupposing that the chief danger attending abandonment is that of incest, a possibility only for surviving children.

The single most characteristic feature of high medieval abandonment literature is its hopefulness. It is predicated, like its ancient antecedents, on a universal belief that exposed children not only survive but flourish; not only overcome the difficulties of being abandoned but rise through them to greatness, becoming popes, missionaries, saints, kings, founders of royal lines, and great heroes, and most often are joyfully reunited with their natal parents in the process. Usually the foster parents or guardians who find the child are wholly devoted to him, in many cases better parents than their biological counterparts.[102] To question the likelihood of these events is to overlook the real message they convey: the need of the societies that composed them, and of individuals within those societies, to believe that abandonment could result in a better life for their children, a need obviously created by an even more basic necessity—the necessity, in the absence of any other acceptable means of family limitation, of abandoning children.

102. James Schultz has pointed out that in a great many Middle High German narrative accounts of childhood biological relationship ("filiation") is terminated or disrupted, and replaced by an adoptive kinship ("affiliation"), which is usually beneficial to the child ("Filiation and Affiliation in Middle High German Narratives," read at the 22nd International Congress on Medieval Studies, Kalamazoo, Mich., May 7, 1987). "Ties of filiation are weakened or broken—by death of a parent, abduction, abandonment, exile, fosterage, oblation, or the free will of the child. But new ties are formed with others that fill the role of parents and are called parents; and these ties of affiliation enable the children to regain the status they had lost. . . . [This] is a myth that puts class and religious affiliation over family. It shows that noble birth and constant faith are invincible: they will be recognized and be able to assert themselves even when the children are completely cut off from family and society. . . ."

PART IV

THE LATER MIDDLE AGES

11

❖   ❖   ❖

CONTINUITIES AND
UNINTENDED
TRAGEDY

BETWEEN THE YEARS 1000 and 1300, child abandonment underwent several dramatic transformations. During the
eleventh and twelfth centuries, a period of unprecedented economic
prosperity and expansion, it was apparently comparatively rare in
continental Europe, except in the form of oblation, practiced mostly
by the upper classes. Poorer elements of the population appear to
have found in the burgeoning social and economic structures of the
age room to place most of their children without overtly abandoning them, although forms of "placement" such as apprenticeship
and "fostering" may have differed little from outright abandonment. Since the Western moral tradition did not condemn it, it remained largely unopposed except in Scandinavia, where a complex
ethical reaction did disparage exposing infants in some contexts.
Both paradoxically and understandably, this was the area of Europe
where abandonment was most common throughout this period.

As the spectacular growth of the twelfth century slowed and became less pronounced in the thirteenth, a much more varied picture
emerged. Oblation waned notably, and secular abandonment re-
appeared as a widespread social problem affecting all social classes
and manifesting itself in both traditional and novel forms. Although
both church and state began to pay more attention to it, absolute
prohibitions were rare and local. The general import of Christian
morality, both civil and ecclesiastical, focused on the consequences

of the abandonment rather than the morality of the act itself: children must be baptized properly, no matter what the circumstances of their birth; parents may not reclaim; efforts must be made to forestall death or accidental incest.

A network of nonnatal parental structures[1]—particularly "spiritual kindred" such as godparents—was consolidated and more clearly defined during these centuries, along with points of dogma bearing on childhood and on parental responsibility. But these were, by and large, exquisitely ambivalent in their impact: the Scholastic decision to place unbaptized children in limbo, for example, removed both any hope that *expositi* might enter heaven if they died before being christened and any fear that they would be consigned to hell.[2] Emphasis on the duty of Christians to baptize their children was probably balanced by much more critical attention to conjugal infractions, rendering parents more anxious about illegitimate and even unhealthy children as reflections on their own past acts. Expanding the family to include spiritual kindred increased the pool of caretakers, but also vastly complicated and often invalidated marriages, rendering many children technically illegitimate, and thus undesirable.[3]

Parents at the close of the thirteenth century were, in the end, probably in much the same situation as parents during the previous thirteen hundred years. Resources, though greater in absolute terms, seemed more and more limited as the vast increase in population filled the cities and countryside, and there was more extravagant

1. I deliberately refrain from using the more common expression "artificial family structures" because it is not clear to me that "nuclear" families are any more "natural" than other kindred patterns, even those not established by biological heritage.

2. At least among those made aware of it by local preachers, a separate and largely insoluble question. There had been a general supposition on the part of theologians from Augustine through the twelfth century that unbaptized infants resided in hell, even if they were not actively tormented. This was increasingly unsatisfactory to the High Middle Ages, and St. Thomas Aquinas articulated (*De malo* 5.3; *Commentary on the Sentences* 2.33, q. 2, a. 2) a belief in "limbo"—a place where unbaptized infants enjoy a limited happiness without the beatific vision afforded the saved—which became the received wisdom among theologians, although not *de fide*. For its relation to more popular beliefs about the afterlife, which may have been partly responsible for it, see Jacques LeGoff, *The Birth of Purgatory*, trans. Arthur Goldhammer (Chicago, 1984).

3. See above, note 76 of chapter 9.

variation in means from family to family. There was no widely known method of limiting birth without forgoing conjugal relations, which presumably enjoyed their enduring personal appeal and, in addition, were adduced by the prevailing morality as the sole purpose and justification of marriage. If they could not afford to retain a child—because they had too many to feed, too many to marry, too many to grant property to; because he would bring shame upon one or both parents; because he was defective or "possessed" of malevolent temperament—they, or some of them at least, abandoned him.

They could do so with optimism, because a host of cultural artifacts (oral, written, and even pictorial) held out the unchallenged hope that the child would survive, would overcome the circumstances of his birth, would become someone worthwhile, perhaps great, and might even someday be reunited with parents. Whether this was more than a hope remains one of the most glaring omissions from the historical record. The testimony of literary witnesses seems so clearly to meet a need that the investigator must maintain skepticism about their accuracy, and the historical record preserves little specific data to confirm or deny the probability of a happier life for abandoned children. That they sometimes died is manifest from a few legal and moral statements, but the bulk of commentary on the phenomenon seems to be predicated on the assumption that they survived. What became of them remains utterly unknown, except for the general connection of foundlings with religion, which may be a reliable indication that many of them entered religious life or at least became dependents of churches or monasteries. And this would be a "happy ending" by the standards of the age. Almost certainly some simply adopted the names of foster parents and pursued ordinary lives among the vast, unrecorded populations of the city and countryside.[4]

---

4. In the fourteenth century, for example, the "adopted" son of a man with no biological heirs had to undertake a long legal action to retain his inheritance, because there was apparently no legal record or recognition of his "adoption." The circumstances of the adoption are not specified beyond the remark "le dit feu avoit norry le dit clerc et l'avoit institué son heretier en son testament," and the assertion that the litigant, a clerk, was the child of two unmarried persons: *Recueil*, 1333, vol. 11, no. 169, pp. 388–94. This is a particularly revealing instance, because the crown does not seem to be informed even of its own rulings about the legality of "natural" children inheriting, and the case is finally resolved through a compro-

For the most part, the High Middle Ages integrated Christian moral concern surrounding abandonment (e.g., about baptism or the possibilities of incest) with relief mechanisms for parents and encouragement of the beneficent intervention of strangers, both of which had been persistent in Europe for more than a millennium.

Some of this picture remained unchanged in later medieval and early modern Europe.[5] Children continued to be exposed at the doors of churches and in other public places,[6] and in the fifteenth century parents were still leaving salt or tokens with their abandoned offspring to indicate ancestry and baptismal status.[7] Although for-

---

mise not following either general French law or the specific concessions the crown had previously granted to Poitou: the adopted son is allowed to retain his inheritance but must pay the king a fixed sum three times a year. Cf. the fifteenth-century case (*Recueil*, vol. 11, no. 909, pp. 32–35) of a twelve-year-old boy ambiguously designated "povre enfant orfelin," who is apparently the ward of the entire community.

5. The classic study of this period and its troubles is that of J. K. Huizinga, *The Waning of the Middle Ages* (London, 1924, and many subsequent editions). H. A. Miskimin, *The Economy of Early Renaissance Europe, 1300–1460* (Englewood Cliffs, N.J., 1969) is the best survey of economic developments. For more detailed and recent approaches to the social history, see, *inter alia*, M. Mollat and P. Wolff, *The Popular Revolutions of the Late Middle Ages* (London, 1972); Gordon Leff, *Heresy in the Later Middle Ages;* Richard Kieckhefer, *Unquiet Souls: Fourteenth-Century Saints and Their Religious Milieu;* Julio Valdeón Baruque, *Los conflictos sociales en el reino de Castilla en los siglos XIV y XV* (Madrid, 1975).

6. See, e.g., the account of a mother abandoning a three-year-old child on the porch of the "hostel" of the bishop of Châlons in Paris on September 6, 1336, published in *Régistre criminel de la Justice de St-Martin-des-Champs à Paris au XIVe siècle,* ed. Louis Tanon (Paris, 1877). The child "cried after her" as she fled, and she was apprehended and prosecuted, although under what sanction is unclear, since neither civil nor ecclesiastical law in the area included an unequivocal penalty for abandonment. Even children destined for foundling homes were abandoned at churches well into the fifteenth century: see, e.g., Richard Trexler, "The Foundlings of Florence," p. 272. For monasteries, see Lorcin, "Retraite," and Schimmelpfennig, "*Ex fornicatione nati,*" p. 34.

7. For example, Ridolfo Livi (*La Schiavitù domestica nei tempi di mezzo e nei moderni*, p. 227, n. 1) publishes a receipt for a foundling accepted at the Innocenti in Florence in December of 1445, the child of a student and a female slave (not the student's), who was wrapped in distinctive cloth and "had a bit of salt on his neck as a sign that he was not baptized." Many of the entries indicate such tokens and most record whether the baptismal status is known or not, as the initial rubric in the register requires (Livi, pp. 226–27). Cf. a similar case of a child deposited at the *maison-Dieu* of Amiens in 1408 with salt to indicate he required baptism, cited in Martin-Doisy, "Enfants," p. 460.

mal oblation became less common,[8] especially for males, the placing of boys in "minor" seminaries made a kind of abandonment to
the church possible well into modern times. Such boys usually remained in contact with their parents, but they ceased being a part of
the family in terms of daily responsibility, and they were removed
from the pool of potential parents of the next generation—helping
to maintain demographic equilibrium.[9] The same was true of nuns,
who often served as teachers to the next generation of children sent
away to religious boarding school—a parallel to "fostering" in the
early Middle Ages. Many of these persons were "destined" for religious life from infancy in the minds of their families, for religious,
economic, or personal reasons; and although the church had taken
strong measures during the thirteenth century to guarantee that religious vocation always involved free consent,[10] it would be naïve to
imagine that children were actually in a position to resist the desires
of their families or the communities to which they were given.
Even in the nineteenth century Manzoni could poignantly examine
the reality of "free choice" for a girl given to a convent.[11]

The lower classes continued to abandon their children in great
number to more prosperous households as servants.[12] Of the ser-

8. But certainly not unknown; see, e.g., the grateful memory of his donation
by Andreas, a fifteenth-century oblate: "Cum a parentibus meis omnipotentis Dei
servitio educandus secundum regularis normam institutionis . . . traditus fuissem,
iuxta miserentis Dei pietatem. . . ." (MGH SS 12.731).

9. The demographic role of celibacy could be considerable: Trexler concludes
that thirteen percent of all females in Florence in the sixteenth century were in holy
orders ("Le célibat à la fin du Moyen Age: Les religieuses de Florence," *Annales* 27
[1972] 1329–50).

10. The decree of Santiago prohibiting priests from taking on boys to be servants was repeated half a century later at a Synod of 1309 (*Synodicon Hispanum*,
Santiago de Compostela, 4, p. 282, canon 8), suggesting that it had not worked.
Two fourteenth-century councils prohibited clerics from keeping their children
with them in monasteries.

11. *I promessi sposi*, chap. 9.

12. Such children, usually servants of the lower clergy or of modest households, appear frequently in documents of the fourteenth and fifteenth centuries,
e.g., the inquisitorial registers of Pamiers in the early fourteenth century (Jacques
Fournier, *Le Registre d'Inquisition de Jacques Fournier, Évêque de Pamiers* 1.243, 488),
discussed briefly by Emmanuel Le Roy Ladurie, *Montaillou, village occitan de 1294 à
1324*, pp. 317–21. Note the English decree of 1388 about child labor in J. Bagely and
P. Rowley, *A Documentary History of England* (London, 1966), 1.218; see also the
discussion in Barbara Hanawalt, "Childrearing Among the Lower Classes of Late
Medieval England," pp. 18–19, and *eadem*, *The Ties That Bound: Peasant Families*

vants recorded in the Florentine *catasto* of 1427, the most detailed premodern European census, more than half were under twelve.[13] In an increasingly money-based economy, poor parents "sold" the services of their offspring to the rich in arrangements which, while not technically constituting slavery, were probably little different, and resembled comparable practices in late antiquity.[14] Families

---

in Medieval England, pp. 156–68 (despite the more general implications of the title, Hanawalt confines her material and observations to the later Middle Ages). It was extremely common in Barcelona in the fifteenth century for poor parents to consign their children to labor in households of the wealthy for periods of four to twelve years, until they had a trade of their own or were married; but the extent to which this involved "abandonment" by the parents is difficult to determine; in some cases it is clear that parents retained involvement with the child, at least to the extent of approving a marriage: see, e.g., Jacques Heers, *Esclaves et domestiques,* p. 150. The infamous fifteenth-century child murderer, Gilles de Rais, was able to perpetrate his crimes on dozens—possibly hundreds—of children between the ages of seven and fifteen who were either already separated from their parents or whose parents were persuaded to part with them for their betterment in his service. This sensational subject has received little scholarly treatment since Eugène Bossard published a study of the trial (*Gilles de Rais Maréchal de France dit Barbe Bleue, 1404–1440* [Paris, 1886], translated by Reginald Hyatte as *Laughter for the Devil: The Trials of Gilles de Rais, Companion-in-Arms of Joan of Arc* [Rutherford, 1984]); Georges Bataille, *Le Procès de Gilles de Rais* (Paris, 1965) is a useful modern summary. Pierre Vallin confessed under torture in 1438 to charges that he had sacrificed his own daughter and eaten the flesh of other children as well; J. B. Russell believes both the charges and confession to be wholly false (*Lucifer: The Devil in the Middle Ages,* p. 296; cf. *idem, A History of Witchcraft* [London, 1980], pp. 78–79).

13. Fewer than 25 percent are adults: Herlihy and Klapisch, p. 136. This is the more striking when one takes into account that the census rarely records servants of any sort, and usually underreports girls (ibid., pp. 135 and 245), so there were probably more children and more girls than it discloses. Boys under twelve are 32.1 percent of the total; girls under twelve are only 23.1 percent. An additional 30.3 percent are boys and girls from thirteen to seventeen. In every age cohort, boys given to service outnumber girls, but this is probably due to underreporting of female servants.

14. This was especially common in Italy (and sometimes called the "Venetian custom"), where such children were known as *anime:* see Verlinden, "L'Enfant esclave," pp. 120–24, and his "La législation vénitienne au bas Moyen Age en matière d'esclavage," pp. 154–59; Heers, *Esclaves,* pp. 156, 231–32; Guido Ruggiero, *The Boundaries of Eros: Sex Crime and Sexuality in Renaissance Venice* (New York, 1985), chap. 7, esp. pp. 151–54; and the cases of fourteenth-century Serbs selling the labor of their children to Italians, in *Acta et Diplomata Res Albaniae Mediae Aetatis Illustrantia,* ed. L. Thallóczy (Vienna, 1913), discussed by Durham (*Some Tribal Origins,* pp. 190–91). Herlihy (*Medieval and Renaissance Pistoia,* p. 98, n. 35)

were driven to abandon, as before, by poverty, by illegitimacy, by defect or ill health of children, and by the church's continued insistence that infant deformity resulted from parental incontinence.[15] Clerics themselves went on producing illegitimate children, which they also went on abandoning.[16] Parents were still said to eat children during famines—and one is no more sure than before whether these should be viewed as a literary topos or reflections of actual incidents.[17] Some extreme religious movements clearly did encourage

---

notes the presence of many unrelated children in the households of the wealthy, some kept specifically "per lavorare," but does not seem to take this into account when speculating on the causes of the "low birth rate" of the poor. In *Tuscans*, he and Klapisch pay much more attention to this phenomenon (e.g., pp. 136–39). The Venetian *Consiglio dei Pregali* tried to regulate the practice in 1386 to prevent it from becoming a form of slavery, declaring that such children were legally free Christians (discussed in Verlinden, "L'Enfant esclave").

15. On the first and second, see material about foundlings, below; for the second it should, nonetheless, be noted that many parents—even peasants—did rear illegitimate children: see, for example, cases cited by Zvi Razi, *Life, Marriage and Death in a Medieval Parish*, pp. 65–71, 138, 139. On bastards among the middle class, see also David Nicholas, *Domestic Life of a Medieval City*, chap. 8. Nobles in many ages have recognized illegitimate children: John of Gaunt recognized four, and succeeded in having them accepted into the peerage; compare cases of legitimation, cited below, notes 16 and 73. For the persistence of ideas about parental sexual behavior and deformity, see, *inter alia*, Bayerische Staatsbibliothek clm 18404 (s. XIV), folio 128r, forbidding the usual constellation of sexual activities (during lactation, menstruation, etc.) and predicting the birth of leprous, lunatic, or possessed children from those engaging in such acts. A. Tenenti ("Témoignages Toscans sur la mort des enfants autour de 1400," ADH [1973] 133–34) cites a case in which parents stopped seeing their dying child and ultimately even abandoned the house.

16. Two children of clerics were brought to a foundling hospital in Florence in 1412: see Trexler, "Foundlings," p. 271; cf. Schimmelpfenning, "Ex fornicatione nati." The king of France granted legitimation in August of 1340 to all three sons of the Bishop of Poitiers, and ennobled the eldest: Archives Nationales, Reg. JJ 72, n. 314, folio 231, published in *Recueil*, vol. 13, no. 273, pp. 177–79; cf. a similar letter legitimating a cleric and his brother a year later: ibid., no. 285, pp. 204–5.

17. Johannes de Trokelow, *Annales* (*Chronica monasterii sancti Albani*), ed. H. T. Riley (London, 1866), p. 94. Hanawalt cites this both in "The Female Felon," p. 260, and in *The Ties That Bound*, p. 102, with suitable reservations in the latter about its accuracy. Cf. note 12, above, for charges of cannibalism in France. That some parents were desperate during this period is certain, but cannibalism hardly seems the only option: in 1374, for example, the French crown issued a full pardon to Jean Mosset for stealing five and a half bushels of grain from a mill to feed his wife and three small children: *Recueil*, vol. 19, no. 578, pp. 351–53.

treatment of children that seems savage by modern standards: in a haunting incident from the fourteenth-century inquisitorial records of Pamiers, a father instructed his wife to impose on their infant daughter the "ultimate fast" (*endura*) of the Catharan religious movement to which they belonged—that is, to deny the child milk and give her only water and vegetables until she died, at which point she would immediately enter heaven. But when the father left the house, the mother was unable to allow her daughter to die of neglect, and nursed her. The father was furious, and subsequently removed his love, the wife lamented to the authorities, from both herself and the child.[18]

Among the higher classes customs of "fosterage" persisted and continued to function in some cases as *de facto* abandonment.[19] Systems to preserve estates—entailment and primogeniture—although more significant in the fourteenth and fifteenth centuries than before, were not uniform or entirely effective even where officially in force, and in some regions the practice of partible inheritance, which they were designed to circumvent, still provoked abandon-

18. *Registre d'inquisition* 2.415; discussed in LeRoy Ladurie, *Montaillou* (cited in note 12, above), pp. 314–15. The child died a year after this incident, of unspecified causes. But the father ultimately renounced Catharism, and was reconciled with his wife. It does not appear to have been the domestic unrest caused by the incident that inspired the change: the whole village (Arques) renounced the faith at the same time (discussed in Ladurie, ibid.).

19. See, e.g., the very casual arrangement involving Lorenzo, son of Ser Niccolò, in Renato Piattoli, "Lettere di Piero Benintendi, mercante del Trecento," *Atti della società Ligure di Storia Patria* 60, 1 (Genoa, 1932), pp. 127–31 (trans. in Lopez, *Medieval Trade*, p. 400). (This is closely related to, if not actually a form of, the "emancipation" of Italian children, discussed below.) A comparable letter reflecting a much more formal arrangement among the English is printed among the "Paston Letters": *Original Letters Written During the Reigns of Henry VI, Edward IV and Richard III*, ed. John Fenn (London, 1787) 1.195–96, no. 50. For discussion of the phenomenon among the English, see Grant McCracken, "The Exchange of Children in Tudor England: An Anthropological Phenomenon in Historical Context," JFH 8, 4 (1983) 303–13, and bibliography. "Fostering" continued to figure prominently in Scandinavian literature, although much of this is consciously archaized and therefore not a reliable indication of contemporary practice (see, e.g., *Ectors saga*, LMIR 1.110, 156, 157; *Nitida saga*, LMIR 5.4; *Sigrgarðs saga ok Valbrands*, ibid., p. 168; *Adonias saga*, LMIR 3.151). On the other hand, it is probably revealing that the author of *Victors saga ok Blávus* mentions that the son of a ruler grew up at his father's court, as if this were a notable fact (LMIR 1.3: "Victor vex nu upp med fodr sinum . . .").

ment among the upper classes: for example, in most of Italy.[20] This may be one of several reasons why exposing was more prominent in Italy during the fourteenth and fifteenth centuries than elsewhere in Europe, although the ancient Roman custom of "emancipation" was also revived there and in other areas of partible inheritance as a means of divesting families of heirs.[21] Civil and canon lawyers in Italy in the later Middle Ages disagreed about whether emancipation was a punishment for a bad son or a reward for a good one: probably it could be either.[22] Sometimes it was simply a means of escaping responsibility for one's children—much like the paid "fostering" of earlier periods.[23] Whether it was tantamount to abandonment in practical and emotional terms depended largely on the circumstances.

Actual slavery (as opposed to feudal servitude or indenturing) became more common in the later Middle Ages than it had been at

20. Lorcin ("Retraite," p. 197), specifically relating inheritance practices to the placing of children in religious life, finds that in the opening decades of the fourteenth century only 40 percent of testators leave their estate to one child, but by the year 1500, 77 percent do. For an overview of Italy, see Herlihy, *Medieval Households,* pp. 94, 136–38; Christiane Klapisch-Zuber, *Women, Family, and Ritual in Renaissance Italy,* pp. 213–14, 284–85, etc.; for England, where primogeniture was most widely practiced, see Hanawalt, *The Ties That Bound,* chap. 4; and bibliography in McCracken (see previous note). The first laws about entailment were passed in Castile in 1505 (Nueva Recopilación 5.7, in *Códigos españoles* 2), although it had clearly been customary in many regions long before this.

21. Roman emancipation was the termination of *patria potestas* by voluntary action of the father (as opposed to the son being released through the father's death, or a daughter through marriage). It might entail *deminutio capitis minima* (loss of family standing) and nullify rights of inheritance, but this varied according to circumstance. See *Institutes* 1.12.6, Dig. 1.7, JC 8.48, for the theory, although practice was more complicated. Revived Roman law was even less uniform: on this see Paolo de Castro, *Commentaria in digesti novi partem secundam* (Lyons, 1553), folio 56v, and Thomas Kuehn, *Emancipation in Late Medieval Florence* (New Brunswick, N.J., 1982), especially pp. 64–69. Even infants could be emancipated, but in late medieval Florence if there was no will an emancipated child could claim his share of an inheritance (Kuehn, pp. 26–27). For early modern parallels see, *inter alia,* the remarks of Flandrin, *Families in Former Times,* pp. 70–79, 241.

22. Kuehn, pp. 25–34.

23. Herlihy notes that many children of the prosperous were "emancipated" as early as age eight and sent to do accounting or other types of work ("Family and Property," in Miskimin et al., *The Medieval City,* pp. 17–18). For emancipation in other areas see, e.g., *Furs de València* 3.18.9, p. 216 (and ibid., 2.13.3, where the

406 · *The Kindness of Strangers*

any time after the fall of Rome,[24] and it is easy to show that then, as in all ages, children constituted a substantial portion of the slave trade, but it is difficult to discover exactly how they came to do so.[25] As in the ancient world, calamities forced some parents with no other recourse to sell. An Italian contemporary described the plight of Jewish parents expelled from Spain in 1492:

> Not long after this, [Ferdinand and Isabella] ordered the re-
> maining Jews to depart their kingdom on a set day. If, because
> of poverty, as was frequently the case, or some other reason,
> they could not obey, they were either burned or pretended to be
> Christians. A few embraced the faith of Christ; the remaining
> throng set out for Italy, Greece, Asia Minor; many went to
> Syria and Egypt. At first this measure seemed laudable, respect-
> ing the honor of our religion; but it was actually rather cruel if
> one considers them human beings created by God rather than
> beasts. It was pitiful to see their sufferings. Many were con-
> sumed by hunger, especially nursing mothers and their babies.
> Half-dead mothers held dying children in their arms. . . . I can
> hardly say how cruelly and greedily they were treated by those
> who transported them. Many were drowned by the avarice of
> the sailors, and those who were unable to pay their passage sold
> their children.[26]

Such horrors were not "typical," but the transition from late medieval to early modern Europe was appallingly turbulent and violent
in some areas, and many elements of society—especially at the bottom—suffered piteously.

Child slaves were particularly common in southern Europe, the

---

opposite of a *fill emancipat* is, interestingly, a *fill familiar,* who might be chronologically an adult); see also *Siete Partidas* 7.4.18.

24. See Verlinden, *L'Esclavage* 1 and 2; *idem,* "La Législation vénitienne,"
pp. 147–72; *idem,* "L'Enfant esclave," pp. 107–25; Livi, *La Schiavitù* (as cited
above); Heers, *Esclaves;* Alfonso Franco Silva, *La Esclavitud en Sevilla y su tierra a
fines de la Edad Media* (Seville, 1979).

25. Piracy was common: see, e.g., the complaint of the Byzantine ambassador
in 1319 about the theft of four children from an island, in G. M. Thomas, *Diplo-
matarium Veneto-Levantinum* (Venice, 1880) 1.125–27; trans. in Lopez, *Medieval
Trade,* p. 315.

26. Bartholomew Senarega, *De Rebus Genuensibus, 1388–1514,* in Muratori,
SSRRII, 24 (Milan, 1738) 531–32.

comparatively rich commercial centers of which absorbed much of the human trade from the Balkans and North Africa.[27] Of the slaves sold in Sicily, Naples, and Venice in the fourteenth century whose age is known, about one-third were under fifteen.[28] The familiarity of servile children from "pagan" lands in the households of the wealthy clearly provided a cover for poor Europeans to sell or place their own children in such situations as well.[29] They were some-

27. There was some specific demand for children, but on the whole they do not appear to have been regarded as more or less valuable than adult slaves. The same fourteenth-century letter mentioning the transfer of the child Lorenzo (above, note 19) includes a reply to a request for a slave girl: "I am informed about the little slave girl you want, and about the age and everything. . . . Whenever ships come from Romania, they should carry some [slave girls]; but keep in mind that little slave girls are as expensive as the grown ones, and there will be none that does not cost fifty to sixty florins if we want one of any value . . ." (trans. in Lopez, *Medieval Trade*, pp. 402–3). Child slaves were less common in northern Europe: see Heers, pp. 211–12. Though there is no evidence that children were particularly valuable, pregnant females or those with milk were: ibid., pp. 202–3. Ten to twenty percent of the female slaves sold in Seville in the fifteenth century were pregnant or breast-feeding, and their infants were usually included with them at no extra cost (Franco Silva, *Esclavitud*, p. 156; cited in note 24, above). Franco Silva found a great preference for young adult slaves in Seville.

28. To be exact, 28.8 percent, although the records themselves are probably not exact; the figure is 21.1 in the fifteenth century. Both are my calculations, using data provided in Verlinden, *L'Esclavage* 2, pp. 180–81, 208–15, 304–5, 307, 309–10, 311–14, 317–29, 575–84, 588–98, 604–11, and 625–36. I excluded one set of tables that did not distinguish the fourteenth from the fifteenth century: the overall figure, including it, is 22.4 percent for the two centuries. (But compare the apparently contradictory statements by Verlinden himself in "L'Enfant esclave," pp. 119–20.) The rough accuracy of these findings is supported by the fact that of 4,465 slaves sold in Seville between 1470 and 1525, 28.1 percent were age fifteen or younger, and 14.5 percent were ten or younger (Franco Silva, p. 161). Most of these had been born in Seville; Franco Silva assumes, perhaps naïvely, that this means they were all the offspring of slave parents (p. 156). Given the known rate of abandonment in Spanish cities a little later, it seems very likely that some, at least, were abandoned by free parents.

29. Heers, pp. 154 ff, documents the presence in Venetian and Florentine households of purchased Italian children in addition to the Adriatic children allowed by law, although he does not draw the conclusions I suggest. Durham (*Some Tribal Origins*, pp. 190–91) found poor Ragusans, Dalmatians, and Serbians still selling their children to more prosperous families as late as the twentieth century. The children were said to be "adopted," although they were sometimes sold as far away as Istanbul, and were often sexually abused by their "adopted" "fathers" and "brothers."

times prostituted, as their ancient counterparts had been.[30] The off-spring of slaves were themselves frequently abandoned, and may then have been found and sold, although better or worse fates might await them if they were taken to foundling homes. Those kept at home were occasionally reared as free.[31]

The evidence, although still fragmentary, continues to suggest a smaller family size in much of Europe than one would expect in societies without effective contraceptive techniques.[32] Records consistently disclose or imply that the wealthy had larger families than the

30. Verlinden, "La Législation," pp. 152–54.

31. Vergerio de Capodistria, a Paduan chronicler, asserted that in the 1350s one could not find any home-born slaves because all had been enfranchised: see Heers, p. 213. Many slave children were certainly emancipated (cases cited in Heers, pp. 229–31), but the offspring of unions between slave mothers and free fathers constituted a major percentage of the children abandoned to foundling homes: see Trexler, "Foundlings," *passim,* and observations below. Men who impregnated female slaves had to pay insurance against the mother's death (Heers, pp. 216–17).

32. In addition to the studies of the fourteenth and fifteenth centuries already cited (e.g., Herlihy, *Medieval Households, Medieval and Renaissance Pistoia;* Razi; Hanawalt, *The Ties That Bound;* Lorcin, "Retraite"; etc.), see Harry Miskimin, "The Legacies of London: 1259–1330," in *The Medieval City,* Miskimin et al., eds., pp. 209–27; Silvia Thrupp, *The Merchant Class of Medieval London* (Ann Arbor, 1962); J. A. Raftis, *A Small Town in late Medieval England: Godmanchester 1278–1400* (Toronto, 1982); Edward Britton, *The Community of the Vill: A Study in the History of the Family and Village Life in Fourteenth-Century England* (Toronto, 1977); Clare Coleman, *Downham-in-the-Isle: A Study of an Ecclesiastical Manor in the Thirteenth and Fourteenth Centuries* (Suffolk, 1984); and, for the East, Angeliki Laiou-Thomadakis, *Peasant Society in the Late Byzantine Empire: A Social and Demographic Study* (Princeton, 1977), and E. A. Hammel, "Household Structure in Fourteenth-Century Macedonia," JFH 5, 3 (1980) 242–73, all of which find relatively small family size among the middle and lower classes. Some of the figures are amazingly low: Miskimin ("Legacies," p. 221) found that the middle class of London in the early fourteenth century had only 1.33 children per testator, and noted that "internal population growth was invariably too small to maintain the urban community" (p. 219). K. B. McFarlane (*The Nobility of Later Medieval England* [Oxford, 1973], pp. 142–76) reported that the families he studied died out in the male line on average in four generations. These trends seem comparable to the decline of Roman population in the second and third centuries of the Christian era, but they were reversed, in England at least, by the seventeenth century: see note 38 of Introduction. On the other hand, Ladurie estimates 4.5 legitimate births per family for the region around Montaillou in southern France from 1280 to 1324 (*Montaillou,* pp. 204–5). He does so "taking into account various imponderables," which are not specified.

poor,[33] and suggest the unusual sex ratios[34] observed in other so-

33. See, e.g., discussion in Razi, pp. 83–93. (But to assess the reliability of Razi's methods, compare L. R. Poos and R. M. Smith, "'Legal Windows onto Historical Populations?' Recent Research on Demography and the Manor Court in Medieval England," *Law and History Review* 2 [1984] 128–52, with response and counterresponse, ibid. 3 [1985] 121–200, 409–29.) In Pistoia in 1427 the official records show a proportion of two to one in the number of children of the wealthy compared with those of the poor, in both rural and urban settings: Herlihy, *Medieval and Renaissance Pistoia*, pp. 117–18; cf. p. 98 for comparison with fertility rates, and *idem*, "Family and Property in Renaissance Florence," *Medieval City*, p. 16, where he finds that the wealthiest 10 percent of urban households include 25 percent of all children under eighteen in Florence; or *Medieval Households*, p. 153, where he says that the top 25 percent of the population rears one-half of the children. The disproportion is reflected even where the class differences are small: Miskimin ("Legacies," p. 218) found that his sample of merchants had 0.88 sons per testator, whereas Thrupp's wealthier sample (*Merchant Class*, p. 200) had 1.3. The disparity increased during the sixteenth century: in some areas in the seventeenth century prosperous households were on average four times larger than poor ones, and the disproportion was accounted for in large measure by the distribution of children: see, e.g., Flandrin, *Families in Former Times*, pp. 82–85, and Laslett, *The World We Have Lost*, pp. 64 ff. All these figures must be read in context to be understood properly; there is insufficient space here to assess their findings in detail. For example, T. H. Hollingworth, "A Demographic Study of the British Ducal Families," *Population Studies* 11 (1957) 4–26, finds an average of 4.6 children per family among the upper classes, but a large percentage of the nobles in his study had no children at all, so the real number of children per family was higher.

34. I.e., generally higher than one would anticipate, and especially so among the wealthy. Herlihy believes that there were more women than men in the population at large from the twelfth century on (he suggests that warfare may account for this [*Medieval Households*, pp. 102–3], but this seems an odd explanation: there was surely as much warfare before the twelfth century as after), yet in *Tuscans* (pp. 135–36) he shows that the sex ratio as well as the number of children rises with affluence. This suggests some form of intervention. Miskimin prefers the dangers of childbirth to infanticide as explanation of the high sex ratio he found among his testators ("Legacies," p. 221). (German grave sites do indicate that about half of all females in the Middle Ages died during "mothering" years—i.e., between early adulthood and age thirty-nine: Arnold, *Kind und Gesellschaft*, p. 37.) Razi's "correction" (especially on pp. 92–93) for sex ratio—i.e., adding children to the numbers in the documents to make up for an assumed failure to record females—begs the question of whether poorer families in fact reared all their children, especially females: underreporting is likely, but counter-distortion by historians through arbitrary manipulation of the numbers obscures rather than clarifies the demography of the period. It is also likely that poor families failed to bring up girls, either exposing them or giving them to other families as servants. This may be either balanced or aggravated by the fact that the documents on which

cieties with widespread abandonment.[35] Abandonment has not been considered as part of the explanation for this. Barbara Hanawalt, for example, lists as causes for the small family size in fourteenth-century England "birth control, infanticide, high infant mortality, late marriages, infertility due to poor diet, high female mortality, and economic limitations on nuptiality";[36] she meanwhile shows that infanticide was negligible and adduces no evidence of effective contraception at the time. Abandonment through exposure or in arrangements of servitude, abundantly evident in English historical sources of the High and later Middle Ages, is a more likely means of family limitation. In some areas covered by her study, servants comprised forty percent of the population, and household service, at least before the great plague of 1348–50,[37] was the obvious option for cadet children even of propertied families.[38] Only David Herlihy recognizes abandonment as an important means of family limitation

---

Razi and others base their conclusions tend to provide information only about those who either occupy some niche in the structure of their society or who have run afoul of those who do. In a review of Razi, M. McIntosh observed that the data on which he relied "are less useful and at times completely silent about those inhabitants who did not hold land from the lord, about poor freeholders, women, servants, and live-in laborers, and about any temporary or transient elements within the community" (*Speculum* 56, 4 [1981], p. 908).

35. There is, of course, no reason to doubt that the upper classes, after primogeniture was widespread, felt freer to rear large families than their poorer fellow citizens, since they could afford to be good Catholics, at least in regard to procreative purpose—which may have helped assuage compunctions about wealth, frequently denigrated in the New Testament. But this only explains the motivation for the disproportion, not how it was achieved: i.e., how did the poor keep their families so much smaller than those of the rich without contraception or infanticide?

36. Hanawalt, *The Ties That Bound*, p. 95.

37. Literature on the Black Death is vast and of uneven quality. Phillip Ziegler, *The Black Death* (London, 1969) is a useful introduction. For demographic consequences and estimates, see, for example, the useful discussion in Razi, pp. 99–113, and for a Continental comparison, Amada Lopez de Meneses, *Documentos acerca de la Peste Negra en los dominios de la Corona de Aragón* (Zaragoza, 1956).

38. Ibid., pp. 164–66. She concludes that "on balance the evidence is against the practice of either having live-in servants or arranging for the majority of young people to undergo a period of servitude," but the evidence she provides implies that live-in servants were common (five out of thirty families had them in one survey; both the houses robbed by a band of thieves on one night had live-in help, etc.). R. H. Hilton, who has studied the question most extensively, decided the evidence was "inconclusive" (*The English Peasantry in the Later Middle Ages* [Oxford, 1975], pp. 31–34; Hanawalt mentions this on p. 164).

in the fourteenth and fifteenth centuries, and he vacillates in his estimation of its importance.[39]

Brissaud believed that infanticide was widespread during the period, but admitted that there is very little evidence of it;[40] Hanawalt's conclusion that it was extremely rare in England in the later Middle Ages is probably accurate for continental Europe as well.[41] On the other hand, the rate of infant mortality may have been exceptionally high during the fourteenth and fifteenth centuries as the result of plague, famine, and other disasters: young children suffer disease

39. In *Medieval and Renaissance Pistoia*, pp. 100, 116–20, it is ignored; in *Medieval Households*, pp. 147–48, he seems to posit contraceptive techniques as the major means of regulating family size, although elsewhere in the work he notes in passing (e.g., pp. 153 and 214, nn. 36–37) that forms of abandonment might have reduced family size. But in *Tuscans* (pp. 145–46) he does address abandonment specifically as a means of divesting the family of unwanted children.

40. Of 1,366 letters of remission for crimes to residents of Poitou between 1302 and 1502, for example, only eleven—less than one percent—deal with infanticide: Brissaud, "L'Infanticide," p. 251, n. 91 bis. For comparable figures in England, see following note, and Helmholz, "Infanticide in the Province of Canterbury," p. 384. Helmholz finds infanticide vigorously prosecuted when it occurs, but this is not very often. It could be said to have been vigorously prosecuted in France as well, but this must not be confused with its being actually *punished*. For two cases of outright, proven infanticide that were simply pardoned, see *Recueil*, vol. 6, no. 860, pp. 352–54, and vol. 11, no. 1515, pp. 343–46. Cf. vol. 6, no. 704, pp. 44–47: pardon of a father whose thirteen-year-old daughter suffocated when he locked her in a casket to punish her. People were often arraigned on charges of infanticide that involved accidental death, but they were always absolved: see, e.g., in vol. 6, no. 856, pp. 341–43, where a woman alone during childbirth was accused of infanticide when the baby died, but she was absolved; or vol. 11, no. 1012, pp. 334–37, where a nineteen-year-old girl seduced by her employer gave birth to a dead child, which she buried out of fear of her husband. She, too, is absolved, as are persons accused of killing children in vol. 6, no. 783, pp. 138–40; vol. 11, no. 907, pp. 26–29; and vol. 11, no. 933, pp. 86–89 (this case involved the use of an abortifacient resulting in stillbirth); cf. vol. 11, no. 907, pp. 26–29, and vol. 6, no. 783, pp. 138–40. Sometimes charges of infanticide were false: see, e.g., *Recueil*, vol. 1, no. 180, pp 425–29. See Introduction, note 111, on the probable proportions of abandonments to infanticides—in the nineteenth century running at as much as 900 to 1.

41. In her data as of 1974 she found that among 2,933 homicides in fourteenth-century English jail-delivery and coroner's roles there was a single case of infanticide (Hanawalt, "The Female Felon in Fourteenth-Century England"; the case is described on p. 259). In a later study she found two cases in 4,000 ("Childbearing Among the Lower Classes of Late Medieval England," p. 9). For a German instance of infanticide in the fourteenth century, see *Annales Colmarienses maiores*, MGH SS 17.231.

and calamity disproportionately, and the poor would have less resistance in many cultures than the wealthy.[42]

Literature of the later Middle Ages, like that of earlier periods, includes abandonments of many sorts, all treated as ordinary aspects of life. Most such themes were similar to those in earlier writings, discussed in the previous chapter, but a few were novel and reflective of the particular conditions of the day. Boccaccio's *Decameron* begins with a graphic description of the terrors of the plague of 1348–50, among which is the fact that "one brother would abandon another, or an uncle a nephew or a sister a brother or sometimes even a wife her husband; and, what is worse and almost beyond belief, fathers and mothers would shun to visit or care for their children—as if they were not theirs."[43] The fourteenth-century English alliterative poem *The Siege of Jerusalem* includes an account of "Mary, a mild wife," who cooks and devours her own son during a siege. The poem is set in a distant time and place, and the incident may be a fanciful invention, but it could also reflect a horror which the fourteenth-century victims of plague, famine, and war had seen or heard about closer to home.[44]

Abandonment under more normal conditions occurs in literature as well. To test his wife, a husband in the *Decameron* disposes of their young children by sending them to a relative, allowing her to believe they have been exposed.[45] Although she is heartbroken, and his subjects deeply disapprove, there is no suggestion that the action violates civil or ecclesiastical law. The wife in the story (Griselda) had herself been given up by her father in an arrangement which could be seen as a form of abandonment, and was common in most of premodern Europe: she was sold to be the bride of a wealthy

42. Arnold (*Kind und Gesellschaft*, p. 36) cites evidence from grave sites suggesting a very high infant mortality rate, although the data cannot be dated very precisely.

43. *Decameron,* introduction.

44. Ed. E. Kolbing and Mabel Day (London, 1932) (Early English Text Society, 188), lines 1077–1092.

45. *Decameron* 10.10. The servant who comes to take the daughter away does not finish explaining the command given him ("e ch'io . . .—e non disse piú"); the narrator says that the wife understood that he was to kill the child, but she asks that the girl not be left to the birds and beasts, implying that she assumed the child was to be exposed. Possibly she thought exposing necessarily resulted in death—an assumption that may have been truer in her day than it had been earlier (see below, pp. 411ff.). The husband's subjects subsequently assume he has had both children killed. See note 49, below.

man.[46] Whether daughters in such cases regarded themselves as abandoned by their families would, of course, depend on how old they were, on physical circumstances (e.g., how they were treated, how near their new home was to that of their parents, etc.), and on their attitude toward the marriage itself. That this could happen to persons who would today be considered "children" is evident in this same story: the husband arranges to test the wife's devotion even further by divorcing[47] her and marrying someone else—a twelve-year-old. There is disgust at his insensitivity to a loving wife, but no one appears the least bit surprised at the age of the replacement.[48] (She is, in fact, the daughter he had previously sent away—a recurrence of the ancient association of abandonment with incest?)[49]

In a late medieval saga the princely hero agrees to trade his firstborn son to a childless commoner for a harp, asking only that the boy be treated well.[50] The new parents become the child's "foster

46. The buying of wives is in need of study. It is obviously difficult to distinguish between social arrangements (dower, dowry, etc.) involving the exchange of money or property as a convention relating to marriage and the actual purchase of a free person from parents or some other authority, but it seems clear enough that many heirs and heiresses were effectively sold throughout the Middle Ages, and commoners were probably bought outright, as this story suggests. Even in the twelfth century, when ecclesiastical concern about the niceties of marriage was probably at its height, Adam of Eynsham records the marriage of a four-year-old peasant girl to a noble—to the horror, it should be added, of the bishop and the narrator—(*Magna vita sancti Hugonis,* ed. Douie and Farmer, 4.5 [2.23–24]). For general discussions of marriage at the time in its social context, see the articles in "Marriage in the Middle Ages," *Viator* 4 (1973) 413–501, and David Herlihy, "The Medieval Marriage Market," *Medieval and Renaissance Studies* 6 (1974) 3–27. In the early Middle Ages older women would marry very young boys, apparently to obtain their property: see above, chapter 4, note 103.

47. See chapter 9, note 84.

48. The king of France granted a remission in 1373 to a couple who had married his son to her daughter by a previous marriage; the girl, whose father was dead, was twelve at the time, and the couple arranged the marriage without consulting her tutor, which seems to have been the aspect objected to by the crown, putatively the protector of all minors (*Recueil,* vol. 4, no. 556 bis, pp. lxxi–lxxii).

49. The story fascinated Boccaccio's contemporaries, though not necessarily because its details about the treatment of children were surprising or unusual. Petrarch translated it into Latin, and Chaucer rendered this in English as "The Clerk's Tale." Although there are subtle and interesting variations on the original in both, none of these seems to bear materially on the issues of interest here.

50. *Sigrgarðs saga ok Valbrands* (LMIR 5, pp. 127–28). Cf. *Vilhjálms saga Sjóðs* (LMIR 4, pp. 6–7), where a king stakes his five-year-old son against a ring in a board game.

414 · The Kindness of Strangers

parents," and although the natal father subsequently regrets the deal, the foster father retains control, loves the boy very much, and is eventually ennobled (p. 187). The boy knows about his background, and there is an *anagnorisis* with his mother and maternal grandfather (pp. 168–69, 174). It seems unlikely that nobles would abandon children publicly to commoners, for reasons discussed previously, and the story may be simply a "quicksand topos." On the other hand, it could be a realistic expression of cynicism about the actual operations and meaning of "fostering" in the later Middle Ages. It is not difficult to believe that selfish motives often moved natal parents, or that "foster parents" of lower status benefited from the position and might even have offered bribes to obtain it.[51]

In addition to these many continuities, however, there was also one dramatic change in abandonment, which altered irrevocably the contours of the phenomenon during the course of the fourteenth and fifteenth centuries, and which entailed its own set of mysteries and historical problems. A hint of it is evident in the projection of likely fates for unwanted children in Boccaccio's *Corbaccio*.

> How many babies, entering life against their [mother's] will, are tossed into the arms of fortune! Look at the hospitals! How many more die[52] before they have tasted mother's milk? How many are abandoned to the woods, how many to the beasts and the birds? So many perish in such ways that, all things considered, the least of [the mother's] sins is having pursued the desires of the flesh.[53]

51. In *Adonias saga* (LMIR 3, p. 89) there is a brutally realistic scene where a king simply refuses to accept a child into his family.

52. "Se n'uccidono": Trexler ("Infanticide," p. 98) translates this sentence as, "How many are killed before they sip the mother's milk!" (cf. the similar translation in *The Corbaccio*, trans. Anthony Cassell [Chicago, 1975], p. 28). This reading is possible, especially if the *ne* is understood to refer to the action of the mothers, hinted at previously. But the reflexive *uccidersi* normally means either "to die" or "to commit suicide," as opposed to *uccidere*, "to kill." Boccaccio's charge seems to me that of indirect responsibility if the children perish, as suggested by his use of the more neutral *periscono* ("perish") just following (also with *ne*), and not an accusation of actual infanticide. Understood this way, the *ne* refers to fortune, through whose unkind offices the children die.

53. "Quanti parti per questo, mal lor grado venuti a bene, nelle braccia della fortuna si gittano! Riguardinsi gli spedali. Quanti ancora, prima che essi il materno latte abbino gustato, se n'uccidono! Quanti a' boschi, quanti alle fiere se ne concedono e agli uccelli! Tanti e in sí fatte maniere ne periscono che, bene ogni cosa considerata, il minore peccato in loro è l'avere l'appetito della lussuria seguíto"

The woods, the beasts, and the birds are a familiar litany, perhaps only *topoi*. But the prominence of hospitals, to Boccaccio the obvious first recourse for an abandoning mother, is striking. It is not even juxtaposed with churches, as it had been in Hugo of Trimberg's poem half a century earlier.

By the close of the thirteenth century, quite a few hospitals accepted foundlings along with the sick, the dying, pregnant women, and sometimes the indigent;[54] by the end of the fourteenth, most urban hospitals in southern Europe probably did so. But during this century an even more important development had taken place: many large German, French, and Italian cities had established institutions specifically for abandoned children.[55] Precise dates of es-

---

(*Opere di Giovanni Boccaccio,* ed. Cesare Segre [Milan, 1966], p. 1212; cf. translation by Trexler, which differs from mine, as noted above). The claim that lechery is the least of the mother's sins is a paraphrase of Juvenal, Satire 6.134–35; cf. Jean de Meun, *Roman de la Rose,* verses 9143–45.

54. There is clear evidence that Santa Maria da San Gallo, the oldest of the Florentine homes, was caring for foundlings in 1294: see G. Pinto, "Il Personale, le Balie e i salariati dell'ospedale di San Gallo di Firenze negli anni 1395–1406," pp. 115–17. Pinto gives a detailed view both of the administration of a late medieval foundling hospital and the kinds of documentation it left behind; the foundlings themselves, by contrast, figure little in the study.

55. The small town of Prato, near Florence, had a foundling home at the beginning of the fourteenth century, and kept records of infants it received from 1333: see Livi, *La Schiavitù,* pp. 111–12. Lucca's foundling hospital was in operation as the fifteenth century opened: see Verlinden, *L'Esclavage,* 2.414. Santo Spirito in Rome was clearly caring for foundlings by the fourteenth century, as were other hospitals of the order of the Holy Spirit in southern France: see following note. In Genoa there was specialized care for the abandoned children of slaves: see Heers, *Esclaves,* p. 227. Luigi Passerini (*Storia,* pp. 660–61) claims that Pisa had a foundling home in 1219, Siena by 1233, and Venice by the fourteenth century, but the documentation for each of these assertions is questionable. Records of foundling care from the hospice in Marseilles date from the beginning of the fourteenth century (some are published in French translation in Remacle, *Hospices,* pp. 45–47; see also A. Fabre, *Histoire des Hôpitaux et des Institutions de Bienfaisance de Marseilles* [Marseilles, 1854] 1.381–439). L'Aumône de Notre Dame in Chartres was caring for abandoned children in 1349, and C. Billot ("Les Enfants abandonnés à Chartres à la fin du Moyen Age," ADH [1975] 167–87) thinks it had been organized to do so "depuis longtemps" (p. 178). In Germany, Ulm, Freiburg, and Nuremberg all had foundling homes in the fourteenth century, as notices in city records indicate, although few details survive: see Ernst Mummenhoff, *Das Findel- und Waisenhaus zu Nürnberg, orts-, kultur- und wirtschaftsgeschichtlich,* in *Mitteilungen des Vereins für Geschichte der Stadt Nürnberg* 21 (1915) 57–336; Ursula Gray, *Das Bild des Kindes im Spiegel der altdeutschen Dichtung und Literatur* (Bern, 1974), pp. 177–78; and Arnold,

tablishment are usually wanting for such homes; the first evidence of their existence indicates that they had been in operation for some time.[56] The easiest to trace are those of Florence: the confraternity of Misericordia took in lost or abandoned children from the mid-thirteenth century; the foundling hospital Santa Maria da San Gallo was established at the end of the thirteenth century; a second foundling hospital, Santa Maria della Scala, was founded in 1316 and received the sick poor as well as infants.[57] By the end of the century, the two together received about two hundred children a year.[58]

Kind und Gesellschaft, pp. 46–47—although the latter two studies must be used with caution.

56. For example, a legend that the hospital of the Holy Spirit (Santa Maria in Saxia) in Rome was created when fishermen brought to Innocent III (1198–1216) the bodies of infants tossed into the Tiber by their mothers is based on a series of beautiful but not necessarily accurate paintings preserved in a fifteenth-century cartulary belonging to the order's hospital in Dijon (see figures 15–17). The story is neither inherently unlikely nor verifiable. The order to which the hospital belonged was founded in Montpellier toward the end of the twelfth century, but there is little documentation about its functions before the end of the thirteenth: see Michèle Revel, "Le Rayonnement à Rome et en Italie de l'Ordre du Saint-Esprit de Montpellier," in *Assistance et charité,* pp. 343–55; *La Carità cristiana in Roma,* esp. pp. 140–52 and 185–87; Pietro De Angelis, *L'Ospedale di Santo Spirito in Saxia,* 1: *Dalle origini al 1300* (Rome, 1960), especially pp. 195–204; Paul Brune, *L'Histoire de l'Ordre Hospitalier du Saint-Esprit* (Paris, 1892), pp. 38–40. Revel is suitably cautious regarding the foundation legend ("si on en croit la légende"), and notes that although the hospitals included foundlings and orphans in their charge, in the documentation "on y parle peu des enfants abandonnés" (pp. 349–50). Cf. the much less critical accounts of Semichon, *Histoire,* pp. 88–89, and Payne, *Child,* p. 297.

57. For San Gallo, see note 54, above. For La Scala, Lucia Sandri, *L'Ospedale di S. Maria della Scala di S. Gimignano nel quattrocento,* esp. pp. 18–19. For the Innocenti, see Trexler, "Foundlings," esp. p. 261.

58. In 1396, San Gallo had about 40 foundlings (Pinto, p. 125) and La Scala about 150 (Trexler, "Foundlings," p. 264). This would be a small number of abandoned children in a city said by a contemporary to have a population of 100,000 and to baptize between 5,500 and 6,000 children a year (Giovanni Villani, *Cronica di Giovanni Villani* [Florence, 1823] 9, chap. 94). Even if the figures—which are suspiciously round, although Herlihy (*Medieval and Renaissance Pistoia,* p. 94) finds them credible—are reliable, there is no reason to assume that the children left at foundling homes during this period constituted even a large percentage of, much less all, the abandoned children. In the 1430s Herlihy finds only 141 foundlings under fifteen at La Scala (*Tuscans,* p. 145), but at the same time another 216 children were being maintained at public expense in private homes (p. 136), and the majority of servants recorded in households were under twelve, amounting to more than 400 children. Moreover, the Innocenti was opened precisely because there were many more *espositi* than the existing hospitals could handle.

Santa Maria degl'Innocenti, exclusively for foundlings, was opened in 1445 to alleviate the burden on the other two.[59] This chronology is fairly typical: in a few areas such institutions may have started a little earlier, in most they were slightly later. Within a century nearly every major European city would have some public institution specifically for exposed children, although southern states embraced this trend more rapidly than northern regions.[60]

Other modes of divesting the family of children did not disappear. The whole panoply of formal and informal arrangements for hiring, lending, or giving children away is amply evident in sources of the period, and babies are still left in churches, beside roads, and in trees, although it is likely that as hospitals became the ordinary recourse of abandoning parents, fewer and fewer people bothered to look for infants in traditional exposing sites; and this may have caused a rise in mortality among the exposed.[61] The accessibility of municipal foundling hospitals and the general presumption that children were well cared for within them caught on with stunning rapidity in the urban centers of Europe, and they quickly came to

59. It was founded by a bequest of 1410 made by Francesco Datini, who had initially left half of his estate to Santa Maria della Scala, plus a sum for his illegitimate daughter, Ginevra, who had herself been secretly placed in a hospital in Florence. This is shown by Philip Gavitt, "Charity and Children in Renaissance Florence: the Ospedale degli Innocenti, 1410–1536," Ph.D. diss., Univ. of Michigan, 1988, pp. 61–62. Gavitt's is the most detailed study available of the Innocenti. See also Trexler, "Foundlings," p. 261; and Klapisch-Zuber, *Women*, pp. 151–53, which draws on Trexler and Pinto.

60. Michel Mollat, agreeing that the exact time of emergence is not discernible in the records, nonetheless places it later: see *The Poor in the Middle Ages*, pp. 288–90. For other areas see, e.g., Rotha Clay, *The Medieval Hospitals of England* (London, 1909), and more recently, Ruth McClure, *Coram's Children: The London Foundling Hospital in the Eighteenth Century*, and other works on abandonment cited above, in the Introduction, note 93.

61. Helmholz ("Infanticide," p. 380) cites a case of 1448 in which an exposed child died; a few decades later a French father and son exposed the illegitimate child of the father's daughter in order to save her reputation. They baptized the child, wrapped him well, and then left him at the Poor House of Pousauges, about two leagues distant, but the baby was dead by the next morning, and they were arraigned and imprisoned. When it was ascertained that they had only intended to abandon the child, however, and not to harm him, all charges were dropped: Archives Nationales Reg. JJ 206, n. 1063, folio 229v, published in *Recueil*, vol. 12, no. 1589, pp. 148–50. Observe that two years later Mauricette Moricau, who had borne a child after being seduced by a monk, actually murdered her illegitimate child, and was also excused from any penalty: JJ 205, n. 114, folio 59 (January 1479), in *Recueil*, vol. 12, no. 1523, pp. 240–41.

seem more desirable than traditional, unregulated and uncertain methods.

Indeed, one could interpret the statistics as showing that the establishment of foundling hospitals encouraged abandonment:[62] the Innocenti was opened in Florence because the two older homes could no longer handle the several hundred children deposited in them annually. Within fifty years it alone was accepting nine hundred children a year.[63] This is not necessarily an indication that parents were abandoning to the new homes children they would otherwise have retained; it is equally possible that the infants would have been disposed of in some other way if there were no foundling hospices, and that the steady increase in admissions represents a shift in the fate of the exposed, not an increase in their numbers.

Most children were conveyed to the hospital by servants, friends, relatives, or clerics, or simply left at its doors.[64] The parents were often known and recorded, even when the baby was left anonymously: communities were small, and pregnancies difficult to conceal, especially among the lower classes, who could afford little privacy.[65] The keeping of records about parents or tokens left with children at hospitals was doubtless intended to enable the hospital to assess any later parental claims for recovery, and perhaps also to help forestall inappropriate marriages.[66] Parents who reclaimed

62. See comments in Trexler, "Foundlings," p. 267.

63. Trexler, "Foundlings," p. 263. Precisely comparable figures for La Scala are not available, but its own history illustrates the same trend. In 1319, three years after it opened, it received sixty babies; by the end of the century, it supported nearly three times that many (p. 264). Gavitt, "Charity," p. 32, finds that 4.9 percent of children baptized in the city were abandoned to the Innocenti in 1451, and 9.3 in 1465.

64. See discussion in Gavitt, "Charity," chap. 5; Pinto, pp. 126–27; table 2 in Trexler, "Foundlings," p. 265; and Sandri, pp. 99–110 (the latter two dealing entirely with the fifteenth century).

65. See discussion in Trexler, "Foundlings" (p. 265), and, *inter alia,* the records of the Innocenti published in Livi (pp. 218 ff), where the identities of either or both parents are usually given. About half of the bearers of children to the Innocenti in the late fifteenth century were willing and able to identify the mother; half refused. About a quarter of them identified the father (Trexler, "Foundlings," p. 265).

66. Sandri discusses fifteenth-century *segni* at some length (pp. 110–28). Few such records have survived, and when they do, the degree of detail they encompass can easily be confused with their "completeness": previous researchers have failed to take into account the great likelihood that the records of such institutions are imperfect, even in years when entries are copious and detailed. Given the severe

would normally be expected to reimburse the hospital for expenses, which may be part of the reason reclamations were extremely rare.[67] The earliest series of such records is from Florence in the first half of the fifteenth century and suggests that (then and there, at least) the children abandoned were usually unweaned infants[68] of urban origin,[69] in good health when they reached the hospital; about sixty percent were female.[70] Approximately half were abandoned as a result of social catastrophe (famine, poverty, war) or personal difficulty: for example, after his wife died and he was unable to care for them, a Florentine weaver abandoned to San Gallo four of his seven children, aged six, five, four, and two.[71] About half were illegitimate,[72] but to infer that "illegitimacy" was the cause of abandonment would be an oversimplification, since among the lower classes irregular unions and illegitimate children were familiar, and even prosperous parents often retained bastards.[73] Those exposed were usually the offspring of parents of very disparate status: about a

---

financial and staffing difficulties most of them suffered, it is unlikely that they kept consistently accurate records even of such basic matters as the number of children admitted. Gavitt notes that the Innocenti, whose records are the most complete of any late medieval foundling home, completely lost track of some of its wards: "Charity," p. 396.

67. Trexler, "Foundlings," p. 270; cf. Sandri, as above. Trexler surmises that the leaving of tokens with the children represented hope or the assuaging of guilt more than a realistic indication of intention to reclaim.

68. In "normal" times, 95.9 percent were unweaned; in "hard" times, as many as a third might be a year old or more (Trexler, "Foundlings," p. 266).

69. In the period 1404–13, only one in twenty children at San Gallo whose provenance can be traced came from a rural area. Two decades later, three-eighths of the known origins were outside the city (Trexler, "Foundlings," p. 266).

70. Over sixty percent at San Gallo; just under at the Innocenti: Trexler, "Foundlings," p. 267. For physical health, ibid., p. 268.

71. Ibid., pp. 273–74.

72. Ibid., p. 274, table 4. Trexler himself seems confused on this issue: in addition to this table, he says specifically, on pp. 266–67, that the majority of abandoned children were not illegitimate, but then appears to contradict this on p. 270.

73. Legitimation by the church was possible for many children, and, in some areas of Europe, by the government as well: see, e.g., the cases cited in notes 15 and 16, above. One need not have been the son of a prelate to merit such a favor: see, e.g., JJ 126, n. 24, folio 13v (January 1385), in *Recueil*, vol. 5 (Poitiers, 1891); and JJ 200, n. 80, folio 45 (April 1468), in *Recueil*, vol. 11 (Poitiers, 1909), no. 942, pp. 113–15. In the latter, a "filius naturalis" legitimated by the king had already become a "magister in artibus et medicinis" before his legitimation, suggesting that bastards could prosper even without this nicety.

third of the first hundred children given to the Innocenti had slave mothers and unidentified fathers—presumably owners or other free members of the household.[74]

Whether or not an infant had been baptized was the first concern of the hospital authorities, and salt, notes, or personal testimony were all taken as indications.[75] In the absence of any clue, babies were baptized conditionally, and then assigned to a wet nurse, sometimes in the hospital, but more commonly in the countryside, following an ancient custom also observed by the wealthier classes of much of Europe.[76] The length of time before weaning, the rules and pay for the nurses, the degree of institutional supervision, and the fate of the child after returning to the hospital varied widely from city to city, and are neither well known nor a subject of easy summary.[77] Boys were generally apprenticed as early as possible and left the hospital to earn a living, while girls were sometimes given a modest dowry and married by institutional authority.[78] Marriage presented difficulties, however, in societies where social standing was of great importance.[79] Children were occasionally "adopted"

74. Pinto, pp. 126–27; Trexler, "Foundlings," p. 270; at the Ospedale della Misericordia of Prato between 1372 and 1394, also a third (eight out of twenty-three) of infants whose parentage is known were the children of slaves. But the majority (sixty-one) were of unknown ancestry: Livi, p. 111.

75. Trexler, "Foundlings," p. 269; Sandri, pp. 122–23. In the absence of other information some authorities considered infants under fifteen days to have been unbaptized; older than this to have been baptized. About 68 percent of the first one hundred admissions to the Innocenti for whom such information is available had not been baptized.

76. "Even the newly born infants of rich families were frequently placed in rural households, to be nursed for their first year of life in the countryside" (Herlihy, *Medieval and Renaissance Pistoia*, p. 91). On the other hand, in the years 1375–85, Guido dell'Antella, a Florentine, employed in his home four nurses (two of them slaves) for his four children, as well as three others outside the home (Heers, *Esclaves*, p. 202). It is tempting to view the placing of exposed children with wet nurses as an ironic assimilation to the status of wealthy children, but, in fact, even very poor women often gave their babies to others to nurse: see, e.g., Fournier, *Registre* 1.382, where an extremely humble peasant girl gives her illegitimate child to someone else to nurse.

77. See Gavitt, "Charity," and individual discussions in works cited in note 55, above, especially Pinto, Sandri, and Billot, who address questions about nursing in some detail. For more general discussion of nursing at Florence, see especially Christiane Klapisch-Zuber, "Parents de sang, parents de lait: la mise en nourrice à Florence (1300–1530)," ADH (1983) 33–64.

78. Pinto, pp. 125–26; Trexler, "Foundlings," p. 261; cf. Billot, p. 169.

79. Trexler, "Foundlings," pp. 261–62.

by childless couples or individuals, but, despite efforts on the part of hospital authorities to ensure the sincerity of the foster parents, most such arrangements were simply a means to obtain cheap labor, as is evident from the fact that when the "adopted" children died their bodies were returned to the Innocenti for burial rather than interred in the adopter's family plot.[80] Older systems of abandonment in which families took personal responsibility for an *alumnus* (or *alumna*), or even a child they had brought up as a servant, probably imposed less stigma on *expositi* than foundling homes, which produced classless, familyless, unconnected adolescents with no claim on the support or help of any persons or groups in the community.

But becoming a nonperson socially was less terrible than a much more common fate of children left at the hospitals. Paradoxically, tragically, and, from a modern point of view, predictably, gathering so many infants in one place in societies with very little awareness of hygiene and almost no real medicine resulted in an appalling death rate. In the later fourteenth century 20 percent of the infants died within a month of their arrival at San Gallo, and another 30 percent within a year. Only 32 percent lived to age five.[81] At La Scala in the next century 25 percent died within a month, and another 40 percent within a year; only 13 percent reached their sixth year.[82] The statistics were less horrifying at the Innocenti when it opened, but within a century an abandoning parent was "consigning his child to death."[83] (Compare a mortality rate of 17 percent among Florentine

80. Gavitt, "Charity," pp. 438–66, discusses this in great detail. Contracts were sometimes made requiring that a boy be taught a trade or a girl given a dowry (see Passerini, *Storia,* pp. 667–68, for such a contract), but more often the children were simply farmed out to work, without any other agreement than that the employer would clothe and feed them; many were returned to the hospital when no longer needed, before they were even old enough to benefit from apprenticeship or dowry (Gavitt, "Charity," pp. 456ff.). The hospitals themselves also made use of the children, through manual labor and other enterprises: sometimes they were taken out begging (ibid., p. 339), and sometimes lent to maintain the milk supply of nurses (ibid., p. 396).

81. Pinto, p. 127.

82. Sandri, p. 161.

83. Trexler, "Foundlings," pp. 275–76. Gavitt, "Charity," found that the mortality rate at the Innocenti in the fifteenth century ranged from 25 to 60 percent (p. 372), but tended toward the latter figure. Billot finds lower figures for older children at Chartres in the fifteenth century, but is suspicious of underreporting, and reports a death rate of "nearly 100 percent" for infants in some years (pp. 176–77). The situation grew worse instead of better in succeeding centuries:

children put out to nurse by their parents between 1300 and 1530.)[84]

The causes of infant death are complex in most circumstances, and given the level of medical sophistication at the time it would be unrealistic to expect the fragmented records of the hospitals to disclose the precise cause of these staggering rates of mortality.[85] The wet nurses were often blamed. Low and erratic pay were constant difficulties for them, occasioned by the limited and fluctuating income of the hospitals themselves.[86] They were often poor, and sometimes nursed several children at once;[87] if they were already

---

the mortality figures for foundling homes of the eighteenth century are appalling. In Reims, 46 percent of abandoned infants died before the age of one. Bardet finds a mortality rate of 91 percent among infants and 86.4 percent among all children admitted to foundling homes in Rouen in the eighteenth century: Jean-Pierre Bardet, "Enfants abandonnés et assistés à Rouen," *Sur la population française au XVIIe et XVIIIe siècles: Homages à Marcel Reinhard* (Paris, 1973) 19–47. In Lyons it was between 62.5 and 75 percent (Garden, *Lyons*, p. 128). In Paris, 77 percent of those in foundling hospices died before the age of twelve (as compared to 28 percent of Parisian children reared at home: both given in d'Angeville, p. 34; cf. Flandrin's estimate that during this period, "between 200 and 300 children out of every thousand died in their first year" [*Families*, p. 53]). In smaller towns the mortality was even worse: in the hospital of St. Yves at Rennes, of 112 children admitted in 1747, only 2 survived for a year (Meyer, "Illegitimates," p. 258). A general inquiry into French foundling hospitals found that between 1770 and 1776 "15,419 of a total of 21,002 children had died before the age of four" (ibid., p. 261).

84. Klapisch-Zuber, "Parents de sang," pp. 48–53, especially p. 51.

85. Sandri (pp. 161–70) discusses the causes of death recorded for infants admitted to La Scala in the fifteenth century, and speculates on what is omitted from the records. No previous investigator of this subject has considered lack of affection and physical touch as important causes, but there is little doubt among modern experts that these alone can cause infants to sicken and die: this subject is explored in Sally Provence and Rose Lipton, *Infants in Institutions* (New York, 1962); see also "The Experience of Touch: Research Points to a Critical Role" (*New York Times*, Feb. 2, 1988, pp. C1 and 4), which summarizes research showing that essential brain chemicals are released by touch, and that children may die without the physical contact necessary for such release. It is, of course, difficult to know how much or little contact babies in foundling homes actually received, but it seems probable that they were often afforded less attention and intimacy than children kept at home.

86. San Gallo preferred rural nurses not only because they were thought to be healthier, but because they could be paid less: Pinto, p. 129. In the middle of the fifteenth century the commune simply stopped funding the Innocenti for a time, resulting in starvation for the children, who could not be put out to nurse: Trexler, "Foundlings," p. 278.

87. In Florence they were not allowed to nurse their own children if they were hired to nurse someone else's, at least not officially (Trexler, "Infanticide," p. 113,

undernourished they may have provided the children little suste-
nance. On the other hand, a nurse would lose a much needed source
of income when a child died, and had therefore every incentive to
keep him as healthy as possible; many became deeply attached to
children they suckled.[88] They were, moreover, the obvious suspects
in the death of a baby and therefore subject to close scrutiny by hospital authorities (even in regard to the quality of their milk).[89] The
frequent difficulty of finding nurses was itself probably a contributing cause, or the transferring of children from one to another.[90]

The primary culprit was certainly communicable disease, en-
demic and deadly, following the children into the hospital, sweeping through its wards, and pursuing its victims out into their
nursing homes. Society's efforts to minimize the possibly tragic
consequences of anonymous abandonment produced, with bitter
irony, a system that guaranteed the deaths of a majority of exposed
children by magnifying their communal vulnerability to ordinary
disease.

Did no one care? In fact, few people could have known. This was
a case in which the mysteries surrounding abandonment obscured it
even from contemporaries. A major benefit of the foundling-home
system was that the problem of unwanted children was removed
from the streets and the view of ordinary citizens. The children disappeared behind institutional walls, where specialists were paid to
deal with them, so that parents, relatives, neighbors, and society
could forget. How would a parent know that the vast majority of
such children died? Even if a father or mother attempted to reclaim
a child and learned that he had died, this would not in itself be sus-

---

n. 3). Such a provision would be hard to enforce in the countryside, and in the city
might lead to the abandonment of the nurse's own children, whom she might then
be paid to nurse: a kind of welfare system with aid to dependent children at the
price of technical abandonment. Cf. Gavitt, "Charity," p. 428.

88. See, e.g., the case cited in Pinto, p. 131, where a woman and her husband
ask to keep the child she has been paid to nurse because they love her.

89. Cf. remarks on this by Pinto, p. 132, and more general issues in Klapisch-
Zuber, "Parents de sang," pp. 48–53. Gavitt ("Charity," pp. 384–85) notes that
the abandoning parents themselves often implored the hospitals not to send their
children out to wet nurses, apparently fearing the consequences.

90. See Pinto, p. 128; goats were sometimes used when wet nurses could not
be found. Nonabandoned children also changed nurses with some frequency: according to Klapisch-Zuber ("Parents de sang," pp. 45–48) about a third changed
nurses at least once.

picious. A high percentage of parents in premodern societies had experienced the death of at least one child.

It seems possible that the upper classes, to whom appeals for support were directed and from whose members staff was drawn, had some notion of the situation in the hospitals, while the lower strata of society, less likely to be accurately informed about institutional matters before the rise of popular news media, would have had little information on the subject. This would, of course, perpetuate the situation to a considerable degree, since the group most likely to abandon children would feel no reluctance to do so, and only those who could afford the luxury of a large family would shrink from delivering their offspring to the mortal dangers of foundling hospices (e.g., Boccaccio).[91]

What of the nurses, the officials, the civil authorities? The wet nurses themselves, of course, faced the deaths individually and could not have had a clear idea of the general rate for the hospital. Moreover, they were in a vulnerable and defensive position, and their primary concern was doubtless to convince the authorities that they were not responsible for any particular demise and could be trusted with future children. They were hardly likely to raise a hue and cry about the system that supported them and their own families.

Civic leaders appear to have been indifferent to the fate of the children themselves, were often hostile to the hospitals, and grudged keenly the large sums of money required to pay nurses and maintain the institutions. No records survive from the fourteenth or fifteenth centuries of any civil inquests or accountings of the health, well-being, or prospects of the children—only of squabbles over expenses, budgets, and procedures.[92]

If Salimbene's account of the hospital administrator who allowed foundlings to die because he resented the expense of maintaining them depicts more than an isolated instance, the staff of the homes may have contributed in some ways to the carnage. In any event, given their precarious position and constant struggles with the civic bureaucracy, it would have been amazingly courageous for them to alert the public to their inability to preserve their charges. And it is difficult to know how clear a picture even they would have had of the horror occurring under their auspices. Often they were un-

91. On the other hand, this did not prevent Rousseau from casually abandoning five children to foundling homes.
92. See Gavitt, "Charity," chap. 3, "Hospital, Guild, and Commune."

married religious, denizens of a world possessed of few statistics and given to colorful exaggerations of numbers; they may have felt that what they witnessed was the normal toll of human frailty, a sad reminder of the fragile nature of sublunary existence.

Life was perilous in the Middle Ages, and never more so than during the tumultuous fourteenth and fifteenth centuries—a period singularly turbulent even by the standards of a continent that had known little sustained peace and many plagues. Governments collapsed, the moral authority of the church failed, the greatest pestilence in European history halved a population already reeling under famine and economic dislocation; internecine wars all over the continent—sometimes lasting a century or more—drew vast numbers into their violence and employed such lethal innovations as gunpowder. It would have been difficult even for a modern actuary to develop a view of "normal" mortality among the institutionalized infants of the time. (The Archbishop of Armagh complained in the middle of the fourteenth century that parents were keeping their children home from school out of fear of their being coerced into joining mendicant orders, and that this was why enrollment at Oxford had dropped from the thirty thousand students of his day to a paltry six thousand.[93] He wrote this in 1357, seven years after the Black Death had swept through Europe, reducing its population by as much as a half: yet this did not occur to him as the cause of the decline.)[94]

Indeed, contemporaries often expressed satisfaction and pride in foundling homes as a sign of the advance of civilization. A Florentine chronicler of the early fifteenth century evinced poignant optimism about communal charity for the exposed:

> Still other hospices receive infants born secretly. One of these is Santa Maria della Scala, another San Gallo, and a third in the Piazza de' Servi is called the "New Hospital" [sc., the Innocenti]. And these will accept any children of either gender, all of whom are given to nurses and cared for; and when the girls are grown they are all married off, and the males are taught a trade, which is a wonderful thing.[95]

93. Oliger, "De pueris oblatis," pp. 443–44.

94. See general discussion in William Courtenay, "The Effect of the Black Death on English Higher Education," *Speculum* 55, 4 (1980) 696–714; Courtenay does not mention this specific instance.

95. *"L'Istoria de Firenze"* of Gregorio Dati, ed. Luigi Pratesi (1905), cited in Herlihy, "Medieval Children," p. 137, n. 50 (my translation).

The paradox of the foundling hospital—neatly organized, modern, civic, discreet, and deadly—was exquisitely calibrated to the times. Like the general ethos of the age that devised it, it was born of despair and hope, resignation and optimism, triumph and disaster. It arose during a time when plague, famine, war, political and religious collapse, urban violence, and enormous social disruptions wasted much of Europe. Yet these were also the centuries of the Renaissance: a period of spectacular growth, accomplishment, intellectual rebirth, and cultural glory.[96] The fourteenth was not only the century of the Black Death, the Hundred Years War, the Babylonian Captivity, and the Great Schism, but also of Dante, Giotto, Petrarch, Boccaccio, and Chaucer, the century of the flowering of vernacular literature all over Europe, an explosion of humanist learning and culture. The relationship of these seemingly opposed trends is not difficult to conceptualize: rebirth is a logical consequence of death and destruction. The disintegration of old structures requires new ones. Creativity must fill the void of collapse and impose new order on chaos.

It is no accident that the Renaissance was most notable in Italy: the destruction of the period was also most pronounced in Italy. It was in Italy that the plague first came ashore from Asia, on an Italian ship; in Italy that political upheaval was most pronounced during the later Middle Ages, leaving the peninsula, by the opening of the sixteenth century, a tattered assemblage of decaying municipalities and foreign colonies. It was in Italy that economic fluctuations were most disruptive, that the catastrophic fortunes of the papacy were most devastating, that the displacement of feudal structures by commercial economies (and of chivalric armies by mercenary troops) was most keenly felt, and where the dislocation of medieval intellectual patterns by new cultural movements was most obvious. Italy experienced rebirth first because Italy died first, both physically and culturally.

And it was in the turbulent, decadent, and creative Italian city-

96. This aspect of the period was immortalized, almost without reference to the darker side, by Jacob Burckhardt in *The Civilization of Renaissance Italy* (New York, 1954), first published in German in 1860. Somewhat more modern approaches can be found in W. K. Ferguson, *The Renaissance in Historical Thought* (Cambridge, Mass., 1948) or G. Duby, *Foundations of a New Humanism, 1280–1440* (Cleveland, 1966). Recent studies of particular merit and relevance are Richard Trexler, *Public Life in Renaissance Florence* (New York, 1980) and Klapisch-Zuber, *Women, Family, and Ritual in Renaissance Italy*.

states that the most significant early modern development in the handling of abandoned children first took hold, and from which it spread, like Renaissance art and literature, to the rest of Europe. The process of the dissemination and its particular evolution in different countries constitute separate chapters in the history of abandonment, outside the range of this study. But it is striking that they begin, like most earlier chapters, in Italy. For more than a millennium the Italian peninsula had been establishing the patterns of European abandonment—creating and disseminating the myths of the founding foundlings, institutionalizing the position of *alumni,* promulgating laws about the status of exposed children and the rights of parents and finders. Roman models, images, legislation, metaphors, and terminology for abandonment influenced the whole of the Mediterranean and much of Europe throughout the Middle Ages. It was Italy that adopted the Middle-Eastern religion Christianity and named it heir to Rome's cultural and political patrimony, transforming imperial modes of abandonment into Christian ones (e.g., by having children left at churches instead of public buildings). It was in an Italian religious community that St. Benedict defined and instituted the most characteristic and singular form of medieval abandonment: oblation. So perhaps it was to be expected that at the end of the Middle Ages, Italy would introduce to Europe yet another way of dealing with her unwanted children, and that the latest Italian innovation, with its tragic, unintended consequences, should be imitated throughout the continent for the next half-millennium.

12

❖   ❖   ❖

CONCLUSIONS

CHILDREN were abandoned throughout Europe from Hellenistic antiquity to the end of the Middle Ages in great numbers, by parents of every social standing, in a great variety of circumstances. The rate of abandonment was probably at its highest from the later empire (beginning around A.D. 250) to the eleventh century, when it declined and remained low for perhaps two centuries. It began to climb again sometime around 1200. In particularly precarious ecologies such as Scandinavia, however, it probably remained largely constant apart from cultural variables, such as the development of religious proscriptions during the twelfth and thirteenth centuries. These may have caused some decrease in practices such as exposing, although they may only have occasioned an increase in parental anguish over actions they felt they could not avoid.

Parents abandoned their offspring in desperation when they were unable to support them, due to poverty or disaster; in shame, when they were unwilling to keep them because of their physical condition or ancestry (e.g., illegitimate or incestuous); in self-interest or the interest of another child, when inheritance or domestic resources would be compromised by another mouth; in hope, when they believed that someone of greater means or higher standing might find them and bring them up in better circumstances; in resignation, when a child was of unwelcome gender or ominous auspices; or in callousness, if they simply could not be bothered with parenthood.

Most abandoned children were rescued and brought up either as adopted members of another household or as laborers of some sort. Whether they were exposed anonymously (in which case the aim was usually to attract attention), sold, donated, substituted, or "fostered," abandoned infants probably died at a rate only slightly higher than the normal infant mortality rate at the time. The death of *expositi* is sometimes mentioned in moral writings as one of the dangers of abandonment, but vastly less often than the perils of survival, such as incest or enslavement; narrative and legal provisions rarely mention actual instances of death. Humans were the major source of power in ancient and medieval Europe, and it would require extraordinary circumstances—for example, a great oversupply of workers and a very high cost of food—to render children valueless to anyone in such a society. And even where economics might have created such a situation, the "kindness of strangers" in every age seems to have been sufficient to rescue most abandoned children.

Despite the fact that there was reason to disguise it, an enormous number of sources yield information about many aspects of abandonment, from parental motives to the feelings of exposed children; and they disclose a fascinating complexity of social and folk customs regarding the modes of abandoning, possibilities of reclamation, legal views of adoptive versus natal ancestry, the consequences of *anagnorisis,* and general social attitudes toward parent-child relations. For the Roman empire and for Europe in the High Middle Ages, it is possible to compare as separate data bases a large corpus of historical writings—laws, ethical treatments, narrative accounts, demographic remains—with an extensive imaginative literature. The juxtaposition discloses a surprising consistency, indicating that, allowing for the obvious needs of plot and genre, creative writings afford extremely valuable clues about many details of abandonment, and usually correspond closely to the facts recoverable from more traditional historical sources. Very rarely do their depictions turn out to be "quicksand stories"; often they are more like eyewitness accounts.

At no point did European society as a whole entertain serious sanctions against the practice. Most ethical systems, in fact, either tolerated or regulated it. Ancient and early Christian moralists sometimes reproached parents for exposing their offspring, but rarely because the act itself was reprehensible: it was usually condemned as a token of irresponsible sexuality, or as a dereliction of some wider duty to state or family. Almost no ancient writers adduced an inherent obligation of procreator to child; and few writers, in law, narrative, or literature, blamed individual parents for exposing children.

Christianity may well have increased the rate of abandonment, both by insisting more rigidly than any other moral system on the absolute necessity of procreative purpose in all human sexual acts, and by providing, through churches and monasteries, regular and relatively humane modes of abandoning infants nearly everywhere on the continent. Although children left at churches were regularly sold, and those donated to monasteries subjected to a kind of servitude, both of these means of regulating the problem of surplus children were conscientious responses to a difficult situation. (Oblation may have originated as a purely religious phenomenon, although it is doubtful that any human institutions are "purely" anything, and complaints from monks about parents using it to dispose of unwanted children are as old as the practice itself.)

Even in the High Middle Ages, when the church began to regulate European domestic life with great exactitude and to give it the form—regarding marriage, for example—it was to retain until modern times, abandonment remained familiar and acceptable, both in its classic form of exposing and in an array of other modes, ranging from outright sale to some kinds of fostering. By the thirteenth century, distinctions had been introduced to some civic and ecclesiastical codes to hold parents responsible if abandoned children died as a result of neglect; but much of this concern was related to the issue of baptism, and to the worry, largely instilled by developments of scholastic theology, that unbaptized infants were excluded from heaven.

The sale of children by parents, common in both ancient and medieval Europe, seems at first startlingly callous, but close attention to the desperate circumstances that often inspired it renders the parents' actions more understandable. If sale was the best hope for the child's survival, it was little different from drastic measures any parent would take to save a child. When it was a selfish decision, it was no more so than many modern forms of parental neglect or exploitation.

Two significant differences between abandonment in antiquity and in the Middle Ages may be noted. One is a gradual increase in organization and regulation occasioned by the intervention of the church. The change was slight, because, apart from oblation, which involved a small minority of abandoned children, the procedures remained somewhat *ad hoc* even when churches acted as clearing-houses, and the process depended still to a considerable extent on local custom and individual initiative, as it had in the ancient world.

The second, more important, difference was that the increasing social significance of lineage and birth in the Middle Ages gradually rendered adoption an inherently troubling and risky concept. As a theological idea it remained an important element of Western religious thought—in the importance of the adoption of the Gentiles, for example, or the adoption of all newly baptized Christians by their "spiritual parents"—but almost no one in medieval Europe idealized it as a social reality. Neither parent nor child wished to acknowledge that a family relationship was not biological. This did not prevent families from rearing abandoned children, but they almost invariably pretended the child was a biological heir. The much idealized, almost transcendent relationship of *alumnus* with foster parent, so admired in the ancient world, had only pale counterparts in medieval Europe: in Germanic "fostering," which was not specifically a means of caring for the abandoned, and in the "fostering" of children by religious leaders in the early Middle Ages. Apart from this, and the open acceptance of foundlings as servants or second-class members of households, there was general pretense that all children were born into their families. Such deceptions doubtless improved the lot of individuals, but ultimately undermined the status of foundlings as a group by implicitly denying the ancient idea that adoptive parent-child relations were not only as good as, but in some ways better than their biological counterparts. By the close of the Middle Ages they were decidedly inferior, except in purely metaphorical applications (e.g., the *alumni* of universities).

Apart from these differences and local variations, the fact of abandonment remained largely unchanged from Roman antiquity to the end of the Middle Ages. The great disjunction in its history was occasioned by the rise of foundling homes sometime in the early thirteenth century. Within a century or two nearly all major European cities had such hospices, which neatly gathered all of the troubling and messy aspects of child abandonment away from view, off the streets, under institutional supervision. Behind their walls, paid officials dealt with society's loose ends, and neither the parents who abandoned them nor their fellow citizens had to devote any further thought or care to the children. Even the foundling homes did not have to care for them for long. A majority of the children died within a few years of admission in most areas of Europe from the time of the emergence of foundling homes until the eighteenth century; in some times and places the mortality rate exceeded ninety percent.[1]

This tragic development substantially altered the demographics of the phenomenon. From imperial times to the later Middle Ages, the abandoning of children had constituted a gentle but important regulator of numerous aspects of European family life: it was a slow brake on demographic increase, removing children from their social niche and limiting their chances of marriage and reproduction; it curtailed the number of heirs without actually eliminating the children (they survived as workers and could often be relocated if heirs died); it enabled parents to correct for gender, and shifted unwanted or burdensome children to situations where they were desired or valued; it provided an opportunity for parents to give up children to a better life, with richer parents or the church. Foundling homes, by contrast, constituted a simpler and more direct means of coping with unwanted children. The intricate, gentle complexities of the systems of transfer developed in ancient and medieval Europe were transformed into a simple technique of disposal—in a hauntingly literal sense. Entrants to foundling homes were removed from the population by isolation or death. A minority returned to society in their teens, anonymous and stigmatized, but more fortunate than the greater numbers who died in infancy or early childhood.[2]

1. The horrifying mortality rates were, in fact, the major argument for closing them. By the nineteenth century, however, the death rate had declined considerably, judging by figures such as those presented in Hügel, *Findelhäuser,* pp. 436–40, and in M. Martin-Doisy, "Enfants trouvés," col. 638. The former finds, for example, that in Vienna the mortality rate for foundlings dropped from 60 percent at the end of the eighteenth century to 27 percent in 1854, almost the normal infant mortality rate for Austria at the time; the latter reports for France a high rate of 1 in 2 children in some areas, but in others rates as low as 1 in 45 (or less than 2 percent).

2. See above, comments on San Gallo, and the Innocenti. For comparable difficulties of *expositi* in later centuries, consult the studies of eighteenth-century abandonment cited in the Introduction. Note also the contrast between the common Italian surname Esposito, meaning "exposed," and the names given foundlings in the ancient world, such as Eutyche, "happily found." In the telephone directory of New Haven, Connecticut, which has about 119,000 names, of all national origins, there are 328 Espositos.

One of the most colorful features of early modern foundling hospitals was a revolving door in a niche in the wall which allowed a parent or servant to deposit a child safely without being observed. In France it was called the *tour;* in Italy, the *ruota.* The *tour* may have originated as early as the fourteenth century, possibly at the hospital of the Holy Spirit in Rome, but it is impossible to trace its origins precisely. Its use and significance evoke, pitifully, the poignant contrast between ancient and modern approaches to the problem of unwanted children. Under the empire their fate had been left to the whim of individuals: they were exposed in public locations in the central city, without any supervision or civic intervention, and no effort was made to regulate their treatment or to guarantee their well-being. But they were gathered up, generally survived to adulthood, reared as children as often as kept for slaves, and frequently achieved considerable success in life, often marrying into their adoptive families. Society relied on the kindness of strangers to protect its extra children, a kindness much admired and prominent in the public consciousness. Even a wild animal could be expected to feel tenderness toward exposed children: Romans looked up to see, in the center of their city, the statue of a wolf who had suckled two abandoned children and in so doing helped to found their empire. Kindness to abandoned children, their culture subtly insisted, redounds to everyone's glory; the child you expose—or take in—may rise to the very top of human society.

A millennium and a half later, their descendants, too conscientious to leave the fate of unwanted children to chance or the kindness of strangers, and too preoccupied with family ties and lineage to admire affective solutions, intervened to establish an orderly public means of handling them—a method that ensured they would not perish of hunger, be devoured by beasts, or commit incest with a relative in a brothel. In Renaissance cities the infants disappeared quietly and efficiently through the revolving doors of state-run foundling homes, out of sight and mind, into social oblivion, or, more likely, death by disease.

Abandonment now became an even greater mystery, hidden from the public behind institutional walls from which few emerged, walls that afforded little opportunity for *anagnorisis,* adoption, or triumph over natal adversity. The strangers no longer had to be kind to pick up the children: now they were paid to rescue them. But because it was their job, they remained strangers; and the children themselves, reared apart from society, apart from families, without lineage either natural or adopted, either died among strangers or entered society as strangers. Mostly they died: unkind fortune, twisting gentle intentions to cruel ends, finally united in the flesh of infants those fates which had hitherto been joined mostly in rhetoric—abandonment and death.

❖   ❖   ❖

A PPENDIX OF
T RANSLATIONS

(Of the translations below, all by the author, only the first
has previously appeared in English. A cross-reference is provided to relevant discussion in the text.)

The Disputed Baby

Greek; A.D. 49
Text: OP 1, Document 37, pp. 89–91[1]
Context: Chapters 1 and 2

From the records of Tiberius Claudius Pasio the tribune: in the ninth year of the emperor Tiberius Claudius Caesar Augustus Germanicus . . . , Pesouris appeared before the tribunal against Saraeus.

Aristocles, the lawyer for Pesouris, argued: "Pesouris, for whom I speak, picked up from a dung heap[2] a male baby named[3] Herakles in the seventh year of the Lord Tiberius Claudius Caesar. This he entrusted to the accused, who was nurse to Pesouris's son. She received her pay for the first year. And when the time came in the second year she again received it. That I speak the truth about these matters is shown by these documents in which she admits to having been paid.

"The baby being underfed, Pesouris took him away. Then she, finding a suitable moment, broke into our house and stole the baby, and wishes to bring him up as a free child.[4] I have here the first receipt for pay, and the second. I think these should be taken into account."[5]

Saraeus replied: "After I had weaned my own child, their baby was entrusted to me. I did receive from them all eight staters. After this the baby died, and [. . .][6] Now they want to take away my own son."

Theon added: "We have the documents relating to the baby."

The tribune ruled: "Since from its look the baby appears to be the child of Saraeus, if she will make a written statement with her husband that the baby entrusted to her by Pesouris died, it seems best to me to follow the decision of the lord prefect allowing her to have the baby once she has returned the money she received."

1. Cf. ibid., document 38, in which the husband of the defendant in this case complains that the plaintiff has failed to comply with the verdict. Grenfell and Hunt also provide translations.

2. ἀπὸ κοπρίαν: see chapter 2, note 108, above.

3. Presumably by Pesouris.

4. Literally, "with a free name." In document 38, Saraeus's husband complains that Pesouris has taken away his son "for servitude," leading most who have studied the case to conclude that Pesouris intended Heracles to be a servant in his household.

5. Possibly, "I thought they were worth saving."

6. The text is damaged; Grenfell and Hunt conjecture, "Then the foundling died and I was left with the money." I am less certain.

ON THE OBLATION OF CHILDREN

Rabanus Maurus
Latin; A.D. 819
Text: PL 107: 419–40 (column numbers are provided in brackets in the translation)
Context: Chapter 5

[419] Anyone who examines the holy scriptures, bestowed on the human race by supernal wisdom through divine inspiration of wise men, will find that they direct us to the destruction of infidelity and cupidity, and to the nurturing of faith and charity: so that renouncing the devil and all his works we may through faith, hope, and charity dutifully serve one God, Father, Son, and Holy Spirit. One wonders, therefore—indeed, one looks with pity—at those who, ignoring the fact that they were professed in infancy and that at the outset of life they abandoned [the world], place it first, as if it were of more eminent and greater dignity.

Some of them learned holy letters from the cradle, and were sustained by the bounty of the church until they were sufficiently well educated to be promoted to the sublimity of holy orders. But ungrateful for such a gift, they oppose the faith of orthodox fathers, and daily attack the mother of all the faithful with the weapons of their iniquity.

. . . The impudent originators of heretical doctrine pompously claim, in fact, that parents have no right to give [*tradere*] small children to the service of God, and that it is wrong to make a freeborn child a slave; they try to impose human law on God, to subordinate [his] will and authority to human sanctions. [420] They fail to recall that the Apostle said, "Whether slave or free, we are all one in Christ,"[7] and, "he that is called, being free, is Christ's slave,"[8] and "he that is called in the Lord, being a slave, is the Lord's freeman."[9] Or that the holy fathers held it a great honor

---

7. Cf. 1 Corinthians 12:13.

8. 1 Corinthians 7:22. I have diverged from the KJV by using "slave" for "servant," here and subsequently, for the Vulgate's *servus*. "Servant" fails to convey to modern readers the lack of freedom intended by New Testament writers and Rabanus. The former certainly had in mind what we would call "slaves," and the latter was probably thinking of something closer to a "serf." Modern readers are most familiar with "servants" who are free persons hired as household laborers. Although *servus* is neither exactly "slave" nor exactly "servant" in the context of this debate, it refers to perpetual, involuntary servitude, and is considerably closer to the connotations of the former.

9. 1 Corinthians 7:22.

to be called the "slaves"[10] of God, which is why Abraham, Isaac, and Jacob were called the highest slaves of God; just as Moses and the prophets Job and David were honorably designated by the name "slaves of God," when the Lord himself said to Satan, "Hast thou considered my slave Job, that there is none like him in the earth . . . ?"[11] And of David he said, "I have found David my slave; with my holy oil have I anointed him."[12]

But perhaps these authors of new dogma will reply that while they do not deny that the entire human race is bound to the service of God, this does not entitle anyone to consign [*tradat*] his son to observe monastic discipline or to follow a religious rule.

[421] . . . We have undertaken to write against those who say that it is not right for parents to commit their freeborn children to the service of God, and against those who, counting as little the oath they swore to God, angrily reject the holy service they have professed, as if they could abandon it without sin: they detest and despise the monastic discipline ordained according to the rules of the holy fathers, [regarding it] as established by human rather than divine authority. We will first show with the testimony of sacred scripture and the example of the holy fathers that it is licit to consecrate one's child to the service of God;[13] then that a vow one has sworn to God cannot be abandoned without grave sin;[14] finally, that monastic life was established not by human design but by divine authority.[15]

[422] . . . Abraham, the unequalled example of faith, obedience, and true piety, at the Lord's call left his land and his kinfolk, and passed to the land the Lord had promised him and his descendants as their own. It is told how there, in obedience to the will of the Lord, he brought his son Isaac, whom the Lord had promised him, to a place the Lord had designated. He built an altar and arranged wood upon it, gathered up his beloved son, placed him on the altar over the pile of wood, stretched out his hand and gripped his sword and was about to sacrifice him, when the angel of the Lord stopped him, saying, "Lay not thine hand upon the lad, neither do thou any thing unto him: for now I know that thou fearest God, seeing thou hast not withheld thy son, thine only son, [423] from me."[16]

. . . What will the importunate defenders of freeborn liberty, they who speak vainly against the Lord, say to this? Will they say that the patriarch acted wrongly

---

10. The normal expression in this context among English-speaking Christians is "servant of God," but this makes a weak and misleading translation here, for the reasons adduced in note 8, above.

11. Job 1:8.

12. Psalm 89 [88]:20 [21].

13. This is dealt with in PL 107.419–33, the bulk of the treatise; all of its main arguments are translated here, although repetitions, rhetorical excursus, and proliferation of biblical examples are reduced or omitted.

14. 433–34.

15. 434–40. Criticism of monastic life and defenses by monks were a long-standing Christian tradition, as Rabanus's treatment itself makes evident.

16. Genesis 22:12.

when he offered[17] his only son and heir, born of a free wife, in fulfillment of the Lord's commandment? Or will they accuse the Lord of impiety for forcing his faithful worshipper to commit infanticide? Is it not a greater evil for them to maintain that a worldly and temporal law should be given precedence over the divine and eternal law, which governs and directs all things at [God's] will? If what the eternal God orders is not right, how could what general vanity teaches be right?

. . . The same Lord who then through his oracle ordered the patriarch to offer his son as a sacrifice, now in his gospel commands the people of his church to offer their offspring to holy service; and he who then praised pious obedience for love of him, now approves holy devotion for love of him. . . . "He that loveth father or mother more than me is not worthy of me: and he that loveth son or daughter more than me is not worthy of me. And he that taketh not his cross, and followeth after me, is not worthy of me."[18] And, "Every one that hath forsaken houses, or brethren, or sisters, or children or lands, for my name's sake, shall receive an hundredfold, and shall inherit everlasting life."[19] Isaac is ultimately the faithful worshipper of God and the most devoted executor of paternal desires, the example of what the Apostle described when he said, "[He] became obedient unto death, even the death of the cross."[20] For he carried the wood for his own sacrificial fire, that he might prefigure Christ's carrying the cross to effect the sacrament of his passion.

[424] . . . Likewise Jacob, a simple man living in tents, provides us an example of greatest humility and gentleness: if we wish to inherit paternal blessing, we must remain in the tents of our simplicity, subject in all things to mother church, submitting ourselves to her rules, rather than serving the vain concerns of the world with the crude and hairy Esau. But why should I narrate the deeds of the patriarchs one by one to demonstrate the power of paternal authority to consign children to the service of God, when the Lord himself commanded Israel, in the law, to consecrate to him the firstborn of everything, saying to Moses, "Thou shalt set apart for the Lord every firstborn that openeth the womb among the children of Israel, of men and of cattle; all are mine."[21] And again, when he wished to substitute for the firstborn [of Israel] the Levites to serve the tabernacle, he spoke to Moses, saying, "Take the Levites from among the children of Israel, and cleanse them."[22] And later:

Thou shalt bring the Levites before the tabernacle of the congregation; and thou shalt gather the whole assembly of the children of Israel together.

And thou shalt bring the Levites before the Lord: and the children of Israel shall put their hands upon the Levites.

And Aaron shall offer the Levites before the Lord for an offering of the children of Israel, that they may execute the service of the Lord. . . .

17. Note that in Latin this is the verb, *offero,* used for oblation.
18. Matthew 10:37, 38.
19. Matthew 19:29.
20. Philippians 2:8.
21. Paraphrase of Exodus 13:12 and 13, 22:30, 34:20, and Numbers 3:12–13, 8:17–19.
22. Numbers 8:6.

And thou shalt . . . offer them for an offering [*oblationem*]. . . .

For they are wholly given unto me from among the children of Israel; instead of such as open every womb, even instead of the firstborn of all the children of Israel, have I taken them unto me.

For all the firstborn of the children of Israel are mine, both man and beast. . . .[23]

Notice that the Lord demands the firstborn from all those obligated to follow his laws—not just of humans, but also the firstborn of the beasts, making clear that we owe him not only what belongs to us but our very selves.

And lest you be able to propose with justice any counterargument, and say that it is not right for any man to offer his son, who is as free as he, to the service of God, he [sc., God] orders the whole people to offer one whole tribe of the twelve to the tabernacle of the convenant, to serve there as an offering to the Lord for his ministry. Who then should have greater authority—the children of Israel who offered their brothers, the Levites, denied after this donation all share of every earthly inheritance by a decree of the Lord (possession being retained among the other tribes), or a father who has determined to devote his own son, still at a tender age and not yet legally competent or responsible, [425] to the service of God according to the regulations of the holy rule, laying aside all wordly cares and business and possessions? It is one thing for an equal to be handed over by an equal, and another for a minor to be subjugated to someone by an elder. Among equals in fact arguments often arise as to whether one side will dominate the other or be relegated to servitude; but between an adult and a minor there is no reason why the younger should not subject himself to the control of the elder. And if the Lord's rule applies even to adults, why do the idle gossipers and instigators of malicious charges not cease criticizing the laws of God?

[426] . . . It is written in the book of Judges that Jephthah the Gileadite, "a most valiant man," moved by the spirit of God, swore a vow to the Lord as he prepared to make war against the Ammonites to rescue Israel from their hands:

If thou wilt deliver the children of Ammon into my hands, whosoever shall first come forth out of the doors of my house and shall meet me when I return in peace from the children of Ammon, the same will I offer a holocaust to the Lord.

And Jephthah passed over to the children of Ammon, to fight against them: and the Lord delivered them into his hands. . . . And the children of Ammon were humbled by the children of Israel.

And when Jephthah returned into Mizpeh to his house, his only daughter met him with timbrels and with dances: for he had no other children.

And when he saw her, he rent his garments, and said, Alas! my daughter, thou hast deceived me, and thou thyself art deceived:[24] for I have opened my mouth unto the Lord, and I can do no other thing.

---

23. Numbers 8:9–17; cf. Numbers 3.
24. *Sic* in Rabanus, following the Vulgate: "decepisti me, et ipsa decepta es."

And she answered him: My father, if thou hast opened thy mouth to the Lord, do unto me whatsoever thou hast promised, since the victory hath been granted to thee, and revenge of thy enemies.

And she said to her father: Grant me only this which I desire: Let me go, that I may go about the mountains for two months, and may bewail my virginity with my companions.

And he answered her: Go. And he sent her away for two months. And when she was gone with her comrades and companions, she mourned her virginity in the mountains. And the two months being expired, she returned to her father, and he did to her as he had vowed, and she knew no man.[25]

And what will they say to this, those friends of mine whose discourse is always directed to criticizing our order? Who is so stupid and perverse that he would accuse Jephthah of sacrilege because he sacrificed his daughter on account of a vow he made to God, when the scripture says that he did this because "the spirit of the Lord came upon him," and especially when the Apostle Paul in the Epistle to the Hebrews counts him among the number of the saints? If it was permitted the parents of that time to sacrifice a son or daughter to the Lord by the knife, how could it not be proper for men of this age to consecrate their offspring to God spiritually, offering them as living gifts, holy and pleasing to God, thus reasonably honoring Christ?

If the offering of Abraham pleased God, and Jephthah's deed earned him the merits of sanctity, why should we not believe that religious oblation instituted by evangelical teaching is much more pleasing to God? Especially when the Apostle James says of Abraham, "Was not Abraham our father justified by works, when he had offered Isaac his son upon the altar?"[26]

[427] . . . The admirable deed of Hanna, recorded in the book of Samuel, also demonstrates this, when it describes her as sterile and ridiculed for this by her rival, the other wife of Elkanah her husband. She turns in prayer to the Lord, and he does not disappoint her hope, but grants her request, as it is written:

O Lord of hosts, if thou wilt look down on the affliction of thy servant, and wilt be mindful of me, and not forget thy handmaid, and wilt give to thy servant a man child: I will give him to the Lord all the days of his life, and no razor shall come upon his head.[27]

. . . And Elkanah knew Hanna his wife: and the Lord remembered her. And it came to pass when the time was come about, Hanna conceived

---

Cf. KJV, which is closer to the Hebrew: "thou hast brought me very low, and thou art one of them that trouble me."

25. Judges 11:30–39. I have used here the Douay-Rheims translation of the Vulgate version quoted by Rabanus, retaining the more common KJV transliterations of names.

26. James 2:21.

27. 1 Samuel [Kings] 1:11, Douay-Rheims.

and bore a son, and named his name Samuel: because she had asked him of the Lord.[28]

. . . And after she had weaned him, she carried him with her, with three calves, and three bushels of flour, and a bottle of wine, and she brought him to the house of the Lord in Shiloh. Now the child was as yet very young:

And they immolated a calf, and offered the child to Eli.

And Hanna said, . . . I am that woman who stood before thee here praying to the Lord.

For this child did I pray, and the Lord hath granted me my petition, which I asked of him.

Therefore I also have lent him to the Lord all the days of his life, he shall be lent to the Lord.[29]

I should like to know what those haters and detractors of monastic oblation would say about this offering [*oblatione*], which is almost identical to the monastic oblation the blessed father Benedict established in his Rule? Just as there he commands parents to offer their infant children at the altar with a gift and a petition, [428] here this holy woman and prophetess solemnly offered her infant son to the Lord in the presence of Eli with a gift of wheat and other items, as recorded in the book of Kings.[30]

Do they think Hanna did this as the result of insolence: swearing this vow to God before the conception of her firstborn child without the consent or command of her husband, as if this lay within her own power? Then, after his birth—although with her husband's consent—it was nevertheless she who took him faithfully to the Lord and there diligently expounded to Eli the priest the whole story of her vow. Who, however, would dare to say that the Lord is wicked for granting this woman, on the merits of her faith and as the effect of her great devotion, the grace of his holy spirit?

And as many examples of this sort may be found in the Old Testament, so also similar testimony to this effect occurs in the New. . . . The Holy Gospel relates that the parents of the Savior deposited Jesus as a boy in the temple with an offering as decreed by the Lord, so that the giver of the law might corroborate and confirm by his own example and might demonstrate that the offerings and devotion of the faithful in his church do not in any way displease him. If Jesus wished to be conveyed to the temple by his parents and there to be offered for them as an offering to God, who will dare to find fault with the oblation of children by their parents, or prevent them from making a living offering to God?

The faith not only of those being offered, but also of those offering is acceptable to God, as the scripture makes clear. This is why the baptism of infants is conferred in holy church by virtue of the faith and profession of the parents:

28. The Hebrew name Samuel is composed of parts which may be interpreted to mean "asked of God."

29. 1 Samuel [Kings] 1:19–20, 26–28, Douay-Rheims.

30. *Sic,* although above, Rabanus had identified it as the book of "Samuel." The Vulgate applies both names to what the KJV calls "Samuel."

[429] And they brought young children to him, that he should touch them, and his disciples rebuked those that brought them.

But when Jesus saw it, he was much displeased, and said unto them, Suffer the little children to come unto me, and forbid them not: for of such is the kingdom of God.

Verily I say unto you, Whosoever shall not receive the kingdom of God as a little child, he shall not enter therein.

And he took them up in his arms, put his hands upon them, and blessed them.[31]

Let them hear these things who oppose the oblation of children, and know that they exert themselves in an evil cause and a vain one, objecting to the age [sc., of oblates], as if it were not the prerogative of parents to offer their infants to God, and to give them over to his service. If he, the very Truth, was indignant with his earthly disciples when they rebuked those that brought the children, even though they had not yet been enlightened and inspired by his passion and resurrection and the coming of the Holy Spirit, what do these people think they are earning for themselves, arguing contrary to the Catholic faith with hearts hardened by earthly desire, even though the church is now spread throughout the world and the truth is everywhere plain, and by introducing into the church new heresies, though the end of the world approaches?

[431] . . . Since they have heard that monastic oblation of very young children is supposed to be confirmed by suitable witnesses, and since they dare not openly gainsay and resist the truth, they seek a way to accomplish through subterfuge the nefarious ends their perverted minds contemplate. So they argue subtly, and, to mislead their followers and subordinates more easily, take as the pretext for their error the argument that it is only licit to call as a witness in confirming the truth of the Christian religion a person of the same people:[32] for example, they say that regarding a Saxon, no Frank or Roman or anyone from any other people—no matter how noble of birth or lofty of character he may be considered among his own people—may be a witness, but only another Saxon. The law of his own people, they say, could not suffer a person of another to be called as witness for limiting someone's legal freedom. As if they lose their freedom and nobility of lineage who profit from the service of Christ, when it is obvious that they are freer who serve one God than are those who are in servitude to many vices and sins.

Clearly they adduce this argument for no other reason than to arouse disrespect among the people for monastic life and religious discipline, saying that those who become monks are made slaves. . . . If respect of persons and national origin were to be considered in every case, and witnesses approved in such a way that one would accept none who were not of his people, how then would the other nations have received the testimony of the Jews for faith in Christ, since they were not similar in religion or heritage [*natione*]? The apostles and prophets were all Jewish.

31. Mark 10:13–16; cf. Matthew 19:13–15, Luke 18:15–17.

32. I have translated both *gens* and *natio* in the following sentences as "people"; "nation" might also be possible, but bears connotations from modern political concepts which are not appropriate to the historical circumstance in question.

LETTER OF POPE NICHOLAS I TO THE FRANKISH BISHOPS CONCERNING INVOLUNTARY RELIGIOUS PROFESSION FOR MINORS

Latin; ninth century
Text: MGH Epp. 4, no. 131, pp. 652–54; PL 161.519–20; cf.
  Decretum 2.20.3.4 (Friedberg, 849–50)
Context: Chapters 5 and 8

A man named Lambert, presently a cleric, came to the Holy See, along with his father Atto, formerly a count and now a cleric. He addresses us personally, stating that his father, while still a layman, had built two monasteries at his own expense, with the intention that after his death, Lambert his son should succeed him. The father then of his own accord and quite irregularly, entirely without the son's consent, put a cowl on [Lambert] when he was still at a tender age, somewhere between eight and eleven.[33]

On account of this, Lambert claims, after a certain period of time, Bishop Salomon forced him unwillingly to accept a monk's habit along with some others— although Lambert himself had not been donated by a parent, nor given the blessing of the abbot—and constrained him, entirely against his will, he says, to remain a regular monk. As a consequence of this he was deprived of his paternal and maternal inheritance by his siblings.

We have carefully investigated this matter and interrogated his father under oath to see if what he said was true. The cleric Atto responded that he considered himself a real monk and had intended that his son should be a real monk and follow in his footsteps. But testifying under oath he admitted that at first whenever he had tried to put a cowl on him Lambert had always resisted and never consented to becoming a monk, but finally he had been forcibly dressed in the habit by retainers. He admitted that Lambert had never sworn obedience, "nor did I, his father, offer him wrapped in the pallium at the altar, nor was he ever made a monk by receiving the blessing of the rule from any priest or abbot, as custom requires."

In relation to this the said Atto the cleric also confided that if he had realized then how severe monastic life was, he would never have forced his son Lambert to wear the cowl.

Wherefore, advisedly recalling those words of the Psalmist with which he announces that he will freely sacrifice himself to the Lord[34] and prays that the "freewill offerings of [his] mouth"[35] should be made acceptable in the sight of the Lord,

---

33. Ten, according to some versions, including Gratian: see Friedberg.
34. Psalms 54 [53]:6.
35. Psalms 119 [118]:108.

we have concluded that the said Lambert ought not to have been made a monk through the use of such force. What someone does not choose he neither desires nor loves; what he does not love he easily despises. There is no good which is not voluntary. This is why the Lord himself commanded that no stave be carried on the way,[36] lest any injury result from it. It would, therefore, have been better advised to have preached contempt of the world and love of God with pious persuasion than to have incited him to celestial love through the use of force.

Wherefore we have determined to send this our apostolic letter to all your graces, warning and directing that, if it is as they say, no bishop or abbot or monastery of other monks should compel him against his will to accept monastic discipline, nor may his siblings on this account have any license whatever to deprive him of his inheritance from either father or mother; rather, until such time as divine inspiration should move him of his own free will to submit to monastic life, let him live in canonical life among religious and churchmen, apart from worldly and secular pursuits and concerns. We do not, indeed, regard religious canons as separate from the fellowship of holy monks, because according to the Apostle "every man shall receive his own reward according to his own labor."[37]

36. Matthew 10:10.
37. 1 Corinthians 3:8.

COMPLICATIONS REGARDING A RENTED CHILD

Latin; late eleventh century; Normandy
Text: P. le Cacheux, *"Une charte de jumièges concernant l'épreuve par la fer chaud (fin du XI siècle),"* Société de l'histoire de Normandie: Mélanges *(Rouen, 1927), pp. 205–16 (page numbers are provided in brackets in the translation)*
Context: Chapter 7

[213] In the days of Richard, Count of Normandy, and of his son Robert, and of William the son of Robert, there was a chaplain of theirs at Bayeux named Ernald, a man rich in goods and real estate both inside and outside the city, which he had bought with his own gold and silver. When he died, during the rule of William, the Duke of the Normans, Stephen, nephew of the said Ernald, inherited according to the laws of succession the estate of his uncle by grant of Duke William. This Stephen had a little son by a widow of Bayeux named Oringa, the sister of a Norman, Ambarius. When the child died, the ingenious woman, without Stephen's knowledge, rented a child from a woman called Ulburga who lived in the village of Merdignac,[38] paying her ten sous a year.

Stephen believed the child his and made him heir of his property, that is, of the homes he had at the Gate of Trees inside the city and of twelve acres of land he held at Gold Spring outside the city and of some fields from which he derived income. Then, after first his wife and later Stephen himself passed away, the said woman from Merdignac, not receiving the rent she was accustomed to getting for her son, demanded the return of the child, but could not get him back from the relatives of Stephen's wife. Word of her claim reached William the duke, who had by now become king, and his wife, Matilda, in the village of Bonneville. The king arranged to have a hearing to determine whether the woman should regain her child. King William, Archbishop John,[39] [214] Roger Belmont, and a number of others decided that the woman claiming the boy should regain her son by means of the ordeal of hot iron if God should preserve her unharmed.

King William and his wife Mathilda sent me, Rainald, their clerk, to Bayeux to witness the ordeal; William the archdeacon, now Abbot of Fécamp, Godselin the archdeacon, Robert of Lille, with his wife Albereda, Evremar of Bayeux, and quite a few other outstanding citizens went with me at the king's behest. When the ordeal was carried out in the little monastery of St. Vigor, the woman reclaiming her

---

38. "Merdiniacus": Le Cacheux gives "Merdigny"; both are conjectural.
39. Jean d'Avranches, archbishop of Rouen from 1067 to 1079..

son was unharmed by the judgment of God, as I and the other named witnesses observed.[40]

And when the king learned this from me and the other witnesses he laid claim to the estate of Stephen and gave it to the queen, who gave me, with the approval of the king, the houses and the twelve acres I mentioned before and the fields and all of Stephen's free holdings. [215] . . . To Geoffrey the cleric, surnamed the Masculine, I gave one field from the estate in return for his service; and another, yielding eleven sous a year, I gave to Evremar, in return for which he is to look out for my interest in court, if necessary, and whenever during the year I come to Bayeux he is to provide me, the first night, with wine and beer and good bread, according to custom, and to feed my horses, and—for this I have the witness of my lady the queen—to advance me up to 100 sous in the city if I should need them. And a third field I gave to Vitale the clerk that he should serve me. . . . All these things which I have described can be verified by Vitale the clerk, who was with me throughout. . . .

40. Note that three of the witnesses—Rainald, Evremar, and Vitale—ultimately came into possession of portions of the disputed property, which could conceivably have had something to do with the outcome..

"THE SNOW CHILD"

Latin; probably eleventh century

Text: The Oxford Book of Medieval Latin Verse, ed. F. J. E. Raby
(Oxford, 1959), no. 120, pp. 167–70[41]

Context: Chapter 7

Pay attention,
all you people,
to a funny story,
and hear how
a Swiss wife
fooled her husband,
and he her.

A Swiss citizen
of Constance,
transporting goods by ship
across the seas,
left at home
a rather
frisky wife.

Scarcely had he
split the somber sea
with his oar,
when suddenly
a storm arose
and the sea raged.
The winds blew,
the waves were tossed,
and long after,
the north wind
deposited the wandering exile
on a distant shore.

Nor, in the meantime,
was his wife idle at home:

41. From *Die Cambridger Lieder,* ed. Karl Strecker (3d edition: Berlin, 1966),
14, pp. 41–44.

actors came by,
young men followed.
Oblivious of her absent husband,
she received them cheerfully,
and the next night was pregnant.
At the proper time
she gave birth
to an improper son.

Two years pass;
the exile
returns.
The faithless wife
comes to meet him,
dragging behind her
a little boy.
They exchange kisses.
"And where,"
the husband asks her,
"did this boy come from?
You'd better explain,
or you'll really get it."

But she,
fearful of her husband,
is always ready
with a trick.
"Dear, dear husband,"
she finally begins.
"I happened to be
in the Alps,
and thirsty,
so I quenched my thirst
with snow.
Filled up [42]
from this,
I then, alas,
gave birth
to this wretched
baby boy."

Five years or more
had passed after this.
The traveling merchant
again takes up his oars.

42. *Gravida*, which means both "full" and "pregnant."

He repairs his damaged vessel,
sets the sails,
and takes the snow child
with him.

Once across the sea,
he puts the child up for sale,
trading him to a merchant
for ready cash;
he gets a hundred pounds.
Having sold the child,
he returns a rich man.

Arriving home,
he tells his wife,
"I'm so sorry, darling,
so sorry, dear.
I have lost your child,
whom you yourself
could not have loved
more than I.

"A storm came up,
and the fury of the winds drove us,
utterly exhausted,
onto the sand banks of North Africa.
The sun beat down heavily [43] on us all,
and the snow child
melted."

Thus the Swiss
fooled
his faithless wife.
So deception triumphed over deception.
For him whom the snow bore
the sun rightly melted.

43. "Nos omnes graviter torret sol"—maliciously expanding the pun of *gravida*.

THE NUN OF WATTON

Aelred of Rievaulx
Latin; mid-twelfth century; England
Text: PL 195.780–96[44]
Context: Chapter 8

[789] To know and conceal the miracles of the Lord and clear indications of divine love is a kind of sacrilege. It is not proper that something which may be a consolation for the living, an example for those to come, an inspiration to all, should escape the attention of any. Too often we are deterred by the stupidity of the multitude, who, either fearing envy or simply languishing in apathy, scarcely believe their own eyes when it comes to a matter of good, but are induced to believe something evil by the lightest touch on the ear. That is why, beloved father, I have thought it particularly desirable to disclose to you a remarkable thing, unheard of in our time: your holy good nature thinks well of everyone, and is inclined to suspect evil of no one without certain proof. Let there be no hesitation about the truth of my words, since part of what I am about to tell you I saw with my own eyes, and all of it was confirmed to me by persons whose maturity and manifest integrity would under no circumstances permit them to lie.

Among the convents of virgins which the venerable father and priest Gilbert,[45] beloved of God, established with remarkable fervor in various provinces of England, one is located in the province of York, in a place which takes its name from the fact that it is surrounded by water and marsh and is therefore called Watton, that is, "wet town."

[791] . . . During the time of Bishop Henry of York,[46] of holy and blessed memory, a certain girl thought to be about four years old was taken in to be reared[47] in this

44. I have adopted the improved readings suggested by Giles Constable in "Aelred of Rievaulx and the Nun of Watton," in Baker, *Medieval Women*, p. 205, n. 1.

45. St. Gilbert of Sempringham (d. 1189), founder of the only English monastic order, for whose canonization now see *The Book of St. Gilbert*, ed. Raymonde Foreville and Gillian Keir (Oxford, 1987). Some Gilbertine houses were double monasteries for men and women. This seems to have been the case at Watton, and Ellen Barrett, in a forthcoming article, will suggest that the context of this story is at least in part the suspicions entertained by contemporaries about such houses and the consequent defensiveness of the nuns about their modesty.

46. Henry Murdac, archbishop of York from 1147 to 1153.

47. *Nutriendam: nutrire* is the normal word for the supervision of oblates during childhood.

convent at the request of this same holy bishop. As soon as she was no longer a little child, she began to display the girlish abandon of girlish age: no love for religious life, no concern for the rule, no inclination to honor God. Her glance was flirtatious, her speech indecorous, and her walk suggestive. She went about with her head covered by the holy veil, but she managed nothing worthy of such raiment in her deeds. She was reproached by words but not corrected; injured by beatings but not chastened. She wasted hours in plain view of her teachers, either doing nothing, or making naughty signs, or telling stories, or persuading others to waste time. She was restrained by the discipline of the order, and forced against her will to maintain some external semblance of decency, but all such constraints worked on her through fear, none through love. By the time she was a teenager she preferred the superficial to the spiritual, play to reflection, and the silly to the serious.

It happened that the brothers who were in charge of the maintenance of the convent had to enter the cloister to do some work. Fascinated, she came close and hung about observing their work and appearance. One of them was a teenager, handsomer than the rest and in the bloom of youth. The unhappy girl fixed her gaze on him, and he stared back at her. While they were admiring each other with languid looks, the insidious serpent, penetrating both their hearts, deposited his fatal venom throughout their vitals. At first it was simply a matter of nods, but signs followed the nods, and finally they broke the silence and exchanged words about the sweetness of love. They spurred each other on, each watering in the other the seeds of desire, the motivations of lust. Although he was thinking about sex, she later said that she thought only of love. Meanwhile, their passion intensified.

[792] They agreed on a time and place to speak more freely and to enjoy each other more fully. Abandoning the defense of light, they preferred the darkness of night, and fleeing the open they sought a secret place. The wicked predator gave a sign to his prey: at the sound of a stone which he promised to throw against the wall or roof of the building in which she usually slept, the unfortunate girl, knowing that he had come, would slip out to meet him.

Where, father,[48] was your most diligent concern for the maintenance of discipline then? Where then were your many ingenious devices for eliminating occasions of sin? Where then was that care so prudent, so cautious, so perspicacious, and that supervision so strict in regard to every door, every window, every corner, that it seemed to deny access even to evil spirits? One girl made a mockery of all of your efforts, father, because "except the Lord keep the city, the watchman waketh but in vain."[49] You did, blessed man, what a man could do, what was called for. But just as no one could justify him whom God has given up, so no one could save him whom he has not preserved.

48. I.e., St. Gilbert, who had established the order. One might conclude from this aside that the letter was written to him, but Constable considers the identity of the addressee "unknown" ("Aelred of Rievaulx and the Nun of Watton," p. 209), and the conclusion of the letter does militate against taking Gilbert as its recipient. The outburst is probably an apostrophe directed to Gilbert as the founder of the order.

49. Psalm 127 [126]:1.

And you, unhappy girl, what were you about? What were you thinking? What made you press your ears so eagerly to the roof tiles? Where was respect, where was love, where was reverence for that holy congregation? Where was the sweet memory of the blessed bishop who had given you to the convent? None of these restrained you from such a sin. All of them forgotten, a base passion alone inhabited your heart. You rose, pitiful one; you answered the door. The divine will prevented your effort to leave; you tried again but did not succeed. You returned and observed the usual vigils of the Virgin Mary with twelve readings. What else should Christ have done for you that he did not do? Oh, remarkable hardness of heart: why would you resume your efforts to leave?

. . . What next? Alas! She goes out. Block your ears, virgins of Christ, and close your eyes. She walks out the virgin of Christ; shortly after she returns an adulteress. She goes out, and like a dove, seduced and spiritless, she is instantly caught in the talons of the hawk. She is thrown down, her mouth covered so that she cannot call out, and she is corrupted in the flesh as she had already been in the spirit.

Wickedness required repetition of the new pleasure. But after this had been going on rather often, the sisters, wondering about the sound they kept hearing at night, began to suspect something was amiss. She, in particular, fell under suspicion, since her behavior had all along seemed questionable to everyone. The flight of the youth aggravated suspicion. For once the fact of her having conceived made itself known to the adulterer, fearing that he also would be betrayed, he left the monastery to return to the world. Then the wiser nuns summoned the girl. Unable to disguise it any longer, she confessed her failing. Shock seized those who heard her. Their feelings overcame them,[50] and looking at each other they clapped their hands together and fell on her, ripping the veil from her head. Some believed that she should be burned, some that she should be skinned alive, and others that she should be tied to a tree and roasted over charcoal.

[793] The elder women restrained the fervor of the younger ones. Even so, she was stripped, stretched out, and whipped without any mercy. A prison cell was prepared, she was chained, and they put her in it. To each of her feet two rings were attached with small chains; in these they inserted two chains of considerable weight, of which one was fastened with nails to an enormous log, the other, drawn through a hole to the outdoors, was held by a bar. She was sustained on bread and water and tormented with daily scoldings.

Meanwhile, her swelling belly gave evidence of pregnancy. What a grief this was to everyone! How many laments arose from the most holy virgins, who, fearing for their honor, worried that the sin of one would be imputed to all. It was almost as if they had already exposed themselves to ridicule in the eyes of everyone, as if they were already given over to be mocked by the lips[51] of all. All wept; every single one. And roused by the intensity of their grief, they fell again on the captive. Had the older women not protected the fetus, the others would scarcely have ceased abusing her for a minute. She bore all these ills patiently, crying out

50. Literally, "zeal burned in their bones."
51. Literally, "to be nibbled by the teeth."

that she deserved yet greater punishment, but that she believed that the others would suffer no ill because of her faithlessness.

They debated what to do. If they expelled her, it would not only redound to their discredit but pose considerable danger to their souls if the destitute mother died alone with her offspring. But if they kept them, they complained, they could not conceal the birth. One said, "It is best that his pregnant whore be given back to the wicked youth with her adulterous child, and let the worries fall on him whose ill deeds occasioned them."

"If it will help you, do so," the unhappy girl responded, "even though I know it will be my ruin: the boy promised me that he would meet me on a certain night at a certain time in the place complicit in our sin. If it is your decision to give me to him, let it be done as it is willed in heaven." Seizing on her suggestion and now panting for vengeance on the youth, they besought her to tell the truth about everything. She told all, and maintained that what she had said was true.

Then the head of the congregation[52] took some of the brothers aside and explained the matter. He ordered that one of them, covering his head with the veil, should sit in the appointed spot that night, with the others hidden nearby so they could catch him when he came, beat him with clubs and hold him. It was accomplished as he directed. Ignorant of what had happened to her, the young man came, now worldly not only in attitude but in dress. Burning with lust, as soon as he saw the veil he pounced like a mindless horse or mule on the man he thought was a woman. Those present, however, administering a bitter antidote with their staffs, managed to extinguish his fever.

The situation was explained to the nuns. Right away some of them, possessed of zeal for God if not of wisdom, wishing to avenge the injury to virginity, asked the brothers to release the young man to them for a little while, as if they needed to learn some secret from him. Once in their hands, he was thrown down and held. The cause of all the evils was brought in as if to a show: they placed in her hands an instrument, and she was forced, unwilling, to unman him with her own hands. Then one of [794] those standing by, grabbing the parts of which he had been relieved, foul and bloody and just as they were, stuck them in the mouth of the sinner. You see what ardor inflamed the guardians of modesty, the avengers of uncleanness, the lovers of Christ before all else! You see how mutilating him in this way and harassing her with insults and injury they avenged the injury to Christ.

. . . I praise not the deed but the zeal; I do not approve of the shedding of blood, but I commend the great outrage of the holy virgins against immorality. What would they not suffer, not do to preserve their chastity, if they would go this far to avenge it? But to return to our subject. The mutilated boy was given back to the brothers, and the troubled woman to her cell. So far, wretched girl, we have written the story of your misfortunes, but from this point we can direct the pen to relate how the most tender mercy of Jesus rained on you: "where sin abounded, grace did much more abound."[53]

Now that vengeance had been exacted, their fervor abated, and the holy vir-

52. St. Gilbert.
53. Romans 5:20.

gins turned to the footsteps of Christ. They wept and prayed that he would spare the place, would look after their virginal modesty, would prevent a scandal, would ward off danger. Every day they appealed to the divine mercy with prayers and tears. The sinner meanwhile moved the tender heart of Jesus with the pains and injuries and insults she suffered. . . . You heeded, kind Jesus, you heeded both the zeal and respect of your many handmaids and the affliction of the single sinner.

Already the infant moved in the womb, the milk flowed from the full breasts; her belly was so large it looked as if she would bear twins. A leaden color surrounded her eyes, her face went white, and as soon as her breasts were emptied they refilled with liquid. Her cell barely accommodated her now: they began to prepare for the birth, taking such precautions as they could that the cries of the baby not give away the birth.

And then in the dead of night, when the unfortunate had fallen fast asleep, she had a dream in which the bishop who had originally committed her to religious life in that monastery (as noted previously) stood beside her, wearing a pallium and dressed in monk's clothing. He fixed her with a stern gaze and asked, "Why is it that you constantly curse me?" Terrified, she shook her head. [795] "It is true," persisted the holy man. "Why do you deny it?" Finding herself caught, she replied, "In truth, lord bishop, because you handed me over to this monastery, in which so many evils found me."

To this he answered, "You are more readily blamed for sins which you have not yet disclosed to your spiritual father as you should. See that you confess as soon as you can, follow my instructions and say these psalms every day in honor of Christ." Then, as soon as he had described the names and numbers of the psalms, he vanished. She awoke, and feeling better, committed to memory both the vision and the psalms.

The next night, when she seemed on the point of giving birth, and the anticipation of that hour was bitter . . . the venerable prelate appeared again in a dream to the desperate girl, bringing with him two women of beautiful visage.[54] The bishop came up to the miserable girl, laid her head on his knees, wrapped her face in the pallium he carried, and exclaimed to her, "If you had purified yourself in confession, you would see clearly what is happening. Now you will perceive the benefit, but you will not be able to understand the mode or nature of what is done." Standing after a little, she saw the women, it seemed to her, carrying the baby wrapped in white linen and following the departing bishop.

Waking, she felt no weight in her belly. She ran her hand over her body and found it completely restored.[55] The next morning when her guards beheld her, they saw that her belly had shrunk to normal, that her face had acquired a girlish if not virginal look, that her eyes were bright and had lost their leaden color. At first they could not believe their own eyes. "What is this?" they said. "Have you now added to all your other crimes the murder of your baby?" Immediately the tiny cell

54. The punctuation of this sentence in the PL is clearly mistaken: the third comma, if needed at all, should follow *desperanti*.

55. Literally, "empty."

in which she sat chained was turned inside out. But the narrow cell, her threadbare clothes, the meager straw bedding could hide nothing. "Wretched girl," they demanded, "have you given birth or not?"

"I don't know," she answered. She related the vision, and said she knew nothing further. Thoroughly frightened, they were unable to believe something so unprecedented. They felt her belly: such slenderness had replaced the swelling that you would have thought her back was stuck to her front. They squeezed her breasts, but elicited no liquid from them. Not sparing her, they pressed harder, but expressed nothing. They ran their fingers over every joint, exploring everything, but found no sign of childbirth, no indication even of pregnancy. They called the others, and they all found the same thing: everything restored, everything proper, everything beautiful.

They dared not, nonetheless, make any decision or judgment without the authority of the father [Gilbert]. She was kept still bound, the iron still chafing her ankles, the chains still clanking. [796] But she saw two ministers of divine mercy come to her: one of them, with the help of his companion, cut the chain by which the captive was most tightly constrained. The sisters noticed in the morning that the chain was missing, and asked for an explanation, but could not believe what they heard, and searched all the bedclothes, finding nothing. After a while they did discover one link of the chain that had fallen from her feet. Since it was intact and still as hard as a toolmaker's die, but disconnected from her feet, they were utterly amazed.

Why should I linger over details? She had been freed in this way from the rest, and only one foot remained bound by one fetter. Meanwhile the holy father [Gilbert] arrived, and when he had learned everything from the obvious signs and most trustworthy witnesses, as becomes a man of remarkable humility, he felt he should consult me, insignificant as I am,[56] about all these things. Coming therefore to our monastery, the servant of Christ disclosed the miracle to me in secret and asked that I should not deny my presence to the handmaids of Christ. I willingly agreed.

When he had received me and my traveling companions most kindly and courteously,[57] we went to the chamber within a chamber where the prisoner sat in her cave. There stood many, maidens as well as widows of advanced years, rich in wisdom and judgment, remarkable in sanctity and greatly experienced in religious discipline. After they had recounted everything to us, I began to feel the fetter with my own hands, and I realized that she could not have gotten free of the other one by herself or with the aid of others except by divine assistance. Some of them, not having yet put aside fear, asked us if more chains should be placed on her. We forbade this, pointing out that this would be harsh and a clear sign of lack of faith. Rather, one should anticipate and hope that whoever freed her from the others would rescue her also from what still held her. Then at the instigation of the father [Gilbert], many things worthy of timeless record were recalled to us, through

56. Literally, "my smallness."
57. At Watton, apparently some time later.

which it was clearly made known that God is pleased with those who fear him, even those who wait upon his mercy.

We, therefore, commending ourselves to their holy prayers and comforting them as we could with the word of the Lord, returned to our monastery, praising and glorifying the Lord for all we had heard and seen and which had been told us by the holy virgins. A few days later we received a letter from that venerable man informing us that the fetter we had seen holding her had fallen off, and asking my unworthy advice about what should be done. I therefore wrote these few among other words: "What God hath cleansed, that call not thou common;[58] and whom He hath loosed, thou shalt not bind."[59]

I therefore thought I should particularly write these things to you, who are dear to me and far removed from these parts, both to deprive the hostile of any advantage[60] and so as not to keep quiet about the glory of Christ.

58. Acts 11:9.
59. Cf. Matthew 16:19.
60. Either the enemies of virtue in general, or those hostile to the Gilbertine order and seeking a scandal such as this to discredit it.

THE ABBESS WHO BORE A CHILD AND WAS SAVED BY THE HOLY VIRGIN

Latin; first half of the twelfth century; England
Text: Hilding Kjellman, la Deuxième Collection Anglo-Normande
   des Miracles de la Sainte Vierge et son original latin *(Paris, 1922)*
   *(Arbeten Utgifna med Understöd af Vilhelm Ekmans Universitetsfond,
   Uppsala, 27), no. 13, pp. 60–61*
Context: Chapter 10

There was a certain nun, an abbess, in a certain convent, who was disliked by all the sisters subject to her because she was immoderately fervent in observance, which by no means redounded to her advantage. Led astray by the instigation of the devil and her own weakness, she became pregnant, and was soon desperate. She tried to think of someone to whom she could reveal her secret, and by a stroke of inspiration, made one of the sisters *praeposita* of the whole convent, gradually becoming more and more intimate with her and finally making her privy to her whole secret.

O trust, never certain! She who should have kept the secret disclosed it, and the facts were made known through her to the archdeacon, and through him to the bishop, as a consequence of which a great scandal arose. Everywhere there was talk of deposing the abbess, or even burning her.

What next? The day of the birth arrives, and the bishop, drawn there by trickery, is in the chapterhouse with all his retinue. A clamor arises from the nuns about having such an abominable crime in their midst. Some cover their ears, others proclaim that the abbess should not be admitted to Christian society. These make fun, those condemn, all hold her in contempt.

What could the abbess do in these circumstances? Words cannot describe the grief, the fear, the trembling she felt all at once in her heart. Inspired by hope— hope, I say, which alone abandons humans not even in death—she fled manfully to our most tender and merciful mistress, Holy Mary. And to whom else would she have gone? To her, I say, who offers aid to all those fleeing to her in need, who is the refuge of every sinner and the solace of all Christians. To her the abbess flees in such straits, praying and weeping before her altar, punctuating her pleas with groans, sobs, and tears.

Nor did the mother lack mercy. For when a deep sleep overtook the abbess, in the great bitterness of her heart, our Lady Holy Mary, the tenderest of the tender, appeared with a retinue of angels, first rebuking the guilty, but, after her sincere confession and vows, consoling her gently with her own loving person. And when the abbess, in this sleep, as it seemed to her and actually was, gave birth to a baby, the gentle lady, standing by just like a midwife, gave orders to the angels that they should take the baby away to a certain hermit much beloved of her, who should bring the baby up in her service.

They, for their part, obeyed and it was done. While these acts of mercy were taking place a great tumult arose in the chapterhouse. The clerics were sent by the bishop to bring the abbess in disgrace to judgment. Once she was present, the bishop ordered representatives to examine carefully her uterus. They, marveling, reported finding no sign whatever of what had been alleged. Others were sent, and still others of rank and gender different from her accusers, who reported the same thing with astonishment. Finally the bishop himself, incredulous, comes and sees her, lively, healthy, and free of pregnancy. Furious, he orders a great fire lit and the accusers of the abbess, male and female, thrown in.

When she hears this, she throws herself at the bishop's feet and recounts the entire affair from beginning to end. The bishop is more amazed than words can tell, and praising with the others in a loud voice the most kind mother of God, goes with the clerics immediately to the hermit where, just as it was told, he finds the child entrusted by the Virgin Mary.

The child was reared there for seven years, and then carefully schooled at the bishop's own court. After the bishop died he succeeded him nobly in his episcopal office, in which he led a most holy life until his end. . . .

REMISSION FROM LOUIS XI OF PENALTY FOR THE
DEATH OF AN EXPOSED INFANT

French; February 1477
Text: Guérin, Recueil, vol. 12, no. 1589, pp. 148–50, from Archives
*   Nationales, Reg. JJ 206, no. 1063, folio 229v*
Context: Chapter 11

Louis, King of France by the Grace of God. Know that we have received the humble supplication of the relatives and close friends of Pierre Barbin, spinner, Julien Barbin, his son, and Jehan Begault, all poor laborers who live in the village of Chauffaye in Poitou, according to which on the Vigil of the Purification of the Virgin Mary, in the year 1474, Marguerite Barbin, the daughter of Pierre and Jeanne Barbin, then his wife, gave birth to a male child around daybreak and would never name the man who had engendered the baby. After the birth the said Pierre and Julien Barbin and the now deceased Morine, then still living, in order to preserve the honor of the daughter, who was not married, baptized the baby in a pan at their home and kept and harbored him until around eight or nine at night. They made plans among themselves to take the baby to the poorhouse of Pousauges, which was about two leagues from their home, and to this end the supplicants took the baby and wrapped him well and suitably in good cloth.

This done, Julien went to look for the said Begault, his neighbor, and explained the circumstances to him, asking if he would be willing to accompany them to the poorhouse, to which he consented. Once Begault had therefore arrived at the house of Barbin, the supplicants took the baby and carried him to the poorhouse or Hôtel-Dieu, and left him there in the arcade or porch in front of the poorhouse, well wrapped, making sure that he was healthy and quite alive, and not noting in him any sign of illness or death.

But the next morning the baby was found dead on the porch, and was buried there at the poorhouse. The case was reported to the castellan and the procurator of Vouvent, where the supplicants lived. As a result of this report about the case, the justice of Vouvent imprisoned there Julien and Begault. Pierre Barbin, the father, who had advised the transporting of the child, disappeared. Later Julien and Begault were released for a period of time on recognizance, and both father and son Barbin were then imprisoned. Begault then disappeared and failed to appear on the day of his arraignment.

And although the supplicants intended no harm in making the determination to take the child to the poorhouse and Hôtel-Dieu and did it solely to protect the honor of the said girl, nonetheless, they fear that, having been so long imprisoned,

they may be treated severely by the courts unless we intervene. . . .[61] Wherefore
we . . . have aquitted the supplicants of every penalty in the matter and case herein
described . . . , and so command the seneschal of Poitou. . . . Given at Paris, in
the month of February, in the sixteenth year of our reign. . . .

61. Ellipses, here and following, are in the original: this document is a record
of the actual charter of acquittal and omits titles and other details..

❖ ❖ ❖

FREQUENTLY CITED WORKS

A list of all the sources employed for this study would be uselessly massive. This list includes only works which are cited repeatedly in the text at sufficient remove from their first occurrence to make it difficult for the reader to locate the full reference. Bibliography in its more common sense (i.e., works relevant to particular topics) is given in the notes.

Standard ancient and medieval works (e.g., writings of Plato or Augustine, scripture, major sagas) are listed only when a specific edition is of importance, particularly for reference to a more accurate text; otherwise they are cited in the notes with standard division numbers and may be located in any modern edition. Full references are provided to less familiar works.

Alexandre-Bidon, Danièle, and Monique Closson. *L'Enfant à l'ombre des cathédrales*. Lyons, 1985.

Altfridi vita sancti Liudgeri episcopi Mimigardefordensis. Ed. G. Pertz. Hannover, 1829. MGH SS 2.

d'Angeville, Adolphe. *Essai sur la statistique de population française, considerée sous quelques-uns de ses rapports physiques et moraux*. Paris, 1876; reprinted with introduction by E. Leroy Ladurie, Paris, 1969.

Antoniadis-Bibicou, H. "Quelques notes sur l'enfant de la Moyenne Époque Byzantine (du VIe au XIIe siècle)." *Annales de démographie historique* (1973) 77–84.

Archibald, Elizabeth. "Apollonius of Tyre in the Middle Ages and the Renaissance." Ph.D. diss., Yale University, 1984.

———. "The Flight from Incest: Two Late Classical Precursors of the Constance Theme." *The Chaucer Review* 20, 4 (1986) 259–72.

Ariès, Philippe. *L'Enfant et la vie familiale sous l'ancien régime*. 2nd ed., Paris, 1970. (English trans.: Robert Boldick. *Centuries of Childhood*. New York, 1962.)

Arnold, Klaus. *Kind und Gesellschaft in Mittelalter und Renaissance: Beiträge und Texte zur Geschichte der Kindheit*. Munich, 1980.

Assistance et charité. Ed. M. H. Vicaire. Toulouse, 1978.

Baer, Yitzhak. *A History of the Jews in Christian Spain*. Philadelphia, 1961.

Baker, Derek, ed. *Medieval Women*. Oxford, 1978.

Barstow, Anne L. *Married Priests and the Reforming Papacy: The Eleventh-Century Debates*. New York, 1982. Texts and Studies in Religion, 12.

de Beaumanoir, Philippe. *Coutumes de Beauvaisis*. Ed. A. Salmon. Paris, 1900.

Belmont, Nicole. "Levana; or, How to Raise Up Children." *Family and Society: Selections from the Annales, Économies, Sociétés, Civilisations*. Ed. Robert Forster and Orest Ranum, trans. Elborg Forster and Patricia Ranum. Baltimore, 1976. Pp. 1–15.

Bennet, H. "The Exposure of Infants in Ancient Rome." *Classical Journal* 18 (1923) 341–51.

Berlière, Ursmer. "Les Écoles claustrales au Moyen Âge." *Académie royal de Belgique: Bulletin de la classe des lettres et de sciences morales et politiques* 5 S, 7 (1921) 550–72.

Bieżuńska-Małowist, Iza. "Die Expositio von Kindern als Quelle der Sklavenbeschaffung im griechisch-römischen Ägypten." *Jahrbuch für Wirtschaftsgeschichte* 2 (1971) 129–33.

Binder, Gerhard. *Die Aussetzung des Königkindes: Kyros und Romulus*. Meisenheim am Glan, 1964. Beiträge zur klassischen Philologie, 10.

Blumstein, Philip, and Pepper Schwartz. *American Couples*. New York, 1983.

Bolkestein, H. "The Exposure of Children at Athens and the ἐγχυτρίστριαι." *Classical Philology* 17 (1922) 222–39.

Boswell, John. *The Royal Treasure: Muslim Communities under the Crown of Aragon in the Fourteenth Century*. New Haven, 1977.

———. *Christianity, Social Tolerance, and Homosexuality: Gay People in Western Europe from the Beginning of the Christian Era to the Fourteenth Century*. Chicago, 1980.

———. "*Expositio* and *Oblatio*: The Abandonment of Children and the Ancient and Medieval Family." *American Historical Review* 89, 1 (February 1984) 10–33.

Bracton, Henry de. *De legibus et consuetudinibus Angliae*. Ed. G. E. Woodbine. New Haven, 1915–42.

Brissaud, Yves. "L'Infanticide à la fin du moyen âge, ses motivations psychologiques et sa repression." *Revue historique de droit français et étranger* 50 (1972) 229–56.

Britton. Ed. and trans. Francis Nichols. Oxford, 1865.

Brooke, C. N. L. *The Monastic World*. London, 1974.

Brundage, James. *Law, Sex, and Christian Society in Medieval Europe*. Chicago, 1987.

Brunt, P. A. *Italian Manpower, 225 B.C.–A.D. 14*. Oxford, 1971.

Bynum, Caroline. *Holy Feast and Holy Fast: The Religious Significance of Food to Medieval Women*. Berkeley, 1987.

Caesar of Heisterbach. *Dialogus miraculorum*. Ed. J. Strange. Cologne, 1951.

Cameron, A. "The Exposure of Children and Greek Ethics." *Classical Review* 46 (1932) 105–14.

Carcopino, Jérôme. "Le droit romain d'exposition des enfants et le Gnomon de l'Idiologue." *Mémoires de la Société Nationale des Antiquaires de France* 7 (1924–27). Paris, 1928. Pp. 59–86.

La Carità cristiana in Roma. Ed. Vincenzo Monachino, Mariano da Alatri, et al. Bologna, 1968. Roma Cristiana, 10.

Coale, A. "The History of Human Population." *Scientific American* 231 (September 1974) 40–51.

La Colección canónica hispana, 2: Colecciones derivadas. Ed. Gonzalo Martínez Díez. Madrid, 1976. *Monumenta Hispaniae sacra,* Serie canónica, 1.

———, *3: Concilios griegos y africanos.* Ed. Gonzalo Martínez Díez and Felix Rodríguez. Madrid, 1982. *Monumenta Hispaniae sacra,* Serie canónica, 3.

———, *4: Concilios galos: Concilios hispanos: Primera parte.* Ed. Gonzalo Martínez Díez and Felix Rodríguez. Madrid, 1984. *Monumenta Hispaniae sacra,* Serie canónica, 4.

Coleman, Emily. "Infanticide in the Early Middle Ages." In Susan Mosher Stuard, ed., *Women in Medieval Society.* Philadelphia, 1976. Pp. 47–71.

Collins, Roger. "Julian of Toledo and the Royal Succession in Late Seventh-Century Spain." In *Early Medieval Kingship,* ed. P. Sawyer and I. Wood. Leeds, 1977.

Colonna, Aristides, ed. *Heliodori Aethiopica.* Rome, 1938.

Concilia Galliae A.314–A.506. Ed. C. Munier. Turnhout, 1963. CCSL 100.

Concilios visigóticos e hispano-romanos. Ed. José Vives. Barcelona-Madrid, 1963.

Constable, Giles. "Aelred of Rievaulx and the Nun of Watton." In *Medieval Women,* ed. Derek Baker. Oxford, 1978. Pp. 205–26.

Corpus Iuris Sueo-Gotorum Antiqui: Samling af Sweriges gamla lagar. Ed. H. S. Dollin and C. J. Schlyter. Stockholm, 1827–77.

Councils and Synods with Other Documents relating to the English Church. Ed. F. M. Powicke and C. R. Cheney. Oxford, 1964. 2 vols.

De Legibus Anglie. Ed. and trans. G. D. G. Hall. London, 1965.

Delasselle, Claude. "Les enfants abandonnés à Paris au XVIIIe siècle." *Annales* (1975) 187–218.

Deroux, M. P. "Les Origines de l'oblature bénédictine." *Revue Mabillon* 17 (1927) 1–16, 81–113, 193–216.

Diehl, E. *Inscriptiones latinae christianae veteres.* Zurich, 1925–61.

Duby, Georges. "The 'Youth' in Twelfth-Century Aristocratic Society." In *Lordship and Community in Medieval Europe,* ed. Frederic Cheyette. New York, 1968. Pp. 198–209.

Duguer, Antoine (Anton Degurov). *Essai sur l'histoire des enfants trouvés.* Paris, 1885.

Dunn, Charles. *The Foundling and the Werewolf: A Literary-Historical Study of Guillaume de Palerne.* Toronto, 1960. University of Toronto Studies and Texts, 8.

Durham, M. E. *Some Tribal Origins, Laws, and Customs of the Balkans.* London, 1928.

L'Enfant au Moyen Âge: Littérature et Civilisation. Paris, 1980.

Engels, Donald. "The Problem of Female Infanticide in the Greco-Roman World." *Classical Philology* 75 (1980) 112–20.

Les Établissements de Saint Louis. Ed. Paul Viollet. Paris, 1883.

Étienne, R. "La Conscience médicale antique et la vie des enfants." *Annales de démographie historique* (1973) 15–46.

Exclus et systèmes d'exclusion dans la littérature et la civilisation médiévales. Paris, 1978.

Eyben, Emil. "Family Planning in Graeco-Roman Antiquity." *Ancient Society* 11–12 (1980–81) 1–82.

Finnboga saga hins Ramma. Ed. Hugo Gering. Halle, 1879.

Flandrin, Jean-Louis. "L'Attitude à l'égard du petit enfant et les conduites sexuelles dans la civilisation occidentale." *Annales de démographie historique* (1973) 152–53.

———. *Families in Former Times: Kinship, Household and Sexuality*. Trans. Richard Southern. Cambridge, 1979. (Orig.: *Familles: parenté, maison, sexualité*. Paris, 1976.)

Flateyjarbok: En Samling af Norske Konge-Sagaer. Oslo, 1860.

Fleta. Ed. and trans. H. G. Richardson and G. O. Sayles. London, 1955. Selden Society, 72.

Formulae. Ed. Karl Zeumer. Hannover, 1886. MGH Legum, 5.1.

Fossati Vanzetti, Maria Bianchi. "Vendita ed esposizione degli infanti da Costantino a Giustiniano." *Studia et documenta historiae et juris* 49 (1983) 179–224.

Fournier, Jacques. *Le Registre d'Inquisition de Jacques Fournier, Évêque de Pamiers*. Ed. Jean Duvernoy. Paris, 1965.

Fuero de Béjar. Ed. Juan Gutierrez Cuadrado. Salamanca, 1974.

Fuero de Teruel. Ed. Max Gorosch. Stockholm, 1950. Leges Hispanicae Medii Aevii, 1.

Furs de València (in 4 vols.). Ed. Germà Colon and Arcadi García. Barcelona, 1970–83.

Garden, Maurice. *Lyons et les Lyonnais au XVIIIe siècle*. Paris, 1970.

Gauthier de Coincy. *Les miracles de Nostre Dame*. Ed. F. Koenig. Droz, 1970.

Gesta Romanorum. Ed. Hermann Oesterley. Berlin, 1872.

Ginzberg, Louis. *The Legends of the Jews* (in 7 vols.). Philadelphia, 1909–38.

Glass, D. V. *Population in History*. London, 1965.

Glauser, Jürg. *Isländische Märchensagas. Studien zur Prosaliteratur im spätmittelalterlichen Island*. Basel, 1983. Beiträge zur nordischen Philologie, 12.

Glotz, G. "L'Exposition des Enfants." *Études Sociales et Juridiques sur l'antiquité grecque*. Paris, 1906. Pp. 187–228. (Taken from the articles "Expositio" and "Infanticidium" in the *Dictionnaire des antiquités* [1892 and 1898 eds., respectively].)

Golden, Mark. "Demography and the Exposure of Girls at Athens." *Phoenix* 35, 4 (1981) 316–31.

Gonzalo de Berceo. *Milagros de Nuestra Señora*. Ed. and trans. Amancio Bolaño e Isla. Mexico City, 1976.

Goodich, Michael. *Vita Perfecta: The Ideal of Sainthood in the Thirteenth Century*. Stuttgart, 1982. Monographien zur Geschichte des Mittelalters, 25.

Goody, Jack. "Adoption in Cross-Cultural Perspective." *Comparative Studies in Society and History* 11 (1969) 550–78.

———. *Production and Reproduction: A Comparative Study of the Domestic Domain*. Cambridge, 1976.

———. *The Development of the Family and Marriage in Europe*. Cambridge, England, 1983.

Der Göttweiger Trojanerkrieg. Ed. Alfred Koppitz. Berlin, 1926. Deutsche Texte des Mittelalters, 29.

Guillaume d'Angleterre. Ed. Maurice Wilmotte. Paris, 1962.

Gunnlaugs saga ormstungu. Ed. Sigurður Nordal and Guðni Jónsson. Reykjavik, 1938. Íslenzk Fornrít, 3.

Habicht, J.-P., Julie CaVanzo, P. Butz, and Linda Meyers. "The Contraceptive Role of Breastfeeding." *Population Studies* 39, 2 (1985) 213–32.

Hadas, Moses. *Heliodorus, An Ethiopian Romance.* Ann Arbor, 1957.

Haddan, Arthur, and William Stubbs. *Councils and Ecclesiastical Documents Relating to Great Britain and Ireland* (in 3 vols.). Oxford, 1869–78.

Hanawalt, Barbara. "The Female Felon in Fourteenth-Century England." *Viator: Medieval and Renaissance Studies* 5 (1974) 253–68.

———. "Childrearing Among the Lower Classes of Late Medieval England." *Journal of Interdisciplinary History* 8, 1 (1977) 1–22.

———. *The Ties That Bound: Peasant Families in Medieval England.* Oxford, 1986.

Harris, William. "The Theoretical Possibility of Extensive Infanticide in the Graeco-Roman World." *Classical Quarterly* 32 (1982) 114–16.

Heers, Jacques. *Esclaves et domestiques au Moyen Âge dans le monde méditerranéen.* Paris, 1981.

Hefele, Charles. *Histoire des conciles d'après les documents originaux.* Paris, 1908.

Helmholz, Richard. "Infanticide in the Province of Canterbury during the Fifteenth Century." *History of Childhood Quarterly* 2 (1975) 379–90.

Henricus de Sugusio, Cardinalis Hostiensis. *Summa.* Lyons, 1537.

Herlihy, David. *Medieval and Renaissance Pistoia. The Social History of An Italian Town.* New Haven, 1967.

———. "Family and Property in Renaissance Florence." In *The Medieval City,* ed. Miskimin, Herlihy, and Udovitch. New Haven, 1977. Pp. 3–24.

———. "Medieval Children." In *The Walter Prescott Webb Memorial Lectures: Essays on Medieval Civilization.* Austin, 1978. Pp. 109–42.

———. "The Making of the Medieval Family: Symmetry, Structure, and Sentiment." *Journal of Family History* 8, 2 (1983) 116–30.

———. *Medieval Households.* Cambridge, Mass., 1985.

Herlihy, David, and Christiane Klapisch-Zuber. *Tuscans and Their Families: A Study of the Florentine Catasto of 1427.* New Haven, 1985.

Hexter, Ralph. *Ovid and Medieval Schooling: Studies in Medieval School Commentaries on Ovid's Ars amatoria, Epistulae ex Ponto, and Epistulae heroidum.* Munich, 1986. Münchener Beiträge zur Mediävistik und Renaissance-Forschung.

Hopkins, Keith. "Contraception in the Roman Empire." *Comparative Studies in Society and History* 8 (1965–66) 124–51.

Hrólfs saga Kraka. Ed. D. Slay. Copenhagen, 1960.

Hugo von Trimberg. *Der Renner.* Ed. Gustav Ehrismann. Tübingen, 1909.

Huillard-Bréholles, Jean. *Historia diplomatica Friderici II.* Paris, 1852–61.

Hunecke, Volker. "Les enfants trouvés: contexte européen et cas Milanais (XVIIIe–XIXe siècles)." *Revue d'Histoire moderne et contemporaine* 32 (1985) 3–29.

Hügel, S. *Die Findelhäuser und das Findelwesen Europa's, ihre Geschichte, Gesetzgebung, Verwaltung, Statistik und Reform*. Vienna, 1863.

Huyghebaert, Nicolas. "Les femmes laïques dans la vie religieuse des XIe et XIIe siècles dans la province ecclésiastique de Reims." *I Laici nella societas christiana dei secoli XI e XII. Atti della terza Settimana internazionale di studio, Mendola, 21–17 agosto, 1965*. Milan, 1968.

Illmer, Detlef. "Zum Problem der Emanzipationsgewohnheiten im Merowingischen Frankenreich." In *L'Enfant* 2, pp. 127–68.

The Irish Pentitentials. Ed. Ludwig Bieler. Dublin, 1963.

Jochens, Jenny. "The Church and Sexuality in Medieval Iceland." *Journal of Medieval History* 6 (1980) 377–92.

Johnson, Penelope. *Prayer, Patronage, and Power: The Abbey of La Trinité, Vendôme, 1032–1187*. New York, 1981.

Jómsvíkinga saga. Ed. N. F. Blake. London, 1962.

Karras, Ruth Mazo. *Slavery and Society in Medieval Scandinavia*. New Haven, 1988.

———. "Concubinage and Slavery in the Viking Age." Forthcoming, in *Scandinavian Studies*.

Kellum, Barbara. "Infanticide in England in the Later Middle Ages." *History of Childhood Quarterly* 1 (1973–74) 367–88.

Keyfitz, Nathan. "The Population of China." *Scientific American* 250, 2 (February 1984) 38–47.

Kieckhefer, Richard. *Unquiet Souls: Fourteenth-Century Saints and Their Religious Milieu*. Chicago, 1984.

Kinsey, Alfred. *Sexual Behavior in the Human Male*. New York, 1947.

Kirshner, Julius, and Suzanne Wemple, eds. *Women of the Medieval World*. Oxford, 1985.

Klapisch-Zuber, Christiane. *Women, Family, and Ritual in Renaissance Italy*. Trans. Lydia Cochrane. Chicago, 1985.

Kortekaas, G. A. A. *Historia Apollonii Regis Tyri: Prolegomena, Text Edition of the Two Principal Latin Recensions, Bibliography, Indices, and Appendices*. Groningen, 1984.

Lacey, W. K. *The Family in Classical Greece*. Ithaca, N.Y., 1968.

Lallemand, L. *Histoire des enfants abandonnés et delaissés*. Paris, 1885.

Langer, W. "Infanticide: A Historical Survey." *History of Childhood Quarterly* 1 (1973–74) 353–74.

Laslett, Peter. *The World We Have Lost*. New York, 1965.

Laslett, Peter, and Richard Wall, eds. *Household and Family in Past Time*. Cambridge, England, 1972.

Laslett, Peter, et al., eds. *Bastardy and Its Comparative History*. Cambridge, Mass., 1980.

Late Medieval Icelandic Romances. Ed. Agnete Loth. *Editiones Arnamagnaeanae*, Series B. Copenhagen, 1962–.

Laws of Early Iceland: Grágás, vol. 1. Trans. Andrew Dennis, Peter Foote, and Richard Perkins. Winnipeg, 1980.

Laws of the Earliest English Kings. Ed. and trans. F. L. Attenborough. Cambridge, England, 1922.

Leclercq, Henri. "Alumni." In *Dictionnaire d'archéologie chrétienne et de liturgie,* vol. 1. Paris, 1907. Pp. 1288–1306.

Leff, Gordon, *Heresy in the Later Middle Ages.* Manchester, 1967.

Leges Burgundionum. Ed. L. R. de Salis. Hannover, 1892. MGH LL 1.2.1.

Leges Visigothorum. Ed. K. Zeumer. Hannover, 1902. MGH LL 1.1.

le Grand, Léon. *Statuts d'Hôtels-Dieu et de Léproseries: Recueil de Textes du XIIe au XIVe siècle.* Paris, 1901.

Le Roy Ladurie, Emmanuel. *Montaillou, village occitan de 1294 à 1324.* Poitiers, 1975.

Leyser, K. J. *Rule and Conflict in an Early Medieval Society: Ottonian Saxony.* London, 1979.

The Liber Augustalis, or Constitutions of Melfi Promulgated by the Emperor Frederick II for the Kingdom of Sicily in 1231. Trans. James Powell. Syracuse, 1971.

Lithell, Ula-Britt. "Breast-Feeding Habits and Their Relation to Infant Mortality and Marital Fertility." *Journal of Family History* 6, 2 (1981) 182–94.

Livi, Ridolfo. *La Schiavitù domestica nei tempi di mezzo e nei moderni: Ricerche storiche di un antropologo.* Padua, 1928.

Lopez, Robert. *Medieval Trade in the Mediterranean World.* New York, 1961.

Lopez de Meneses, Amada. *Documentos acerca de la Peste Negra en los dominios de la Corona de Aragón.* Zaragoza, 1956.

Lorcin, M.-T. "Retraite des veuves et villes au couvent: Quelques aspects de la condition féminine à la fin du Moyen Âge." *Annales de démographie historique* (1975) 187–204.

Lutz, Cora. *Musonius Rufus, "The Roman Socrates."* New Haven, 1947. Yale Classical Studies, 10. Pp. 96–101.

Lyman, Richard. "Barbarism and Religion: Late Roman and Early Medieval Childhood." *The History of Childhood.* Ed. Lloyd deMause. New York, 1974. Pp. 75–100.

Lynch, Joseph. *Simoniacal Entry into Religious Life from 1000 to 1260.* Columbus, Ohio, 1976.

———. *Godparents and Kinship in Early Medieval Europe.* Princeton, 1986.

McClure, Ruth. *Coram's Children: The London Foundling Hospital in the Eighteenth Century.* New Haven, 1981.

McLaughlin, Mary. "Survivors and Surrogates: Children and Parents from the Ninth to the Thirteenth Centuries." *The History of Childhood.* Ed. Lloyd deMause. New York, 1974. Pp. 101–82.

McNeill, John, and Helena Gamer. *Medieval Handbooks of Penance: A Translation of the Principal "Libri Poenitentiales" and Selections from Related Documents.* New York, 1938.

Mansi, Joannes D. *Sacrorum conciliorum nova et amplissima collectio.* Paris, 1902. 53 vols.

Martin-Doisy, M. "Enfants trouvés, abandonnés et orphelins pauvres." In *Encyclopédie théologique,* 3. *Dictionnaire d'économie charitable,* 4. Paris, 1864. Pp. 440–736.

Metz, René. "L'Enfant dans le droit canonique médiéval: Orientations de recherche." In *L'Enfant* 2.

Meyer, Jean. "Illegitimates and Foundlings in Pre-Industrial France." In *Bastardy and Its Comparative History*. Ed. Peter Laslett et al. Cambridge, Mass., 1980.

Le miroir de Souabe. Ed. George Matilde and K. Eckhardt. Aalen, 1973.

Miskimin, Harry, David Herlihy, and A. Udovitch, eds. *The Medieval City*. New Haven, 1977.

Da Molin, Giovanni. "Les enfants abandonnés dans les villes italiennes aux XVIIIe et XIXe siècles." *Annales de démographie historique* (1983) 103–24.

Mollat, Michel. *The Poor in the Middle Ages: An Essay in Social History*. Trans. Arthur Goldhammer. New Haven, 1986.

Muratori, Ludovico. *Rerum italicarum scriptores*. Milan, 1725–51.

Murray, Alexander. *Reason and Society in the Middle Ages*. Oxford, 1978.

Murray, Alexander. *Germanic Kinship Structure: Studies in Law and Society in Antiquity and the Early Middle Ages*. Toronto, 1983.

Nani, Teresa. "ΘΡΕΠΤΟΙ." *Epigraphica* 5–6 (1943–44) 45–84.

Nelson, Janet. "Queens as Jezebels: The Careers of Brunhild and Balthild in Merovingian History." In Derek Baker, ed., *Medieval Women*. Oxford, 1978. Pp. 31–78.

Nicholas, David. *The Domestic Life of a Medieval City: Women, Children, and the Family in Fourteenth-Century Ghent*. London, 1985.

Noonan, John. *Contraception: A History of Its Treatment by the Catholic Theologians and Canonists*. Cambridge, Mass., 1965.

Ólafs saga Tryggvasonar. In Snorri Sturluson, *Heimskringla*, ed. Bjarni Aðalbjarnarson. Reykjavik, 1941. Íslenzk Fornrít, 26.

Oliger, Livario. "De pueris oblatis in ordine minorum." *Archivum franciscanum historicum* 8. 1915.

Orlandís, José. "Notas sobre la 'Oblatio puerorum' en los siglos XI y XII." *Anuario de historia del derecho español* 31 (1961) 163–68.

———. "La Oblación de niños a los monasterios en la España Visigótica." In *idem*, ed., *Estudios sobre instituciones monásticas medievales*. Pamplona, 1971.

Pactus legis salicae. Ed. Karl A. Eckhardt. Hannover, 1962. MGH LL 1.41.

Paris, Matthew. *Chronica majora*. Ed. H. R. Luard. London, 1876.

Parisse, Michel. *Noblesse et chevalerie en Lorraine médiévale: Les Familles nobles du XIe au XIIIe siècle*. Nancy, 1982.

Passerini, Luigi. *Storia degli stabilimenti di beneficenza e d'istruzione elementare gratuita della città di Firenze*. Florence, 1853.

Patlagean, Evelyne. "L'Enfant et son avenir dans la famille byzantine (IVe–XIIe siècles)." *Annales de démographie historique* (1973) 85–93.

———. "Birth Control in the Early Byzantine Empire." *Biology of Man in History: Selections from the Annales, Économies, Sociétés, Civilisations*. Baltimore, 1975.

———. *Pauvreté économique et pauvreté sociale à Byzance: 4e–7e siècles*. Paris, 1977.

Patterson, Cynthia. "'Not Worth the Rearing': The Causes of Infant Exposure in Ancient Greece." *Transactions of the American Philological Association* 115 (1985) 103–23.

Payne, George. *The Child in Human Progress.* New York, 1916.

Pentikäinen, Juha. *The Nordic Dead Child Tradition.* Helsinki, 1968.

Perry, B. E. *The Ancient Romances.* Berkeley, 1967.

Peyronnet, Jean-Claude. "Les enfants abandonnés et leurs nourrices à Limoges au XVIIIe siècle." *Revue d'Histoire moderne et contemporaine* (1976) 418–41.

Pharr, Clyde, trans. *The Theodosian Code and Novels and the Sirmondian Constitutions.* Princeton, 1952.

Pinto, G. "Il Personale, le balie e i salariati dell'Ospedale di San Gallo di Firenze negli anni 1395–1406." *Ricerche storiche: Rivista semestrale del Centro Piombinese di Studi storici* 4, 2 (1974) 113–68.

Pomeroy, Sarah. *Goddesses, Whores, Wives, and Slaves: Women in Classical Antiquity.* New York, 1975.

———. "Infanticide in Hellenistic Greece." In *Images of Women in Antiquity.* Ed. Averil Cameron and A. Kuhrt. London, 1983. Pp. 207–22.

———. "Copronyms and the Exposure of Infants in Egypt." In *Studies in Honor of A. Arthur Schiller.* Ed. Roger Bagnall and W. Harris. Leiden, 1986. Pp. 147–62.

"Quaestio Johannis Pecham." Ed. Livario Oliger, in "De pueris oblatis in ordine minorum." *Archivum franciscanum historicum* 8 (1915) 414–39.

Radin, Max. "The Exposure of Infants in Roman Law and Practice." *Classical Journal* 20 (1925) 337–43.

Rank, Otto. *Das Inzest-Motif in Dichtung und Sage.* Leipzig, 1912.

Rawson, Beryl. "Children in the Roman *Familia.*" In *eadem, The Family in Ancient Rome: New Perspectives.* Ithaca, N.Y., 1986. Pp. 170–200.

Razi, Zvi. *Life, Marriage, and Death in a Medieval Parish: Economy, Society, and Demography in Halesowen, 1270–1400.* London, 1980.

Redford, Donald. "The Literary Motif of the Exposed Child." *Numen: International Review of the History of Religions* 14 (1967) 209–28.

Regino of Prüm. *De synodalibus causes et disciplinis ecclesiasticis.* Ed. F. Wasserschleben. Leipzig, 1840.

Remacle, Bernard-Benoît. *Des Hospices d'enfans* [sic] *trouvés en Europe, et principalement en France.* Paris, 1838.

Riché, Pierre. "Problèmes de Démographie historique du Haut Moyen Âge (Ve–VIIIe siècles)." *Annales de démographie historique* (1966) 37–55.

———. "L'Enfant dans le Haut Moyen Âge." *Annales de démographie historique* (1973) 95–98.

———. *Les Écoles et l'enseignement dans l'Occident chrétien de la fin du Ve siècle au milieu du XIe siècle.* Paris, 1979.

Rigaud, Eudes. *Regestrum visitationum archiepiscopi Rothomagensis, Journal des visites pastorales d'Eudes Rigaud, archevêque de Rouen.* Ed. Thomas Bonnin. Rouen, 1852. English trans.: *The Register of Eudes Rigaud.* Ed. Jeremiah F. O'Sullivan, trans. Sydney M. Brown. New York, 1964.

Ring, Richard. "Early Medieval Peasant Households in Central Italy." *Journal of Family History* 4, 1 (1979) 2–25.

Ríus Serra, José. *Cartulario de Sant Cugat del Vallés.* Barcelona, 1947.

Robert of Flamborough. *Liber poenitentialis*. Ed. J.-J. Firth. Toronto, 1971. Pontifical Institute of Mediaeval Studies, Studies and Texts, 18.

Rozière, Eugène de. *Recueil générale des formules usitées dans l'empire des Francs du Ve au Xe siècle*. Paris, 1859–1871.

Russell, Jeffery Burton. *Lucifer: The Devil in the Middle Ages*. Ithaca, 1984.

Rychner, Jean. *Lais*. Paris, 1966.

Salimbene de Adam. *Cronica*. Ed. G. Scalia. Bari, 1966.

Sandri, Lucia. *L'Ospedale di S. Maria della Scala di S. Gimignano nel quattrocento. Contributo alla storia dell'infanzia abbandonata*. Florence, 1982. Biblioteca della "Miscellanea storica dell Valdesa," 4.

Schimmelpfennig, Bernhard. "*Ex fornicatione nati*: Studies on the Position of Priests' Sons from the Twelfth to the Fourteenth Century." *Studies in Medieval and Renaissance History* 2 (OS 12) (1979) 1–50.

Schmitt, Jean-Claude. *The Holy Greyhound: Guinefort, Healer of Children Since the Thirteenth Century*. Trans. Martin Thom. New York, 1983.

Schmitz, H. J. *Die Bussbücher und die Bussdisciplin der Kirche*. Mainz, 1883 (reprinted Graz, 1958).

Sears, Elizabeth. *The Ages of Man: Medieval Interpretations of the Life Cycle*. Princeton, 1986.

Semichon, Ernest. *Histoire des enfants abandonnés depuis l'antiquité jusqu'à nos jours. Le tour*. Paris, 1880.

Shahar, Shulamith. *The Fourth Estate: A History of Women in the Middle Ages*. Trans. Chaya Galai. London, 1983.

Las Siete Partidas. In *Los Códigos Españoles*. Madrid, 1847.

Sigal, Pierre-André. "Le vocabulaire de l'enfance et de l'adolescence dans les recueils de miracles latins des XIe et XIIe siècles." In *L'Enfant au Moyen Age*. Paris, 1980.

Stacey, Robin. "Contract and Legal Enforcement in Celtic Law." Ph.D. diss., Yale University, 1985.

Statuts, chapitres généraux et visites de l'ordre de Cluny. Ed. Gaston Charvin. Paris, 1965.

Les Statuts synodaux français du XIIIe siècle, 1: *Les Statuts de Paris et le Synodal de l'Ouest (XIIIe siècle)*. Ed. and trans. Odette Pontal. Paris, 1971. Collection de Documents Inédits sur l'Histoire de France. Section de Philologie et d'Histoire jusqu'à 1610, 9.

———. 2: *Les Statuts de 1230 à 1260*. Ed. Odette Pontal. Paris, 1983. Collection de Documents, 15.

Stein-Wilkeshuis, M. W. "The Juridical Position of Children in Old Icelandic Society." In *L'Enfant* 2. Pp. 363–79.

Steinwenter, Artur. "Zum Problem der Kontinuität zwischen antiken und mittelalterlichen Rechtsordnungen." *Iura* 2 (1951) 15–43.

Sturluson, Snorri. *Heimskringla*, vol. 1. Ed. Bjarni Aðalbjarnarson. Reykjavik, 1941. Íslenzk Fornrít, 26.

Synodicon Hispanum. Ed. Antonio García y García. Madrid, 1981.

Syrisch-Römisches Rechtsbuch aus dem fünften Jahrhundert. Ed. Karl Georg Bruns and Eduard Sachau. Leipzig, 1880.

Terme, Jean, and J.-B. Monfalcon. *Histoire des enfants trouvés.* Paris, 1840.

Thorne, S. E. *Bracton on the Laws and Customs of England.* Cambridge, Mass., 1968.

Trexler, Richard. "The Foundlings of Florence, 1395–1455." *The History of Childhood Quarterly* 1 (1973) 259–84.

———. "Infanticide in Florence: New Sources and First Results." *History of Childhood Quarterly* 2 (1975) 98–117.

Tubach, Frederic. *Index Exemplorum: A Handbook of Medieval Religious Tales.* Helsinki, 1969. FF Communications, 86, no. 204.

Urschwabenspiegel. Ed. Karl Eckhardt. Aalen, 1975. Studia Iuris Suevici, 1.

Vadin, Béatrix. "L'absence de représentation de l'enfant et/ou du sentiment de l'enfance dans la littérature médiévale." *Exclus et systèmes d'exclusion dans la littérature de la civilisation médiévale.* Aix-en-Provence, 1978. Pp. 363–84.

van Hook, La Rue. "The Exposure of Infants at Athens." *Transactions of the American Philological Association* 41 (1920) 36–44.

van N. Viljoen, G. "Plato and Aristotle on the Exposure of Infants at Athens." *Acta Classica* 2 (1959) 58–69.

Verlinden, Charles. "L'Enfant esclave dans l'Europe médiévale." In *L'Enfant* 2. Pp. 107–25.

———. *L'Esclavage dans l'Europe médiévale,* 1: *Péninsule ibérique-France.* Brugge, 1955. Vol. 2: *Italie, Colonies Italiennes du Levant, Levant Latin, Empire Byzantin.* Ghent, 1977.

———. "La Législation vénitienne au bas Moyen Age en matière d'esclavage." In *Ricerche storiche ed economiche in memoria di Corrado Barbagallo,* ed. Luigi de Rosa. Naples, 1970. Pp. 147–72.

Vitae sanctorum Hiberniae. Ed. C. Plummer. Oxford, 1910.

Waiblinger, Franz. *Historia Apollonii regis Tyri.* Munich, 1978.

Wailes, Stephen. "The Romance of Kudrun." *Speculum* 58, 2 (April 1983) 347–67.

Waltner, Ann. "The Adoption of Children in Ming and Early Ch'ing China." Ph.D. diss., University of California, Berkeley, 1981.

Wasserschleben, Hermann. *Die Irische Kanonensammlung.* Leipzig, 1885.

Wolfdietrich A. Ed. Hermann Schneider. Halle, 1931. Altdeutsche Textbibliothek, 28.

Wolff, Philippe, Michel Labrousse, et al. *Histoire de Toulouse.* Toulouse, 1974.

Index